Travel
Perspectives

A Guide to Becoming a Travel Professional

Fourth Edition

Thomson Delmar Learning

Hospitality, Travel, and Tourism

Options.

Thomson Delmar Learning offers comprehensive and up-to-date teaching, learning, and professional education resources to help you prepare for professional and support careers in hospitality, travel, and tourism.

Careers.

Explore our hospitality, travel, and tourism education specializations to find textbooks, laboratory manuals, software, and online companions.

Service.

Customer service and satisfaction should be the highest priority for any successful business. If you have questions or comments regarding any of our products, or if you have a product proposal, please contact us at the address below.

Air Fares and Ticketing • Catering and Banquet Services • Conducting Tours Cruising • Customer Service • Dining Room and Banquet Management • E-Commerce and Information Technology • Food and Beverage Cost Control Front Office Operations and Management • Geography for the Travel Professional • Hospitality and Travel Marketing • Hospitality Sales • Hotel, Restaurant, and Travel Law • Hotel Operations • Human Resources Management Ice Sculpting • Internet for the Retail Travel Industry • Introduction to Travel and Tourism • Math Principles • Selling Cruises • Selling Tourism • Training Design

---

Thomson Delmar Learning
5 Maxwell Drive
Clifton Park, New York 12065-2919

For additional information, find us online at
http://www.delmarlearning.com or
http://www.hospitality-tourism.delmar.com

Travel Perspectives

A Guide to Becoming a Travel Professional

Fourth Edition

Ginger Gorham and Susan Rice

Travel Careers Incorporated
Indianapolis, Indiana

THOMSON

DELMAR LEARNING

Australia   Brazil   Canada   Mexico   Singapore   Spain   United Kingdom   United States

THOMSON
———————— ™
DELMAR LEARNING

Travel Perspectives: A Guide to Becoming a Travel Professional, 4th Edition
by Ginger Gorham and Susan Rice

Vice President, Career Education Strategic Business Unit:
Dawn Gerrain

Acquisitions Editor:
Matthew Hart

Managing Editor:
Robert Serenka, Jr.

Product Manager:
Patricia M. Osborn

Editorial Assistant:
Patrick B. Horn

Director of Production:
Wendy A. Troeger

Senior Content Project Manager:
Matthew J. Williams

Director of Marketing:
Wendy E. Mapstone

Marketing Channel Manager:
Kristin McNary

Marketing Coordinator:
Scott Chrysler

Cover Design:
Joe Villanova

Cover Images:
© Mint Photography / Alamy
© George Carruthers / Alamy
© Dennis MacDonald / Alamy

For permission to use material from this text or product, contact us by
Tel   (800) 730-2214
Fax   (800) 730-2215
www.thomsonrights.com

Library of Congress Cataloging-in-Publication Data

Gorham, Ginger.
  Travel perspectives : a guide to becoming a travel professional / Ginger Gorham and Susan Rice.—4th ed.
      p. cm.
  Includes bibliographical references (p.   ) and index.
  ISBN-13: 978-1-4180-1649-4 (alk. paper)
  ISBN-10: 1-4180-1649-7 (alk. paper)
  1. Travel agents—Vocational guidance. I. Rice, Susan, 1949- II. Title.
  G154.T63 2006
  910.23'73—dc22
                                    2006025055

NOTICE TO THE READER

The publisher does not warrant or guarantee any of the products described herein or perform any independent analysis in connection with any of the product information contained herein. The publisher does not assume, and expressly disclaims, any obligation to obtain and include information other than that provided to it by the manufacturer.

The reader is notified that this text is an educational tool, not a practice book. Since the law is in constant change, no rule or statement of law in this book should be relied upon for any service to any client. The reader should always refer to standard legal sources for the current rule or law. If legal advice or other expert assistance is required, the services of the appropriate professional should be sought.

The publisher makes no representation or warranties of any kind, including but not limited to, the warranties of fitness for particular purpose or merchantability, nor are any such representations implied with respect to the material set forth herein, and the publisher takes no responsibility with respect to such material. The publisher shall not be liable for any special, consequential, or exemplary damages resulting, in whole or part, from the readers' use of, or reliance upon, this material.

Contents

● Preface   xi

● Acknowledgments   xiii

● About the Authors   xv

Section I   Today's Travel Industry   1

● Chapter 1   Your Place in Travel   3
- ○ An Overview   4
- ○ Careers in Travel   4
- ○ The Successful Travel Professional   4
- ○ Spotlight on Careers   6
  - ▪ Travel Counselor   6
  - ▪ Independent or Home-Based Travel Counselor   7
  - ▪ Meeting Planner, Event Planner, Meeting Facilitator   7
  - ▪ Reservation Sales Agent   8
  - ▪ Sales Representative   8
  - ▪ Tour Escort, Tour Guide, Tour Conductor, and Tour Director   9
  - ▪ Flight Attendant   10
  - ▪ Cruise Industry Jobs   10
  - ▪ Journalist or Photographer   11
- ○ Getting a Job   11
  - ▪ Your Resume   12
  - ▪ Cover Letter   14
  - ▪ Job Interview Skills   14
- ○ Professional Certification and Continuing Education Opportunities   15
- ○ Summary   16
- Review Questions   17

● Chapter 2   Technology and the Travel Professional   19
- ○ Airline Computer Reservations and Ticketing   20
- ○ The Internet and the World Wide Web   20
- ○ The Internet Connection: Modems, Browsers, and ISPs   21
  - ▪ URLs and Search Engines   21
- ○ The Internet and Travel Professionals   21
  - ▪ The Internet as a Reference Tool   22
  - ▪ E-mail   22

- ▪ Advertising via the World Wide Web   22
- ▪ Making Bookings on the Web   23
- ○ E-Commerce and E-Marketing   24
  - ▪ Advantages of E-Marketing   24
  - ▪ E-Marketing and the Impact on Travel Agencies   24
  - ▪ Developing a Web Site   25
  - ▪ About Dot Com and Dot Travel   26
- ○ Summary   26
- Review Questions   29

● Chapter 3   Travel in the Twenty-First Century   31
- ○ Increasing Global Awareness   32
- ○ Traveling Safely   32
  - ▪ The Government and Our Security   32
  - ▪ Airport and Airline Security   34
  - ▪ Security for Ships, Trains, and Hotels   34
  - ▪ Security at Parks and Monuments   35
  - ▪ Border Security   35
  - ▪ Being Prepared   35
- ○ Take Precautions Against Travel Scams   35
  - ▪ Travel Purchase Scams   36
  - ▪ Scams while Traveling   37
- ○ Ecotourism   37
  - ▪ Defining Ecotourism   38
  - ▪ Who's Who in Ecotourism   38
  - ▪ Certifying the "Ecolabel"   38
  - ▪ The Ecotourist   39
- ○ Summary   39
- Review Questions   41

Section II   Geography for Travel Professionals   43

● Chapter 4   Basic Travel Geography   45
- ○ Using Maps   46
  - ▪ Geographical Terms   47
- ○ Winds, Water, and Weather   47
  - ▪ Common and Proper Spelling Chart   48
- ○ Summary   48
- Review Questions   49

● Chapter 5   Travel Destinations   51
- ○ Archeological Sites and Mysterious Places   52
- ○ Beaches   54

◦ Buildings, Structures, and Gardens   55
  ▪ Castles, Palaces, and Mansions   55
◦ Gaming   58
◦ Golf   58
◦ Historical Sites   59
◦ Museums, Theatre, Music, and Art   60
◦ National Parks   60
◦ Natural Treasures   62
◦ Religious Sites   63
◦ Scuba and Snorkeling   64
◦ Theme Parks   64
◦ Winter Sports   65
◦ Summary   65
Review Questions   67

Section III United States Air Travel   69

● Chapter 6 Air Travel Basics   71
◦ The Travel Agency and Air Travel   72
  ▪ Agency Automation   73
  ▪ Agency Revenue   75
  ▪ U.S. Air Travel Safety   76
◦ The Airlines   76
  ▪ Airline Codes   77
  ▪ Airline Policies   78
  ▪ Airline Operations   79
◦ Commercial Aircraft   80
◦ Airports   83
  ▪ Departures   83
  ▪ Arrivals   84
  ▪ Airport Services   84
◦ Airport Codes   84
◦ Summary   86
Exercises   89
Review Questions   95

● Chapter 7 Planning United States
  Flight Itineraries   97
◦ Establishing Priorities   98
◦ Flight Patterns   98
◦ Types of Trips   99
  ▪ One-Way Travel   99
  ▪ Round-Trip Travel   100
  ▪ Open-Jaw Travel   100
  ▪ Circle-Trip Travel   100
  ▪ Open-Jaw with Side Trip   100
◦ Flight Schedule Selection   101
  ▪ Using the *OAG*   101
  ▪ GDS Flight Availability Displays   101
◦ Time Comparison   101
◦ Elapsed Flying Time   104
◦ Making Flight Reservations   105
  ▪ GDS Reservations   105
  ▪ Unethical Booking and
    Ticketing Practices   105

◦ Finding the Answers   106
◦ Summary   107
Exercises   109
Review Questions   115

● Chapter 8 United States Airfares
  and Other Charges   117
◦ Normal and Excursion Fares   118
◦ Inventory Control   118
◦ Fare Basis Codes and Booking Classes   119
  ▪ Sister Fares   120
◦ Fare Construction   120
  ▪ Fare Construction—One-Way Travel   120
  ▪ Fare Construction—Round-Trip Travel   121
  ▪ Fare Construction—Open-Jaw Travel   121
  ▪ Fare Construction—Circle Trip   122
  ▪ Fare Construction—Open-Jaw
    with Side Trip   122
◦ Combinability Rules   123
◦ Airline Computer Fare Display   123
◦ Taxes and Other Fees—United States, Canada,
  and Mexico   125
  ▪ Within the 48 Contiguous States, Alaska,
    or Hawaii   125
  ▪ From the 48 Contiguous States
    to Alaska and Hawaii   125
  ▪ The Buffer Zone   126
  ▪ Within Canada or Within Mexico   126
  ▪ Too Many Taxes   126
◦ Summary   128
Exercises   129
Review Questions   133

● Chapter 9 Ticketing and Reporting   135
◦ Ticketless air Travel   136
◦ Electronic Ticketing   137
◦ Paper Ticket   137
  ▪ Ticket Stock   138
  ▪ Validation   138
  ▪ Basic Ticket Information   139
◦ Refunds and Exchanges   140
◦ Travel Agency Service Fees   140
◦ Reporting Air Sales   140
◦ Summary   141
Review Questions   143

Section IV Selling Other Travel
Products and Services   145

● Chapter 10 Accommodations   147
◦ The Lodging Industry at a Glance   148
◦ Types of Accommodations   148
◦ Property Organization, Ownership, and
  Management   149

○ Accommodation Rating Systems	150
○ Accommodation Rates	151
○ Lodging Language	151
○ Using Reference Tools	153
○ Selecting the Right Accommodation	155
○ Making Reservations	155
○ Hotel Safety	156
○ Summary	156
Exercises	157
Review Questions	161

● **Chapter 11 Rental Cars** **163**

○ The Car Rental Industry at a Glance	164
○ Rental Car Class and Size Groups	164
■ Rate Plans and Extra Charges	165
■ Insurance	166
■ International Rentals	166
■ Making Car Rental Reservations	167
■ Requirements for Renting a Car	167
■ What Happens at the Rental Counter	167
○ Summary	168
Exercise	169
Review Questions	171

● **Chapter 12 Traveling by Rail** **173**

○ Selling Rail Travel	174
○ Amtrak: A Brief History	174
○ The Amtrak Route System	175
○ Traveling with Amtrak	177
■ Service on Corridor Trains	177
■ Long-Distance Trains	178
○ Amtrak's Auto Train	179
○ Amtrak Fares	179
○ Amtrak Discounted and Promotional Fares	180
○ Making Reservations on Amtrak	181
■ Security	181
○ Other Railroads Around the World	181
■ VIA Rail Canada	181
■ Trains of Europe	182
■ Trains in Japan	184
○ Private Rail Cars and Private Luxury Trains	184
○ Summary	185
Exercises	187
Review Questions	189

● **Chapter 13 Consolidators, Charters, Group Sales, and Travel Insurance** **191**

○ Consolidators	192
■ Profit from Consolidators	193
■ Consolidator Policies	193
○ Charters	194
■ Aircraft Charters	194
■ Motorcoach, Rail, and Cruise Charters	195
■ Travel Agency Charters	195
○ Group Sales	195

○ Insurance	196
■ Trip Cancellation or Interruption Coverage	196
■ Health and Accident Coverage	197
■ Baggage Coverage	197
■ Flight Coverage	197
■ Coverage for Bankruptcies and Defaults	197
■ Coverage for Terrorist Acts or Identity Theft	198
■ Other Means of Coverage	198
■ Insurance Waiver	198
○ Summary	198
Review Questions	201

● **Chapter 14 Tours of the World** **203**

○ Types of Tours	204
■ Independent Tours	204
■ Hosted Tours	204
■ Escorted Tours	204
■ Special-Interest Tour	205
■ Dynamic Tour Packaging	205
○ Tour Benefits	206
■ The Best Type of Tour	207
○ The Language of Tours	207
○ Selecting Tour Operators	208
○ Reading Tour Brochures and Web Sites	209
○ Selling Tours	210
○ Making Tour Reservations and Payments	212
○ Confirmation and Follow-up	214
○ Summary	215
Exercises	217
Review Questions	223

Section V Selling the Cruise Experience   225

● **Chapter 15 The Basics of Cruising** **227**

○ Cruise Benefits and Disadvantages	228
■ Benefits to the Client	228
■ Benefits to the Travel Professional	229
■ Disadvantages of Cruising	229
○ Sources for Cruise Information	229
■ CLIA	229
■ Other Information Sources	229
○ Major Cruise Lines and Cruise Types	230
○ Cruise Areas of the World	230
○ The Language of Cruising	234
■ The Ship	234
■ Onboard	234
■ Accommodations	234
■ Coming and Going	235
■ Other Terms	235
○ Facilities, Features, and Food	235
■ Bars and Lounges	235
■ Casino	235
■ Electricity	235

- Entertainment   236
- Finances   236
- Food, Food, and More Food   237
- Hair Salons   238
- Laundry   238
- Library   238
- Medical Services   238
- Phone, Fax, and Computer   238
- Religious Services   239
- Ship's Shops   239
- Spa, Sports, Health, and Fitness   239
- Tipping   239
- Selling Other Types of Sea Travel   240
- Summary   240
- Exercises   241
- Review Questions   243

● Chapter 16 Cruise Pricing and Selling   245
- What Does a Cruise Cost?   246
- Basics of Cruise Fare Calculation   247
- Making the Calculations   248
- Making Reservations   248
- Keeping Records   249
- After the Sale   249
- Setting Sail   249
- Embarkation   250
- Debarkation   250
- Cruise Line Security   250
- Summary   250
- Exercises   253
- Review Questions   255

Section VI International Air Travel   257

● Chapter 17 Practical Advice for
International Travelers   259
- Entry Requirements for International Travel   260
- Proof of Citizenship   260
- Tourist Card   261
- Passport   261
- Visa   264
- Entry Documentation in the GDS   265
- State Department's Role in
International Travel   265
- Traveling in Good Health   266
- Required and Recommended Vaccinations   266
- Jet Lag (Desynchronosis)   267
- Intestinal Problems   267
- Altitude Sickness   268
- Medical Assistance Abroad   268
- Money Matters   268
- Money Tips   269
- Embassies and Consulates   269
- Entry into a Foreign Country   270

- At the Destination   270
- Duty-Free Allowance   271
- Returning Home   271
- Summary   272
- Review Questions   273

● Chapter 18 International Air Travel Basics   275
- Travel Differences   276
- IATA and Traffic Conference Areas   277
- Twenty-Four-Hour Clock   278
- International Date Line (IDL)   279
- Time Comparison   279
- Elapsed Flying Time   280
- International City, Airport, and Airline Codes   280
- Summary   285
- Exercises   287
- Review Questions   291

● Chapter 19 International Airfares, Taxes,
Schedules, and Ticketing   295
- IATA Trip Classifications   296
- SITIs, SOTOs, and Split Ticketing   296
- International Fare Terms   297
- Booking Classes and Fare Basis Codes   299
- International Taxes and Fees   300
- Airline Rate Desk   301
- International Flight Schedules   301
- OAG Flight Guide   301
- GDS Flight Availability   302
- Reference Sources for Additional Information   302
- Basic International Ticketing   303
- Summary   304
- Exercises   305
- Review Questions   309

Section VII Selling and Servicing
the Travel Client   311

● Chapter 20 Sales Skills for the Travel
Professional   313
- The Importance of Sales   314
- Being an Effective Communicator   314
- The Sales Process   314
- Initial Contact   315
- Ask the Right Questions   315
- Match the Product to the Need   317
- Recommend a Product   318
- Answer Questions and Handle   318
- Ask for the Business   318
- Support the Customer   319
- Telephone Selling   320
- Summary   321
- Exercises   323
- Review Questions   327

● Chapter 21 Customer Service for the Travel
Professional   329
  ○ Defining Customer Service   330
    ■ What do Customers Want?   330
    ■ Commitment to Excellence   330
    ■ What Can Travel Professionals Do?   331
    ■ Follow-up   331
  ○ Handling Complaints   331
  ○ Handling Irate Customers   332
  ○ Telephone Etiquette   332

  ○ Can You Judge a Book by Its Cover?   333
  ○ Summary   334
  Review Questions   335

● Endnotes   337

● References   339

● Glossary   341

● Index   355

 For additional Travel and Tourism resources, go to http://www.hospitality-tourism.delmar.com.

Preface

NEW FOURTH EDITION COVERAGE

In recent years, the travel industry has been buffeted by significant international events such as terrorist attacks; the expanding war on terrorism; outbreaks of contagious diseases, such as Bird Flu and SARS; and hurricanes, floods, and tsunami. In addition to these issues, travelers have concerns about security in airports, at hotels, on cruise ships, and on trains; travel scams, thieves; pickpockets; and identity theft. The ease and speed of global communications and greater media focus on global issues have given consumers a heightened awareness of all issues surrounding travel.

As professionals in travel and tourism, it is more imperative than ever before that we be knowledgeable about the global marketplace and global pressures on our industry. As recently as the mid-1990s, we had no concept of how much the Internet would change the way in which travel products and services are bought and sold. The pace of technology, and the change it has brought, have been breathtaking. Nor did we realize the full extent to which global events and catastrophes would affect our industry. During this event-filled period, some travel businesses have decided not to compete, some are struggling to compete, and some have embraced newness and dramatically changed the way in which they interact with their customers.

Consistent with the events that have buffeted and changed the travel industry forever, the authors have made many significant changes in the fourth edition. Every chapter has been updated, and content added, to reflect the changes inherent in doing business in this Internet-driven economy. It is our hope that readers of this textbook will gain a necessary perspective on the global nature of our business and an excitement for the future of travel and tourism.

The Internet

Consumers have displayed their acceptance of online retail ("e-tail") as witnessed by the huge growth of Internet sales of all kinds, especially travel. Travel professionals have also gained in many ways from the Internet. Discussion of the Internet has been expanded to include ways that travel professionals can effectively utilize the World Wide Web.

An informative section on the e-commerce economy has been added to this edition. Here the student will find e-commerce basics as well as tips on developing a Web presence and utilizing the dot travel designator.

The Web Activities and Important Industry Web Sites have been retained and updated to develop fluency in the workings of the Internet. Whatever the student's current level of familiarity with the Internet, it is our hope to impart an interest in, and increased knowledge of, this most important resource.

Terrorism and Other Travel Concerns

Travelers have, of necessity, become much more sensitive to concerns about their health and safety when they leave home. The governments of the United States and other countries have implemented stringent security measures at airports, borders, national monuments, hotels, cruise ships, and train stations. It has been, and continues to be, a daunting task.

While these new measures have given us added security, they also mean that travelers must adapt. Travelers have had to develop an increased awareness plus a few new coping skills. Often the best coping strategy is preparation. Travel professionals can play an important role in seeing that their clients are well prepared for any travel experience. Coverage is given to government agencies and their functions in protecting travelers and changes travelers can expect to see at airports, on trains and cruise ships, and at hotels and borders.

An individual traveler is much less likely to be a victim of terrorism than a victim of a crime or a scam. Travel scams consistently rank near the top of the list of complaints received by the Federal Trade Commission (FTC). Students will be aided in understanding the most common types of travel scams and how to deal with them.

Ecotourism

With increased global awareness has come more emphasis on how travel and tourism affect the world's environment. Tourism is not passive. Tourists interact with their travel destination and its resources, and without a focus on sustainable tourism, some of the places we love will be in danger of being changed forever by tourism. Since the United Nations designated 2002 as the International Year of Ecotourism, ecotours have become much more prevalent. Ecotourism is one of the fastest growing segments of the industry with millions of tourists seeking out such products. Without many rules in place for certifying a location or accommodation as fit to use the ecolabel, it falls in the lap of travel professionals, and ultimately the ecotourist, to make informed decisions and demand high standards.

Career Opportunities

Career areas that have increased in importance during the past 10 years have been expanded. More emphasis has been given to home-based travel counselors and available options for Internet careers, both career areas made possible by advances in technology. A case study asks students to choose a career area of interest and research it extensively. Students are also given the task of writing a professional resume for the travel industry and developing job interviewing skills.

Geography

A section on geography has been added to the fourth edition. The global nature of travel and tourism has made it paramount for students to develop a fundamental understanding of geography. While it is not possible to provide comprehensive coverage of geography in just two chapters, we do hope to spark an interest in geography that will lead to lifelong curiosity and promote further study. In our global world, we cannot stress enough the importance of developing an understanding of our world—physically, socially, economically, and politically. In these chapters, students will focus on using maps, understanding distances, travel patterns of U.S. tourists, and features of major tourist attractions. Attention is focused on major world cities and their locations, reasons why travelers want to visit particular destinations, major sightseeing attractions, the best time of year to visit, and so on. Interest in, and knowledge of, geography will be a lifetime asset to the travel professional, and it needs to begin now.

Focus on Building Skills

The format continues to reflect the skill-based approach of previous editions. Each major product sold by a travel *professional* is covered in depth. The student is acquainted with terminology, product features, reference materials, and given a focus on what it takes to sell the product to a client. The entire text is built around selling. Not only have we described a product, we have also given the student ideas on how and when to sell it. In addition to this overlay, a separate section is devoted to building selling skills.

Each chapter has been significantly updated to reflect the many changes that have occurred in the industry. Many new photographs and illustrations have been added to reinforce concepts learned.

Critical Thinking

Case studies have been added to most chapters to give students further exposure to situations that may be encountered. These brief studies give the student a look at actual situations related to selling a product. Students are encouraged to approach problem solving with the attitudes and concerns of a travel professional.

Instructional Aids

Chapter objectives and key terms are an important feature in the fourth edition. A list of objectives and key terms begins each chapter. Exercises and Review Questions allow the student to put into practice newly acquired knowledge and skills. Case studies assist students in developing critical thinking. Selling skills are an integral part of the content, exposing students to not only product information, but also tips on selling the products to a client.

Organization and Content

The fourth edition includes 7 sections and 21 chapters. The first section provides an overview of today's travel industry, including careers, technology, and special issues of interest to the twenty-first-century traveler. Section II focuses entirely on geography in order to give students an important foundation. Sections III through VI examine the features and benefits of various products and services sold, and Section VII takes an in-depth look at the sales process and skills necessary to turn a potential customer into a buying customer.

THE INSTRUCTOR GUIDE

The Instructor Guide provides instructors with guidelines and ideas for teaching from this textbook. The tools provided include

- complete objectives
- teaching tips
- suggestions for videos and other resources
- transparencies
- classroom exercises and instructional materials
- answers to student exercises
- chapter-by-chapter exams and exam keys

Acknowledgments

The authors wish to express their appreciation to the following individuals for their contributions to this text.

Barbara Conner, B.A., M.A.
Instructor with Hospitality Management
Normandale Community College
Bloomington, MN

Carol Weissert
Livengood & Associates
Indianapolis, IN

David Schoenberg, Ph.D.
Director of Travel and Tourism
LaGuardia Community College
Long Island City, NY

Debra Barnick, B.S., M.A.
Program Chair of Travel and Tourism
Lakeland Community College
Kirtland, OH

Juline Mills, Ph.D.
Assistant Professor of Hospitality and Tourism
    Management
Purdue University
West Lafayette, IN

Michael Freiband, B.A., M.B.A.
Adjunct Faculty of Travel and Tourism
Northern Virginia Community College
Annandale, VA

President Rex Yentes, B.A., M.A.
Webber International University
Winter Haven, FL

Richard Hindman, B.A., M.A.
Director of Hospitality Management/Culinary Arts
Central Texas College
Killeen, TX

Saba Alhadi, B.A., M.A.
Photowalks
Natick, MA

Tina Blanchet, C.T.C., C.H.E., D.S.
Program Director of the Tourism Department
Bay State College
Boston, MA

About the Authors

GINGER GORHAM

Ginger Gorham chose the travel industry as a second career and has worked as a travel counselor, agency manager, author, and teacher. As the child of a career military officer, she has had a long history of travel, living in England for several years. She has traveled extensively in the United States, the Caribbean, South America, and Europe. Her interests include archaeology and ancient Roman and Egyptian history, and she has a cursory knowledge of five languages. She and her husband operate an online antique business.

SUSAN RICE

Susan Rice began her career in the travel industry with Amtrak, where she spent nearly 14 years in sales and marketing. With a master's degree in adult education, plus her experience in travel, it was a natural fit to create and operate a postsecondary travel school that included a travel agency. She has also served as a part-time instructor and travel program organizer at Indiana-Purdue University at Indianapolis. Her most recent entrepreneurial adventures are a retail store and a commerce Web site. She and her husband renovated a historic home that they share with two Labrador Retrievers. Ms. Rice is listed in *Who's Who in American Education* and *Who's Who of Business Leaders*.

SECTION

I

Today's Travel Industry

CHAPTER 1
Your Place in Travel

CHAPTER 2
Technology and the Travel
Professional

CHAPTER 3
Travel in the Twenty-First Century

Your Place in Travel

OBJECTIVES

At the conclusion of this chapter, you should be able to

- understand the reasons why people travel, and how travel products and services are purchased.
- understand the many segments of the travel and tourism industry, and the corresponding career options.
- realize the personal skills and abilities that will lead to a successful career in-travel.
- develop an in-depth understanding of several career areas.
- write an effective resume and cover letter.
- apply for and interview for a job.
- recognize opportunities for professional certification and continuing education.

KEY TERMS

confidentiality

cover letter

entrepreneur

familiarization (FAM) trip

Travel Institute

reservation sales agents

resume

tour escorts

tour guide

trade publications

trade shows

Travel Agent Proficiency (TAP) test

travel counselor

AN OVERVIEW

Every time a person travels, whether for business or pleasure, he or she needs to purchase a variety of goods and services. Can you quickly name five things a traveler will need? The list might start like this: a reservation on an airline or train, a ticket, security, a place to sleep, a car to drive, restaurants, entertainment, information, and so on. In the United States alone, it takes 10 million workers to provide the goods and services a person needs every time he or she travels. Who are these people? They are the airline reservation agent, the hotel front desk clerk, the waiter, the brochure or Web site producer, the computer specialist, the travel agent, the entrepreneur—millions of people working at diverse and interesting endeavors.

One reason that a career in travel is attractive is the great diversity within the industry. Some people will begin their career in one segment of the industry and find that the skills and experiences gained in that area allow them to move easily into another segment of the industry. A flight attendant who becomes a tour guide is one example of this.

Others take the more traditional route and concentrate on one industry sector, going on to achieve a series of specific career goals. A hotel career may take this route, beginning at the front desk, moving on to other hotel departments, and then into management.

We also cannot forget the entrepreneur. The travel industry supports many small business owners whose creativity and ideas are the basis for exciting new enterprises. Entrepreneurs often begin as employees, gaining knowledge and expertise before going on to be a business owner. A travel agent who starts a home-based travel agency is an example of this. Entrepreneurs can find a place in most segments of travel.

CAREERS IN TRAVEL

To better assess the diversity and areas of career opportunity, we have divided the travel industry into eight business segments. In Table 1–1 we list several types of businesses that one might find in that segment, and several career choices within those businesses. Later in this chapter, we will focus on a few specific career choices with job descriptions, education requirements, advantages and disadvantages, and other helpful information.

THE SUCCESSFUL TRAVEL PROFESSIONAL

Job skills and product expertise can be learned by taking specialized training before entering the job market and through on-the-job training provided by an employer.

Personal interests and abilities are what will make the job successful for each individual. For example, a person who does not enjoy meeting and helping people will not be happy in a career as a travel counselor or flight attendant. Taking a personal inventory of your interests and abilities should be an important part of your decision to enter a new career. Compare your interests and abilities to the following list.

- *Are you self-motivated?* Self-motivation is the ability to determine what should be done and decide how to accomplish it. This is an invaluable skill, especially if you are working without any direct supervision, as does an independent sales representative.

- *Do you have a genuine desire to help people?* Foremost for success in most travel careers is a genuine desire to help people. Customers are the reason the travel industry exists. Even if you are in a position that does not have direct contact with the public, you will probably be supporting those who do work directly with customers. Working with the public is often like being an actor with a critical audience, yet it is also rewarding.

- *Do you have an awareness of the world around you?* Do you have an awareness of the world around you and an interest in finding out everything you can about it? Will you make a constant effort to gain product knowledge? You can never be satisfied that you "know it all."

- *Do you have a positive attitude?* Customer service professionals must have a positive attitude—sometimes under difficult circumstances. The success of your employer will depend on your ability to handle both good and bad days with the same positive approach. Your co-workers and customers alike appreciate and expect this.

- *Are you good at handling change?* The travel industry is in a constant state of change. You must be able to keep up with the product changes, as well as procedural changes. The changing demands of customers also keep things interesting. In other words, you will have to adapt easily to change.

- *Are you patient?* Patience is a virtue in most things. In a travel career, it is a necessity. Your customers will not always make up their minds quickly; your suppliers may put obstacles in your path to making a sale; your supervisor may make what seem to be ridiculous demands; and just when you think you know everything, someone will change it. Patience can make your job easier and can make you more efficient if you take the time to get all the facts and chart your course before taking action.

- *Can you work as part of a team?* The decisions you make and the way you handle your job responsibilities will affect other people. Working as part of a team means that you consider the impact of your behavior on those around you and that you do your job in a way that enhances your company's image.

SEGMENT	TYPE OF BUSINESS	CAREER CHOICES
• Accommodations and lodging	Hotel, motel, bed and breakfast, resort	Front desk clerk, front desk supervisor, reservationist, group sales manager, night auditor, catering manager, food and beverage manager, concierge, activities director, assistant manager, general manager
• Transportation	Airline, railroad, cruise line, motorcoach, rental car	Reservationist; customer service representative; ticketing agent, clerical specialist; accounting specialist; social director; scheduling director; marketing director; flight attendant; automation specialist; director of group, tour, and convention sales; operations specialist
• Tourism support	Retail travel agency, corporate travel agency, tour company	Travel counselor, corporate travel agent, independent sales agent, reservation sales agent, automation specialist, tour escort, tour guide, tour/group sales manager, international specialist, accounting supervisor, travel manager, travel agency owner, entrepreneur
• Special events and conferences	Festivals, trade shows, conventions	Meeting planner, event planner, convention service manager, convention sales representative, convention planner
• Internet-based travel	Airline, travel agency, Amtrak, tour operator, commerce Web site, hotel, resort	Computer specialist, Web site developer, content editor, reservationist, entrepreneur
• Journalism	Trade magazine, guidebook, travel book, Web site developer	Travel writer, guidebook writer, photographer, freelance writer, freelance photographer, advertising or public relations specialist, trade publication writer, brochure copywriter
• Recreation	Theme park, museum, natural attraction, ski resort, golf and tennis resort, casino	Marketing sales representative, reservationist, group sales specialist, guide service, manager
• Government	Federal, state, and local governments	National Park Service staff, customs, security specialist, airport director, Convention and Visitors Bureau staff, U.S. Travel and Tourism staff

TABLE 1–1 Business segments and career choices in the travel industry. (*Note:* This is not intended to be a comprehensive list.)

• *Can you be trusted with confidential information?* Medical, legal, and financial professionals understand that client information is strictly confidential and never discussed with anyone outside the office. Travel plans are also highly personal and should be treated with the same confidentiality. The travel professional never discusses a client's travel arrangements with anyone (including the client's spouse) unless that person has been involved in the planning process. Never leave messages at the office or home about travel plans if you are unable to reach the traveler. It may be tempting to tell a friend about the famous person you met, but it violates the privacy of your client to do so.

• *Are you good at organizing your time?* In most travel industry jobs, no two days are alike. Because your job duties are varied, you must be able to set priorities, organize your time to accomplish your responsibilities, and recognize changing demands. This requires a high degree of organization.

• *Are you always on time?* Airlines are evaluated on their on-time performance, and you will be, too. It is absolutely necessary that you arrive at your job and at other functions when you are scheduled to arrive. Your manager, co-workers, and customers depend on your presence at work to handle everyday responsibilities. If your personal circumstances interfere with your ability to be on the job and on time, your career will suffer.

• *Do you have basic office skills?* Skills in the areas of typing, computers, letter writing, telephone systems, accounting, filing, and record keeping are a definite advantage for the person entering the travel field. Computer skills have become mandatory, not just for airline reservation systems, but for business and Internet applications as well.

• *Do you have an interest in geography?* The need to be familiar with and interested in the world around you cannot be overemphasized. A travel professional must have an understanding of the geography of important destinations, as well as major world events, and cultural and social characteristics.

SPOTLIGHT ON CAREERS

Whether you are working toward your first job or changing careers in midlife, there are many things to consider. Few industries offer as much opportunity or diversity as does travel, but what about working conditions, chances for advancement, salaries, work hours, required training, benefits, responsibilities, and other related concerns? We take an in-depth look at several career options to provide answers to these questions.

Travel Counselor

The travel agency functions as a middleman channeling products from suppliers (e.g., airlines, cruise lines, tour operators) to customers. Some suppliers pay a commission (usually a percentage of the selling price) to the travel agency. Commission rates vary from 5 percent to more than 10 percent, depending on the product and the volume of that product sold by the agency. Most assess a consulting or service fee.

Travel agencies may sell business travel, leisure or vacation travel, or a combination of both. Specialized agencies that focus on a single product or market, such as cruises, luxury, or group travel, are increasing.

JOB DESCRIPTION A travel counselor's job is a varied one. In fact, most travel counselors say this is what they like best about their job. A typical day can include conferring with suppliers and customers, issuing tickets, making reservations, and giving advice on tourist attractions, weather conditions, customs, travel documents, and much more. Providing counseling, customer service, and selling activities account for over 50 percent of a counselor's time. The counselor uses a variety of information sources, including the Internet and airline computers, to assist clients.

TRAINING Specialized training is important for prospective travel counselors. Many vocational and proprietary schools offer travel certificate programs lasting from six weeks to six months. Travel courses are offered through adult education programs at public high schools or universities, and some colleges and universities offer degree

programs in travel and tourism. Home study and Internet-based courses are also available.

Training programs provide an excellent foundation for beginning travel counselors, but on-the-job training is also important. A job candidate with training, but no other experience, may start in a job requiring less skill and responsibility; however, in smaller agencies, a new employee may start out with full responsibilities.

SALARY AND BENEFITS According to the United States Bureau of Labor Statistics in 2002, a travel counselor could expect annual earnings ranging from $20,800 to $41,660.[1] In 2004, the fourteenth Annual Retailer Salary and Compensation Survey conducted by the Travel Institute,[2] found the average income for a travel counselor is $32,500. This study also found that increased levels of training and specialization added considerably to annual salaries. The majority of travel counselors are paid salary, but some receive compensation based on their level of sales or commission. Most travel agencies provide basic health insurance for their employees.

Travel counselors are encouraged to travel, and when they do, it is often discounted substantially. Travel is viewed as part of a counselor's ongoing education and as a reward for being a productive employee. Familiarization (FAM) trips are offered by destinations or suppliers as a way to acquaint a counselor with that product. FAM trips are open only to counselors, and although they often are not free, they are very inexpensive. When using discounts to travel, especially when on a FAM trip, a counselor is expected to dress and act as a business professional.

ADVANTAGES AND DISADVANTAGES Most travel counselors consider the variety of the work and customer contact to be advantages of their job. Travel discounts are another. A travel counselor may work under stressful conditions during busy times. Some consider this to be a disadvantage, while others work better under stress. Leisure agencies usually experience more fluctuation in service demand but may have a more relaxed work atmosphere than a corporate agency.

Some agencies operate during normal business hours or Monday through Friday from 8:00 A.M. to 5:00 P.M., but many others have weekend and evening hours in order to be available when their customers are. Agencies that do business over a wide geographical range may have longer workdays to compensate for time zone differences.

CAREER ADVANCEMENT In a small travel agency, there may be little or no room for career advancement. In larger agencies, there are opportunities to move into management at various levels. Travel counselors may also consider using their skills in other segments of the industry, such as transportation.

RELATED CAREERS

• *Corporate travel counselor and corporate travel manager.* Many companies use a travel agency to handle business travel arranging for their employees. A corporate travel counselor is expected to work with the employee to make the best and least expensive travel arrangements, while at the same time, enforcing the company's travel policies. The corporate travel counselor is often responsible for *only* business travel (no vacation planning). Sometimes a corporate travel counselor works with employees of more than one company. However, in some larger corporations, a corporate travel agency may be contracted to work with only that company's employees. Corporate travel counselors generally receive higher salaries and better benefits than leisure counselors. At the next level, a corporate travel manager oversees all employee travel and ensures that corporate travel policies are enforced.

• *Secretaries.* Many secretaries handle travel arrangements for their immediate supervisor, and sometimes for an entire department or small company. The secretary may work closely with a travel agency when making reservations and ticketing, or do the entire process alone. It is beneficial to have knowledge of the day-to-day responsibilities of a travel counselor.

• *Travel agency owner.* Opening a full-service travel agency requires approval by the Airline Reporting Corporation (ARC). An agency will usually be accessible to the public and clearly identified as a travel agency. There are, however, full-service travel agencies located in large corporations or private homes, or on the Internet. ARC sets the standards for appointing travel agencies, and ensures compliance with their regulations. Agency owners have often been travel counselors and continue to act in that capacity while owning their agency. Some agency owners have not had agency experience, nor do they wish to handle the day-to-day agency functions. ARC requires this type of owner have a manager who has experience either as a travel counselor, or ticketing agent for an airline.

Independent or Home-Based Travel Counselor

Over the past ten years, the number of travel counselors who work from home has increased substantially. This has been due in large part to changes in technology, but it is also an attractive cost-cutting measure for some agencies to have part- or full-time counselors who work from home. A home-based agent can, therefore, be an employee of a travel agency, maintain an agency affiliation but not as an employee, or be truly independent.

The major choice for the independent home-based agent is whether to be appointed by the Airlines Reporting Corporation (ARC) and thus be able to issue airline tickets, or to be an affiliate of a travel agency "host" that is already ARC appointed and will issue airline tickets for her. A further option is not to issue airline tickets at all. Because issuing airline tickets has become less profitable over the years, many home-based agents choose not to undertake the expense of an ARC appointment. Many travel agencies act as "host" agencies, allowing the independent agent to utilize their computer system and their ARC number for issuing airline tickets and making other reservations. In a later chapter ARC will be discussed in more detail.

Although there are many advantages of working at home, sometimes it can be difficult not to have co-workers to ask for help and support. There are, however, other places for the independent agent to find support. The Outside Sales and Support Network (OSSN) (http://www.ossn.com) is a trade organization that helps home-based agents by providing such things as a study program, liability insurance, surety bond, discounts on computer access, and help with constructing a Web site. By its affiliation with TRUE (Travel Retailer Universal Enumeration), OSSN members can receive a numeric identification that is recognized throughout the industry allowing independent agents to make bookings directly with suppliers. **NACTA**, or the National Association of Commissioned Agents, (http://www.nacta.com) provides similar services as well as an identification number through http://www.TravelSellers.com.

It is important for the independent agent to be aware of legal and financial requirements of operating a home-based business. Among other requirements, there are bank accounts, business licenses, tax and insurance requirements, and credit card merchant accounts that need to be established. While pay may be low to begin, being on your own can provide financial, as well as personal, rewards.

Meeting Planner, Event Planner, Meeting Facilitator

Meetings, large or small, require considerable planning. The meeting planner's job is to coordinate all facets of a meeting from contract negotiations to airline and hotel reservations to meeting rooms, meals, and entertainment. Some large travel agencies and hotels employ meeting planners, and many more work for large corporations or associations. Some are self-employed and work independently. Meeting planners, especially those with many years of experience, are likely to earn upwards of $50,000.

Meetings include trade shows, sales meetings, motivational or informational meetings, and many other types of gatherings. It is the meeting planner who researches the destination, its facilities and costs, ease of transportation to various locations, and area attractions. The planner will then recommend a site that best fits the meeting requirements. Once a site is selected, the planner is responsible for putting all the details together and making certain the meeting arrangements do not exceed budget. Obviously, this is a job that requires considerable detail orientation, creativity, and flexibility.

Reservation Sales Agent

Some jobs, such as reservation sales agent, are very similar across several segments of the industry. Reservation sales agents are employed by airlines, cruise lines, tour operators, hotels, resorts, rental car companies, and others. (See Figure 1–1.)

JOB DESCRIPTION Reservation sales agents work in large central offices and answer customer telephone or Internet inquiries. A computer terminal is used to obtain the necessary information to make reservations, answer questions, or offer information on routes, time schedules, rates, or accommodations.

TRAINING Usually a minimum of a high school diploma or its equivalent is required. A travel certificate is not mandatory but is often preferred by employers.

Some type of instruction is usually given on the job. Trainees will be taught company policy, government regulations, ticketing procedures, fare calculations, passenger itinerary planning, and how to use the computer reservation system. Learning how to conduct a conversation in an organized, yet pleasing, manner is an important part of the training. After training, new agents may work with a supervisor or experienced agent for several days or weeks.

SALARY AND BENEFITS Reservation sales agents are usually paid an hourly wage and a package of benefits that typically includes free or very low-cost travel, health and life insurance, vacation, and sick leave.

ADVANTAGES AND DISADVANTAGES Because the travel industry operates at all hours, reservation sales agents may have irregular schedules. Those sales agents with the least seniority often work nights, weekends, and holidays. Many reservation sales agents begin on a part-time basis and then move into full-time work.

CAREER ADVANCEMENT Because reservation sales agents are employed by large companies, there is potential for advancement, although it may be in different departments of the company. A reservation call center is a good place to learn some valuable skills and to gain information about all facets of the company's operation.

RELATED CAREERS
- *Ticket agent, passenger agent, ticket seller, or reservation clerk.* These various job titles have similar responsibilities, such as selling tickets, handling passenger inquiries and complaints, checking baggage, examining visas, and ensuring passenger seating.
- *Gate agent.* The gate agent assists passengers in airports by making boarding announcements, directing passengers to the correct boarding areas, and issuing boarding passes.
- *Travel clerk.* A travel clerk may work for an automobile club planning surface travel routes for club members. Part of the responsibilities will include indicating routes on road maps, and pointing out restaurants, hotels, and sightseeing en route.
- *Front desk clerk.* In a hotel, motel, or resort, the front desk clerk handles guest registrations, reservations, room assignments, switchboard, and sometimes accounting. (See Figure 1–2.)
- *Customer service agent or passenger services agent.* The responsibilities of this job may include solving customer complaints and problems, and acting as a liaison between the company and its customers to ensure customer satisfaction.

Sales Representative

Most major suppliers (e.g., airlines, cruise lines, car rental agencies, Amtrak, hotels, and tour operators) employ sales representatives. State and local convention and visitor's bureaus may also employ sales representatives.

FIGURE 1–1 Reservation Sales Agents are employed by airlines, cruise lines, tour operators, hotels, rental car companies, and others.

FIGURE 1–2 The front desk clerk in a hotel handles guest registrations, reservations, room assignments, switchboard, and sometimes accounting.

JOB DESCRIPTION Sales representatives are responsible for promoting their company to travel agencies, business travel departments, meeting planners, tour operators, and others in a position to increase the sales of the company's product. Sales representatives also participate in trade shows and other functions to promote the image of their company and its products. Some travel within an assigned territory is usually required.

TRAINING A college degree may not be required, but some college is usually preferred. Prior experience in sales or in travel and tourism is also preferred. Training is usually on the job.

SALARY AND BENEFITS Salaries vary widely, but may be expected to start in the $30,000 range. A sales representative is usually (although not always) paid a salary (without commissions), and benefits may include a company car and expense account. Travel benefits are often included, as is insurance coverage.

ADVANTAGES AND DISADVANTAGES The ability to set and maintain one's own work schedule is considered by most sales representatives to be an advantage. Depending upon the size of an assigned territory, travel may consume considerable time away from home.

CAREER ADVANCEMENT Because of their knowledge of and experience with their company, sales representatives may move to other positions within their company's marketing department, or to other departments within the company.

RELATED CAREERS

• *District Sales Manager (DSM).* Cruise lines employ DSMs to work with travel agencies and to promote the cruise line at trade shows or other types of activities. In other travel companies, the DSM manages a territory and usually several sales representatives who work in the territory.

• *Multiline Sales Representative.* Many companies want field sales representation but do not want to employ their own representatives. They may turn to a sales representative who represents several companies at the same time, called a multiline sales representative. Sales for multiple businesses can be made with the same customer, often on the same call. For example, several hotels and/or car rental companies may be represented by one sales rep. During a sales call with a travel agency, the rep provides information and materials for each company she represents. Multiline reps may work on commission and they may pay their own expenses in return for a contractual agreement to be the exclusive "agent" in a given territory or market or for specific accounts.

Tour Escort, Tour Guide, Tour Conductor, and Tour Director

These are all names for jobs that have many similar components and responsibilities.

JOB DESCRIPTION A tour guide may take people on sightseeing excursions of limited duration. Sometimes called a *step-on guide,* this person provides specialized knowledge about a particular place or topic. Tour escorts, tour conductors, and tour directors travel with and assist a tour group over several days or for the duration of the tour. There are part-time, as well as full-time, opportunities working for a tour operator or wholesaler. Escorting a tour requires many of the same personal skills required of a travel counselor, and an understanding of the travel industry is very helpful. A tour escort or director may be called upon to solve problems ranging from lost luggage to a hurricane.

TRAINING A tour director or tour escort will often have expertise in a certain subject, such as architecture, language, history, or ecology, and many have background in the travel industry or professions like teaching. Although much of the training is on-the-job, some community colleges, universities, and postsecondary schools provide courses in tourism management and tour guiding. The National Tour Association, a trade organization for tourism professionals, awards a Certified Tour Professional (CTP) certificate. You must have five years of experience in the tour industry, and take specified courses to qualify.[3]

SALARY AND BENEFITS Wages may range from $10 to $20 per hour, but that usually includes no benefits, such as health insurance or sick leave. Gratuities are an important source of income for a tour escort or guide. The more credentials and experience you have, the greater the pay.

ADVANTAGES AND DISADVANTAGES If traveling is what you dream of doing, this is a great job. Consider, however, that you will be gone all of the time you are working. If you work full-time, you will be gone full-time. This may not be attractive to everyone.

CAREER ADVANCEMENT There is opportunity for advancement, but it is often limited to being assigned to larger groups or more prestigious tour destinations. Using your contacts and experience to start your own tour operation might be another way to advance your career.

RELATED CAREERS
• *Tour coordinator.* The responsibility of a tour coordinator is to package a tour. This might include negotiating with suppliers, planning itineraries, advertising, preparing brochures, and possibly visiting the tour sites to ensure quality.

Flight Attendant

Good health, good vision, neat and attractive appearance, friendly personality, and high moral character are mentioned by airlines as necessary qualifications for flight attendants. Height and weight restrictions and overall fitness are also considered.

JOB DESCRIPTION Flight attendants are responsible for the safety of passengers as well as their comfort. They may care for unaccompanied children, or passengers who become ill on a flight. In an emergency, flight attendants handle safety procedures and administer first aid.

TRAINING All airlines require a high school diploma as the minimum education, but two years of college is preferable, along with some experience in customer service. A second language can be an asset for working on international flights. All airlines provide training for their flight attendants. Training may range from two to six weeks initially, and cover emergency procedures, grooming, preparation and service of food, and the types of aircraft the company flies. In-service training is also required.

SALARY AND BENEFITS Salaries vary by carrier but are generally calculated as a base salary plus an hourly rate for flying time over a specified minimum number of hours.

According to the U.S. Bureau of Labor Statistics (www.bls.gov), median annual earnings of flight attendants were $43,140 in 2002, with a range of $20,890 to more than $91,000. The Association of Flight Attendants indicates that beginning flight attendants had median earnings of about $15,338 a year in 2002. Travel expenses while on duty (accommodations and food) are paid by the airline. The best routes, schedules, and pay go to the most senior employees. A coveted incentive for flight attendants and their immediate families is free travel on their own airline and reduced fares on most other airlines.

ADVANTAGES AND DISADVANTAGES Constant travel can be either an advantage or a disadvantage for different people. Schedules, especially on international flights, can be long and can interfere with "normal" sleep schedules. Attending to the needs and well-being of passengers is the first priority of a flight attendant. Even those who love this aspect of the job say this is usually demanding and can be difficult.

CAREER ADVANCEMENT Flight attendants may choose to move "inside" their company to train or manage other flight attendants. Other career opportunities within their airline or with other travel companies are also possibilities.

Cruise Industry Jobs

The cruise ship industry is one of the fastest growing areas in the travel industry. Major cruise lines have introduced 64 new ships in just the past few years, and predictions are that several will be built every year for the foreseeable future. Most industry jobs are on luxury liners, but you can also find employment on smaller vessels such as steamboats and sailing yachts. If being at sea is not your choice, there are many cruise jobs available "on land," too.

JOB DESCRIPTION A wide array of jobs is available on board a cruise ship, ranging from deckhands, ship officers, and maintenance crews to room stewards, housekeepers, entertainers, bartenders, waiters, gift shop clerks, casino workers, and recreation and fitness directors, just to name a few.

There are many cruise jobs for which you never have to leave your home city. These jobs include reservations, secretaries, customer service, crew travel coordinators, accounting, and so on. As you might expect, these jobs are concentrated in locations such as south Florida where cruise lines have corporate headquarters, and in some port cities as well.

TRAINING Preparation for a cruise job may consist of specialized education for jobs in reservations, accounting, bartending, entertainment, and so on. However, you may still need to start out in a position requiring less skill and move up to your desired position by proving your abilities.

FIGURE 1–3 Working on a Cruise Ship Provides opportunities to see the world and meet people.

Because many large cruise ships are registered outside the United States, some jobs will be awarded to citizens of the country of registry, but your ability to speak English is imperative since the majority of cruise passengers are English speaking. The Internet is an excellent resource for jobs in the cruise industry. Each major cruise line has its own requirements and procedures for application, so do the research.

SALARY AND BENEFITS The pay varies among different cruise lines and for different jobs. Salaries may seem low, but consider that you get free travel, room, and food. The work environment is comfortable and there are activities for the crew and usually a gathering place to meet your crew mates on your free time. Other benefits include medical insurance and reduced-price cruise vacation for family and friends.

ADVANTAGES AND DISADVANTAGES Since being "at sea" is mandatory for all on-board cruise jobs, a tendency toward motion sickness could make any on-board job a miserable experience. The work is demanding, the hours are long, and living quarters are small and not very private. However, the chance to see the world and meet interesting people may outweigh the disadvantages for you. Although you are working, there are opportunities to get off the ship and sightsee, and you will have time off between cruises.

Journalist or Photographer

The travel industry offers many opportunities for travel writers and photographers. Many major suppliers have advertising agencies that are responsible for promotional materials such as brochures and media advertising. Public relations firms may handle press inquiries, arrange interviews, and write press releases. The supplier (e.g., airline, cruise line) may also handle these functions internally.

JOB DESCRIPTION Travel writers and photographers are employed by travel publications both full-time and in a freelance capacity. There are many publications on travel, from trade magazines and guidebooks to general magazines and newspapers.

The competition in this field is intense. Experience is a valuable asset. Writing for newspapers or developing travel brochures are often good places to start.

TRAINING Courses in creative writing plus continuous practice of your craft provide the best training. Because most employers want people with experience, start wherever you can get it.

SALARY AND BENEFITS Freelance travel writers are often paid "by the piece," and the pay is often not high—perhaps $15 for an article printed by a newspaper. Traveling is, of course, a major benefit, and travel writers and photographers can often take advantage of industry FAMs or other discounts. Working for a newspaper or magazine, beginning salaries will be comparable to those of a travel counselor.

ADVANTAGES AND DISADVANTAGES Opportunities to travel are sought after by most travel writers and photographers. While travel may be considered by some people to be an advantage, others see it as a disadvantage. Because competition is intense, so is pressure to have an article or photograph accepted by a publisher, and deadlines are a fact of life. Pay, even for those employed by newspapers or magazines, is not high.

CAREER ADVANCEMENT Advancement may be simply moving from one employer to another where you can work on projects that are more to your personal liking or more prestigious. Working as a freelance journalist or photographer may also be a desirable career move for some.

RELATED CAREERS
- Jobs in public relations and advertising for a major hotel, cruise line, or the like, require firsthand experience and the ability to expertly communicate information.
- Reporters for newspapers, radio, and television must travel in search of a story. Travel may be across town or across the globe.

GETTING A JOB

Once you have focused on the type of job you would like, you have to begin thinking about the things you must do to get it. Start by collecting necessary materials such as copies of diplomas or travel certificates, grade transcripts, awards, letters of recommendation, references, your resume, and a cover letter. Assemble these items in a portfolio that can be given to an employer. Also, each specific employer may have an application form that must be completed perfectly.

Your Resume

A great resume can be one of the best selling tools you have when looking for a job in travel. The primary purpose of a resume is to persuade the reader to grant you an interview. Sounds simple, doesn't it? Not so! Writing a great resume requires considerable thought, dedication, and time, but it will be well worth your efforts. A good resume will convince the reader that your experience has taught you many things that the reader will find valuable. Keep in mind that you will have about 20 seconds to make an impact on the reader.

You will find several hundred books and Web sites offering a host of conflicting advice on writing a resume. There are a few common threads, however. A well-written resume should focus on what the reader wants to know about you. You should omit needless items, use action verbs and short sentences, and keep the resume to one page if possible. Use bulleted items for emphasis.

The first task is to outline the information that is to be included on your resume. Complete your outline over a period of days, taking time to jot down bits and pieces of your past experience as you think of them. Don't be concerned about how you say things; just get them down on paper. Focus on your work experience, travel experience, personal and business skills, volunteer experience, interests, talents, and accomplishments. From this initial list, develop an outline for your resume that includes the following categories.

CAREER OBJECTIVE Give a short (one sentence), but specific, statement of what type of job you are seeking. If you are interested in several types of positions, you may want to have more than one resume with different objectives on each.

EDUCATION List your most recent training first, focusing on travel-related courses or degrees. List the school name, address, dates attended, and degree received. Include your grade point average if it was very good, and list any awards or achievements.

EXPERIENCE Include work and volunteer experience—if it relates to the job you want. There is no hard and fast rule that requires you to list jobs in chronological order. If you have had several jobs of the same type, you may wish to group them together, rather than separately, under a heading such as *customer service*.

SKILLS List your best characteristics that are important to the type of job you are seeking. Examples might be "quick learner, organized, interacts well with people, customer oriented, proven ability to increase sales." You may choose to name this section Professional Skills and include items such as Sabre system, Microsoft Word, or Microsoft Access.

REFERENCES "Available on request" is appropriate, but be sure to have a separate page with your references that is actually available if an employer inquires. Always get permission before listing a person as a reference.

Study the sample resume in Figure 1–4.

You have spent considerable time creating your resume. All your hard work must now be presented in first-rate fashion. When laying out your resume, leave a one-inch margin at each edge of the page. Double-space between paragraphs or sections. Use larger or bold type for section headings. If you do not have access to appropriate computer software and a quality printer, have your resume professionally typeset and printed.

Use quality paper. White is the preferred color, but light shades of gray, tan, or even mauve can look very impressive. Some employers may ask you to fax a resume. Avoid this if at all possible because the product the employer receives is usually not very good. Hand-delivery is the best route, or simply mail your resume if you cannot appear in person. If you must fax a resume, use only white paper because colors look even worse.

Electronic transfer has become an acceptable way of transmitting your resume to a prospective employer. There are many Web sites that will, for a fee, create a resume and format it for electronic transfer. You may choose to e-mail to employers of your choice.

Proofread carefully; then, proofread again. Have a friend review your resume. It must be perfect!

MORE THAN JUST A RESUME Your resume is important, but a resume alone will not get you a job. It will, of course, be necessary to spend time locating potential employers and researching the employment scene. Be prepared to use the yellow pages and newspaper classified advertisements. Several Internet sites list job openings, but usually few are entry-level.

Talk to everyone you know about your job search, and ask them for recommendations or referrals. You never know when someone might have the perfect connection.

After making a list of potential employers, the most effective approach is a personal visit to the company. If you telephone ahead, it is easy to be put off. If you show up on the doorstep, resume in hand, and ready to complete an application, it will be harder for someone to turn you away. Positions have been filled simply because an applicant appeared when a vacancy suddenly became available in a company that was "not hiring."

Madeline Diaz
482 Louisville Drive
Columbus, Ohio 43012
(555) 565-5555 mdiaz@aol.com

Career Objective

To secure a position as a travel counselor with a customer service- and sales-oriented travel agency.

Skills

- Extensive travel in the United States and Caribbean; knowledgeable about many tourist attractions and sites
- Skilled in the use of Sabre Computer Reservation System, Microsoft Word, and the Internet
- Efficient, organized, and a quick learner
- Interact well with people and believe in team work

Education

Travel Certificate; August 2000; Travel Careers, Inc., Columbus, Ohio
- 98 percent grade average
- Student member of American Society of Travel Agents
- Gained knowledge of geography and destinations; skills in selling cruises, tours, rail, and air travel; and familiarity with the Sabre Computer Reservation System.

Experience

8/04–present   Travel Agency Intern, ABC Travel, Springfield, Ohio
- Increased knowledge of agency operations and counselor responsibilities
- Developed skills with Sabre system

9/00–7/04   Sales Associate, Nordstrom Department Store, Columbus, Ohio
- Exceeded sales quotas by an average of 15 percent
- Provided courteous service
- Created displays

6/00–8/00   Hostess, Walt Disney World, Lake Buena Vista, Florida
- Satisfied all requirements of Walt Disney World training program
- Handled guest relations for theme restaurant
- Interacted with customers and staff to ensure smooth operation and customer satisfaction
- Provided courteous service

1/00–5/00   President of Student Council, Columbus North High School
- Planned and implemented student functions

References

Available on request

FIGURE 1–4 A great resume can be one of the best selling tools you have when looking for a job.

Cover Letter

Each resume you mail or fax to a prospective employer must be accompanied by an original cover letter. The cover letter is your introduction when you are not there in person. Get the name and title of the person within the company who is responsible for hiring. The inside address of your letter will contain this information.

The first paragraph should show the reader that you know something about the company, and should mention the job you are seeking. The second paragraph should highlight one or two of the major points from your resume and why you think these things will make you a great choice. Try to show how and why you are just the person the company needs.

In the final paragraph, ask for an interview. Give some specific dates for follow-up so you will have a good reason to call later. A sample cover letter is shown in Figure 1–5.

Job Interview Skills

The purpose of a job interview is to give the company an opportunity to see whether you have the right "product" to sell to them. The interview also gives you a chance to see if this is the employer you want. Be prepared to ask questions as well as answer them.

Most interviewers are looking for *confidence* first and *competence* second. The way you dress communicates a great deal about your self-concept and about the type of person you are. Your image is especially crucial during job interviews and the first few weeks on the job. Once on the job, you will find out how much leeway you have, but until then, follow a few simple guidelines.

- take a conservative approach; wear clothing with simple lines, classic styles, and neutral colors
- wear simple jewelry or none at all
- choose simple, neat, natural hairstyles

Before you go to a job interview, *get prepared*. No one likes being interviewed. We all get nervous, which leads to sweaty palms, tripping over your tongue, and forgetting what you want to say. Being prepared is your best defense, and *the best way to be prepared is to practice*. Have someone ask you interview questions. Prepare and then rehearse your answers. How would you answer the following questions?

1. *Tell me about yourself.* Be prepared to focus on the aspects of your background that qualify you for this job. The interviewer isn't interested in knowing that you have two cats and love pasta.

2. *What is your major strength?* Talk about your strength that is especially important for success on this job. You will be much more impressive if you talk about your

June 28, 200X

Ms. Jan Karaker
Apollo Travel
206 Market Street
Columbus, OH 43020

Dear Ms. Karaker:

After talking with several people, I have learned that your company has earned a reputation for being customer-service oriented, and that you have just opened a new office. It is my goal to become a travel counselor and to utilize my travel education and marketing and customer service experience.

The enclosed resume shows that I have maintained a high grade average. My travel experience has given me the opportunity to learn about several popular destinations. My work experience has helped me develop patience and understanding when working with customers.

I have just completed my travel training, and am anxious to begin working. May I meet with you within the next two weeks to discuss the possibility of joining your agency? I will call you on or before July 8. Thank you for taking the time to consider my resume.

Sincerely,
Madeline Diaz

FIGURE 1–5 The Cover Letter is your introduction when you are not there in person.

interest in geography rather than your abilities on the golf course.

3. *What is your major weakness?* Don't fall for this one. It is up to you to present your best self at an interview, so turn this negatively phrased question into a positive by saying something like, "I prefer that things be done correctly, and sometimes push myself too hard."

4. *What did you like least about your last job?* Turn this negative into a positive. "My last job limited my ability to use all of my skills." Avoid saying anything negative about any person, organization, or previous employer.

5. *What salary do you expect to make?* Answer this question by reconfirming that you have considerable talent to offer and that you feel certain you will start at a level commensurate with your abilities. You will work hard to advance. You should have a general idea of the range of pay for the position; you may give this information to the interviewer as well.

PROFESSIONAL CERTIFICATION AND CONTINUING EDUCATION OPPORTUNITIES

Today's travel professional knows that keeping skills and knowledge current requires a constant search for educational opportunities and information. There are many such opportunities and resources in travel. Keep in mind higher levels of pay often go hand-in-hand with more education.

Every industry has its journals and other publications. These are called trade publications, and the travel industry has many. Nearly all are available online, and include http://www.travelweekly.com, http://www.modernagent.com, http://www.travelagentcentral.com, and http://www.travelagewest.com. You can also choose to receive e-mails that provide highlights of the latest travel news, allowing you to pick and choose which information you wish to pursue in depth. These are provided by ASTA Smart Brief, Travel Weekly Daily Bulletin, Travel Agent Digital Editor, and Mailpound, to name a few. These are an important way for travel professionals to keep up with new products, legal issues, what other professionals are doing, vendors who are having problems, and other important issues.

Trade shows provide a means for industry suppliers to exhibit their products and services. Exhibitors pay the show organizers for a booth and sometimes to set up and staff the exhibits. The show attendees then have the chance to pick up new materials and to learn about products in which they are interested. Trade show organizers are responsible for promoting the show to a potential audience.

FAM trips are organized by a travel supplier to offer travel professionals an inexpensive way to familiarize themselves with a destination or product. Although FAM trips usually are not free, the charges are minimal. FAM trips may be organized by airlines, resorts, tour operators, tourist offices, or others who wish to educate travel professionals about their products. Those who take advantage of FAM trips are not on vacation. They are expected to act and dress as professionals and to attend all scheduled functions. The agenda is usually very full because the supplier wants to impart as much information as possible. FAM trips are, of course, the best way to gather information about a destination.

Travel associations and professional organizations actively work to improve the travel industry. Some of these groups offer educational programs designed to address the needs of travel professionals. The Travel Institute is one such group. The *Certified Travel Associate (CTA)*, the *Certified Travel Counselor (CTC)*, and the *Destination Specialist* are some of the educational programs available through the Travel Institute to assist industry professionals at all career levels. After *18 months'* experience in the travel industry, and completion of required course work focusing on counseling, selling, and other core competencies, a candidate for the the Travel Institute must then pass an exam in order to attain the designation.

The CTC designation requires at least *five years'* experience in the industry plus completion of required course work. It has been shown that the travel counselors with the CTC designation often earn more and advance further than those without it.

Destination Specialist programs offer comprehensive study on specific regions of the world. The Travel Institute also offers other educational programs with a focus on the development of selling skills.

The Travel Institute's Destination Specialist programs cover Africa, the Caribbean, China, Eastern and Western Europe, Latin America, the Pacific Rim, North America, and Hawaii, plus corporate travel geography and a special interest travel program that studies 21 of the fastest growing specialties for niche marketing.

The American Society of Travel Agents offers the *Certified Travel Specialist (CTS)* in three areas: family travel, mature adult travel, and special interest travel. In addition to course work in niche marketing, a two-day course in the area of specialization must be completed.

For some years, the travel industry sought a standard to define the term "travel professional." The national Travel Agent Proficiency (TAP) test is a basic competency test that measures the entry-level knowledge of travel professionals within all aspects of the travel industry. The test was developed by the travel Institute and the American Society of Travel Agents (ASTA) to provide a national standard of entry-level proficiency for the travel industry. Additional information on this test may be obtained from http://www.thetravelinstitute.com. Results from the TAP test are now used by many employers to screen applicants for entry-level travel positions.

The International Airline Travel Agent Network (IATAN) Education Program provides many learning opportunities about the world and its political and cultural distinctions.

The Cruise Lines International Association (CLIA) Cruise Counselor Certification Program allows travel counselors to develop extensive cruise industry knowledge as well as cruise selling skills. There are three levels of achievement: the Accredited Cruise Counselor, the Master Cruise Counselor, and the Elite Cruise Counselor. Accredited (ACC) and Master (MCC) credits are earned by completing a combination of training seminars, video training, online training, and cruise experience, as well as textbook and case studies. Elite Cruise Counselor (ECC) requires the successful completion of any 10 (15-credit) CLIA live or online seminars and exams, and additional product knowledge requirements including cabin sales, ship inspections, and personal cruises not utilized for prior certification levels. CLIA also offers Management and Sales Institutes. Information is available from www.cruising.org.

The *Certified ARC Specialist (CAS)* designation is offered by the Airlines Reporting Corporation. This certification was suggested by travel counselors and developed with the assistance of several airlines and travel counselor organizations. The CAS tests knowledge of ARC-related functions like ticket security and sales reporting and is required for all new travel agency locations seeking ARC approval. More information can be obtained from ARC's Web site (http://www.arccorp.com).

Industry suppliers, such as Walt Disney Company and the tourist bureaus of several foreign countries, have developed training programs. These programs provide the opportunity for travel professionals to develop expertise in a specific product or geographic area. The *Disney Specialist* is offered through the College of Disney Knowledge and is ICTA accredited. Tourist boards that offer programs include Austria, Ireland, Jamaica, and Scotland.

SUMMARY

The travel and tourism industry is an extremely varied and interesting place to pursue a career. Different segments of the travel industry, such as transportation, tourism support, or accommodations, offer many interesting career choices. Which type of career you choose depends on your own personal interests and abilities.

Some travel industry careers require advance training and experience, while others can provide on-the-job training. Once in the travel industry, there are many varied educational programs to enhance professionalism and knowledge.

Finding the right career in travel requires some research to determine which is best for you. It might also require some training if special skills are required for that job. A job search plan is another necessary element for success. A resume is one of the best selling tools you have when seeking a job. A cover letter must accompany your resume whenever it is mailed or faxed to a prospective employer. The cover letter is your introduction.

Interviewing for a job requires preparation and special attention to the image you present. Know what questions an interviewer may ask, and prepare your answers in advance so nervousness does not cause you to forget what to say.

Professional certifications and continuing education are important to the travel professional to keep skill and knowledge current, and to achieve increased pay. Many opportunities exist. Which you choose will depend upon your interests and goals.

 For additional Travel and Tourism resources, go to http://www.hospitality-tourism.delmar.com.

PLEASE COMPLETE THE CHAPTER REVIEW QUESTIONS NOW.

Case Study

Now that you have read about several careers in the travel industry, you probably have some ideas of your own. Select a career that you find very interesting, and research it thoroughly. You will need to answer the following questions in depth:

Give the job title of your chosen career and describe the job responsibilities.

What type of personal skills will lead to your success in this career?

What type of education is required?

What are the advantages of this career?

What are the disadvantages of this career?

What is the pay range for this career?

List six employers you plan to contact. Describe in detail the procedure you will use to apply for this job.

Make a list of the Web sites you found most useful in your research. Why was each one useful?

Do you feel the same about this career as you did when you began to research it? Why or why not?

Review Questions

Complete the following questions using the information in Chapter 1.

1. Your friend just returned from a week's vacation to Disney World. He traveled via air to Orlando and stayed in a hotel. He came into contact with many travel professionals. List as many as you can.

    _____

    _____

    _____

2. "Your resume is important, but a resume alone will not get you a job." Respond to this statement by describing what other things you might need to do to find a job.

    _____

    _____

    _____

3. Results from the TAP test are now used by many employers to screen applicants for entry-level travel positions. Describe this test and why you think employers use it to screen job applicants.

    _____

    _____

    _____

4. Which of the following organizations provide continuing education opportunities for travel professionals? Mark all that apply.

    a. The Travel Institute

    b. Cruise Line International Association

    c. American Society of Travel Agents

    d. Travel Weekly

    e. Walt Disney Company

5. What can you do to prepare for a job interview?

    _____

    _____

    _____

6. Go to http://www.careerbuilder.com. In the "Find Jobs" section, enter a travel job and location you are interested in. Discuss the results you found and whether or not you think they will be helpful to you in your job search.

    _____

    _____

    _____

7. As a travel professional, you would like to improve your knowledge of certain destinations. What educational opportunities are available to you?

    _____

    _____

    _____

8. What types of certification does CLIA provide?

   _____

   _____

   _____

9. Visit American Airline's Web site (http://www.aa.com). Go to the AA Careers section. What is the company's application procedure?

   _____

   _____

   _____

10. At the same site (http://www.aa.com) locate a job in which you might be interested. Describe the job. What qualifications are required for this job? Where is it located?

   _____

   _____

   _____

Technology and the Travel Professional

OBJECTIVES

At the conclusion of this chapter, you should be able to

- understand the enormous growth and change associated with the Internet.
- understand the impact of the Internet on the travel industry.
- identify major airline computer reservation systems and understand their advantages to a travel counselor.
- recognize the force of e-commerce on the travel industry.
- outline several ways in which a travel counselor can utilize the Internet.
- appreciate factors involved in Web site development, including the significance of dot travel.

KEY TERMS

browser
Computer Reservation
   Systems (CRS)
dot travel
e-commerce
e-mail

Global Distribution
   System (GDS)
hubs
Internet
Internet scam
Internet Service Provider (ISP)

online
search engine
Uniform Resource
   Locator (URL)
Web banners
World Wide Web (www)

Just the word Internet inspires a wide array of perceptions and emotions. It's everywhere, whether you are an investor in Internet stocks, or a user of Internet technology; whether you love it or hate it, you can't get away from the Internet in today's economy. There is no question that the Internet has transformed much of the travel industry, but its effect is relatively recent. The influence of technology on the business of travel actually began in the 1950s with the development of airline computer reservation and ticketing systems. This chapter looks at the beginning of technology in the travel industry, as well as modern implications of technology and the Internet for the travel professional.

AIRLINE COMPUTER RESERVATIONS AND TICKETING

Computerized airline reservation and ticketing systems, or Computer Reservation Systems (CRS), have been around since the 1950s. Originally these systems were owned and used only by airlines. Travel agencies were granted access to them in the 1960s. It was a miraculous thing to be able to type in a few commands and retrieve a fare or make a reservation. What a time saver! Prior to the CRS, airlines and travel agents relied on printed references for fare and schedule information, and each reservation was booked manually.

At first, only the largest travel agencies could afford access to airline computers, so by the early 1980s, only a handful of travel agencies used airline computer systems. By 1993, just over a decade later, things had changed. Ninety-five percent of travel agency locations had become automated, and there was no turning back. Automated reservation and ticketing, now known as the Global Distribution System (GDS), had become a business necessity.

Some say the technology of the original airline systems is basically unchanged, inflexible and unable to adequately serve those who use it. Others argue that although the technology is over 50 years old, it has been upgraded constantly and is still the only system that can adequately support the level of transactions that are currently demanded of a reservation and ticketing system. In fact, Internet newcomers like Orbitz and Expedia, two of the largest travel Web sites, utilize GDS technology for their bargain fare search and reservation functions.

Sabre, Worldspan, Amadeus, and Galileo are the largest of the Global Distribution Systems. Amadeus is the only one that retains airline ownership. A GDS offers the travel professional access to travel information, reservations, and ticketing across the country or around the world. Flights, hotels, rental cars, Amtrak, Via Rail Canada, tours, cruises, and much more are available in a GDS. In order to stay competitive with the Internet, and with each other, each system has developed its own enhanced search and booking features that make it more efficient for travel professionals to easily and quickly find and utilize information on various travel products and services. For example, *Sabre® Cars* provides rates, availability, and product information for more than 37 car rental companies in more than 150 different country destinations. Worldspan CruiseSelect^{SM} allows cruise lines to distribute comprehensive cruise content via the Web to travel agencies in the United States and Canada. Each GDS also offers versions specially designed for home-based and corporate travel agents that are easier to learn and navigate.

There are several "high-tech" software companies that are developing alternatives to the GDS, new approaches to reservations and ticketing that (they promise) will make it easier for travel counselors to do their job, and be less expensive to operate. One of these is Farelogix, Inc. They promise travel agencies the ability to bypass the GDS, yet have access to the content of all four GDSs, and at 10 percent of the current cost for a GDS. Farelogix also promises to be a less expensive distribution alternative for airlines and other suppliers. Another is Genesis Travel Distribution which combines GDS and Web fares from airline and consumer Web sites into a single consolidated system.

THE INTERNET AND THE WORLD WIDE WEB

The next destination in the technology journey is the Internet. In 1994 almost no travel Web sites existed. Since then, the number of Web sites and online consumer purchases of travel products and services has skyrocketed. Online sales are expected to reach $91 billion by 2009, from $58 billion only five years previously.[1] There is no doubt that the Inernet changed the behavior of travel consumers, as well as the business of travel. (See Figure 2–1).

Suddenly (or so it seemed), any person and any business from the smallest travel agency to a major airline could

FIGURE 2–1 Online consumer purchases of travel products and services are expected to reach $91 billion by 2009.

utilize information, communication, marketing, advertising, and commerce via cyberspace. How has this been possible? As we will see, the development of the personal computer, the Internet, and the World Wide Web was key.

In the mid-1970s we saw the development of the personal computer or PC. The PC revolutionized the use of computers. They were now available for use in homes as well as businesses. Smaller desktop hardware and specially designed software could manage a customer list, business correspondence, accounting, newsletters, and a whole lot more. It was no longer necessary to have a computer that filled a large room or an entire floor of a business. Nor was it prohibitively expensive to own and operate a computer. Because the hardware became so inexpensive, each employee could have a computer terminal at his or her desk. It was now possible for anyone to benefit from the power, expediency, and convenience of the computer.

The Internet was developed to electronically link information networks of the military, universities, governments, and research facilities around the world. Between 65,000 and 75,000 worldwide information networks in over 100 countries were linked by the Internet. Although begun in the 1960s, the Internet was used by only a handful of people until the early 1990s. It was not until the **World Wide Web** (**www** or the "Web") was made public in 1992 that much of the information on the Internet became available to virtually anyone who had a PC and a modem. By the mid-1990s, PCs were widely used and the World Wide Web was fast becoming indispensable.

The World Wide Web is not synonymous with the Internet. The Web is simply one way of accessing information over the medium of the Internet. The Web uses the HTTP (Hyper Text Transfer Protocol), which is only one of the languages spoken over the Internet to transmit data. Web documents called *Web pages* are linked to each other via *hyperlinks*. Web documents may contain graphics, sounds, text, and video.

> If you see HTTPS you'll know you're on a "secure" server and can safely use your credit card online.

The Internet Connection: Modems, Browsers, and ISPs

Once connected to the Internet, the PC user has access to an incredible catalog of information via the Web, but first the user has to make the connection. To make the connection to the Internet and the Web, the PC user needs a *modem* (except for a wireless connection), a **browser**, and an **Internet Service Provider (ISP)**. A modem is a device that makes it possible for computers to exchange data over phone or cable lines. An ISP is a technical service company that has the necessary equipment and know-how to connect customers (people with home or office computers)

to the Internet for a fee. An ISP can be a "dial-up" service, so called because it provides access to the Internet via a phone line. Some well-known dial-up ISPs are America Online, Juno, Earthlink, and Net Zero. Dial-ups are inexpensive but also known for their slowness in connecting. ISPs can also be DSL (digital subscriber line), cable, or wireless. These options are more expensive than dial-up, but the time required to connect to and navigate around the Web is considerably reduced. A cable connection is the fastest option, while wireless is the most convenient. Wireless Internet hook-up has alleviated the need to physically connect your computer to a modem, phone line, or cable modem. Many public places, such as airports and hotels, now have wireless access. Browsers are software programs that allow the user to access and display information on the Web. Popular browsers include Microsoft Explorer and Netscape Navigator.

URLs and Search Engines

Faced with the enormous volume of data that is available via the World Wide Web, locating what you want is its own challenge. One way to locate information on the Web is to type the exact location or "address" of the information using a **Uniform Resource Locator (URL)**. A URL is attached to every Web site, just as you have a distinctive address or telephone number. A typical URL looks like this: http://www.expedia.com. If you know the URL, finding the site is simple.

However, if you don't know the *exact* URL, it would be difficult (if not impossible) to find specific information without the assistance of a **search engine** (such as Google or Yahoo!). A search engine is a software program that searches the huge Internet database for files that fit specific guidelines you have set up. Developing "search" criteria has become an important skill for extracting information you need from the vast resources that are available on the Internet. A nonspecific "search" for a general term like "travel" might yield millions of Web locations (URLs) at which you would find some type of information about travel. Most of them are probably not relevant to your needs. A more effective search uses specific key terms or phrases that will produce more relevant results. There are books and **online** *help* sections of your favorite search engine to assist you in developing search skills. If you choose to read a book, http://www.amazon.com lists over *six thousand* books on the best way to use Google.

THE INTERNET AND TRAVEL PROFESSIONALS

To retain their business edge, most travel professionals have developed skills in using the vast resources of the Internet. The Internet can be used by travel professionals as a reference tool, to communicate with customers and other professionals (e-mail), as an advertising medium, a booking tool, and to sell travel products ("e-commerce").

The Internet as a Reference Tool

Research has never been so easy! At your desktop you now have the equivalent of several libraries of information. Gone are the days of searching through books and brochures for answers. Information is so easily available that it has become a challenge to know more than your customer. Need passport information? A map to a restaurant in Seattle? Tours for motorcycle enthusiasts in Europe? Currency conversion? It's all there on the World Wide Web. The downside is that searching for it can be time consuming. A search for "passport information" using Google yielded 37 million sites containing passport information, some obviously more relevant than others! As mentioned earlier, being able to utilize search engines and search criteria has become an important skill. It is important to learn some solid search practices.

Once you find a site with the information you need, look at it critically. Seek out sites that are sponsored by travel organizations you are familiar with (such as ASTA, CLIA, or ARC), or travel industry publications (such as *Travel Weekly* or *Travel Agent*). Many industry suppliers (airlines, cruise lines, hotels, Amtrak, etc.) have extremely informative Web sites. Watch out for sites that may look official but are published by an individual or organization with an agenda that may or may not have the benefit of truth and accuracy. If you don't recognize the source of information, move on to a more reliable site. Some travel industry sites have consolidated information into hubs. Each hub is a collection of links to other Web sites. ASTA Smart Briefs and Travel Pulse Daily from Modern Agent e-mail subscribers daily with news briefs that are linked to the publication that authored the news article. If you want more details, just click on the link to read the full story. Travel Weekly sponsors http://www.travelweekly.com with daily news stories, articles on destinations, and links to other informational sites such as http://www.hotelandtravelindex.com.

E-mail

According to several studies, e-mail has replaced the telephone as the primary source of business communication. Business e-mail is used to communicate with customers and with co-workers. There are several advantages to using e-mail. It can be sent at your convenience and the receiver can read it at his convenience; no more "phone-tag." E-mail provides a written record of the communication, usually an advantage in business communication. It is sometimes all too easy to forget that like a business letter, what is written in an e-mail leaves a permanent trail. We dash off an e-mail message or delete one with equal ease, not thinking

much about its permanence. According to one former federal prosecutor, many careless e-mails have been used as the basis for lawsuits from criminal cases to sexual harassment.

As when writing a business letter, communicating with e-mail requires that appropriate etiquette be followed. Business e-mail should be clear and accurate. Avoid jargon and saying things that might be misconstrued by a reader. Something as simple as using all capital letters might be seen as the virtual equivalent of shouting at your reader. Always proofread e-mail for errors in spelling and grammar. Just because it's fast, doesn't mean e-mail can be sloppy. The "subject" line of your email should describe the content of the e-mail. E-mails with missing or nondescript subject lines are less likely to be read. If you want someone else to see an e-mail that was sent to you, always get permission from the sender before forwarding it.

Learn how to use "attachments." Attaching a document or photograph to your e-mail can save time and lengthy explanations, but be aware that attachments on incoming e-mail can be a source of viruses that have the potential to damage your computer. Don't open e-mail attachments that are not familiar to you. It pays to be cautious even with familiar names. Sometimes scammers may use the name and logo of a well-known entity to elicit a response from an unsuspecting e-mail recipient. The recipient may be asked for private information (account numbers or passwords), or simply opening the e-mail may provide the vehicle for a virus to be carried to your computer. Many e-mail providers have features that scan incoming messages and attachments for viruses, but they are not foolproof.

E-mail is successfully used as a marketing tool. E-mail marketing is the use of e-mail to promote your business through newsletters, announcements of specials, and the like to customers. The American Society of Travel Agents (ASTA) endorses GreatBIGnews.com as a tool to help travel agents and suppliers create electronic promotional pieces for instant e-mail distribution to their clients. Every business should collect e-mail addresses, as well as *permission* to use them, for all current customers. E-mail is a fast and inexpensive way to reach many consumers with your message.

Advertising via the World Wide Web

Many questions revolve around Web advertising. It is generally inexpensive for advertisers (it is possible to advertise directly to consumers worldwide for only a few hundred dollars a month), but consumers often complain about how annoying it can be. Its effectiveness is debated, yet it is a preferred advertising medium for many.

Web advertisers often prefer "interruption" marketing, sometimes called interstitials. Interstitials can be Web banners, partial or full-page pop-up ads. A Web banner is placed at the top and/or sides of a Web page. The banners act like small billboards to encourage the viewer to "click

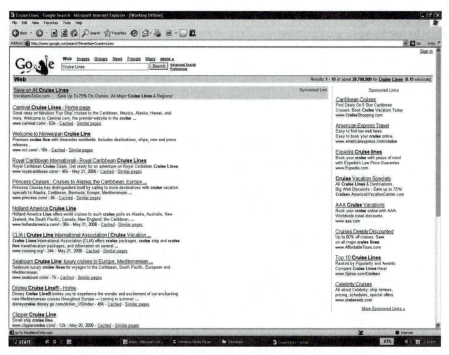

FIGURE 2–2 Sponsored Links are paid for by the advertiser on a "pay per click" basis.

here" to visit another Web site. It is fairly common to see travel-related content in banners and pop-up ads.

Pop-up ads are those uninvited ads that appear over whatever Internet content the viewer is reading at the time. A pop-up may be a partial page ad or a full-page ad that interrupts content, forcing the viewer's attention before he can continue. These advertising forums attempt to grab a consumer's attention with placement, bold color, size, and animation, and they locate themselves on Web sites that are likely to be visited by their targeted consumers.

Another form of Web advertising is the "sponsored links or sponsored results" offered by some search engines. When you query a search engine, the search results page may show small ads along the side of the page. These ads are sponsored by search engines like Google or Yahoo and paid for by the advertiser on a "pay per click" basis. In other words, each time an interested viewer "clicks" his mouse on a sponsored ad in order to view the advertised site, the owner of that site pays a small fee. The ads appear to Web users who are searching for information that may be related. For example, a Google search for "Caribbean cruise" listed several sponsored links from businesses selling cruises. While these advertisements may be helpful to the person searching for information, it's important to keep in mind that the sites advertised are not necessarily more legitimate than any other sites. Search engines that sponsor links place some restrictions on the type of site that may advertise, but the ads are placed to draw your attention to a Web site so you will "visit." Determining the site's quality is largely up to the user. (See Figure 2–2.)

Making Bookings on the Web

Travel counselors are making more and more frequent use of the World Wide Web to make travel reservations for their clients. Supplier sites are well designed and informative. Many suppliers encourage travel agents to use their sites for bookings with *agent only* sections on their Web sites. These private areas offer travel agents access to information and reservation capability that may not be available to the general public.

Internet Case Study

You have spent quite a bit of time quoting prices for a cruise to a new customer. On a call to follow up, the prospective client tells you he has made the reservation online with Carnival Cruise Lines. What would you do?

1. Will you explain to the customer that because he booked his cruise online, you will not receive any commission on the sale even though you have spent considerable time gathering information for him?

2. Will you thank him for contacting you and offer your assistance on future travel arrangements?

3. Will you tell the customer he made a big mistake and hang up on him?

4. None of the above. I would do the following:

_____

_____

E-COMMERCE AND E-MARKETING

Travel suppliers quickly recognized the power of the Internet to reach consumers and began to do business in ways that had never before been attempted. Internet commerce, or e-commerce, is defined as the sale and purchase of products and services over the Internet. The impact of e-commerce on the travel industry has been enormous. One of the industry's largest e-tailers is Expedia. Expedia, and others, have seen enormous growth in a short period. Overall, e-tail sales of travel products and services account for more online sales than any other product.

Advantages of E-Marketing

The major advantages that e-commerce offers are its *global reach* and its *availability twenty-four hours a day, seven days a week.* Customers are not just from down the block anymore. They may not even be in the same city; perhaps not in the same country. Because nearly everything is handled electronically, it's possible for the business to have only minimal staffing. This kind of global marketing and staffing 24 hours per day, 7 days per week (24/7), would be prohibitively expensive for a traditional storefront.

Consumers have displayed their acceptance of online retail as witnessed by the huge growth of Internet sales of all kinds, especially travel. The question facing the travel industry is not *whether* travel consumers will buy online, but *how much.* There are many reasons we have so readily taken to shopping online. *It saves us time.* What previously took a few days of comparison shopping at traditional outlets now requires only a few mouse clicks. We can shop whenever and wherever we want. *We can exert more control* over our shopping experience. For travel consumers, this means we can check prices, availability, details on places to go and things to do, and read reviews by journalists and Web logs (*blogs*) by other travelers before making travel decisions. We *can make changes* to a booked flight and make our own seat assignments. We can print our own boarding pass. No longer must consumers rely solely on travel professionals to provide these things.

Of course, one of the primary advantages the Internet offers to travel consumers is the ability to make their own travel arrangements. Reservations can be made on supplier Web sites (for example, American Airlines, Carnival Cruise Line, or Hertz). In some cases, suppliers offer special online discounts to consumers who book directly via their Web site. Another online option is a large travel agency site like Expedia, Travelocity, or Orbitz. There are also auction sites like http://www.Priceline.com. On an auction site, you first supply your credit card number, then you state the price you are willing to pay for a service such as air transportation between Washington D.C. and Orlando.

If Priceline is able to match your price, you have purchased the tickets. What you cannot do is back out of the purchase if you don't like the flight times, number of stops, or the airline. If Priceline is unable to meet your price, you are not charged, and you have the opportunity to try again using a higher price.

E-Marketing and the Impact on Travel Agencies

Will consumers' ability to make online travel arrangements eventually overtake travel agencies? Some say if the current trend is maintained, the Internet will become the primary source of travel information and reservations in a very short time. On the other hand, the American Society of Travel Agents (ASTA) holds that the majority of business travelers and leisure travelers still prefer to use a travel agent and will most likely continue to do so.

We cannot debate the fact that the number of travel agency locations declined by 31 percent between 2001 and 2005, while at the same time Internet sales continued to grow. Online travel sites have definitely had an impact on the way many travelers make their arrangements.

Yet, there are still many consumers who admit they are just not comfortable doing business online, and many others who simply don't have the necessary hardware, software, or inclination. Some consumers become easily frustrated by slow access, low-quality sites, and sometimes just too much information. A sizable number of travelers say they want and need help sorting through the options and finding the best prices. Further, studies of online travel buyers have found an almost complete lack of loyalty to one Web site. Most use multiple sites when making travel arrangements. Many consumers use the Internet only to gather information about travel without ever making a purchase online.

There are certainly some disadvantages to consumers in buying products and services online. For many consumers, *the lack of personal contact* is problematic. A sizable number of travelers still want help sorting through the options and finding the best prices. Especially when travel planning becomes complicated and expensive, consumers are finding that the Internet isn't for them.

On the Internet, everyone looks the same. To the online consumer viewing only a Web site, a small company appears the same as a big one; a reputable company does business right alongside an unethical one. A beautiful Web site may well be the thing that hooks an unsuspecting consumer into paying for an expensive travel service, only to realize he has been part of an Internet scam.

An ongoing concern for consumers who would like to purchase products on the Internet is the safety of putting personal information, like credit card numbers, on the

Internet. Although most Web sites say their sites are safe, there is still a perception among consumers that this may not be the case.

Some travel agencies have addressed these problem areas by combining the traditional functions of a personalized, storefront business with the convenience and reach of e-commerce. Consumers who know a business exists as a physical store feel more confident turning to its Web site for making a purchase. In combination with a traditional travel agency operation, a Web site can be an attractive addition to a marketing plan.

For their part, travel counselors work hard to address consumers' concerns by providing the personal touch, expert advice, and professional service that are sometimes lacking in online transactions. Despite the surge in online bookings, there remain over 20,000 travel agencies in the United States. We will no doubt learn to exist with multiple distribution channels, including both traditional and new.

Developing a Web Site

It has become almost an imperative for a business to have a presence on the Web. According to some, a small business without a Web site can expect slower growth than the business that develops its e-commerce potential. True or not, a Web site is no longer something we can do tomorrow. Our customers expect us to have a Web site today!

TYPES OF WEB SITES Creating a Web site can be fairly simple to extremely complex. A Web site can be simply *informational*, a one page or multipage site that provides consumers with your location, your product(s), hours of operation, refund policies, and so on. Information Web sites are sometimes called electronic brochures.

A *commerce* site allows customers to purchase products and services directly from a business using its Web site. A commerce site requires complex databases as well as the ability to conduct secure online transactions.

The type of Web presence a business chooses will depend upon its basic business and marketing plan. Before beginning a Web site, it is important to decide who you want to reach with your Web site, and what you want to accomplish.

NAMING AND REGISTERING A WEB SITE A domain name (http://www.mydomain.com) is your unique Web address (URL). Once registered, it cannot be used by anyone else. Because your domain name is the way your customers find you on the Web, choosing an appropriate and memorable name could well be the most important thing your business does. Generally, the shorter your domain name, the better. Not only is a shorter name easier to remember, but it's also easier to type. It's also a good idea to avoid hyphens and underscores in a domain name.

Once you decide on a domain name, you must register it. A simple online search will locate hundreds of companies that register domain names. There is a small annual fee to register each name, but once registered, the name cannot be issued to anyone else as long as you pay this fee. Conversely, you may not use a domain name that is already registered by someone else. The Web site www.whois.net is a domain-based research company that allows anyone to locate available domain names, or to look up information about any domain name such as whom it is registered to, who hosts it, and when the registration expires.

Most people prefer a ".com" domain, because it is so well known, but the travel industry has been instrumental in the development of a ".travel" domain. This will be described in more detail later.

WEB HOSTING You do not need to have a Web host to register a domain name, but you must have a *host* if you want customers to be able to view your site. A Web host stores your Web site's HTML (Hyper Text Markup Language) files and graphics on their servers, generally for a monthly fee. *Server* is the tech name for the remote computer that stores the Web page you want to see. The host's server allows your Web site to be viewed over the World Wide Web. A simple online search will locate hundreds of Web hosting services. A good Web host should offer things like a money back guarantee, 24/7 customer support, access to statistics about your site's visitors, e-mail accounts, and secure servers.

DESIGN A WEB SITE Web site design options include hiring a Web developer (which can be expensive), or designing your own Web site. If you will be selecting a Web developer, look for one that understands something about your business. There are Web developers such as TA Edge (http://www.taedge.com) and Online Agency (http://www.online agency.com) that specialize in developing travel sites. Before deciding on a developer, look at other Web sites the consultant has created to see if they are fully functional, well designed, and if you like them.

If you choose to design your own site, design template software such as Microsoft Front Page, Microsoft Publisher, or travel-specific templates such as those provided by Online Agency (http://www.onlineagency.com), makes it unnecessary for you to be conversant in the Internet language known as HTML. You can write your content, insert it into a template, and the software converts it into HTML text. Design software ranges from free to over $300, but the primary cost of building your own site is your time. The initial creation can be very time consuming, especially if you are creating a commerce site. The job isn't done when the site is completed either. Your site must be edited, refined, and updated on a continuing basis. If this isn't feasible, it's time to hire a professional.

INCREASING YOUR VISIBILITY Unfortunately, just making your Web site available online does not necessarily mean that anyone will see it! It's very easy to get lost in the vast content of the Web. Here is an example: A Google search for "ski vacations" yielded 3½ million responses! If your Web site is among those, how on earth does someone find it?

Your first effort should be to *register your site with several search engines*, such as Google and Yahoo. This can be done at each search engine for free, or you can use a service that will, for a fee, register your URL with several search engines at once. A Web developer should do this as part of a Web site development package.

After you register your site with a particular search engine, it can take months before they actually list you and you begin to see increases in traffic at your site, so promoting your site will be a long-term effort. There are ways to optimize the chances that your Web site will be found in a search, and there are many Web sites available to teach you some of the techniques. If your major goal is to have high rankings and traffic right away, you can pay for the traffic by using sponsored ads or other Internet advertising techniques such as banner ads aimed at consumers who are looking at similar Web sites.

> According to *TravelCLICK,* provider of e-commerce solutions for hotels, they will guarantee subscribing hotels prime positions toward the top of the display of the travel distribution system.

You may never succeed in getting your Web site listed at the top of every search, but some basic marketing can assist your efforts to direct customers to your site. *Display your Web address* on every piece of material that is seen by your customers: business cards, brochures, and letterhead. If you have a storefront, display your Web address on your exterior sign and/or store window. If you advertise in the yellow pages, newspapers, or other print media, list your Web site prominently in the ads. Display your Web address on promotional items you give to customers: coffee mugs, pens, key chains, passport holders, luggage tags, and so on. Link your URL to other sites such as online Yellow Pages, your local Chamber of Commerce, or complimentary travel sites. These suggestions are very low cost and/or free ways to promote your Web site.

If this all sounds a bit overwhelming, hire a professional who may know a few tricks to getting your Web site noticed! With any e-commerce site, giving customers access to your business is only part of the equation. The real power is in finding a way to combine the advantages of e-tail with security, accuracy, value, and excellent customer service.

About Dot Com and Dot Travel

Dot com (.com) was the original domain for commerce Web sites. It has become so common that most Web site developers prefer to have the .com designation. Other common domains are .net, .org, .gov, and .edu. In January 2006, dot travel (".travel") became an official domain. Before .travel could be launched, it had to be approved by ICANN, the Internet Corporation for Assigned Names and Numbers. ICANN is an international nonprofit corporation that maintains oversight responsibility of the Internet.

This was an important development in the travel industry as a way to prescreen owners of the .travel domain, thus lessening the potential that scam artists could possess one. Internet travel scams are a serious concern for the industry. A professional looking Web site can lure customers who pay for vacation packages, hotel rooms, RV and car rentals, and other tourist amenities that are never delivered. In Alaska, a scammer used a URL that was nearly identical to that of the state's Travel Industry Association.

Consumers, believing they were dealing with the state, had no reason to be skeptical, and many ended up being parted with their money. When consumers lose their money in an Internet scam, it is often difficult for law enforcement to track down the origin of the phony Web sites because the scammers deliberately use complicated technology to elude detection.

Unlike the dot-travel domain, a dot-com or dot-net domain name is registered on a first-come-first-served basis, and there are no requirements for registrants to meet any kind of criteria, or to even be legitimate. On the other hand, to hold a .travel domain name, the registrant must be preauthenticated before being granted the right to use a .travel domain. Over 30 travel trade associations around the world, as well as Dunn & Bradstreet, can perform this authentication for any organization that requests a .travel domain.

Consumers can have confidence that the operators of .travel Web sites meet clear, standard, and objective criteria. Thus, consumers can have greater confidence purchasing travel over the Internet through .travel Web sites. Travel businesses will also benefit by being able to more confidently do business with a .travel domain nameholder with which they are not familiar. More information is available at www.tralliance.travel.

SUMMARY

The influence of technology on the business of travel actually began long before the Internet with airline computer reservation and ticketing systems. These systems transformed travel transactions in the 1960s and 1970s, the way the Internet and the World Wide Web have transformed the way travel products and services have been bought and sold in the last 20 years. Online consumer purchases of travel-related services are expected to reach $91 billion by 2009.

The Internet has become an important tool for travel professionals, too. The Web is used as a reference tool, to communicate with customers and other professionals, as an advertising medium, as a booking tool, and to sell travel products.

E-Commerce is the sale and purchase of products and services over the Internet. The impact of e-commerce on the travel industry has been enormous. A Web site has become part of most business plans. A business can choose a simple information site, or a full-blown commerce site, but unless it's promoted in a combination of ways, it's unlikely to be noticed in the vastness of the Internet. To address the issues of security and Internet scams, a dot-travel domain registration exists. Any business using the .travel designator has been preauthenticated and is a legitimate travel business. Only if combined with customer service can a commerce Web site fulfill customer needs.

For additional Travel and Tourism resources, go to http://www.hospitality-tourism.delmar.com.

> PLEASE COMPLETE THE CHAPTER REVIEW QUESTIONS NOW.

Internet Case Study

A small dude ranch in Arizona wants to increase its off-season visitors and encourage repeat business. They want to develop a Web site to meet this goal, but need your help to decide what to do.

1. Develop realistic goals for (a) increasing off-season visitors to the hotel, and (b) encouraging existing customers to return to the hotel.
2. What information should be included on the Web site? Should customers be able to make reservations online?
3. How should the site be promoted?
4. What features of the Web site can be used to maintain contact with current customers?
5. How will you evaluate whether or not the site is successful?

Review Questions

Complete the following questions using the information in Chapter 2.

1. What do you think accounts for the rapid growth of online travel sales?

   _____

   _____

   _____

2. Discuss the following statement: *"The use of e-mail requires that appropriate etiquette be followed."*

   _____

   _____

   _____

3. As a travel professional, how will you utilize the Internet to assist you in selling travel?

   _____

   _____

   _____

4. What is your response to the following statement?: *"Web advertising is generally inexpensive for advertisers, but often annoying to Internet users."*

   _____

   _____

   _____

5. Are the Internet and the World Wide Web the same thing? Explain.

   _____

   _____

   _____

6. Do a Web search for "Web hosts." Compare the prices and features of two hosts and explain why you would select one over the other.

   _____

   _____

   _____

7. Why would a Web site developer want to obtain a dot-travel designation?

   _____

   _____

   _____

8. The Web site http://www.GreatBIGnews.com promotes "e-mail marketing made simple." As a travel professional, why would you want to use e-mail marketing? Go to this Web site and explain the services it offers to travel professionals.

   _____

   _____

   _____

9. *"To the online consumer viewing only a Web site, a small company appears the same as a big one."* Explain how this statement can be an advantage to a small business, but a disadvantage to a consumer.

_____

_____

_____

10. What are some basic marketing techniques that could be used to direct customers to your Web site?

_____

_____

_____

11. Why is it important to improve search precision when using a search engine such as Google?

_____

_____

_____

12. Go to http://www.google.com and browse "Web search help." From the information you find, select and discuss four things a person can do to make a Google search more precise.

_____

_____

_____

13. Go to http://www.smartbrief.com/about. Describe this tool and its importance for travel professionals.

_____

_____

_____

CHAPTER
3

Travel in the Twenty-First Century

OBJECTIVES

At the conclusion of this chapter, you will be able to

- communicate the importance of, and the government's role in, safe travel.
- recognize security precautions, such as biometrics, and know why there is controversy surrounding their use.
- understand common travel scams and how to deal with them.
- express the philosophy of ecotourism, and understand its importance in travel and tourism.

KEY TERMS

biometrics
Department of Homeland
  Security (DHS)
ecotourism
geotourism

identity theft
prohibited items
sustainable tourism
United States Transportation Security
  Administration (TSA)

travel insurance
travel scams
U.S. State Department

INCREASING GLOBAL AWARENESS

In recent years, the travel industry has been buffeted by significant international events such as terrorist attacks, the expanding war on terrorism, outbreaks of contagious diseases such as "Bird Flu" and SARS, hurricanes, floods, and tsunamis. In addition to these issues, travelers have concerns about airport security, security at hotels, security on cruise ships and trains, travel scams, thieves, pickpockets, and identity theft. The ease of global communications and greater media focus on global issues have given consumers a heightened awareness of all health and safety issues, and an increased need to protect themselves while traveling both at home and abroad.

Not only do global events affect tourism, but tourists also interact with the destinations to which they travel. With increased global awareness has come more emphasis on how travel and tourism affect the world's environment. Since the United Nations designated 2002 as the International Year of Ecotourism, "ecotours" have become much more prevalent. Ecotours are one of the fastest growing segments of the industry with millions of tourists seeking out such products.

It is imperative that travel professionals be knowledgeable about global phenomena. In this chapter, we will examine some twenty-first century travel issues: how health and safety issues affect the business of travel, and how the traveler interacts with the world in which he travels.

TRAVELING SAFELY

Attitudes and practices surrounding travel safety changed drastically with the terrorist attacks of September 11, 2001. Until September 11, 2001, travel in the United States and internationally had grown steadily for many years. The terrorist attacks on the World Trade Center and the Pentagon stopped us in our tracks. Travel fell by more than 40 percent for several weeks after the attacks. In 2001 travel agency sales fell 16 percent from 2000 levels—only the second time since 1985 that total annual sales did not increase.

Industry experts predicted a full recovery for the travel industry, and, as predicted, the numbers began to slowly rise. Increased security precautions at airports, along with great travel bargains, encouraged people to start traveling again. Since that catastrophic incident, the world has experienced others. Yet, except for brief downturns, travel has continued on a fairly steady course. To Americans, and many others in the world, travel is a value we cherish. We simply cannot imagine giving it up.

Travelers have, however, become much more sensitive to concerns about their health and safety. The governments of the United States and other countries have implemented stringent security measures at airports, borders, national monuments, hotels, cruise ships, and train stations. It has been, and continues to be, a daunting task.

While these new measures have given us added security, they have also meant that travelers must adapt to some degree of inconvenience. Travelers have had to develop an increased awareness plus a few new coping skills. Often the best coping strategy is preparation. The more we know and the better we prepare, the less we will be affected by circumstance. Travel professionals can play an important role in seeing that their clients are well prepared for any travel experience.

The Government and Our Security

Immediately following a terrorist attack, security naturally tops the list of traveler concerns. Travelers may choose to avoid large metropolitan areas, air travel, cruise ships, major sporting events, or anything perceived as likely terrorist targets. Often, the most immediate effect is the fear of flying. A number of people will avoid air travel for some time after a major catastrophe. The **United States Transportation Security Administration (TSA)** was created in response to the terrorist attacks of September 2001 as part of the Aviation and Transportation Security Act signed into law by President George W. Bush on November 19, 2001. TSA was originally in the Department of Transportation but was moved to the Department of Homeland Security (see next page) in March 2003.

TSA's mission is to protect the nation's transportation systems by ensuring the freedom of movement for people and commerce. In February 2002, TSA assumed responsibility for security at the nation's airports and by the end of the year had deployed a federal workforce to meet challenging Congressional deadlines for screening all passengers and baggage.

TSA's Pledge to Travelers consists of seven points:

- We pledge to do everything we can to ensure that your flight is secure.
- We pledge to treat you with courtesy, dignity, and respect during the screening process.
- We pledge that if additional screening is required, we will communicate and explain each step of the additional screening process.
- We pledge to honor your request for a private screening at any time during the screening process.
- We pledge that if additional screening of your person is required, it will be provided by a screener of the same gender.
- We pledge to accept all feedback and to consider your input as a vital part of our effort to continually enhance the screening experience.
- We pledge to respond to your comments in a timely manner.[1]

FIGURE 3–1 The Department of Homeland Security was created in 2002 as an executive department of the United States.

The **Department of Homeland Security (DHS)** (see Figure 3–1) was created in 2002 as an executive department of the United States. Its mission is stated as follows:

a. Prevent terrorist attacks within the United States.
b. Reduce the vulnerability of the United States to terrorism.
c. Minimize the damage, and assist in the recovery, from terrorist attacks that do occur within the United States.

DHS inherited the professional workforce, programs, and infrastructure of the Coast Guard, Customs Service, Immigration and Naturalization Service, and the Transportation Security Administration. Collectively these public servants are responsible for protecting our nation's transportation systems and supervising the entry of people and goods into the United States. This is no easy task given that 730 million people travel on commercial aircraft each year and that there are now more than 700 million pieces of baggage being screened for explosives each year. Additionally, there are 11.2 million trucks and 2.2 million railcars that cross into the United States each year. Also, 7,500 foreign flagships make 51,000 calls in U.S. ports annually.

DHS is responsible for protecting the movement of international trade across U.S. borders, maximizing the security of the international supply chain, and engaging foreign governments and trading partners in programs designed to identify and eliminate security threats before these arrive at U.S. ports and borders.[2]

The Transportation Security Administration has published these guidelines for air travelers. Following these tips will help you reduce your wait time at the security checkpoint.

Before the Airport

- Do not pack or bring **prohibited items** to the airport. Read the *Permitted and Prohibited Items* list at the TSA Web site.
- Place valuables such as jewelry, cash, and laptop computers in carry-on baggage only. Tape your business card to the bottom of your laptop.
- Avoid wearing clothing, jewelry, and accessories that contain metal. Metal items, sometimes even small ones like hair clips or belt buckles, may set off the alarm on the metal detector.
- Avoid wearing shoes that contain metal or have thick soles or heels. Many types of footwear will require additional screening even if the metal detector does not alarm.
- Put all undeveloped film and cameras with film in your carry-on baggage. Checked baggage screening equipment will damage undeveloped film.
- Declare firearms and ammunition to your airline and place them in your checked baggage.
- If you wish to lock your baggage, use a TSA-recognized lock.
- Do not bring lighters or prohibited matches to the airport.
- Do not pack wrapped gifts and do not bring wrapped gifts to the checkpoint. Wrap on arrival or ship your gifts prior to your departure. TSA may have to unwrap packages for security reasons.

At the Airport

- Each adult traveler needs to keep available his or her airline boarding pass and government-issued photo ID until exiting the security checkpoint. Due to different airport configurations, at many airports you will be required to display these documents more than once.
- Place the following items *in* your carry-on baggage or in a plastic bag prior to entering the screening checkpoint:
  - Mobile phones
  - Keys
  - Loose change
  - Money clips
  - PDAs (personal data assistants)
  - Large amounts of jewelry
  - Metal hair decorations
  - Large belt buckles
- Take your laptop and video cameras with cassettes *out* of their cases and place them in a bin provided at the checkpoint.
- Take *off* all outer coats, suit coats, jackets, and blazers.[3]

Airport and Airline Security

Security measures of one type or another are here to stay. The exact methods of examining airline passengers to determine whether they carry dangerous materials will no doubt change many times as technology catches up with the demand for better and faster methods. Airlines and airports are considering several options for business travelers, frequent fliers, and others who wish to speed their progress through security checkpoints. Privacy advocates, on the other hand, warn that we must scrutinize security methods for their degree of personal invasiveness. The Federal Aviation Administration, International Air Transport Association (IATA), airlines, and other industry groups are searching for the best compromise. Meanwhile, businesses are rushing to develop the best and quickest screening devices.

Although the amount of time varies widely among airports, anyone who flies will, at some point, have to wait at an airport security checkpoint (Figure 3–2). To speed the security process, new technology is being explored for use in airport security applications to provide faster and more reliable screening. "Puffer" machines can be used to detect trace amounts of explosives with a brief puff of air directed at a passenger during a security screening. "Image interpretation" software is used at security checkpoints to spot dangerous objects that passengers may attempt to carry on the aircraft. The software, taken from the medical field, provides three-dimensional color images that can be rotated 360 degrees.

A promising science is called **biometrics**. This is the digital analysis of biological characteristics such as facial structure, fingerprints, iris patterns, or voice recognition using cameras or scanners. These characteristics are then matched to profiles contained in large databases. Some experts say face recognition may be the most promising biometric technique for crowded airports.

Another technique involves securing an individual's biometric data and then comparing the data to existing databases of known or suspected terrorists. The prescreened information is placed on a chip on a thin card, which can then be used by the cardholder to pass through security checkpoints without further screening. A few private companies are offering programs of this type for a fee of about $80 annually.

Although promising, biometrics has been the subject of much controversy among privacy advocates who claim there are not enough safeguards to keep information private and prevent mistakes. The question that remains for travelers is one of priority: Will we trade personal privacy for personal security?

Security for Ships, Trains, and Hotels

Cruise lines, railroads, and hotels have also tightened security. The changes may not be as apparent as those at airports, but here are some things you may notice.

- *On cruise ships.* Cruise lines are working closely with law-enforcement officials and federal agencies, including the U.S. Coast Guard, the U.S. Citizenship and Immigration Services, and the Federal Bureau of Investigation. Cruise ship personnel train for all kinds of emergencies, including hijacking and terrorist attack. A change in itinerary is always a possibility to avoid danger areas. In most cases, passengers must show a passport or a birth certificate plus government-issued photo ID prior to embarkation. Luggage and carry-on articles are much more likely to be searched, and security personnel are more visible on board. The American Association of Port Authorities (AAPA) has seen significant increases in its funding from the Department of Homeland Security for port security.

- *At hotels.* Working with local authorities, some U.S.-based hotel chains have heightened security at their properties in the United States and abroad. According to hotel officials, most of the changes are "behind the scenes," meaning that hotel guests are not likely to see many overt security measures. Some high-profile locations have added bomb sniffing dogs to their security patrols, and some utilize biometric data for hotel safes.

- *On the train.* Amtrak now requires passengers to show a photo ID when purchasing tickets from station ticket agents or when checking baggage or sending packages. There are more uniformed officers in stations and aboard trains, and increased security inspections and patrols around bridges and tunnels.

FIGURE 3–2 Anyone who files, will, at some point have to wait at airport security checkpoint.

Security at Parks and Monuments

The National Park Service has heightened security at a number of parks and monuments, particularly in the New York City and Washington, D.C., areas. Theme parks have also stepped up security. At Walt Disney parks and resorts, for example, visitors will see more patrols and can expect to have their bags searched at entry points. Parking structures may be closed early or access may be limited after hours.

Border Security

Travel between the United States and Canada, Mexico, and the Caribbean has become more complicated and time consuming. U.S. Customs officers are searching everyone and everything entering the United States. This means delays, sometimes long ones, when crossing borders. Canada, Mexico, and most of the Caribbean require U.S. travelers to carry a U.S. passport. Information and estimated waiting time at key crossings are available on a government Web site, http://www.cbp.gov.

Being Prepared

As private industry and government scramble to find better ways to thwart terrorism and more reliable ways to make travelers secure, passengers will be faced with an increased level of inconvenience. Minimizing the inconvenience may be a simple matter of being prepared. There are some things that a traveler can do.

- *Plan to arrive early.* Most airlines are suggesting that travelers arrive at least two hours before a scheduled domestic departure, and three hours prior to an international flight. Call the airline in advance to find out how much time should be allowed.
- *Carry proper identification.* IDs are closely scrutinized, so carry a photo ID (such as a passport or driver's license), or two forms of ID, one of which must be government issued.
- *Pack smart.* The TSA publishes an extensive list of permitted and prohibited items on their Web site. Don't take questionable materials; buy hairspray or a disposable razor at your destination.
- *Pack light.* The trip through security will go more quickly if everyone carries less stuff. Be especially aware of cameras, DVDs, radios, laptop computers, and cell phones as these items are being closely scrutinized.

It is always smart to do some research on general travel information and on the destination to which you will be traveling. The United States Bureau of Consular Affairs offers several publications to assist travelers. Some publications are more general in nature, such as "A Safe Trip Abroad," or "Medical Information for Americans Traveling Abroad." Others offer specific information for travel to various parts of the world, such as "Tips for Travelers to Canada," "Tips for Business Travelers to Nigeria," or "Tips for Travelers to China." A complete list of Consular Affairs publications can found be on the Government Printing Office Web site (http://bookstore.gpo.gov).

TAKE PRECAUTIONS AGAINST TRAVEL SCAMS

The security precautions we are most often faced with are those designed to prevent terrorism. The governments of most countries have many programs in effect to minimize the threats of terrorism to travelers. However, an individual traveler is much less likely to be a victim of terrorism than a victim of a crime or a scam. Travel scams consistently rank near the top of the list of complaints received by the Federal Trade Commission (FTC). By mail, e-mail, fax, phone solicitation, or your own Internet research, the promise is the same: a marvelous travel experience for very little money. Being a victim of a scam can just as easily occur while traveling. Understanding common scams can be a helpful tool for tourist and travel professionals alike. It is important to take precautions, and to make some conscious decisions about behavior while traveling. Some basic precautions may well be the difference between being a victim of a scam or a crime or not.

- First, be informed about the destination. Check the U.S. State Department's travel Web site to make sure there aren't warnings, advisories, or announcements that might affect travel plans.
- Purchase travel insurance. Travel insurance can protect a traveler from many types of calamities, but not all policies are created equal. Look for coverage of such events as medical emergencies, including medical evacuation, trip cancellation/interruption, baggage damage, and identity theft. Identity theft has been identified by the Federal Trade Commission as American's fastest growing consumer crime. It affects thousands of travelers annually with an average loss of $11,000.
- Photocopy all documentation, including passport, flight tickets, hotel reservation confirmation, medical insurance policies—anything with your name on it. Make two copies, one set to leave at home, in case your family needs to come to your rescue, one set to take with you. An added precaution is to e-mail yourself any information you may need in case of an emergency, such as contact information

for consular offices where you are staying, emergency numbers for lost or stolen credit cards, insurance help lines, and so on. If you have a Web-based e-mail account (e.g., Hotmail or Yahoo!), you can access your e-mail from any computer in any cybercafe worldwide.

• Be smart about money. Carry a minimal amount of cash. Use debit and/or credit cards instead of cash. Keep some of your money in a separate place, so if your wallet or purse is stolen, you'll still have some money. Don't advertise the fact that you have money (or jewelry or possessions). That's an open invitation to criminals.

• Be alert. Criminals and scam artists look for people who are not paying attention to their surroundings. Make it a habit to be aware of people around you—a pickpocket can be anyone from a child to a woman holding a baby. Use simple precautions like carrying your money next to your skin and in front of you, not in back.

• Carry a cell phone. If you are unable to communicate emergency contact information, a quick check of your cell phone directory can product a wealth of information—if a stranger knows what to look for. Enter your emergency contact under "I.C.E." (*In Case of Emergency*) so that a stranger could easily locate it.

• Be aware of health concerns. If traveling internationally, call the International Travelers Hot Line at the Centers for Disease Control in Atlanta, Georgia at 404-332-4559. Information includes vaccination requirements, food and water precautions and reports on current disease outbreaks worldwide. Pack your prescription medications with care and include information on the prescription. Some doctors suggest packing a back-up supply and storing it separately in case your original is lost or stolen. Include your favorite nonprescription pain relievers, cold medicines, antidiarrheal medications, and so on. Consider what you will do if you become sick traveling abroad. If an American citizen becomes seriously ill or injured abroad, a U.S. consular officer can assist in locating appropriate medical services and informing family or friends. If necessary, a consular officer can also assist in the transfer of funds from the United States. However, payment of hospital and other expenses is the responsibility of the traveler. Before going abroad, learn what medical services your personal health insurance will cover overseas. If your health insurance policy provides coverage outside the United States, carry both your insurance policy identity card as proof of such insurance and a claim form. Although many health insurance companies will pay "customary and reasonable" hospital costs abroad, very few will pay for your medical evacuation back to the United States. Medical evacuation can easily cost $10,000 and up, depending on your location. Travel insurance may cover some or all of these costs for as little as $3 or $4 per day. An extensive listing of over 50 medical evacuation and travel insurance companies can

be found at the U.S. State Department Web site. A traveler going abroad with any preexisting medical problems should carry a letter from the attending physician, describing the medical condition and any prescription medications, including the generic name of prescribed drugs. Any medications being carried overseas should be left in their original containers and be clearly labeled. Travelers should check with the foreign embassy of the country they are visiting to make sure any required medications are not considered to be illegal narcotics.

Travel Purchase Scams

A few of the more common scams involved in selling travel follow.

• E-mails, faxes, or mail announcing that you have been "chosen" to win a free vacation, free airfare, or a hotel stay—especially when you know you haven't entered anything. Recently, the FTC has noted an increase in fraudulent travel promotions advertised through unsolicited faxes—sometimes disguised to look as if they're from a travel company the consumer may recognize.

• Advertisements for bargain basement prices or "discount travel certificates" available if you agree to a presentation from a "time-share" company. These presentations are usually extremely high-pressure sales pitches designed to sell a few weeks of "ownership" in a vacation property.

• Travel clubs that require you to pay a fee for participation and in return promise travel discounts for all cardholders. While there are many legitimate travel clubs, this is a very common scam.

• Two-for-one or "companion" scams that offer you two tickets for the price of one when in reality the cost of one ticket is as much, if not more, than you would have paid for two separately.

• Telemarketers who promise great travel packages if you agree to pay now, over the phone. These are often skilled salespeople who know how to put the pressure on and avoid answering specific questions about the offer until after you fork over a credit card number.

• Fraudulent Web sites are often quite elaborate, making it difficult to differentiate between a quality vendor and a travel scam artist. The Internet has given travelers incredible access to travel information, but with that has come the necessity to constantly be on guard against the possibility of being scammed.

The American Society of Travel Agents provides the following suggestions when evaluating travel offers:

• "Be extremely skeptical about postcard and phone solicitations that say you've been selected to receive a fabulous vacation."

- "Never give out your credit card number unless you initiate the transaction and you are confident about the company with which you are doing business."
- "You should receive complete details in writing about any trip prior to payment. These details should include the total price; cancellation and change penalties, if any; and specific information about all components of the package."
- "If you insist on calling a 900 number in response to a travel solicitation, understand the charges and know the risks."
- "Walk away from high-pressure sales presentations that don't allow you time to evaluate the offer, or that require that you disclose your income."
- "Be suspicious of companies that require that you wait at least 60 days to take your trip."[4]

There is another scam that travel professionals and travelers should be especially aware of. Consumers can fall victim to "instant travel agent" offers. Some companies may offer to sell identification that will "guarantee" discounted rates from cruise lines, hotel companies, rental car companies, or airlines. In reality, the companies that sell this identification have no control over discounts. Only the actual supplier of the services can extend professional courtesies such as discounted rates to true travel professionals.

Scams while Traveling

Awareness of possible scams and staying alert are often the best preventative, but even those who are frequent travelers can fall victim to a well-orchestrated scam. Scammers are very inventive and are constantly developing new ways to part a traveler from his money. It pays to be alert to a few common themes.

LOCAL TRANSPORTATION Travelers are dependent upon local transportation. Nearly everyone has heard about the scenic tour by taxi. In this scam a taxi driver takes advantage of the fact that you don't know the city and drives the long way to the hotel or other destination, thus running up a large fare. You can't learn every city in advance, but it might pay to ask the hotel what the usual taxi fare is to your destination.

Drivers may be paid "commissions" by hotels and attractions to deliver tourists. Don't rely upon information given by local drivers, and if you are concerned, insist upon your original destination.

Another common scam is being cheated for the price of a journey. Often this is done by people who hang around the bus or train pretending to be drivers or conductors. They ask for the fare and then disappear. Avoiding this one is as simple as asking for a ticket. If they won't give you a ticket, don't give them any money.

TRANSACTIONS INVOLVING MONEY, CREDIT CARDS, AND VALUABLES Don't rely on anyone who changes currency to do it accurately and honestly. It's important to have at least a reasonable idea of how much money you expect to get back. And count your change. This means you must know how much an item costs, and how much you should get back.

Overcharging for goods and services is institutionalized in some countries. A traveler should have at least a general idea of hotel prices and the like. You may be expected to bargain for a better price, but not always. The best way to avoid being overcharged is to walk away if you think the price is out of line.

Credit card transactions are usually the safest way to make purchases, but even so, card numbers can be stolen, or the card itself can be stolen. Keep receipts and check them against the card statement after you return home. Report any discrepancies to the credit card issuer.

Using hotel safes may not always be safe. While *all* of your valuables may not be stolen from a "safe," a few notes or travelers checks may be removed, making it difficult to prove that they were ever there. Your credit cards may be removed for a short time while the thief goes on a shopping spree. The best practice is to keep money, credit cards, and travelers checks on you, and don't bring "valuables" when you travel.

TAKING ADVICE OF LOCALS In general, these scams are based on offering you free advice or assistance that may result in your paying for something you otherwise would not want, or going someplace you may not want to go. If it sounds "too good to be true," don't do it. Travelers often don't want to offend a friendly local citizen, and unfortunately scam artists prey upon that. It isn't necessary to be rude; just walk away if the conversation makes you uncomfortable. If that doesn't work, feel free to yell for help.

ECOTOURISM

Tourists often have a huge impact upon the destinations they visit. That impact can be a financial blessing for the economy, but it can also cause devastating damage to fragile environments. There is a tenuous balance between the travel industry and those who want to retain the ecology and conserve resources. The travel industry on one side is seen as promoting unlimited travel of the globe, which if badly managed, can overrun and ruin a destination; conservationists, on the other hand, are seen to be promoting environmental concerns over all others. Somewhere in the middle is ecotourism or sustainable tourism. Since the United Nations designated 2002 as the International Year of Ecotourism, interest in ecotourism has developed in many directions. It is currently one of the fastest growing segments of the tour industry.

Defining Ecotourism

Tourism is not a passive activity. When we visit a destination, we interact with the destination and its resources. Well-managed tourism can provide an area with jobs and other financial incentives for wildlife and historic preservation and cultural enrichment. The hope is that by promoting sustainable tourism, local people will have not only income, but also a powerful incentive to conserve and protect their own resources.

The International Ecotourism Society (TIES) was founded in 1990 and they describe themselves as the oldest and largest ecotourism organization in the world. TIES has defined ecotourism as *"responsible travel to natural areas that conserves the environment and improves the well-being of local people"* (Figure 3–3). The organization further states that "those who implement and participate in ecotourism activities should follow the following principles:

- Minimize impact
- Build environmental and cultural awareness and respect
- Provide positive experiences for both visitors and hosts
- Provide direct financial benefits for conservation
- Provide financial benefits and empowerment for local people
- Raise sensitivity to host countries' political, environmental, and social climate
- Support international human rights and labor agreements"[5]

A related concept is geotourism, which the Travel Industry Association of America and the National Geographic Society define as tourism that sustains or enhances the geographical character of a place—its environment, culture, aesthetics, heritage, and the well-being of its residents. Geotourism encompasses all tourism to the extent that residents of a location have a vested interest in protecting the resources that people are coming for, whether historic, cultural, gastronomic, environmental, or other.

Who's Who in Ecotourism

There are many organizations, public and private, working to further the goals of sustainable tourism. A few noteworthy organizations are the United Nations Environmental Program (UNEP); United Nations Educational, Scientific, and Cultural Organization (UNESCO); World Tourism Organization (WTO); World Travel and Tourism Council (WTTC); the World Conservation Union; and National Geographic. Business Enterprises for Sustainable Tourism (BEST), a program of the International Tourism Partnership, is an international consortium of educators committed to furthering the development and dissemination of knowledge in the field of sustainable tourism.

It is evident from only this small list that there are many influential organizations contributing to the effort to define, promote, and certify ecotourism. There are many hundreds of less well known organizations and people who contribute their resources toward the goals of sustainable tourism.

Certifying the "Ecolabel"

Although there are possibly hundreds of ecocertification programs in existence, there are no universal standards to determine how legitimate the certification really is or on what standards it is based. This causes difficulty for a travel professional or traveler who is shopping for a destination, tour, or accommodation that adheres to the standards of ecotourism. Just having an "ecolabel" is not a guarantee of anything.

Both Green Globe 21 and the World Heritage Convention are two organizations that have developed high performance standards for ecotourism. Green Globe 21 was developed by the World Travel and Tourism Council. Since 1999, it has certified accommodations, destinations, and tour operators around the world. While not actually a certification program, the World Heritage Convention, administered by UNESCO, has chosen 700 sites worldwide based on rigorous evaluation of their standards to conservation.

There are many other groups that use responsible guidelines before applying the ecolabel. If you are unfamiliar with the certifying organization, do a bit of online research to determine its credentials before trusting its

FIGURE 3–3 Ecotourism means conserving and respecting the environment.

certification. Despite all the certification programs that exist (good and bad), only 1 percent of the world's tourism products carry any ecocertification. It's fairly obvious that one of the great difficulties with certification is that there is so little of it.

The Ecotourist

By some estimates there are more than five million ecotourists—the majority come from the United States, Europe, Canada, and Australia. There is very little statistical data on who can be classified as an ecotourist. In general, we can probably assume that these are travelers who have made some definite choices about their travel experience: the type of travel they purchase, the destinations they choose, the tour operators they use, and the ways in which they conduct themselves while traveling.

Because the goals and concepts of ecotourism are not widely understood, it often gets confused with "adventure" tours or any tour related to a nature experience. These do not necessarily promote the goals of sustainable tourism. In fact, some tour operators may use the terms "ecotourism" and "green-friendly" and behave in environmentally irresponsible ways.

Without rules for certifying a location or accommodation as fit to use the ecolabel, it falls in the lap of travel professionals, and ultimately the ecotourist, to make informed decisions and demand high standards. Understand the goals of ecotourism and get detailed information about any organization you intend to use. Determine whether the businesses you patronize have environmentally friendly policies with regard to water, waste disposal, energy, and so on. Know the features of the tour and judge for yourself whether the activities are such that local people and cultures are respected and will benefit from your having been there, or whether the environment has been compromised by your presence.

Tourists can make a difference by making conscientious choices. The Ecotourism Society, National Audubon Society, American Society of Travel Agents, and other concerned organizations have developed guidelines for travelers. They include in part

- Travel in the spirit of humility, showing appreciation for things you see.
- In wilderness areas remain on marked trails; keep 20 to 30 feet (6 to 9 meters) from wildlife; do not take anything (plants, rocks, shells, seeds, animals); do not introduce anything (plants, seeds, animals) to the environment.
- Never litter or leave waste in a wilderness area; when at sea, don't dump plastic or nonbiodegradable garbage overboard.

- Remember your cultural background is one among many; show respect for the way other people think and do things. Don't expect or demand special privileges because you're American.
- Study before you go, learning local customs and several phrases so you can be courteous and communicate with local people.
- Respect the privacy and dignity of local people; ask before taking photos.
- Never purchase products made from endangered plants or animals, including orchids, cacti, sea turtles, crocodiles, snakes, lizards, pangolin (anteaters), ivory, wild birds and their skins and feathers, coral, furs of spotted cats, marine mammals, and polar bears.
- Don't give local kids candy or encourage them to ask for handouts.
- Don't make promises to local people that you cannot keep.
- Do support and contribute to local conservation efforts.

SUMMARY

The twenty-first century traveler must be more prepared and more aware than ever before. It is the responsibility of every travel professional to assist travelers in developing these skills. The governments of many countries have structured policies and practices that they believe will help to protect tourists, but ultimately it becomes the traveler's responsibility to stay safe. A traveler is much more likely to be a victim of a scam or crime than of terrorism. Being aware of scams involving travel purchases and those that can happen while traveling can be the difference between being cheated or not.

We now understand that tourism is not just a passive activity. It is an interaction with a destination and its resources. Ecotourism seeks to promote responsible travel that conserves the environment and promotes the wellbeing of people. Because ecotourism is not yet well understood, and certification is not prevalent, it is up to each of us to be familiar with the goals of sustainable tourism and make conscientious decisions about the travel experiences we choose. If unchecked, tourism can lead to the depletion of an area's resources.

For additional Travel and Tourism resources, go to www.hospitality-tourism.delmar.com.

PLEASE COMPLETE THE CHAPTER REVIEW QUESTIONS NOW.

Review Questions

Complete the following questions using the information in Chapter 3.

1. Do you think measures taken by the U.S. government to protect travelers are sufficient? Explain.

   _____

   _____

   _____

2. A client, who is a frequent traveler, tells you that time spent waiting in security lines at the airport is getting longer and longer. Do you have any information that might help your client?

   _____

   _____

   _____

3. Although promising, biometrics has been the subject of much controversy among privacy advocates. What is your response to this concern?

   _____

   _____

   _____

4. What is an "instant travel agent" offer?

   _____

   _____

   _____

5. What does it mean when we say, "Tourism is not a passive activity"?

   _____

   _____

   _____

6. Tourists can make a difference in promoting sustainable tourism by making conscientious choices. What are some of these choices? Is it realistic to expect tourists to travel responsibly?

   _____

   _____

   _____

7. An individual traveler is much less likely to be a victim of terrorism than a victim of a crime or a scam. Discuss precautions a traveler can take against being victimized.

   _____

   _____

   _____

SECTION II

Geography for Travel Professionals

CHAPTER 4
Basic Travel Geography

CHAPTER 5
Travel Destinations

Basic Travel Geography

OBJECTIVES

At the conclusion of this chapter, you should be able to

- identify the various aspects that make up geography.
- identify the continents, oceans, and navigation lines.
- define various geographical terms.
- understand the effects wind, ocean currents, and weather have on various destinations.

KEY TERMS

continents	hemispheres	oceans
equator	International Date Line (IDL)	parallels of latitude
Greenwich Meridian	jet stream	trade winds
Gulf Stream	Meridian of Longitude	

Ask twelve different people to define the word *geography* and you will undoubtedly receive twelve different answers. Interestingly enough, each answer may be correct, as far as each answer goes. Most dictionaries and encyclopedias define geography as "the study of spatial variation on the Earth's surface and of humankind's relation to its environment," or something similar. Think of the world's great oceans, deep gorges, majestic mountains, and raging waterfalls. Think of humankind's development and migration throughout the centuries and how we have adapted to particular terrains and weather conditions. These are part of the study of geography as well.

Knowing the height of various mountains and the length of particular rivers will certainly be helpful to the game-show contestant, but what geographical knowledge is important for the travel counselor? Knowing where major cities are located, why travelers want to visit particular destinations, major sightseeing attractions, and the best time of the year to visit are certainly all part of the study of geography viewed from a travel perspective. However, as you advance your study of geography, you will find that understanding each destination's history, culture, ethnic groups, religion, and art is of great benefit to your clients.

This chapter covers only the most basic elements of travel geography that will give you a firm grounding of the subject. There are a few excellent books about travel geography from which you can acquire a much more thorough knowledge of the subject. One of the best books available to travel students is *Travel Around the World,* published by Weissmann Travel Reports. To learn more about this book, use the Web site http://www.travelaroundtheworld.net.

USING MAPS

Maps come in all sizes, shapes, and colors, but all of them show, to one degree or another, the world's land masses, known as **continents**, and the four major **oceans**. It is interesting to note that some maps, or rather those who make the maps (cartographers), do not always agree on the number of continents. Everyone agrees on the first five: Africa, Antarctica, Australia, North America, and South America. But some maps identify two more, Europe and Asia, while others show these two combined into one continent called *Eurasia*. Of the oceans, everyone agrees that there are four: Atlantic, Arctic, Indian, and Pacific.

When looking at different types of maps, it is important to know about *land mass distortion*. Depending on the map, areas of land in the northern and southern regions may appear larger than they actually are. For example, look at any rectangular flat map of the world and compare the size of Greenland to that of Australia. You would say that Greenland is most definitely larger. Now compare the size of Greenland and Australia on a globe. Which is larger? The correct answer is Australia. Why? Because the world is a globe, land masses become enlarged as they are stretched to fit into a flat rectangular map. The only true way to judge size is by using a globe.

> If you compare a map that was prepared in the United States to one published in Europe, for example, you will notice that certain locations do not have the same names. A typical example of this is Vienna, Austria. Vienna is the English spelling; the correct spelling is actually *Wien!* At the end of this chapter you will find a list that details many similar spelling differences.

Depending on the type of map you are viewing, you may see horizontal and vertical lines, some of which have names. You may also notice that these lines are marked with degrees. These degrees, both horizontally and vertically, equal 360, the total number of degrees in a circle. All of these are used for navigation and location.

The horizontal lines are called **parallels of latitude**. Of the five lines that are named, the **equator** (0 degrees) is the most important. By following the equator around the world, you see that the Earth is divided into two halves, called **hemispheres**, and you see the Northern and Southern Hemispheres. Starting at the North Pole and moving south, the other named lines are the Arctic Circle, the Tropic of Cancer, the Tropic of Capricorn, and the Antarctic Circle.

Because the Earth is tilted on its axis, the seasons are reversed in the Northern and Southern Hemispheres. During June, July, and August, the Northern Hemisphere is warmer because it is tilted toward the sun, and thus these months are considered summer. But during December, January, and February, the Southern Hemisphere is closer to the sun. If your client says he wants to go snow skiing in August, don't discreetly laugh at him; send him to New Zealand, Chile, or Argentina!

Of the vertical lines, called **Meridian of Longitude**, two are named. At zero degrees, you will see the **Greenwich Meridian**, also known as the Prime Meridian. On the opposite side of the Earth at 180 degrees is the **International Date Line (IDL)**. By starting at the North Pole and following these two lines to the South Pole, the Earth is once again divided into halves. These are the Eastern and Western Hemispheres. Which is which? Because time is measured in relationship to the Greenwich Meridian, everything from this meridian west to the International Date Line is the Western Hemisphere, which includes North and South America. From the Greenwich Meridian east to the International Date Line you see the Eastern Hemisphere, including Europe, Africa, Asia, and Australia.

> The United States and a handful of other countries measure map distances in miles. The vast majority of the world uses kilometers. A *kilometer* is .6 of a mile.

By studying maps in closer detail, you also see a variety of terms, some of which may be familiar to you.

Geographical Terms

archipelago (say "are-keh-*pel*-ah-go"): an island group

atoll: a coral island, generally shaped like a ring or a horseshoe

bay: a body of water that is open to the sea and mostly surrounded by land

canyon: a gorge or deep chasm that has steep sides

cape: a narrow strip of land that projects into the sea

cay or caye (usually pronounced "key"): a low coral or sand reef or island

delta: the area at which a river or stream empties into a larger body of water

fjord (say "fee-*ord*"): a sea inlet bordered by high cliffs

glacier: a mass of slowly moving ice that has formed over thousands of years

gulf: a body of water, usually circular in shape, that is part of a larger body of water

isthmus (say "*is*-mus"): a narrow strip of land that connects two larger land masses

peninsula: a landform, larger than a cape, that extends into the sea

plain: a large area of flat land that usually has few trees

plateau (say "pla-*toe*"): an area of flat land that is elevated from the land around it

reef: a line of coral or rock formations located under the sea

strait: a narrow channel of water that connects to larger bodies of water

WINDS, WATER, AND WEATHER

Wind patterns and water currents, in addition to land topography, help determine our weather. These factors are instrumental in understanding the best time to visit various parts of the world.

Oceanic currents in the Northern Hemisphere generally move in a clockwise direction. If you look at a map of the North Atlantic, you can visualize water known as the Gulf Stream, moving from the northwest coast of Africa toward the equator, along the northeast coast of South America, past the southeast coast of North America, and on toward Europe. The water is warmed near the equator and carries this warmth as it moves north. This warmth gradually dissipates, so we can understand why the water off the coast of Florida is warmer than off the coast of northwest Africa.

The United States measures temperature in Fahrenheit, but the rest of the world uses Celsius, also known as *centigrade*. To convert Celsius to Fahrenheit, use Celsius $\times$ 2 + 32. To convert Fahrenheit to Celsius, use Fahrenheit $-$ 32 $\div$ 2. Please note: These conversion formulas result only in approximate temperature, but they are quick and easy.

In other parts of the Northern Hemisphere, similar movement of water is taking place: the cold California Current in the eastern part of the Pacific and the warm Japan Current in the western Pacific. In the Southern Hemisphere, oceanic currents generally flow in a counterclockwise direction. These currents include the cold Humboldt, which is located off the coasts of Peru and Chile in South America, and the cold Benguela current off the coast of southwest Africa.

Air currents generally move in an eastwardly direction north of the Tropic of Cancer in the Northern Hemisphere and south of the Tropic of Capricorn in the Southern Hemisphere. These winds are called the jet stream, or the *westerlies*. Have you ever wondered why a flight from Washington, D.C., to San Francisco might take four hours, while the return flight only three and one half hours? The answer is the jet stream!

Winds between the two tropics typically flow in a westwardly direction and are known as the trade winds. This air movement is usually very humid and is especially noticeable in Central and northern South America as well as northern Australia because there are no major mountains or other features to disrupt the air flow.

Mountains have an effect on both weather and temperature. As damp winds run into mountains, precipitation is released on the side of the mountains the wind first hits, known as the windward side. The leeward, or opposite side of the mountains, receives less rain and/or snow. As damp winds hit very high mountains, the direction of the wind turns back on itself and fog is often the result.

As one climbs a mountain or simply travels to a higher elevation, the air becomes less oxygen-rich and cooler. For every 1,000 feet/305 meters in elevation, the air cools

Important Industry Web Sites

Mapblast: **http://www.mapblast.com**

Time Zone Converter: **http://www.timezoneconverter.com**

Weatherbug: **http://www.weatherbug.com**

Weather Worldwide: **http://www.intellicast.com**

Worldclock: **http://www.timeanddate.com**

World Tourism Office: **http://www.towd.com**

Common and Proper Spelling Chart

Variations of Major European Place Names

Common Name - Proper Name - Country

Antwerp - Antwerpen - Belgium *	Epidavros - Epidauros - Greece	Naples - Napoli - Italy
Athens - Athinai - Greece	Florence - Firenza - Italy	Nessebur - Nessebăr - Bulgaria
Balearic Islands - Islas Baleares - Spain	Geneva - Genéve - Switzerland	Nuremberg - Nürnberg - Germany
Belgrade - Beograd - Serbia	Genoa - Genova - Italy	Oostend - Ostend - Belgium *
Bourgas - Burgas - Bulgaria	Ghent - Gent - Belgium *	Padua - Padova - Italy
Breslau - Wroclaw - Poland	Hamelin - Hameln - Germany	Patras - Pátrai - Greece
Brunswick - Braunschweig - Germany	Heraklion - Iraklion - Greece	Pilsen - Plzeň - Czech Republic
Brussels - Bruxelles - Bruges - Belgium *	Hydra - Idhra - Greece	Prague - Praha - Czech Republic
Bucharest - Buchuresti - Romania	Ieper - Ypres - Belgium *	Rhodes - Rodhos - Greece
Canary Islands - Islas Canarias - Spain	Ithaca - Ithaki - Greece	Rome - Roma - Italy
Carlsbad - Karlovy Vary - Czech Republic	Kazanlik - Kazanlăk - Bulgaria	Rousse - Ruse - Bulgaria
Chios - Khíos - Greece	Kortrijk - Courtrai - Belgium *	Santorini - Thira - Greece
Coblence - Koblenz - Germany	Kyustendil - Kjustendil - Bulgaria	Seville - Sevilla - Spain
Cologne - Köln - Germany	Lesbos - Lesvos - Greece	Slunichev Bryag - Slančev Brjag - Bulgaria
Constance - Konstanz - Germany	Leuven - Louvain - Belgium *	Sparta - Sparti - Greece
Copenhagen - København - Denmark	Liège - Luik - Belgium *	Stettin - Szczecin - Poland
Corfu - Kérkyra - Greece	Lisbon - Lisboa - Portugal	The Hague - Den Haag - Netherlands
Courtrai - Kortrijk - Belgium *	Lucerne - Luzern - Switzerland	Thessaloniki - Salonika - Greece
Cracow - Krakow - Poland	Majorca - Mallorca - Spain	Turin - Torino - Italy
Crete - Kriti - Greece	Milan - Milano - Italy	Tournai - Boomik - Belgium *
Danzig - Gdańsk - Poland	Minorca - Menorca - Spain	Vienna - Wien - Austria
Doomik - Tournai - Belgium *	Moscow - Moskva - Russia	Venice - Venezia - Italy
Drouzhba - Družba - Bulgaria	Munich - München - Germany	Vojens - Skrydstrup - Denmark
Eleusis - Elvsís - Greece	Mycenae - Mikínai - Greece	Warsaw - Warszawa - Poland

* *Note:* French and Flemish are both official languages of Belgium. The variations of place names in this country are not a matter of common and proper names but are of the two languages.

3.5 degrees F/1.5 degrees C. Air temperature reduction due to altitude is know as *lapse rate*. The reduction in oxygen is not usually a problem below 5,000 feet/1,524 meters, but at higher elevations, travelers may experience altitude sickness. (See Chapter 16 for more on altitude sickness.)

In many parts of the world, weather determines the best or the worst time of the year to visit. There are some very good weather-related Web sites that you can use to learn about weather trends and conditions for any destination. You will also find this information in many of the travel reference sources and guides.

maps and the general dispersion of land and water upon our planet.

The equator creates the Southern and Northern hemispheres, and because of the Earth's tilt on its axis, the seasons are reversed. Because of this, so-called "high-season" is not the same time of the year worldwide. Being aware of other factors such as air and oceanic currents helps us to understand why weather conditions in a particular location are what they are. All of these are within the study of geography and understanding them is crucial to helping travelers select appropriate destinations.

SUMMARY

Knowing the length of a river, height of a mountain, or population of a country is fine, but the successful travel counselor knows that the subject of geography is much more varied. To adequately assist their clients, travel professionals must have an understanding of how to use

For additional Travel and Tourism resources, go to http://www.hospitality-tourism.delmar.com.

PLEASE COMPLETE THE CHAPTER REVIEW QUESTIONS NOW.

Review Questions*

1. Identify the seven continents. _____
   _____

2. Identify the four oceans. _____

3. Why is a globe usually more accurate than a flat map when comparing the sizes of land masses? _____
   _____
   _____

4. What are the Parallels of Latitude? _____
   _____

5. What are the Meridians of Longitude? _____
   _____

6. What two lines create the Eastern and Western Hemispheres? _____
   _____

7. What line creates the Northern and Southern Hemispheres? _____
   _____

8. Are the seasons the same throughout the world? Why or why not? ___
   _____
   _____

9. How is distance measured in most of the world? _____

10. Convert 30 kilometers into miles. _____

11. In your own words, define these terms.
    a. plateau _____
       _____

    b. cay or caye _____
       _____

    c. peninsula _____
       _____

    d. glacier _____
       _____

    e. delta _____
       _____

    f. fjord _____
       _____

*Source: "A Guide to Becoming a Travel Professional" Student Workbook.

12. What is the Gulf Stream? _____

_____

13. How is temperature measured in most of the world? _____

14. Convert 27 degrees Celsius to Fahrenheit. _____

15. What is the jet stream? _____

_____

CHAPTER

5

Travel Destinations

OBJECTIVES

At the conclusion of this chapter, you should be able to

- identify many of the world's most important tourist areas.
- name various tourist attractions and discuss why they are popular.
- locate the most important tourist attractions and sites.
- discuss in detail various tourist designations and define their popularity.

Why do travelers select the destinations they do? What makes a destination popular? There are as many answers as there are possible destinations. Considering that entire books have been written that cover only one country or portion of a country, we cannot cover this topic in depth here. However, the following gives you a basic understanding of some of the more popular destinations of the world and why they are so.

Each list includes sites and attractions that are arranged alphabetically. Each listing includes its location, and many listings also include pertinent information and a brief description. Where relevant, dates are also included, identified as either B.C.E. (before the common era) or C.E. (common era). These identifiers replace B.C. and A.D., and you will see these new identifiers in all of the newer texts and reference sources.

In the following lists, we have tried to include areas and attractions that are the most important and popular. However, although we have made every effort to remain objective, it is difficult, if not impossible, to do so. For example, if you ask two people to name the most impressive tourist area or attraction, you will no doubt receive two different answers. We apologize if we have omitted your favorite in any of these lists.

ARCHEOLOGICAL SITES AND MYSTERIOUS PLACES

- *Abu Simbel, Egypt.* Built by the Pharaoh Ramses II in 1300 B.C.E., the site includes the Great Temple and the Temple of Nefertari (favorite wife of Ramses II). The Great Temple is sculpted from living rock and is faced by four statues of Ramses II that are 65 feet (20 meters) high. Inside are three major halls, the largest of which is 58 feet (17.4 meters) deep and 54 feet (16.2 meters) wide. Thanks to the efforts of UNESCO and many supporting nations in 1959, these temples were saved from flooding when the Aswan High Dam was built; the entire complex was cut into blocks and moved to higher ground.

- *Altun Ha, Belize.* Mayan city, trading, and ceremonial center, dating from about 550 C.E., abandoned around 1000. Notable structures include the Temple of the Green Tomb and the Temple of the Masonry Altar (60 feet/18.3 meters high).

- *Ankor Wat, Cambodia.* King Jayavarman II began this Hindu temple complex (later converted to Buddhist) in the 9th century C.E. By 1431, it was all but abandoned by the Khmer Empire. The walls of the complex are 2 1/2 miles (4 kilometers) in circumference. The central block measures 717 by 620 feet (215 by 186 meters) and is 200 feet (60 meters high). The entire complex is covered with delicate bas relief carvings and magnificent friezes.

- *Carthage, Tunisia.* Dating from 814 B.C.E., this major Phoenician city and home of Hannibal was destroyed by the Romans in 146 C.E. The site includes baths, dwellings, temples, theatres, villas, shrines, and the naval port.

- *Chaco Ruins, New Mexico, U.S.* Remains of the Anasazi cliff-dweller structures dating from 750 C.E. Important areas include the 800-room, four-story Pueblo Bonito and the Great Kiva, which is 53 feet (16 meters) in diameter.

- *Chan Chan, Peru.* Located in a desert region between the Pacific Ocean and the Andes Mountains, this city covers nine square miles (23.3 square kilometers). At its zenith, Chan Chan boasted nine royal compounds and a population of 50,000 people.

- *Chichén Itzá, Yucatán, Mexico.* One of the primary Mayan centers dating from 432 C.E., occupied by the Toltecs from 982. Important sites include the Cenote Sagrado (sacred well); Ball Court; Temple of the Jaguars; El Castillo; 1,000-column court; and other pyramids, temples, and towers.

- *Colloseum (Flavian Amphitheatre), Rome, Italy.* Constructed in 70 C.E., this arena could hold 55,000 spectators. It measures 620 by 513 feet (186 by 154 meters) and is 157 feet (47 meters) high. Originally, spectators were sheltered from the sun by a retractable roof as they watched gladiators, slaves, and exotic animals fight to the death.

- *Copan* (say "koh-*pahn*"), *Honduras.* Mayan city dating from 436 C.E. Important buildings include the Stairway of the Hieroglyphs (2,500 individual glyphs), Ball Court, plazas, pyramids, stelae, and huge sculpture of humans.

- *Delphi, Greece.* Dating from 1400 B.C.E., this site has been one of prophecy. The Oracle (Pythia) was believed to have divine sight and was consulted by Hercules, Oedipus, and Alexander, among others. Other important buildings include the Athenian Treasures, which was used for offerings, the Theatre, and the Temple of Apollo.

- *Easter Island (Rapa Nui), Chile.* Two thousand miles (3,218.7 kilometers) off the coast, the primary draw of this location is the statues. Called *Moai*, these statues are of unknown origin, and there are over 1,000 of them. Quarried in the central part of the island, they were dragged to the coast and stood upright, facing inland. The Moai range in height from 12 to 32 feet (3.7 to 9.8 meters) and weigh between 20 and 30 tons.

- *Ephesus, Turkey.* Founded between 1500 and 1000 B.C.E., this city is noted for the House of the Virgin Mary; the Temple of Artemis; the theatre, gymnasium, and baths; and the Library of Celsius.

- *Giant's Causeway, Northern Ireland, United Kingdom.* Along a 3½ mile (5.6 kilometer) stretch of coastline are some 40,000 octagonal basalt pillars that are joined to each other. Caused by magma eruptions, they range from 50 feet (15.3 meters) in height.

- *Great Pyramids, Giza, Egypt.* The largest was built for the Pharaoh Cheops (Khufu). Each side measures 756 feet (230 meters). It is 481 feet (147 meters) high and contains 2½ million blocks that weigh from 2 to 15 tons each. Inside are granite chambers and passageways; originally, the outside was faced with Tura limestone. The other two major pyramids in the complex were built for Pharaohs Chephren (Khafre) and Mycerinus (Menkaure).

- *Great Zimbabwe, Zimbabwe.* Built of dry-fit stone blocks, this ancient city and trade center is of unknown date and origin. The enclosure measures 830 feet (253 meters) in circumference and ranges in height from 16 to 35 feet (4.9 to 10.78 meters). Within the enclosure is a mysterious conical tower, 30 feet (9 meters) high, with no doors, windows, or stairs.

- *Knossos, Crete (Kriti), Greece.* Here you will see the 1,500-room palace of King Minos. Dating from about 1600 B.C.E., the palace was three stories high and covered 237,000 square feet (22,018 square meters). It was the reputed site of the Labyrinth and the Minotaur who roamed within.

- *Leptis Magna, Libya.* Begun by the Phoenicians in the 10th century B.C.E., this city of 80,000 people was later under the control of the Numidians, followed by the Romans. Interesting sites include the law courts, forum (over 100 columns), shops, triumphal arches, temples, baths, amphitheatre, and harbor.

- *Machu Picchu* (say "mah-*shoo* pea-*shoo*"), *Peru.* Known as the "Lost City of the Incas," Machu Picchu is located in the Andes Mountains at an altitude of 8,000 feet (2,438.4 meters). Rediscovered in 1911, the site includes over 200 houses, palaces, the Temple of the Sun, and the Temple of the Three Windows (trapezoidal in shape). All of the structures were constructed of finely hewn stone without the use of mortar.

- *Mesa Verde, Colorado, U.S.* The Anasazi arrived here in the sixth century, and by 1200 C.E., there were over 600 dwellings. By 1300, the site was abandoned. The dwellings were multistory apartment complexes and were originally painted with red and white designs. To reach their homes, these cliff-dwellers used ladders or hand and toe holds in the rock.

- *Ming Tombs, near Beijing, People's Republic of China.* The site contains the tombs of 13 Ming Emperors, the most noted of which is that of Emperor Wan Li (Zhu Yijun) and his wives. The tomb is surrounded by beautiful gardens, pagodas, and statuary. Each tomb is linked by huge archways along the Sacred Way.

- *Moenjodaro, Pakistan.* The world's first planned city, Moenjodaro began in 2500 B.C.E. of kiln-fired brick. By 1900 B.C.E., the city was in decline. Today we see the remains of the Great Bath, homes, Assembly Hall, and Granary. Strangely, there are no known temples or religious structures in Moenjodaro.

- *Mycenae, Greece.* Dating from 1500 to 1200 B.C.E., this is one of Greece's oldest cities. Structures of note include the Treasury of Athens, Royal Burials, Amphitheatre, and the Lion Gate.

- *Nazca Lines, Peru.* This mysterious site is estimated to date from 900 B.C.E. to 630 C.E. and covers the Nazca Plateau. On this plateau are hundreds of dead straight lines, geometric shapes, fish, birds, and insects. The drawings in the earth are so large (100 yards/90 meters up to several miles/kilometers) that they can be clearly seen only from the air.

- *Palenque* (say "peh-len-*kay*"), *Chiapas, Mexico.* One of the most beautiful Mayan sites, it is surrounded by jungle with a stream running through it. Notable structures include the Temple of the Sun, the Temple of the Count, and the Temple of the Foliated Cross. Perhaps the most important is the Temple of the Inscriptions, which contains the tomb of Pacal. The lid of Pacal's sarcophagus weighs five tons.

- *Parthenon, Athens, Greece.* Located on the Acropolis, the Parthenon is the most famous of several temples on the site. It was constructed in 438 B.C.E. of white marble and was originally brightly painted. The magnificent friezes (Elgin Marbles) can be seen in the British Museum in London.

- *Persepolis, Iran.* Begun by Darius I in 515 B.C.E., this city was the ceremonial center of the Persian Empire. The Palace Audience Chamber could hold 10,000 people and was reached by a double reversed staircase, which was designed for people to mount while seated upon their horses. Other areas of note are the monumental statues and gateways, harems, and barracks.

- *Petra, Jordan.* Dating from 4000 B.C.E., this Nabatean city was carved from solid rock and supported a population of 30,000 people. Known as the "Rose City," it actually appears orange, purple, vermilion, and yellow as the sun's angle changes. The city is entered through a 1-mile- (1.6-kilometer-) long ravine with sheer rock walls that soar to a height of 328 feet (100 meters). Once a popular rest stop on six caravan routes, Petra is now famous for its ten-story high building known as the Treasury.

- *Pompeii, Italy.* This city of 20,000 people was buried under 20 feet (6 meters) of ash when Mt. Vesuvius erupted in 79 C.E. Today's visitors can see homes, shops, theatres, the amphitheatre, baths, mosaics, frescoes, temples, and tombs.

- *Roman Forum, Rome, Italy.* From about 600 B.C.E., this was the center of the city and included the law courts, temples, civic buildings, shops, markets, and courtyards. What you see today was buried under 30 to 50 feet (9 to 15 meters) of rubble and is the result of excavations that began in the 1700s.

- *Sphinx, Giza, Egypt.* Thought to be the face of King Chephren, the Sphinx has the body of a lion. The paws are

50 feet (15 meters) long and the total length is 150 feet (45 meters). Originally brightly painted, the Sphinx has suffered badly from erosion. Its missing nose is the result of Turkish gunfire.

- *Stonehenge, England, United Kingdom.* Estimated to date from 3500 B.C.E., these giant megaliths make up one of the most mysterious places on Earth. The primary stones were quarried in Northern Wales, weigh approximately 26 tons each, and are 16 feet (5 meters) high. Arranged in a horseshoe, there are ball-and-socket joints on two so that the lintels (flat top stones) could be held in place. In the center is the altar stone and outside the primary horseshoe are lesser stone circles. Of unknown origin (the site pre-dates the Druids by many centuries), the Druids use the site for modern-day rituals.

- *Temple of Karnak, Karnak, Egypt.* Approached by the Avenue of the Sphinxes, this series of temples dates from about 1500 B.C.E. Of particular note are the Hypostyle Hall (54,000 square feet/5,000 square meters), the Sacred Lake, and temples dedicated to various Egyptian gods.

- *Temple of Luxor, Luxor, Egypt.* Begun in 1400 B.C.E. by Amenhotep III, the temple has been expanded by each of his successors. Within the complex are courtyards, massive statues, colonnades, and hypostyles. Originally dedicated to the god Amun, today's visitors may be surprised to see the remains of an ancient Christian Church and the Abu Haggag Mosque.

- *Teotihuacan* (say "tay-ah-tee-wah-*kahn*"), *near Mexico City, Mexico.* At its peak (300 to 600 C.E.), the city covered over eight square miles (20.7 square kilometers) and was home to approximately 150,000 people. Aztec and Toltec influences can be seen in the primary structures, including the Pyramid of the Sun (216 feet/65.8 meters high), Pyramid of the Moon (150 feet/45.8 meters high), the Avenue of the Dead, and the Temples of Tlaloc and Quetzalcoatl.

- *Tikal* (say "tih-*kahl*"), *Guatemala.* Mayan city covering 50 square miles (80.5 square kilometers) with a population of 45,000 at its height; deserted about 900 C.E. Tikal is noted for its ornately carved stelae (upright stone shafts), the Temple of the Jaguar Priest, Temple of the Giant Jaguar (187 feet/57 meters high), the Great Plaza, Plaza Mayor, and the Temple of the Masks.

- *Tulum* (say "too-*loom*"), *Quintana Roo, Mexico.* Enclosed Mayan fortress-city on the coast dating from about 600 C.E., although most of the structures date after 1200. Tulum is a popular shore excursion for cruise passengers. Important buildings include El Castillo, Temple of the Descending God, and Great Palace.

- *Ur, Iran.* This Sumarian ziggurat (stepped temple) was built of solid brick. It measures 210 by 140 feet (63 by 42 meters) and is 54 feet (16 meters) high. On top is the Sacred Shrine, which is reached by a triple staircase. The walls that separate the temple from the city were built by Nebuchadnezzar.

- *Uxmal* (say "oosh-*mahl*"), *Yucatán, Mexico.* One of the most important later Mayan cities, dating from 600 C.E. Major buildings include the Temple of the Magician, the Nunnery, the Great Pyramid, Ball Court, the Governor's Palace, and House of the Turtles.

- *Valleys of the Kings, Queens, and Nobles, Egypt.* The most famous of these rock-cut tombs is that of Tutankhamun. It was discovered in 1922, and many of the tomb's riches can be seen in the Cairo Museum or in traveling exhibits. Other important tombs include those of Seti I, Amenhotep II, Amenophis II, Ramses III, Ramses IV, Horemhep, and Tutmosis III.

- *Xi'an Tomb, People's Republic of China.* The tomb of China's first emperor, Qin Shi Huangdi, covers close to 6 acres (2.4 hectares) and was built in 200 B.C.E. To guard the tomb's entrance, the emperor ordered that 8,000 life-sized warriors be crafted in terra cotta, each one armed with wooden and bronze weapons along with hundreds of horses. It is estimated that the entire complex covers 20 square miles (51.8 square kilometers).

- *Xunantunich* (say "zsoo-*nan*-too-*neech*"), *Belize.* Mayan city that flourished between 300 and 900 C.E. Includes the 130-foot- (39.6-meter-) high El Castillo, beautiful stucco friezes, and the vaulted palace known as "A-11."

BEACHES

Almost every state, province, or country that has a coastline may also have beaches. All of them are not necessarily popular with tourists. All of the islands in the Caribbean offer beaches and are visited to one degree or another by leisure travelers. The beach areas listed here represent many of the most frequently visited destinations in the world.

- Acapulco, Mexico
- Algarve, Portugal
- Amalfi Coastal Region, Italy
- Ambergris Caye, Belize
- Bali, Indonesia
- Bondi Beach, Sydney, Australia
- Bora Bora, French Polynesia
- Cable Beach, New Providence Island, Bahamas
- Cancun, Mexico
- Cannes, France
- Caragena, Colombia
- Copacabana, Rio de Janeiro, Brazil
- Costa del Sol, Spain
- Cozumel, Mexico
- Daytona Beach, Florida, United States
- Fort Lauderdale, Florida, United States

- Fort Myers, Florida, United States
- Gold Coast, Queensland, Australia
- Hawaii, United States
- Hilton Head, South Carolina, United States
- Huatulco, Mexico
- Ipanema, Rio de Janeiro, Brazil
- Ixtapa/Zihuatanejo, Mexico
- Jerbi Island, Tunisia
- Lucaya Beach, Great Bahama Island, Bahamas
- Mar del Plata, Argentina
- Margarita Island, Venezuela
- Mazatlan, Mexico
- Miami Beach, Florida, United States
- Montego Bay, Jamaica
- Moorea, French Polynesia
- Myrtle Beach, South Carolina, United States
- Negril, Jamaica
- Nice, France
- Ocho Rios, Jamaica
- Pattaya, Thailand
- Phuket, Thailand
- Seychelles
- St. Croix, U.S. Virgin Islands
- St. Petersburg, Florida, United States
- St. Thomas, U.S. Virgin Islands
- St. Tropez, France
- Tahiti, French Polynesia
- Tampa, Florida, United States
- Virginia Beach, Virginia, United States

BUILDINGS, STRUCTURES, AND GARDENS

Castles, Palaces, and Mansions

- *Alcazar, Segovia, Spain.* Eleventh-century castle that includes the Throne Room, Tower of John II, Salon de la Galera, Pieze del Cordon, and Royal Apartments.

- *Alhambra Palace, Grenada, Spain.* This thirteenth-century walled fortress was built by Mohammed I. Important areas include the Puerta de la Justitia, Court of Myrtles, Court of Lions, Generalife Gardens, Hall of the Ambassadors, and Hall of Kings. Considered by many to be the star of the palace is the Room of the Two Sisters, with its celestial ceiling containing over 4,400 tiny plaster honeycomb cells.

- *Atomium, Brussels, Belgium.* Replica of an iron molecule, 165 billion times actual size.

- *Big Ben, London, England, United Kingdom.* Although the clock tower of the Houses of Parliament is usually referred to as "Big Ben," Big Ben is really the 13-ton bell in the 316-foot- (96-meter-) high tower. As the clock strikes every quarter hour, Big Ben's sound is heard all over the city.

- *Biltmore Mansion, near Asheville, North Carolina, United States.* Modeled after a French chateau, George W. Vanderbilt began his 250-room mansion in the 1890s, setting it within an 8,000-acre (3,237-hectare) park. On the estate are approximately 75 acres (30.4 hectares) of formal gardens and a winery.

- *Blarney Castle, Republic of Ireland.* In the upper level of the castle suspended over a shaft is a special stone, reputed to give those who kiss it the "gift of gab." To kiss the stone you must lie on your back, bending your head backwards, with someone holding your feet. Other areas of interest on the grounds are a Druid stone circle, the Witch's Stove, and the Dungeon.

- *Blenheim* (say "*blehn*-hem"), *England, United Kingdom.* Begun as a hunting lodge for King Henry I, Blenheim became the home of John Churchill, Duke of Marlborough, and the birthplace of Sir Winston Churchill. Noted areas include the formal gardens, Long Library, Green Writing Room, Red Drawing Room, and the State Bedrooms.

- *Bognor Botanical Garden and Orchid House, Jakarta, Indonesia.* Garden featuring over 12,695 plant species.

- *Breakers, Newport, Rhode Island, United States.* In 1893, Commodore Cornelius Vanderbilt began work on his Italian Renaissance "summer cottage." On an 11-acre (4.5-hectare) estate sits his 70-room mansion with its roofed central courtyard. Entire rooms were crafted in Europe, imported to the site, and reassembled. Of particular note are the Library and Grand Dining Room.

- *Brooklyn Bridge, New York City, New York, United States.* Suspension bridge built in 1889 at a total length of 5,989 feet (1,825 meters).

- *Buckingham Palace, London, England, United Kingdom.* Built in 1703 for the Duke of Buckingham and Candos, the palace is now the official royal residence in London. For a limited time each year, the palace is open to the public, but the most popular attraction takes place outside: the Changing of the Guard. Important rooms include the Queen's Picture Gallery, Queen's Gallery, and the lavishly furnished State Rooms.

- *Butchart Gardens, Victoria, British Columbia, Canada.* Founded in 1904 and covering about 50 acres (20 hectares), this is one of the most impressive gardens in the world.

- *Capiland Suspension Bridge, Vancouver, British Columbia, Canada.* Soaring 230 feet (70 meters) over the river, this bridge really does swing.

- *Chambord, France.* Built between 1519 and 1541, this was the royal hunting lodge of Francois I who spent only 27 days there. The roof has a profusion of towers, chimneys, gables, turrets, and pinnacles. Within this 440-room "lodge" is a magnificent double spiral staircase.

- *Chenonceaux, France.* This summer house was built in 1515 for Thomas Bohier. The house is attached to a five-arched bridge over the River Cher with a gallery above.

- *Chrysler Building, New York City, New York, United States.* This art-deco building was begun in 1928 and is 1,048 feet (319 meters) tall. The top is eclipsed by a seven-story pinnacle.

- *CN Tower, Toronto, Ontario, Canada.* Built in 1976, this 1,820-foot- (555-meter-) high tower is topped by a seven-story Sky Pod, which houses a 400-seat revolving restaurant.

- *Doge's Palace, Venice, Italy.* Built for Doge Francesco Foscari in the 1340s, the façade is covered with arches, carved pillars, and a colonnaded balcony. The palace is connected to the law courts and prison by the Bridge of Sighs. Major sites in the palace include the Staircase of Gold and the Hall of the Great Council.

- *Eiffel Tower, Paris, France.* Built in 1883, this tower is 985 feet (300 meters) tall; there are three observation levels. The huge base measures 410 feet (125 meters) on each of the four sides.

- *Ellis Island, New York City, New York, United States.* Landing site for 12 million immigrants from between 1897 and 1938.

- *Empire State Building, New York City, New York, United States.* Built in 1931, this skyscraper has 102 floors and is 1,252 feet (381 meters) tall.

- *Faneuil Hall Marketplace, Boston, Massachusetts, United States.* Restored historic district offering a variety of shops and restaurants.

- *Fisherman's Wharf, San Francisco, California, United States.* Dating to 1846, the wharf area now offers a variety of restaurants, shops, and recreational opportunities.

- *Fontainebleau Palace, near Paris, France.* Built in 1270 for King Louis IX, the palace boasts the White Horse Courtyard with double staircase, Great Pavilion, Galerie Francois Ier, Marie Antoinette's Apartments, Red Room, Council Room, and Throne Room.

- *Forbidden City, Beijing, People's Republic of China.* Home of the Imperial Family from 1368 through 1911. The complex includes six palaces and 800 other buildings. The palaces are identified as the Halls of Earthly Peace, Union and Peace, Heavenly Peace, Protective Harmony, Medium Harmony, and Supreme Harmony.

- *Gateway Arch, St. Louis, Missouri, United States.* At its base, the arch's width is the same as its height: 630 feet (192 meters) wide.

- *Golden Gate Bridge, San Francisco/Sausalito, California, United States.* Built in 1933, this suspension bridge is 1.7 miles (2.7 meters) long.

- *Gota Canal, Sweden.* This 300-mile- (485-kilometer-) long canal connects the Baltic and North Seas via rivers, lakes, and manmade structures.

- *Grand Central Station, New York City, New York, United States.* Built in 1913, this is one of the most spectacular train stations in the world.

- *Hearst Castle, California, United States.* The fancy of William Randolph Hearst, the estate's buildings cover 90,080 square feet (8,368 square meters). The buildings incorporate 41 fireplaces and 61 bathrooms. In the main "house" there are 38 bedrooms, a wine cellar, Hidden Terrace, Private Suite, and libraries.

- *Hofburg Palace, Vienna, Austria.* This thirteenth-century palace includes the Grand Staircase, Festival Hall, Ceremonial Hall, Marble Hall, Radetzky Apartments, Ambassador's Staircase, Chamber of the Guards, and Hall of Knights.

- *Hoover Dam, Nevada/Arizona, United States.* Built in 1931 on the Colorado River, it is the highest concrete dam in the Western Hemisphere at 726 feet (221.3 meters). At the base, the dam is 660 feet (201 meters) thick.

- *Jantar Mantar, Jaipur, India.* Observatory built by Jai Singh II in 1726.

- *Jardin Botanique, Montreal, Quebec, Canada.* Founded in 1931, this botanical garden boasts over 21,000 plant species.

- *Jardin du Luxembourg, Paris, France.* Originally laid out in the seventeenth century, it is the only surviving Renaissance garden in Paris. Of interest are the numerous statues, monuments, and fountains.

- *Keukenhof (Kitchen) Garden, Netherlands.* Sixty-five-acre (25-hectare) garden boasting over 6,000,000 flowering plants.

- *Khalili Bazaar, Cairo, Egypt.* Ancient section of the city with narrow, winding streets and alleyways offering a variety of shops, stalls, and carts.

- *Le Jet d'Eau, Geneva, Switzerland.* Europe's tallest fountain at 476 feet (145 meters) high.

- *Leaning Tower of Pisa, Pisa, Italy.* Built in 1173 as the cathedral's bell tower, it is 200 feet (60 meters) tall and leans at a precarious angle. The 297-step circular staircase can be climbed to the top, but the stairs have been (and probably will be again) closed at various times due to structural problems.

- *Linderhof Palace, Germany.* Built in 1870 for King Ludwig II of Bavaria, this palace is high rococo with gold gilding everywhere. In front is the gold Neptune Fountain and on the grounds are the Grotto and Moorish Kiosk.

- *Mann's Chinese Theatre, Hollywood, California, United States.* Built in 1927 and formerly known as Graumann's, the theater is bordered by the foot and hand prints as well as the autographs of over 200 stars of stage and screen.

- *Marble House, Newport, Rhode Island, United States.* In 1888, William K. Vanderbilt began work on his "summer cottage." The result includes the Ballroom, the Gold Room, and the Gothic Room, all filled with medieval and Renaissance objects of art and magnificent stained glass windows.

- *Monet's House, Giverny, France.* The artist's home and gardens, many of which are subjects of his paintings.

- *Neuschwanstein* (say noi-*schvahn*-stine), *Germany.* Built by King Ludwig II of Bavaria in 1869, the fairy-tale castle was used by Walt Disney as a model for Sleeping Beauty's Castle. Ludwig used Wagnarian themes, heavy Gothic decor, and ornate and delicate woodcarving throughout the castle. Visitors can see the Royal Bedroom and the Throne Room as well as the artificial stalactite grotto.

- *Nijo Castle, Kyoto, Japan.* Home of the Shogun Tokugawa Ieyasu, the castle was built in 1601. The main structure has 33 rooms, including the magnificent Audience Chamber. On the grounds are gardens and the Karamon Gate.

- *Nymphenburg Palace, Munich, Germany.* The palace and pavilions were built in 1664 for the Electress Henrietta Adelaide and are laid out around gardens, artificial lakes, and streams. The baroque Amalienburg Pavilion features the rococo Central Hall and Mirror Room. Other pavilions include the Pagodenburg and the Badenburg.

- *Oxford University, Oxford, England, United Kingdom.* Of outstanding architecture, the first college was founded in 1263. Today there are 35 colleges.

- *Panama Canal, Panama.* Link built in 1914 between the Atlantic and Pacific Oceans, the canal is 50 miles (80.5 kilometers) long. In the center is Gatun Lake. The entire crossing takes between eight and ten hours.

- *Picadilly Circus, London, England, United Kingdom.* This circular intersection of six major streets is the center of the West End and southern boundary of the Soho District.

- *Ponte Vecchio, Florence, Italy.* Built in 1345 over the River Arno, shops jut out from the sides, just as they did in its early years.

- *Potala Palace, Lhasa, Tibet, People's Republic of China.* The present palace was begun in 1645 by the fifth Dalai Lama, and it covers 1,399,308 square feet (130,000 square meters). The palace was the seat of Tibetan government until Tibet was annexed by China. Within the palace are the tombs of past Dalai Lamas, ceremonial rooms, and religious schools for monks.

- *Royal Palace, Madrid, Spain.* Built in 1738 for Philip V. Noted areas include the Royal Apartments, Main Staircase, Throne Room, Porcelain Salon (walls and ceiling are of fine porcelain), Armeria Real, and Sala del Gasparini.

- *Royal Palace, Stockholm, Sweden.* Built in 1692 for Carl XI, this is the largest palace in the world. It contains 600 furnished rooms on three floors, all decorated in baroque or rococo. Within the Royal Apartments are exceptionally fine porcelains, portraits, tapestries, and a solid silver throne. Within the vaults are the Royal Armory and Treasury.

- *Schönbrunn Palace, Vienna, Austria.* Seat of the Habsburg Austrian Empire, built for Maximilian II in 1569. The palace is of baroque architecture and features the Great Courtyard and Gloriette Triumphal Gate. Important rooms include the Blue Salon, Salon of Million, and the Hall of Mirrors where six-year-old Mozart and his sister entertained with a concert.

- *Sears Tower, Chicago, Illinois, United States.* At 1,450 feet (492 meters) and 110 stories, this is the tallest building in the United States.

- *Space Needle, Seattle, Washington, United States.* Constructed for the Seattle World's Fair, the needle is 605 feet (184 meters) high.

- *Space Tower, Rotterdam, Netherlands.* Tower topped by a revolving restaurant.

- *Spanish Riding Academy, Vienna, Austria.* Home to the fabulous Lipizzaner stallions.

- *St. Mark's Square, Venice, Italy.* Laid out around 1050 C.E., the famous square is bordered on three sides by palatial arcades.

- *Statue of Liberty, Liberty Island, New York City, New York, United States.* Given as a gift from France in 1884, the statue is 151 feet (46.5 meters) high. The adventuresome can climb the 192 steps to the top of the pedestal for a magnificent view.

- *Summer Palace of Catherine the Great, near St. Petersburg, Russia.* Although completely gutted by the Nazis in World War II, the palace has been lovingly restored but for the Amber Room. This room was sheathed in finely carved amber and these panels have never been found. The façade is blue, white, and gold, and is about 950 feet (290 meters) long. Of particular note are the gardens with the Rastrelli Pavilion.

- *Taj Mahal, Agra, India.* Mausoleum built by Shah Jahan in 1630 for his wife, Arjuman Banu Begum. The white marble structure was originally encrusted with precious gemstones (now gone on the lower levels).

- *Tiergarten, Berlin, Germany.* Several hundred acres of park, gardens, and the famous Berlin Zoo.

- *Topkapi Palace, Istanbul, Turkey.* Built in 1453 for the Sultan Mehmet II. The kitchen building (fed over 5,000 people daily), Gate of Happiness (Bab i Saadet), white marble library, Harem, and Treasure House can be visited. In the Throne Room is the captured throne of Shah Ismail, which is covered with more than 25,000 jewels.

- *Tower Bridge, London, England, United Kingdom.* Built in 1886, the bridge has a center section that hydraulically raises and lowers to allow ships through. The upper gallery provides spectacular views of the city.

- *Tower of London, London, England, United Kingdom.* Built by William the Conqueror in 1078 as a royal residence, the castle was later used as a prison, and is now one of the most popular tourist attractions in the city. Yeoman Warders, known as Beefeaters, patrol the grounds and give visitors insightful historical information. Of particular interest are the White Tower, Traitor's Gate, the Bloody Tower, the Banqueting Hall, and the Crown Jewels.

- *Trafalgar Square, London, England, United Kingdom.* The square was laid out in 1829 and is now famous for Nelson's Column, bronze lions, and watching passersby.

- *Trevi Fountain, Rome, Italy.* Built in 1732, the fountain is most well known for Bernini's sculpture of Neptune in his winged chariot.

- *Versailles* (say "*vair-sye*") *Palace, near Paris, France.* Begun as a chateau for King Louis XII, Versailles is usually associated with King Louis XIV. Noted areas include the Hall of Mirrors, King's Apartments, Queen's Great and Small Apartments, Orangery, Temple of Love, gardens with hydraulic water works, and the Grand Canal (200 ft/ 61 meters wide and 1 mile/1.6 kilometers long).

- *Warwick* (say "*war*-ick") *Castle, England, United Kingdom.* Built by William the Conqueror in 1068, Warwick is one of the largest and best-preserved castles in Europe. Primary sections of the castle include the Dungeon, Chapel, Guy's Tower (128 feet/39 meters tall), and Caesar's Tower (147 feet/44.8 meters tall). Within the castle are towers with very narrow spiral staircases, the Royal Apartments, the Library, the Music Room, the Great Hall, and Kenilworth Bedroom. On the grounds are the Conservatory and Peacock Garden and Victorian Rose Garden.

- *White House, Washington, DC, United States.* Begun in 1799 as the home and office of the President of the United Sates, important rooms include the elliptical Blue Room, the Library, the China Room, the East Room, the Red Room, the Green Room, the Map Room, the State Dining Room, and the Diplomatic Reception Room.

- *Windsor Castle, England, United Kingdom.* Built by William the Conqueror in 1100 and surrounded by the 4,800-acre (1942-hectare) Great Park. Important areas include St. George's Chapel, the Round Tower, the State Apartments with treasures from the Royal Collection, semi-state rooms, the Drawings Gallery, and Queen Mary's Doll House.

- *Winter Palace, St. Petersburg, Russia.* Finished in 1754 for the Empress Elizabeth and her pet cats (over 100 of them), the palace is now the main building of the world-class Hermitage Museum. Of note are the Malachite Room and Carrara Marble Staircase. In Russian baroque, the palace has 1,057 rooms and 117 staircases.

- *Würzburg Residence, Germany.* Built for Prince-Bishop Johann Philipp von Schönborn in 1720, the palace boasts 300 rooms with wonderful German baroque design, frescoes, and plasterwork.

- *Zen Garden of Emptiness, Kyoto, Japan.* One of, if not the, premier rock garden in the world.

GAMING

Gaming can now be found in many U.S. states, especially on Native American land and along major rivers. A wide variety of countries worldwide also offer gaming. Listed here are some of the major gaming destinations.

- Atlantic City, New Jersey, United States
- Biloxi, Mississippi, United States
- Deadwood, North Dakota, United States
- Gulfport, Mississippi, United States
- Las Vegas, Nevada, United States
- Macau, People's Republic of China
- Monte Carlo Casino, Monaco
- Reno, Nevada, United States
- Sun City, South Africa
- Tunica, Mississippi, United States

GOLF

Practically all major cities in the United States and throughout the world offer golf courses that are open to the public. In fact, almost all smaller towns in the United States have courses as well. The courses listed here represent some of the highest-rated public courses worldwide.

- #4 (Cog Hill), Lemont, Illinois, United States
- Banff Springs–Rundle/Sulphur, Alberta, Canada
- Big Sky Course, Pemberton, British Columbia, Canada
- Cascades, Hot Springs, Virginia, United States
- Challenger-Champion (Bay Hill), Orlando, Florida, United States
- Cordova Bay Course, Victoria, British Columbia, Canada
- Cotton Bay Course, Rock Sound, Eleuthera, Bahamas
- Dorado Beach–East Course, Dorado, Puerto Rico
- East Sussex–East Course, Uckfield, England, United Kingdom
- Gallagher's Canyon, Kelowana, British Columbia, Canada
- Gary Player Course at Sun City, Sun City, South Africa
- Gleneagles–King's Course, Auchterarder, Scotland, United Kingdom
- Half Moon Golf Club, Montego Bay, Jamaica
- Harbour Town, Hilton Head Island, South Carolina, United States
- Jasper Park Golf Course, Alberta, Canada
- Kawana–Oshima Course, Kawana, Japan
- Lahinch–Old Course, Lahinch, Republic of Ireland
- Mauna Kea, Kohala Coast, Hawaii, United States

- Mid Ocean Club, Tucker's Town, Bermuda
- Mirage Golf Course, Port Douglas, Queensland, Australia
- Monument (Troon North), Scottsdale, Arizona, United States
- Palmilla–Nicklaus Signature, Cabo San Lucas, Mexico
- Pasatiempo, Santa Cruz, California, United States
- Pebble Beach, Pebble Beach, California, United States
- Penina Championship Courses, Algarve, Portugal
- Pine Barrens (World Woods), Brooksville, Florida, United States
- Pinehurst #2, Pinehurst, North Carolina, United States
- Port Royal Course, Southampton, Bermuda
- Pumpkin Ridge (Ghost Creek), Cornelius, Oregon, United States
- River Course (Blackwolf Run), Kohler, Wisconsin, United States
- Royal Dornoch, Dornoch, Scotland, United Kingdom
- Royal St. Georges, Sandwich, England, United Kingdom
- Royal Westmoreland, Westmoreland, Barbados
- Spyglass Hill, Pebble Beach, California, United States
- St. Andrews–Old Course, St. Andrews, Scotland, United Kingdom
- St. Mellion–Nicklaus Course, Saltash, England, United Kingdom
- Stadium Course (TCP Sawgrass), Ponte Vedra Beach, Florida, United States
- Sunningdale–Old Course, Sunningdale, England, United Kingdom
- Whistler–Palmer, Whistler, British Columbia, Canada
- Woburn–Dukes Course, Bow Brickhill, England, United Kingdom

HISTORICAL SITES

- *Alamo, San Antonio, Texas, United States.* This Spanish Franciscan Mission (circa 1722) was converted into a fort in 1793 and is the site where Davy Crocket and a handful of men resisted 5,000 Mexican troops.

- *Ann Frank House, Amsterdam, Netherlands.* House where she hid from the Nazis for two years and wrote her famous diary. Ann Frank died at Bergen-Belsen on March 3, 1945 at the age of 16.

- *Arc de Triomphe, Paris, France.* Commemorating Napoleon's victories, the arch was commissioned in 1806 and finished in 1836. There are magnificent views of Paris from the top, and underneath the arch is the Tomb of the Unknown Soldier.

- *Arizona Memorial, Honolulu, Oahu, Hawaii, United States.* Memorial to the 1,000 men who lost their lives when the ship was sunk on December 7, 1941.

- *Auschwitz, Poland.* Site of one of the most infamous Nazi concentration camps of World War II, where millions of Jews, Poles, Slavs, and others were exterminated. The gallows, crematoriums, barracks, and gas chambers are now a memorial to those who died there.

- *Battle of the Bulge, Bastogne, Belgium.* Memorial to the American division who surrounded the town December 22, 1944, and pushed the Nazis back by January of 1945.

- *Boston, Massachusetts, United States.* Sites include the Old State House, Paul Revere's House, Granary Burial Ground, Old North Church, Freedom Trail, and Black Heritage Trail.

- *Caraquet, New Brunswick, Canada.* Established by the Acadians in 1758, the site now has about 40 restored buildings that re-create the original settlement.

- *Dacau, Germany.* Site of the first Nazi concentration camps, it is now a memorial to the thousands who perished there.

- *Fort Sumter, South Carolina, United States.* The site where the Civil War began on April 12, 1861.

- *Gambia, West Africa.* Location of the village Juffure, made famous by Alex Haley's magnificent work *Roots*.

- *Gettysburg, Pennsylvania, United States.* The largest battlefield site in the United States; the battle on July 1, 1863, was the turning point in the Civil War.

- *Gorée Island, Senegal.* Primary embarkation site for the millions of slaves bound for Europe and the New World.

- *Great Wall of China, People's Republic of China.* Begun in 221 B.C.E. by the Emperor Qin Shi Huangdi as a defense against the northern tribes, the wall was extended and enlarged throughout several centuries. The wall is estimated to be 3,750 miles (6,000 kilometers) long. In places, it is 25 feet (7.6 meters) high and is wide enough for five horsemen to ride abreast.

- *Hadrian's Wall, England, United Kingdom.* Remains of a defensive wall (73 miles/117 kilometers long), forts, and watchtowers built in 120 C.E.

- *Halifax Citadel, Halifax, Nova Scotia, Canada.* Guards in period dress (kilts) patrol the grounds of this 1828 star-shaped fort.

- *Kanchanaburi, Thailand.* Site of the Bridge over the River Kwai. Some 8,000 Allied POWs died during the forced labor operation to build the bridge. Many of them are buried in the nearby cemetery.

- *Kennedy Space Center, Cape Canaveral, Florida, United States.* Visitors enjoy the rocket displays, command center, IMAX films, and launch pads.

- *Little Big Horn National Monument, Montana, United States.* Site where the Sioux defeated Custer on June 25, 1876.

- *Mt. Rushmore, South Dakota, United States.* On this 5,600-foot- (1707-meter-) high peak are the carved heads (1927) of George Washington, Abraham Lincoln, Thomas Jefferson, and Theodore Roosevelt.

- *Normandy Beaches, France.* Site of the Allied landing on D-Day during World War II. The beaches include Juno, Sword, Omaha, Utah, and Gold. In the area are several memorials, museums, and cemeteries for the Allied Forces.

- *Old Royal Observatory, Greenwich, England, United Kingdom.* Built by Charles II in 1675 to develop our current system of location and navigation. Here you can stand with one foot in the Eastern Hemisphere and the other foot in the Western Hemisphere.

- *Philadelphia, Pennsylvania, United States.* Sites include Independence Hall with the Liberty Bell, Graff House, Congress Hall, Betsy Ross House, and Penn's Landing.

- *Plaza Boliva, Caracas, Venezuela.* Park dedicated to Simón Bolivar, "The Great Liberator" of much of northern South America from Spanish rule.

- *Richmond, Virginia, United States.* Sites include the Richmond Capitol Building, Museum and White House of the Confederacy, and the Richmond National Battlefield Park.

- *Roman Baths, Bath, England, United Kingdom.* Site of ancient hot springs around which the Romans built a spa in the first century C.E.

- *Southern Mississippi River Valley, United States.* Numerous Civil War battle sites, former plantation homes, and antebellum mansions.

- *Stone Mountain, near Atlanta, Georgia, United States.* Granite monolith carved with Robert E. Lee, Stonewall Jackson, and Jefferson Davis on their horses.

- *Stratford-upon-Avon, England, United Kingdom.* Sites include the birthplace of William Shakespeare, the Royal Shakespeare Theatre, and Shakespeare's tomb at Trinity Church.

- *Tiananmen Square, Beijing, People's Republic of China.* Sites include the tomb of Mao Zedong and the Monument to the People's Hero.

- *Washington, D.C./Baltimore, Maryland/Arlington, Virginia area, United States.* Sites include the Jefferson Memorial, the Lincoln Memorial, the U.S. Capitol, the U.S. Holocaust Memorial Museum, the Vietnam Veteran's Memorial, the Washington Monument, the White House, Arlington National Cemetery, and Fort McHenry.

- *Waterloo, Belgium.* Site of Napoleon's defeat by Wellington and Blücher on June 18, 1815.

MUSEUMS, THEATRE, MUSIC, AND ART

- Ballet Folklorico, Mexico City, Mexico
- Bolshoi Ballet, Moscow, Russia
- Branson, Missouri, United States
- British Museum, London, England, United Kingdom
- Broadway, New York City, New York, United States
- Carnegie Hall, New York City, New York, United States
- Frogner Park, Oslo, Norway
- Glyptotek Art Museum, Copenhagen, Denmark
- Grand Ole Opry, Nashville, Kentucky, United States
- Guggenheim Museum, New York City, New York, United States
- Heard Museum, Phoenix, Arizona, United States
- Hermitage, St. Petersburg, Russia
- Hollywood, California, United States
- La Scala Opera House, Milan, Italy
- Louvre, Paris, France
- Metropolitan Museum of Art, New York City, New York, United States
- Moulin Rouge, Paris, France
- Museum of Anthropology, Mexico City, Mexico
- National Museum, Taipei, Taiwan
- Opera—Bastille, Paris, France
- Opera House, Sydney, Australia
- Prado, Madrid, Spain
- Pushkin Art Museum, Moscow, Russia
- Radio City Music Hall, New York City, New York, United States
- Rock and Roll Hall of Fame, Cleveland, Ohio, United States
- Shin-Kabuki-za, Osaka, Japan
- Smithsonian Institution, Washington, D.C., United States
- Soho District, London, England, United Kingdom
- Tate Gallery, London, England, United Kingdom
- Times Square, New York City, New York, United States
- U.S. Holocaust Memorial Museum, Washington, D.C., United States
- Uffizi Gallery, Florence, Italy
- Van Gogh Museum, Amsterdam, Netherlands
- Victoria and Albert Museum, London, England, United Kingdom

NATIONAL PARKS

- *Aberdare National Park, Kenya.* 297 square miles/770 square kilometers. Visitors to the park may travel through highlands and bamboo rain forests, viewing spectacular waterfalls. On safari, one may see warthogs, monkeys, elephants, leopards, and lions.

- *Amboselli National Park, Kenya.* 1,235.5 square miles/3,200 square kilometers. Park animals include rhino, elephant, buffalo, wildebeests, and cheetahs.
- *Banff National Park, Alberta, Canada.* 1885; 1,640,960 acres/664,073 hectares. The park includes glaciers, Icefields Parkway, summer and winter sports, and the game sanctuary for grizzly bear, caribou, and wolves.
- *Bryce Canyon National Park, Utah, United States.* 1928; 35,835 acres/14,502 hectares. This canyon has curiously eroded pinnacles of various colors that are known as "hoodoos."
- *Carlsbad Caverns National Park, New Mexico, United States.* 1930; 46,753 acres/18,920 hectares. This series of huge limestone caverns contains the largest known underground room in the world. The Big Room is .5 mile/.8 kilometers long by 650 feet/198 meters wide by 285 feet/87 meters high.
- *Denali National Park, Alaska, United States.* 1917; 1,939,493 acres/784,885 hectares. The most recognizable feature of the park is Mt. KcKinley (20,320 feet/6,194 meters), the highest peak in North America. Wildlife include white Alaskan mountain sheep, grizzly bears, wolves, and caribou.
- *Everglades National Park, Florida, United States.* 1934; 1,400,533 acres/566,776 hectares. This park offers vast marshlands and mangrove swamps with wildlife that includes manatees, ibis, herons, snowy egrets, and alligators.
- *Fjordland National Park, New Zealand.* 3,224,725 acres/1,305,000 hectares. The landscape of the park includes snowcapped mountains, glacial lakes, valleys, fjords, waterfalls, and dense forest. Wildlife include penguins, seals, and dolphins.
- *Grand Canyon National Park, Arizona, United States.* 1919; 1,218,375 acres/493,059 hectares. Throughout the millennia, the Colorado River has carved out the canyon to a depth of over 1 mile (1.6 kilometers) in places. Throughout the main canyon are many smaller canyons. The rock layers are a virtual history of the area because of the many aquatic fossils.
- *Great Smoky Mountains National Park, Tennessee/North Carolina, United States.* 1930; 516,626 acres/208,923 hectares, most visited park in the United States. The park is densely forested and offers a wide variety of flowering shrubs and flowers. The park was so named because the valleys are often shrouded in mist that looks "smoky."
- *Jasper National Park, Alberta, Canada.* 1907; 2,688,000 acres/1,087,795 hectares. Sites include a big-game sanctuary, Mt. Columbia (12,293 feet/3,748 meters), forested valleys, mountains, lakes, and glaciers. Wildlife include bighorn sheep, mountain lion, grizzly bear, caribou, wolves, and mule deer.
- *Kakadu National Park, Australia.* 19,000 square miles/49,210 square kilometers. This park is famous for its Aborigine art on the rock formations, Aboriginal Cultural Center, high cliffs, waterfalls, woodland forests, and various reptiles.
- *Kruger National Park, South Africa.* 1926; 8,000 square miles/20,720 square kilometers. The park's animals include rhinos, buffalo, lions, leopards, and elephants.
- *Mammoth Cave National Park, Kentucky, United States.* 1941; 51,354 acres/20,782 hectares, world's longest cave system stretching over 150 miles/241.4 kilometers. Sites include caves on five levels, Bottomless Pit, Crystal Lake, Mammoth Dome, onyx cascades, gypsum flowers, stalactites, and stalagmites.
- *Masai Mara Game Reserve, Kenya.* 645.5 square miles/1,672 square kilometers. Park animals include cape buffalos, civets, zebras, jackals, hyenas, baboons, lions, hippos, crocodiles, antelopes, giraffes, wildebeests, and warthogs.
- *Monteverde Cloud Forest Reserve, Costa Rica.* Situated on steep mountains with deep valleys, volcanoes, waterfalls, thermal streams, and mineral baths, the park is famous for its emerald toucans and quetzal birds.
- *Mt. Cook National Park, New Zealand.* 270 square miles/699 square kilometers. Sites include glaciers, snowfields surrounded by some 3,000 peaks, and rain forests.
- *Ngorongoro Crater, Tanzania.* The crater of an extinct volcano, it is 2,000 feet (610 meters) deep and 12 miles (19 kilometers) wide. On the rich grassland live hippos, elephants, lions, jackals, wildebeests, hyenas, zebras, cape buffalo, black rhinos, and cheetah.
- *Rocky Mountain National Park, Colorado, United States.* 1915; 263,809 acres/106,760 hectares. This is the heart of the Rockies. Of particular note are Long's Peak (14,526 feet/4427.5 meters), Trail Ridge Road, and the Continental Divide. Wildlife include coyote, moose, elk, mule deer, and big horn sheep.
- *Royal Chitwan National Park, Nepal.* 360 square miles/932 square kilometers. With grass standing over 20 feet (6 meters) tall, this lush park is known for its tigers, leopards, rhinos, crocodiles, and monkeys.
- *Serengeti National Park, Tanzania.* 5,600 square miles/14,504 square kilometers. The landscape of the park varies between rain forests and plains and offers rivers and volcanoes. Wildlife include wildebeests, zebras, lions, hyenas, and gazelle.
- *Torres del Paine, Chile.* 1959; 447,261 acres/181,000 hectares. Sights include forests, lakes, glaciers, icebergs, craggy mountains, guanaco, puma, condor, and black-necked swan.
- *Virunga National Park, Republic of Congo.* 1925; 3,088 square miles/7,998 square kilometers. With varied landscape, the park offers swamps, steppes, snowfields, and lava plains. Virunga is most famous for its mountain gorillas, the subject of the film *Gorillas in the Mist.*

- *Wolong Natural Reserve, People's Republic of China.* With rolling mountains and bamboo forests, this park is famous for its giant pandas.

- *Wood Buffalo National Park, Alberta/Northern Territories, Canada.* 1922; 11,072,000 acres/4,480,679 hectares. The vast area is covered by forests and plains and is a buffalo preserve.

- *Yankari National Park, Nigeria.* 1956; 794.6 square miles/2,058 square kilometers. Park animals include elephants, baboons, crocodiles, hippos, buffalo, and monkeys.

- *Yellowstone National Park, Wyoming/Montana/Idaho, United States.* 1872 (first national park in the U.S.); 2,221,773 acres/899,199 hectares. Sites include Mammoth Hot Springs, Grand Canyon of Yellowstone, Yellowstone River, lakes, waterfalls, and geysers. (Old Faithful erupts 17 to 21 times a day with water jets up to 130 feet/40 meters high.)

- *Yosemite National Park, California, United States.* 1890; 760,917 acres/307,937 hectares. Sights include high cliffs, lofty waterfalls, giant sequoia trees, and the rock formations of Half Dome, Cathedral Spires, and El Capitan.

- *Zion National Park, Utah, United States.* 1919; 147,035 acres/59,502 hectares. The sandstone cliffs of remarkable colors were carved by the Virgin River. Of interest are the Narrows (the cliff walls are 2,000 feet/610 meters high and as close together as 20 feet/60 meters), towering rock formations, and the abundant wildlife.

NATURAL TREASURES

- *Amazon River, Brazil.* Second longest river in the world, it begins high in the Andes and flows some 4,000 miles (6,437 kilometers) to the Atlantic Ocean. Along the basin are rich rain forest and various tribal groups.

- *Angel Falls, Venezuela.* World's highest waterfall at 3,212 feet (979 meters).

- *Black Forest, Germany.* This region of rolling hills, lakes, mineral springs, and dense forest is known for wood carvings and cuckoo clocks.

- *Cappadocia, Turkey.* Site noted for its rock pinnacles, carved rock dwellings, caves, and ravines.

- *Crater Lake, Oregon, United States.* 6 miles/9.6 kilometers wide by 5,217 feet/1,590 meters deep, this is the crater of the extinct volcano, Mt. Mazama. Of particular note is the rich blue water.

- *Diamond Head, Honolulu, Oahu, Hawaii, United States.* Promontory of an extinct volcano, there are ancient Hawaiian burial grounds along the rim.

- *Fern Grotto, Kauai, Hawaii, United States.* This lush green grotto is a popular site for weddings.

- *Fjords, Norway.* Narrow arms of the sea bordered by high mountains and cliffs, the most famous ones are Sognafjord, Geirangerfjord, Trollfjord, and Hardangerfjord.

- *Galapagos Islands, Ecuador.* Located 600 miles/1,970 kilometers from the mainland, this island group is famous for its pristine ecosystem. Native animals include giant tortoises, red- and blue-footed boobies, marine iguanas, penguins, sea lions, seals, herons, flamingos, pelicans, and flightless cormorants. The islands inspired Charles Darwin to write *Origin of Species*.

- *Hell's Canyon, Idaho, United States.* The deepest canyon in North America (7,900 feet/2,400 meters), it was carved out by the Snake River.

- *Iguazu Falls, Brazil/Argentina.* Over a 2.5-mile/4-kilometer stretch are more than 20 cataracts separated by masses of rock and tree-covered islands that create approximately 275 waterfalls, some of which are 1,300 feet (91 meters) high.

- *Inside Passage, British Columbia, Canada/Alaska, United States.* Protected channel between the mainland and the offshore islands. Along the 1,000-mile/1,600-kilometer length are snowcapped mountains, glaciers, fjords, whales, bear, and moose.

- *Lake Titicaca, Peru/Bolivia.* This huge lake is the highest navigable lake in the world, located at an altitude of 12,500 feet (3,810 meters). It was the center of the ancient civilization at Tiahuanaco.

- *Matterhorn, Switzerland.* The most famous Alpine peak, it is 14,690 feet/4,475.5 meters high.

- *Mauna Kea, Hawaii Island, Hawaii, United States.* This volcano is the highest point in Hawaii at 13,796 feet (4,205 meters).

- *Mauna Loa, Hawaii Island, Hawaii, United States.* 13,680 feet/4,169 meters high, the central pit of this volcano is sometimes active. Recent lava flows have burst through the sides of the volcano.

- *Milford Sound, New Zealand.* Inlet of the Tasman Sea, it is noted for its scenery and magnificent fjords.

- *Mt. Everest, Nepal.* The highest mountain in the world, 29,028 feet/8,847.7 meters.

- *Mt. Fuji (also FujinoYama or Fujisan), Japan.* This sacred mountain is the almost-perfect cone of a volcano. It is 12,388 feet (3,744 meters) high.

- *Mt. Kilimanjaro, Tanzania.* The highest point in Africa at 19,340 feet (5,895 meters), it is the snowcapped peak of a dormant volcano.

- *Niagara Falls, New York, United States/Ontario, Canada.* On the Canadian side is Horseshoe Falls, 158 feet/48 meters high with a crest of 2,600 feet/729 meters. The American Falls are 167 feet/51 meters high with a crest of 1,000 feet/305 meters. At the base of the American Falls is the Cave of the Wind, and downstream are the whirlpool rapids in the gorge.

- *Outback, Australia.* The vast and desolate interior of Australia, where huge cattle and sheep ranches (stations) are found.

- *Pampas, Argentina.* Grassland covering 294,000 square miles (761,457 square kilometers), the area is famous for cattle and sheep ranches and the Argentine cowboys known as *gauchos.*

- *Ring of Kerry, Republic of Ireland.* This spectacular circular drive around the Dingle Peninsula passes old monasteries and ruined castles.

- *Sahara Desert, Northern Africa.* This region consists of deserts and oases and covers an area of 3,500,000 square miles (9,064,958 square kilometers).

- *Uluru (also Ayers Rock), Australia.* Part of the Olgas, this 1,143-foot- (348.4-meter-) high monolith is sacred to the Aborigines. At different times of the day, the rock appears orange, red, and purple. The outcrop measures 9 miles (13 kilometers) in circumference.

- *Victoria Falls, Zambia/Zimbabwe.* This series of falls on the Zambezi River is broken by islands and stretches over a distance of 5,580 feet (1,700 meters).

- *Yangtzee River Gorges, People's Republic of China.* These gorges are most notable between I-ch'ang and Feng-chieh, with cliffs 1,000 feet (320 meters) high.

RELIGIOUS SITES

- *Ajanta Caves, near Mumbai (Bombay), India.* This series of caves have religious carvings and paintings that date from the second century B.C.E.

- *Anuradhapura, Sri Lanka.* Dating from the eighth century, this Buddhist temple complex is hewn from solid rock and is larger than the Pyramids of Egypt.

- *Baha'i Temple, Haifi, Israel.* Center of the Baha'i faith and the tomb of Baha Allah.

- *Blue Mosque, Istanbul, Turkey.* One of the most famous mosques in the world, it is noted for its massive rounded structure and delicate minarets.

- *Borobudur, Java, Indonesia.* Dating from 1000 C.E., this Buddhist temple complex includes a truncated pyramid covered with carvings that illustrate the life and teachings of Buddha.

- *Buddha's Universal Church, San Francisco, California, United States.* The largest Buddhist temple in the United States, the five-story building has lovely murals and delicate mosaics.

- *Cathedral of San Giovanni, Turin (Torino), Italy.* Home of the Holy Shroud, said to be the cloth in which Jesus was wrapped after crucifixion.

- *Chartres Cathedral, Chartres, France.* This 22,000-square-foot (2,044-square-meter) cathedral was built in Gothic style in 1194. Of particular note are the 176 stained glass windows that are exceptional for their quality and brilliance.

- *Christ the Redeemer, Rio de Janeiro, Brazil.* This 130-foot/40 meter tall statue of Jesus sits atop Corcovado Mountain and provides magnificent views of the city.

- *Church of the Holy Sepulcher, Jerusalem, Israel.* Built on the site of the burial and resurrection of Jesus, this church is one of the most holy in Christendom.

- *Church of the Nativity, Bethlehem, Israel.* The original church was built in 325 on the site of Jesus' birth. The church was rebuilt in the sixth century and was later repaired in the twelfth century by the Crusaders.

- *Dome of the Rock (Mosque of Omar), Jerusalem, Israel.* One of the most holy sites in Islam, the mosque contains the rock from which Mohammed ascended to heaven.

- *Ganges River, India.* This holy river is 1,560 miles (2,510 kilometers) long and is sacred to the Hindu. Although it is highly polluted, Hindus bathe in it as a purifying ritual. Note: It is not uncommon to see floating corpses of both humans and animals in the river.

- *Jokhang, Lhasa, Tibet, People's Republic of China.* This is the holiest of Tibetan Buddhist temples.

- *Juma Mosque, Durban, South Africa.* The largest mosque in the Southern Hemisphere.

- *La Sagrada Familla, Barcelona, Spain.* Constructed in 1882, this church is a surreal mixture of a castle and a dragon's cave.

- *Lourdes, France.* In 1858, a peasant girl saw the Virgin Mary and a spring came forth on the spot. Today, pilgrims travel from all over the world to visit the underground basilica, which was completed in 1958.

- *Masada, Israel.* Atop a 1,300-foot (400-meter) mesa-shaped rock are the remains of a centuries-old fortress. It was here in 73 C.E. that 900 Jews withstood 10,000 Roman soldiers for seven months. When defeat was imminent, the Jews committed suicide. Masada is now a site of Jewish pilgrimage.

- *Mecca, Saudi Arabia.* The Great Mosque marks the site of Mohammed's birth in 570 C.E. It is the goal of every Moslem to make a holy journey (*hajj*) to Mecca, the most holy site in Islam.

- *Medina, Saudi Arabia.* One of the most holy cities in Islam. Here are the Prophet's Mosque, place of his death in 632 C.E., and Mohammed's Tomb.

- *Meiji Shrine, Tokyo, Japan.* One of the most well known shrines of the ancient religion of Shinto.

- *Mormon Tabernacle, Salt Lake City, Utah, United States.* Headquarters of the Church of Jesus Christ of Latter Day Saints.

- *Notre Dame Cathedral, Paris, France.* Probably the most famous cathedral in the world, it was built in 1163 on the

Ile de la Cite. Of French Gothic architecture, the cathedral is noted for the flying buttresses that disperse the pressure from the height of the nave.

- *Notre Dame de la Paix, Yamassoukro, Cote d'Ivoire.* Built in the 1990s, it is said to be the largest church in the world. It is noted for its magnificent stained glass windows that illustrate stories from the Bible.

- *Pagan, Myanmar.* Dating from 849 C.E., this area contains thousands of Buddhist shrines, pagodas, and monasteries.

- *Passion Play, Oberammergau, Germany.* The first Passion Play was performed in this tiny village in 1634 because of a vow made to God during the plague of 1633. The vow has been kept and the play is performed every 10 years, reenacting the suffering, death, and resurrection of Jesus.

- *Sacré-Coeur, Paris, France.* This Byzantine-Romanesque basilica was built in 1875 on Montmartre Hill. Visitors can begin in the crypts and climb all the way to the dome for a spectacular view of Paris.

- *Sistine Chapel, Vatican City.* Built for Pope Sixtus IV in 1473, the chapel is most famous for the works of Michelangelo. Over a four-year period, Michelangelo painted nine episodes from Genesis on the ceiling and the *Last Judgment* on the altar wall. The chapel also includes magnificent marble floors, delicate mosaics, and frescoes by Botticelli and others.

- *St. Basil's Cathedral, Moscow, Russia.* Built in the sixteenth century, this church is a landmark with its brightly colored onion-domes and surrounding cupolas.

- *St. Catherine's Monastery, Sinai, Egypt.* The cathedral was built in the sixth century on the site of the Burning Bush. It contains a huge library with early Christian manuscripts and relics.

- *St. Patrick's Cathedral, New York City, New York, United States.* Built in 1858, it is the largest Roman Catholic church in the United States. The marble structure is cruciform in shape and has 12 side chapels. Of particular note are the many stained glass windows and the 19-bell chimes.

- *St. Peter's Basilica, Vatican City.* Headquarters of the Roman Catholic faith and home of the Pope. Consecrated in 1626, the most notable areas include Michelangelo's *Pieta* and magnificent dome, the grotto-tomb of St. Peter, and the tombs of many popes. The basilica holds 50,000 people and is 700 feet (313 meters) long by 450 feet (137 meters) wide.

- *Todai-ji Temple, Nara, Japan.* This temple contains the largest bronze Buddha in the world (53.5 feet/16.3 meters high).

- *Vishvanatha Temple, Varanasi (Kasi), India.* The most holy city to those who follow the Hindu faith. The temple offers several sites to ritually bathe in the Ganges River, sprinkle ashes of the deceased, or pass on to the next life.

- *Wat Phra Keo (Temple of the Emerald Buddha), Bangkok, Thailand.* This famous temple is within the compound of the Grand Palace.

- *Western Wall (also Wailing Wall), Jerusalem, Israel.* Once part of King Solomon's Temple, the wall is one of the most holy sites in Judaism.

- *Westminster Abbey, London, England, United Kingdom.* Built in 1042 by King Edward I (the Confessor), the church has an octagonal chapter house and is the coronation site of kings and queens. Eighteen former monarchs are buried here as well as Chaucer, Browning, and Tennyson in "Poet's Corner."

SCUBA AND SNORKELING

As with some of the other lists, this one could include thousands of sites. In fact, any body of water could be considered a destination for travelers who are interested in scuba and snorkeling. Listed here are some of the top-rated sites in the world.

- Ambergris Caye, Belize
- Aruba
- Bahamas
- Cancun, Mexico
- Cayman Islands
- Cozumel, Mexico
- Eilat, Israel
- Great Barrier Reef, Australia
- Micronesia
- Palau
- Red Sea, Egypt
- Samoa
- Solomon Islands

THEME PARKS

- Alton Towers—England, United Kingdom
- Blackpool Pleasure Beach—England, United Kingdom
- Busch Gardens—Tampa, Florida; Williamsburg, Virginia, United States
- Cedar Point—Sandusky, Ohio, United States
- Disneyland—Anaheim, California, United States
- Disneyland Paris—near Paris, France
- Disneyland Tokyo—near Tokyo, Japan
- Dollywood—Pigeon Forge, Tennessee, United States
- Euro-Park—Germany
- King's Domain—Doswell, Virginia, United States
- Kings Island—Cincinnati, Ohio, United States
- Knott's Berry Farm—Los Angeles, California, United States

- Middle Kingdom—Hong Kong, People's Republic of China
- Opryland—Nashville, Tennessee, United States
- Port Aventura—Cost Daurada, Spain
- Sea World—Orlando, Florida; San Diego, California; San Antonio, Texas; and Aurora, Ohio, United States
- Six Flags—Valencia, California; Arlington, Texas; Gurnee, Illinois; Atlanta, Georgia; Jackson, New Jersey, United States
- Tivoli Gardens—Copenhagen, Denmark
- Universal Studios—near Orlando, Florida; Hollywood, California, United States
- Walt Disney World—near Orlando, Florida, United States

WINTER SPORTS

- Alberville, France
- Angelfire, New Mexico, United States
- Aspen, Colorado, United States
- Bariloche, Argentina
- Big Four Ski East, Quebec, Canada
- Blackcomb Ski Mountain, British Columbia, Canada
- Bolzano (Bozen), Italy
- Cypress Bowl, British Columbia, Canada
- Garmish-Partenkirchen, Germany
- Grenoble, France
- Grouse Mountain, British Columbia, Canada
- Gstaad, Switzerland
- Innsbruck, Austria
- Interlaken, Switzerland
- Jackson Hole, Wyoming, United States
- Killington, Vermont, United States
- Lake Louise, Alberta, Canada
- Lake Tahoe, California, United States
- Laurentian Mountains, Quebec, Canada
- Lillehammer, Norway

- Loon Mountain, New Hampshire, United States
- Pyrenees Mountains, Spain/France
- Seymour Mountain, British Columbia, Canada
- Snowbird, Utah, United States
- Snowmass, Colorado, United States
- Southern Alps, New Zealand
- Squaw Valley, California, United States
- St. Moritz, Switzerland
- Steamboat Springs, Colorado, United States
- Sun Valley, Idaho, United States
- Taos, New Mexico, United States
- Telluride, Colorado, United States
- Vail, Colorado, United States
- Waterville Valley, New Hampshire, United States
- Whistler, British Columbia, Canada
- Zermatt, Switzerland

SUMMARY

In this chapter, you have read about a variety of attractions and destinations. You have learned some interesting facts about them, and have hopefully developed an interest in finding out more about some of them. Remember that each list contains only the most important and popular sites; there are thousands and thousands more sites in each category. The most important thing to remember is that a destination's history, culture, religion, art, and ethnicity all serve to make a destination what it is.

 For additional Travel and Tourism resources, go to http://www.hospitality-tourism.delmar.com.

PLEASE COMPLETE THE CHAPTER REVIEW QUESTIONS NOW.

Review Questions*

1. Uluru (Ayers Rock) is sacred to what group of people? _____

2. What ancient temple was moved to avoid being flooded when the Aswan High Dam was built? _____ _____

3. Where are the four Disney parks located? _____

4. Name the Paris arch that commemorates the victories of Napoleon. _____

5. The famous Biltmore Mansion is located near this city in South Carolina. _____

6. Name five famous ski resort areas in Colorado. _____ _____

7. What Canadian national park is known for its glaciers, year-round spots, and game sanctuary? _____ _____

8. This region in Germany is densely forested and is known for its mineral springs and wood carvings. _____ _____

9. This castle is famous for its stone, which gives those who kiss it the "gift of gab." _____

10. The Old North Church, Black Freedom Trail, and Paul Revere's House can be visited in this historical city. _____ _____

11. Name two national parks in Utah that are famous for their canyons and rock formations. _____ _____

12. Famous sites at this palace include the Changing of the Guard, State Rooms, and the Queen's Picture Gallery. _____

13. This famous garden was founded in 1904 in Victoria, British Columbia, Canada. _____

14. Name two famous beaches in the Bahamas. _____

15. Name two areas in Mexico that are famous for snorkeling and scuba diving. _____ _____

16. Begun in 1519, this former royal hunting "lodge" has 440 rooms. _____

17. Who were the three pharaohs who built the Great Pyramids? _____ _____

18. What archeological site includes the Temple of the Jaguars, Ball Court, and Cenote Sagrado? _____ _____

19. What church is built on the site of Jesus' burial and resurrection? _____

20. The Hoover Dam, located in Nevada and Arizona, spans this river. _____

21. On what island can visitors see the remains of King Minos's Palace? _____

---

*Source: "A Guide to Becoming a Travel Professional" Student Workbook.

22. Name the structure that was built on the site where Mohammed ascended to heaven. _____ _____

23. What island is famous for its huge Moai statues? _____

24. At 985 feet/300 meters tall, this is the most famous site in Paris. _____

25. What Kauai location is a popular site for weddings? _____

26. This area of San Francisco is famous for its shops, restaurants, and recreational opportunities. _____ _____

27. Name the island group that is famous for its pristine ecosystem and was the inspiration for Charles Darwin. _____

28. In what country is the village of Juffure made famous in Alex Haley's *Roots*? _____

29. In what country are the remains of the city of Petra located? _____

30. Name two Nevada cities known for world-class casinos. _____

31. What archaeological site is known as the "Lost City of the Incas"? _____

32. What Hollywood site is famous for hundreds of celebrity hand and foot prints? _____ _____

33. This queen's doll house is one of the most loved attractions at Windsor Castle. _____

34. This area of New Zealand is known for its spectacular scenery and magnificent fjords. _____ _____

35. The heads of four presidents are carved in stone on this South Dakota mountain. _____

36. What castle in southern Germany was Walt Disney's inspiration for Sleeping Beauty's Castle? _____

37. This Paris cathedral is noted for its Gothic architecture and flying buttresses. _____

38. What structure in Central America connects the Atlantic and Pacific Oceans? _____

39. The tomb of Emperor Qin Shi Huangdi, including 8,000 life-sized terra cotta warriors, is located in this country. _____

40. The largest Buddhist temple in the United States is located in this city. _____

41. Gleneagles and St. Andrews are world-renown golf courses in this country. _____

42. What author and playwright is linked with the town of Stratford-upon-Avon? _____

43. The Western Wall was once part of this king's temple. _____

44. In what state is Hilton Head located? _____

45. In what city is the Hermitage Museum located? _____

46. One of the most famous sites in England is this ancient stone circle. _____

47. One of India's most famous landmarks is this mausoleum that was built by Shah Jahan for his wife. _____ _____

48. Name the palace that is famous for its Treasure House, Harem, and Library. _____

49. Name the national park that is famous for its mountain gorillas. _____

50. In what city can the Smithsonian Institution be visited? _____

SECTION III

United States Air Travel

CHAPTER 6
Air Travel Basics

CHAPTER 7
Planning United States Flight
Itineraries

CHAPTER 8
United States Airfares and Other
Charges

CHAPTER 9
Ticketing and Reporting

CHAPTER 6

Air Travel Basics

OBJECTIVES

At the conclusion of this chapter, you should be able to

- explain U.S. travel agency appointment procedures.
- discuss travel agency automation choices.
- detail how travel agencies earn money.
- understand current safety and security procedures.
- define the relationship between the airlines and specific government agencies.
- identify the codes for selected airlines.
- describe airline policies and operations.
- explain the relationship between aircraft configuration and passenger comfort.
- identify the various areas of airports, available services, and arrival and departure procedures.
- identify selected airport codes.

KEY TERMS

air traffic control

Air Transport Association (ATA)

airline clubs

Airlines Reporting Corporation (ARC)

airport authority

ARC appointment

ARC number

bias

boarding pass

bulkheads

bumping

cabin

carousels

child

code sharing

commuter airlines

concourse

conference

configuration

consortium

denied boarding compensation (DBC)

Department of Transportation (DOT)

dual-designated carrier

Federal Aviation Administration (FAA)

KEY TERMS *continued*

frequent flyer programs
fuselage
gate
Global Travel Distribution System (GDS)
ground control
hub and spoke
IATAN ID card
infants
interline agreements
International Air Transport Association (IATA)
International Airlines Travel Agent Network (IATAN)
jetways
load factor
major airline

markup
meet and assist
Miscellaneous Charges Order (MCO)
narrow-body aircraft
National Transportation Safety Board (NTSB)
net rate
no-rec
no-shows
overbook
override
passenger name record (PNR)
pitch
pressurize
pseudocity code
reconfirm

regional airlines
seat assignments
service fees
sine or sign
skycaps
tarmac
taxiway
terminal
Transportation Security Administration (TSA)
Travel Agency Service Fee (TASF) document
unaccompanied minors
vendors
wait-list
wide-body aircraft

THE TRAVEL AGENCY AND AIR TRAVEL

The Internet, airline reservation centers, and airline city ticket offices notwithstanding, travel agencies are selling more air travel than ever before. Travel agents reported $7.3 billion in sales through June 2005. This represents an 8 percent increase over the same time the previous year. These sales figures are impressive in spite of the fact that the number of travel agencies has steadily been decreasing over the past several years. But, before a travel agency can sell air travel, it must enter into an agreement with each airline it wants to sell. These agreements can be accomplished in one of two ways or a combination of both.

First, the travel agency can contact each airline individually for authorization to sell air travel. Each airline will set in writing its requirements and regulations for the travel agency as well as booking and ticketing procedures. Each airline's contract will clearly state the airline's responsibility to the travel agency.

A much easier way is for the travel agency to request appointment by the **Airlines Reporting Corporation (ARC)**. Everyone in the travel industry refers to the Airlines Reporting Corporation simply by saying "ark," as if it were a word. ARC was founded in 1984 as a close corporation; it can have no more than 30 shareholders and there are restrictions on the transfer of its stock. Presently, there are 14 shareholders and they are all major

Materials for planning a trip.

airlines. In addition to the 14 stockholders, there are 130 airlines (United States and international), 4 railroads, and 27 travel vendors that are members of ARC.

ARC is perhaps the most important organization, also known as a conference, to U.S. travel agencies. The functions of ARC include

- travel agency accreditation
- ticket and ticket number assignment, distribution, and control
- travel transaction reporting and financial settlement
- continuing education for ticket issuance and reporting

From recommendations by its members, Advisory Counsel, and Joint Advisory Board-Agent Reporting Agreement, ARC has established a standardized set of regulations and requirements for U.S. travel agencies. By accepting ARC's approval, the agency agrees to abide by ARC regulations for selling, ticketing, and record keeping, and to follow agency security and ticket security procedures.

When a travel agency is approved by ARC, the agency is said to receive ARC appointment. In other words, the travel agency has been approved to sell travel for all airline, rail, and travel vendor members of ARC. At the time of appointment, ARC assigns an identification number to the travel agency. The first two digits of the number identify the state where the agency is located. The next five digits identify the agency. The sixth, and last digit, is called a check digit. An agency's ARC number would be written as 15 99988 7.

Once the ARC number has been assigned, the travel agency may sell travel on most U.S. and international airlines. There are, however, a few U.S. airlines that are not members of ARC. Generally these non-ARC airlines are small and have very limited route systems. A travel agency that wants to sell non-ARC airlines must contact each non-ARC airline directly.

The International Airlines Travel Agent Network (IATAN), another conference, is also important to U.S. travel agencies. IATAN is said like "i-uh-*tan*." After a U.S. travel agency has been appointed by ARC, it may elect to apply to IATAN for appointment to sell travel on its member airlines. IATAN has approximately 265 international airline members, some of which are not members of ARC.

Although IATAN's regulations and standards for appointment are very similar to those of ARC, IATAN is concerned solely with international air travel. IATAN does not issue a separate ID number; rather, it uses the number assigned by ARC. One of IATAN's most important functions is training in international fare calculation, taxes, and ticketing.

IATAN also issues identification cards to travel professionals who have fulfilled specific requirements for employment or earnings. The IATAN ID card is required by most airlines, rental car companies, hotels, cruise lines, and tour operators before travel discounts will be given.

Web Activity

1. Using the Internet, find out all of the requirements for a travel counselor who wants to apply for the IATAN ID card.
2. Access ARC's Web site and find out which nonair and nonrail vendors are members of ARC.

IATAN is a division of another conference, the International Air Transport Association (IATA), said like "i-*ah*-tah." IATA is the governing and appointing body for travel agencies outside the United States, and before IATAN was founded, U.S. travel agencies were appointed by IATA as well.

It is not uncommon for a travel professional who has been in the industry for many years to refer to the ARC number as an IATA number. Years ago, every agency's identification number was an IATA number. Some travel professionals may refer to the agency's IATA number. No matter what it's called, an agency's identification is the ARC number.

Agency Automation

Over 95 percent of all travel agencies in the United States are automated. A reservation, known as a passenger name record (PNR), for air travel, car rental, hotel, or other product is made in the computer rather than by phone. Almost all of the automated travel agencies subscribe to a Computer Reservation System (CRS), more commonly known as a Global Travel Distribution System (GDS). There are four main GDSs used in the United States (see Figure 6–1).

The GDS provides the software, or program, that allows travel counselors to make reservations, issue tickets, and so on. The travel agency may also use other software such as programs for word processing, databases, spreadsheets, Internet access, and e-mail. Most travel agencies use standard PCs to run the GDS software. PC hardware consists of a monitor, CPU, keyboard, and printer. Some travel agencies

Important Industry Web Sites

Airlines Reporting Corporation: **http://www.arccorp.com**

International Airlines Travel Agent Network: **http://www.iatan.org**

International Air Transport Association: **http://www.iata.org**

System Name	U.S. Host(s)	International Hosts	Publicly Traded	Agency Installations	Web Site
Amadeus	Continental	Air France Iberia Lufthansa	yes—IBEX	Over 220,000 terminals in 210 markets worldwide	http://www.amadeus.com
Galileo, subsidiary of Cedent (marketed as Apollo in the United States)	United	Alitalia British Air KLM Swissair	yes—CD	Over 43,500 agencies in 105 countries	http://www.galileo.com
Sabre	American	none	yes—TSG	Over 50,000 agencies wolrdwide	http://www.sabre.com
Worldspan, owned by Travel Transaction Processing	Delta Northwest	none	no	Over 18,000 agencies in 70 countries	http://www.worldspan.com

FIGURE 6–1 Global Travel Distribution Systems (GDSs) used in the United States.

own their PCs, but most agencies lease their hardware from the GDS.

Each travel agency has a special identification in the GDS called a **pseudocity code**. The pseudocity code is assigned at the time the travel agency contracts with the GDS. By using this identification, all reservations are secured to the booking agency, making access to the reservations by other agencies impossible. Everyone who uses a GDS is given an identification, called a **sine** or **sign**. The sine identifies the travel counselor or airline employee to the GDS.

The principle airline developers or owners of a GDS are called hosts. Does that mean that an agency can only sell its GDS host airline(s)? No, almost all of the other airlines will pay each GDS so that their flight schedules, fare information, and so on are accessible to all travel counselors. These airlines are called cohosts. Each GDS has several levels of participation for the cohosts. A high level of participation means greater expense to the cohost and more data will be available to travel counselors. All major U.S. airlines and many international airlines have the highest level of participation in all four GDSs used in the United States.

One of the most important features of the highest level of GDS participation is last seat availability. This means that the participating airline provides the GDS with up-to-the-minute flight availability. An airline with a lower level of GDS participation will send a "sold-out" message to the GDS before the flight is actually sold out, giving booking messages in transit time to reach them.

Direct access is another important feature of the higher levels of GDS participation. Direct access is comparable to the travel counselor reaching into the participating airline's computer and getting firsthand information.

In doing so, the travel counselor has access to last seat availability. Direct access also helps reduce the chance of a reservation being electronically lost in transit to the booking airline. A lost reservation is referred to as a **no-rec**, which means no record. Figure 6–2 shows the relation between hosts, cohosts, and direct access capability.

Each GDS offers travel agencies a variety of reservation platforms. Some are considered "dedicated," others are "dial-in," and still others are "Internet-based." In all cases, a phone line and modem are required. Regardless of the platform, the basic GDS functionality is the same. Airlines, car rental, hotels, cruises, and tours can be booked in all GDSs as well as a variety of other suppliers. Added features of the GDS include e-mail, fax, and ARC reporting.

Host . . . . automatic direct access, last seat availability

Cohost level 1 . . . . . automatic direct access, last seat availability

Cohost level 2 . . . . . direct access and last seat availability requires secondary format

Cohost level 3 . . . . . direct access not available; must call the airline for last seat availability

Cohost level 4 . . . . . schedule and fare information displayed but not flight availability; must call the airline to make a reservation

FIGURE 6–2 GDS host, cohost, direct access, and last seat availability.

As you can see, the GDS is a most valuable tool in the travel industry.

Agency Revenue

Travel agency revenue falls into four categories: commission, commission overrides, markups, and service fees.

Most nonair travel suppliers, known as vendors, pay the travel agency a commission for selling their products. The standard commission percentage varies from one vendor to another.

Some travel agencies will join a consortium as a means of increasing revenue. By pooling the sales volume of all member travel agencies, the consortium has increased bargaining power with the vendors. A vendor may contract with the consortium to pay all member travel agencies a certain percentage over and above the standard commission. These additional commission points are called override.

In addition to consortia, there are also franchise, marketing, and cooperative groups. Although these groups function much like consortia, agency membership is usually more expensive. Some examples of national or international franchise and cooperative groups include American Express, Carlson Wagonlit, Cruise Holidays International, Empress Travel, Hickory Travel Systems, National Association of Commissioned Travel Agents (NACTA), Thor, Travel Professionals International, and Uniglobe.

A large travel agency may approach a vendor with the agency's sales figures. Based on those figures, the vendor may agree that the agency is aggressively promoting the sale of that vendor's products. As a result, the vendor may agree to pay the agency an override percentage. Override percentages can be any amount, but 1 to 5 percent over the standard commission rate is common.

Important Industry Web Sites

Travel Trade: **http://www.traveltrade.com**

Travel Weekly: **http://www.travelweekly.com**

Some products are sold to the travel agency at a net rate; that is, without a commission being included. Before the counselor quotes a price to the client, the counselor must markup the net rate; in other words, the agency profit must be added. Group space, full aircraft charters, convention hotel rates, and some air consolidator fares are often quoted as a net rate.

The fourth area of agency revenue is service fees. Practically all travel agencies in the United States charge their customers for certain services. Each travel agency has a schedule of services and associated fees. As a general rule, the less commission the sale of a product generates, the higher the fee. Some agencies charge fees only for the sale of products that pay low commission percentages. For example, because air travel does not earn commission, an agency will charge a fee, whereas the standard commission on a cruise or tour is 10 percent, so the agency may not charge a fee on these products. Service fees can be processed electronically on an ARC document called a

Selected Consortia and Marketing Groups

Name	Year Founded	Approximate Membership Locations	Approximate Cost	Web Site
Cruise Shoppes	1986	250	$300	http://www.cruiseshoppes.com
Ensemble Travel Group	1968	1,500	$600 initial; yearly fee based on sales	http://www.ensembledirect.com
eTravCo	1996	1,400	$200 to $300 per year	http://www.etravco.com
MAST	1969	138	$450 to $1,550 depending on type of membership	http://www.mast.org
The Travel Authority	1970	Over 40	Varies	http://www.thetravelauthority.com
Travelsavers	1970	2,800	None	http://www.travelsavers.com
Vacation.com	1998	8,000	$350	http://www.vacation.com

Airline ticket or electronic ticket processing charge	$30–$60
Voluntary ticket or electronic ticket reissue, refund, or void	$36–$50
Voucher transaction	$25
Domestic tour research	$25–$50
International tour research	$50–$100

FIGURE 6–3 Sample Fee Schedule.

Miscellaneous Charges Order (MCO) or a Travel Agency Service Fee (TASF) document may be used.

Travel agency service fees can be any amount the agency selects, and they usually vary depending on the product (see Figure 6–3).

The combination of the standard commission, overrides, markups, and service fees represent the travel agency's revenue. From this revenue, the agency must pay rent, salaries, memberships, utilities, GDS expenses, and so on. To increase revenue sources, some travel agencies are now selling travel-related products such as luggage, electrical appliances, books, maps, and other items.

Web Activity

Access one of the travel counselor trade publications. What are the most recent news stories that deal with agency commission?

With so many travel-buying venues available today, it is no wonder that travel agencies put strong emphasis on developing and keeping customer loyalty. Your knowledge and experience coupled with your people skills are the foundation of a solid relationship with your clients.

A recent study found that 7 out of 10 U.S. adults are more comfortable booking travel with a traditional travel counselor instead of making arrangements by phone or online with the vendor. According to the study, more than half of the respondents cited the counselor's understanding of the traveler's needs and their willingness to find appropriate travel products as the number one advantage to using a travel counselor.

With all this in mind, it is easy to understand why most travel agencies are putting greater emphasis on customer service and the sales ability of their counselors. As you begin your career in travel, never lose sight of the following:

- Without customer service, customers will disappear.
- Without customers, sales will disappear.
- Without sales, revenue will disappear.
- Without revenue, the travel agency and its employees will disappear.

PLEASE TURN TO PAGE 89 AND COMPLETE EXERCISE 6–1 NOW.

U.S. Air Travel Safety

As a result of the terrorist attacks of September 11, 2001, the U.S. government signed into law the Aviation and Transportation Security Act. This act provided for the creation of the Transportation Security Administration (TSA). As of March 2003, the TSA is part of the Department of Homeland Security.

The TSA has programs, in various stages of development, covering aviation, mass transit, rail, highway, pipeline, postal and shipping, and support of the U.S. Coast Guard.

As part of the TSA's efforts to provide for safer and more efficient air travel, the Registered Traveler program is in its pilot stages. This program is designed for certain personal information to be stored about a traveler and this information is rapidly checked and verified during the flight check-in procedure.

Testing, training, and maintenance of airport security screeners will become more efficient and standardized through the TSA program known as Screening Partnership Program, known as SPP. The SPP is a joint effort between the government and the private sectors.

THE AIRLINES

Every airline operating in the United States is governed by two federal agencies, the Department of Transportation and the Federal Aviation Administration.

The Department of Transportation (DOT) regulates all air transportation within the United States. An example of DOT's regulation is that before an airline can begin service between two cities, the airline must apply for DOT approval. Another function of DOT is to monitor GDS displays to ensure that one airline is not given preferential treatment over another. Preferential placement of airline information in a GDS is called bias and it is an illegal practice.

The Federal Aviation Administration (FAA) is a division of the DOT and is a very important organization to all of us. The FAA is responsible for air traffic control, aircraft certification, passenger safety, and pilot licensing. Without the FAA, air travel could not exist.

Another important government agency is the National Transportation Safety Board (NTSB). There are two primary areas of functionality within the NTSB: safety and investigation. The NTSB recommends safety enhancements to the airlines, DOT, and FAA. It is the NTSB's responsibility to investigate all airline accidents, determine the cause if possible, and make recommendations as to how the problems could have been avoided. The NTSB publishes accident statistics on a yearly basis.

Most U.S. airlines are members of the **Air Transport Association (ATA)**. This organization represents the commercial air travel industry before Congress and is a lobby group for the airlines. The primary purpose of the ATA is to promote safety and efficiency in air travel.

Important Industry Web Sites

Air Transport Association (United States): **http://www.air-transport.org**

Air Transport Association of Canada: **http://www.atac.ca**

Department of Transportation: **http://www.dot.gov**

Federal Aviation Administration: **http://www.faa.gov**

Federal Trade Commission: **http://www.ftc.gov**

Homeland Security: **http://www.dhs.gov**

National Transportation Safety Board: **http://www.ntsb.gov**

Transportation Security Administration: **http://www.tsa.gov**

All airlines are divided into three main categories: major, national, and regional. Since the enactment of the Airline Deregulation Act of 1978, the distinction between the classifications has become somewhat blurred, and in some cases, barely exists.

An airline that operates flights from one country to another country or long-distance routes within its home country is considered a **major airline**. Generally, a major airline has revenue over $1 billion annually. A somewhat obsolete term for a major airline is trunk airline.

The classification of a national airline, in the true sense of the term, has almost disappeared. A national airline maintains schedules within one country exclusively and operates both long- and short-haul routes. Some industry references define a national airline based strictly on revenue, between $100 million and $1 billion annually.

Regional airlines, commonly called **commuter airlines**, generally limit their routes to short-haul flights. As a rule, a regional airline operates within a specific area of the country and often utilizes turbo-prop or propeller aircraft accommodating from 19 to 103 passengers.

Without an interline agreement . . .

1. Your client is traveling to his destination on Airline A, but returning home on Airline B. You would have to issue separate tickets, one for each airline.

2. Your client is traveling on Airline A to Pittsburgh where she must change to Airline B for her trip to Manchester, New Hampshire. Your client would have to claim her baggage in Pittsburgh from Airline A and recheck it with Airline B.

3. Your client wants to ship some freight to Lafayette, Indiana. The quickest way is with Airline A to Chicago, then Airline B. It cannot be done without an interline agreement.

FIGURE 6–4 Sample interline agreement provisions.

Almost all U.S. and international airlines have Web sites. A comprehensive list of these sites can be found at http://www.quickaid.com/links/airlines.cg.

Thankfully for all of us who travel, most airlines have agreed to work together by signing **interline agreements**. An interline agreement is between two airlines that agree to transfer baggage, cargo, and passengers from one airline to the other (see Figure 6–4). Without an interline agreement, it would not be possible for both airlines' flights to appear on a single ticket.

Airline Codes

Every airline in the United States has been assigned a two-character code by ARC. International airlines also have two-character codes, which are assigned by IATA. In the early days of air travel, all airline codes were a combination of two letters. Several years ago, ARC and IATA exhausted the supply of two letter combinations. So, today, several airlines have codes that consist of a letter and a number.

In addition to the two-character code, each airline has a three-character code, although this code is seldom used in the travel industry. Every airline also has a numeric code that appears on airline identification plates. The numeric code is used on tickets and refund transactions.

Everyone in the travel industry, including travel counselors, airline reservationists, baggage handlers, and air traffic controllers, uses the two-character airline codes. All reference sources, flight timetables, and computer displays use the two-character airline code, not the airline name. Travel counselors can locate airline codes in their GDS, and a complete list of airline codes can be found in the *OAG (Official Airline Guide) Flight Guide*. It is interesting to note that as part of the interview process, some employers test the job applicant's knowledge of these codes. Here is a list of selected U.S. airlines and their codes.

Airline Name	Airline Code
Alaska Air	AS
Aloha Air	AQ
American Airlines	AA
America West	HP
ATA	TZ
Continental Airlines	CO
Delta Airlines	DL
Frontier Airlines	F9
Hawaiian Air	HA
Jet Blue	B6
Midwest Airlines	YX
Northwest Airlines	NW
Southwest	WN
United Airlines	UA
USAirways	US

It has become common, if somewhat confusing, for one airline to contract to use the code of another airline. This practice is called code sharing. The airline that uses the code of another airline is called a dual-designated carrier. In the early days of code sharing, a smaller airline would contract to use the code of a larger airline. Today, it is common for a large airline to use the code of another large airline.

Although printed flight schedules and computer displays indicate a code-share situation, it can be easily overlooked. The practice of code sharing (see Figure 6–5) means that travel counselors must pay careful attention when making reservations so that the client is advised of a dual-designated carrier. For example, a passenger's ticket shows a flight on Continental Airlines but the flight is a code share with American West Airlines. At which airline's counter does the

Airline Name	Code Share Partners
American	American Eagle, Alaska, Horizon, Hawaiian, Horizon, and Mexicana.
Continental	Atlantic Southeast, Delta, Northwest, and Hawaiian.
Delta	Alaska, Continental, Comair Northwest, Aeromexico, Air Jamaica, and El Al Israel.
Northwest	American Eagle, Horizon, Mesaba, Hawaiian, Continental, Delta, Sky West, and Atlantic Southeast.
United	Aloha, Air Canada, and USAirways.
USAirways	Bahamasair, Mesaba, Sky West, and United.

FIGURE 6–5 Examples of code sharing.

client check in? Without the travel counselor explaining the situation to the client, major problems can easily arise.

The positive side of code sharing means that small airports are now served by major airlines through their code-sharing partners. From an airfare perspective, this means that a single fare on one airline can be used instead of two separate fares on different airlines. Travelers who are members of an airline's frequent flyer program benefit because air miles are accumulated on the entire trip, even on the dual-designated airline's portion.

Airline Policies

Most U.S. airlines have comparable policies for special services and situations, although each airline's cost for a particular service may differ a bit. Each airline has a special area of data in the GDS where travel counselors can learn about the services, costs, and any special procedures that must be followed.

Infants (under two years of age) who do not occupy a seat are called lap-held infants and on flights within the United States, there is no cost. A lap-held infant traveling internationally pays 10 percent of the adult fare. For safety, many passengers want to use an infant seat and secure the infant in the seat next to the adult. Most airlines charge one half of the adult fare for an infant in a seat.

Each child (over two years of age but under 14 years) must have a seat. There are special fares for children under 12, but they are usually a reduction of the full coach fare, the most expensive type of coach fare. Because most passengers use discounted coach fares, it is usually less expensive for the child to use the same fare as the adult. Please note that under certain circumstances a few airlines may consider a passenger under 17 years of age to be a child.

Each airline has strict requirements for unaccompanied minors (children under 14 years of age traveling alone). As a general rule, the child must be at least five years old; eight years old if a change of planes is required. Information about the adult meeting the child at the destination must be given to the airline. This information includes the name, address, phone number, and relationship to the child. The airline is very strict about verifying the identity of the adult meeting the child. An unaccompanied minor pays the applicable adult fare and the airline charges an additional fee of $60 to $100.

Passengers traveling with *pets* must advise the travel counselor so that the counselor can make a special request to the airline. All pets must be in an approved carrier. Generally, the airlines will allow one dog and one cat to travel in the passenger compartment. Pets who will travel in the passenger compartment must be small enough so that the carrier fits under the seat in front of the passenger.

Larger or exotic pets must travel in the cargo section of the aircraft, but they will be the last to be loaded at the origin city, and the first to be removed at the destination. Please note that some airlines will not carry live animals in cargo for safety reasons. The airline charge for pets in the cabin or in cargo ranges from $75 to $150 each way.

Service animals, such as seeing-eye dogs, are allowed to travel with their masters and sit at their masters' feet. The dogs must be harnessed and be free of disease and odor. It is a good idea for a passenger traveling with an animal to carry a certificate of vaccination on the trip.

Some passengers may not be able to walk distances and this can be a problem in larger airports. Other passengers may be easily confused and need help. Most airlines offer a service called **meet and assist**. An airline or airport employee meets the passenger at a designated location in an electric cart, much like a golf cart. This service can be requested to take the passenger from the ticket counter area to the gate area, from one gate to another gate, or from the gate to the baggage claim area. Not all airlines offer this service but those that do do not charge for this service, although a tip to the attendant is appreciated.

The travel counselor can request a wheelchair for a passenger who is unable to walk and board the aircraft. Unlike a meet and assist, an airline or airport employee takes the passenger onto the aircraft and assists the passenger into his seat. Almost all airlines offer this service and there is usually no charge, although a tip to the attendant is appreciated.

Some passengers are prohibited from eating certain foods due to dietary, cultural, or religious restrictions. The travel counselor can request a special meal for these passengers. Some of the more frequently requested special meals include diabetic, no salt, low calorie, vegetarian, kosher, Hindu, and Moslem. Most snacks and meals are no longer free but are available for purchase. Depending on the airline, snacks and meals may be complimentary in first and business classes.

Most airlines allow seats to be assigned in advance of travel. **Seat assignments** indicate the specific row and seat the passenger will occupy on each flight. Each airline specifies how far in advance of the flight seats can be assigned. When possible, the travel counselor should make the seat assignments in the GDS. Boarding passes, the physical evidence of the seat assignments, are usually issued by the airline when the traveler checks in for his flight.

For flights within the United States, passengers should call the airline 24 hours before the flight to **reconfirm** the reservation. At this time, the passenger learns if the flight number, departure time, or arrival time has changed. This process should be repeated at the destination, before the trip home. Internationally, reconfirmation should be done two to three days before each flight.

Each airline sets limitations on the number of pieces, size, and weight of baggage that can be carried on board a flight as well as baggage that will be in the cargo compartment. Carry-on baggage must be small enough to be stored under the seat or in the overhead compartments. In addition to the free baggage allowance, each airline has established a policy for excess baggage. Never assume that the baggage allowance on Airline A's flight from Boston to Atlanta is the same as the allowance for Airline B's flight from Chicago to London. Each airline provides baggage information in the GDS and this information can also be found in the *OAG Flight Guide* and on airline Web sites.

For most flights within the United States, passengers should arrive at least one or two hours before flight time. At the airport check-in, the airline may issue a **boarding pass**, a card for each flight showing the row and seat that has been assigned. Some airlines simply write the row and seat on the ticket or ticket jacket instead of using cards. A few airlines do not assign specific seats; rather, they assign passengers to a boarding group, identified by a group number or color.

Most of the larger airlines have **frequent flyer programs** and membership in them is free. Each airline's program includes partner airlines, hotels, rental car companies, and other vendors. When a frequent flyer member travels on one of the partner airlines, or uses the services of the other vendors, "miles" are accumulated into the frequent flyer member's account. These "miles" can be used for air travel upgrades, free air travel, and other products. Travel counselors and clients can access data about frequent flyer programs on each airline's Web site, or see combined information at http://www.webflyer.com.

When the flight the traveler wants is sold out, the traveler may ask to be put on a **wait-list**. A wait-list is the airline's list of people who hope to be confirmed on a particular flight as cancellations are received. When a travel counselor puts a traveler on a wait-list, the counselor usually confirms an alternate flight in case the wait-list does not clear. If the airline can clear, or confirm, a wait-listed passenger, the airline notifies the travel counselor who, in turn, notifies the traveler. It is important to note that almost all of the lower-priced fares do not allow wait-listing.

Airline Operations

All U.S. airlines have established their route systems using the **hub and spoke** principle. Each airline selects one or more airports to be hubs and these act as the home base for the airline. The spokes are the cities around the hub. Flights from the spokes act as feeder routes into the hub.

Have you ever wondered why you had to change planes in Chicago O'Hare, for example? Almost all changes of planes take place at hub airports. Chicago O'Hare was a hub for the airline you were flying. Figure 6–6 shows some of the major hubs in the United States and the airlines that use them as such.

One of the most important statistics for an airline is **load factor**. Load factor is the relationship of the number of seats on a specific flight to the number of booked seats.

Airline Name	Hub City and Airport
American	Chicago O'Hare, Dallas–Ft. Worth, Miami, San Juan, St. Louis
Continental	Houston George Bush Intercontinental, Detroit Metro, Cleveland, Memphis
Delta	Atlanta, Dallas–Ft. Worth, Cincinnati, Salt Lake City
Northwest	Detroit Metro, Memphis, Minneapolis
United	Chicago O'Hare, Denver
USAirways	Pittsburgh, Charlotte, Philadelphia, Baltimore, Washington Dulles

FIGURE 6–6 Selected U.S. airlines and their hubs.

For example, if 78 seats were booked on a flight that could accommodate 139, the load factor is 56 percent. Included in the 78 booked seats are a certain number of people who will not show up for the flight and will not cancel their reservations. These people are called **no-shows**.

Over a period of time, the airline will monitor the number of no-shows on a specific flight. This information helps the airline determine by what percentage it can safely **overbook** the flight. Overbooking means allowing more seats to be booked than are actually available.

On a full flight, if the number of no-shows and the number of overbookings are equal, everyone travels. However, if the number of overbookings exceeds the number of no-shows, there are too many passengers and not enough seats. In this situation, the airline first asks for volunteers who are willing to give up their seats and take a later flight. These volunteers are given a voucher for a certain dollar value that can be used toward future travel. This voucher is called **denied boarding compensation (DBC)**.

If there are not enough volunteers on an overbooked flight, the airline removes off-duty airline personnel and those travel counselors who are traveling free or on a travel counselor's discounted fare. These passengers are accommodated on the next available flight, but no compensation is given.

If there are still too many passengers for the flight, **bumping** begins. Bumping means removing regular passengers. The bumped passengers are booked on the next available flight and are given DBC. How does an airline decide which passengers to bump? That is a bit of a mystery. The airline may use any of the following criteria:

- fare—the lower the fare, the greater the chance of being bumped.
- purchase date—the closer to the day of the flight the travel is purchased, the greater the chance of being bumped.
- check-in time—the closer to flight time the passenger checks in, the greater the chance of being bumped.
- passenger status—a senator, for example, might have a lesser chance of being bumped.
- frequent flyer member—by virtue of their loyalty to the airline, frequent flyer members may have a lesser chance of being bumped.

PLEASE TURN TO PAGE 90 AND COMPLETE EXERCISE 6–2 NOW.

COMMERCIAL AIRCRAFT

Today's aircraft come in many different sizes and designs. Some aircraft carry fewer than 20 passengers, while other aircraft can accommodate more than 350 people. Some aircraft have one passenger compartment, known as a **cabin**; others have three or four cabins. The passenger cabin(s) on some aircraft are pressurized; others are not. Some aircraft are powered by jet engines, some have turbine engines with propellers (turbo-prop), while still others have piston engines with propellers (prop). A full list of commercial aircraft and statistical information can be found in the *OAG Flight Guide*. Some of the more popular aircraft are shown in Figure 6–7.

All aircraft, regardless of size, fall into one of two categories: narrow-body or wide-body. A **narrow-body aircraft** has one aisle that runs down the center of the aircraft. All regional airlines use narrow-body aircraft and the larger airlines use them on many of their routes. A **wide-body aircraft** has two aisles and each row of seats is divided into three sections. Large airlines use wide-body aircraft on some long-distance U.S. routes and flights to foreign countries.

It is important to note that passengers traveling with personal wheelchairs cannot take them onboard the aircraft. Personal wheelchairs are too wide for all aircraft aisles and must be carried in cargo. Passengers who cannot walk onboard use wheelchairs belonging to the airline or airport.

When an airline places an order with an aircraft manufacturer, the airline specifies the configuration. The **configuration** is the floor plan or interior design of the aircraft. The airline can specify the number of cabins, the

 Web Activity

Access three major U.S. airlines' Web sites. On each site, locate an aircraft diagram for a Boeing 727. Are the three airlines' configurations the same?

Aircraft	Code	Wide-Body	Engine Type, Number, & Location	Pressurized	Passengers	Coach Seat Configuration
Aerospatiale Alenia (all series)	ATR	no	turbo-prop, 2, wings	yes	42–74	2/2
Aerospatiale Alenia ATR 72	AT7	no	turbo-prop, 2, wings	yes	64–74	2/2
Airbus Industrie A300	AB3	yes	jet, 2, wings	yes	220–375	2/4/2
Airbus Industrie A320	320	no	jet, 2, wings	yes	131–156	3/3
Beechcraft 1900 (all series)	BE1	no	turbo-prop, 2, wings	yes	19	1/1
Boeing 717	717	no	jet, 2, fuselage	yes	106–117	2/3
Boeing 727 (all series)	727	no	jet, 3, fuselage and tail	yes	125	3/3
Boeing 737 (all series)	737	no	jet, 2, wings	yes	103	3/3
Boeing 747 (all series)	747	yes	jet, 4, wings	yes	452–548	3/4/3
Boeing 757-200	757	no	jet, 2, wings	yes	178–239	3/3
Boeing 767 (all series)	767	yes	jet, 2, wings	yes	216–290	2/3/2
Boeing 777	777	yes	jet, 2, wings	yes	231–375	2/5/2
British Aerospace Jetstream 31	J31	no	turbo-prop, 2, wings	yes	8–19	1/2
British Aerospace Jetstream 41	J41	no	turbo-prop, 2, wings	yes	29	1/2
Canadair Regional Jet	CRJ	no	jet, 2, fuselage	yes	50	2/2
DeHaviland DHC-8 (all series)	DH8	no	turbo-prop, 2, wings	yes	36–56	2/2
Dornier 328	D38	no	turbo-prop, 2, wings	yes	30	1/2
Embraer EMB-120 Brasilia	EM2	no	turbo-prop, 2, wings	yes	24–30	1/2
Fairchild Metro Merlin	SWM	no	turbo-prop, 2, wings	yes	6–20	1/1
Fokker 100	100	no	jet, 2, fuselage	yes	107–119	2/3
Fokker F28 (all series)	F28	no	jet, 2, fuselage	yes	55–85	2/3
Lockheed L-1011 (all series)	L10	yes	jet, 3, wings and tail	yes	256–400	3/4/3
Lockheed L-1011-500	L15	yes	jet, 3, wings and tail	yes	256–400	2/5/2
McDonnell Douglas MD-80	M80	no	jet, 2, fuselage	yes	172	2/3
McDonnell Douglas DC-10 (all series)	D10	yes	jet, 3, wings and tail	yes	255–380	2/5/2
McDonnell Douglas DC-9 (10 & 20 series)	DC9	no	jet, 2, fuselage	yes	90	2/3
McDonnell Douglas MD-11	M11	yes	jet, 3, wings and tail	yes	250–400	2/5/2
Saab SF340	SF3	no	turbo-prop, 2, wings	yes	35	1/2

FIGURE 6–7 Popular aircraft in use today.

number of seat rows in each cabin, the distance between each row of seats (called **pitch**), and so on.

Several travel counselor reference sources illustrate the aircraft configuration for a variety of airlines and aircraft types. Each diagram shows the body of the aircraft, known as the **fuselage**; the passenger cabins; and the **bulkheads**, the wall or partition between cabins. An aircraft configuration also shows the wing location; flight deck (cockpit);

seating areas; and the location of lavatories, the galley (kitchen), storage areas, and emergency exits. Figure 6–8 shows a narrow-body aircraft configuration and Figure 6–9 shows a wide-body aircraft.

Narrow-body aircraft generally have one or two passenger cabins, first class and coach. Wide-body aircraft usually have a first-class cabin, business-class cabin, and three coach-class cabins.

First class is very expensive but offers wider seats, greater pitch, and more elaborate food and beverage choices. On international flights, first-class seats may be "sleeper seats" that fully recline.

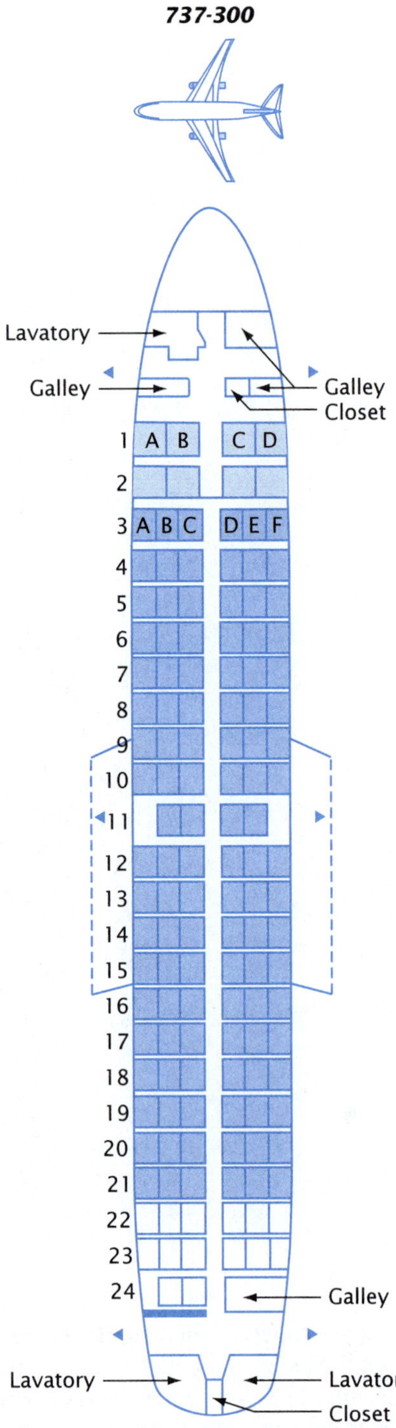

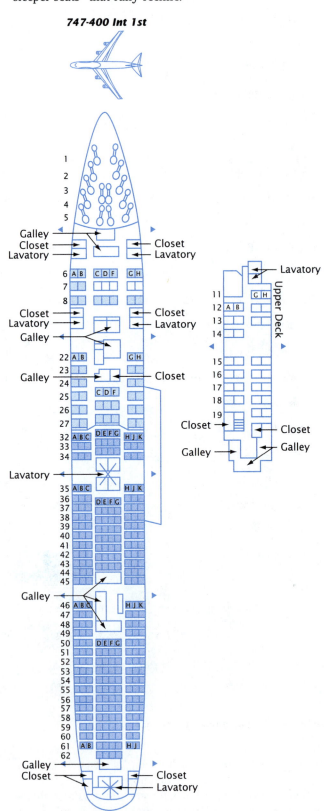

FIGURE 6–8 Example of narrow-body aircraft configuration.

FIGURE 6–9 Example of wide-body aircraft configuration.

Business class is less expensive than first class, but more expensive than coach class. Business class offers wider seats, greater pitch, and enhanced food and beverage service.

On most airlines, the coach-class cabin(s) has narrow seats and very little pitch. Meal service on flights within the United States has greatly decreased over the past few years, but beverage and snack service is still available on some flights and meals are available for purchase.

The size and configuration of an aircraft directly impacts passenger comfort and seat preference. Very small aircraft may not **pressurize** the passenger cabin according to flight altitude. The lack of pressurization can cause pain in the inner ear and neck, especially in infants and small children. It is vitally important that the travel counselor advise the passenger if the proposed itinerary utilizes a smaller aircraft, especially if it is not pressurized.

When making seat assignments for your clients, consider the following:

- Seats immediately in front of an emergency exit do not usually recline because they would block the exit area.
- Seats over the wing provide more stability but may experience increased engine noise on certain aircraft.
- Seats in the rear may experience increased vibration, motion, fumes, and engine noise on certain aircraft.
- The bulkhead row (the row of seats just behind the bulkhead) usually offers increased legroom, but carry-on baggage must be stored in the overhead compartments.
- On some international flights, the rear section of the aircraft may allow smoking.
- Seats behind an emergency exit sometimes offer increased leg room.
- Only passengers who are at least 16 years old and are capable of and willing to take responsibility during an emergency can be seated in an emergency exit row.
- Some airlines will preassign seats in the first several rows to frequent flyer members only.

PLEASE TURN TO PAGE 91 AND COMPLETE EXERCISE 6-3 NOW.

AIRPORTS

For inexperienced travelers, the thought of finding one's way around the airport can be a scary thing. Even people who have traveled extensively are sometimes intimidated by the thought of having to change planes at very large airports such as Chicago O'Hare or Dallas–Ft. Worth. Airports can be confusing, but with guidance from the travel counselor many of the traveler's anxieties can be relieved. The *OAG Flight Guide,* the *OAG Travel Planner* series, and many airline Web sites have diagrams of major airports. These can easily be copied or printed and given to the passenger as an added service.

Departures

Airports around the world come in all sizes, shapes, and designs. But the center or heart of any airport is the **terminal** building. Small airports have one terminal, while large airports may have more than one. Passengers arriving at the airport to board a flight enter the terminal at the *departure area*. At some airports, the passenger is able to check his baggage outside the terminal with airline employees called **skycaps.** Some airlines charge $2.00 per bag for curbside check-in.

Important Industry Web Sites

Directory of Airport Web Site Links:
http://www.quickaid.com/airports/

This site offers information about airport ground transportation, information about hotels and yellow pages, and includes maps of airport terminals.

Most departing passengers go into the terminal to the airline *ticket counters* to *check in*. For many travelers, this is their first contact with the airline. At the ticket counter, the passenger gives her photo ID or passport and ticket (if she has one) to the ticket counter agent.

Depending on the airline, passengers may be able to check in at a self-serve kiosk. A credit card number may also be required to verify passenger name and identity. By entering the reservation number, the computer screen displays the passenger's booking, followed by step-by-step instructions for completing the check-in process. Another option for travelers who have booked their flights on an airline's Web site is online check-in. Before leaving home, the traveler displays the booking on the airline's Web site and then follows the directions for check-in. However, with security procedures as they are today, these two options may not save the traveler much time in the long run.

The ticket counter agent displays the traveler's reservation in the computer and compares the name to the ID and ticket. At this time, the ticket counter agent tags checked baggage, assigns a seat if it was not done previously, and issues a boarding pass. The boarding pass identifies the row and seat that has been assigned to the passenger. The ticket counter agent also tells the passenger where to go for his flight.

The passenger may have to walk down a long corridor, called a **concourse**, to get to her **gate**. In the concourse area are the security check points. Only those with tickets or boarding passes are allowed beyond this point. All carry-on baggage, purses, laptop computers, and so on are checked, either in the x-ray machine or by security personnel. Depending on the type of shoes the passenger is wearing, she may be asked to remove them for inspection. Each traveler must empty all pockets and place the contents into a tray for inspection. When all this is done, each passenger walks through the metal detector. If any metal is detected, the traveler will be scanned by a hand-held devise and in extreme circumstances, could be physically searched. The gate is the area where she waits to board her flight and has the doorway she uses to exit the airport. At each gate area, there is a counter staffed by airline personnel called gate agents. Gate agents can make seat assignments and issue boarding passes, just like ticket counter agents. This is especially helpful for passengers who checked their luggage with the skycaps and for travelers who have only carry-on baggage.

Most airports use connecting devices, called jetways, to connect the airport door to the aircraft door. The passenger walks through the jetway and onto the plane. Some airports do not have jetways and some aircraft cannot use them. In these circumstances, passengers walk from the airport onto a paved area, known as the tarmac, to where the aircraft is parked. In other situations, an airport vehicle is used to transport passengers from the gate area to the aircraft.

After all passengers have boarded the aircraft, baggage has been stowed, all fuel and catering has been loaded, and the flight-deck crew have completed their preflight checks, the flight is ready to depart. When the flight receives clearance from ground control, it begins to move along the taxiway toward the assigned *runway*. At busy airports, it is common for the flight to have to wait in line for takeoff. After takeoff, ground control "hands off" the flight to air traffic control and the passengers are finally on their way.

Arrivals

When a traveler arrives at his destination, he exits the aircraft through the jetway and walks through the concourse to the baggage claim area. Baggage is off-loaded from the aircraft and brought to a baggage handling area. From this area, the luggage is put onto conveyor belts, called carousels, which move the luggage to the baggage claim area.

Many airports have rental car companies located in the baggage claim area. Taxis, airport shuttles, and limos are available at all but the smallest airports. Hotels located near major airports may have shuttle service available for hotel guests arriving at the airport.

Airport Services

Today's airports try to make the time spent there as pleasant as possible. Waiting passengers can shop in a variety of stores, eat in restaurants, grab a snack at food stalls, or visit observation areas. Some airports even have health clubs with complete workout areas. All airports offer restroom facilities, baggage storage areas, and information centers. International airports have duty-free (tax-free) shops, as well as currency exchange, customs, and immigration areas.

A special amenity found in most major airports is the airline clubs, such as American's Admirals Club, United's Red Carpet Club, and Delta's Crown Room Club. Each airline club charges a membership fee of between $150 and $200 per year. Club members enjoy the benefits of a private waiting area, business center, complimentary refreshments, and the service of an airline representative. Many clubs have shower facilities and exercise areas. For someone who spends a good deal of time in airports, these clubs certainly make the experience more pleasant.

Airports are not owned by the airlines; rather, they are owned and operated by city, county, or state authorities, generally known as the airport authority. The airlines rent counter space and gate space and pay fees for every flight that arrives or departs. Stores, food outlets, and other vendors located within the airport pay rent to the airport authority. Rental car companies located in the baggage claim area or on airport property also pay rental fees. As flight service increases at a specific airport, more people use the facilities, more jobs are created, and more revenue is generated for the airport authority.

After the terrorist attacks of September 11, 2001, airport security has dramatically changed. Prior to these attacks, each airport authority was responsible for security. Now, it is the combined efforts of the National Security Administration (NSA), the airport authority, and private enterprise. Thanks to the dedication, hard work, and innovative new programs, security at U.S. airports has not only improved but has also become more consistent throughout the country. All airport security in the United States includes baggage x-ray, metal detectors, patrol personnel, and canine units.

Internationally, security tends to be stricter than we see in the United States. Some airports do not have trash receptacles because they can be used to hide explosive devices. Security personnel usually carry rifles. This can come as a great surprise to first-time travelers. By advising clients of what they might encounter, the travel professional is preparing the client for new situations. Remember, no one likes surprises.

AIRPORT CODES

Every city and airport has a three-letter code assigned by the International Standards Organization (ISO), located in Geneva, Switzerland. ARC and IATA have adopted the codes established by the ISO. These codes are used for everything from reservations to the tags put on checked baggage to air traffic controllers' radar screens.

Cities served by only one airport use the same code for the city as for the airport. Cities or major metropolitan areas that have more than one airport are assigned a city code and each airport has a separate code. It is interesting to note that, in some cases, the city code is the same as the code for one of the airports serving the metropolitan area.

U.S. Cities Served by Multiple Airports

- Chicago, Illinois
  - Chicago (city) — CHI
  - Chicago O'Hare Airport — ORD
  - Chicago Midway Airport — MDW

- Dallas–Ft. Worth, Texas metropolitan area
  - Dallas (city) — DFW
  - Dallas Love Field Airport — DAL
  - Dallas–Ft. Worth International Airport — DFW

- Detroit, Michigan
  - Detroit (city) — DTT
  - Detroit Wayne County (Metro) Airport — DTW
  - Detroit City Airport — DET

- Houston, Texas
  - Houston (city) — HOU
  - Houston George Bush Intercontinental Airport — IAH
  - Houston Hobby Airport — HOU

- Los Angeles, California metropolitan area
  - Los Angeles (city) — LAX
  - Los Angeles International Airport — LAX
  - Burbank Airport — BUR
  - Long Beach Airport — LGB
  - Ontario Airport — ONT
  - Orange County Airport — SNA

- New York, New York–Newark, New Jersey metropolitan area
  - New York (city) — NYC
  - New York LaGuardia Airport — LGA
  - New York Kennedy Airport — JFK
  - Newark Airport — EWR

- San Francisco, California metropolitan area
  - San Francisco (city) — SFO
  - San Francisco International Airport — SFO
  - Oakland Airport — OAK

- Washington, D.C.–Baltimore, Maryland metropolitan area
  - Baltimore (city) — BAL
  - Washington, D.C. (city) — WAS
  - Baltimore International Airport — BWI
  - Washington Dulles Airport — IAD
  - Washington Reagan National Airport — DCA

As part of the job interview, some travel agencies test the applicant's knowledge of these codes. See Figure 6–10 for a list of U.S. airport codes.

As you may have noticed, many of the codes seem logical. In many cases, the code is the first three letters of the city name. Others, however, seem to make no sense at all. Many times, knowing the reason for a seemingly bizarre code will help you to memorize the code more easily. The following code list indicates the reason for the code used.

- Hartford, Connecticut (BDL)—formerly known as Bradley Field
- Chicago O'Hare, Illinois (ORD)—formerly known as Orchard Field
- Spokane, Washington (GEG)—formerly Geiger Army Air Field
- Knoxville, Tennessee (TYS)—formerly McGee Tyson Airport
- Cincinnati, Ohio (CVG)—is actually located in Covington, Kentucky
- New Orleans, Louisiana (MSY)—originally called Moisant International Airport. Moisant is pronounced "Moy-San"
- Nashville, Tennessee (BNA)—originally called Berry Nashville Airport
- Orlando, Florida (MCO)—formerly McCoy Air Force Base
- Ft. Myers, Florida (RSW)—the new airport is called Regional Southwest
- Harrisburg, Pennsylvania (MDT)—the airport name is Olmsted State
- Louisville, Kentucky (SDF)—the airport name is Standiford Field

PLEASE TURN TO PAGE 92 AND COMPLETE EXERCISE 6–4 NOW.

? What Would You Do?

Your client wants to bring her mother from Lima, Peru, to Milwaukee. The best fare requires plane changes at both Miami and Atlanta. Your client is concerned about these plane changes because her mother speaks only Spanish.

1. Should you try to convince your client to book her mother on a direct flight, assuming one exists, even though it is more expensive?
2. Are airport signs in the United States typically in Spanish as well as English, thus eliminating the language problem?
3. Might the airline be of assistance to your client's mother in some way?

How does the travel professional know which code to use, the city or the airport code? The answer is simple: Always use the applicable airport code. City codes are not specific enough to use on flight schedules. Of course, there is an exception, and that is on ticket fare calculation. Here, city codes are used.

There are literally thousands and thousands of codes worldwide. It is impossible to learn all of the codes, so thankfully, an alphabetical list can be found in the *OAG Flight Guide*. City, airport, airline, and even aircraft codes can be obtained in the GDS.

ABE	Allentown, PA	DTW	Detroit, MI; Wayne County	MKE	Milwaukee, WI
ABQ	Albuquerque, NM		(Metro) Airport	MKK	Hoolehua, Molokai Island, HI
ABY	Albany, GA	ELP	El Paso, TX	MSN	Madison, WI
AGS	Augusta, GA	EWR	Newark, NJ	MSP	Minneapolis, MN
AIY	Atlantic City, NJ	EYW	Key West, FL	MSY	New Orleans, LA
ALB	Albany, NY	FAI	Fairbanks, AK	MYR	Myrtle Beach, SC
ANC	Anchorage, AK	FLL	Ft. Lauderdale, FL	OAK	Oakland, CA
ASE	Aspen, CO	GEG	Spokane, WA	OGG	Kahului, Maui Island, HI
ATL	Atlanta, GA	GNV	Gainesville, FL	OKC	Oklahoma City, OK
AUG	Augusta, ME	GRB	Green Bay, WI	OMA	Omaha, NE
AUS	Austin, TX	GRR	Grand Rapids, MI	ONT	Ontario, CA
AVL	Asheville, NC	GSO	Greensboro, NC	ORD	Chicago, IL; O'Hare Airport
BDL	Hartford, CT	GTF	Great Falls, MT	ORF	Norfolk, VA
BGR	Bangor, ME	HLN	Helena, MT	PBI	West Palm Beach, FL
BHM	Birmingham, AL	HNL	Honolulu, Oahu Island, HI	PDX	Portland, OR
BIL	Billings, MT	HOU	Houston, TX; Hobby Airport	PHL	Philadelphia, PA
BIS	Bismark, ND	IAD	Washington, DC; Dulles Airport	PHX	Phoenix, AZ
BNA	Nashville, TN	IAH	Houston, TX; George Bush	PIE	St. Petersburg, FL
BOI	Boise, ID		Intercontinental Airport	PIT	Pittsburgh, PA
BOS	Boston, MA	ICT	Wichita, KS	PNS	Pensacola, FL
BTR	Baton Rouge, LA	IDA	Idaho Falls, ID	PSP	Palm Springs, CA
BTV	Burlington, VT	IND	Indianapolis, IN	PWM	Portland, ME
BUF	Buffalo, NY	ITO	Hilo, Hawaii Island, HI	RAP	Rapid City, SD
BWI	Baltimore, MD	JAN	Jackson, MS	RDU	Raleigh–Durham, NC
BZN	Bozeman, MT	JAX	Jacksonville, FL	RIC	Richmond, VA
CAE	Columbia, SC	JFK	New York, NY; Kennedy Airport	RNO	Reno, NV
CAK	Akron/Canton, OH	JNU	Juneau, AK	ROA	Roanoke, VA
CHA	Chattanooga, TN	KOA	Kona, Hawaii Island, HI	RSW	Ft. Myers, Fl
CHS	Charleston, SC	LAS	Las Vegas, NV	SAN	San Diego, CA
CID	Cedar Rapids, IA	LAX	Los Angeles, CA; International	SAT	San Antonio, TX
CLE	Cleveland, OH		Airport	SAV	Savannah, GA
CLT	Charlotte, NC	LEX	Lexington, KY	SDF	Louisville, KY
CMH	Columbus, OH	LGA	New York, NY; LaGuardia	SEA	Seattle/Tacoma, WA
COS	Colorado Springs, CO		Airport	SFO	San Francisco, CA;
CRW	Charleston, WV	LIH	Lihue, Kauai Island, HI		International Airport
CVG	Cincinnati, OH	LIT	Little Rock, AR	SLC	Salt Lake City, UT
DAB	Daytona Beach, FL	LNK	Lincoln, NE	SMF	Sacramento, CA
DAL	Dallas, TX; Love Field Airport	MCI	Kansas City, MO	SRQ	Sarasota, FL
DAY	Dayton, OH	MCO	Orlando, FL	STL	St. Louis, MO
DCA	Washington, DC; Reagan	MDT	Harrisburg, PA	SYR	Syracuse, NY
	National Airport	MDW	Chicago, IL; Midway Airport	TOL	Toledo, OH
DEN	Denver, CO	MEM	Memphis, TN	TPA	Tampa, FL
DET	Detroit, MI; City Airport	MGM	Montgomery, AL	TUL	Tulsa, OK
DFW	Dallas–Ft. Worth, TX	MHT	Manchester, NH	TUS	Tucson, AZ
DSM	Des Moines, IA	MIA	Miami, FL	TYS	Knoxville, TN

FIGURE 6–10 U.S. Airport Codes.

SUMMARY

There are many agencies that appoint, govern, or oversee all facets of U.S. air travel. These agencies, sometimes known as conferences, are directly related to the operation of U.S. travel agencies, airlines, and airports. It is important for the travel professional to understand how these agencies interact and affect each other.

A basic understanding of how a travel agency functions, contracts for its computers, and generates revenue is vitally important. Armed with this knowledge, even the entry-level travel counselor can easily see how everything he does and the manner in which he does it can ultimately affect the travel agency's bottom line.

The travel industry, and especially air travel, has various codes for airlines, cities, airports, and aircraft. In addition to the codes, there is a plethora of acronyms and terms. Travel professionals must be well versed in these codes, acronyms, and terms if they are to do their jobs in a timely and efficient manner.

To better serve the traveler, it is important for the travel professional to understand the various airline policies and programs. It is also important to understand what happens at an airport and the procedures the traveler will encounter. Much of the travel professional's value to his clients is found in his knowledge and ability to explain air travel procedures to his clients, thereby avoiding potential problems the client may face. The primary difference between one travel professional and another is in the service that supplements the sale of travel products.

 For additional Travel and Tourism resources, go to http://www.hospitality-tourism.delmar.com.

PLEASE COMPLETE THE CHAPTER REVIEW QUESTIONS NOW.

EXERCISE 6–1 The Travel Agency and Air Travel

1. Identify the four GDSs and the U.S. airline(s) that hosts each system.

   _____

   _____

   _____

2. Why do many travel agencies find it beneficial to join a consortium? _____

   _____

3. Explain the two methods in which a new travel agency can gain airline approval to sell air travel. _____

   _____

4. What is a travel agency's GDS identification called? _____

5. What types of vendors are members of ARC? _____

6. What are the four types of agency revenue? _____

7. How is an agency's survival directly linked to customer service? _____

   _____

8. Identify two reasons why many U.S. travel agencies apply for appointment by IATAN in addition to ARC accreditation? _____

   _____

9. What is a passenger name record? _____

10. What types of travel sales usually earn commission for the travel agency? _____

11. What is an override commission? _____

12. To what conference would a new travel agency in Italy apply for appointment? _____

13. Identify four functions of ARC. _____

    _____

    _____

    _____

14. Why might a travel agency charge a service fee for one type of travel product but not another? _____

    _____

15. What type of computer hardware is used by most travel agencies? _____

16. What type of computer hardware is used by many airline ticket counter agents? _____

17. What does an ARC number identify? _____

18. What is a cohost? _____

19. Why do all travel agencies charge service fees when selling air travel? _____

    _____

20. Name the two documents used for processing service fees through ARC. _____
_____

EXERCISE 6-2 The Airlines

1. What does NTSB stand for? _____

2. What does the NTSB do? _____

3. What areas of air transportation are affected when two airlines have an interline agreement? _____
_____
_____

4. What are the conditions under which an airline will carry an unaccompanied minor? _____
_____
_____

5. What is the difference between an assigned seat and a boarding pass? _____
_____

6. To what agency must an airline apply before it can begin operating a new flight? _____

7. Where could a travel counselor obtain the code for Continental Airlines? _____

8. What is the airline practice of code sharing? _____
_____

9. A client tells the travel counselor that he will be traveling with his cat. What should the counselor do? _____
_____
_____

10. From an airline's perspective, what is the purpose of a frequent flyer program? _____
_____

11. From a traveler's perspective, what are the benefits of being a frequent flyer member? _____
_____

12. What is the hub and spoke system? _____
_____

13. What are the functions of the FAA? _____
_____

14. Why must travel counselors pay careful attention when selecting flight schedules involving dual-designated carriers? _____
_____
_____

15. What is overbooking? _____

16. Explain the procedure that takes place when a flight is overbooked. _____
_____
_____
_____

17. What is bias? _____

18. What is a wait-list? _____
_____

19. Decode these airlines: NW _____ AA _____
YX _____ US _____ CO _____

20. Identify the code for these airlines: United _____ Northwest _____
ATA _____ Southwest _____ Delta _____ Alaska Air _____

EXERCISE 6-3 Commercial Aircraft

1. What separates passenger cabins on an aircraft? _____

2. What is the difference between narrow- and wide-body aircraft? _____
_____

3. Why might some passengers wish to avoid flights on regional airlines? _____
_____
_____

4. Where can travel counselors find detailed statistical data about all types of aircraft? _____

5. Why can't a personal wheelchair be taken onboard a flight? _____

6. Why is pitch important to passenger comfort? _____

7. What areas of an aircraft are shown on a configuration? _____
_____

8. What is business class? Is it offered on all flights? _____
_____
_____

9. Why might some passengers prefer seats in the bulkhead row? _____

10. Are all aircraft of the same model configured in the same way? Why or why not? _____
_____

11. In what way is pressurization related to passenger comfort? _____
_____

12. What types of passengers cannot be seated in an emergency exit row? _____
_____

13. Why should travel counselors avoid assigning seats directly in front of an emergency row? _____
_____

14. Why might the first few rows of seats on a flight be unavailable for assignment? _____
_____

15. Identify the three types of aircraft engines. _____

16. What are the advantages of first-class seating? _____
_____

17. Why might clients wish to avoid seating in the rear of the aircraft or over the wings? _____

18. How many engines are on the 727 aircraft and where are they located? _____

19. What is the passenger capacity of the J31 aircraft? _____

20. Identify by name as many wide-body aircraft as you can. _____

_____

_____

_____

EXERCISE 6-4 Airports

1. What is a jetway? _____

2. What are the advantages of being an airline club member? _____

_____

3. Where can travel counselors find airport diagrams and other helpful information about airport services? _____

_____

4. What happens when a traveler checks in for her flight at the airport ticket counter? _____

_____

_____

5. What is the difference between the tarmac, taxiway, and runway? _____

_____

_____

6. Indicate the city name, and the airport name where needed. Please print.

ALB	_____	IAD	_____
AUS	_____	RDU	_____
BUF	_____	BNA	_____
LEX	_____	TUL	_____
GEG	_____	LGA	_____
ROA	_____	CRW	_____
MEM	_____	TUS	_____
RNO	_____	BDL	_____
BOS	_____	CHS	_____
BWI	_____	CLE	_____
MDW	_____	IAH	_____
DCA	_____	GRR	_____
DFW	_____	DSM	_____
RAP	_____	FLL	_____
ORF	_____	BOI	_____
PBI	_____	ATL	_____
SMF	_____	TPA	_____

DAB _____   CAE _____

JFK _____   CMH _____

JAX _____   PHL _____

SAN _____   BIL _____

7. Indicate the three-letter airport code. Please print.

_____ St. Louis	_____ Orlando	_____ Colorado Springs
_____ Dallas Love Field	_____ Detroit Metro	_____ San Antonio
_____ Phoenix	_____ Ft. Myers	_____ Little Rock
_____ Dayton	_____ Seattle	_____ El Paso
_____ Cincinnati	_____ Portland, Oregon	_____ Chicago O'Hare
_____ Indianapolis	_____ Pittsburgh	_____ Salt Lake City
_____ Las Vegas	_____ Palm Springs	_____ Charlotte, North Carolina
_____ Los Angeles	_____ Sarasota	_____ San Francisco
_____ Kansas City	_____ Richmond	_____ Minneapolis
_____ Newark	_____ New Orleans	_____ Miami
_____ Honolulu	_____ Maui	_____ Kauai

Review Questions

1. What do these acronyms stand for?

   ARC _____

   ATA _____

   CRS _____

   CRT _____

   DBC _____

   DOT _____

   FAA _____

   GDS _____

   IATA _____

   IATAN _____

   NTSB _____

   OAG _____

   PNR _____

   TSA _____

2. Indicate the airline name represented by these codes. Please print.

   DL _____   NW _____

   TZ _____   AA _____

   AQ _____   F9 _____

3. Indicate the airline code for each of these airlines. Please print.

   _____ USAirways   _____ United   _____ Continental

   _____ Alaska Air   _____ Midwest   _____ Hawaiian Air

4. Indicate the city name, and airport name where needed, for each of these codes. Please print.

   BTR _____   DCA _____

   HNL _____   TYS _____

   MIA _____   OKC _____

   CID _____   FAI _____

   ASE _____   LIH _____

5. Indicate the code for each of these airports. Please print.

   _____ Lexington   _____ Sarasota   _____ Atlantic City

   _____ Anchorage   _____ New York LaGuardia   _____ Buffalo

   _____ Houston Bush Intercontinental   _____ Hilo   _____ Maui

   _____ Washington Dulles   _____ Minneapolis   _____ Reno

   _____ Tucson   _____ Louisville   _____ Oakland

6. Indicate the appropriate term for each of these definitions.

- the travel agency identification to the GDS _____
- the counselor or reservationist's identification to the GDS _____
- the airline(s) that developed or owns a GDS _____
- payment from a vendor to an agency for selling the vendor's products _____
- an organization to which agencies belong to increase revenue _____
- extra commission paid by some vendors to a travel agency _____
- a rate that does not have commission built into it _____
- an extra charge made by the agency to the clients _____
- an agreement between two airlines for the purpose of transferring passengers, baggage, and cargo _____
- an airline policy that allows one airline to use the code of another _____
- the airline that uses the code of another airline _____
- a list of passengers that hope to be confirmed on a sold-out flight as cancellations are received _____
- the airline policy of using an airport as a home base and feeding flights from other airports into it _____
- the ratio of filled seats to total seats on a flight _____
- a traveler who does not show up for his flight _____
- an airline practice of selling more seats on a flight than are available _____
- removal of paid passengers from an oversold flight _____
- diagram of an aircraft _____
- the body of an aircraft _____
- a wall or partition between cabins on an aircraft _____
- the distance between the rows of seats on an aircraft _____
- the main airport building(s) _____
- an airline employee who checks baggage curbside _____
- the portion of an airport where the gates are located _____
- the waiting and boarding area of an airport _____
- the connecting device between the gate and aircraft _____
- the people who direct aircraft movement on the ground _____
- the conveyor belt that moves baggage from the back of the airport to the public area _____
- the organization responsible for airport operations _____

Planning United States Flight Itineraries

OBJECTIVES

At the conclusion of this chapter, you should be able to

- determine the air client's wants and needs.
- identify the various flight patterns.
- recognize the different types of trips.
- interpret a basic GDS flight availability display.
- calculate time comparison and elapsed flying time.
- make flight reservations.
- recognize unethical booking practices.
- use reference sources to assist in planning air travel itineraries.

KEY TERMS

ARUNK or ARNK	en route stops	normal fare
back-to-back ticketing	excursion fare	offline connection
booking classes	fictitious bookings	one-way trip
churning	fictitious return	online connection
circle trip	Greenwich Mean Time (GMT)	open-jaw trip
city pair	inbound	open-jaw with side trip
connection	International Date Line (IDL)	optional PNR fields
direct flight	itinerary field	outbound
double connections	leg	phone field
duplicate bookings	minimum connecting time	qualify the traveler
elapsed flying time	name field	received from field
end transaction	nonstop flight	record locator

KEY TERMS *continued*

round-trip

segment

single connection

speculative bookings

surface segment

ticket date field

time comparison

time zones

A traveler calls a Chicago travel agency and says, "I want a flight to New York in two weeks. I don't want to change planes and I want the cheapest fare." The travel counselor immediately accesses fares and flight schedules in the GDS and within a minute or two, the travel counselor is rattling off fares and flight times. Is it likely that this transaction will be concluded quickly? Is it likely that this prospective client will purchase travel at all from this travel counselor?

ESTABLISHING PRIORITIES

The travel counselor in the scenario did almost everything wrong. The travel counselor simply did not have enough information to begin researching flights and fares. The traveler said that he wanted a flight to New York, but the counselor does not know into which New York airport he wants to arrive. The travel counselor assumed he will depart from Chicago, but even if this is true, the agent does not know from which Chicago airport.

The traveler said that he wants a flight in two weeks. This is too vague and an actual travel date should have been established. Is he returning or is he traveling one-way? Again, the travel counselor does not know. This information is very important because round-trip fares are almost always less expensive than one-way fares.

The travel counselor has failed to understand that the traveler's primary priority, "cheapest fare," and the fact that he does not want to change planes may be contradictory. An airline with schedules that require a change of planes may have lower fares than an airline that offers direct flights. If that is true in this scenario, what is more important to the prospective client?

During the initial contact with a prospective client, the travel counselor must qualify the traveler by asking the right questions. These questions should result in specific information about what the client wants and how willing he is to be flexible in order to satisfy his primary priority. For most air travelers, the primary priority is either getting the lowest fare or obtaining the most convenient schedule.

Leisure travelers, those visiting family or taking a vacation, will usually put greater emphasis on obtaining the lowest fare. People traveling on business or for family

Important Industry Web Sites

Association of Business Travelers:
http://www.abt-travel.com

International Association of Conference Centers:
http://www.iacconline.com

International Association of Convention & Visitors Bureaus:
http://www.iacvb.org

National Business Travel Association: **http://www.nbta.org**

Society of Incentive and Travel Executives:
http://www.site-intl.org

---

emergencies generally select convenient schedule as the primary priority. It is the travel counselor's responsibility to establish what is more important to the traveler.

What questions should the travel counselor have asked in the previous scenario?

_____

_____

_____

_____

_____

After the travel counselor knows clearly what the potential client wants, then the travel counselor can select the correct flight pattern, type of trip, flight schedule, and airfare.

FLIGHT PATTERNS

All flight schedules fall into one of three categories: nonstop, direct or through, or connection. The action of the flight after it departs the origin city determines the category into which it falls.

A nonstop flight, as the term implies, makes no stops between the origin and destination cities. For example, a nonstop flight is shown as

LAX ⟶ BOS

A direct flight, sometimes called a through flight, makes one or more en route stops between the origin and destination cities, but there is no change of planes. At the en route stop, passengers may get off or on the flight, and the flight may take on fuel or catering. Many travelers will say they want a direct flight when. In fact, what they want is a nonstop. A direct flight is shown as

LAX ⟶ STL ⟶ BOS

A connection schedule requires at least one change of planes between the origin and destination cities. Schedules with one plane change are called single connections whereas schedules with two plane changes are called double connections. Every connection is either an online connection, that is, the same airline is used on all flights, or it is an offline connection and different airlines are used. The least convenient type of connection schedule involves the use of different airports at the connection point. A single connection is shown as

LAX ⟶ STL
STL ⟶ BOS

Every connection has a minimum connecting time; that is, the least amount of time that must be allowed for a change of planes. The minimum connecting time is based on the airline(s) used and the airport where the connection will be made. For example, a plane change from one Delta flight to a different Delta flight at CVG may require a minimum of 20 minutes. But, changing from an American flight to a United flight at SFO may require a minimum of 60 minutes. Internationally, security procedures, immigration, and customs increases minimum connecting time to as much as two hours or more.

All flight schedules shown as connections in the GDS as well as in the *OAG (Official Airline Guide) Flight Guide* have been checked to be sure the minimum time has been met. If the travel counselor obtains flight schedules on a flight-by-flight basis and constructs his own connection, minimum connecting time must be verified. The travel counselor can access minimum connecting time requirements in the GDS or in the *OAG Flight Guide*.

When making flight reservations, each flight, commonly referred to as a leg or segment, is booked separately. Each segment is identified by a city pair, that is, the origin city and the city where the passenger first deplanes. Nonstop and direct flights consist of one segment and one city pair. Connection service consists of two or more segments and city pairs.

From the perspective of passenger convenience,

- select a nonstop flight first
- select a direct flight second
- select an online connection third
- select an offline connection fourth
- select a multiple airport connection fifth

However, if obtaining the lowest fare is the traveler's primary priority, keep in mind that the most convenient schedule may not result in the lowest fare. Perhaps the most important fact to remember when selecting flight schedules is that none of the lowest airfares allow different airlines to be combined.

TYPES OF TRIPS

Understanding the types of trips and being able to recognize each type of trip directly affects the travel counselor's ability to price the trip correctly. In some cases, the definition of a type of trip depends on the type of fare that will be used. To better understand the trip definitions, you should understand one aspect of fares. That aspect is that all airfares are identified as either a normal fare or an excursion fare.

A normal fare is priced at a one-way amount and if it is to be used for a round-trip, the amount is doubled. Generally, normal fares carry very few, if any, restrictions or limitations and are the most expensive type of fare.

An excursion fare is priced at a round-trip amount and can *never* be sold on a one-way basis for half the amount. Excursion fares are usually the least expensive type of fare, but they can be very restrictive. All excursion fares, with very few exceptions, have the following requirements:

- the same airline must be used on all segments
- reservations must be made and travel purchased in advance
- there is a minimum stay requirement
- there is a maximum stay limitation
- travel is nonrefundable and there is a penalty for making changes
- all flight segments must be confirmed (no wait-listing or open segments)

Now we can discuss the five basic trip types: one-way, round-trip, open-jaw, circle trip, and open-jaw with side trip.

Having said all that, the current trend in airfares is rather different that it has been over the past few decades. Today, excursion fares are few and far between. Actually, they exist only in a few markets. Most airfares can presently be purchased on a one-way basis and have only a few restrictions. But, because airline policies, airfares in particular, can be rather fickle, we will cover fare construction with the idea that excursion fares are the least expensive.

One-Way Travel

The one-way trip is the most simple of the five trip types, and it is also the most expensive. A one-way trip is always defined as a trip from the origin city to the destination city. Figure 7–1 illustrates a one-way trip.

SFO ————————→ PIT

FIGURE 7–1 One-way trip example.

Keep in mind that the one-way trip can utilize a non-stop, direct, or connection service. It is only the fact that the traveler is not returning to the origin city that makes this a one-way trip.

Round-Trip Travel

The round-trip is the most common type of trip. Perhaps 85 percent of all travel takes the form of a round-trip. A round-trip is defined as a trip from the origin city to the destination city and back to the origin. The portion of the trip from the origin to the destination is known as the outbound. The portion of the trip from the destination back to the origin is known as the inbound. Figure 7–2 illustrates a round-trip.

SFO ————————→ PIT
SFO ←———————— PIT

FIGURE 7–2 Round-trip example.

In most cases, it does not matter if nonstop, direct, or connection service is used, especially if using normal fares. If excursion fares are used, the same airline must be used on the complete trip, the restrictions listed previously may apply, and there may be restrictions on the routing.

Open-Jaw Travel

An open-jaw trip consists of the origin city and two destination cities and travel between one of the city pairs must be other than air. Figure 7–3 illustrates two examples of open-jaw trips.

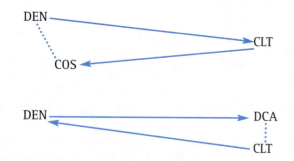

FIGURE 7–3 Open-jaw trip examples.

The nonair segment of an open-jaw trip is called a surface segment. In reality, travel between the city pair on the surface segment can be by train, private jet, hot air balloon, or even roller blades. The point is that there is no commercial flight on this segment.

When normal fares are used, the airline, flight pattern, and distance between the cities are of no consequence. But, when excursion fares are used, all of these factors are important.

A travel counselor who cannot recognize an open-jaw trip sees it as two one-way trips. This oversight causes the counselor to use normal fares. Overlooking the possibility of using excursion fares could cause the traveler to pay a much higher fare than is necessary.

Circle-Trip Travel

A circle trip has two distinct definitions, both determined by the type of fare that is used. If normal fares are used, a circle trip is defined as a trip that has two or more destinations and all segments are by commercial air. The airlines and flight patterns do not matter.

If excursion fares are used, a circle trip is defined as a trip that has two destinations (no more, no less) and all segments are by commercial air. As with round- and open-jaw trips, using excursion fares on a circle trip means that certain flight patterns or routing may be required. Figure 7–4 illustrates the circle trip for excursion fares.

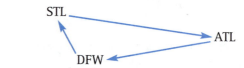

FIGURE 7–4 Circle-trip example.

Travel counselors who are unable to recognize a circle trip for what it is may not realize that in certain circumstances excursion fares can be used. If a circle trip qualifies for excursion fares, but the travel counselor sees the trip as a combination of one-way trips, the counselor will likely use normal fares, charging far more than is necessary.

Open-Jaw with Side Trip

An open-jaw with side trip is the combination of the standard open-jaw and one-way trips. Of the five trip types, this is the least common. If normal fares are used, each segment is priced as a one-way and choice of airlines and routing do not matter. If excursion fares are used, the open-jaw portion is priced like any open-jaw trip, but the side trip must be priced as a one-way. Figure 7–5 illustrates an open-jaw with side trip.

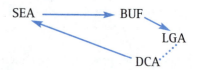

FIGURE 7–5 Open-jaw with side trip example.

PLEASE TURN TO PAGE 109 AND COMPLETE
EXERCISE 7–1 NOW.

FLIGHT SCHEDULE SELECTION

After the travel counselor has determined the traveler's needs and priorities and visualized the type of trip the traveler is proposing, the next step is to offer flight options. Flight schedules are usually obtained in the GDS, and various Web sites, but nonautomated agencies, may select schedules from the *OAG Flight Guide,* known simply as the *OAG.*

Using the *OAG*

The *OAG* is offered in two volumes: the North American edition and the worldwide edition. The North American edition contains flights between cities in North America, Central America, and the Caribbean and is published bimonthly. The worldwide edition contains flights worldwide including those listed in the North American edition and is published monthly. Depending on the edition, an annual subscription costs between $300 and $600. The worldwide edition is also available on a stand-alone CD-ROM with monthly updates and costs approximately $350 per year.

The *OAG* is also online with free access to flight schedules at http://www.oag.com. This site can also be accessed via *Travel Weekly,* directories section, at http://www.travelweekly.com.

Web Activity

Your GDS is down and isn't expected to be functional for several hours, and your agency does not subscribe to the *OAG.* You have several bookings that must be made right away. Do any of the major U.S. airlines have an area on their Web site where travel agency bookings can be made?

GDS Flight Availability Displays

As you learned in Chapter 6, there are four GDSs used by U.S. travel agencies: Amadeus, Galileo, Sabre, and Worldspan. Each GDS has its own format that must be typed before flight availability will be displayed, but fortunately, all GDS availability displays look basically the same. So, if you can interpret a flight availability display from one, you can interpret them all.

The GDS arranges schedules by showing nonstop and direct flights first. Because the GDS format usually includes a desired departure time, the GDS arranges these flights so that those departing nearest the requested time are shown first. As the travel counselor scrolls, or moves down, flights further away from the requested departure time are shown.

After nonstop and direct flights are shown, connection service begins. Again, the requested departure time is a factor in determining the order in which the connections are shown. As the travel counselor scrolls the connections,

offline connections and connections using multiple airports may be shown. Generally, the most convenient schedules are shown on the first or second screen.

It is important to note that each travel agency can change its GDS display and sort criteria. For example, an agency that has an override commission agreement with a particular airline may set the GDS to display that airline before showing flights on other airlines.

Figure 7–6 is a GDS flight availability display from Washington Reagan National to Los Angeles. Because the first few screens include nonstop and direct flights only, Figure 7–6 is actually a compilation of the data from multiple screens.

Before we can take our first look at GDS flight schedules, a brief discussion about booking classes is in order. Each flight listing indicates the booking classes that are offered. Each booking class indicates the aircraft cabin category and a fare type:

> F or P = first class
> A = discounted first class
> C or J = business class
> Y, S, or W = coach class
> M, K, V, L, Q, etc. = discounted coach class

A thorough explanation of booking classes can be found in the next chapter. For now, all you have to know about booking classes are the listed codes.

PLEASE TURN TO PAGE 110 AND COMPLETE EXERCISE 7–2 NOW.

TIME COMPARISON

At some point in our lives, we have all had to know what time it is in another part of the country. Calculating the time difference between two locations is called time comparison. As a travel counselor, airline reservationist, or other travel professional, you will be working with passengers traveling to all points in the United Sates, as well as internationally. It is, therefore, extremely important to understand time zones and their effect on travel.

In the United States, the 48 contiguous states are divided into four time zones: Eastern, Central, Mountain, and Pacific. Alaska and Hawaii have their own time zones (see Figure 7–7).

Each time zone around the world is referenced to the *Greenwich Meridian,* an imaginary vertical line near London, England. The Greenwich time zone is called Greenwich Mean Time (GMT), and is shown as a zero. Each time zone west of GMT is expressed as a negative number because the time is earlier than it is at GMT. Each time zone east of GMT is expressed as a positive number because the time is later than it is at GMT. The stopping point for

15JUN-FR-10A	DCALAX (WASQLA)			ET PT		AC1								①
DCA ALTERNATE BWI IAD/LAX ALTERNATE BUR LGB ONT SNA														
1	#DL1019	F9	A9	Y9	B9	M9	H9	Q9	K9	DCALAX-	945A	211P	7	757	1
2	#NW 41	F7	A7	Y7	B7	M7	H7	K7	V7	DCALAX-	615A	1039A	8	757	1
3	#CO 171	F9	Y9	B9	Q9	K9	V9	T9	H9	DCALAX-	800P	1223A#1	8	757	1
4	#AA1885	F7	Y7	B7	H7	M7	Q7	K7	V7	DCADFW-	950A	1150A	N	M80	0
5	#AA2433	F7	Y7	B7	H7	M7	Q7	K7	V7	LAX-	1230P	131P	8	757	0
6	#UA 609	F9	A9	Y9	B9	M9	H9	Q9	V9	DCAORD-	1000A	1051A	6	320	0
7	#UA 117	F9	A9	Y9	B9	M9	H9	Q9	V9	LAX-	1145A	157P	6	757	0

②   ③   ④   ⑤   ⑥   ⑦   ⑧

1. Header lines. This display is for June 15, Friday, departing around 10:00 a.m. The city codes, if different from the input codes, are shown. Notice that QLA is used instead of LAX because LAX also indicates Los Angeles International Airport. The departure city is in the eastern time zone and the arrival city is in the pacific time zone. AC1 indicates that more classes can be viewed. The second header lists possible alternate airports for both origin and destination.
2. Line number, symbol indicating the level of GDS participation, airline code, and flight number.
3. Classes and availability. Based on the level of GDS participation, each airline has a maximum number of seats that will be shown in availability; 9, 7, and 4 are common.
4. City pair. A dash after the arrival city indicates there are more classes that can be viewed.
5. Departure and arrival times. A flight that arrives the next day is shown as "#1," two days later as "#2," and the day before as "1."
6. On-time frequency. The number 6 indicates that the flight is on time 60 to 70 percent of the time; 5 indicates 50 to 60 percent; "N" indicates there is no on-time data available.
7. Aircraft equipment code.
8. Number of en route stops.

FIGURE 7-6 Sample GDS flight availability display.

determining east and west is another imaginary line called the International Date Line (IDL) (see Figure 7–8).

By looking at Figures 7–7 and 7–8, you can see that all U.S. time zones are expressed as negative numbers, each number representing the number of hours the zone is behind, or earlier than, the time at GMT. To determine the number of hours difference between two cities in the United States, you simply subtract the smaller number from the larger. For example, Boston is expressed as −5 and San Francisco is expressed as −8; therefore, there is a three-hour time difference between the two cities.

If the current time in Boston is 9:30 A.M., what time would it be in San Francisco? First, you must understand that because San Francisco is west of Boston, it is earlier in San Francisco. Armed with that information, you now know that you must subtract the three-hour time difference from 9:30 A.M. So, it is 6:30 A.M. in San Francisco.

The expressions shown in Figures 7–7 and 7–8 represent standard time, which is used throughout this text. Most of the world observes daylight savings time, gener-

ally between March and October, and during that period the expressions are different. For example, during daylight savings time, GMT is shown as +1, U.S. Eastern time is −4, Central is −5, Mountain is −6, and Pacific is −7.

U.S. Time Comparison

Step 1: Determine how each city is expressed in relation to GMT.

Step 2: Subtract the smaller number from the larger number to determine the number of hours difference between the two cities.

Step 3: Is the city where you do not know the time west or east of the known city? If the unknown city is west, you subtract the number of hours difference from the known time. If the unknown city is east, you add the number of hours difference to the known time.

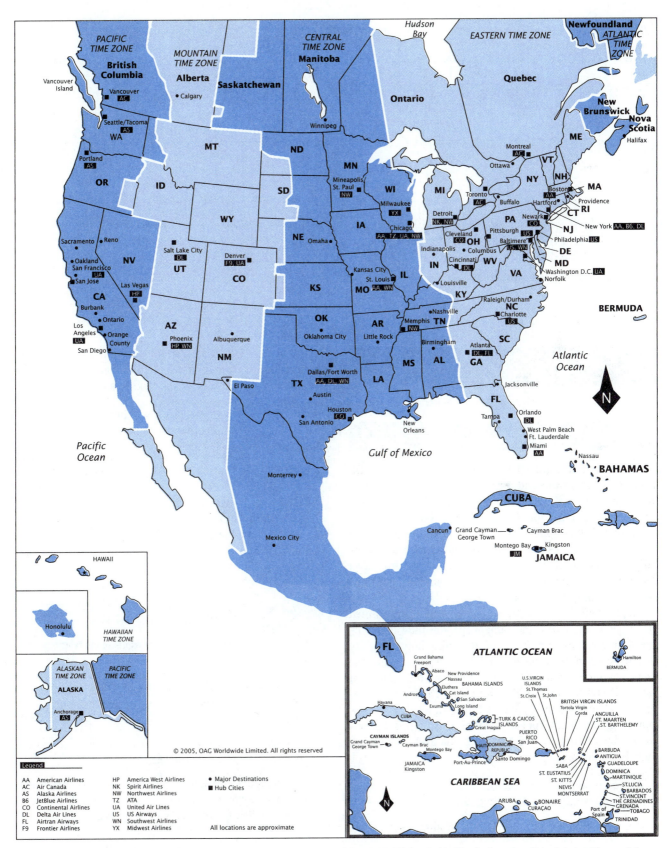

FIGURE 7–7 Time zone map. Page 599 from July 01, 2005 edition of the *OAG Flight Guide North America*. Reprinted with special permission from OAG Worldwide.

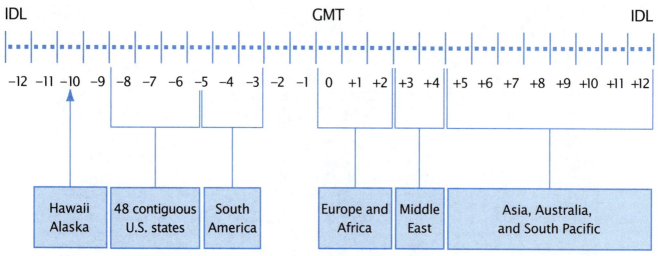

FIGURE 7–8 GMT time-line illustration.

PLEASE TURN TO PAGE 111 AND COMPLETE EXERCISE 7–3 NOW.

ELAPSED FLYING TIME

When looking at flight schedules in the *OAG* or in a GDS display, the departure and arrival times are local. That is, the departure time is local for the departure city and the arrival time is local for the arrival city. For this reason, eastbound flights appear to take much longer than they actually do and westbound flights appear to take practically no time at all. That is why it is important for travel counselors to know how to calculate the actual flight time, known as elapsed flying time.

To calculate elapsed flying time within the United States, you begin with the same steps you used to calculate time comparison. First, you determine how each city is expressed in relationship to GMT. Then, subtract the smaller number from the larger to calculate the number of hours difference between the two cities. The next step involves calculating the apparent flying time; that is, how long does the flight appear to take? This step is accomplished by subtracting the departure time from the arrival time. For example,

Arrival time	10:55 A.M.
Departure time	−8:22 A.M.
Apparent flying time	2 hours, 33 minutes

When calculating apparent flying time, there are some important points to remember. Because time is based on the number 60, you cannot use a calculator for math

calculations. Always add or subtract minutes from minutes, and hours from hours. To demonstrate another potential problem, take a look at the next example.

Arrival time	8:15 P.M. (borrow 1 hour and convert it to minutes)	7:75 P.M.
Departure time	6:55 P.M.	−6:55 P.M.
Apparent flying time		1 hour, 20 minutes

The last step in calculating elapsed flying time is to add or subtract the number of hours difference between the two cities from the apparent flying time. If the flight is westbound, add the hours and if the flight is eastbound, subtract the hours.

Elapsed Flying Time

Step 1: Determine how each city is expressed in relationship to GMT.

Step 2: Subtract the smaller number from the larger number to determine the number of hours difference between the two cities.

Step 3: Subtract the departure time from the arrival time to determine the apparent flying time.

Step 4: If the flight is westbound, add the hours difference to the apparent flying time. If the flight is eastbound, subtract the hours difference from the apparent flying time.

PLEASE TURN TO PAGE 111 AND COMPLETE EXERCISE 7–4 NOW.

MAKING FLIGHT RESERVATIONS

After the client and travel counselor have selected appropriate flight schedules, a reservation can be made. Although most flight reservations are made in the GDS, there are circumstances when they must be made on an airline Web site.

Regardless of how the reservation is made, either in the GDS or by phone, the finished product is a *passenger name record,* or *PNR.*

GDS Reservations

Each area of PNR data is known as a *PNR field* and each field contains the same type of data. The primary PNR fields are itinerary, name, phone, ticket date, and received from.

When making a GDS reservation, the flights are booked in the computer, creating the PNR's itinerary field. This field can also contain rental cars, hotels, tours, and cruises that have been booked, or sold, in the GDS. A surface segment, as in an open-jaw trip, is part of the itinerary field and is shown as ARUNK or ARNK.

The travel counselor enters the passenger's name, exactly as it appears on his photo ID or passport, creating the PNR's name field. This field can also contain titles or passenger type codes, known as PTCs.

The phone field should contain at least two items, the agency's phone and a home number for the traveler. It is also a good idea to include the traveler's business phone number and a contact for the passenger at his destination.

The ticket date field indicates the date when a ticket or electronic ticket will be processed and paid for. Depending on the GDS, this field may also show the validating airline or other ticketing-related information.

Depending on the GDS, the received from field may be mandatory for the completion of a PNR. This field identifies the name of the person from whom the travel counselor received the booking instruction. This could be the passenger herself, or an other person such as a family member, business associate, secretary, or personal assistant.

Other fields are considered optional PNR fields because they are not required before a PNR can be saved. Optional fields include form of payment, passenger address, seat assignments, special requests, and remarks. It is important to note that although these fields may be considered optional to the GDS, the travel agency may consider them mandatory for all PNRs.

Finalizing or saving the PNR after it is completed is called end transaction. Without this step, nothing has actually been booked. When the travel counselor ends the transaction, the PNR is saved and booking messages are electronically sent to the appropriate airline.

At this point, the GDS selects a combination of six letters or numbers, called a record locator. The record locator is the GDS's unique identification for the particular

```
1.1MEIJER/JULIUS   2.1SCHAFFER/OLIVER
1 UA 576Q 05JAN W  DFWORD HK2 805A 1013A HRQ //DCUA /E
3 AA2339H 07JAN F  ORDDFW HK2 330P 600P  HRS //DCAA /E
TKT/TIME LIMIT
  1. TAW08AUG/
PHONES
  1. DFW214-555-1834-ABC TRAVEL/TAMMY
  2. DFW214-555-1134-H JULIUS MEIJER
  3. DFW214-555-8162-B JULIUS MEIJER
REMARKS -
  1./JULIUS MEIJER AND OLIVER SCHAFFER
  2/KEYSTONE CORPORATION
  3./3319 EASTGATE DRIVE
  4./DALLAS TX 75220
  5.-*AX111112223334444‡12/09
RECEIVED FROM - SECY. LISA
  GT63.GT63*A12 0915/01OCT06
```

FIGURE 7–9 Sample Sabre PNR.

PNR. Figure 7–9 shows a completed PNR that was booked in Sabre.

Unethical Booking and Ticketing Practices

Every booking made in the GDS creates revenue for the GDS because each vendor (airline, hotel, car rental, cruise, and tour company) pays the GDS a booking fee. Unethical booking practices cause the vendors to pay booking fees without generating revenue for the vendor.

Some travelers and travel counselors may make two or more reservations for the same trip, called duplicate bookings. When the traveler decides which booking he wants, the other bookings may or may not be cancelled. This practice not only creates additional booking fees, but can also create a no-show problem if the unwanted reservations are not canceled.

Another unacceptable booking practice is the creation of fictitious bookings, also called speculative bookings. In this instance, one or more reservations are made in the hope that the traveler will purchase one of the trips. Again, this practice results in unnecessary booking fees and if the fictitious bookings are not cancelled, the no-show factor is increased. Many travel agents use the 50/50 guideline: If the agent is more than 50 percent sure that the client will purchase travel, a booking can ethically be made.

Most of the lower airfares require the purchase be made within 24 hours of when the reservation is made. If the traveler has not made a final decision within that time, the travel counselor may cancel and immediately rebook the flights. This practice is called churning. Churning causes airline fees for the initial booking as well as for every cancellation and rebooking. Some airlines have begun billing travel agencies for the fees incurred as a result of churning.

One-way airfares are generally more expensive than round-trip fares. Because of this, a traveler may ask that a fictitious return be booked for her one-way trip so that she can pay the lower, round-trip fare. She uses the first portion of the trip, but not the return. Not only does this practice create unnecessary airline booking fees and a no-show situation on the return, it also can create problems for the travel agency. Some airlines are now charging the travel agency for the one-way fare that should have been used on the trip in addition to penalty amounts. Do not confuse this unethical practice with the legitimate pricing technique of breaking the fare that is discussed in Chapter 8.

Some travel counselors use a practice called back-to-back ticketing for clients who are traveling round-trip but do not qualify for the lower fares. This practice involves booking and ticketing two round-trips, each with a fictitious return. The client uses the first portion of each ticket but not the second. This practice creates the same problems as the fictitious return, multiplied by two. Do not confuse this unethical practice with the legitimate pricing technique, back-to-back excursions, which is described in Chapter 8.

PLEASE TURN TO PAGE 112 AND COMPLETE EXERCISE 7–5 NOW.

FINDING THE ANSWERS

In any travel counselor–traveler transaction, a variety of questions may arise. The true travel professional does not know all of the answers but does know where he can find them. The GDS can be used to obtain a variety of information but in many cases, the travel counselor relies on other sources.

In addition to flight schedules, the *OAG* contains a wealth of information. Many questions the travel counselor and traveler may have can be answered by turning to the appropriate section of the *OAG*. Here are some examples:

Other *OAG Flight Guide North American Edition* Information

- aircraft seating information
- aircraft performance statistics including passenger capacity, number and type of engines, body style, and pressurization
- airline codes and abbreviations
- airline corporate offices
- city and airport code list
- flight itineraries showing where each flight originates, stops en route, and terminates
- minimum connecting times
- toll-free phone numbers for airlines

Another excellent source of travel information is the *Business Travel Planner,* published by Northstar Travel Media. This reference tool is available online at http://www.btp24.com and it also comes in a printed version. Most users of this resource prefer the online version because it can be updated quickly as situations change. A single user access for the online site is $149 per year.

In addition to information on breaking news and risk assessments, this site features detailed and comprehensive destination data. You can obtain information on virtually every country and over 8,000 cities. The data includes a brief history, currency, climate, travel warnings, official Web site links, visa and passport information, air and ground transportation, airport diagrams, travel advisories, hotels, dining, and local attractions.

In addition to the *Business Travel Planner,* Northstar Travel Media publishes *Travel Weekly, Hotel & Travel Index, Official Meeting Facilities Guide, Official Hotel Guide,* and *Travel Management Daily.*

Some Important Industry Web Sites

Arthur Frommer's Budget Travel Online: **http://www.frommers.com**

City guides: **http://www.excite.com**

City links: **http://www.usacitylink.com/**

Conde Nast Traveler: **http://www.cntraveler.com**

Festival Finder: **http://www.festivalfinder.com**

Fodor's Guides: **http://www.fodors.com**

International Protocol: **http://www.home3.americanexpress.com**

Las Vegas Show Guide: **http://www.lvol.com**

Lonely Planet Guides: **http://www.lonelyplanet.com**

Map Blast: **http://www.mapblast.com**

Map Quest: **http://www.mapquest.com**

OAG: **http://www.oag.com**

Rough Guides: **http://www.travel.roughguides.com**

Time Out: **http://www.timeout.com**

Time Zone Converter: **http://www.timezoneconverter.com/**

The Travel Channel Online: **http://www.travel.discovery.com**

Tourism Offices: **http://www.towd.com**

U.S. Destination Guide:
http://www.twcrossroads.com/directories/
usdestindex.html

Weather Forecasts: **http://www.intillicast.com**

World City Guide:
http://travel.lycos.com/destinations

World Clock: **http://www.timeanddate.com/worldclock**

Worldwide Destination Guide:
http://www.twcrossroads.com/directories/wdestindex.html

? *What Would You Do?*

Your client tells you that he can depart from Nashville on either Saturday or Sunday for his trip to Omaha. He wants to stay three or four days and wants the least expensive fare.

1. What other information do you need from this client?
2. Do you think it would be less expensive for him to depart on Saturday or Sunday?
3. Based on your answer to question 2, why do you think so?

SUMMARY

Each client has different wants and needs. Additionally, the level of travel knowledge and experience varies from one client to another. The first step in any client transaction is learning this type of information. It is the most important job for the travel professional. Although some clients are flexible and will consider all options, others must depart and arrive at very specific times. A first-time traveler may need much more explanation than a person who has traveled many times in the past. The choices clients make affect the way in which the travel professional proceeds.

Being able to identify the types of air trips, such as one-way, round-trip, open-jaw, or circle trip, and using resources, such as the *OAG Flight Guide* or airline GDS, contributes to the counselor's accuracy and creativity in assisting clients. Accurately pricing itineraries depends on the counselor's ability to obtain information from the client and match airline flight schedules and fares to the client's objectives. The process of making flight reservations for clients must be accomplished efficiently and accurately, otherwise, the client will simply find another travel counselor and take her business elsewhere.

 For additional Travel and Tourism resources, go to http://www.hospitality-tourism.delmar.com.

PLEASE COMPLETE THE CHAPTER REVIEW
QUESTIONS NOW.

EXERCISE 7-1 Establishing Priorities, Flight Patterns, and Types of Trips

1. PIT ——→ CVG ——→ RSW is an example of what type of trip? _____

2. PIT ——→ CVG ——→ RSW is an example of what type of flight pattern? _____

3. Your client says that he must arrive in Omaha in time for a noon meeting and he wants the lowest fare. What do you think his priority probably is? _____

4. SDF ——→ CHS is an example of what type of flight pattern? _____

5. BIL ——→ CLE is an example of what type of trip? _____
   ATL

6. Your client says that she needs a flight to Washington, DC. One of the first questions you ask is _____

7. What is the difference between an online connection and an offline connection? In what way are they the same? _____

8. MCI ——→ BDL is an example of what type of trip? _____
   LGA

9. Your client says that he wants to go Milwaukee on Tuesday or Wednesday, return after staying seven days, and he wants the lowest fare. What do you think his priority probably is? _____

10. DEN ←—— IND is an example of what type of trip? _____
    COS

11. Your client says that she does not want to change planes and she wants the lowest fare. How will you handle this? _____

12. In what way is determining the client's flexibility relevant to obtaining the lowest fare? _____

13. ONT ——→ IAH is an example of what type of trip? _____
    ONT ←—— IAH

14. Asking the right questions at the initial client contact is called _____

15. Fly from PSP to ELP, fly from ELP to AUS, surface from AUS to DFW, and fly from DFW to PSP is an example of what type of trip? _____

16. TPA ——→ ATL   is an example of what type of flight pattern? _____
    ATL ——→ CLE

17. Under what circumstances must you verify that a connection complies with minimum connecting time? _____
_____

18. Define the term "city pair." _____
_____

19. Each flight on an itinerary is commonly called _____

20. What is the difference between the outbound flight and the inbound flight? _____

EXERCISE 7-2 CRS Flight Availability Displays

Directions: Answer questions based on the following display.

```
20MAY—MO—8A   PHXSEA   MT   PT         AC1
1$WN2844      F4 Y4 H4 W4 B4 Q0 L4 K4      PHXSEA-      737A      1035A     N     733     0
2$AS  721     F4 Y4 B4 M4 H4 Q4 V4         PHXSEA       630A      918A      8     M80     0
3#UA2106      F6 A6 Y9 B9 M9 H9 Q9 V9      PHXSEA-      600A      1034A     8     735     1
4#CO2786      A8 F8 Y9 H9 K9 B9 V9 Q9      PHXPDX-      742A      1025A           733     0
5#CO8768      Y4 H4 K0 B0 V0 Q0 T0         SEA          1200N     1250P           DH8     0
     CO2786 OPERATED BY AMERICA WEST
     CO8768 OPERATED BY HORIZON AIR DBA ALASKA AIRLINES
6$AS  707     F4 Y4 B4 M4 H4 Q4 VR         PHXPDX       650A      932A      N     M80     0
7$AS2248      Y4 B4 M4 H4 Q0 V0 K0         SEA          1030A     1120A           DH8     0
     AS2248 OPERATED BY HORIZON AIR
8#UA2258      F0 A0 Y9 B9 M9 H9 Q9 V9      PHXSFO-      918A      1121A     N     733     0
9#UA1010      F7 A7 C7 Y9 B9 M9 H9 Q9      SEA-         1211P     209P      6     733     0
```

1. What airline code and flight number represents the earliest nonstop flight from origin to destination? _____

2. How many nonstop flights are offered from origin to destination? _____

3. How many connections are offered from origin to destination? _____

4. Identify, by airline codes and flight numbers, the connection that would be the most convenient for the client. _____

5. Your clients want to use a QE21NR fare. Could you book them on HP 2844? _____

6. How often does AS 721 arrive on time? _____

7. How often does UA 2258 arrive on time? _____

8. Your clients want to travel in first class. Could you book them on the AS connection? _____

9. Identify by airline codes and flight numbers the two flights using regional aircraft. _____

10. This availability display is for what date and day of the week? _____

11. Your clients want to use a KXE14IP fare. Could you book them on the CO connection? _____

12. In what time zone is Seattle? _____

13. Identify by airline code and flight number the latest nonstop flight from origin to destination. _____

EXERCISE 7-3   Time Comparison

1. All locations are expressed as a plus or minus number. This number represents the location's relationship to _____

2. Why are all U.S. locations shown with negative numbers? _____

3. Name the four time zones, west to east, in the 48 contiguous states. _____

4. It is 2:00 P.M. in Miami (−5). What time is it in Chicago (−6)? _____

5. It is 3:15 P.M. in San Diego (−8). What time is it in Dallas (−6)? _____

6. It is 9:45 A.M. in Phoenix (−7). What time is it in Seattle (−8)? _____

7. It is 9:25 P.M. in New York (−5). What time is it in Boston (−5)? _____

8. It is 2:00 A.M. in Atlanta (−5). What time and day is it in Los Angeles (−8)? _____

9. It is 11:30 P.M. in Spokane (−8). What time and day is it in Pittsburgh (−5)? _____

10. It is 11:47 P.M. in Reno (−8). What time and day is it in Minneapolis (−6)? _____

11. It is 8:16 A.M. in Charleston, SC (−5). What time is it in Boise (−7)? _____

12. It is 2:07 P.M. in Bismark (−6). What time is it in Oklahoma City (−6)? _____

13. It is 8:19 P.M. in Richmond (−5). What time is it in El Paso (−7)? _____

14. It is 4:09 P.M. in Colorado Springs (−7). What time is it in Hartford (−5)? _____

15. It is 1:15 A.M. in Washington, DC (−5). What time and day is it in San Diego (−8)? _____

16. It is 4:48 P.M. in Chicago (−6). What time is it in Denver (−7)? _____

17. It is 1:30 A.M. in Palm Springs (−8). What time and day is it in Honolulu (−10)? _____

18. It is 11:25 A.M. in Sacramento (−8). What time is it in Salt Lake City (−7)? _____

19. It is 10:15 P.M. in Anchorage (−9). What time and day is it in Charlotte (−5)? _____

20. It is 9:15 A.M. in New Orleans (−6). What time is it in Maui (−10)? _____

EXERCISE 7-4   Elapsed Flying Time

1. A flight departs Dallas (−6) at 1:07 P.M. and arrives in Pensacola (−6) at 3:36 P.M. What is the actual elapsed flying time?

2. A flight departs Baltimore (−5) at 10:00 A.M. and arrives in Las Vegas (−8) at 1:32 P.M. What is the actual elapsed flying time? _____

3. A flight departs Detroit Metro (−5) at 5:30 P.M. and arrives in Ft. Myers (−5) at 10:10 P.M. What is the actual elapsed flying time? _____

4. A flight departs Atlanta (−5) at 12:01 P.M. and arrives in Austin (−6) at 1:07 P.M. What is the actual elapsed flying time?

5. A flight departs Seattle (−8) at 8:45 A.M. and arrives in Calgary (−7) at 12:30 P.M. What is the actual elapsed flying time?

6. A flight departs Chicago O'Hare (−6) at 8:00 P.M. and arrives in Sarasota (−5) at 11:39 P.M. What is the actual elapsed flying time? _____

7. A flight departs Newark (−5) at 12:42 P.M. and arrives in Tampa (−5) at 3:37 P.M. What is the actual elapsed flying time? _____

8. A flight departs Boston (−5) at 4:05 P.M. and arrives in Los Angeles (−8) at 6:22 P.M. What is the actual elapsed flying time? _____

9. A flight departs Phoenix (−7) at 10:15 A.M. and arrives in Des Moines (−6) at 2:03 P.M. What is the actual elapsed flying time? _____

10. A flight departs Houston Bush Intercontinental (−6) at 8:52 A.M. and arrives in Boston (−5) at 12:06 P.M. What is the actual elapsed flying time? _____

11. A flight departs Anchorage (−9) at 7:00 A.M. and arrives in Seattle (−8) at 11:28 A.M. What is the actual elapsed flying time? _____

12. A flight departs Honolulu (−10) at 1:30 P.M. and arrives in Boston (−5) at 9:10 A.M. the next morning. What is the actual elapsed flying time? _____

13. A flight departs Los Angeles (−8) at 8:30 A.M. and arrives in Honolulu (−10) at 11:03 A.M. What is the actual elapsed flying time? _____

14. A flight departs New York (−5) at 1:05 P.M. and arrives in St. Johns, Newfoundland (−3½) at 6:55 P.M. What is the actual elapsed flying time? _____

15. A flight departs Indianapolis (−5) at 9:45 A.M. and arrives in Cancun (−6) at 12:50 P.M. What is the actual elapsed flying time? _____

EXERCISE 7-5 Making Flight Reservations

1. Why might a travel counselor make flight reservations on an airline's Web site rather than in the GDS? _____ _____

2. What is a PNR? _____

3. One type of unethical booking practice is called a speculative booking. What is it? _____ _____

4. Each PNR consists of areas or sections known as _____

5. Give some examples of optional PNR fields. _____

6. What is the purpose of a res sheet? _____

7. The primary PNR fields are _____

8. One type of unethical booking practice is called a fictitious return. What is it? _____ _____

9. How is a surface segment shown in a PNR? _____

10. What information is or might be shown in the ticket date field of a PNR? _____ _____

11. What types of items are included in a PNR itinerary field? _____

12. Explain how unethical booking and ticketing practices are costly to the airlines. _____ _____

13. What is the purpose of the received from field in a PNR? _____

14. What two items should always be included in the PNR phone field? _____

15. In what way might unethical booking and ticketing practices be costly to the travel agency? _____

_____

_____

16. What is a record locator? _____

17. Finalizing a completed PNR in the CRS is called _____

Review Questions

1. What questions might you ask during the qualification process with a potential air client?_____
   _____
   _____

2. Identify and explain five types of unethical booking and ticketing practices. _____
   _____
   _____
   _____
   _____
   _____

3. It is 9:37 A.M. in Honolulu (−10). What time is it in Wichita (−6)?_____

4. It is 11:45 P.M. in Cincinnati (−5). What time is it in Anchorage (−9)? _____

5. Using airport codes, draw examples of
   • a one-way trip
   • a round-trip
   • an open-jaw trip
   • a circle trip
   • an open-jaw with side trip

6. Identify the five primary PNR fields and explain the data contained in each field. _____
   _____
   _____
   _____
   _____

7. A flight departs Vancouver (−8) at 8:50 P.M. and arrives in Atlanta (−5) at 5:40 A.M. the next morning. What is the elapsed flying time?_____

8. A flight departs Anchorage (−9) at 12:45 A.M. and arrives in Seattle (−8) at 5:07 A.M. What is the elapsed flying time?
   _____

9. Using airport codes, draw examples of
   • a nonstop flight
   • a direct flight
   • a single online connection
   • a single offline connection
   • a double connection
   • a multiple airport connection

10. In order, list the data given when making a flight reservation by phone. _____
    _____

11. What is an excursion fare? _____

12. What are the typical restrictions and limitations of an excursion fare? _____

_____

_____

13. What is a normal fare? _____

14. The portion of a trip from the origin to the destination is called _____

15. The return portion of a round-trip is called _____

16. Identify the booking classes that represent

    coach class _____   first class _____

    business class _____   discounted coach class _____

17. What is a change of gauge flight? _____

CHAPTER 8

United States Airfares and Other Charges

OBJECTIVES

At the conclusion of this chapter, you should be able to

- understand the difference between normal and excursion fares.
- understand the inventory control principle.
- understand fare basis codes and booking classes.
- know how to use fare construction concepts.
- understand a GDS rule and fare display.
- calculate fares, taxes, PFCs, segment fees, security fees, and fuel surcharges.
- understand Alaskan and Hawaiian tax principles.
- understand tax features of the Buffer Zone.
- understand taxes for travel within Canada.

KEY TERMS

Alaskan tax
Alaska/Hawaii International Travel Facilities Tax
back-to-back excursion fares
booking code
breaking the fare
fare basis code (FBC)

fare based
fuel surcharge
Hawaiian tax
inventory control
mileage based
Passenger Facility Charge (PFC)
point-to-point fares

restricted inventory
security fee
segment fee
sister fares
splitting and combining excursion fares
U.S. Transportation Tax
unrestricted inventory

For a travel counselor selling air travel, the task of coping with the myriad of airfares is probably the most difficult. From the air traveler's point of view, understanding fare construction is perhaps the most important skill the counselor can possess. The first question asked by most clients is, "What is the cheapest fare to . . . ?" or "Do you have any specials to . . . ?"

At first glance, GDS fare displays appear incomprehensible. Fortunately, it is not quite as bad as it seems.

NORMAL AND EXCURSION FARES

As you learned in the last chapter, all airfares fall into one of two categories: normal or excursion. A *normal fare* is priced one-way and if it is to be used on a round-trip, the amount is doubled. Normal fares are usually the least restrictive and in most markets are also the least expensive.

A fare priced for round-trip is called an *excursion fare*. Excursion fares, when they exist, are generally the least expensive type of fare as well as the most restrictive. Excursion fares can never be sold on a one-way basis for half the cost. Typical restrictions or limitations of excursion fares include:

- the same airline must be used on all segments.
- reservations must be made and travel purchased in advance.
- there is a minimum stay requirement.
- there is a maximum stay limitation.
- travel is nonrefundable and there is a penalty for making changes.
- all flight segments must be confirmed (no wait-listing or open returns).

INVENTORY CONTROL

Between any given city pair, each airline may have 10, 20, 30, or more fares, each with its own set of rules. The airline principle of inventory control (see Figure 8–1) is the allocation of a specific number of seats per flight that can be sold at each of the fare amounts. Each inventory is either unrestricted or restricted to a particular number of seats that can be sold at a given fare.

To avoid confusion, the term restricted inventory means that the number of seats that can be sold at that price has been limited, or restricted to a specific number. It has nothing to do with the restrictions or limitations of the fare, such as advance purchase or minimum stay. Along the same lines, the term unrestricted inventory means that the number of seats that can be sold at that price has not been limited to a specific number.

> Unrestricted Inventory includes first class (F or P), business class (C or J), and coach class (Y, S, or W).
>
> Restricted Inventory includes discounted first class (A), discounted business class (D or Z), and discounted coach classes (B, Q, M, K, V, L, H, T, N, etc.).

Have you ever seen an advertisement in the newspaper or on television that says "Fly to Orlando for $200"? You may have gone to the airline's Web site only to learn that that fare is sold out, but there is a fare for $350 available. This is inventory control in action. If we use the example in the chart below, we see that only 10 seats can be sold at $200 and, of course, they will be sold out before the higher fares. Once that inventory has been sold, the next higher, *available* fare is offered.

Passenger cabin	Booking class	Fare	Total seats in cabin	Type of inventory	Comments
First Class	F	$800	28	Unrestricted	All 28 seats can be sold at $800 each
First Class—discounted	A	$650	10 of 28	Restricted	Only 10 of the 28 first-class seats can be sold at $650 each
Coach Class	Y	$600	92	Unrestricted	All 92 seats can be sold at $600 each
Coach—discounted	Q	$400	20 of 92	Restricted	Only 20 of the 92 coach seats can be sold at $400 each
Coach—discounted	V	$350	20 of 92	Restricted	Only 20 of the 92 coach seats can be sold at $350 each
Coach—discounted	M	$300	20 of 92	Restricted	Only 20 of the 92 coach seats can be sold at $300 each
Coach—discounted	K	$250	10 of 92	Restricted	Only 10 of the 92 coach seats can be sold at $250 each
Coach—discounted	L	$200	10 of 92	Restricted	Only 10 of the 92 coach seats can be sold at $200 each

FIGURE 8–1 Example of inventory control.

All travel counselors know that travel at the lower fares during peak times (holidays, spring break, major events) sells out months in advance. The airlines know this as well, but it is common to see advertisements for low fares just before these popular travel times. It is no wonder that many people feel cheated when they attempt to purchase travel at the advertised price. As long as the airline publishes that fare, regardless of whether seats are available on all flights, the airline can advertise the fare.

To confound the situation of inventory control even further, each airline may alter the number of seats allocated to each fare inventory. Each flight is monitored to see how sales are going. As the date of the flight nears, seats may be taken from coach class and added to the discounted coach inventories as a means of boosting sales. The theory is that it is better to sell all of the seats at a discount than to take off with the aircraft less than full.

On the other hand, if a flight is selling out quickly, the airline may take a portion of the lower-fare inventory and add it to the inventory of a higher fare. The purpose of this is to generate as much revenue from the flight as possible.

Should the travel counselor suggest that the client wait to see if more inventory is added to a lower-fare category? Most travel counselors agree that this is not wise. If the airline added inventory, the counselor would have to check flights for this client repeatedly throughout the day, every day. The possibility of the counselor finding a seat in the lower-priced inventory as seats are added and before they sell out is very slim. Also, remember that none of the lower-priced fares allow for wait-listing.

It is important to note that when a traveler purchases a restricted inventory type of fare, he can be seated anywhere within the applicable passenger cabin. For example, a traveler buying a $250 fare with a K booking class can sit anywhere within the coach class cabin. In fact, it is very common for a $250 K class passenger to be seated next to a $600 Y class passenger. How could this happen?

Perhaps the $250 passenger could comply with all of the restrictions and limitations of the fare, but the $600 passenger could not. Or, it may be that the $250 passenger purchased travel months in advance and by the time the $600 traveler made reservations, all of the lower-priced inventories had been exhausted. It is easy to see why the best airfare advice travel counselors can give their clients is to make their reservations and purchase travel as soon as their plans are firm.

FARE BASIS CODES AND BOOKING CLASSES

During the days of federal airline regulation (before 1978), there may have been as few as five or six basic fare types between any given city pair. These consisted of one-way, round-trip, Super Saver, senior citizen, child, and military.

Today, there may be 100 or more different fares for that same city pair, each with its own set of rules and regulations. If this sounds like a jungle of confusion to you, you are quite right, it is. But, by learning about booking classes and fare basis codes, the jungle becomes a bit more civilized.

Every fare has been assigned a fare basis code (FBC), either a single letter or a combination of letters or numbers. The first letter, or in some cases the only letter, of the FBC is the booking code, also called booking class or primary code. The booking code identifies the inventory that must be sold in order to obtain the desired fare. Any additional letters or numbers in an FBC may or may not represent particular features of the fare. Figure 8–2 illustrates some of the features found in typical fare basis codes.

- FBC first position: booking code
  - R = supersonic (international only)
  - P or F = first class
  - A = discounted first class
  - J or C = business class
  - D or Z = discounted business class
  - Y, S, or W = coach class
  - B, H, K, L, M, N, Q, T, V, etc. = discounted coach class
- FBC other positions:
  - Day of the week
    - W = weekend
    - X = weekday
    - X67 = except Saturday and Sunday
    - D67 = Saturday and Sunday only
    - Z23 = Tuesday and Wednesday only
    - O = off-peak travel days
    - P = peak travel days
  - Time of the day
    - O = off-peak travel times
    - P = peak travel times
    - N = night, usually before 6 a.m. and after 9 p.m.
  - Season (varies by destination)
    - H = high season
    - L = low season
    - O = shoulder season
  - Type of trip
    - R = round-trip
    - E = excursion
  - Refundability/Change Penalty
    - NR = nonrefundable
    - N = nonrefundable
    - R50 = change penalty of $50
  - Advance purchase
    - IP = instant purchase
    - 7 = 7-day advance purchase
    - 14 = 14-day advance purchase
    - 21 = 21-day advance purchase
  - Minimum stay
    - 1 = 1-day minimum stay

FIGURE 8–2 Examples of features found in U.S. fare basis codes.

By looking at Figure 8–2 you can see some logic in the meanings of each feature. Other restrictions may not be indicated in the FBC. An additional complication is that the meaning of letters and numbers in an FBC can be quite different for international fares and they can vary from one airline to another.

Sister Fares

Sister fares are two fares offered by the same airline for the same city pair and the restrictions are identical but for one feature. This one feature can be the day of the week, time of day, or season (usually international only) in which the fare can be used. By reading each fare's rule in the GDS, the differing feature is explained. Figure 8–3 demonstrates sister fares.

By studying Figure 8–3, you can see that each pair of sister fares has identical rules but for one item. In the first and second example, the item is the days of the week in which the fare can be used and the third example demonstrates differing times of day.

In what way are sister fares used? Let's say that a client wants to travel from Little Rock to Philadelphia on a Tuesday and return the following Sunday. If we use the first two examples shown in Figure 8–3, we see that neither of the fares by itself applies to this client's trip. If normal fares are to be used, the travel counselor can simply add the two applicable one-way sister fares together. If excursion fares are used, the travel counselor splits and combines the excursion fares to create a customized fare for the client.

```
Using normal sister fares for round-trip travel:
LIT—PHL Tuesday:        VX67NR                    $215
PHL—LIT Sunday:         VD67NR                  + $255
Customized round-trip fare                        $470

Using excursion sister fares for round-trip travel:
LIT—PHL Tuesday:     TXE14NR    $200 ÷ 2 =      100
PHL—LIT Sunday:      TWE14NR    $250 ÷ 2 =  + $125
Customized round-trip fare                       $225
```

PLEASE TURN TO PAGE 129 AND COMPLETE EXERCISE 8–1 NOW.

FARE CONSTRUCTION

Obtaining the best fare is fairly straightforward in most circumstances. The travel counselor makes a GDS request for fares, either one-way or round-trip, reads the appropriate rule to check for applicability, checks flight availability, offers choices to the client, and makes the booking. Depending on the GDS and the agency, finding the lowest applicable fare can be simpler still.

Each GDS has developed functions that can search all fares, rules, and flights for the client's dates of travel. One or more itineraries that represent the lowest fare are displayed and the travel counselor selects and books one of the options. These functions go by different names depending on the GDS: Power Shopper, Bargain Finder Plus, Best Buy Quote, or Value Pricer.

With this capability, should the travel counselor still understand fare basis codes and fare construction principles? Absolutely—for two very important reasons!

1. These functions are not usually part of the basic GDS cost to the agency and because of the extra expense, not all agencies can afford this capability.
2. Although these functions are usually accurate, there are times when they fail to produce the lowest fare. Along the same lines, travel counselors can utilize their knowledge of fare construction to price certain trips creatively; something these functions cannot usually do.

Fare Construction—One-Way Travel

The simplest type of fare is a one-way fare. As you have already learned, a one-way fare has the fewest restrictions and limitations. The travel counselor can request that normal fares be shown in the GDS for a client's city pair, find

```
Pair #1 (excursion fares)
   UA   TWE14NR   T = discounted coach, W = weekend, E = excursion, 14 = 14-day advance purchase, NR = nonrefundable. $250 round-trip.
   UA   TXE14NR   T = discounted coach, X = weekday, E = excursion, 14 = 14-day advance purchase, NR = nonrefundable. $200 round-trip.
Pair #2 (normal fares)
   AA   VD67NR    V = discounted coach, D67 = Saturday and Sunday only, NR = nonrefundable. $255 one-way, $510 round-trip.
   AA   VX67NR    V = discounted coach, X67 = except Saturday and Sunday, NR = nonrefundable. $215 one-way, $430 round-trip.
Pair #3 (excursion fares)
   CO   QEO7IP    Q = discounted coach, E = excursion, O = off-peak travel times, 7 = 7-day advance purchase, IP = instant purchase. $300 round-trip.
   CO   QEP7IP    Q = discounted coach, E = excursion, P = peak travel times, 7 = 7-day advance purchase, IP = instance purchase. $350 round-trip.
```

FIGURE 8–3 Examples of sister fares.

Pricing from origin to destination:
    DTW to FLL—$275

Breaking the fare at a connection point:
    DTW to CVG $ 49
    CVG to FLL   + $175
              Trip total $224

Savings by breaking the fare: $51

FIGURE 8–4 Breaking the fare at the connection point.

Pricing as a simple round trip—$398

    1. CLT-STL   15JUN
    2. STL-PSP   15JUN   (connection)
    3. PSP-STL   22JUN
    4. STL-CLT   22JUN   (connection)

Pricing using back-to-back excursions

    1. CLT-STL   15JUN
    2. STL-PSP   15JUN
    3. PSP-STL   22JUN $239 + $119 = $358
    4. STL-CLT   22JUN

Savings by using back-to-back excursions: $40

FIGURE 8–5 Regular excursion fare compared to back-to-back excursions.

Pricing by using two normal fares:

    MSP/PHX normal fare $335
    TUS/MSP normal fare   + $350
              Trip total $685

FIGURE 8–6 Using normal fares on an open-jaw trip.

the least expensive one-way fare, read the appropriate rule to check for applicability, and make the booking. However, is it possible to be creative with the fares to save money? Perhaps.

Suppose the client is traveling from Detroit Metro to Ft. Lauderdale and does not mind changing planes en route. The travel counselor knows that possible cities for a connection (hubs) between DTW and FLL include Chicago O'Hare, Atlanta, and Cincinnati. The travel counselor requests normal fares in the GDS from DTW to the connection point and another fare display from the connection point to FLL and adds them together. Figure 8–4 shows an example of this technique, which is called breaking the fare.

As you can see in Figure 8–4, the normal fare from DTW to FLL is $275. But, if the counselor uses a connection in CVG and uses two point-to-point fares added together, the total is $224. In other words, the client saves $51 because the travel counselor knew how and took the time to be creative. Do not confuse this pricing technique with the unethical practice, fictitious return, described in Chapter 7.

Fare Construction—Round-Trip Travel

In almost all cases, the least expensive round-trip fare is priced from origin to destination and back to origin. It usually does not matter if a nonstop, direct, or connection service is used or the city in which a connection is made. In a few instances, using the technique called back-to-back excursion fares results in a lower fare. This technique requires that a connection be made in both directions and that the change of planes take place in the same city. Do not confuse this pricing technique with the unethical practice of back-to-back ticketing described in Chapter 7.

The principle of back-to-back excursions means that two excursion fares are used and added together instead of using just one. The first excursion is from the origin to the connection point and back to the origin. The second excursion is from the connection point to the destination and back to the connection point. Figure 8–5 compares a regular round-trip price to back-to-back excursions.

Because the special GDS pricing functions may not have found the back-to-back scenario, it is important that

the travel counselor know how to test this possibility. As you can see in Figure 8–5, using this technique saves the client $40.

Fare Construction—Open-Jaw Travel

When normal fares are used, the cities used in an open jaw make no difference in the fare construction. For example, a client is traveling from Minneapolis to Phoenix, spends a few days traveling by car in Arizona, then returns from Tucson back to MSP. The surface segment of this typical open jaw is between PHX and TUS.

Pricing on this trip is simple: The one-way MSP/PHX fare is added to the one-way TUS/MSP fare, resulting in the total fare for this open-jaw trip. This pricing construction is valid providing the client is using first class, business class, coach class, or one-way discounted coach class fares (see Figure 8–6).

If this same client's priority is obtaining the lowest fare, the counselor may need to approach pricing in a completely different fashion. Almost all excursion fare rules allow usage on an open-jaw trip provided that the cities being used pass a simple test. When excursion fares are used on an open-jaw trip, the pricing technique is called *splitting and combining excursions*. This test is usually mileage based, although it can be fare based.

A mileage-based test requires that the air miles on the surface segment be equal to or less than the air miles on

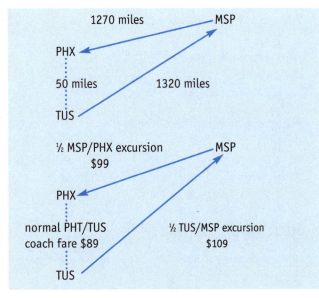

FIGURE 8-7 Mileage and fare tests on an open-jaw trip.

Pricing by splitting and combining excursion fares:

MSP/PHX $198 excursion ÷ 2 =	$99
TUS/MSP $218 excursion ÷ 2 =	+ $109
Trip total	$208

Savings by splitting and combining excursions: $477

FIGURE 8-8 Splitting and combining excursion fares on an open-jaw trip.

each of the flown segments. The fare-based test requires that the one-way coach fare on the surface segment must be equal to or less than the split excursions on each of the flown segments. Figure 8-7 demonstrates an example of both tests for the MSP/PHX, TUS/MSP itinerary.

As you can see in Figure 8-7, it does not matter which test was stated in the fare rule, the proposed itinerary passes both tests. Because the itinerary passes, the travel counselor can split and combine excursion fares as long as all fare restrictions and limitations are met. Figure 8-8 demonstrates splitting and combining excursion fares.

As you see in Figure 8-6, the price using normal fares was $685. By splitting and combining excursion fares, the travel counselor has created a fare of $208—a savings to the client of $477!

Fare Construction—Circle Trip

As you learned earlier, a circle trip can consist of any number of destinations when normal fares are used.

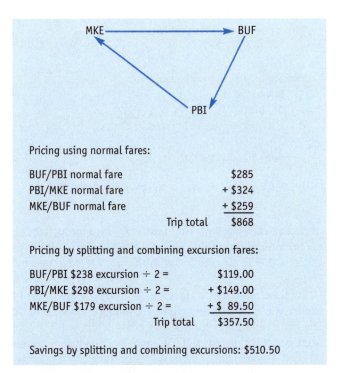

Pricing using normal fares:

BUF/PBI normal fare	$285
PBI/MKE normal fare	+ $324
MKE/BUF normal fare	+ $259
Trip total	$868

Pricing by splitting and combining excursion fares:

BUF/PBI $238 excursion ÷ 2 =	$119.00
PBI/MKE $298 excursion ÷ 2 =	+ $149.00
MKE/BUF $179 excursion ÷ 2 =	+ $ 89.50
Trip total	$357.50

Savings by splitting and combining excursions: $510.50

FIGURE 8-9 Using normal fares on a circle trip compared to splitting and combining excursion fares.

Almost all fare rules allow excursion fares to be used on a circle trip (splitting and combining); however, the circle trip can have only two destinations—no more, no less.

Anytime excursion fares are used, all restrictions and limitations as detailed in the fare rules must be met. There is, however, a new question we must now ask ourselves. What about the minimum stay requirement that almost all excursion fares have? Must the client satisfy the minimum stay in both of his destinations? The answer is no. Almost all fare rules state that when splitting and combining excursion fares on a circle trip, the minimum stay requirement must be met at the destination that is farthest away from the origin city.

Figure 8-9 demonstrates a circle trip from Buffalo to West Palm Beach, PBI to Milwaukee, and MKE to BUF. Notice the difference in cost when normal fares are used compared to splitting and combining excursion fares.

If the travel counselor saw this client's itinerary as three one-way trips and priced it using normal fares, the counselor would quote $868. However, by seeing the circle trip for what it is, the counselor knows that using excursion fares is a possibility. By splitting and combining excursion fares, the client's total is now $357.50; a savings of $510.50!

Fare Construction—Open-Jaw with Side Trip

All features of open-jaw pricing hold true when working with an open-jaw with a side trip. **Splitting and combining**

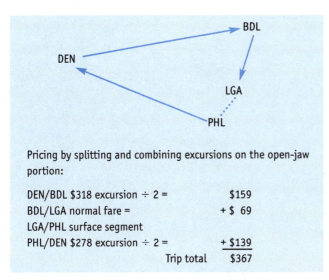

Pricing by splitting and combining excursions on the open-jaw portion:

DEN/BDL $318 excursion ÷ 2 =	$159
BDL/LGA normal fare =	+ $ 69
LGA/PHL surface segment	
PHL/DEN $278 excursion ÷ 2 =	+ $139
Trip total	$367

FIGURE 8-10 Open-jaw with side trip fare construction.

excursion fares must be verified in each fare rule for mileage or fare tests and for all other restrictions. The difference in this trip is the side trip.

For example, a client wants to fly from Denver to Hartford, BDL to New York LaGuardia, surface to Philadelphia, and PHL back to DEN (see Figure 8–10). The travel counselor could use three point-to-point normal fares on this itinerary, but that would be very expensive. For pricing purposes only, let's look at this itinerary in a different way: one open-jaw trip, and one one-way (side trip).

If you look only at the DEN/BDL and PHL/DEN portion of this trip, you can easily see an open-jaw. This portion, as long as all restrictions and limitations are met, can be priced using excursion fares (splitting and combining). The remainder of the itinerary is the BDL/LGA portion. For this leg, the travel counselor finds and uses the least expensive normal fare.

COMBINABILITY RULES

Regardless of whether the travel counselor is splitting and combining sister fares or using the technique on an open-jaw or circle trip, certain guidelines must be followed. Every fare rule can be viewed in the GDS and combinability is always listed in the rule. Figure 8–11 is a fare rule displayed in the Worldspan GDS.

Anytime fares are split and combined, the most restrictive fare rules govern the entire trip. For example, combining a 7-day advance purchase fare with a 21-day advance purchase requires that all segments of the itinerary meet the 21-day advance purchase rule. Combining one fare that has a 1-day minimum stay with another fare

that has a 7-day minimum stay requirement means that the 7-day minimum governs the trip.

It is important to note that almost all fares can be combined as long as all fare rules are met and the same airline is maintained. A travel counselor can use one half of an excursion fare for the outbound and a normal Y class fare for the inbound. Or, a travel counselor can use one half of a BE21XNR combined with one half of a QE7NR. Why might a travel counselor do this? Primarily, this sort of combination is done because the lowest fare is not available in one direction or the other.

PLEASE TURN TO PAGE 130 AND COMPLETE EXERCISE 8–2 NOW.

AIRLINE COMPUTER FARE DISPLAY

Nearly all U.S. travel agencies are automated and obtain both domestic and international airfares from the GDS. Although each system's display is slightly different in appearance, the fare information provided is quite similar. For example, a counselor who uses Galileo would probably be able to interpret a display from Sabre, Amadeus, or Worldspan.

Each GDS groups the lowest fares among all airlines and shows them first. It is interesting to note that each time a counselor requests a display for the same city pair and dates, the airline order is different. If this were not true, the GDS would be guilty of bias. Figure 8–12 is a Worldspan fare display from Indianapolis to Ft. Lauderdale.

By looking at Figure 8–12, you can see that the least expensive round-trip fare is $196 and is offered by DL, JI, UA, and NW. The symbol "#" preceding some of the fare basis codes is called an *End Item* in Worldspan. In this position, the End Item indicates that blackout dates apply. An End Item in the advance purchase column means that the advance purchase rule is too complex to be shown; the counselor must go to the fare rule. Notice that some of the fares do not have a minimum stay requirement and others have a minimum of one day. A minimum stay of "SUN" is somewhat deceptive; it means that the minimum stay is one Saturday night and the return cannot commence until Sunday. If an actual number of days is not specified for the maximum stay limitation, 365 days is assumed.

The fare display header lines provide additional information. "NLX" indicates that normal and excursion fares are shown. Notice the comment about U.S. taxes that is followed by "SEG/PFC CHARGES MAY APPLY." All GDS fare displays for cities in the United States include tax, but as you will learn shortly, there are other charges that must be added to the amounts shown in the display.

```
INDFLL-DL    5APR06    *RULE DISPLAY*    TARIFF 011    RULE 4040
001-FARE BASIS        USD     TAX     TOTAL     PTC   FT
L14SLEXP             91.16    6.84    98.00     ADT   NL
L14SLEXP/IN00        0.00     0.00    0.00      INF   NL
L14SLEXP/IN50        45.58    3.42    49.00     INS   NL
BOOKING CODE         L
FIRST TRAVEL         - 9MAR06    LAST TRAVEL—9JUN06
TRAVEL COMPLETE      - 9JUN06
SEASONS              - NO RESTRICTIONS
PENALTIES            - CHANGE—50.00 USD    CANCEL—NON REF
DAY/TIME             - NO RESTRICTIONS
ADV RES/TKT          - RES REQ 14 DAYS BEFORE DEPART
                       TKTG WITHIN 1 DAY AFTER RESERVATIONS OR AT LEAST
                       14 DAYS BEFORE DEPART WHICHEVER IS EARLIER
MIN STAY             - NO RESTRICTIONS
MAX STAY             - NO RESTRICTIONS
BLACKOUTS            - 18FEB06   27FEB06   21APR06   30APR06   26MAY06   30MAY06
                       05JUL06   01SEP06   05SEP06   21NOV06   26NOV06   22DEC06
SURCHARGES           - NONE
STOPOVERS            - NOT PERMITTED
TRANSFERS            - NO RESTRICTIONS
FLT APPLIC           - DL FLT 2300-2599 DL FLT 9650-9654 DL FLT 9425-9444
CHILD DIS            - 1ST INF UNDER 2 YRS FREE NO SEAT
                       1ST INF UNDER 2 YRS 50 PCT IN SEAT
COMBINABILITY        - COMBINATIONS PERMITTED ONLY WITH DL FARES
                       OPEN JAW PERMITTED—MILEAGE BASED
                       CIRCLE TRIP PERMITTED—2 COMPONENTS ONLY
ELIGIBILITY          - NO RESTRICTIONS
ACCOM PSGR           - NO RESTRICTION
TVL RESTR            - RETURN BY 09JUN06 MIDNIGHT
                       PTA ALLOWED AND CONSTIUES TKTG
INDUSTRY FARE TYPE   - IP—INSTANT PURCHASE
PFCS MAY VARY BY RTG
ROUTING 2    FROM-TO    IND-DL-ORL-DL-FLL
```

FIGURE 8–11 Worldspan fare rule display.

```
INDFLL  NLX FARES FOR TRVL 15JUN06 AND TKTG 05APR
      US TAXES VARY
          * SEG/PFC CHARGES MAY APPLY
```

LN	A/L	F.B.C. USD	OW	RT	EFF	LTK	AP	MIN/MAX
1	DL	#L14SLEXP	98.00	196.00	9MAR06	-	##	-/-
2	JI	MR14NR		196.00	11APR06	-	##	1/-
3	UA	VRA14FN		196.00	23MAR06	-	##	-/-
4	DL	#LR14M1SN		196.00	22MAR06	-	##	1/-
5	JI	#MLE14SL		196.00	12MAR06	-	##	SUN/ 30
6	NW	KR14OMN		196.00	24MAR06	-	##	1/-
7	JI	W7SLEXP	99.00	198.00	3APR06	7APR06	##	-/-
8	DL	#L7SALEXP	99.00	198.00	27MAR06		##	-/-

FIGURE 8–12 Partial fare display from Worldspan GDS.

TAXES AND OTHER FEES—UNITED STATES, CANADA, AND MEXICO

When it comes to air travel, fares are seldom exactly what they seem. In almost all cases, the fare amounts shown in the GDS must have other items added before the travel counselor can quote a cost. Which taxes and other fees are included depends on where the client is going, and in some cases, where the client is originating.

Within the 48 Contiguous States, Alaska, or Hawaii

All air travel within the 48 contiguous states, completely within Alaska, or completely within Hawaii is taxed; currently the rate of *tax is 7.5 percent*. The U.S. Transportation Tax, also called the ticket tax, is included in the amounts shown in a GDS fare display. Because GDS fares and fares quoted by an airline include this tax, the travel counselor must know how to break down the fare into base (commissionable) and tax (noncommissionable) amounts before a ticket can be written (see Figure 8–13). The 7.5 percent tax is shown in one of the ticket tax boxes with the code *US*.

Fare amounts shown in the GDS are referred to as total fares, even though they include tax but no other charges. The word "total" is a misnomer because, in most cases, other fees must be added before an amount can be quoted to the client. Exercises in this text use the phrase "total fare" to indicate inclusive of tax. We use the term "grand total" to indicate an amount to which all other fees have been added.

At every board point and at every en route stop point, a segment fee of $3.20 applies. Segment fees are com-

bined and the total is shown in one of the ticket tax boxes with the code *ZP*. Each segment fee is also identified in the fare ladder portion of a ticket. The amount of the segment fee is subject to change by the government at any time.

At many board points, a Passenger Facility Charge (PFC) may apply. Depending on the airport, the PFC can be $1.00, $2.00, $3.00, $4.00, or $4.50; however, the vast majority of airports charging PFCs charge $3.00 or $4.50. PFCs for the itinerary are combined and the total is shown in one of the ticket tax boxes with the code *XF*. Like segment fees, PFCs are identified in the fare ladder portion of a ticket.

A fuel surcharge applies at many board point airports and the amounts range from $10.00 to $20.00. Fuel surcharges are the result of fuel shortages or escalating fuel prices. Shown in a GDS fare rule display as a base amount, fuel surcharges are taxed at 7.5 percent. Fuel surcharges do not appear in a ticket tax box; rather, they are added to the base fare and are shown in the fare box of the ticket. Each fuel surcharge is also listed in the fare ladder portion of a ticket with the code *Q*.

After the terrorist attacks of September 11, 2001, the U.S. government initiated a new security fee to help cover the cost of added security for all travelers boarding flights in the United States. This fee is $2.50 per embarkation up to a maximum of $5.00 for one-way trips and $10.00 for round-trips. The security service fee is shown on tickets with the code *AY* and is not taxable.

From the 48 Contiguous States to Alaska and Hawaii

Tax structures for travel from the 48 contiguous states to Alaska are based on the client's origin and destination cities. Each city pair has a unique tax factor. Tax on travel to Hawaii from the 48 contiguous states is based on the client's origin city only; each city has its own tax factor.

In addition to the Alaskan tax or the Hawaiian tax, another tax applies. This tax is called the Alaska/Hawaii International Travel Facilities Tax. Because a flight from the 48 contiguous states to Alaska or Hawaii leaves U.S. air space and enters international air space, the flight has technically left the United States. On return flights from Alaska or Hawaii back to the 48 contiguous states, the same thing happens. So, on one-way trips, a $6.90 U.S. departure tax is charged once; on round-trips the tax is charged twice. The combination of Alaskan or Hawaiian tax and the U.S. departure tax is shown in one of the ticket tax boxes with the code *US*. Figure 8–14 illustrates a variety of Alaskan and Hawaiian tax calculations.

Alaskan, Hawaiian, and U.S. departure taxes are included in the amounts shown in a GDS fare display. Additionally,

---

Total Fare ÷ 1.075 = Base Fare
    For example: $350 total fare ÷1.075 = $325.58 base fare
Total Fare − Base Fare = Tax
    For example: $350 total fare − $325.58 base fare = $24.42 tax
Note: If you begin with a grand total, you must subtract PFCs and segment fees before you divide by 1.075.

Base Fare × 1.075 = Total Fare
    For example: $325.58 base fare × 1.075 = $350 total fare

Base Fare × .075 = Tax
    For example: $325.58 base fare × .075 = $24.42 tax

Base Fare + Tax = Total Fare
    For example: $325.58 base fare + $24.42 tax = $350 total fare

FIGURE 8–13 Tax calculation on air travel within the 48 contiguous states.

If the Alaskan or Hawaiian tax factor is .0329:

Total Fare ÷ 1.0329 = Base Fare

For example: $638 total fare ÷ 1.0329 = $617.68 base fare

Total Fare − Base Fare = Tax

For example: $638 total fare − $617.68 base fare = $20.32 tax

Note: If you begin with a grand total, you must subtract PFCs, segment fees, and the U.S. departure tax before you divide by 1.0329.

Total Fare + PFCs + segment fees + U.S. departure tax = Grand Total

For example: $638 total fare + $12 PFCs + $10 segment fees + $6.40 U.S. departure tax outbound + $6.40 U.S. departure tax inbound = $672.80 grand total.

FIGURE 8–14 Tax calculation for travel between the 48 contiguous states and Alaska or Hawaii.

segment fees, PFCs, security fees, and fuel surcharges may also apply.

Both the *OAG Flight Guide* and the *ARC Industry Agents' Handbook* include charts for Alaskan and Hawaiian tax percentages as well as information about the U.S. departure tax.

The Buffer Zone

The buffer zone is the area from the U.S. border 225 miles north into Canada and from the U.S. border 225 miles south into Mexico. Travel from the 48 contiguous states into the buffer zone is not considered domestic or international with regard to tax principles. The buffer zone is a unique tax area.

Flights to cities in the Canadian and Mexican buffer zone are taxed at U.S. 7.5 percent and segment fees, PFCs, and fuel surcharges also apply. On itineraries that return to the United States, a $7 U.S. Immigration Fee, code *XY,* is charged.

Currently there is no Canadian tax applicable for travel from the United States into the buffer zone. If the itinerary includes a departure from Calgary (YYC), the Calgary Airport Improvement Fee is charged. This fee is identified by the code *SQ* and is 12 Canadian dollars (CAD).

Travelers from the United States to cities in the Mexican buffer zone must pay a Mexican Tourist Tax of 170 new Mexican pesos (MXN), and a Mexican airport departure tax, code *XD,* that varies by airport. On itineraries that return to the United States, a $3.10 Animal Plant and Health Inspection Service (APHIS) Fee, code *XA,* and a $7 U.S. Immigration Fee are also charged.

Fare amounts shown in a GDS display for travel from the 48 contiguous states to a city in the buffer zone are shown as base amounts. The *ARC Industry Agents' Handbook* includes sections dealing with tax principles for travel to the buffer zone.

Within Canada or Within Mexico

Itineraries that are totally within Canada are taxed at 7 percent. This tax is called the Goods and Services Tax (GST) and is shown in one of the ticket tax boxes with the code *XG.* Flights from a city in the province of Quebec to other Canadian cities are subject to the Quebec Sales Tax, which is currently 7.5 percent. The Quebec Sales Tax is shown in one of the ticket tax boxes with the code *XQ.* As mentioned earlier, any flight departing the Calgary Airport is subject to the $12 CAD Calgary Airport Improvement Fee.

For travel sold in the United States for itineraries that begin in Canada, the GST applies. GST is shown in one of the ticket tax boxes with the code *XG.* The GST does not apply when travel originates in the provinces of Nova Scotia, New Brunswick, or Newfoundland. Travel originating in these areas is subject to the 15 percent Harmonized Sales Tax (HST). The HST is shown with the code RC in one of the ticket tax boxes.

Flights from cities in the province of Quebec to other Canadian cities are also subject to the Quebec Sales Tax, shown on the ticket with the code *XQ.* Passengers departing the Calgary Airport (YYC) are subject to the Calgary Airport Improvement Fee of $12, identified by the code *SQ.* All travelers flying from a Canadian city into the United States are subject to the U.S. Immigration Fee of $7, identified by the code *XY.*

As mentioned earlier, Mexican airports have a departure tax and the amount varies by airport. The codes for the Mexican airport departure tax are *XV* and *XD.* The Mexican International Transportation Tax, code *MX,* is 2.5 percent to 3.75 percent depending on the origin airport. Again, depending on airport, the Mexican Domestic Transportation Tax ranges from 2.5 to 15 percent, code *XO.*

As strange as it may seem, the 7.5 percent U.S. ticket tax applies for itineraries from one Canadian buffer zone city to another Canadian city in the buffer zone when travel is purchased in the United States. The same thing is true for Mexican cities that are both in the buffer zone. Even though no U.S. city is part of the itinerary, segment fees apply to cities in the Canadian and Mexican buffer zones.

Too Many Taxes

If after reading the last few sections your head is spinning from all of the taxes and other fees, you are not alone. Most travel counselors cannot imagine facing all of these charges without help from their GDSs. It is no wonder that the traveling public is completely baffled by fares, taxes, fees, and surcharges. To help us get a handle on all of this,

Tax Name	Tax Code	Cincinnati to Pittsburgh RT	Honolulu to Maui RT	Fairbanks to Anchorage RT	Los Angeles to Honolulu RT	Seattle to Anchorage RT	Chicago to Montreal RT	Boston to Toronto RT	Toronto to Vancouver RT	Montreal to Calgary RT	Houston to Monterrey RT	Halifax to Toronto RT
7.5% U.S. Ticket Tax	US	√	√	√			√	√	√	√	√	√
$3.20 Segment Fee	ZP	√	√	√	√	√	√	√	√	√	√	√
PFC	XF	√	√	√	√	√	√	√				
Alaskan Tax	US					√						
Hawaiian Tax	US				√							
$3.10 APHIS Fee	XA										√	
$7 Immigration Fee	XY						√	√			√	
$6.90 U.S. Departure Tax	US				√	√						
7% Goods & Services Tax	XG								√	√		
15% Harmonized Sales Tax	RC											√
7.5% Quebec Sales Tax	XQ									√		
$10 CAD Calgary Airport Fee	SQ									√		
170 MXN Tourist Tax	UK										√	
Mexico Airport Departure Tax	XD										√	
Fuel Surcharge	Q	√	√	√	√	√	√	√	√	√		√
U.S. Security Service Fee $2.50	AY	√	√	√	√	√	√	√			√	

FIGURE 8–15 Tax and fee chart for the United States, Buffer Zone, Canada, and Mexico.

Figure 8–15 brings everything into perspective. All items in Figure 8–15 represent a purchase in the United States and no additional stopovers.

With all of these taxes and additional fees, you may be wondering just how many tax boxes are available on tickets. There are only three tax boxes on automated tickets and four on handwritten tickets. So, what happens when more than three or four taxes or other charges apply? The answer is a combined tax item, shown with the code *XT*. Anytime a combined tax amount appears in one of the ticket tax boxes, each tax is listed separately with its respective code in the fare ladder portion of the ticket.

PLEASE TURN TO PAGE 132 AND COMPLETE
EXERCISE 8–3 NOW.

? What Would You Do?

A traveler calls your agency about a $149 fare he saw in the newspaper. You check the GDS fare display and see that the fare requires "Q" booking class. On checking flight availability, you see that the noon flight on that airline is sold out in Q class.

1. Would the best option be to offer the best available fare on the noon flight?
2. Would the best option be to find another flight that has Q class available?
3. How would you explain this situation to your caller?

SUMMARY

Working with airfares is perhaps one of the most complicated tasks that a travel professional faces. Each airline has its own fare structure and each fare has its own set of rules and regulations. Although the travel counselor cannot memorize each and every fare he has to contend with, he must understand how and where to obtain this information. Regardless of the amount of additional service the travel professional provides, a client may choose to go elsewhere if the counselor feels that the counselor is not pricing the itinerary in the best way.

In addition to the myriad of airfares, travel counselors must also contend with and understand the various taxes, fees, and surcharges that apply to air travel. The applicable taxes and fees depend on the client's destination, and in some cases, his origin city as well. Understanding which taxes and fees are to be added to the client's airfare is important for the accurate quotation of the client's trip.

 For additional Travel and Tourism resources, go to http://www.hospitality-tourism.delmar.com.

PLEASE COMPLETE THE CHAPTER REVIEW
QUESTIONS NOW.

EXERCISE 8-1 Fare Basis Codes and Booking Classes

1. Interpret these fare basis codes.

   KEX234IP _____

   FXR30 _____

   QWE21NR _____

   YN _____

   VXRIP _____

   BED236NR _____

2. Identify the usual features of normal fares. _____

   _____

3. Identify the booking classes that represent unrestricted inventory. _____

4. What are sister fares? _____

   _____

5. Identify the typical restrictions and limitations of excursion fares. _____

   _____

6. Do excursion fare restrictions mean the same thing as restricted inventory? _____

7. What is the difference between a booking class or code and a fare basis code? _____

   _____

8. Explain the airline principle of inventory control. _____

   _____

9. If a client does not qualify for either one of a pair of sister fares because of the client's travel dates, what should you do? ____

   _____

10. Today is Monday, June 10, 2006, and you have obtained the following fare basis codes, amounts, and restrictions or limitations. Reservations and ticketing will take place on June 10, 2006. Calculate the fare for each client based on this information. Write down the airline code(s), fare basis code(s), and amount(s). If you must make any calculations, be sure to write them down as well.

A/L	FBC	OW	RT	ADV. PUR.	DAYS	MIN. STAY	MAX. STAY
NW	TXE21NR	200.00	21 days	M—F	1 Sat. night	30 days	
CO	QE07IP	200.00	7 days	M—F	1 day	n/a	
CO	QEP7IP	250.00	7 days	Sa & Su	1 day	n/a	
NW	TWE21NR	250.00	21 days	Sa & Su	1 Sat. night	30 days	
HP	VX67NR	150.00	300.00	none	M—F	n/a	n/a
HP	VD67NR	180.00	360.00	none	Sa & Su	n/a	n/a

a. Depart Tuesday, August 13; return Friday, August 16. _____

b. Depart Sunday, July 21; one-way. _____

c. Depart Friday, October 11; return Monday, October 21. _____

_____

d. Depart Sunday, August 25; return Saturday, August 31. _____

e. Depart Tuesday, November 12; one-way. _____

f. Depart Wednesday, June 12; return Saturday, June 15. _____

g. Depart Saturday, August 24; return Tuesday, October 15. _____

h. Depart Friday, December 13; return Sunday, December 15. _____

EXERCISE 8-2 Fare Construction

1. Depending on GDS, functions that automatically check fares, rules, and flight availability are called _____

_____

2. Even though the functions mentioned in question 1 are available, why must travel counselors be well versed in interpreting fare and fare rule displays? _____

_____

3. Your client is flying from PHL to SMF round-trip with a connection in ORD in both directions. What fare technique might you check in an attempt to lower the fare? _____

_____

4. Your client is flying from DTW to MIA, driving from MIA to JAX, and flying from JAX to DTW. What fare technique will you attempt to use in order to save money? _____

_____

5. Based on the itinerary in question 4, what test(s) determines if excursion fares can be used? _____

_____

6. Your client is flying from DCA to LAS, one-way. Explain what you might check in hopes of saving your client money. _____

_____

7. The three excursion fares that you want to use for your client's circle trip have different advance purchase and minimum stay rules. Fare 1 is a 7-day advance purchase and a 7-day minimum stay. Fares 2 and 3 have a 21-day advance purchase and a Saturday night minimum. Which rules apply to your client's trip? _____

_____

Directions: The remaining questions are based on the following rule display.

FARE BASIS		USD	TAX	TOTAL	PTC	FT
WE14SA1N	R	184.19	13.81	198.00	ADT	EX
WE14SA1N/INF100	R	00.00	00.00	00.00	INF	EX
WE14SA1N/INF50	R	92.09	6.91	99.00	INS	EX
WE14SA1N/SD10	R	165.77	12.43	178.20	SRC	EX
WE14SA1N/SD10C	R	165.77	12.43	178.20	CMP	EX

```
BOOKING CLASS      W WN
FIRST TRAVEL       - 20APR02      LAST TRAVEL      - 14JUN02
TRAVEL COMPLETE    - 14JUN02
SEASONS            - NO RESTRICTION
PENALTIES          - CHANGE – 75.00 USD              TKT NON REF
DAY/TIME           - TUE/WED/SAT ALL DAY
ADV RES/TKT        - RES REQ 14 DAYS BEFORE DPTR—TKT WITHIN 1 DAY
                     AFTER RESERVATIONS OR AT LEAST 14 DAYS BEFORE
                     DPTR WHICHEVER IS EARLIER
MIN STAY           - RETURN AFTER 1 DAY AFTER DPTR FROM ORIGIN
MAX STAY           - 30 DAYS AFTER DEPARTURE FROM ORIGIN
BLACKOUTS          - NO RESTRICTIONS
SURCHARGES         - NONE
STOPOVERS          - NOT PERMITTED
COMBINABILITY      - MAY BE COMBINED WITH ANY OTHER UA FARE
                     THAT ALLOWS COMBINATION
ROUTING  2   DTW IAH ORD
```

8. How much is the adult (ADT) total fare? _____

9. Can your client use this fare and change planes in Denver? _____

10. What class must you book in flight availability in order to use this fare? _____

11. Is this a normal or excursion fare? _____

12. How much is the penalty to change a ticketed booking? _____

13. What is the minimum stay requirement? _____

14. On what days of the week can this fare be used? _____

15. Are there any blackout dates? _____

16. By what date must all travel be completed? _____

17. How much is the total fare for an infant in a seat (INS)? _____

18. If your clients cannot travel, can they get their money back? _____

19. Today is March 15 and your client has made reservations for a May 15 departure. By what date must he purchase his ticket/e-tkt?

_____

20. Today is April 10 and your client wants to make a reservation for travel on April 20 using this fare. What will you say?

_____

_____

_____

_____

_____

EXERCISE 8-3 Fare, Tax, and Total Calculation

1. How much is the base fare and tax on a total fare of $347?   _____

2. Your client's round-trip grand total cost on WN is $427, inclusive of $6 PFCs, $6.40 in segment fees, and $5.00 security fees. How much is the base fare and tax?   _____

3. Your client's one-way base fare on HA is $441.86. PFCs are $6, there is $6.40 in segment fees, and $2.50 security fees. What grand total amount will you quote?   _____

4. Your client's total round-trip fare on DL is $350. PFCs are $9, there is $12.80 in segment fees, and $10.00 security fees. The PTA service charge is $75. What grand total do you quote?   _____

5. The round-trip base fare from Brownsville to Anchorage is $714.15. The Alaskan tax factor is .0502. PFCs are $16.00, segment fees are $12.80, and $10.00 security fees. How much is the grand total?   _____

6. The one-way trip base fare from Buffalo to Honolulu is $769.60. The Hawaiian tax factor is .0395. PFCs are $6, segment fees are $6.20, and security fees are $5.00. How much is the grand total?   _____

7. Your client's grand total for her round-trip DL ticket is $385, inclusive of $12 in PFCs, $12.80 in segment fees, and $5.00 security fees. How much is the base fare?   _____

8. Your client's grand total for his round-trip UA ticket is $1242, inclusive of $9 in PFCs, $12.80 in segment fees, and $10.00 security fees. How much is the base fare?   _____

Review Questions

Directions: Answer questions 1–10 based on the following fare display.

```
MIACVG NLX FARES FOR TRVL 20AUG06 AND TKTG 23MAR
US TAXES VARY * SEG/PFC CHARGES MAY APPLY
```

LN	A/L	F.B.C. USD	OW	RT	EFF	LTK	AP	MIN/MAX
1	HP	#HE21NR		232.00	09MAY06	-	##	SUN/30
2	NW	QE14QNR		247.00	09MAY06	27JUN	##	SUN/30
3	DL	LE14NR		247.00	09MAY06	-	##	SUN/-
4	AA	NE14NR		247.00	09MAY06	-	##	SUN/30
5	UA	VE14NR		262.00	20MAR06	-	##	1/30
6	CO	QE14NRIP		277.00	16MAR06	-	##	SUN/45
7	CO	V7N	173.00	346.00	09MAY06	-	##	-/-
8	UA	H7N	185.00	370.00	17MAR06	-	##	-/-

1. Explain as much as you can about the advance purchase requirement for American's fare. _____

_____

2. How much is the least expensive one-way fare? _____

_____

3. How would you explain HP's minimum stay requirement to your client? _____

_____

4. What is the maximum stay limitation for the QE14NRIP fare? _____

5. By what date must Northwest's fare be booked and ticketed? _____

6. How much is the least expensive round-trip fare? _____

7. What does the symbol "#" in front of the fare basis code indicate? _____

_____

8. What is the maximum stay limitation on Delta's fare? _____

9. What is the minimum stay requirement on the VE14NR fare? _____

10. This display shows fares between what two cities? _____

11. Identify these tax and surcharge codes by name and indicate the appropriate amount or percentage for each item.

Q _____

US _____

XF _____

ZP _____

AY _____

12. What is the buffer zone? _____

13. Identify these tax codes by name and indicate the appropriate amount or percentage for each item.

MX _____

RC _____

SQ _____

XA _____

XD _____

XG _____

XO _____

XQ _____

XV _____

XY _____

14. Your client is traveling from Spokane to Vancouver round-trip. Identify by name the taxes or fees that may or will apply.

_____

_____

15. Your client is traveling from Kona to Honolulu round-trip. Identify by name the taxes or fees that may or will apply.

_____

_____

16. Your client is traveling from Halifax to Toronto round-trip. Identify by name the taxes or fees that may or will apply.

_____

_____

17. Your client is traveling from Montreal to Boston round-trip. Identify by name the taxes or fees that may or will apply.

_____

_____

Ticketing and Reporting

OBJECTIVES

At the conclusion of this chapter, you should be able to

- distinguish among the three types of "ticketing."
- identify accountable and nonaccountable ARC ticket stock.
- understand the mechanics of e-ticketing.
- understand the use of a Prepaid Ticket Advice.
- define the reasons for refund and exchange transactions.
- accurately discuss how travel agency service fees can be processed.
- have a basic understanding of ARC reporting and cash flow.

KEY TERMS

agency identification plate
airline identification plate
ARC report
Area Settlement Bank
Credit Memo

Debit Memo
electronic ticket (e-tkt)
fare ladder
Interactive Agent Reporting (IAR)
Prepaid Ticket Advice (PTA)

Refund-Exchange Notice (REN)
Sales Report Settlement Authorization
ticketless air travel
validation

Everything you have learned thus far culminates with the issuance of a ticket. City and airport codes, flight patterns, types of trips, and itinerary planning all come into play at this point. As discussed earlier, the sale of air travel does not earn commission for the travel agency.

The term "ticketing" is broken down into three categories: ticketless, electronic ticket (known as e-tkt), or paper ticket.

TICKETLESS AIR TRAVEL

Only a few U.S. airlines handle their business as ticketless air travel. Depending on the airline being booked, the reservation may be made in the GDS or on the airline's Web site. The travel counselor makes the reservation, entering all the mandatory information. The credit card information is entered and the airline processes the charge. Regardless of whether the booking is made in the agency's GDS or on the airline's Web site, no ticket and no ARC accounting coupons are produced. This type of booking is not processed through ARC; rather, it is a direct sale between the customer, agency, and airline. The travel counselor can print an itinerary (Figure 9–1) for the traveler, which includes the booking number, also called the confirmation or reservation number or record locator.

The travel counselor will then process the travel agency's service fee by using either the Travel Agency Service Fee (TASF) document or a Miscellaneous Charges Order (MCO). Both of these documents are available through ARC in manual and automated versions. This transaction will be a

---

ABC Airlines

TICKETLESS TRAVEL

1-800-435-9792

NON TRANSFERABLE. POSITIVE IDENTIFICATION REQUIRED.

Receipt and itinerary as of 01/28/xx 08:27AM

Confirmation Number: ZIX9K3   ARC no: 00123456   Received: TAMMY/T
Confirmation Date: 01/28/xx
Passenger(s):
   DOUGLAS/DARWIN 526-2701883501-6

Itinerary:	Flt#	Date	Depart	Arrive
Indianapolis/Las Vegas	1651 M	28MAY06	06:35AM	08:35AM
Las Vegas/Indianapolis	309 M	05JUN06	05:50PM	11:30PM

****

Cost:	Total for 1 Passenger(s)	AIR:	223.26
		TAX:	16.74
		OTHER FEES:	20.40
		Total Fare:	$260.40

****

Payment Summary:
   Current payment(s):
      28JAN09 VISA 111122223333xxxx   Ref 526-2701883501-6 $260.40
                                              Total Payments: $260.40

****

Fare Rule(s):
   VALID ONLY ON ABC AIRLINES
   NON REFUNDABLE / STANDBY REQ UPGRADE TO FULL Y FARE
All travel involving funds from this Confirm no. must be completed by 01/28/07
Fare Calculation:
   ADT-1 INDABLAS Q22.00 142.00 LASABIND Q 15.00 135.00 $277.00 END XT ZP INDLAS 6.40 AY 5.00 XFIND4.50LAS4.50
BOARDING PASS DISTRIBUTION AT GATE.

FIGURE 9–1 Sample airline itinerary for ticketless booking.

ITINERARY RECEIPT
PAGE NO. 1

KAREN WILSON
2439 WESTPORT DRIVE
WASHINGTON DC 20007

WILSON/KAREN

* ELECTRONIC TICKET *   POSITIVE IDENTIFICATION REQUIRED AT CHECK-IN
** REQUEST TERMS/CONDITIONS OF TRAVEL AND CARRIER LIABILITY NOTICES FROM TRAVEL AGENCY OR THE TRANSPORTING
CARRIER. **
RESTRICTIONS-NON-REFUNDABLE/PNLTY FOR CHGS. ISSUED BY ABC TRAVEL WASHINGTON DC

28JAN06

A   FR   23FEB   LV INDIANAPOLIS   828A   AMERICAN AIR   156V   OK
                    AR DALLAS–FT WORTH   955A   BAGS ALLOWED-   3PIECE   0STOP   M80
                                                        SEATS *14C* RESERVED WILSON/KAREN

NOT VALID FOR TRAVEL-BEFORE 23FEB/AFTER 23FEB

A   TH   01MAR   LV   DALLAS–FT WORTH   1241P   AMERICAN AIR   872V   OK
                    AR   INDIANAPOLIS   349P   BAGS ALLOWED-   3PIECE   0STOP   M80
                                                        SEATS * 23D * RESERVED WILSON/KAREN

NOT VALID FOR TRAVEL BEFORE 01MAR/AFTER 01MAR

                                               TICKET NUMBER(S):   E0018400222333
                                               AIR FARE   390.69
                                               TAX   51.31
                                               TOTAL AIR FARE   442.00
                                               TOTAL AMOUNT DUE   442.00

THIS AMOUNT HAS BEEN CHARGED TO VI **** **** **** 4444

FIGURE 9–2 Sample itinerary for an electronic ticket.

separate charge on the client's credit card, in addition to the purchase of the ticketless air travel.

ELECTRONIC TICKETING

An electronic ticket (e-tkt) is the same thing as ticketless air travel in the client's eyes because the client does not have a paper ticket. From the travel counselor's perspective, the two are quite different.

All e-tkt transactions are booked in the travel counselor's GDS, just like any other PNR. Seat assignments can and should be made at this time. The travel counselor issues the accounting coupons of the ticket and the passenger receipt coupon, but no flight coupons. The charge to the credit card is processed at the time the accounting coupons are issued. Approximately 85 percent of all agency ticket transactions are electronic.

Because the travel counselor has a PNR in his GDS, an itinerary receipt is easily produced for the client (see Figure 9–2). The client also may be given a confirmation number. At the airport, the client shows her photo ID or passport, and the airline reservationist retrieves the PNR in his computer and issues boarding passes.

All domestic and most international itineraries can be handled as an e-tkt transaction.

Some clients prefer having a paper ticket even when an e-tkt is possible. Many airlines charge from $5.00 to $25.00 for a paper ticket and it's very common for the agency's service fee to be higher as well.

PAPER TICKET

Regardless of who issues the paper ticket, the travel counselor or the airline, it is produced by one of two methods: by computer or written by hand. Please note that most airlines no longer accept handwritten tickets and many travel agencies do not keep manual stock on hand.

Selected ARC Documents

Accountable Documents
Automated Tickets
Manual Tickets
Prepaid Ticket Advice
Miscellaneous Charges Order
Tour Order

Nonaccountable Documents
Refund/Exchange Notice (REN)
Universal Credit Card Charge Form
Agent Automated Deduction
Sales Summary Adjustment Request
Sales Report Settlement Authorization

FIGURE 9–3 Airlines Reporting Corporation (ARC) stock.

Ticket Stock

All tickets and other airline documents are called *ticket stock* and are issued by ARC. All ticket stock is purchased from ARC using an ARC Ticket Requisition form. The cost for ticket stock varies from agency to agency, depending on the number and type of documents ordered.

Ticket stock falls into two categories: accountable documents and nonaccountable documents (see Figure 9–3). As the documents are used, accountable ticket stock must be carefully logged by number, either by hand or in the CRS.

Every accountable document must be tracked by document number and kept at the agency. *Never* throw away an accountable document! If you should make an error and have to start over, write the word "VOID" in large letters on all copies or coupons of the document. A voided document is kept in the travel agency's files for at least two years. If an accountable document should be discovered missing during a routine ARC audit, the travel agency could face heavy fines or ARC could close the agency indefinitely.

Should the travel counselor make a mistake while completing a nonaccountable document and have to start over, the counselor may discard the document. As the term implies, these documents are not logged or audited by ARC. Before throwing a nonaccountable document away, check with the agency manager. It is possible that the agency has a policy of monitoring these documents as well, even though they are not required to do so by ARC.

Validation

The term validation refers to the imprinting of certain data on an ARC accountable document, and in so doing, the document becomes valid for use. When an automated ticket is issued, the computer automatically validates it on

printing. All hand-issued (manual) documents are validated by hand in a machine that looks very similar to a credit card imprinter. This machine is called a ticket validator or ticket imprinter.

When a document is validated, it is imprinted with three very important types of information: the date of issue; the travel agency data consisting of name, agency location, and eight-digit ARC number; and the airline data consisting of name and the three-digit numeric code plus the "check" digit.

The date of issue, whether imprinted by hand or by the computer, is done in a specific way; for example, 01 JUN 06.

The agency ARC number is imprinted as 00 12345 6. Notice the spacing in the ARC number. The first two digits identify the state where the agency is located. The series of five digits identifies the specific agency and the last digit is called a check digit. ARC assigned this number when your agency was appointed and provided the agency with an agency identification plate (see Figure 9–4). The ARC number is also recognized by IATAN and IATA.

On appointment by ARC, each airline supplied the agency with an airline identification plate. Each plate is stamped with the airline information that imprints on validation. The travel counselor decides which airline's plate to use for validation. An airline ticket or other document can be validated on *one* airline's plate only, even if the trip involves several airlines.

What if the passenger's itinerary contains more than one airline? How does the travel counselor decide which airline's identification plate to use? As a general rule, the outbound airline should be used as the validating carrier. However, the counselor may use any airline within the itinerary.

Each airline wants to be the validating carrier for one very important reason: cash flow. All money from an airline ticket, e-tkt, or other document goes to the validating carrier. This airline holds the money until the passenger has traveled. Then, the validating airline sends the applicable amounts, if any, to the other airlines that appeared on the ticket.

Because of the cash flow situation, airlines have been known to tell an agency, "If you validate all your tickets, e-tkts, and other documents on us (even though we may not be the outbound carrier), we will give you free travel for yourself." As you might expect, this practice doesn't precisely follow the rules; however, it is not illegal.

Now, let's look at cash flow from another point of view. What if the outbound airline is on very shaky financial

ABC TRAVEL

WASHINGTON, DC

00   12345   6

FIGURE 9–4 Sample travel agency identification plate.

ground? By validating the ticket on this airline, it holds the passenger's money until the flights have taken place. If, before the flights are taken, this airline files for bankruptcy, what happens to the passenger's money? Can he get a refund?

A refund from a bankrupt airline is unlikely. Usually, all assets are frozen, meaning no refunds are allowed. If this airline chooses to liquidate its assets, the passenger can make a claim in bankruptcy court, and maybe, in a year or two, get a small portion of his money back.

When the outbound carrier is financially unstable, the agency manager may request that counselors validate on one of the other airlines on the itinerary. This protects the passenger's money. On the other hand, it stops the cash flow to an airline that is already unstable, perhaps forcing a bankruptcy. There is no clear-cut answer when you are dealing with an airline that is in financial trouble. Trust the travel agency manager's experience and knowledge.

Basic Ticket Information

A travel counselor who is processing a ticket transaction will generate up to eight coupons, or parts of an actual ticket. These include the airline's Notice of Incorporated Terms, Auditor's Coupon (for ARC), Agency Coupon, up to four flight coupons, and the Passenger Receipt. An e-tkt transaction may result in three or less coupons being issued: Notice of Incorporated Terms, Auditor's Coupon, and the Passenger Receipt. Some agencies may issue the Agency Coupon, but most do not.

All tickets and e-tkts contain the same areas of information and these areas of information are always presented in the same way. You have already learned about the three areas of validation. Here are the other primary areas of information:

• Passenger's full name, for example, Wilson/Jennifer. Remember that the way the name appears on the booking, ticket, or e-tkt must match the traveler's photo ID. You may also see "ADT" to indicate an adult traveler, "CHD" for child, "UM" for an unaccompanied minor child, or "INF" for infant.
• Flight data lines contain the from and to airports, carrier (airline code), flight number, class (F, Y, K, etc.), flight date (15JUN, for example), departure time (725P, for example), and status (OK for a confirmed flight, RQ for wait-listed, SA for space available). At the beginning of each flight data line, you will see an "O," which indicates a stopover city or an "X" to indicate a connection point.
• Fare Basis Code, such as H14EDN.
• Fare ladder line contains a full breakdown of how the fare was constructed and includes fuel surcharges, PFCs,

security fees, special taxes that are being combined, and segment fees.
• Fare, three Tax, and Total boxes
• Form of Payment: CASH, CHECK, or the credit card two-letter code followed by the card number and expiration date. Use AX for American Express, VI for Visa, CA for MasterCard, and DS for Discover.

All tickets and e-tkts can accommodate a total of four flights. If your client's itinerary consists of less than four flights, the remaining flight coupons are marked "VOID." This is true even on e-tkts, even though your client is given no flight coupons at all. When an itinerary contains more than four flights, two or more tickets or e-tkts are processed as a conjunction ticket or e-tkt.

In the case of an itinerary that has a surface segment, such as in an open-jaw trip, the term "ARNK" is entered during the booking process. For example, your client is traveling from Boston to Tucson and is returning from Phoenix to Boston. The first flight data line on the ticket or e-tkt would show the BOS/TUS flight. The second line would be marked "VOID," because there is no flight departing from Tucson. The third line would show the flight from PHX back to BOS.

Now let's look at the above itinerary in a different way. Your client is traveling from Boston to Tucson. She will need a flight from Tucson to Phoenix, but she does not know exactly when. Her flight from Phoenix to Boston is booked and confirmed. In this situation, the second flight data line would show "OPEN." This means that the second leg of the trip will be booked at a later time. When making this type of reservation, an airline and fare must be established for the TUS/PHX leg and the cost of this flight is included in the total price of the trip.

In rare situations, a traveler may need a Prepaid Ticket Advice (PTA). This is more common on international itineraries and with airlines that do not have or allow e-tkts. For example, the traveler is in LaPaz, Bolivia, and must travel to DFW. Reservations are being made by a relative in Dallas and payment is being made there as well. Assuming that an e-tkt is not possible, a PTA will be needed. The steps are as follows:

1. A reservation is made as usual in the GDS.
2. Payment is collected.
3. The PTA is processed in the GDS or can be handwritten. If a handwritten document is being used, the travel counselor must phone the airline, giving them the details of the payment.
4. The traveler is issued a ticket by the airline in LaPaz.

Most airlines charge a service fee for PTA transactions, ranging from $75 to $150. The travel agency may charge a higher service fee for a PTA because of the additional work involved.

REFUNDS AND EXCHANGES

Refunds and exchanges are usually processed in your GDS, but they can be handled on a handwritten document called a Refund-Exchange Notice (REN). Tickets, e-tkts, PTAs, MCOs, and Tour Orders can be refunded or exchanged provided that the fare used allows for refund or exchange. Additionally, a travel counselor may exchange an airline-issued voucher toward travel. A travel agency can never refund or exchange a document that was issued by a different travel agency.

? What Would You Do?

Your client purchased a refundable ticket on Monday and paid for it by check. Three days later, he tells you that he has to cancel his trip and would like his money back.

1. Will you process a REN and write a refund check to your client?
2. Will you process a REN and tell him that in 10 to 14 days you can refund his money?
3. Will you void the ticket transaction and issue a refund check?

Refund transactions can be full or partial, depending on the type of fare originally used. However, there may be an airline fee for a refund transaction as well as one charged by the travel agency.

Exchange transactions can be even exchanges, exchanges with additional collection, or exchanges with refund. Again, there may be airline service fees in addition to those charged by the travel agency.

TRAVEL AGENCY SERVICE FEES

Almost all U.S. travel agencies charge their customers for services rendered, especially when selling air travel. As you know, airlines no longer pay commission to travel agencies for selling their services so this revenue must be obtained elsewhere.

When a client purchases air travel and pays by cash or check, the travel counselor simply adds the agency fee to the amount being collected. When payment is made via credit card, the agency fee can be collected by using a Travel Agency Service Fee (TASF) or an MCO, both processed through ARC. Both of these documents are available in automated and handwritten versions, although most travel agencies now use only the automated versions.

The TASF and MCO documents have areas for the flight information, passenger name, credit card type code, number, expiration date, and fee amount. As these are processed through ARC, they act as a reduction in the amount of money owed to ARC each week.

REPORTING AIR SALES

One of the most important functions of ARC is the centralization of reporting sales and making payments to the airlines. Each week, the travel agency reports sales of tickets, e-tkts, MCOs, PTAs, and Tour Orders, as well as TASFs. There are two ways this weekly reporting can be processed:

1. ARC Interactive Agent Reporting (IAR) in the GDS or on ARC's Web site—no paperwork is sent to ARC.
2. Third-party software, computerized printout, Sales Report Settlement Authorization, and the auditor's ticket or e-tkt coupons are sent to ARC.

ARC does still allow for manual reporting but charges a hefty fee for doing so. In manual reporting the agency must organize all auditor's and agency coupons numerically, run adding machine tapes, and complete a Sales Report Settlement Authorization form. All this paperwork is then mailed to ARC for processing. This is hardly an efficient way of reporting.

Regardless of how the reporting is done, the cash flow is handled in the same manner, through ARC's Area Settlement Bank. The travel agency pays ARC for all cash and check transactions and ARC, in turn, pays the appropriate airlines. ARC collects payment from the credit card companies for charge transactions and distributes these funds to the airlines. ARC collects travel agency service fee transactions from the credit card companies and pays them to the travel agency. If a travel agency has high cash or check sales, it will probably owe ARC. ARC will automatically withdraw the appropriate amount from the agency's bank account via an electronic funds transfer (EFT). If the agency has had few or no cash or check sales, ARC will probably owe the agency. ARC will transfer funds into the agency's bank account via EFT.

To ARC, a reporting week begins at 12:01 A.M. Monday and goes through midnight on Sunday. Sales during this time must be reported no later than Tuesday of the following week, although special consideration is given when a national holiday falls on Monday.

In addition to agency-generated documents, there are two other documents that are included in the weekly ARC report. These are generated by the airlines and are the Credit Memo and Debit Memo. The credit memo is issued when the airline owes the agency money and the debit memo is used when the travel agency owes the airline.

Important Industry Web Sites

Airlines Reporting Corporation: **http://www.arccorp.com**

Alpha: **http://www.sectormicro.com**

GlobalWare: **http://www.globaludyog.com**

Lanyon: **http://www.lanyon.com**

Trams: **http://www.trams.com**

TravCom: **http://www.travcom.com**

Unisys: **http://www.unisys.com/travel**

Each GDS has special sections dealing with ARC reporting. These sections include various training opportunities and the reporting programs themselves. Complete reporting information can also be obtained on ARC's Web site and in the *ARC Industry Agents' Handbook?*

SUMMARY

Much of the information you learned in previous chapters is put into use in this chapter. Airline codes, airport codes, types of trips, fare and tax calculation, and so on are all part of ticketing. All of a travel professional's knowledge and customer service is fine, but if it fails to result in a booking and sale of travel, it has produced no revenue for the travel agency.

Almost all air travel within North America and many international trips are handled as electronic ticket transactions. To the client, this means ticketless. To the travel professional, electronic ticket transactions and ticketless air travel are two very different things. Each requires that booking and agency-produced documentation be handled in different ways.

In today's world, all travel agencies charge service fees for the sale of air travel, given that the airlines no longer pay commission to the agencies. Fortunately, ARC has provided a ways of processing these fees, along with the reporting of sales. Accounting is part of every business and travel is no exception. Almost all air sales are reported to ARC on a weekly basis and to this end, ARC provides efficient automated ways of processing payments.

For additional Travel and Tourism resources, go to http://www.hospitality-tourism.delmar.com.

PLEASE COMPLETE THE CHAPTER REVIEW
QUESTIONS NOW.

Review Questions

1. From the client's perspective, what is the difference between an e-tkt and ticketless air travel? _____
_____

2. From the travel counselor's perspective, what is the difference between an e-tkt and ticketless air travel? _____
_____

3. Identify five examples of accountable ticket stock.

   a. _____   b. _____

   c. _____   d. _____

   e. _____

4. Describe the primary difference between accountable ticket stock and nonaccountable ticket stock in regard to record keeping.
_____

5. Identify and define the three areas of validation on a standard airline ticket.

   a. _____   b. _____

   c. _____

6. Explain why every airline wants to be the "validating carrier." _____
_____

7. On an itinerary consisting of more than one airline, which airline is usually selected as the validating carrier? _____
_____

8. Who set the rules and procedures for issuing domestic airline tickets? _____
_____

9. What status code is used on an airline ticket to indicate a confirmed flight? _____
_____

10. What status code is used on an airline ticket to indicate a wait-listed flight? _____
_____

11. What status code is used on an airline ticket to indicate a space-available or standby flight? _____
_____

12. What word appears on the flight data line when an open segment exists? _____

13. You are making a reservation for your client. You ask her name and she says, "Jenny Anderson." What should you do? _____
_____

14. List as many documents as you can that are or could be included in the ARC report. _____
_____

15. What is the name of ARC's electronic reporting program? _____
_____

16. What two documents can be used to process travel agency service fees? _____
_____

17. How often must the ARC report be submitted? _____

_____

18. What is the deadline for transmitting the ARC report? _____

_____

19. What does the term "authorized amount" mean? _____

_____

20. How are funds owed the travel agency paid? _____

_____

SECTION IV

Selling Other Travel Products and Services

CHAPTER 10
Accommodations

CHAPTER 11
Rental Cars

CHAPTER 12
Traveling by Rail

CHAPTER 13
Consolidators, Charters, Group Sales, and Travel Insurance

CHAPTER 14
Tours of the World

CHAPTER 10

Accommodations

OBJECTIVES

At the conclusion of this chapter, you will be able to

- realize the impact of the Internet on the lodging industry.
- identify types of lodging accommodations and relate to customer needs.
- select reference sources and understand rating systems.
- understand the language of the lodging.

KEY TERMS

adjoining rooms
affiliated property
airport hotel
all-inclusive resorts
all-suite hotels
amenities
bed & breakfast
cancellation policy
chain property
city-commercial hotel
concierge

confirmation number
connecting rooms
convention hotels
franchise properties
frequent guest programs
guarantee
guesthouses
hostels
hotel
Hotel and Travel Index
housing bureau

independent property
motel
pensions
representative company
resorts
self-catering
STAR Service
supply-and-demand
transient
walking the guest

THE LODGING INDUSTRY AT A GLANCE

The lodging industry has seen its share of changes over the past quarter century as it has grown from just over 2 million rooms in 1980 to well over 4 million rooms today. Although there are still many wonderfully individual independently owned properties, a great number of lodging properties are now owned by large companies such as Cendant Corporation, Intercontinental Hotel Group, or Marriott International. For example, Cendant's Hospitality Services group has over 6,400 properties with names such as Amerihost Inn, Days Inn, Ramada, Super 8, and Travelodge. Intercontinental Hotel Group operates such properties as Candlewood, Holiday Inn, and Crown Plaza.

As in other segments of the travel industry, the Internet has brought many changes to the lodging industry. Most lodging facilities have their own online booking sites, and many also utilize large booking sites such as Expedia and Travelocity. Smaller properties, such as bed and breakfast lodging, had a difficult time making their presence known to potential guests prior to widespread usage of the World Wide Web. Now a simple online search will find almost anything a guest desires. The lodging industry has seen a steady increase in online bookings, which surpassed GDS bookings for the first time in 2004. Another change brought about by Internet usage has been the complete array of business services now offered by many properties, both large and small. These services include Internet connections in rooms, wireless Internet, and free on-site computers for guests to use.

For a travel agency, recommending and booking lodging is an important source of income since commissions from hotel sales range from 5 to 10 percent. (See Figure 10–1.) There are, however, those who predict that commissions paid to travel agencies by hotels will shrink over time to 5 percent, in the end becoming a flat fee of $5 to $10. Historically, there has been an uneasy alliance between travel agencies and the lodging industry over the commission issue, many on the travel agency side claiming that too many earned commissions go unpaid by too many hotels. Overall, the lodging industry still views travel agencies as an important component of their ability to fill rooms largely because many travelers still rely on travel counselors for lodging recommendations.

In this chapter, you will learn about the diverse types of accommodations available in the lodging industry, how to determine what type of accommodation will best suit the client, and the mechanics of completing the reservation transaction.

TYPES OF ACCOMMODATIONS

Lodging is a key component of travel that can enhance the quality of the experience or turn the trip into a complete

FIGURE 10–1 For a travel agency, recommending and booking lodging is an important source of income.

disaster. There are as many types of accommodations, at all levels of price and amenity, as there are guests to stay in them. Determining the type of accommodation a customer prefers is the first step toward matching the lodging experience to the guest.

The least expensive type of accommodation, hostels, began in Europe and can now be found worldwide. Hostels are dormlike accommodations with shared bathroom facilities and, possibly, a shared kitchen. Originally established for younger travelers (youth hostels), these accommodations are available to everyone and, in some cases, cater to older travelers (elder hostels).

The bed & breakfast concept, also known as B&B, began in the United Kingdom and has since spread to the United States and many other countries. B&Bs are usually family homes with one or more guest rooms and, generally, with a shared bathroom. Clients looking for a taste of the local culture, charming surroundings, and personal attention appreciate the type of accommodation B&Bs offer. B&Bs are found in rural areas, small towns, and sometimes in major cities. As you might expect, B&Bs offer a unique environment, but they do not offer the variety of activities and guest services found in other types of accommodations.

A motel, also known as a motor inn or motor lodge, is typically a one- or two-story property that caters primarily to motorists. Cars are parked around the perimeter of the property and room access is from the outside. Motels with more than two stories may have elevators. However, motels with only one or two stories may not. Most motels do not have a restaurant on site but may offer a light breakfast in the lobby area.

Generally, motels have very limited guest services but an outdoor swimming pool is not uncommon. Motels are usually located in smaller towns and along major highways in and around large cities. Because of the location and limited guest services, motels tend to be less expensive than other types of accommodations.

Internationally, there are very few motels. Outside the United States, motel accommodations are usually called pensions (pronounced "pen-see-*owns*") or guesthouses. Pensions are generally small, family-run properties that offer a minimum of guest services. Most pensions offer meal plans where guests can have one, two, or three meals per day included in the room rate. It is important to note that pensions may have shared bathroom facilities, unlike motels in the United States that always offer private facilities.

Travelers who stay in a property for only one night are referred to as transient guests. Because of the short length of stay, these travelers may prefer motels, pensions, or guesthouses, which are commonly called transient lodgings. These types of accommodations do not lend themselves to longer stays because of the limited facilities, activities, and services.

Self-catering accommodations can be found worldwide and are popular with travelers staying in one location for a week or more. This type of accommodation can be anything from a one-room apartment to a suite of rooms in a castle to an entire house. Generally, self-catering accommodations are rented by the week and include everything that is necessary with the exception of food.

Most people define the word hotel as a property in which guest rooms are accessed via interior corridors. Hotels come in all shapes and sizes and guest services and activities vary widely from one hotel to another.

Sometimes a hotel is classified by its location and by the clientele to which it caters. An airport hotel, for example, is located near the airport and caters to travelers with early morning departures or late night arrivals. Airport hotels may also be chosen by meeting planners because of the hotel's convenient location, both for in-town attendees as well as for attendees arriving by air.

A city-commercial hotel is located in the downtown or business district of a city and caters primarily to business travelers. These hotels usually offer meeting rooms, business centers, and in-room computer connections. City-commercial hotels have one or more restaurants and may also offer a variety of activities. Hotels located in the downtown area of a city also attract leisure travelers interested in city activities such as museums, theatre, and shopping.

Convention hotels are located near convention or exposition sites or they have these facilities within the property. Generally, convention hotels offer the same guest services and activities as city-commercial hotels. Properties that have on-site convention facilities are often centrally located within a city, providing easy access to convention attendees. This central location also affords convention attendees the opportunity to enjoy a variety of the city's dining and entertainment options.

All-suite hotels can be found in all major cities in the United States as well as in many other countries. Instead

Praia do Carvoeira Beach, Portugal.

of just a bedroom and bathroom, all-suite properties offer separate sleeping, bath, and living areas as well as a kitchenette. It is common for all-suite hotels to offer a variety of guest services and activities and, in many cases, a full breakfast is included in the room rate.

Resorts are designed to be destinations unto themselves and can be found in cities, near beaches, in the mountains, near golf centers, and in almost all popular tourist destinations. A variety of dining options, recreational activities, and guest services are available at resort hotels. Sometimes a resort hotel has a specific focus; for example, golf, gambling, skiing, water sports, or spa facilities.

An all-inclusive resort includes all food, drinks, and activities in the room rate. Some resorts in the United States, the Caribbean, and other popular destinations are all-inclusive. This type of accommodation is popular because all of the major expenses are known up front, making budget planning easier. In locations where dining is very expensive, an all-inclusive resort may be less expensive than paying for the features separately. This fact can be easily overlooked when simply comparing rates and not taking into consideration all that is included.

PLEASE TURN TO PAGE 157 AND COMPLETE EXERCISE 10-1 NOW.

PROPERTY ORGANIZATION, OWNERSHIP, AND MANAGEMENT

Regardless of the type of accommodation property, each is classified based on the ownership and management of the property. In years past, these classifications were clear-cut, but today, some hotel groups fall into more than one classification.

Property Organization Summary

	Hostels and Small Independent	Large Independent	Affiliated	Franchise	Chain
Available in printed reference sources	probably not	yes	yes	yes	yes
Available in GDSs	probably not	probably	yes	yes	yes
Available on the Internet	probably	probably	probably	probably	probably
Toll-free reservation number	probably not	yes	yes	yes	yes
Agency commission	probably not	probably	probably	yes	yes

An independent property is privately owned and operated. Other than abiding by state and federal regulations, the independent property owner decides everything from the level of service to the manner in which the accounting is done. You may think that only the smallest motels and inns are independent, but some of the world's largest and most prestigious hotels and resorts are operated independently.

An affiliated property is an independent accommodation property that has elected to make use of a representative company, or *rep company*. For a set annual fee, the rep company provides marketing and sales assistance; a central reservations center; and inclusion in GDSs, printed reference sources, and the Internet. When an independent property becomes affiliated with a rep company, it becomes much more accessible for travel counselor bookings and the commission is usually paid through the rep company. Examples of rep companies include Utell, Leading Hotels of the World, and Preferred Hotels. It is interesting to note that although Best Western is a rep group, it is a not-for-profit organization, unlike all of the other rep companies.

Franchise properties are independently owned and operated but are guided and served by the franchise group. By paying the franchise fee, the property owner can use the franchise name, advertising and sales force, reservation center, and central commission processing program. The franchise fee is much higher than that of a rep company but provides much more guidance and assistance. All properties in a franchise group are expected to maintain a certain level of service and quality to remain in the group. Two major franchise groups are Choice Hotels International (Sleep Inn, Comfort Inn, Quality Inn, Clarion, Rodeway, EconoLodge, and Main Stay Suites) and Hospitality Franchise Systems (Days Inn, Howard Johnsons, Park Inn International, Ramada, and Super 8).

In years past, a chain property was owned by the chain and managed locally. Today, this is still true at some properties but there are also chain properties that are privately owned and managed. When a property belongs to a chain, name recognition and consistency of quality are important features.

Because names like Holiday Inn, Hilton, Marriott, and Hyatt are known by almost everyone, it is logical for a traveler to select a property based on a name he knows over one he does not know. It is also logical for a traveler to expect the same level of service and quality at a Hilton in Chicago as he would at a Hilton in Milwaukee. Typically, all properties are the same with regard to organization, management, booking procedures, and commission payment. Basic levels of guest services should be consistent at all properties within a chain.

PLEASE TURN TO PAGE 158 AND COMPLETE EXERCISE 10–2 NOW.

ACCOMMODATION RATING SYSTEMS

Rating systems vary by reference source. Terms or symbols such as stars, diamonds, or crowns, are used to indicate the rating. For example, *The Mobile Guide,* available in bookstores, uses stars, and the *AAA Guidebooks,* available to AAA members, use diamonds to rate accommodations. Generally, the more symbols used, the more deluxe the property and the more expensive the room rate. It is generally accepted that accommodations are rated as one of ten categories from Superior Deluxe to Moderate Tourist Class, in descending order (see Accommodation Rating Terms, as used in the *Hotel and Travel Index*).

The country in which the property is located can change the meaning of the rating terms. All ratings are based on the perception of the citizens of the country. That indicates that the standard of living in a particular country could influence the perception. For example, a property in a developing nation might be listed as "first class," based on that country's citizen's perception. But, a citizen of the United States or Canada might consider that same property as "tourist class." Travel counselors should be mindful of this when researching hotels in foreign destinations, away from the so-called tourist areas.

Accommodation Rating Terms used in *Hotel and Travel Index*

Superior Deluxe—elegant, luxurious, and expensive; highest standards of service

Deluxe—outstanding property offering many of the same features as Superior Deluxe

Moderate Deluxe—fine accommodations and public rooms but slightly less grand than Deluxe

Superior First Class—above average property with some outstanding features

First Class—dependable and comfortable property with good standards of service

Limited First Class—a first-class property with regard to accommodation quality, but limited public areas, food service, and facilities

Moderate First Class—basically a first-class property but with slightly fewer services and more standard rooms

Superior Tourist Class—budget property, well maintained, possibly a few additional services

Tourist Class—budget property, basically just a place to sleep

Moderate Tourist Class—low-budget property, often old and not well kept

HOTEL CASE STUDY

Your clients, Stephan and Katarina Smolensky, are having trouble deciding where they want to stay in Scottsdale, near Phoenix. They play tennis and golf and would appreciate having spa facilities available. They are considering the Hyatt Regency Scottsdale Resort, the Phoenician, and the Radisson Resort & Spa Scottsdale. From information obtained on the Internet, prepare a fact sheet for each property detailing the accommodations, facilities, services, and rates. Based on the information you have obtained, which property do you think best meets your clients' needs?

ACCOMMODATION RATES

Many factors come into play when pricing hotel rooms. The supply-and-demand principle has much to do with pricing. In a city that has thousands of rooms but few travelers, the average room rate is lower. On the other hand, in a city that has few rooms but many travelers, the average room rate is higher.

The *location of a hotel* in a city has a bearing on the price of the rooms. For example, a hotel in the suburbs is usually less expensive than an airport or downtown location. The *location of the room* within the hotel also affects the price. Rooms near the pool and rooms with a view (e.g., ocean, pool, scenic) command a higher price than rooms in the back of the hotel.

The *size of the room and the furnishings* are factors in establishing room rates. Larger rooms and those with more elaborate decor and furnishings are more expensive than the basic four walls with a bed and bath. The *number and type of beds* in a room can affect the rate; for example, a room with a king-sized bed may be more expensive than a room with a double bed. As you might expect, rooms with a kitchenette, mini-bar, VCR, or a jacuzzi tub are priced higher than standard rooms.

Room rates are affected by the *time of year* and *length of stay*. In resort areas of the United States, as well as

international destinations, rates are determined by season. High season is not the same time of year worldwide. For example, high season in the Caribbean is the winter months, while Bermuda's high season is the summer months. A stay of a week or longer may result in a lower per-night rate than the rate for a one-night stay.

In some destinations, the *day of the week* has a bearing on the room rate. Some properties offer one rate for weekend stays and another rate for weekdays. For example, a property in Las Vegas may charge a higher rate for weekend stays, while a property in Chicago may charge a higher rate for weekday stays.

If the guest is traveling on business, a *corporate rate* may be available. Guests who are part of a convention are generally offered a preferred *convention rate*, as are *members of certain organizations*, such as AAA or AARP. Guests who are part of a *group* (usually 10 or more rooms) staying at the same hotel may be given a group rate that is lower than the normal rate. *Children* staying in the same room with parents are usually free. Numerous hotels around the world offer from 10 to 50 percent discount to guests who are employed in the *travel industry*.

Travel agencies that are members of a consortium may have access to special *negotiated hotel rates*. Negotiated rates are lower than the regular rates and are fully commissionable to the travel agency.

All rates for accommodations are priced per room, not per person. A hotel may offer one rate for single occupancy, another rate for double occupancy, and an extra-person charge for third or fourth guests. All printed reference sources and the CRS indicate occupancy and many other terms with codes.

LODGING LANGUAGE

As you have learned, accommodations vary widely; some are very basic and others are ultra-deluxe. An important factor to consider when assisting the client with

Room Rate and Other Charge Codes

1P, 2P—one person, two people

APT—apartment; separate sleeping, bath, living, and kitchen or dining rooms

Comp—complimentary; a room provided free of charge

DWB—double with bath; room with private bath, priced for occupancy by two people

EFF or Efficiency—a room that includes sleeping, living, and kitchen or dining areas, usually with private bath

EP or EAP—extra person or each additional person; supplementary charge for occupancy over the stated number

Net rate—a rate that does not include agency commission. Rates for groups and conventions are often quoted as net. Before the travel counselor quotes a rate to the client in these circumstances, agency profit is added.

PP—per person; meal plans are always per person as are some other charges

Rack rate—standard published rate for a room

ROH—run of house; an inexpensive rate without a specified grade of room. The guest may be given any room grade from minimum to deluxe, depending on what is available at the time of check-in.

SC—service charge; extra charge that may be listed as a percentage or as a flat amount per person

STE—suite; separate sleeping, bath, living, and kitchen or dining rooms

SWB—single with bath; room with private bath, priced for occupancy by one person

TD—trade discount; discount offered for travel industry employees

TPL—triple; room with private bath, priced for occupancy by three people

TWB—twin with bath; room with private bath, priced for occupancy by two people. On rare occasions, TWB can mean "triple with bath."

VAT—value added tax; tax charged in some foreign countries, similar to a sales tax

WKLY—weekly; rate for a seven-night stay

FIGURE 10–2 Amenities, such as in-room Internet connection, are important to guests.

Many hotels and resorts offer the special services of a concierge. A concierge can be an area in the main lobby where a hotel employee, also called a concierge, assists guests. Or, the concierge can be available to guests staying on a particular floor or floors. The concierge is very knowledgeable about the city and surrounding areas. Typical concierge duties include reconfirming flights, arranging a rental car, making dinner reservations, obtaining theatre tickets, giving directions, and making sightseeing and shopping suggestions.

Most chains and franchise groups have frequent guest programs. These programs encourage brand loyalty and provide a variety of benefits to the member. Each time a member stays in a participating hotel, points are accumulated. The points can be redeemed for free hotel stays or merchandise. Many airline frequent flyer programs are tied in with certain hotel chains. By giving the hotel the client's airline frequent flyer membership number, "miles" are added to the client's account for each night of the client's hotel stay.

Properties where room access is via a common corridor as well as motel-type properties may have rooms with a communicating door between them. These rooms are called connecting rooms. Rooms that are simply side-by-side and do not have room-to-room access are called adjoining rooms. It is common for a group or large family to request these types of rooms. It is important to note that clients often confuse adjoining and connecting.

Regardless of how accommodations are reserved, a confirmation number is given. This number is very important and should be on the client's itinerary or given verbally to him. It is this number that confirms the room type, length of stay, room rate, and other features of the booking.

accommodation selection is the amenities offered by the property (Figure 10–2). Amenities can be extra features within the room, such as TV, movies, hair dryer, and minibar. A swimming pool, restaurant, bar, casino, spa, private beach, golf course, health club, airport shuttle, and shopping venues are examples of property amenities.

Some hotels will hold a reservation until 4:00 P.M. or 6:00 P.M. on the day of arrival. Other properties require a guarantee, usually in the amount of one night's rate. The travel counselor can guarantee a reservation by using the client's credit card, sending an agency check for the deposit, or sending full prepayment. It is common for hotel stays during special events, high season, or at resort properties to require a guarantee of three or more nights' rate. When a reservation has been guaranteed, the room will be held all night.

When a hotel reservation has been guaranteed, it is especially important to understand the property's cancellation policy. Many hotels require cancellation before 6:00 P.M. the day of arrival, while others may have a cancellation policy of two or more days before arrival. If the cancellation policy is not followed or the guest is a no-show, the hotel charges the guest's credit card or the deposit is forfeited.

It is common practice for hotels, especially during busy times, to overbook, just like the airlines. Sometimes, a hotel becomes overbooked because guests do not depart as planned. So, what happens when a traveler arrives at his hotel but there are no rooms available, even though he has a reservation? Most hotels arrange accommodations at another hotel of equal or greater quality and absorb any price differential. This policy is called walking the guest and it includes transportation to the new hotel.

When a convention is in town, the city's visitor's bureau may act as a housing bureau. Convention organizers, working through the housing bureau, block rooms at one or more hotels within the city. To take advantage of the lower priced convention rates, the convention attendee must make hotel reservations with the housing bureau.

The housing bureau acts as a clearinghouse for hotel space during the convention, distributing the reservations among the contracted hotels.

Some hotels, especially resorts and properties in the Caribbean, offer a variety of meal plans. The most important fact to remember about meal plans is that when *meal plans are offered as an additional item, they are priced per person.*

How does the travel counselor know whether meals are included in the room rates or if the meal plans are offered as an additional feature? Reference sources usually indicate included meal plans as follows: MAP SWB $$$.$$ DWB $$$.$$. In this example, the property includes a full breakfast and dinner (MAP) daily in the room rate. The single room rate (SWB) includes the room and meals for one person. The double room rate (DWB) includes the room and meals for two people.

Meal plans that are offered as an additional feature are shown as follows:

EP SWB $$$.$$ DWB $$$.$$
PP CP +$$.$$ BP +$$.$$ MAP +$$.$$ AP +$$.$$

In this example, the room rates do not include meals (EP). The meal plans are per person (PP) and the plans offered include Continental Plan (CP), Bermuda Plan (BP), Modified American Plan (MAP), and American Plan (AP).

The meals included in these plans can be one of two types, *table d'hôte* or *à la carte*. Table d'hôte is a set menu without choices, and substitutions are probably not allowed. An à la carte meal is one in which the guest may select anything from the menu.

USING REFERENCE TOOLS

There are two references used by travel counselors for worldwide lodging information. Both are owned and published by Northstar Travel Media, but each provides a different approach to the information it carries.

- *Hotel and Travel Index* and http://www.hotelandtravelindex.com
- *STAR Service* available only online at http://www.starserviceonline.com

The Hotel and Travel Index (HTI) printed version is published quarterly and is usually free to qualified travel agencies. Over 45,000 properties have a basic two- or three-line listing in the printed version. Many properties purchase additional advertising in the printed volume. The advertisement, of course, contains much more detailed information, including photographs of the property. There are also "Travel Tools" such as airport diagrams, city maps, and locator maps.

Its online companion, http://www.hotelandtravelindex.com, is also available free of charge. After combining

Meal Plans

EP	European Plan	No meals.
CP	Continental Plan	Light breakfast. In the United States, a light breakfast is usually a selection of breads or muffins, juice, and coffee.
		Internationally, a light breakfast can include a selection of meats, cheeses, cereals, fruits, breads, and boiled eggs.
BP	Bermuda Plan	Full breakfast.
MAP	Modified American Plan	Full breakfast and dinner. In Europe, this plan is sometimes called half-board or demi-pension.
AP	American Plan	Three full meals daily. In Europe, this plan is sometimes called full-board or full-pension.

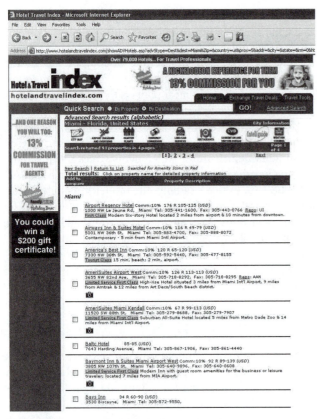

FIGURE 10–3 The *Hotel and Travel Index* has basic two- or three-line listings or more detailed listings with pictures. Reproduced with permission from http://www.hotelandtravelindex.com.

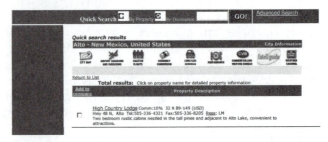

FIGURE 10–4 Intelliguide from *HTI* provides a mini report on destinations around the world. Reprinted with permission from http://www.starserviceonline.com.

forces with the *Official Hotel Guide,* the *Hotel and Travel Index* Web site now has information on over 70,000 properties, and offers great flexibility to the user. Figure 10–3 shows an example of a basic listing plus two listings that have purchased different amounts of advertising space.

Through a partnership with http://www.hotels.com, *HTI* online offers booking in nearly 4,000 hotels worldwide. By booking this way, travel agencies receive guaranteed lowest rates and access to last-room availability at these properties. In addition, IATA agents will receive 5 percent commission on bookings made with http://www.hotels.com.

HTI also includes a helpful feature called *Intelliguide,* which provides a minireport on destinations around the world including history, tourist sites, geostats, transportation, currency, and a calendar of events. *Intelliguide* minireports are only a fraction of what's available by subscription (printed or online) through Weissman World. The complete resource provides comprehensive destination information on every country in the world and 10,000 cities. See Figure 10–4 for a portion of a typical listing from *Intelliguide.*

STAR Service is a completely different type of lodging resource. Available only online (http://www.starserviceon-

line.com), it covers more than 10,000 hotels in 100 countries and accepts no advertising. STAR Service travel correspondents personally visit each hotel and provide their candid opinion of the property. They tell you what it's actually like to be a guest—right down to the decor in the lobby and how big the closets are. *STAR Service* also includes commission information for travel agents, rates, and contact information. This type of information can be extremely valuable, but keep in mind that the reports are subjective and contain considerable editorial comment. Figure 10–5 provides a look at *STAR Service* commentary.

"Female-friendly" hotels are proving to be a great marketing technique for some deluxe hotels. An example is Miami's Sanctuary Hotel which offers single women an ongoing 25 percent discount and special amenities like beach jogging, yoga companions, a chic in-house salon and spa, and personal shoppers. Bathrooms are miniretreats equipped with steam showers and jacuzzi tubs.

🌐 Helpful Industry Web Sites

Accommodation Resources on the Web

Accommodation Search Engine: **http://www.ase.net.** Search by price, type, facilities, and activities.

All Hotels: **http://www.all-hotels.com/index.asp**. Directories of hotels and B&Bs—search by country, city, or area within a city.

B&Bs: **http://www.bedandbreakfast.com**

B&Bs and Inns of Canada: **http://www.cantravel.ab.ca**

Hostelling Internet Guide: **http://www.hostels.com/hostel.menu.html**

Hotel Chains/Franchises/Rep. Companies: **http://www.hotelstravel.com/chains.html**

STAR Service: **http://www.starserviceonline.com**

FIGURE 10–5 *STAR* Service accepts no advertising and provides a subjective report on each hotel. Reprinted with permission from http://www.starserviceonline.com.

SELECTING THE RIGHT ACCOMMODATION

As we stated before, lodging can make or break a trip. Hotels are well aware of the importance of offering amenities that are important to guests. According to one study, amenities that rate high with hotel guests are complimentary breakfast, in-room refrigerators and coffee makers, pillow top mattresses, and high-speed, wireless Internet access. Another study found that location is the single most important factor that travelers use to decide where to stay. Some hotels have determined that being "child-friendly" is important to their business. Matching your client to the many variations in accommodations is a challenge, but a very important part of the process. You will have to gather some information about your client and his preferences:

- the purpose of the trip (business, vacation, family emergency, etc.)
- price range (moderate, deluxe, budget)
- specific needs (handicapped accessible, nonsmoking)
- specific preferences (pool, exercise facilities, meeting rooms, restaurant, etc.)
- type of property (bed and breakfast, resort, downtown hotel)

Armed with answers to these questions, it's time to consult one of the references we have discussed. Offer the client a small selection (three or four) from which to choose.

> More people than ever before are traveling with their pets. In one survey, 67 percent of respondents reported traveling with their pet. Of these, 43 percent said they stayed in a hotel or motel while on the road. Some hotels have begun capitalizing on this trend by offering amenities for pets such as special pet beds with a doggie biscuit on the pillow and gourmet dinners to order. Many Web sites such as http://www.petswelcome.com and http://www.takeyourpet.com list hundreds of pet-friendly lodging sites.

Many new travel counselors believe that they are expected to select a specific hotel for the client. This is not true and, in fact, it is not a good idea in most cases. Selecting a property for the client places a heavy responsibility on the counselor's shoulders. It also opens the door for the client to return and say, "Why did you book me in that hotel? It was terrible!" It is far better to show the client three or four properties that meets the client's needs as well as to help the client to form a final decision. Of course, if the counselor has personal experience with a property or has clients who recently stayed there, the counselor can certainly pass this information on to the client.

PLEASE TURN TO PAGE 158 AND COMPLETE EXERCISE 10–3 NOW.

MAKING RESERVATIONS

After selecting the preferred accommodation, it's up to the travel counselor to secure the reservation. This is done in any number of ways, depending on the circumstances. Travel counselors often prefer to make reservations in the GDS, although this isn't always possible because many properties are not included in any GDS.

A lodging reservation can be completed by contacting the hotel directly by phone, fax, or e-mail. There are times that it's just plain simpler to make a phone call to make a reservation, and there are times when having the request in writing (fax or e-mail) is important so that the details of the reservation are made clear to everyone.

Many hotels have booking capabilities on their Web sites (e.g., http://www.choicehotels.com). Some have "agent-only" sections that guarantee lowest rates and commissions to encourage travel counselors to use Web sites, such as http://www.hotels.com. A grouping of several hundred hotels on one site may also be an efficient method of making reservations, such as http://www.hotels.com.

There may also be circumstances in which it's most efficient to make the reservation through a third party such as a housing bureau or convention and visitors bureau, or a consolidator, especially for unusual properties or remote destinations, or in situations in which local rooms have been blocked for a convention.

Whichever way you choose, there is some basic information that's necessary before you begin:

- property name, location, and contact information
- client name
- number of guests
- number and age of children
- senior citizens
- arrival date and time and check-out date
- grade of room (e.g., standard, deluxe, ocean view)
- number and type of beds
- special requests (e.g., crib, wheelchair accessible)
- discount numbers (membership in AARP or AAA, corporate, hotel frequent guest, airline frequent flyer)

It is also important, as part of the reservation process, to check with the property on their specific guarantee and cancellation policies. To avoid potential problems, make certain the client understands all the details on guarantees and cancellations.

> **PLEASE TURN TO PAGE 159 AND COMPLETE EXERCISE 10-4 NOW.**

HOTEL SAFETY

The American Hotel and Lodging Association (AH&LA) (http://www.ahla.com) actively promotes hotel safety and asks its members to not only make sure guests stay safe, but also to educate guests on what they can do to assure their own safety. The following 10-point list is provided by AH&LA:

1. Don't answer the door in a hotel or motel room without verifying who it is. If a person claims to be an employee, call the front desk and ask if someone from their staff is supposed to have access to your room and for what purpose.

2. Keep your room key with you at all times and don't needlessly display it in public. Should you misplace it, please notify the front desk immediately.

3. Close the door securely whenever you are in your room and use all of the locking devices provided.

4. Check to see that any sliding glass doors or windows and any connecting room doors are locked.

5. Don't invite strangers to your room.

6. Do not draw attention to yourself by displaying large amounts of cash or expensive jewelry.

7. Place all valuables in the hotel or motel's safe deposit box.

8. When returning to your hotel or motel late in the evening, be aware of your surroundings, stay in well-lighted areas, and use the main entrance.

9. Take a few moments and locate the nearest exit that may be used in the event of an emergency.

10. If you see any suspicious activity, notify the hotel operator or a staff member.

SUMMARY

The lodging industry has seen many changes and has more than doubled in size over the past 25 years. Most lodging facilities have their own Web sites, and many also utilize large booking sites such as Expedia. It is very important to determine the customer's needs and preferences for such things as the type of accommodation and its location, amenities, and price before recommending accommodations. There are references in which to find information about accommodations. These include the *Hotel and Travel Index* and *STAR* Service, as well as many Web sites. Lodging should be viewed as a key component of travel that can enhance the quality of the travel experience or turn the trip into a disaster.

 For additional Travel and Tourism resources, go to http://www.hospitality-tourism.delmar.com.

> **PLEASE COMPLETE THE CHAPTER REVIEW QUESTIONS NOW.**

EXERCISE 10-1 Types of Accommodations

In your own words, briefly describe the following accommodation types.

Airport hotel _____

_____

All-inclusive resort _____

_____

All-suite hotel _____

_____

Bed & breakfast _____

_____

City-commercial hotel _____

_____

Convention hotel _____

_____

Guesthouse _____

_____

Hostel _____

_____

Motel _____

_____

Pension _____

_____

Resort hotel _____

_____

Self-catering _____

_____

Transient _____

_____

EXERCISE 10-2 Property Organization and Accommodation Rating Systems

1. Arrange these rating terms by ranking the most deluxe first (1–10). Briefly describe each rating.

Rank ( ) Deluxe _____

Rank ( ) First Class _____

Rank ( ) Limited First Class _____

Rank ( ) Moderate Deluxe _____

Rank ( ) Moderate First Class _____

Rank ( ) Moderate Tourist Class _____

Rank ( ) Superior Deluxe _____

Rank ( ) Superior First Class _____

Rank ( ) Superior Tourist Class _____

Rank ( ) Tourist Class _____

2. Identify the features of each accommodation classification.

Affiliated _____
_____

Chain _____
_____

Franchise _____
_____

Independent _____
_____

EXERCISE 10-3 Selecting Accommodations

Use the Web site http://www.hotelandtravelindex.com to answer the following questions.

1. Your client is traveling to Memphis, Tennessee and has requested an inexpensive hotel near the airport. Select two hotel choices for your client and answer the following questions for each:

Hotel (A) _____   Hotel (B) _____

- Does this hotel pay commission to travel agents?
  ◦ Hotel (A) _____
  ◦ Hotel (B) _____
- If so, how much?
  ◦ Hotel (A) _____
  ◦ Hotel (B) _____
- Does this hotel have Internet access?
  ◦ Hotel (A) _____
  ◦ Hotel (B) _____

- What is the standard rate for a room?
  - ○ Hotel (A) _____
  - ○ Hotel (B) _____
- What discounts are available?
  - ○ Hotel (A) _____
  - ○ Hotel (B) _____
- What exercise facilities are available?
  - ○ Hotel (A) _____
  - ○ Hotel (B) _____
- What is the cancellation policy?
  - ○ Hotel (A) _____
  - ○ Hotel (B) _____
- How would a travel counselor make a reservation for this hotel?
  - ○ Hotel (A) _____
  - ○ Hotel (B) _____

2. A family is traveling by car from Cincinnati to Orlando (Disney World). They need accommodations near Atlanta for one night. What type of accommodation do you think would best suit their needs and why do you think so?

_____

_____

_____

3. Four friends want to go to the Phoenix/Scottsdale area and play golf for a week. What type of accommodation would best suit their needs and why do you think so?

_____

_____

_____

4. A couple is traveling to New York City for three days. They are interested in the theatre, museums, and shopping. What type of accommodation do you think would best suit their needs and why do you think so?

_____

_____

EXERCISE 10-4   Making Reservations

1. Why is qualifying a client before attempting to offer lodging products important? _____

_____

2. What information do you think would be helpful to assist the client's selection of appropriate accommodations? _____

_____

3. What do you think is the best method a travel counselor can use to make lodging reservations and why? _____

_____

4. Why is it better for a travel counselor to show the client several lodging choices instead of recommending just one?

_____

_____

5. When making reservations at properties such as Hilton, Hyatt, and Marriott, why must the travel counselor know and identify the exact location being booked? _____

_____

6. Why do you think giving the hotel confirmation number to the client, preferably in writing, is important? _____

_____

7. Many hotels do not require a guarantee to hold a reservation. Do you think it is a good idea to make it a habit of guaranteeing all reservations? If yes, why? _____

_____

_____

Review Questions

1. Identify the factors that can affect the cost of a hotel room. _____

   _____

2. What client information do you think would be helpful in assisting the client to select appropriate accommodations?

   _____

3. What safety advice would you give to a hotel guest? _____

   _____

4. Identify the term or code that fits each description.

   a. hotel room priced for occupancy by two people _____

   b. hotel rate that does not have commission built in _____

   c. meal plan that includes breakfast and dinner _____

   d. regular published rate for a hotel room _____

   e. size group of rental car also known as midsize _____

   f. tax in some countries, similar to a sales tax _____

   g. identification given to a hotel booking _____

   h. accommodating a guest at another hotel when the reserved hotel is sold out _____

   i. meal plan that includes a light breakfast _____

   j. dorm-like accommodation with shared bathroom facilities _____

   k. motel-like accommodation outside the United States _____

   l. accommodation rate priced for occupancy by one person _____

   m. swimming pool, restaurant, in-room hair dryer, etc. _____

   n. hotel rooms that are side-by-side and have a door between them _____

   o. special hotel rate for clients traveling on business _____

   p. hotel employee who provides extra guest services _____

   q. meal plan that includes three meals daily _____

5. Under what circumstances might a self-catering accommodation be the best choice? _____

   _____

6. List the two primary references for the hotel industry. Discuss the kinds of information each provides. _____

   _____

   _____

7. Visit the following Web sites: http://www.hotels.com and http://www.expedia.com. Would you find either of these Web sites useful as a travel counselor? Why or why not?

   _____

   _____

   _____

8. It is generally accepted that accommodations are rated as one of ten categories. List each category and provide a brief description of each.

_____

_____

_____

_____

_____

_____

9. Why do you think it is important to rate accommodations?

_____

_____

CHAPTER 11

Rental Cars

OBJECTIVES

At the conclusion of this chapter, you will be able to

- realize the impact of the Internet on booking rental cars.
- understand the language of the rental car industries.
- identify types of rental cars and relate to customer needs.
- outline differences for international car rentals.

KEY TERMS

collision damage waiver (CDW)	intermediate	special equipment
compact	loss damage waiver (LDW)	standard
daily rate	personal accident insurance (PAI)	weekend rate
drop charge	proof of financial responsibility	weekly rate
economy	refuel charge	

THE CAR RENTAL INDUSTRY AT A GLANCE

Traveling by air, rail, or motorcoach means that when you arrive at your destination you are dependent upon public transportation. In some locations, like New York City or London, public transportation is so easily arranged and driving a private vehicle is so stressful, that many people wouldn't even consider renting a car during their stay. However, public transportation is not so readily available in other locations; in fact it would be downright impossible to access some spots without a car. On an average day, the car rental industry has nearly 2 million cars on the road. Let's face it, some travelers simply prefer the freedom and flexibility of having their own vehicle.

Generally, rental car companies are indistinguishable in terms of their product. The industry is, however, extremely competitive, so it pays to compare rates and promotions offered by each company. Some renters shop only for the least expensive rate, while others, especially business travelers, prefer the personalized service, and often higher prices, from companies like Hertz and Avis. Check for money-saving programs like Alamo's Pre-Pay & Save option which saves the customer 10 percent if he pays prior to arriving at the counter.

RENTAL CAR CLASS AND SIZE GROUPS

All rental cars are categorized by size or style. There are four size categories and several style groups. The smallest of the size categories is economy, also called subcompact (see Figure 11–1). In the United States, cars in this category are usually equipped with an automatic transmission and air conditioning. Internationally, an economy-class car has a manual transmission and no air conditioning. Economy cars can accommodate four people and have room for two or three pieces of luggage.

FIGURE 11–1 Economy cars can accommodate four people and have room for two or three pieces of luggage.

Compact size is the next larger class (see Figure 11–2). Again, a compact car in the United States usually has an automatic transmission and air conditioning, but internationally, a manual transmission and no air conditioning is

FIGURE 11–2 A compact car has room for four or five people and three suitcases.

usual. Compact cars have room for three suitcases and can accommodate four or five people.

Intermediate size, also called midsize, is the next larger class (see Figure 11–3). In the United States, intermediate-size cars always have automatic transmissions and air conditioning and these features may be available internationally as well. Intermediate cars can seat five passengers and carry four pieces of luggage.

FIGURE 11–3 An intermediate or midsize car can seat five passengers and carry four pieces of luggage.

Cars in the largest size group are called standard, although many people refer to them as full-size (see Figure 11–4). Generally, this class is equipped with automatic transmission and air conditioning, both domestically and internationally. Standard cars are usually offered with no choice between two- or four-door models. Most rental car companies use the term full-size to indicate a standard four-door model. Standard cars can accommodate five people and carry four or five suitcases.

FIGURE 11–4 Cars in the largest size group are called standard or full-size, and are usually 4-door models.

Vehicles that are categorized by style rather than size include *minivans, premium, luxury,* and *special.* Within these four categories can be found everything from a heavy truck to a sports car to an all-terrain vehicle.

Minivans can usually carry seven people and have room for eight pieces of luggage.

The premium category includes cars that can carry five or six people and six suitcases.

In the United States, the luxury category can include Cadillac and Lincoln Continental, while, at international locations, this category can include Mercedes and BMW. As you might imagine, the U.S. vehicles in this category can accommodate more people and suitcases than their international counterparts.

Most other types of vehicles fall into the special category. These vehicles include convertibles, sports cars, four-wheel drive vehicles, limos, pick-up trucks, all-terrain vehicles, and heavy trucks. In some locations, the special category includes exotic cars such as Jaguar, Lamborghini, Rolls Royce, Bentley, and Maserati.

Rate Plans and Extra Charges

All car rentals are priced as either daily, weekend, or weekly. The daily rate is the most expensive and is charged per 24-hour period. The weekend rate is also charged per 24-hour period, but the rental must begin after noon on Thursday and be completed by noon on Monday. A Weekly rate is the least expensive and, depending on the company, a week is considered five, six, or seven 24-hour periods.

Most rental car companies offer special discounts to the daily, weekend, and weekly rates. These discounts can be given because the renter is a member of the American Automobile Association (AAA) or American Association of Retired Persons (AARP). Many major corporations and government agencies negotiate special discounts with one or more rental car companies. Travel professionals renting a car are usually given a discount, although many rental car companies require the renter to have an IATAN ID card.

Depending on the rental car company and the destination, there may be an additional charge for mileage. A rate that does not have a mileage charge is called an unlimited mileage rate. Some rates allow a specific number of miles per day or per week free and then charge for all additional miles. Other rates have a mileage charge beginning with the first mile driven.

When a daily or weekend rate involves a certain number of free miles, it is important to note that this number is multiplied by the number of days the car is used. Remember, daily and weekend rates are priced per 24-hour period and the free mileage is stated the same way.

Generally, rental car companies give renters a grace period of one to two hours over the scheduled return time. Cars returned after the grace period incur a charge for an extra hour or even an extra day. When making reservations, it is important for the travel counselor to advise the client that extra hour or extra day charges may apply. These extra charges, the actual amounts, and when they apply can easily be checked in the GDS.

Car rentals in the United States are subject to state and local *taxes* and possibly an airport tax or other fees. International rentals in countries that have a Value Added Tax (VAT) are subject to this tax as well as any local tax.

Depending on the rental car company and the rental location, special equipment such as a luggage rack, ski rack, bicycle rack, CB radio, hand controls, trailer hitch, snow chains, mobile phone, child seat, and infant seat may be available. The cost for these extras can range from $5.00 to $10.00 per day. If someone other than the renter may drive the car, an extra charge per day may be applicable.

Helpful Industry Web Sites

Selected Rental Car Web Sites

Alamo: **http://www.alamo.com**

Avis: **http://www.avis.com**

Budget: **http://www.budgetrentacar.com**

Car Rental Web Sites

Dollar: **http://www.dollar.com**

Enterprise: **http://www.enterprise.com**

Hertz: **http://www.hertz.com**

National: **http://www.nationalcar.com**

Payless: **http://www.paylesscar.com**

Rent-A-Wreck: **http://www.rent-a-wreck.com**

Thrifty: **http://www.thrifty.com**

Car Rental Rate Examples

$29.59 per day with unlimited free mileage

$25.59 per day, 100 free miles, $.25 for each additional mile over 100

$99.00 per week, unlimited free mileage

$129.00 per week, 700 free miles, $.25 for each additional mile over 700

$79.00 per week, $.13 for each mile driven

It is important to note that many states in the United States, as well as other countries, require child safety seats for children under five years of age. There may also be requirements regarding the minimum age of passengers riding in the front seat.

One-way rentals usually have an extra charge, known as a drop charge, and this fee can be substantial. The drop charge is usually based on the distance between the rental and return locations and can easily amount to $500 or more. It is important to note that not all companies and not all rental locations allow a one-way rental.

Some rental car companies want vehicles returned with a full tank of gas. If the tank is not full when the car is returned an additional fee is charged. This refuel charge is usually more expensive than filling the tank. Other companies want cars returned empty; that way, they can automatically charge for refueling. The counselor should always ask about this policy when making the reservations or advise the client to ask at the rental counter.

Insurance

All rental car companies offer two types of insurance: personal accident insurance (PAI) and supplemental liability insurance (SLI).

Both of these insurances are optional when renting a car in the United States In fact, many travelers' personal auto insurance or credit card companies include the same coverage as PAI and SLI. Travel counselors should always advise their clients to check with their insurance or credit card company to see if they already have coverage.

Collision damage waiver (CDW), also called loss damage waiver (LDW), costs between $10 and $20 per day and releases the renter from paying for repairs or replacement should an accident occur. It is no wonder that travel counselors and renters refer to CDW and LDW as insurance. PAI costs between $5 and $10 per day and covers the renter and her passengers in the case of injury.

It is unfortunate that some car rental companies have been known to use unnecessary pressure and intimidation to sell these packages. Rental counter agents earn a commission when they sell CDW, PAI, and SLI, so high-pressure tactics are understandable, but still unfortunate for the renter. Some states have passed legislation prohibiting the sale of CDW, PAI, and SLI altogether; the insurances must be included automatically with the rates.

PAI, SLI, and CDW are perhaps much more important when renting a car outside of the United States. All personal auto insurance policies do not include coverage beyond the U.S. borders, although special additions can be purchased to add the coverage. Given that insurance is mandatory in all foreign countries, it is usually easier and less expensive for the client to purchase CDW, PAI, and SLI directly from the car rental company.

International Rentals

Renting a car in most countries simply requires that the renter have a valid U.S. or Canadian driver's license, proof of financial responsibility (such as a credit card), and proof of insurance. A few countries, however, require that the renter have an International Driver's Permit (IDP).

The IDP is obtained at any AAA office and costs $10. Two passport-type photos are needed and the applicant must have a valid U.S. driver's license. The permit is valid for one year; less if the U.S. driver's license expires earlier. As strange as it may seem, a traveler does not have to read any manuals or take any tests to obtain an IDP.

Travel counselors making reservations for international car rentals should inform the client that there may be some monumental differences in driving rules and regulations. Consider the following differences.

1. In many countries, *traffic moves on the left side of the road.* This affects not only driving, but walking as well. Imagine preparing to cross the street and not knowing in which direction to look for oncoming traffic! Countries with left-side driving include Antigua, Australia, Bahamas, Barbados, British Virgin Islands, Cayman Islands, Cyprus, Dominica, Fiji Islands, Guyana, India, Indonesia, Jamaica, Japan, Kenya, Malaysia, Malta, Montserrat, New Zealand, Republic of Ireland, Singapore, South Africa, Sri Lanka, St. Kitts/Nevis, St. Lucia, St. Vincent, Suriname, Tanzania, Thailand, Trinidad and Tobago, Uganda, United Kingdom (England, Scotland, Wales, and Northern Ireland), U.S. Virgin Islands, Zambia, and Zimbabwe.

2. *Gas is sold in liters* instead of gallons. One liter is equal to .264 gallons. In many countries, it is common to pay as much as $5.00 for the equivalent of one gallon of gasoline.

3. *Speed limits are in kilometers per hour* instead of miles per hour. 100 kph is the same as 62.137 mph.

4. *Map distances are shown in kilometers* instead of miles. One kilometer equals .6 miles.

5. *Road signs are international* and a few are quite different than those seen in the United States. To complicate matters, some countries have added some signs that are unique to that country.

6. *Seat belts are mandatory for all passengers,* even in the back seat. Children under five years of age cannot ride in the front seat.

7. *Stop signs and red lights are interpreted as* "you might want to slow down" in many countries. Traffic jams in cities such as Rome and Tokyo make U.S. traffic jams look like a walk in the park. In many countries, lane lines do not mean anything at all, and it is not uncommon to see three or even four cars abreast on a two-lane road.

Making Car Rental Reservations

As with lodging reservations, there are several choices for making car rental reservations. Travel counselors can reserve rental cars through their GDS, by telephone or fax, and on the Internet.

Regardless of how the reservation is made, the travel counselor needs certain information before he can begin the booking process:

1. renter's name
2. pick-up location, date, and time
3. return location, date, and time
4. size/class of car
5. incoming flight data
6. discount numbers, if any

Confirmation information should be given to the client, preferably in writing. GDS bookings make this easy because the rental car information is automatically included when an itinerary is printed for the client.

Requirements for Renting a Car

Each rental car company has a minimum age policy. Depending on the company and circumstance, *the minimum age to rent a car is 18, 21, or 25,* although most companies require that the renter be at least 25 years old. Sometimes when the renter is traveling for company and has a corporate ID and discount number, the minimum age may be lower than 25. A maximum age may also be enforced, especially internationally. Again, depending on the rental car company and circumstance, the maximum age may be 65 or 70 years.

A valid driver's license is always required, although some countries may require an IDP. For all rentals, the renter must show proof of financial responsibility in the event that the car is damaged, lost, stolen, or destroyed. The easiest way of showing proof of financial responsibility is by having a major credit card (not a debit card) that is issued in the renter's name. A department store or gas company credit card will not suffice, nor will Mom and Dad's credit card!

FIGURE 11–5 The client without a credit card is often in for a long wait at the rental counter.

The client without a credit card is in for a wait at the rental counter and an outlay of cash (Figure 11–5). A cash deposit of up to $500 is required. Then, the counter agent must call the renter's employer and bank for references. This means, of course, that the rental must take place during normal business hours.

Many rental car companies also check the renter's driving record with the Department or Bureau of Motor Vehicles. If the renter has had an excessive number of tickets, been convicted of driving while under the influence (DUI), or has outstanding warrants against him, he will not be rented a car even though a reservation exists. Because the driving record check is not done until the client is at the rental counter to pick up the car, it is a good idea to advise the client of this at the time the booking is made. In this way, a client with a poor driving record will not be taken by surprise should the rental car company deny him a car.

What Happens at the Rental Counter

The actual location of the counter varies by rental car company and city. The rule of thumb is the more conveniently located the rental counter and vehicles are, the higher the rates.

Rental Car Location Options

Airport locations include rental counters located in the airport terminal, rental counters located on airport property, and rental counters located near airport property. A free shuttle to the cars or rental counter is provided.

Off-airport locations include locations throughout the city and locations at major hotels. Transportation to the rental location is the client's responsibility.

When the client arrives at the rental counter, she should give the counter agent her name or confirmation number so that the agent can retrieve the client's reservation in the computer. The counter agent asks to see the renter's driver's license and credit card. An imprint of the credit card is made and held at the counter until the car is returned. In many cases, a portion of the renter's credit line is held in case the car is damaged. If the renter does not have a credit card, the deposit is taken and the employment and banking references are obtained. In many circumstances, the renter's driving record is also checked.

The counter agent offers CDW (or LDW), SLI, and PAI if state law permits. The renter is asked to initial the insurance and waiver items and then sign the rental agreement. Travel counselors should always advise their clients never to sign the rental agreement until they fully understand and agree with all items on the agreement.

If more than one make and model of the class reserved is on hand, the renter may be given a choice of vehicles. Before leaving the rental location, the renter should inspect the vehicle for any damage and confirm that the spare tire is present and in good condition. If any problems are found, they should be reported to the counter agent immediately. The renter should also write down the car's mileage before leaving. At the end of the rental, the mileage is written down on the agreement even though a mileage charge may not apply.

When the car is returned, the renter should again inspect the vehicle for damage. At the counter, the agent needs the rental agreement to calculate the total charges and the car keys are returned. Travel counselors should advise their clients never to finalize the rental until the client understands and agrees with the total charges. It is very difficult, if not impossible, to recover overcharges after the client has returned home.

If payment is to be by credit card, the counter agent completes the charge form and asks for the renter's signature. If payment is to be by other means, the charge form is destroyed and payment is made in cash or by traveler's cheques.

Case Study

You booked a **car** for your clients' trip. When they picked it up, they were told the rate was $10 per day higher than indicated on the itinerary you gave them. The rental car agent maintained they were quoted an incorrect rate. They reluctantly accept the rate and complete their trip. When they return home, they contact you about the difference in rates.

1. Would you give the client the difference between the quoted rate and the charged rate?
2. Would you write a letter to the car rental company explaining the situation and ask for a refund on your clients' behalf?
3. Would you contact your GDS account representative and fax a hardcopy of the PNR and the client's bill?

SUMMARY

Reserving rental cars is an integral part of the services provided by a travel counselor. As with any other travel product, learning about the customer's needs and preferences is the only way to find the right product. It's equally important to be well versed in the many variations of cars that exist. You should now be familiar with the reference sources and the various types of rental cars, the rental procedures, and the differences in international car rentals. The Internet has added a dimension to researching and reserving these products and has, in many cases, significantly changed our procedures.

For additional Travel and Tourism resources, go to http://www.hospitality-tourism.delmar.com.

PLEASE COMPLETE THE CHAPTER REVIEW QUESTIONS NOW.

EXERCISE 11-1 Rental Cars

1. Define the three rental car rate plans.

   a. daily _____

   b. weekend _____

   c. weekly _____

2. Describe the three ways in which mileage may be handled on rental car rates. _____

   _____

   _____

3. Identify some vehicles that may be offered in the "special" category. _____

   _____

4. What types of clients might receive a discount from the standard rental car rate? _____

   _____

5. What items might be offered as special equipment on a rental car? _____

   _____

6. What is a drop charge? _____

7. Name the two insurances associated with rental cars. _____

   _____

8. What is a refuel charge? _____

9. Identify four differences a client might encounter when renting and driving a car outside of the United States. _____

   _____

10. Name some vehicles that are usually categorized as luxury class. _____

    _____

11. What charge may apply when a car is returned several hours after the scheduled time? _____

    _____

12. Are taxes usually included in the rate for a rental car? _____

13. Your clients will be renting a car in France. They want a small car to keep the cost down and they must have an automatic transmission. What will you tell them? _____

    _____

14. Your clients are traveling to South Africa next summer. Air conditioning is very important to them and they are thinking about a compact-size car. What will you tell them? _____

    _____

Review Questions

1. What two items must a client always have in order to rent a car? _____
   _____

2. Why should the client inspect the car for damage both before and after the rental? _____
   _____

3. An older couple wants to rent an inexpensive car in Seattle for a week. They will be visiting several family members and they have several large packages for them in addition to their luggage. What size car do you think would best suit their needs and why do you think so? _____
   _____

4. Six friends are traveling together. They want to rent a car in San Francisco to explore northern California for two weeks. What type of car do you think will best suit their needs and why do you think so? _____
   _____

5. A businesswoman wants to rent a car after her 11:00 P.M. flight arrival in Boston. For safety reasons, what will you suggest?
   _____
   _____

6. Your client is renting a car in Tanzania and it is his first trip to that country. Of what will you advise him? _____
   _____

7. Why are rental car companies with counters located in the airport terminal often more expensive than companies located outside of the terminal? _____

8. Depending on rental car company, the minimum age to rent a car can be _____

9. At the rental car counter, the client will be offered what type(s) of insurance? _____

10. After proof of financial responsibility and a valid driver's license have been verified, what else might the rental car counter agent check? _____

Traveling by Rail

OBJECTIVES

After completing this chapter, you should be able to

- recognize the advantages and disadvantages of traveling by rail.
- understand Amtrak's route system and types of equipment.
- understand the types of fares available on Amtrak.
- understand railroads around the world and their most interesting features, fares, and discounts.

KEY TERMS

Acela	Flexipass	Superliner
Auto Train	Japanese National Railway	timetable
Canrailpass	Metroliner	VIA Rail Canada
corridor trains	North America Rail Pass	Viewliner
Eurailpass	promotional fares	
Explore America	rail fare	

SELLING RAIL TRAVEL

Trains conjure up visions of nostalgia for a more leisurely era. Traveling by train is, indeed, nostalgic—plus it offers an opportunity like no other to meet the "locals" and to see the sights in whatever country you happen to be traveling. But rail travel is even more than that; it can also be very practical. Especially for traveling distances of 200 to 400 miles, trains have several distinct advantages over other modes of transportation. Trains usually arrive at and depart from the central business district of a city, thus saving transit time between city and airport, which can be considerable in some cities. The rail passenger also avoids time spent sitting in airport lounges or on airport runways. The air travel time between New York and Washington, D.C., is approximately 1¼ hours, but when you add the time spent in traffic getting to and from these busy airports, the time spent at the airport to check in, and the time spent on the runway or circling the airport, the total travel time can be increased by one to three hours. Amtrak makes this trip from center city to center city in just under three hours. An additional advantage is the cost. Airfares for short-distance trips may be higher than rail fares.

So, even though trains don't move as fast as planes, they can still be a practical alternative in the right situation. In addition to being practical, they are safe, interesting, comfortable, and an excellent way to sightsee. Train travel also provides a great chance to meet people (Figure 12–1).

FIGURE 12–1 Intercity rail travel is a great way to sightsee and meet people.

Traveling by train can, however, be confusing to the uninitiated. Train stations are "do-it-yourself." Unlike airports, in which the traveler is told exactly where and when to go, the rail traveler has to locate the correct train on a video display or indicator board, discover procedures for checking his own bags, locating the correct platform, car, seat, and accommodations. Locating the correct car is imperative because trains are often split en route—what you thought was the right car may end up in the wrong destination. Sometimes your fellow passengers are the only ones available to ask for information, and if you don't speak the language, this may not be much help.

Trains are seeing a resurgence of interest among travelers, and with innovative fare programs, new modern trains, and increased marketing, this interest will most likely continue to grow. In this chapter, we focus on selling Amtrak. Because there are many similarities in rail travel around the world, understanding Amtrak should help you to understand other railroads, too.

AMTRAK: A BRIEF HISTORY

The railroad's share of passengers showed an enormous decline between 1929 and 1970. In response to this disastrous decline in passenger numbers, Congress passed the Rail Passenger Service Act of 1970. This legislation created the National Railroad Passenger Corporation (Amtrak) to manage the national rail network and to be responsible for operating all intercity passenger trains (excluding commuter trains) under contracts with the nation's railroads.

On May 1, 1971, Amtrak began operation of intercity passenger trains in the United States. Amtrak is financed by a combination of earned revenues from passenger service operation and federal government assistance. With government subsidies reaching over $1 billion per year, funding has not always come easily for Amtrak. There is a belief by some that passenger rail service should be profitable and government assistance unnecessary. Others, however, strongly disagree on the feasibility of a profitable passenger rail system. Former Amtrak president David L. Gunn addressed this issue in a column written February 25, 2003: "The first myth is that Amtrak or passenger rail can be profitable. It can't, and others have gotten into a lot of hot water saying it can. In some regions with enough population density, some services can be profitable on an incremental basis—what railroaders call 'above the rails.' But it takes enormous public investment in track, signals, equipment and so on for a reliable system, which cannot be recovered from fares. Public dollars build airports and public dollars should build rail corridors, too."

On-time performance continues to be a challenge for Amtrak. Except in the Northeast (and a few other small areas throughout the country), Amtrak leases tracks belonging to other railroads. These railroads, not Amtrak, are responsible for track conditions and the flow of rail traffic. As a result, Amtrak sometimes faces less than optimum track conditions and train speeds.

Departing: Milwaukee, WI (MKE) to East Glacier Park, MT (GPK)

Service	Departs	Arrives	Duration	Amenities	Seats/Rooms
7 Empire Builder	**Milwaukee, WI** (MKE) **3:55 pm** 10-AUG	**East Glacier Park, MT** (GPK) **6:45 pm** 11-AUG	27hr 50mn	Checked baggage, Dining Car, Lounge, Non-smoking, Sleeping cars	2 Reserved Coach Seats

TABLE 12–1

Except for these lingering problem areas, Amtrak has made vast improvements in equipment and service since its inception in 1971. The fleet has been upgraded with new modern equipment. Superliner and Acela are among the best and newest equipment on the Amtrak system. Amtrak has focused on technology that will continue to improve service and on innovative marketing techniques to improve its share of the travel market. Amtrak reservations can be made through the major airline computer reservation systems, and Amtrak is a member of the Airlines Reporting Corporation (ARC), giving travel professionals complete access to selling and ticketing Amtrak travel. Amtrak's Web site is a full-featured, easy-to-use booking site.

Proponents of rail passenger service believe Amtrak must be a part of a balanced transportation network in the United States. Others push to eliminate Amtrak subsidies completely. Yet, with an uncertain future, Amtrak continues to make strides toward providing a quality travel alternative to a growing market of rail travelers.

THE AMTRAK ROUTE SYSTEM

Amtrak offers over 500 destinations. Nearly 22,000 miles of track makes this possible (see Figure 12–2).

Amtrak service can be broadly divided into two categories: *long-distance* trains and *short-distance* or corridor trains. Long-distance trains are thought of as overnight trains on trips of more than 600 miles. Long-distance trains consist of many types of services and accommodations: coaches, lounge cars, full meal service dining cars, and sleeping accommodations. Reservations are always required for travel on long-distance trains.

Corridor trains are those that travel less than 600 miles per trip. Corridor trains are an efficient way for passengers to travel between many well-traveled city pairs, such as Chicago and St. Louis, Los Angeles and San Diego, or Philadelphia and Washington, D.C. Coach seating is available on all corridor trains.

The development of high-speed rail corridors is a major focus for Amtrak. The first high-speed corridor service

between Boston and New York made its premier run in early 2000. The all-electric Acela trains travel 150 miles per hour and significantly reduce travel times in the corridors they serve. Amtrak's Metroliner trains also provide premier service in the Northeast. All *Acela Express* and *Metroliner* trains provide only reserved first-class and business-class seating for an additional charge.

Amtrak utilizes hub cities to make connections more convenient for passengers. Short-distance trains connect to long-distance trains so that most train service is easily accessible from most points on the Amtrak system. In the midwest, Chicago is the hub city. Notice on the map in Figure 12–2 that from Chicago you can travel to almost anywhere on the Amtrak system.

Finding the departure and arrival times for an Amtrak route is simply done by first checking the route system map, choosing a pair of Amtrak cities, then querying your computer for the schedule of that city pair. The schedule between Milwaukee and Glacier Park will look something like the one in Table 12–1 above.

Service is available on Train number 7, the Empire Builder, which departs from Milwaukee at 3:55 P.M. Travel duration is 27 hours and 50 minutes, so the arrival at the East Glacier Park station is at 6:45 P.M. *the next day*. This is a long-distance train, so in addition to coach seating, it will have a dining car, lounge car, and sleeping accommodations.

For detailed information on the Amtrak route system, the Amtrak National Timetable is the best resource to use. Even though schedule information, as you saw in the above example, is easily accessible online, details on such things as exact routings, intermediate stations, and connecting service are lacking. The timetable should be a constant companion to your computer.

Look carefully at Figure 12–3, "How to Use the Timetable." On this sample, train number 91, the Silver Star, departs from New York at 11:35 A.M. By reading down the left side of the timetable, you see that this train arrives in Washington, D.C., at 4:15 P.M. To travel in the opposite direction, read up the right side of the timetable. The Silver Star, train number 92, departs Washington, D.C., at 11:24 A.M. and arrives in New York at 3:48 P.M. *Be*

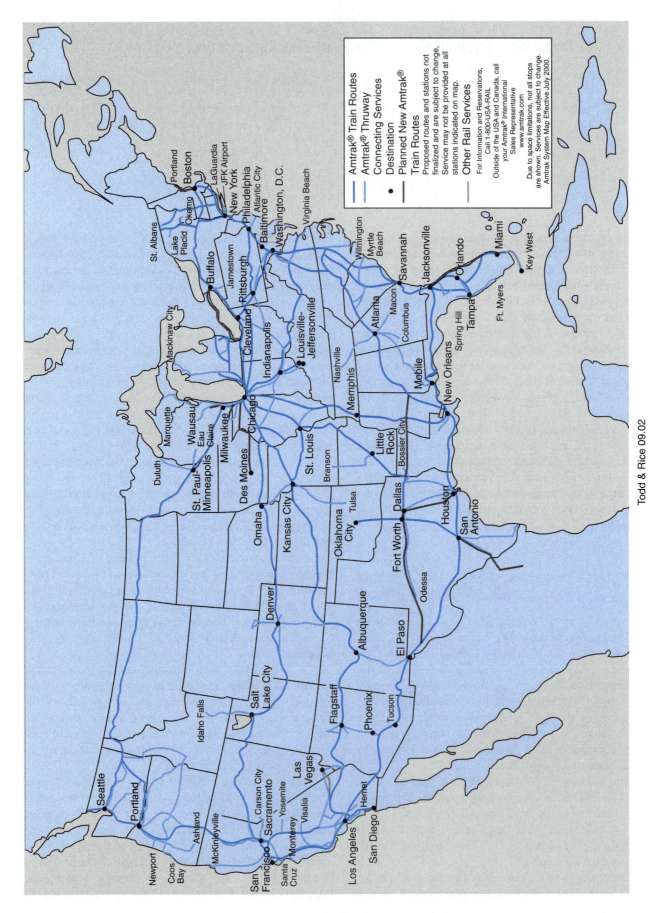

FIGURE 12-2 Amtrak offers 500 destinations and nearly 22,000 miles of track. Courtesy of Amtrak.

Todd & Rice 09.02

HOW TO USE THE TIMETABLE

STEP-BY-STEP TRAVEL PLANNING

1. Locate your destination on the alphabetical list of stations on pages 8–21.

2. Turn to the page indicated to find your schedule.

3. Locate your starting point in the column of cities. **NOTE:** If the schedule does not list your starting point, turn to the map on the inside back cover. Find your starting point on the map and trace the route(s) to your destination. The number blocks along the route(s) indicate the page(s) where the schedule can be found.

4. Read across to determine which trains arrive and/or depart from your station at which times.

5. Some schedules list trains going in one direction only. Others list trains going in both directions. Simply check the arrows at the top of the column to determine whether to read *up or down,* and you can easily determine what time the train you have chosen arrives at your destination and where it stops along the way.

(EXAMPLE ONLY)

A Normal days of operation—during holiday periods, days of operation may vary—be sure to check "Will Also Operate" and "Will Not Operate" areas to determine holiday schedules.

B On-board service symbols—services applicable to each train are noted by symbols across the top of each train schedule. See the Glossary of Amtrak Services and Amenities on pages 6 and 7 for explanation of symbols.

C Italic type indicates connecting services. A blue background indicates a connecting Amtrak or VIA Rail train. Motorcoach, ferry or other rail services appear on a grey background.

D Nearby cities and points of interest are listed in parentheses. ✻ Amtrak Vacations available at these destinations.

E Station service symbols—see the Glossary of Amtrak Services and Amenities on pages 6 and 7 for explanations.

F ▣ Amtrak® Express Shipping and Checked Baggage Service—this baggage symbol indicates stations and trains offering both Express Shipping and Checked Baggage Service. The baggage symbol without a box 🛄 indicates stations and trains offering Checked Baggage Service only. These will be displayed in either the symbol column or in the train time column.

Other Reference Marks are explained on the same page as the schedule, or on the facing page.

1-800-USA-RAIL

(Boston) • New York • Philadelphia • Washington • Richmond • Raleigh • Charleston • Savannah • Jacksonville

Silver Star	Silver Meteor		◄ Train Name ►				Silver Meteor	Silver Star
91	**97**		◄ Train Number ►				**98**	**92**
Daily	Daily		**A** ◄ Days of Operation ►				Daily	Daily
▣🚌✕ 📷✻	▣🚌✕ 📷✻		**B** ◄ On Board Service ►				▣🚌✕ 📷✻	▣🚌✕ 📷✻
Read Down		▼		Mile	Symbol	▲	Read Up	
▣95/191/195	175/163		*Connecting Train No.*		**E**		▣ 84/164	▣132/134
6 30A	1 30P	Dp	*Boston, MA—South Sta.* ✻ (ET)	0	⚹	Ar	5 15P	8 30P
	6 20P	Ar	*New York, NY—Penn Sta.* ✻	231	⚹	Dp	12 30P	4 30P
2 45P	10 10P	Ar	*Washington, DC* ✻	457	⚹	Dp	9 05A	1 05P
📷11 35A	📷 7 05P	Dp	New York, NY—Penn Sta. ✻ (ET)	0	⚹	Ar	📷 9 40A	📷 3 48P
📷R11 52A	📷R 7 23P		Newark, NJ—Penn Sta. **D**	10	⚹		📷D 9 18A	📷D 3 22P
			Metropark, NJ	25	⚹			
R12 40P	R 8 01P		Trenton, NJ	58	⚹		D 8 41A	D 2 32P
📷R 1 55P	📷R 8 37P		Philadelphia, PA—30th St. Sta. ✻	91	⚹		📷D 8 00A	📷D 1 25P
📷R 2 23P	📷R 9 01P		Wilmington, DE	116	♿		📷D 7 34A	📷D12 58P
📷R 3 32P	📷R 9 53P		Baltimore, MD—Penn Sta.	185	⚹		📷D 6 44A	📷D12 02P
			BWI Rail Station, MD	196	⚹			
			New Carrollton, MD	216	⚹		**F**	
📷R 4 15P	📷R10 30P	Ar	Washington, DC ✻	225	⚹	Dp	📷D 6 10A	D11 24A
📷R 4 35P	📷R10 59P	Dp				Ar	📷D 5 45A	📷D11 09A
📷 4 54P			Alexandria, VA	233	♿			📷10 38A
			Franconia/Springfield, VA	240	●			
			Quantico, VA	260	●			
			Fredericksburg, VA	279	●			

SERVICES ON ATLANTIC COAST ROUTE TRAINS

Coaches: Reservations required on all trains.
Sleeping Cars:
- First Class Viewliner® Service on Trains 89, 90, 91, 92, 97 and 98.
- First Class Superliner® Service on Trains 1 and 2.
- Amtrak's Metropolitan Lounge® available in New York, Philadelphia and Washington, and private waiting area available in Miami, for First Class Service passengers.

Carolina Business Class Service: On Trains 79 and 80. Complimentary beverages, newspaper and audio and visual entertainment offered between Washington and Charlotte.

FIGURE 12–3 Amtrak's timetable offers a wealth of information about trains and services across the U.S. Courtesy of Amtrak.

careful not to confuse the schedule for the Silver Meteor, trains number 97 and 98, with the Silver Star. The timetable offers a wealth of information. Every small symbol has meaning and should not be overlooked. Amtrak's timetables are available free of charge from Amtrak.

TRAVELING WITH AMTRAK

Amtrak operates a variety of equipment. The type of equipment on a particular route is determined largely by the length of time it takes the train to travel from its origin to its final destination.

Service on Corridor Trains

A short-distance train, or corridor train, which has a running time of less than six hours, has coach cars and café cars. Amtrak coach seats are available on all corridor trains. Coach seats have ample legroom, fold-down trays, and individual reading lamps. Some corridor trains offer reserved coach seats. These require advanced reservations. On certain short-distance routes, coach seating is unreserved. Unreserved seats are available to boarding passengers on a first-come, first-served basis. Seating is not guaranteed, although every effort is made to provide seats for every passenger on unreserved trains.

There will also be short-order food service available on café or lounge cars. While providing informal food and beverage service, these cars also provide comfortable, casual seating for sightseeing and socializing and have tables for writing or playing cards and other games. A few short distance trains do not have food service cars, but passengers are always welcome to bring their own food on-board.

Long-Distance Trains

Amtrak's cross-country, or long-distance trains, offer the traveler a much different experience from the corridor trains. Vacation travelers who value amenities and on-board experiences as an important part of their vacation are the typical overnight passenger. In addition to reserved coach service, lounge cars, various sleeping accommodations, long-distance trains offer dining cars complete with

service and menus (Figure 12–4). Overnight trains in the eastern United States feature single-level cars and the Viewliner cars that have an additional row of windows above the main windows. This unique feature gives added light during the day, and in sleeping rooms, the upper-berth passenger has a window. In the western United States, bilevel Superliner equipment is available.

Traveling in coach on overnight trains is the most economical way to go. All coach seats must be reserved in advance. Most coach seats on overnight trains are extra-spacious and have a leg rest. Each coach car has well-appointed restrooms.

Private sleeping accommodations may appear expensive when compared with coach fares (or even airfares). It is important to remember that the price of a sleeping accommodation includes all meals while onboard the train, plus complimentary juice, tea, or coffee and a newspaper delivered to your room each morning. Your sleeping room is your hotel on a long-distance train trip.

All sleeping accommodations provide comfortable seats that convert to beds, a sliding door for privacy, and a private window on the world. Depending upon the type of accommodation, sink, toilet, and sometimes shower will be in your room. Restroom facilities, some with showers, are located at the end of each car for rooms that do not provide toilet facilities. Figures 12–5 and 12–6 illustrate two types of sleeping accommodations. Figure 12–7 lists sleeping accommodations and their amenities.

Breakfast

Starters

Screwdriver *(vodka and orange juice)*	$4.00
Bloody Mary *(vodka and tomato juice, seasoned with herbs & spices)*	4.00
Chilled Orange or Apple Juice	1.00

Eggs, Etc.

Two Farm Fresh Eggs* — 4.25
Prepared up. over or scrambled. Served with your choice of grits or hashed brown potatoes and breakfast breads.

The American Bounty Omelet* — 5.50
Each trip, our chefs create a three-egg omelet with various fillings, served with your choice of grits or hashed brown potatoes and breakfast breads. Your server will describe this morning's offering.

French Toast — 4.50
An Amtrak Tradition. Two thick slices, egg dipped and served with syrup or fruit topping.

Classic Pancakes — 4.25
A stack of three pancakes fresh from the griddle, served with syrup or fruit topping.

The American — 4.50
Fresh fruit and non-fat fruited yogurt, served with a toasted bagel and light cream cheese.
Note: *Hot oatmeal or dry cereal with milk can be substituted for the yogurt.*

On the Side

Bacon or Sausage — 1.75
Four grilled bacon slices or two pan sautéed sausage patties.

Beverages

Freshly Brewed Coffee *(regular or decaffeinated)*	1.00
Tea *(hot, iced or herbal)*	1.00
Cold Milk	1.00

Water available upon request. Prices include all taxes. Amtrak accepts major credit cards.

*FDA Consumer Advisory: If you are especially vulnerable to food borne illness, you should only eat seafood, meat and eggs that have been thoroughly cooked.

29830 W. 00

FIGURE 12–4 Amtrak's Dining Cars are full-service restaurants that offer a wide selection of cuisine. Courtesy of Amtrak.

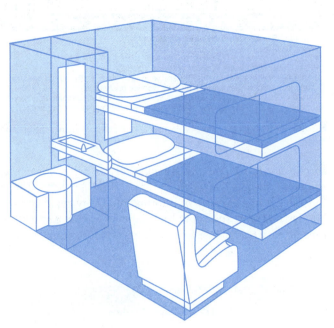

FIGURE 12–5 The Amtrak Viewliner bedroom provides comfortable seats that convert to beds. Courtesy of Amtrak.

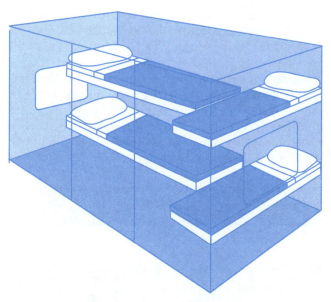

FIGURE 12–6 The Amtrak Superliner family bedroom has beds for 2 adults and 2 children, but no toilet in the room. Courtesy of Amtrak.

AMTRAK'S AUTO TRAIN

How convenient it would be to have your own car to use when you reach your vacation destination without having to actually drive it there! Amtrak's Auto Train service lets you do just that. Auto Train takes cars, vans, SUVs,

motorcycles, small boats, jet skis, passengers, and baggage nonstop from the northeast (Lorton, Virginia) to Sanford, Florida (north of Orlando). While passengers relax in roomy coach seats or private sleeping rooms, Amtrak manages the rest. The price of a ticket includes dinner and breakfast. Amenities include a bilevel lounge car and feature movies. Vehicles are protected in enclosed car carriers.

AMTRAK FARES

Like the airlines, Amtrak has a variety of fare plans, and, as with airfares, Amtrak's fares and fare plans change often. Amtrak offers discounted fares and promotional fares like the Explore America fare. *The best way to get the lowest fare is to travel off peak.* Off-peak fares are offered throughout the year and vary by time of year, time of departure, or day of the week. Online discounts can be found on the Amtrak Web site, http://www.amtrak.com.

A few basic rules apply when calculating Amtrak fares. The first thing to remember about Amtrak fares is that there is always a rail fare for travel on Amtrak. If the passenger travels in a coach seat, the rail fare is all he pays. The rail fare may be discounted in any of the ways mentioned previously. If, however, the passenger chooses to travel in a sleeping room or in business class, there is an additional charge added to the rail fare. This is an easy calculation when there is only one person traveling. Simply add the rail fare to the additional charge to arrive at

Amtrak Sleeping Accommodations

On Superliner Trains	Recommended Capacity	Number of Beds	In-room Toilet	In-room Shower
Roomette	👤👤	2 Adult	none	none
Bedroom	👤👤	2 Adult	1	1
Bedroom Suite	👤👤👤👤	4 Adult	2	2
Family Bedroom	👤👤👤👤	2 Adult 2 Child	none	none
Accessible Bedroom	👤👤	2 Adult	1	none
On Viewliner Trains				
Roomette	👤👤	2 Adult	1	none
Bedroom	👤👤	2 Adult	1	1
Bedroom Suite	👤👤👤👤	4 Adult	2	2
Accessible Bedroom	👤👤	2 Adult	1	none

FIGURE 12–7 Amtrak Superliner sleeping accomodations are similar, but vary from Viewliner Train's accommodations.

General Tips About Amtrak Travel

TIPPING

Tipping is not required for any Amtrak service. Sleeping car passengers who wish to tip their car attendant may use the following guideline: $1 per person per night.

BAGGAGE

Two pieces of carry-on luggage and three pieces of checked, each weighing up to 50 pounds, are allowed. Free red-cap service is provided for baggage assistance.

PETS

The only animals permitted on Amtrak are guide dogs for blind, deaf, or disabled passengers.

HANDICAPPED TRAVELERS

Almost every train has specially equipped seats, sleeper rooms, and restroom facilities especially for handicapped travelers. Wheelchair accessibility varies.

STATIONS

Each Amtrak station is unique. Many are located in center city areas and vary considerably in size and quality. Many stations are historic, while others are new and modern. Information on Amtrak stations, including directions, is available at http://www.amtrak.com.

CELL PHONES

Amtrak welcomes passengers to bring and use cell phones, except in designated "Quiet Cars." Cell phones will work in most places, subject to signal strength.

SMOKING

All Amtrak trains and stations are nonsmoking, except for a designated smoking area on the Auto Train. Passengers may smoke on station platforms during longer stops (subject to state or local laws).

Train travelers usually have many questions about their trip. Amtrak offers these general tips about Amtrak travel. Courtesy of Amtrak at http://www.amtrak.com.

the total fare. For example, the rail fare between Boston and New York is $50 one-way; to upgrade to business class there is an additional charge of $88. One person pays $50 + $88 or a total of $138.00.

When you have more than one person traveling in a sleeping room, it gets a bit more complex. *Remember the rail fare is paid per person, but the additional charge for the sleeping room is paid per room.* A sleeping room may accommodate from one to five people. Each person in the room pays a rail fare, but the charge for the sleeping room is paid only one time.

Let's calculate a fare for two passengers who are traveling together in a Bedroom. If the rail fare is $150 and the sleeping room charge is $250, how much is their total fare? If you said $550, you are correct! ($150 × 2 passengers = $300 + $250 for the room = $550).

If it takes two nights to reach a destination, the stated room charge is not paid per night. Sleeping room charges are always quoted per room for the *entire trip.* Discounts usually do not apply to sleeping room charges, although there are some exceptions to this. The travel counselor FAM fare is one of those exceptions. This fare allows a travel counselor to travel for a 75 percent discount off the rail fare *and* sleeping room charge.

PLEASE TURN TO PAGE 187 AND COMPLETE EXERCISE 12–2 NOW.

AMTRAK DISCOUNTED AND PROMOTIONAL FARES

Several types of individuals may benefit from Amtrak's discounted fares: senior citizens, veterans, active military, students, members of the American Automobile Association (AAA), and members of the National Association of Retired Persons (NARP). Families also benefit from Amtrak's discounts for children. Children ages 2 through 15 ride for half-price when accompanied by an adult paying full fare. Each adult can bring two children along with this half-price discount. One child under age two may travel free with each ticketed adult. Child discounts apply any day, all year.

In addition to the above discounted fares, Amtrak may offer various types of promotional:

- *North America Rail Pass:* Get 30 days, two countries (United States and Canada), and 28,000 miles of track—at one low price with North America Rail Pass.

- *USA Rail Passes:* Rail travel options in the United States for *international* travelers.

- *Rail 2 Rail:* Amtrak, Metrolink, Pacific Surfliner and Coaster offer the Rail 2 Rail program to make traveling in Southern California a breeze.

- *California Rail Pass:* Get 7 days of travel in a 21-day period for $159.

- *Florida Rail Pass:* One year of unlimited travel throughout Florida for $249.

- *Explore America Fares:* Amtrak Explore America fares are flat-rate fares allowing for 45 days of travel within one (or more) of four geographic regions in the United States: west, central, Florida, and east. Passengers may travel from any point to any other point, using the routes of their choice, within the region or regions purchased, with a maximum of three stopovers along the way. There are peak and off-peak passes, and on some trains, the pass can be upgraded to sleeping car or business class. Reservations must be secured for all reserved trains prior to ticket issuance. Tickets for the entire trip must be obtained prior to departure. In general, Explore America fares are not available online.

MAKING RESERVATIONS ON AMTRAK

Reservations are always required for sleeping accommodations, business class, first class, and for coach travel on all long-distance and some corridor trains. For peak travel times, especially the summer months, it is wise to make reservations well in advance. A reservation on Amtrak is completed much the same as an airline reservation, and Amtrak tickets are printed on the agency's ticket printer.

Amtrak tickets are issued using ARC ticket stock, and most of the same rules apply to Amtrak tickets as to airline tickets. Amtrak pays commissions on tickets that are reported through ARC.

Security

As with other modes of transportation, Amtrak has responded to the increased need for the security of its passengers. To this end, valid photo identification is a necessity and must be produced when obtaining, exchanging, and refunding tickets; storing baggage at stations; checking baggage; sending Amtrak Express shipments and on board trains in response to a request by an Amtrak employee. Following federal Transportation Security Administration (TSA) guidelines, Amtrak will conduct random ticket verification checks on board trains to ensure that passengers are properly ticketed. Baggage limitations are strictly enforced.

Amtrak's security guidelines state that identification must be current and in force. The following forms of identification are acceptable for persons 18 and older:

- One piece of photo identification issued by a government authority.
- Two pieces of identification, at least one of which is a nonphoto ID issued by a government authority.

Examples of acceptable forms of ID include:

- State or provincial driver's license
- Passport
- Official government-issued identification (federal, state, or county government or legitimate foreign government)
- Canadian provincial health ID card with photo
- Military photo ID
- Student identification (university, college, or high school photo ID)
- Job Corps photo ID

Amtrak offers service into three popular Canadian cities: Montreal, Toronto, and Vancouver. When crossing the border between the United States and Canada, Amtrak passengers must provide both a proof of citizenship and proof of identity. Amtrak recommends that U.S. and Canadian citizens carry a passport. If a passenger does not have a passport, a certified copy of a birth certificate and current valid government-issued photo identification is required. Citizens of other countries are required to carry a passport, and in many cases, a visa. Customs officials may also board trains at the border. Passengers may be asked to identify and open their baggage.

Additional information on requirements for U.S. citizens when crossing borders can be obtained on the Internet at http://www.travel.state.gov or by phone at 1-800-FED-INFO.

OTHER RAILROADS AROUND THE WORLD

VIA Rail Canada

Most passenger rail service in Canada is operated by VIA Rail Canada, a corporation of the Canadian government. Like rail service in the United States, Canadian rail service is dependent on the financial support of the government.

Because of its proximity to the United States and because Amtrak offers convenient service into several points on the U.S.–Canada border, Canadian trains are popular with American travelers. Like Amtrak, VIA Rail is a member carrier of the ARC. That means it is a simple matter for U.S. travel counselors to sell VIA Rail products and services. VIA Rail pays travel counselors a commission on ARC sales. Information on VIA Rail is available in airline CRSs and by accessing their Web site at http://www.viarail.ca.

The rail system in Canada is coast to coast, serving approximately 400 communities, largely in the southern part of the country. Canada, like the United States, offers some breathtaking scenery and has many routes that take maximum advantage of the countryside. The Canadian Rockies has always been a popular trip with U.S. visitors to Canada.

In general, equipment and accommodations on VIA Rail are very similar to Amtrak. VIA Rail's equipment is well maintained and comfortable. They operate high-speed trains on short-distance routes around major cities such as Toronto and Montreal, and transcontinental service linking eastern and western provinces. The Canrailpass (with adult, student-youth, and senior 60+ versions) may be purchased at both low- and high-season rates for a fixed price. The Pass, which is available only to non-Canadians, allows 12 days of unlimited travel in *Comfort* class (Economy) during a 30-day period. The card can be used anywhere VIA goes, from the Atlantic to the Pacific, and up to Hudson Bay, and allows unlimited stops. It is also possible to add up to three extra days' travel during the 30-day validity period.

Canada's most famous train is the *Canadian,* which travels between Toronto and Vancouver, crossing the picturesque lakelands of northern Ontario, the western plains, and the Canadian Rockies and finishing its journey on the Pacific coast. Other stops include Sudbury Junction, Winnipeg, Saskatoon, Edmonton, Jasper, and Kamloops. Passengers enjoy three days aboard beautifully restored 1950s art-deco-styled equipment. Outdoor enthusiasts who want to get off the train in the middle of a forest *can request their own special stop between Sudbury Junction and Winnipeg!*

Eastern Canada has two scenic routes. The *Ocean* travels between Montreal and Halifax, and the *Chaleur* from Montreal to Gaspé. These trains depart at night as one train. Early in the morning, at the Baie des Chaleurs, the *Ocean* and the *Chaleur* separate. The *Ocean* continues southward across New Brunswick and Nova Scotia, reaching Halifax in midafternoon. The *Chaleur* stays in Québec, heading for Gaspé. At Gaspé, boat tours to the renowned wilderness park area of Bonaventure Island are very popular.

Trains of Europe

European train service is often thought of as the standard to which all railroads should aspire. Passenger train service in Europe is comprised of 23 rail lines (including both eastern and western Europe). There are intracountry and intercountry routes. A high degree of coordination and cooperation exists between individual European railroads so that travel between major cities is reliable and efficient. Further cooperation exists in a growing number of cities where the airports are connected by rail to the central stations. Connecting ferries also play an important role in the overall rail system; in some cases rail coaches are actually loaded aboard ferries for transport. Although overall service standards do vary from country to country, many European countries have excellent train service.

The European rail network offers several premier trains that combine high speed with excellent service and comfort (Figure 12–8). Each train has slightly different amenities.

Artesia: Also known as the France-Italy day train, it covers many routes including Paris to Milan in under five hours.

AVE: For fast and efficient travel in Spain; the AVE travels from Madrid to Seville in just two hours, 30 minutes.

Cisalpino: Connects Switzerland, Southern Italy, and Southern Germany. Links Zurich and Milan in under four hours.

Eurostar: Rail Europe's most famous Premier Train. Also called the Channel Tunnel train, it set the standard

FIGURE 12–8 Rail Europe's most famous Premier Train is the Eurostar High Speed Train, also called the Channel Tunnel train.

in rail travel, smoothly transporting passengers from London to Paris in three hours, and London to Brussels in two hours, 40 minutes. Here are some Eurostar basics:

- Eurostar runs almost hourly between London and Paris (18–21 times a day).
- Eurostar also serves Ashford, Calais-Frethun, Lille, and Disneyland Paris, with seasonal service to the Alpine towns of Moutiers and Bourg St. Maurice.
- Eurostar features three classes of service: Premium First (London-Paris only, with a dedicated car and high level of service); first class (includes complimentary food and beverages); and standard class (for comfort and convenience).

ES: Offers a variety of city combinations in Italy, including Rome to Florence in just one hour, 30 minutes.

ICE: Connects all major German cities, plus parts of Austria and Switzerland.

Riviera Day Trains: International trains operating between the French Riviera Italy and Switzerland.

Spanish Trains: Madrid to Seville.

TGV: Serving over 150 cities in France and Switzerland. This train holds the world speed record at 320 mph!

Talgo 200: Extends the AVE line from Madrid to Malaga and Cadiz in five hours or less.

Thalys: Links Paris to Brussels, Cologne, Dusseldorf, and Amsterdam.

EUROPEAN TIMETABLES The best source of information about European rail service is the Thomas Cook European

Timetable. It is published monthly and can be purchased by subscription or by single issue from http://www.thomascookpublishing.com. Travel counselors can utilize a Web site that specializes in rail products: http://ra.railagent.com. Commission checks are sent immediately with each booking. According to its developers, Railagent.com is intended to be a one-stop worldwide rail distribution system offering point-to-point tickets and rail passes in Europe, Canada, Australia, and New Zealand.

For travelers and travel professionals, comprehensive worldwide timetables, instant booking, and payment are also available at http://www.internationaltrainline.com. The site includes European rail and individual country rail passes; rail travel in Canada, the United States, Australia, New Zealand, and Japan.

Cook's *Timetable* contains schedules for European trains and connecting ferry/bus routes, features of the trains and maps of the train routes, plus additional information such as visa requirements and time zones.

EQUIPMENT AND ACCOMMODATIONS ON EUROPEAN TRAINS

Seating on European trains is divided into first- and second-class sections. First class is more expensive than second class and offers the passenger more room and usually fewer passengers.

Intracountry trains rarely need to travel overnight, so sleeping accommodations are usually only found on long-distance trains. For overnight trips, the following types of sleeping accommodations are available: second-class couchette, first-class couchette, first-class bedrooms, or second-class bedrooms.

The *couchette* is an open bunk with pillow and blanket. For a small charge, you have room to stretch out, but no privacy. In a second-class couchette, there are six couchettes per compartment, three on each side of the aisle. In a first-class couchette, there are four couchettes per compartment, two on each side of the aisle. Couchettes are reserved without regard to sex of the individuals occupying them.

First-class *bedrooms* sleep one or two passengers; second-class bedrooms sleep two or three. All bedrooms have a washstand. Toilets are located at either end of the car (look for "WC" or water closet).

RESERVATIONS ON EUROPEAN TRAINS

Seat reservations are not required on many European trains, and an additional fee is charged when a seat reservation is made. This fee is not refundable should the passenger have a change of plans. Reservations are recommended, however, during holiday periods, in the summer, or if the trip exceeds two hours. It is not possible to make a reservation on some trains; on other trains, reservations are mandatory. Reservations are required on the Rapidos in Italy, Express trains in Spain, and the TGV in France. It is absolutely necessary to make advance reservations for bedrooms or couchette accommodations.

FOOD SERVICE ON EUROPEAN TRAINS

Most long-distance trains serve food onboard. Dining cars require a reservation. Other food service options include a self-service meal in a buffet car or a snack in the bar car. There are also vendors who roll miniselections of snacks and sandwiches past your seat on the train.

At many stations en route, there are buffets where passengers can dine if they are changing trains. You may find vendors selling food and drink through the train windows as the train rolls through a station. It is also common to see passengers who have packed a lunch and brought it onboard with them. Bottled drinking water is a good idea because some trains do not have potable water available.

FARES

From the earlier discussion of Amtrak fares, you remember that the basic fare buys a coach seat. This is comparable to second class in Europe. On Amtrak, an additional accommodation charge buys club car seating or a sleeping accommodation. In Europe, this additional charge, which is usually a percentage increase, buys first-class seating. Many of the premier long-distance trains also charge a supplement above basic fares. Sleeping accommodations are, of course, an extra charge. As a general rule, you should usually expect to pay more for comfort and speed.

Most European railroads offer many discounted fares. If your client is traveling in only one country, check with that railroad for its discount plans. Many individual countries have passes for travel within that country. If the itinerary calls for several countries to be visited, the Eurailpass is probably the best buy, rather than piecing together several point-to-point tickets or rail passes from several different countries.

EURAILPASS AND FLEXIPASS

The Eurailpass is good for unlimited first-class train travel for adults (second-class for youth) in 17 countries: Austria, Belgium, Denmark, Finland, France, Germany, Greece, Hungary, Italy, Luxembourg, Netherlands, Norway, Portugal, Republic of Ireland, Spain, Sweden, and Switzerland. It can be purchased as a consecutive-day pass or a Flexipass. The consecutive-day pass is valid for a number of days (e.g., 15 or 21 days) in a row. The Flexipass, on the other hand, allows travel within a time period, such as five days within a two-month period.

The Eurail Select Pass provides unlimited rail travel in the five most popular countries—Germany, Switzerland, France, Italy, and Spain. A traveler may choose 5, 6, 8, 10, or 15 days of first-class travel (second-class for youth) within a two-month period. For an extra fee, two additional countries from a list of associated countries may be added.

Eurailpass must be purchased in North America. To validate the pass, it must be presented at a ticket window prior to the first journey.

A rail pass does not guarantee a seat. Most trains are open seating and a seat reservation is not mandatory. Seat reservations are required on most high-speed trains, such as the TGV, and on many long-distance trains. It is also wise to consider making a seat reservation for travel during peak travel periods. Sleepers or couchettes always require advance reservations and additional charges.

The Eurailpass is an excellent buy for travelers planning to visit several European countries. Its advantages include unlimited travel on more than 100,000 miles of rail lines, plus the ability to go where and when desired. Because the pass is all you need to travel, there is no need to wait in line at stations to get tickets for the next leg of the trip. European railroads service the smallest hamlets to the largest tourist spots, and the passenger has an unequaled opportunity to enjoy the scenery and meet the local people when traveling by train. The passes are commissionable at 10 percent to travel counselors.

An information-packed Web site is http://www.raileurope.com. Rail Europe is a distributor of European rail products in North America. Their Web site contains information on rail passes, point-to-point tickets, the Eurostar channel train, and rail networks of every European country. Find train schedules, destinations, frequencies, fares, and much more.

BRITRAIL PASS You may have noticed that England, Scotland, Wales, and Northern Ireland are excluded from the Eurailpass. British Railways offers its own BritRail pass for travel in the United Kingdom.

Like the Eurailpass, a BritRail pass is flexible and economical for travel on British Rails' 15,000 daily trains. The pass must be purchased outside of Great Britain.

The BritRail pass may be purchased for 4 days, 8 days, 15 days, 22 days, or one month for either first-class or standard travel. Seat reservations are additional and, although not usually required, reservations are recommended for travel on certain peak days, holidays, and summer Saturdays. Supplements for overnight accommodations are a flat fee per person. Reservations for overnight accommodations are required, and it is recommended that these be made well in advance of travel.

British Rail offers special prices for three, four, or seven days of unlimited travel around London by bus or on the "Tube" (underground or subway). This pass is called the London Plus Pass. Escorted rail tours through England, Scotland, and Wales, as well as sailing trips to Ireland and the Continent, a Paris adventure, and the BritFrance Railpass are more of the options offered by British Rail. The BritRail pass is commissionable.

Trains in Japan

The Japanese National Railway is known for its size, speed, and service. In a country about the size of California, there are 26,000 trains a day. Travel on any express train requires payment of a surcharge (which is refunded if the train arrives at its destination more than two hours late).

Japan's most famous Express trains are the *Shinkansen* or "*Bullet Trains.*" Shinkansen trains travel at speeds of 300 kilometers per hour, and in nearly 40 years of service, serious accidents are very rare. While carrying over 6 billion passengers during those 40 years, these trains also manage to be extremely punctual.

An extensive network of Limited Express (L'EX) trains link the Shinkansen with many other cities. Japan Railways (and other companies) operate at least 30,000 trains daily. In urban areas you will find crowded but efficient commuter lines that link suburbs with downtown areas. In metropolitan areas, trains run with astonishing frequency. For example, on the Yamanote Line, a loop line circling downtown Tokyo, trains run every three minutes, all day. Services on Bullet Trains include dining cars as well as food vendors who sell both Japanese and "western" food.

Long-distance trains in Japan have sleeping accommodations in addition to seating. Class A consists of roomettes for one person and double compartments. Class B provides two-berth and three-berth compartments.

The traveler on Japan's rail system may choose from an array of discounted fares or a Japan Railpass. The Railpass, which must be purchased outside of Japan, allows unlimited travel on trains, buses, and ferries of the Japanese National Railway. Passes are valid for 7, 14, or 21 days. Tickets and rail passes are commissionable to travel counselors.

PRIVATE RAIL CARS AND PRIVATE LUXURY TRAINS

The early to mid-1900s were a period of romance and glamour for the railroads. Today, rail enthusiasts are purchasing and restoring some of the most elegant of the equipment from this era to its original, historic beauty. Privately owned rail cars and entire trains can now be enjoyed by anyone seeking to relive these days of luxury rail travel. An example of one of these projects is the *American Orient Express.* This train is a collection of vintage cars assembled from museums and private collections throughout America. Since 1997, these beautifully restored cars have made several scheduled trips annually with tours that include Colonial Mexico and the Copper Canyon, the American Southwest, National Parks of the west, the antebellum South, and a coastal culinary adventure. Although this type of experience will not appeal to the price conscious, it is becoming increasingly popular not only for its history, but also for the elegance and excellent service that are part of the trip.

Luxurious train travel is not exclusively American, nor is it new. Perhaps the most famous train in the world, the *Orient Express,* was known as the ultimate in luxury. Its first journey was made in 1883 from Paris to Istanbul, an 1,800-mile trip that took almost four days! Due to the general decline in interest in rail travel, the *Orient Express* made its final run in 1977. It has since been returned to its original splendor and is now a part of the Orient Express Hotels, Ltd. Group. In addition to the Venice-to-London rail routes, Orient Express operates the Royal Scotsman luxury rail in Scotland, the Eastern and Oriental Express in southeast Asia, rail journeys through Peru, and several luxury rail trips in the United Kingdom.

South Africa's *Blue Train* is so named because of its sapphire-blue carriages. Its history goes back to the 1880s, but it became today's splendid luxury train in 1997. Since then, it has won "World's Leading Luxury Train" four consecutive years.

The train's most frequent route is between Pretoria and Cape Town, where on average it travels three times a week. This journey is a distance of about 1,000 miles through some breathtaking scenery. The *Blue Train* also operates between Pretoria and Victoria Falls in Zimbabwe, Cape Town and Port Elizabeth (Garden Route), and Pretoria and Hoedspruit in Mpumalanga/Eastern Transvaal (Valley of the Olifants/Safari land) on a less-frequent basis.

Approximately 80 passengers can be accommodated on each train. Each suite has its own shower or bath, and the beds have been custom designed for the *Blue Train*. An interesting feature of the train is a camera mounted on the engine that broadcasts "engineer's eye" pictures to a wide screen in the Club Car.

There are many other luxury and specialty trains throughout the world. *The Andalusian Express,* a restored luxury train, makes two- and three-day trips beginning and ending in Barcelona, Spain, and including the Basque country. The *Great South Pacific Express* travels Eastern Australia and offers its passengers great comfort and incomparable viewing of Australia's wild treasures such as kangaroos, crocodiles, Great Barrier Reef, tropical birds,

? What Would You Do?

Michele and her sister Megan really want to take the train from their home in Chicago to Seattle. When you tell them it will take two nights on the train each way, they decide they can't take that much time. What would you do?

1. What is the objection that Michele and Megan have with the trip you offered them?
2. Because Michele and Megan have expressed this objection, would you assume they are not interested in taking Amtrak and end the conversation?
3. What is another way you could handle this objection?
4. How could you arrange a trip for Michele and Megan so it doesn't take them as much time, but still uses Amtrak?

? What Would You Do?

Mr. and Mrs. Alan Kanervo have asked you to plan an Amtrak trip for them. They wish to depart from Chicago on July 14, stopping in St. Paul, MN, to visit Mrs. Kanervo's brother for two days and going on to Seattle where they plan to stay for five days. On their return trip, they would like to stop in Salt Lake City to visit their granddaughter before returning to Chicago. They must be back in Chicago by July 31. What would you do?

1. What type of Amtrak fare do you recommend for this trip? Why did you choose this fare?
2. The Kanervos ask you to price both coach accommodations and the least expensive sleeping accommodation. Which type of sleeping accommodation do you recommend? Why?
3. Can the fare you recommended in question 1 be combined with the sleeper? What is the total cost for their Amtrak trip?
4. Are meals included in the fare you recommended in question 1? Are meals included in the sleeping accommodation you recommended in question 2?

and urban centers as well. Although not luxury service, the *Flam Line* in Norway is interesting because it is a tribute to modern engineering. Eighty percent of the Flam railway has a gradient of 55 percent, and there are 20 tunnels, many constructed as loops winding in and out of mountains. Each carriage is equipped with five different brakes, each capable of stopping the entire train!

SUMMARY

Trains are a travel option that will not appeal to everyone, just as a cruise will not appeal to every traveler. However, rail travel is worth considering for a number of reasons. No matter what country you may be in, train travel is a great way to see the local sights and meet the local people. Train travel also offers scenic experiences that are not available by any other mode of transport.

Some trains, such as Amtrak's Metroliner and Acela, are extremely practical and efficient. Often trains are the better economic alternative to other forms of transportation. Still other trains are known for the richness of their tradition and service. History buffs, and others, relish the refurbished trains that take us back to the luxury age of train travel.

Fares, accommodations, and services vary depending on the part of the world in which you are traveling. In general, rail passengers can expect to find coach travel as well as sleeping accommodations. The distance the train travels often dictates the type of accommodations that are available. For example, the longer the distance, the more likely it is that the train carries sleeping cars.

All Amtrak trains, and most of the world's trains, offer food service, from full dining car service to lounge cars with snacks and sometimes both. Again, the distance the train travels usually dictates the type of food service available.

Amtrak's climbing ridership and record-breaking revenues are evidence that many of today's travelers are seeking alternatives. There is perhaps no other form of transportation that brings the traveler closer to the spirit of history and of going places.

For additional Travel and Tourism resources, go to http://www.hospitality-tourism.delmar.com.

PLEASE COMPLETE THE CHAPTER REVIEW QUESTIONS NOW.

EXERCISE 12-1 Amtrak Case Study

Mr. and Mrs. Birany heard from their neighbor about a trip they took "out west" on Amtrak. Mrs. Birany contacts her travel consultant for more information. These are her questions:

1. Can we go from Milwaukee to Seattle on the train?

2. How long will it take to get there?

3. Do we have to sit up the whole way or are there beds?

4. Do we have to bring our own food?

Go to http://www.amtrak.com to answer these questions. You may also order Amtrak timetables and other materials from the Web site.

EXERCISE 12-2 Amtrak Fares

Use the fare display below to answer the questions in this exercise.

```
CHILAX09SEP
TH   09SEP     320P FARES VALID CHI-LAX
ONE WAY ACCOMMODATION CHARGE
Roomette              322.00
Bedroom               661.00
Accessible Bedroom    432.00
Family Bedroom        493.00
FULL RAIL FARE CALCULATED
     AMOUNT         MAX    LSTTVL
1    142.00   OW    180    07MAR    NOT AVAILABLE 1JUN-31AUG
2    174.00   OW    180    07MAR    ONE-WAY SPECIAL FARE
3    259.00   OW    45     08SEP    ONE-WAY REGULAR FARE
4    299.00   ZN    45     23OCT    NO TRVL 16JUN-20AUG 15DEC-2JAN
5    359.00   ZN    45     23OCT    ALL-YEAR EXPLORE AMERICA
```

1. A family bedroom (FB) is $493. The rail fare is $259. How much will it cost Mr. and Mrs. Lucas and their two children, ages 6 and 10, to travel one-way between Chicago and Los Angeles in a family bedroom? _____

2. Does the fare you gave to the Lucas family include meals? _____

_____

3. If the Lucas family decides to take their one-year-old son, Joe, is there an additional rail fare? _____

_____

4. Describe the differences between a family bedroom and a bedroom to Mr. and Mrs. Lucas. _____

_____

_____

5. What is the price *difference* between a family bedroom and a bedroom? _____

_____

6. Using the Explore America fare between Chicago and Los Angeles allows round-trip travel with three stopovers for $359. Could Mr. and Mrs. Lucas use this promotional fare for their trip in July? _____ Why or why not? _____

_____

7. If their date of travel is March 15, could the Lucas family use the special one-way rail fare of $174? _____

Why or why not? _____

_____

Review Questions

1. What is the name of the Amtrak service that carries both passengers and automobiles? _____

   Between what two cities does this service operate? _____

2. List four features of the Eurailpass:

   a. _____   b. _____

   c. _____   d. _____

3. When traveling on a long-distance train in the United States, is it necessary to get off the train to eat meals? _____

4. The Japanese National Railway is famous for its _____ trains that often travel at speeds of 156 mph.

5. What city is Amtrak's "hub" in the Midwest? _____

6. High-speed rail corridors are a major focus for Amtrak. What is the name of the all-electric train that services the corridor between Boston and New York? _____

7. Does the price of a sleeping accommodation on Amtrak include meals? _____

8. Describe the difference between a standard bedroom and a family bedroom on Amtrak's Superliner equipment. _____

   _____

9. If the one-way rail fare between Los Angeles and Seattle is $265 per person and the price of a deluxe bedroom is $250 each way, what is the total cost for two adults to travel round-trip between these cities in the deluxe bedroom? _____

10. Using the fares given in question 13, what is the cost for one adult and a 12-year-old child? _____

11. What is the name of the pass that allows rail travel on over 28,000 miles of railways in the United States and Canada?

    _____

12. Does the Eurailpass guarantee a seat on any train? _____

13. Name the luxury train that travels between Venice and London. _____

14. List three reasons to travel by rail. _____

    a. _____

    b. _____

    c. _____

CHAPTER 13

Consolidators, Charters, Group Sales, and Travel Insurance

OBJECTIVES

At the conclusion of this chapter, you should be able to

- explain the pros and cons of using consolidators.
- describe the positives and negatives of charter travel.
- understand the sales potential for groups.
- define the general steps of making a group sale.
- explain the importance of travel insurance.
- understand the agency's liability when travel insurance is declined and the importance of an insurance waiver.

KEY TERMS

American Society of Travel Agents (ASTA)
bulk rates
consolidator
Cruise Lines International Association (CLIA)
dry lease
insurance waiver
National Tour Association (NTA)

passenger contract
preexisting conditions
preferred vendor list
private charter
public charter
rider
socialized medicine
trip protection

United States Air Consolidators Association (USACA)
United States Tour Operators Association (USTOA)
vacation protection
vendor bankruptcy
waiver of responsibility
wet lease

CONSOLIDATORS

A consolidator, is a company that purchases inventory from travel vendors at reduced rates and offers them for sale to travel counselors and the traveling public.

The consolidator can obtain these reduced rates, also known as bulk rates, because it enters into a special agreement with the travel vendor. The agreement between the vendor and consolidator identifies the rates, obligations, responsibilities, and a minimum sales volume. The vendors are not interested in working with a consolidator unless the consolidator can sell a substantial volume.

Another way a consolidator obtains seats, rooms, and cabins is by purchasing unsold inventory, usually close to the departure date. As you might imagine, an airline would not assume that the inventory on a flight, for example, would not sell out six months in advance. However, the airline may want to release unsold inventory two weeks before departure because there is less chance of this inventory being sold through regular channels.

Consolidators can handle any travel products: airline seats, hotel rooms, cruise cabins, rental cars, and even space on tours. However, most consolidators concentrate on air travel and do not offer other types of travel products. The vast majority of air consolidators offer international destinations only, but a few companies handle flights within the United States as well.

It is also possible for a travel agency to become a consolidator. Agencies that have high international air sales may contact one or more airlines. Negotiations take place and topics covered include fare, sales quotas, liability, responsibility, booking procedures, and so on. Because most travel agencies cannot commit to the sales volumes required under these circumstances, most travel agencies simply use existing consolidators rather than becoming one themselves.

Although having the potential for substantial savings, *using consolidators may also have a negative side.* Consider the following:

- Consolidators usually have cancellation or change penalties in addition to those of the airline being used.
- Advance seat assignments may not be allowed.
- Tickets may not count toward the client's frequent flyer membership.
- The client may have to use an airline with which he is not familiar.
- An unusual routing may be required, possibly with more than one plane change.
- Refunds may not be possible if the consolidator goes out of business.
- The airline on the ticket may not accept the ticket if the consolidator goes out of business.

Does this mean that it is a good idea to avoid consolidators? No! There are many reputable consolidators, ones that have been in business for many years and consistently provide value and service, and using a consolidator makes it possible for a small travel agency or independent agent to compete with the larger agencies in offering low fares for international travel. Most travel agencies have a preferred vendor list and certain consolidators are included. This list identifies companies the agency deals with on a consistent basis because these vendors offer value, quality, and service. However, if the travel counselor is considering a new consolidator, the counselor must do appropriate research on the company.

A reliable consolidator reference source can be found at http://www.jaxfax.com. This reference includes information such as departure frequency, type of transportation (scheduled air or charter), minimum and maximum fares, and booking information.

One of the most important indicators of a consolidator's stability is the length of time the company has been in business. Obviously, a company would not still exist if it failed to offer products at a good value and provide customer service along the way. The length of time the consolidator has been in business should not be the only criterion the travel counselor uses, but it is certainly an important one.

Travel counselors should also take into consideration a consolidator's annual sales volume and sales policy. A large sales volume indicates that many agencies are using the consolidator, which would not be the case if the product or service were not acceptable. Some consolidators sell to the general public as well as through travel agencies. In other words, these consolidators are in direct competition with travel agencies. Most travel experts agree that travel agencies should avoid consolidators that sell to the general public and support consolidators that work with agencies exclusively. Following is a list of a few of the largest consolidators:

Consolidator	Year Begun	Sales in Millions	Web address
Air Tickets	1952	25 +	http://www.airtickets.com
American Travel Abroad	1946	25 +	http://www.amta.com
C & H International	1982	25 +	http://www.cnhintl.com
DER Travel Service	1977	25 +	http://www.dertravel.com
Goway Travel	1970	25 +	http://www.goway.com
McAbee Tours	1988	25 +	http://www.mcabee.com
Overseas Express, Inc.	1985	10–25	http://www.ovex.com
Pacific Gateway, Inc.	1986	35 +	http://www.pacificgateway.com
Solar Tours	1984	25 +	http://www.solartours.com
Sunny Land Tours	1969	10–25	http://www.sunnylandtours.com
Trans Am Travel	1980	25 +	http://www.transamtravel.com
TraveNet, Inc.	1989	10–25	http://www.travnet.net

Another important indicator of a consolidator's stability is the organizations to which it belongs. Appointment by the Airline Reporting Corporation (ARC), International Air Transport Association (IATA), and International Airlines Travel Agent Network (IATAN) means that the consolidator has fulfilled and complies with a variety of strict regulations and policies.

To be a member of the United States Tour Operators Association (USTOA), the consolidator must comply with a specific code of ethics, maintain $1 million liability insurance, and $1 million bond for USTOA's Consumer Protection Plan. It is interesting to note that many consolidators hold individual bonds as well. Other organizations to which a consolidator may belong include the American Society of Travel Agents (ASTA), National Tour Association (NTA), United States Air Consolidators Association (USACA), Cruise Lines International Association (CLIA), and Pacific Asia Travel Association (PATA).

Profit from Consolidators

Using consolidators can, in many cases, save the client a great deal of money, but it can be very lucrative for the travel agency as well. Some consolidators state airfares as a *net rate,* not including commission. The travel counselor adds his profit and quotes the total to the client. Depending on the travel agency, the profit can be a fixed dollar amount or a percentage. How much the travel agency earns on a net consolidator fare is totally up to the travel agency.

Web Activity

Your clients, Matsuka Takahashi and Noriyuki Shigeru, will be traveling from Los Angeles to Tokyo one month from today. They have asked for business class and will be staying in Tokyo for 14 nights. Research at least five consolidators' Web sites for the lowest business class fare, additional costs, if any, and credit card fees. If possible, list the airline, flight number, and flight times. Also attempt to learn by what method and when the tickets will be sent to your travel agency.

Other consolidators use airfares that include a *commission.* Depending on the consolidator and airline being used, the commission can be up to 10 or 15 percent.

Consolidator Policies

Typically, consolidators may have a variety of rules and policies that are different from simply selling an airline ticket through regular channels. A travel counselor who frequently sells the same consolidator is already familiar with this consolidator's policies. However, when a consolidator is used only occasionally or is being used for the first time, the travel counselor should ask about and be comfortable with several points including:

- Are agency checks accepted, and if so, is an escrow account used? An escrow account requires that funds remain on deposit until the service has been provided.
- Are all classes (e.g., first, business, and coach) offered?
- Does the agency receive credit with the airline for the sale? Future airline override commissions are dependent on the travel agency's sales volume.
- How far in advance of travel are the tickets sent to the agency?
- Is the fare net or does it include commission?
- Is there a delivery charge for tickets and what delivery method is used?
- Is there a fee for credit card transactions?
- Must travel originate in the United States?
- Of what organizations is the consolidator a member (ARC, IATA, IATAN, ASTA)? A non-ARC appointed consolidator probably obtains tickets from another consolidator.
- What fare amount is shown on the ticket (e.g., actual fare, full fare, zero, "bulk")?
- What methods can be used for booking (e.g., GDS, Internet, phone, fax)?
- When is the flight confirmed, at the time of booking or when payment is received?
- Which company's name appears on the ticket, the consolidator or the travel agency?

Helpful Industry Web Sites

American Society of Travel Agents: **http://www.astanet.com**

Association of British Travel Agents: **http://www.abta.com**

Association of Retail Travel Agents: **http://www.artaonline.com**

Australian Federation of Travel Agents: **http://www.afta.com.au**

Canadian Institutes of Travel Counselors: **http://www.citc.ca**

National Association of Commissioned Travel Agents: **http://www.nacta.com**

Outside Sales Support Network: **http://www.ossn.com**

Travel Agents Forum: **http://www.travelhacker.com**

United States Tour Operators Association: **http://www.ustoa.com**

There are many things to consider when using consolidators. However, consolidators can be a source of low-cost travel and increased travel agency revenue. Using consolidators simply requires a bit more thought and investigation to ensure the lowest risk and inconvenience to both the client and the agency.

As an added precaution for travel agencies, it is not uncommon for travel counselors to ask clients purchasing consolidator tickets to sign a waiver of responsibility. This waiver states that the client fully understands and agrees to all policies regarding purchase, payment, cancellation, and so on. The waiver of responsibility should protect the agency against loss from client litigation.

CHARTERS

All charters fall into one of two categories, public or private. A public charter is usually organized by a tour operator or airline and is then marketed to travel counselors or the general public. Space on the charter is booked on an individual basis and the selling price generally has the agency's commission built in. A private charter can be organized by the group leader, travel counselor, or vendor and is for the exclusive use of the group. Any type of transportation, air, motorcoach, rail, and cruise can be chartered.

Both types of charters have the possibility for reasonable fares and more convenient schedules than those offered by scheduled vendors. However, there are some drawbacks.

Charter airlines may offer a flight to any given destination only on certain days of the week or on a once-a-week basis. This feature allows little client choice or flexibility. Because there is usually only one flight each day, any flight delay means that passengers must simply wait. There is no option of taking a later flight. Sometimes a flight delay can easily run into the following day, especially if an aircraft must be replaced.

Generally speaking, charter airlines and scheduled airlines have no agreements to work together. This fact indicates that should a charter flight be cancelled or should the charter company go out of business, it is unlikely that scheduled airlines will transport the passengers without requiring the purchase of a ticket. When flight departures are delayed because of weather, scheduled airlines usually have priority over charter airlines. Thus, charter passengers will probably wait far longer for departure than those traveling on scheduled airlines.

Aircraft Charters

A private aircraft charter provides an aircraft and crew for a specific group that shares an affinity or common bond. The group leader can go directly to the charter or

scheduled airline or can make arrangements through a travel counselor.

A private charter affords the group several distinct advantages. The group selects the departure time and the flight can be nonstop or direct, even to obscure destinations. The group can decide if in-flight meals and beverages are desired and select what is served. The group can have preassigned seating. Ground transportation at the destination for the group can be ready and waiting and hotels, sightseeing trips, and meals can be part of the charter package.

Under normal circumstances, each member of the group pays less than if regular scheduled air transportation were used. If, however, the group decreases in size, the per-person cost will go up. The price given by the charter or scheduled airline is for the aircraft without regard to how full or how empty it may be.

From a travel counselor's point of view, arranging a private aircraft charter may sound difficult; it isn't! Once the travel counselor has determined the client's needs and desires, a call to the charter or scheduled airline company for a price quote and to check availability is the next step. The company may have to do extensive calculations and call the counselor back with the quote. Remember, this quote is the net amount. If the travel agency intends to make any money for the services the counselor is providing, the counselor must *mark up* the quote. In other words, the counselor must add the agency's profit to the quote before giving the group the total price. Because charters are usually substantially less expensive than scheduled service, the markup can be 10 to 40 percent and still result in a savings to the client.

The airline prepares a contract that details all aspects of the charter, responsibilities and limitations between the airline and agency, and payment schedules. The travel counselor reviews, signs, and returns a copy of the contract to the airline.

On a date dictated by the airline, a deposit is required. The amount of deposit is set forth in the contract and is usually a flat dollar amount per person. The group prepares a check payable to the travel agency. The agency deposits the check and issues an agency check to the airline.

As departure day nears, the final payment is required. Again, the group writes a check to the agency and the agency deposits the check. Before the agency pays the airline, the agency's profits are deducted. Yes, it really is that simple and can be quite profitable.

A public aircraft charter is quite different from a private group. The charter company organizes and markets a flight to Cancun, Mexico, for example. Brochures are printed and distributed to travel agencies. The trip may have a price for air only, and a choice of hotel packages. Because this is a public charter, anyone may purchase a seat or package. The prices on the brochure have the travel counselor's commission built in—usually 10 percent.

Again, the advantages are price and convenience. In most cases, the flight is less expensive than scheduled service and the flight may often be direct or nonstop. This feature is especially nice if the passenger lives in a city where flights to Cancun (or other destinations) are all double connections.

Each public charter traveler is required to sign a passenger contract. The contract includes information about cancellation by the operator, cancellation by the passenger, deposit, final payment, liability, baggage allowance, and responsibility. It is the travel counselor's responsibility to advise the passenger of this information before obtaining his signature.

Payments by cash or check between the client, travel agency, and charter company are handled in the same way as for private charters. The travel agency's commission is withheld before the agency issues its check for final payment. When clients pay by credit card, the card type and number are given to the charter company. Usually the charter company obtains the approval code and processes the charge. Commission checks from the vendor are usually sent to the travel agency after the client has completed travel.

Motorcoach, Rail, and Cruise Charters

The same basic principals apply to motorcoach, rail, and cruise charters as with aircraft charters. Motorcoach, rail, and cruises are usually chartered by a private group and afford the group a good price, selected departure times, en route hotels, sightseeing, meals, and so forth.

Private charters of these modes of transportation require negotiation and contracts between the vendor and travel agency. Payment schedules are defined and all-included features, responsibility, liability, etc. are in the contract details.

The price quoted by the motorcoach, rail, or cruise company may be net, so the travel counselor must add on any profit the agency wishes to make. The percent of markup is up to the agency. Deposits and final payments are handled the same as with aircraft charters.

Yachts, sailboats, and barges can be chartered without a crew, commonly called a dry lease. A charter that includes the services of a crew is often called a wet lease. In fact, these two terms are used for any mode of transportation being chartered to identify the inclusion of crew services. For these charters, the client may have to produce a license to operate the boat or take a short training course from the charter operator. This type of charter company can be located through local tourist boards, visitor's bureaus, and chambers of commerce.

It is an excellent idea when dealing with charter companies to make sure the company is a member of the National Tour Association (NTA). NTA members are required to hold a $1,000,000 bond, which protects the passengers against financial loss. Members are also required to hold a $1,000,000 liability insurance policy, again protecting the passengers. By not verifying the financial reliability of the charter company, the travel agency is opening itself up to potential lawsuits from passengers who have suffered a loss. Membership in other organizations, such as USTOA, is a definite plus.

Travel Agency Charters

Some travel agencies organize and market their own charter trips. When this is done, the agency is gambling on the sale of the seats. If all seats are sold, the agency stands to make a handsome profit. On the other hand, the agency could lose a substantial sum of money if all seats are not sold.

Once the origin, destination, and departure date have been determined, the agency contacts one or more transportation vendors. All aspects of transportation, such as cost, included features, departure time, and payment schedules, are negotiated and decided. A contract is signed and returned to the vendor.

Arrangements with other travel suppliers may be necessary to complete the package. These include accommodations, ground transportation, sightseeing and entrance fees, and meals. Concluding these arrangements is much the same as for the transportation vendor.

After all arrangements are made and a per-person price is determined, the travel agency designs and produces brochures and arranges for advertising. As the travel agency receives bookings and payments, individual client information is compiled into master lists. At a date established by each vendor, the travel agency provides the vendors with specific client information and name lists.

As you can see, much work goes into a travel agency charter; however, the agency has greater control over its profit percentage, and if all seats are sold, the agency revenue is substantial.

Helpful Industry Web Sites

Charter Airlines: **http://www.aircharternet.com**

National Motorcoach Directory: **http://www.motorcoach.com**

United Motorcoach Association: **http://www.uma.org**

GROUP SALES

The potential for selling group travel is everywhere. Schools, churches, business organizations, athletic clubs, historical societies, and senior citizens are only a few of the hundreds of existing groups. Groups travel together for many reasons, but most often a common interest is the impetus behind a group's desire to travel. Travel for group members is an opportunity to explore their interest with others who share it. Most groups have one person, or perhaps a few people, who are given the responsibility for setting up the trip. For the travel counselor, selling to a group can be rewarding, both financially and personally.

Because of the enormous amount of work that goes into marketing to groups and making all of the travel arrangements, some travel agencies choose not to handle group travel, or if they do, they choose to work through a tour operator to make the actual travel arrangements. A tour operator works with groups all the time and has the necessary contacts to negotiate group rates and arrangements. A smaller group might be booked into an existing tour package. A larger group may have a "custom package." The tour operator takes care of hotel reservations, sightseeing, and other local arrangements. The travel agency handles the pretravel details such as making the group proposal to the group leaders, making a presentation to group members to sell the trip, and taking reservations, deposits, and final payments from group members.

Some travel agencies prefer to handle the entire group sales process themselves. This involves marketing to potential groups, making group presentations, putting together a proposal based upon the group's composition and interests, handling all travel arrangements, and may also involve personally escorting the group to its destination. As you can imagine, the potential for profit is greater, but so is the investment of time.

Regardless of the way group travel is organized, communication is an extremely important part of the process. In order to avoid misunderstandings, contracts are required between the travel agency and the tour operator, and between the travel agency and the group. A group contract details all aspects of the group sale and establishes a payment schedule. Keeping meticulous records for a group is essential. Every transaction and conversation should be documented. A group sale, by its very nature, requires that hundreds of details must be handled efficiently and perfectly.

One of the things group organizers often look for are *perks*. A perk can be anything from a tote bag or passport wallet imprinted with the group's name to private receptions or tours for group members. Sometimes a travel agency will pay the cost of perks, but more often, a tour operator or other vendor may have special local arrangements for a list of perks that can be offered for little or no cost. The larger or more high-end the group, the more deluxe will be the perk.

INSURANCE

Demand for travel insurance has been steadily increasing due to such global happenings as terrorist attacks, natural disasters, and financial instability in the industry. The first ever study of the purchase of travel insurance by consumers was conducted in 2005 on behalf of the U.S. Travel Insurance Association. The survey revealed that 17 million travelers spent over $1 billion on travel insurance in 2004.

Travel insurance is one of the most important, and sometimes, most overlooked value-added products a travel professional can offer. There are some very important reasons to offer travel insurance to every client:

1. Insurance protects the client's travel investment against financial loss.
2. Insurance protects the travel professional against claims stemming from the client's financial loss.
3. Insurance commissions to the travel professional range from 10 to 40 percent.

Cruise lines and tour operators together sell 40 percent of travel insurance, usually called trip protection or vacation protection. Insurance offered by cruise lines and tour operators is usually based on the length of the trip and is quite reasonably priced. Some airlines offer "Ticket Protector" insurance that will, for about 4 percent over the ticket price, provide a refund of the ticket price if cancellation is for a "covered reason." Insurance companies offer a wide array of travel insurance policies that can be sold by travel agencies. Travel agencies sell about 35 percent of all travel insurance policies. These policies generally cover trip cancellation or interruption, health and accidents, baggage, flights, vendor bankruptcy, identity theft, and terrorist acts.

Helpful Industry Web Sites

Major Travel Insurance Companies

CSA Travel Protection: **http://www.csatravelprotection.com**

Travel Ex Insurance Services:
http://www.travelex-insurance.com,
http://www.totaltravelinsurance.com,
http://www.1travelinsurance.com

Travel Guard International: **http://www.travel-guard.com**

Trip Cancellation or Interruption Coverage

As you have learned, almost all travel products, including air, carry penalties for change and cancellation. Insurance that includes this coverage should be recommended for any travel product that carries a penalty, even an inexpensive excursion airfare. Typically, a client who purchases a $300 excursion fare (nonrefundable, $75 or more penalty for change) is not interested in insurance. However, a family of five buying the same type of ticket may look at insurance in a different light because they stand to lose a total of $1,500.

Generally, travelers are covered if they must cancel or interrupt their trip due to. . . . or the traveler's death, death of a traveling companion, an immediate family member, or business partner; or if the traveler is called for jury duty. It is interesting to note that some insurance covers trip cancellation simply if the traveler changes their mind and cancels the trip.

Medical situations that have existed prior to the purchase of insurance are called preexisting conditions. Insurance may not cover preexisting conditions so travel counselors must read the policy carefully. Of those insurance companies that do cover preexisting conditions, the purchase of the insurance must usually take place within one week of the trip purchase.

Health and Accident Coverage

While traveling inside the United States, most personal health insurance policies are effective. But, is the client covered while traveling outside the United States? In many cases, the traveler is not covered, not even by Medicare, unless he has purchased a special rider, which is added to his personal health insurance policy. Many U.S. corporations purchase this coverage for their employees who frequently travel internationally. However, the vast majority of travelers have no health insurance once outside the United States.

Almost all countries of the world have socialized medicine, where health care is free or available at a nominal cost to *citizens of that country*. There are usually reciprocal agreements between countries that have socialized medicine; that is, one country agrees to treat citizens of the other country, and vice versa. Because the United States does not have socialized medicine, the United States cannot have reciprocal agreements with other countries. This means that, legally, a U.S. citizen traveling abroad must pay for health care. However, as a gesture of good will, the country being visited may care for a U.S. citizen at no cost, but the government of that country is not legally bound to do so.

To be absolutely safe, additional health insurance for anyone traveling abroad is a must. Unfortunately, most people, including many travel counselors, do not seem to realize this fact.

Generally, most routine health matters are covered by insurance packages offered by vendors or purchased through major insurance companies. Typical exclusions include loss due to acts of war, suicide, armed forces training maneuvers, pregnancy, childbirth, and participating in dangerous activities.

The coverage of preexisting conditions must also be confirmed with regard to health and accident insurance. The travel counselor should read the policy carefully before attempting to explain the coverage to the client. Remember, each insurance company's policy on preexisting conditions varies.

Baggage Coverage

Common carriers, such as airlines, cruise lines, motorcoach companies, and so on, carry a certain amount of insurance on their passengers' baggage.

Generally, additional baggage coverage is included with insurance packages offered by travel vendors and major insurance companies. This coverage usually includes lost, damaged, or delayed baggage. Standard items not usually covered include cameras, jewelry, furs, money, credit cards, tickets, animals, and computer hardware and software. Additionally, baggage is not usually covered if the claim stems from acts of war, government seizure, or illegal transportation of goods.

Flight Coverage

As an added service to their clients, some travel agencies automatically provide flight insurance with every ticket or e-tkt they sell, at no cost to the client. Flight insurance is usually included in packages offered by major insurance companies, or it can be purchased as a separate item.

Generally, flight insurance covers the traveler while on a scheduled airline, military transport, transportation operated by a scheduled airline, and while on airport premises before boarding or after deplaning a scheduled airline's flight. If the client is traveling on a charter flight, the travel counselor should read the policy carefully because the client may not be covered.

Flight insurance does not cover loss due to acts of war, suicide, or participating in dangerous activities, such as parachute jumping. As you might imagine, the insurance is void if the client is committing or attempting to commit a felony.

Coverage for Bankruptcies and Defaults

The likelihood that a traveler will encounter difficulties resulting from a vendor bankruptcy or default seems to be increasing. Travelers who do not take out specific insurance are not protected. Although U.S. airlines are required to honor tickets for an airline that ceases operation, they can charge ticket holders up to an additional $50 each way, and flights are on a "space available" basis only. While some travel insurance covers bankruptcy or default, not all policies do. Be sure you know what coverage the customer is buying.

Coverage for Terrorist Acts or Identity Theft

According to the U.S. Travel Insurance Association, about 30 percent of leisure travelers purchase terrorism insurance. Incidents of terrorism in popular tourist destinations have created a demand for insurance. Many policies excluded terrorist attacks, but because of increased demand, have expanded their coverage to cover personal possessions, travel delays, and cancellation for a traveler caught up in a terrorist attack.

Identity theft and the personal expenses from the resulting turmoil are covered by a few travel insurance policies. Because identity theft has become much more of a concern for travelers, many more insurers are offering it. Policies include financial reimbursement as well as assistance to the traveler in untangling the damage that can result from having one's identity stolen. Coverage can be in effect for up to six months after returning home.

Other Means of Coverage

It is prudent to make any travel purchase using a credit card. Many credit card companies offer automatic coverage such as lost baggage insurance, flight insurance, or health and accident insurance just for using the card for purchasing travel. In addition, if a travel product is not delivered, such as in the case of a bankruptcy or default, the credit card company does not require its customer to pay for the product.

Sometimes personal homeowner's or renter's insurance will cover lost or damaged baggage while traveling. However, it is important to note that this coverage may extend only as far as the U.S. borders.

If travel is booked through a member of either the United States Tour Operator's Association or the National Tour Association, travelers may receive a refund for the cost of service not provided. The refund may be provided even if the member company does not declare bankruptcy or close its doors.

Insurance Waiver

Many travel agencies have learned, some the hard way, that they must protect themselves from client litigation that stems from financial loss. You can probably imagine a variety of sticky situations that could arise between a client and counselor. Some ways to accomplish this agency protection is to:

- require that all travel counselors fully discuss the vendor's policies regarding cancellation

- require that all travel counselors fully explain available insurance options
- require that all travel counselors obtain a signed waiver if insurance is declined

Generally, the insurance waiver states that the client has been advised of cancellation penalties, health care responsibilities, and so on; has been offered insurance; and has declined to purchase the insurance. The waiver includes space for the client's signature, counselor's signature, and date. As you might imagine, the insurance waiver can be the saving grace for the travel agency when a client is set on a lawsuit.

Case Studies

Marcus Tyler has purchased a cruise from you for himself and his wife, Carlotta. After you have explained the cruise line's cancellation policy and recommended insurance, Mr. Tyler mentions that his father had a heart attack last year and still isn't well.

1. Do you immediately sell insurance to Mr. Tyler?
2. Do you explain to Mr. Tyler that a cancellation due to his father's illness is not covered?
3. Do you learn more about insurance coverage for preexisting conditions?

Your clients, Pamela Griffin and Paulette Newman, have had to cancel their tour. Ms. Griffin and Ms. Newman purchased the tour and insurance from you three months ago. Ms. Griffin has been a diabetic since she was 10 years old and now she is in the hospital. She had a cut on her leg that didn't heal and all of the surrounding tissue is badly infected.

1. In what way, if any, is the current hospitalization related to Ms. Griffin's diabetes?
2. Will insurance offered by the tour operator cover the loss from this cancellation?
3. If you did not know about the diabetes when you sold the insurance, can you be held liable if your clients suffer a loss from this cancellation?

SUMMARY

Using a consolidator or charter for air travel can result in benefits to both the client and the travel professional. Consolidators and charters often earn the agency higher commissions than regular air sales, and the airfare offered by consolidators may be considerably less expensive than that found through regular channels. However, there are usually additional rules and limitations to travel sold by consolidators and charters, so it is extremely important that the travel professional be aware of all variations from regular airline rules. Because of these special features, many travel agencies require that consolidator and charter clients sign a waiver of liability.

Group sales can be a very lucrative niche for travel professsionals. For effective group sales, the travel professional must have excellent organizational, communication, and presentation skills. Successful group sales counselors know that this type of sale is a win-win situation.

An important factor of any travel product sale is insurance. Most of the lower-priced airfares, tours, and cruises usually carry penalties for change or cancellation, hence the need for insurance. Clients traveling outside of the United States may find that their health insurance is no longer valid, but fortunately, there is insurance for these circumstances. Understanding the various types of insurance coverage and the protection they provide gives travel professionals another way to be of service to their clients.

 For additional Travel and Tourism resources, go to http://www.hospitality-tourism.delmar.com.

PLEASE COMPLETE THE CHAPTER REVIEW QUESTIONS NOW.

Review Questions

1. How are consolidators able to obtain low airfares? _____
_____
_____

2. What reference sources are available for travel counselors selling consolidators? _____
_____
_____

3. Identify some possible negative aspects of using consolidators. _____
_____
_____
_____

4. Name as many indicators as you can that demonstrate a consolidator's stability. _____
_____
_____
_____

5. Identify some fees or charges that may be in addition to a consolidator's airfare. _____
_____

6. Why do some travel agencies require a waiver of responsibility for consolidator sales? ____
_____
_____

7. In what ways is a private aircraft charter beneficial to the client as well as the travel agency? ____
_____
_____

8. In what ways is selling a public charter beneficial to the client as well as the travel agency? ____
_____
_____

9. What modes of transportation can be chartered? _____
_____

10. What is a passenger contract? _____
_____

11. Explain the payment procedure between client, agency, and charter company when the client pays by check. ____
_____
_____

12. How does the agency receive its commission when the client pays for a charter package by credit card? _____

_____

_____

13. Why is the sale of travel insurance important to the client and the agency? _____

_____

_____

14. What does insurance offered by major insurance companies include that vendor policies do not? _____

_____

15. What are preexisting conditions and how might they affect insurance coverage? _____

_____

_____

GROUP SALES CASE STUDY

Your agency is making a presentation to a large senior citizens' group in your city. While talking to the club's president, you have learned that most of the members are quite active, and the group travels frequently. Many members are interested in American history and enjoy gambling and shopping. They try to travel economically but don't like to be uncomfortable. Trips of five to seven days are the most popular.

Your presentation must include two possible trips and answer the following questions:

1. What two destinations would you suggest?
2. What mode of transportation do you suggest?
3. What activities would be included in a five- to seven-day trip?
4. What type of lodging do you suggest?
5. What is the estimated cost of each trip per person?

Tours of the World

OBJECTIVES

At the conclusion of this chapter, you should be able to

- understand the importance of matching a tour product to the client.
- identify the different types of tours and the unique features of each type.
- understand what the client is actually purchasing.
- identify the benefits to the client who purchases a tour and to the counselor who makes the sale.
- define the terms associated with tours.
- know how to compare and select tour operators.
- read and interpret tour brochures and Web sites.

KEY TERMS

air add-on	escorted tour	local guide
cancellation fee	final payment	option date
components	gateway city	revision fee
deposit	ground operators	single supplement
document packet	host	special-interest tour
dynamic packaging	hosted tours	tour operator
escort	independent tours	triple reduction

A tour is made up of components, usually including transportation, transfers, lodging, meals, and sightseeing, with varying degrees of structure and varying numbers of components. A tour can be as simple as a day-trip to Atlantic City that includes a flight and transfers from the airport to a hotel, or as complex as a month-long around-the-world tour on a private jet that includes every necessity (and a great deal more). Between these two extremes is a vast selection of tour packages to suit any individual or group.

It is the business of a tour operator (sometimes referred to as a "tour wholesaler") to select places of interest and "package" them for travelers and then sell the package either directly to the consumer or through a travel agency. Sometimes travel agencies package and sell their own tours for an individual client or a group. Now, with assistance from the Internet, individual travelers and travel counselors can create a dynamic package, combining the best deals on flight (including charter flights), hotel, and car rental. The tour industry has never been a "one-size-fits-all" business, but today, with huge Internet search capabilities, tours offer more options and more customization than ever before. Understanding the tour industry means being able to assist your client in selecting the "right" tour or the best tour components. As with lodging, the wrong fit can ruin a vacation. The destination, budget, comfort level, and previous travel experience can all affect the *type of tour* that is appropriate.

TYPES OF TOURS

Independent Tours

Independent tours are the least structured tours available and participants are basically on their own. In fact, participants may not even realize that they are on a tour. Travel counselors and travelers alike refer to an independent tour as a package because no actual touring is involved.

Clients interested in an independent tour decide on the destinations, and the appropriate brochures offer a variety of departure dates, lengths of stay, and choice of hotels. Prices are listed for each hotel and length of stay; the departure date may affect the price. It is not uncommon for a tour brochure to show higher prices for departures on the weekend, days near a holiday, during high season, or during special events (e.g., Mardi Gras, Indianapolis 500).

Independent tour participants are completely free to do what they want. Travelers who want to relax on the beach for a week, shop at all the local establishments, or spend hours in the museums and galleries prefer independent tours because there is no set schedule. Many clients traveling to destinations in the United States, Mexico, and the Caribbean select independent tours instead of the other two types.

Hosted Tours

Hosted tours have minimal structure and offer the services of a host. The host is an employee of the tour company who is available during certain times, usually in an area of the hotel lobby. The host can assist with dinner reservations, theatre tickets, rental cars, and offer suggestions about sightseeing, shopping, and dining. The duties of a tour host are much like the duties of a hotel concierge.

Hosted tours include the same features as an independent tour but may also include some basic sightseeing. The host may go along during the sightseeing or a local guide may perform this duty. A tour guide lives in the destination area and joins the group only for a short period of time. Usually, the included sightseeing provides an overview of the area or city and generally lasts only a few hours. Famous sites are pointed out along the way and an inside visit to a popular attraction may be included.

Travelers who want the freedom to explore but realize that a tour representative would be helpful prefer hosted tours. Destinations in the United States, Mexico, the Caribbean, and major European cities are popular choices for hosted tours.

Escorted Tours

Escorted tours are the most structured and a tour company employee, called an escort, is with the group throughout the trip. Travelers selecting escorted tours usually do so because they appreciate the fact that the escort is always present and all sightseeing has previously been arranged. In fact, almost all details of the trip have been prearranged and the participants have nothing to worry about or plan on their own.

Escorted tours are usually very regimented and it is common for the day to begin with breakfast at 8:00 A.M. and conclude with dinner and a show at 9:00 P.M. Participants do not have to attend each planned activity, but there is no refund if they choose to skip an activity. Of course, if tour members want to spend an extra hour shopping and the group is moving on to another city, flexibility is not an option.

Sightseeing on escorted tours is very comprehensive and includes many of the most popular sites and attractions. Participants are usually taken to the attraction entrance and admission has already been paid. Even though the escort stays with the group, local tour guides may join the group for short periods of time. Local guides are experts on particular sites and enjoy sharing their knowledge and answering questions.

Travelers to most international destinations may prefer an escorted tour, simply for the peace of mind. Escorted tours are offered throughout the United States as well and may include visits to several states. Ground transportation on escorted tours is usually by motorcoach (see

FIGURE 14–1 Tourists enjoy experiencing local features, such as this double decker bus.

Figure 14–1) and in some destinations, ferries, trains, cruise ships, and other modes of transportation are used.

Special-Interest Tour

Another type of tour is the special-interest tour. These tours focus on a particular topic, activity, or type of client. A special-interest tour can be independent, hosted, or escorted, but most of them tend to be hosted or escorted.

Dynamic Tour Packaging

Sometimes a traveler wants a custom-fitted tour package that includes activities or components that are not part of a prepackaged tour. For example, a client wants to visit all of the national parks in Utah or all the pyramids in Egypt. Prepackaged tours may include some of these sites, but not all. For this client, a travel counselor would create a customized tour known as an FIT or foreign independent tour. (Although originally created for customized "foreign" tours, FIT is used to identify a domestic customized tour, too.) Arranging an FIT is time consuming and requires a great deal of expertise. The travel counselor has to know, or know how to find, companies to contact for each component, then make reservations, send payments, and so on. Because of the time involved in creating the FIT, and because each component is purchased individually instead of in bulk, FITs can often be more expensive than a prepackaged tour.

Once again, the Internet and the World Wide Web are changing things. Improvements in search engine capabilities have spurred the creation of dynamic packaging. Comparison services, such as http://www.travelsupermarket.com and others like it, are capable of searching a large group of suppliers to locate the best price for a flight, hotel, and car rental simultaneously and in less than 30 seconds! Travel professionals can utilize similar technology through a GDS. Travel counselors (and individuals) are able to customize a tour package in far less time than it took to arrange the FIT. Before dynamic travel comparison, hours of time were involved in locating the best components for the best prices.

Dynamic packaging appeals to anyone who is seeking to create his own tour package by choosing the components he wants and getting them at the best prices available. Also, those looking for a package, but not necessarily interested in a custom tour, are able to use the same Web sites, like http://www.travelsupermarket.com, to compare prepackaged tour offerings of several tour operators to make sure they get the best price available.

Like other segments of the travel industry, the tour industry is changing. The market for custom tour packaging is growing. Some tour operators, feeling the pinch of competition from dynamic packaging, have cut travel agent commissions in order to lower package prices for

Types of Special-Interest Tours

Types of Special-Interest Tours

- literary, famous authors
- archaeology
- ecology
- history
- art
- music
- special event (e.g., Mardi Gras, motor racing, Olympics)

Special-Interest Tours—Activities

- ecotours
- photography
- adventure (e.g., mountain biking, rock climbing, backpacking)
- sports (e.g., skiing, tennis, golf, scuba)
- shopping

Special-Interest Tours—Types of Clients

- physically challenged
- senior citizens
- gay and lesbian
- 18–35 year olds
- religious
- student

Types of Tours and Their Components

	Transportation	Transfers and Porterage	Accommodations	Meals	Sightseeing
Independent	probably	possibly	yes	no	no
Hosted	probably	probably	yes	no	minimal
Escorted	yes	yes	yes	yes	yes

consumers. Travel counselors have to decide whether to promote tour operators that pay the best commissions, or to make their profit by adding a service fee to the tour operator's package price. There remains, however, a large market for the traditional independent, hosted, and escorted prepackaged tours. The remainder of our discussion about tours will focus on these.

TOUR BENEFITS

Clients who purchase packaged tours enjoy several distinct benefits. One of the most important benefits is *volume discount*. Tour operators purchase components at bulk rates from airlines, hotels, attractions, restaurants, and so on. Of course, the tour operator adds his profit to the rates before establishing a tour price, but even so, the price is almost always less expensive than if the traveler purchased each component separately.

The fact that tours are *prepaid* is a benefit to the client for two reasons. First, the client can better plan budgeting around the known price of the tour. The total cost of the trip is more obvious when more components are included in the tour price. Secondly, by prepaying a tour to an international destination, the price may not be affected by currency fluctuation. Generally, once a tour is paid in full, the rate does not increase.

Travelers purchasing hosted or escorted tours enjoy a peace of mind not found in independent travel. Having a host or escort available for questions, problems, and advice is reassuring and comforting to many travelers. Escorted tour members have the added convenience of being taken to each attraction, hotel, or restaurant with all arrangements previously made. By relieving the tour members of the decision making and worrying about arrangements, peace of mind is increased.

Clients who purchase escorted tours receive the benefits of *reliable sightseeing* and *guaranteed entrances* (Figure 14–2). Experience has taught tour organizers which sites and attractions travelers prefer and should be included in the tour. For example, it is a sure bet that sites such as the Eiffel Tower, Arc de Triomphe, and Notre Dame will be included in a tour of Paris. Tour organizers also know when attractions are open and schedule visits accordingly. Entrance

fees are arranged and paid in advance by the tour operator, relieving the tour participant of yet another concern.

It is important to note that tour brochures must be read carefully with regard to sightseeing. Not all attractions include an inside visit. For example, a tour may stop at the Sydney Opera House for 10 minutes, long enough for photos, but not long enough to go inside. Most tour brochures indicate inside visits by using bold or italicized print. Experienced travel counselors have learned never to assume that an inside visit will be made and are careful not to read more into a brochure item than is there.

Selling tours provides travel counselors with benefits as well. Imagine counseling a client about transportation, making the booking, counseling about accommodations, making the booking, and so on. You are correct if you feel this is very time consuming. Selling a tour

FIGURE 14–2 Many cities provide street directories to assist tourists.

instead of arranging each component separately is far more *time efficient.*

Selling a packaged tour, as opposed to selling individual components, allows the travel counselor to maximize earnings. Commission, if it is paid, will be paid on the *total cost* of the tour. Since some elements of a tour, such as meals, sightseeing, and admissions are included in the total cost, they are commissionable. If purchased separately from the tour package, the travel counselor would not benefit.

The Best Type of Tour

The best type of tour is the one that suits the client's needs and wants as well as his level of travel experience and knowledge. A traveler who wants a package to the Bahamas so that he can relax on the beach all week would certainly be unhappy with an escorted tour. On the other hand, a client who wants to see the sights of India might appreciate all the benefits an escorted tour has to offer.

As with all areas of travel, the counselor must qualify the client. The traveler's level of travel experience and knowledge are particularly important when selling tours. For example, a traveler who has been to Hawaii several times may want an independent or hosted tour, whereas a client visiting Hawaii for the first time may prefer an escorted tour. The answers to the qualifying questions should establish:

- destination
- activities to be included (sightseeing, dining, water sports, and so on)
- length of trip
- season of travel (high, low, or shoulder)
- grade and price range of tour (budget, moderate, or deluxe)
- type of tour (independent, hosted, escorted, FIT, or special interest)
- preferred tour members (no one, adults, children, seniors, or special interest)
- pace (leisurely, moderate, or fast)
- traveler's level of travel knowledge and past experience

In addition to asking the right questions, travel counselors must listen carefully, not only to the traveler's answers, but also to their tone of voice. A client who sounds apprehensive or nervous about being on their own may be telling the counselor that an escorted tour would be best.

Another trap the travel counselor must avoid is injecting the counselor's preferences into the scenario. For example, a client tells the counselor that he wants to go to Alaska, but the travel counselor says that the Caribbean would be a much better destination. This counselor's reply is not only rude, it may also cause the traveler to go to another agency to book his trip to Alaska.

The client's destination can influence the type of tour selection. Most travelers going to Las Vegas, Florida, the

FIGURE 14–3 These tourists decided on an escorted tour to enable them to go on a safari.

Bahamas, Caribbean, and Mexican resort areas prefer independent or hosted tours. These destinations are chosen primarily for their individual activities rather than group sightseeing. Other destinations such as Africa, Asia, Australia, South America, and Europe lend themselves to escorted tours (Figure 14–3). Most travelers consider these destinations more exotic than the others mentioned, and as such, the security and comfort of being with a group is preferred.

THE LANGUAGE OF TOURS

There are hundreds of companies worldwide that arrange and market tours. These companies are commonly referred to as tour operators. Tour operators, sometimes called tour wholesalers, can market tours strictly through travel agencies or they also can sell directly to the consumer. Tour operators may also utilize ground operators to arrange specific components such as city sightseeing, special meals, and attraction entrances.

All tour operators establish prices on a per-person basis with the idea that two people will be traveling together. Everything in a brochure—the tour, airfare, extensions, discounts, and insurance—is priced per person.

Independent and hosted tours may offer travelers a choice of accommodation room type. It is common to see two or three prices for the same tour, each price representing a different type of room. For example, a three-night hotel package in a Honolulu hotel may show Garden View $375, and Ocean View $450.

Another factor that should be considered when comparing prices for escorted tours and packages using all-inclusive accommodations is meals. Tours can include continental breakfast, buffet, table d'hôte, or à la carte meals. Some tours utilize a dine-around program, which gives tour members a choice of restaurants.

If a client is traveling alone, there is a single supplement. Single supplements may be expressed as a flat dollar amount or as a percentage of the tour price. A client traveling alone pays the per-person price plus the single supplement.

When three people are traveling together and will share accommodations on a tour, there is usually a triple reduction. The triple reduction is per person and applies to each person in the party of three.

Some tours show a *land-only price* or a *land-air price*. The land-only price includes all tour components, including surface transportation, but not air. The land-air price includes all tour components and air transportation, usually from a gateway city. The gateway city is generally an airline hub and it is the city from which an international flight begins or ends. Many tour brochures include a chart that lists the airfare from various cities to the gateway. This airfare is called an air add-on.

Most tours are booked by travel counselors and, in fact, a few tour operators will not take bookings directly from the traveler. When a tour booking is made, a *confirmation number,* also called a booking or reservation number or record locator, is given. This number identifies the booking to the tour operator. The confirmation number must be used on all future communication with the tour operator.

Some tour operators require a deposit at the time a booking is made. The deposit can be a flat dollar amount per person or a percentage of the tour price. Other tour operators may give the travel counselor an option date. The option date is the date by which the tour operator must have the deposit. Option dates vary by tour operator, but seven days from the date of the booking is common.

At a later time, usually 45 to 60 days before the trip, final payment must be made. The method of payment used for the deposit and the final payment depend on the tour operator. Most tour operators accept credit cards for the deposit and the final payment.

After a tour has been booked and deposit taken, most tour operators charge a revision fee for any changes that are made. Usually revision fees are a flat dollar amount, sometimes per person, sometimes per booking. When a tour must be cancelled, there may be a cancellation fee. The amount of the fee depends on when the cancellation was made and varies by tour operator. A tour operator's cancellation policy is clearly detailed in the brochure.

Almost all tour operators offer an insurance package that covers trip cancellation or interruption, baggage, and health or accident. Often called *trip protection,* this insurance is priced per person, and may vary in price based on the length or type of the trip. Insurance offered by the tour operator does not usually cover loss due to carrier (e.g., airline, tour operator) bankruptcy.

Sometime after the final payment has been made, usually two to three weeks before departure, the tour operator sends a document packet to the travel agency. This packet can include airline tickets, tour tickets, baggage tags, nametags, itinerary, hotel vouchers, guidebooks, discount coupons, and general information. The travel counselor should check the tickets and vouchers over carefully to make sure all information is correct.

Some independent and hosted tours, especially in the United States, may be handled as "ticketless." The tour operator may send or fax an itinerary to the travel agency but no other documents are sent. Vouchers, coupons, and other information may be given to the client at the airport or at the destination.

PLEASE TURN TO PAGE 218 AND COMPLETE EXERCISE 14–2 NOW.

SELECTING TOUR OPERATORS

Tour operators come in all shapes and sizes, and the Internet makes it easy for the unscrupulous among them to take advantage of unsuspecting consumers. Anyone can set up a Web site and make claims to do anything. Now that more consumers are booking their own tours, the United States Tour Operators Association (USTOA) reports a constant stream of complaints about fraudulent activities and misrepresentation online. It is understandable that consumers make these sorts of mistakes when booking tours. It would be inexcusable for a travel counselor to do the same.

Many travel agencies have a *preferred vendor list* that includes tour operators, cruise lines, airlines, hotel chains, and car rental companies. These companies are included on the list because they have proven to offer quality products, excellent service, and value for the price. Tour operators included on a preferred vendor list are financially stable.

Membership in the USTOA and the National Tour Association (NTA) is a good indication that the tour operator is financially stable and is concerned with protecting the clients' personal and financial security. To be accepted as a member of the USTOA, a tour operator must:

- supply a variety of travel industry and banking references
- comply with the established Code of Ethics
- maintain a certain volume of bookings
- have had the same ownership and management for at least three years
- carry $1 million in liability insurance
- obtain a $1 million bond for USTOA's consumer protection plan

At http://www.ustoa.com, travel agents may download information on how to select a tour or vacation package, a traveler's glossary, and a chart of all USTOA members and the destinations they serve. If a client comes to you with a tour operator you are not familiar with, check it against the USTOA list.

NTA members are primarily motorcoach tour operators but can be any type of tour operator. Membership in the NTA requires tour operators to

- carry $1 million in liability insurance
- comply with the NTA Code of Ethics

Some tour operators also elect to become members of the American Society of Travel Agents (ASTA). Although membership in ASTA does not have the financial requirements of the other organizations, ASTA membership is often seen as a statement that the tour operator is anxious to work with travel agencies.

 Helpful Industry Web Sites

Membership Organizations

American Society of Travel Agents: **http://www.astanet.com**

National Tour Association: **http://www.nta.com**

Pacific Asia Travel Association: **http://www.pata.org**

United States Tour Operators Association: **http://www.ustoa.com**

READING TOUR BROCHURES AND WEB SITES

Almost all tour brochures are arranged using the same format. The first several pages include a table of contents, information about the tour operator, special features and discounts, and information about the modes of transportation and accommodations. These pages are designed to excite the reader and convince him that choosing a tour from this company is the correct decision.

Travel counselors can learn a great deal about the company and the clientele to which the company caters simply by reading the text and looking at the pictures. Take a look at any tour brochure and see if you can answer these questions:

1. What is the average age of the tour members?
2. Do children seem to be welcome or do the pictures feature adults only?
3. How are the tour members dressed: casually or formally?
4. Is the focus on activities and sightseeing or on leisure time and relaxation?
5. Of what organizations is the tour operator a member?

6. From the brochure, do you feel the tour operator would be considered upscale, moderate, or budget? (Hint: consider the quality of the photographs and the paper on which the brochure is printed.)

The bulk of the brochure or Web site contains the various tour products. Depending on the type of tour, each may be covered on one page to as many as four or five pages. Each tour product shows a day-by-day itinerary, usually indicating included meals and sightseeing. There may be a boxed area for each tour that details special features and sightseeing. Each tour product may have a price chart showing rates based on departure date, hotel choice, or hotel room type.

Tour Brochure Pricing Formula

	$$$	Per-person brochure price
+	$$$	Single supplement, if applicable
−	$$$	Triple reduction, if applicable
+	$$$	Upgrades, add-ons, additional features, insurance, if any
−	$$$	Discounts or reduction in features, if any
=	$$$$	Total per-person tour price

For two people traveling together, multiply the total per-person tour price by two.

For three people traveling together, multiply the total per-person tour price by three.

The final pages of a tour brochure, and a prominent section of a tour operator Web site, deal with important information such as deposits, final payments, documents, cancellation policies, insurance, and liability. It is in this section of the brochure that every tour operator disclaims responsibility or liability for things like loss or delays or events outside their control. It is here that you will usually find answers to frequently asked questions. A very important point to remember is that one tour operator's policies are not necessarily the same as another tour operator's policies (Figure 14–4). In fact, a tour operator may change policies from one year to the next.

When a traveler looks at a tour brochure, the eyes generally go to the price first. The traveler may not take into consideration all that is included. Travel counselors looking at a tour brochure usually look at the tour features: number of days, places visited, and what is included. It is very important that the travel counselor explain all of these details so that the client understands exactly what is being offered.

One of the indicators of a tour's price is the quality of the hotels used. A deluxe tour includes the best hotels, often more centrally located. Less expensive tours may offer a lower grade of hotels that are farther from the city center or popular sightseeing attractions.

	Deposit	Final Payment	Cancellation	Insurance
Tour Operator A	$100 per person paid at time of booking	45 days prior to departure	46+ days—$50/person 45–30 days—$100/person 29–15 days—$150/person less than 14 days—no refund	$30 to $40/person based on tour—must be paid at deposit
Tour Operator B	$200 per person paid within 7 days of booking	45 days prior to departure	46+ days—$200/person 45–16 days—20% of total price 15–1 days—35% of total price day of departure—no refund	$69 to $79/person based on tour—must be paid prior to final payment
Tour Operator C	$400 per person paid within 7 days of booking	60 days prior to departure	75+ days—no penalty 74–46 days—$400 per person 45–15 days—50% of total price 14–3 days—75% of total price less than 3 days—no refund	$99 to $199/person based on tour—must be paid prior to final payment

FIGURE 14–4 Each tour company establishes its own policies. A comparison indicates many differences in regard to deposits, final payments, and cancellations.

A second factor that can greatly affect a tour's price is meals. How many meals are included? Which meals are included? (Breakfast is far less expensive than dinner.) Are the meals buffet, table d'hôte, or à la carte?

One of the most important aspects of a tour is the pace. Pace can affect a tour's price; generally, the faster the pace, the less expensive the tour. Does the client want to see eight European countries in five days? If so, he must understand that he may have to be up at 6:00 A.M. and may be on the motorcoach until late at night each evening. He will be hustled on and off the motorcoach 20 times each day; the rest he sees from the motorcoach window as it drives by. This pace is not a vacation—it is hard work!

Moderately priced tours generally allow some free time but not much. Deluxe tours often set aside an afternoon in each city or location as free time. Tour members can use the free time how they wish: exploring, shopping, or just relaxing by the hotel pool.

Again, there is no right or wrong tour pace as long as the travel counselor listens to what the traveler wants and then follows his lead. Some clients want to see eight European countries in five days, so for them, the fast-paced tour is perfect. But for those travelers who want to take things a bit slower, selling the same fast-paced tour is a major mistake, and the traveler will be dissatisfied with the tour and the travel counselor.

SELLING TOURS

A traveler comes into a travel agency and says, "I'm interested in European tours." What does the travel counselor do? Does traveler counselor do; jump up and grab some brochures from the files or brochure rack? If so, does the counselor has no concept of what being a good travel counselor is all about. As with all areas of selling travel, specific information must be learned before any brochures can be selected.

First, the travel counselor should convey an interest in the client's request and make the client feel comfortable

Web Activity

Your clients, Esther and Hernando Gonzalez, have traveled to Europe several times, but they have never had the opportunity to spend time in London. They are interested in doing a two-week independent tour in June. Mr. and Mrs. Gonzalez enjoy shopping, museums, history, and theatre. Using the Internet to research things to do in London, prepare a fact sheet for your clients that includes everything you think your clients will appreciate knowing.

Caravan Tours Terms of Travel

- Meals
- Rooms
- Transportation
- Travelers Needing Special Assistance
- Luggage
- Gratuities
- Not Included
- Passports and Visa Requirements
- Final Documents
- Management and Responsibilities
- Travel Protection Plan
- Travel Protection Plan Part A
- Travel Protection Plan Part B
- Cancellation Fees
- Site Usage Agreement
- Copyrights
- Trademarks
- Use of Site
- Comments, Feedback, and Other Submissions
- Privacy Policy

Meals

All meals in Latin America are included. Most meals are included in the United States and Canada. Full, buffet, or deluxe continental breakfasts are included everywhere. Coffee and tea are provided at all meals. In Latin America, bottled water is provided free on the motor coach and purified water is provided at the meals.

Rooms

Accommodations in the hotels, lodges, and ships listed are rooms with two beds and private bath or shower. A limited number of single rooms are available. Triple rooms are usually two beds, sometimes with a cot or roll-away. Changes in type of room due to cancellation by a roommate (a twin changed to a single, a triple to a twin, etc.) will result in the higher tour price for the remaining client(s).

FIGURE 14–5 A tour operator Web site will have a complete list of its policies. Caravan Tours Terms of Service is an example of what type of information will be available. Reprinted from http://www.caravantours.com, with permission of Caravan Tours.

and important. The travel counselor might say something like, "Europe, that's wonderful! I'm sure we can find the perfect tour for you."

Many sales experts suggest that the travel counselor immediately introduce himself and, hopefully, the client

will do the same. If the client does not offer their name, the counselor should ask. The travel counselor should make note of the client's name and use it during the conversation.

The next step is to ask questions in order to learn exactly what type of tour the traveler has in mind. All of the questions that the travel counselor asks should be designed to help the counselor determine what tour operators and brochures are likely to offer products that suit the client.

What questions would you ask? What would you hope to learn from each question?

_____

_____

_____

_____

_____

After the travel counselor understands what the client wants, the counselor should select two or three brochures that offer appropriate products. A mistake some travel counselors make is overloading the client with dozens of brochures and options. The client is overwhelmed and may end up quite frustrated by the vast array of choices. In this case, remember that more is not better.

Tours are best sold face-to-face. In this way, the counselor can sit down with the client with brochures, point out a tour from each brochure, and show the client how each tour satisfies the client's needs. The travel counselor should use the pictures, the day-by-day itinerary of the tour, and the highlighted features as selling tools.

The traveler may have questions about the tour and the counselor should answer them immediately if possible. If the counselor does not know the answer to the client's question but can quickly find it, the counselor should do so. For answers that take a bit of time, there is nothing wrong with saying, "I don't know but I will be happy to find out and let you know." If the counselor does not already have the client's name, now is a good time to ask for it as well as the traveler's phone number.

The travel counselor should help the traveler compare the tours being suggested, both for included features and price. The counselor should make sure the client understands the price and what it includes as well as any additional charges or add-ons. It is a good idea to highlight brochure text dealing with deposits, final payments, cancellation policies, and insurance. Once the traveler has the brochure at home, these important sections may easily be reread.

Rarely will a tour actually be sold during the first contact with the client, unless all travelers are in the agency together. Usually the client takes the brochures home to discuss the options with any traveling companions. Before the client leaves the agency, the travel counselor should suggest that he will call the client in a few days to see if the client has any questions or concerns about the tour.

If the travel counselor was not well versed on the brochures during the first contact with the client, now is the time to brush up on them. Most clients devour the tour brochure information and can very easily end up knowing more about the tour than the travel counselor. If the travel counselor wants to appear professional, knowledgeable, and avoid embarrassment, he will take the brochures home and study them thoroughly.

MAKING TOUR RESERVATIONS AND PAYMENTS

Once a specific tour has been chosen by the client, the travel counselor makes the reservation. Most tour reservations are still made by phone to the individual tour operator, even though most are available through the various GDSs and/or their own Web sites. Many of the tour operator Web sites have "agent only" sections and may even pay an extra percent or two for Web site bookings. Automated bookings have the advantage of taking far less time than booking by phone, but there is no opportunity to ask for clarifications or discuss options unless you phone.

Most clients pay for their tour with a credit card, and almost all tour operators accept payment by credit card, either given by phone or entered into a GDS or Web site. In most cases, the tour operator obtains the credit card approval code and processes the charge. With credit card payments, the total amount goes to the tour operator, who must then issue a check to the booking travel agency for any commissions. Commissions may not be received for several days or weeks after the tour departs.

If the client prefers to pay by check or cash, the travel agency would then pay the tour operator with an agency check. When writing an agency check for final payment on a tour, the agency's commission is simply deducted from the final payment. This method obviously results in the agency receiving its commissions several days or weeks earlier, and can be a sizable advantage for some travel agencies.

Regardless of how the reservation is made, the travel counselor must be prepared with specific information about the client and the desired tour. This information includes:

- tour name or number
- departure and return dates
- special requests, add-ons, discounts, or feature reductions
- client names (as shown on the photo ID or passport)
- form of payment to be used for the deposit or full payment

Helpful Industry Web Sites

Apple Vacations: **http://www.applevacations.com**

Blue Sky Tours: **http://www.blueskytours.com**

Celtic Tours: **http://www.celtictours.com**

Central Holidays: **http://www.centralholidays.com**

Classic Custom Vacations: **http://www.classicvacations.com**

Collette Tours: **http://www.collettetours.com**

Contiki: **http://www.contiki.com**

Delta Vacations: **http://www.deltavacations.com**

Gate 1 Travel: **http://www.gate1travel.com**

General Tours: **http://www.generaltours.com**

Globus & Cosmos: **http://www.globusandcosmos.com**

GoGo Tours: **http://www.gogowwv.com**

Isram World of Travel: **http://www.isram.com**

Maupintour: **http://www.maupintour.com**

Mayflower Tours: **http://www.mayflowertours.com**

Pleasant Holidays: **http://www.pleasantholidays.com**

Sunny Land Tours: **http://www.sunnylandtours.com**

Trafalgar Tours: **http://www.trafalgartours.com**

Travel Impressions: **http://www.travelimpressions.com**

Because the travel counselor has to be in contact with the client, the counselor should also have the client's telephone number, fax, e-mail address, and mailing address. You may wish to use a reservation form (see Figure 14–6) to assist in gathering all the necessary information. This form is also used to record the confirmation number and reservationist's name (phone bookings only) at the time the reservation is made and to record all payment information, both from the client as well as to the tour operator.

Invariably, clients call with questions about the tours they booked, making these forms very handy. If the booking travel counselor is out of the office at the time a client calls, another counselor can look at the form and see exactly what has transpired. If the form is complete, it is possible that the other counselor can answer the client's questions, eliminating the need for a call back.

Most travel agencies maintain a file folder on each tour booking. The file contains the reservation form, action

Passenger Name(s) _____

Passenger Address _____

Passenger Work Phone _____ Passenger Home Phone _____

Frequent Flyer Number(s) _____

Passport Number(s) _____

Seating Preference: Non-Smoking? _____ Smoking? _____ Window? _____ Aisle? _____

Dining Preference: First? _____ Second? _____ Table Size? _____ Smoking? _____ Non-Smoking? _____

Vendor Name _____ Vendor Phone _____

Vendor Address _____

Booking Date _____ Departure Date _____ Return Date _____

Ship/Cabin #/Tour Name _____ Confirmation Number _____

Air Travel: Vendor to ticket (date)? _____ Agency to ticket (date)? _____

Res Agent's Name _____ Commission % _____ Special Requests _____

_____

Total Amount of Sale $ _____ Commissionable Sale Amount $ _____

PAYMENTS BY THE CLIENT

Deposit Amount $ _____ Date Due/Paid _____ Client FOP _____

Final Amount $ _____ Date Due/Paid _____ Client FOP _____

PAYMENTS TO THE VENDOR

Deposit _____

Final Payment: _____

FIGURE 14–6 Most travel agents maintain detailed information on each tour booking. A Reservation Form is an efficient way to record important data.

summary, tour brochure, payment receipts, and any other pertinent data about the booking. Every communication with the client and tour operator should be documented on the action summary and each tour file should contain the same types of paperwork.

CONFIRMATION AND FOLLOW-UP

As an added touch to the service the travel counselor is providing the client, a confirmation letter puts what has been done on the client's behalf in writing (Figure 14–7). The most appropriate time to send a confirmation letter to the client is after the deposit has been processed. If an error has been made during the booking process (e.g., incorrect date, tour, name), the confirmation letter may bring it to the travel counselor's attention.

There are four main subjects that should be covered in the confirmation letter. It is always nice to begin by thanking the client for his business. After all, where would the travel counselor be without the client? Next, state what has been done (e.g., reservation made, deposit sent). Confirm to the client the features that are and are not included in the price. If the client did not purchase insurance, briefly outline the tour operator's cancellation policy and recommend insurance.

Most travel counselors believe that staying in touch with their clients is a very important part of doing business, and rightly so. An excellent way to achieve and maintain a solid counselor–client relationship is by a follow-up letter or phone call to the client after he has returned from his tour. A waste of time? Definitely not!

FIGURE 14–7 These tourists can relax on the beach, knowing their agent is there if needed.

A follow-up letter or phone call accomplishes two very important things:

- lets the client know that the counselor cares about more than just making a sale
- provides the counselor with vendor and product feedback

The counselor has taken great pains to satisfy the client during the sales process of the tour. The clients have spent hundreds, perhaps thousands, of dollars on the tour that the counselor suggested. They have returned home; now is not the time to abandon them. Showing that the counselor cares about the services they did or did not receive, the way they were treated, and their overall opinion solidifies the counselor–client relationship.

If there were problems with the tour or tour operator, they have to be questioned. Were the problems avoidable? Were they the counselor's fault? Did the tour operator perform less than efficiently? A letter to the tour operator might be in order, expressing the client's dissatisfaction and the counselor's concern. Perhaps, the clients should be reimbursed by the tour operator for services not received. If the problems were severe, it may be that the agency's manager will reconsider selling this tour operator in the future.

The point is to never lose sight of the fact that this is a service industry. Without satisfied clients, counselors and their agencies cannot survive.

? *What Would You Do?*

You have been working as a travel counselor for several months and your boss has offered you a choice of familiarization trips: Las Vegas, which you love and have been to several times; Hawaii, which you have sold but never visited; and Kenya, which you have never sold or visited.

1. In what way(s) is Las Vegas the best choice?
2. In what way(s) is Hawaii the best choice?
3. In what way(s) is Kenya the best choice?

SUMMARY

A tour consists of several components including transportation, hotels, meals, and sightseeing. There is a wide variety of tour types that can be matched to each individual traveler, depending on his or her preferences. By understanding the types of tours, the tour operators, and their products, the travel professional can accurately match clients to appropriate products. Improved Web search capabilities have resulted in the growth of dynamic tour packaging and changed the way tour packages are marketed.

There are many benefits to selling and booking tours, both for the client and for the travel agency. For clients, benefits include paying a set price and paying less for the tour than they would for the individual components. With an escorted tour, the client has the added benefit of someone else taking care of the details. For the travel counselor, selling tours is an efficient way of generating higher revenue and making more efficient use of time.

It is important to understand the language of tours and each part of a tour brochure as it relates to use as a selling tool. Selecting a tour operator is based upon several factors such as membership in professional organizations, longevity, and preferred vendor status. Most tour payments are done by credit card, and travel counselors should be especially aware of the importance of consistent record keeping between the time a reservation is made and when the client departs. Selling tours involves the ability to match the client's needs with the tour products.

 *For additional Travel and Tourism resources, go to http://www.hospitality-tourism.delmar.com.*

PLEASE COMPLETE THE CHAPTER REVIEW QUESTIONS NOW.

EXERCISE 14–1 Types of Tours and Their Benefits

1. Identify the two unique features of escorted tours. _____

2. Name the five products and services being purchased when an escorted tour is selected. _____
_____

3. What are the benefits to the client when an escorted tour is purchased? _____
_____

4. Identify the two unique features of an independent tour. _____

5. Name the components typically included in an independent tour. _____
_____

6. What are the benefits to the client when an independent tour is purchased? _____
_____

7. Identify the two unique features of a hosted tour. _____

8. Name the products and services being purchased when a hosted tour is selected. _____
_____

9. What are the benefits to the client who purchases a hosted tour? _____
_____

10. What are the differences between a host, an escort, and a guide? _____
_____
_____

11. What subjects might be the focus of special interest tours? _____
_____

12. What client groups might be the focus of special interest tours? _____
_____

13. What activities might be the focus of special interest tours? _____
_____

14. What is the advantage of dynamic packaging? _____
_____

15. In detail, explain why it is to the travel counselor's advantage to sell a tour instead of air, hotel, and rental car separately.
_____
_____

16. Identify the type of tour that you think best suits the needs of these clients.

a. Young couple, inexperienced travelers, have saved for three years to go to Hawaii, want to see everything in 10–14 days.

   _____

b. Four college friends, inexperienced travelers, want to go to Jamaica as a graduation treat. _____

   _____

c. Older couple, well traveled, want to return to France to visit the Normandy beaches and wine regions. _____

   _____

d. Middle-aged couple, well traveled but first time to Egypt and Israel, interested in the main tourist sites. _____

   _____

e. Young couple, first time to Las Vegas, want to see a couple of shows, gamble, and relax by the hotel pool. _____

   _____

EXERCISE 14–2 The Language of Tours

1. Define these terms in your own words.

   a. air add-on _____

   b. confirmation number _____

   c. deposit _____

   d. final payment _____

   e. gateway city _____

   f. ground operator _____

   g. option date _____

   h. revision fee _____

   i. single supplement _____

   j. tour operator _____

   k. triple reduction _____

2. Are prices shown in tour brochures per person or for a party of two? _____

3. In what way do the hotels used and type of included meals have a bearing on a tour price? _____

   _____

   _____

4. What methods of payment can be used to pay for a tour? _____

   _____

5. What is usually included in the insurance package that is offered by the tour operator? _____

   _____

6. What items may be included in a tour document packet? _____

   _____

9-Day Hawaii Tour

Day 1: Arrive Honolulu, Oahu
Transfer to the Sheraton Waikiki Hotel

Day 2: Oahu
Sightseeing: Polynesian Cultural Center
Included Meals: Breakfast and Dinner
Hotel: Sheraton Waikiki Hotel

Day 3: Honolulu
Sightseeing: Iolani Palace, Punchbowl National Memorial,
Pearl Harbor National Memorial
Included Meals: Breakfast and dinner
Hotel: Sheraton Waikiki Hotel

Day 4: Oahu
Day at leisure
Included Meals: Breakfast
Hotel: Sheraton Waikiki Hotel

Day 5: Oahu–Maui
Flight from Oahu to Maui
Sightseeing: Lahaina, Iao Needle, and Kaanapali Beach
Included Meals: Breakfast and Dinner
Hotel: Maui Marriott Beach Resort

Day 6: Maui
Day at Leisure
Included Meals: Breakfast
Hotel: Maui Marriott Beach Resort

Day 7: Maui
Day at Leisure
Included Meals: Breakfast and Dinner
Hotel: Maui Marriott Beach Resort

Day 8: Maui—Depart for Home
Morning at Leisure
Transfer to Maui Airport
Included Meals: Breakfast
Depart for Home

Day 9: Arrive Home

Land Rates Per Person

	Twin	Single	Triple
Jan.–Mar.	$1599	$2199	$1569
Apr.–Dec.	$1569	$2169	$1539

Payments
Within 5 days of booking, a nonrefundable deposit of $100 per person must be sent. The balance is due 60 days before departure. Payment may be made by American Express, Discover/Novus, Mastercard, or Visa, or by sending a travel agency check. All rates are guaranteed upon deposit.

Revision Fees
A handling fee of $50.00 per transaction will be assessed for any change or revision made to a reservation. A change of departure date within 90 days of departure will be considered a cancellation and cancellation charges will apply.

Cancellation Charges
If you have not purchased waivers and you need to transfer or cancel for any reason prior to tour departure, the cancellation fees will be:
- More than 60 days prior to departure: a nonrefundable deposit will be retained.
- 60–16 days prior to departure: 25% of the total price.
- 15–1 day prior to departure: 50% of the total price.
- Day of departure and after: 100% of the total price.

Waivers
The purchase of waivers will guarantee full refund on all payments except the waiver fee for cancellation for any reason. However, the Land Waiver does not cover the return of air costs nor does the Air Waiver cover the return of land costs. Waivers must be paid with deposit.
- Land Waiver: $50 per person
- Air Waiver: $10 per person

EXERCISE 14–3 9-Day Hawaii Tour

Using the above information, answer the following questions:

1. How many nights are spent in Maui? _____

   _____

2. What forms of payment are accepted? _____

   _____

3. On what island is the Pearl Harbor National Memorial visited? _____

   _____

4. How many meals are included on this tour? _____

_____

5. When must the deposit be paid? _____

_____

6. At what time are the tour rates guaranteed? _____

_____

7. How much will be charged if your client changes departure dates 45 days prior? _____

_____

8. How many days on this tour are spent at leisure? _____

_____

9. How much is the per-person deposit? _____

_____

10. On what island can your client enjoy Kaanapali Beach? _____

_____

11. What hotels are used on this tour? _____

_____

12. What is the cancellation fee for an April 5 departure if it is cancelled on March 28? _____

_____

13. On what island is the Polynesian Cultural Center visited? _____

_____

14. Your clients are two adults who will depart on February 12. Air cost is $900 per person and will be booked with the tour operator. Your agency will earn 10 percent commission on the land tour and 3 percent on the air.
   - Total cost? _____
   - Total amount paid at deposit? _____
   - Total final payment amount? _____
   - Commission amount? _____

15. Your clients are three adults booking the October 18 departure. They do not need air included, but they do want to purchase the Land Waiver. Your agency earns 7 percent commission on the land tour and 10 percent on the waiver.
   - Total cost? _____
   - Total amount paid at deposit? _____
   - Total final payment amount? _____
   - Commission amount? _____

EXERCISE 14-4 Tour Price and Commission Calculation

Using the Britain and Ireland Tour information, answer the following questions:

1. Two adults, June 20 departure, air from Salt Lake City, Travel Protection.
   - Total cost? _____
   - Total amount paid at deposit? _____
   - Total final payment amount? _____
   - Commission amount? _____

16-Day Britain & Ireland Tour

Land: $1720 Land & Air: $2160	Land: $1840 Land & Air: $2345	Land: $1920 Land & Air: $2460	Land: $1950 Land & Air: $2470	Land: $1980 Land & Air: $2490
April 1–April 16	May 6–May 21	June 10–June 25	July 6–July 21	August 3–August 18
April 20–May 5	May 9–May 24	June 15–June 30	July 11–July 26	August 7–August 22
April 27–May 12	May 13–May 28	June 20–July 5	July 17–August 1	August 10–August 25
April 29–May 14	May 27–June 11	June 29–July 14	July 29–August 13	August 15–August 30

All prices are per person based on double occupancy. Land & Air prices include air transportation from New York. For add-ons from your city and nonincluded taxes, fees, and surcharges, see the chart below.

Departures	Pittsburgh	Salt Lake City	Tampa	Washington DC
April 1–April 29	$110	$215	$145	$65
May 6–May 27	$125	$245	$170	$80
June 10–June 29	$145	$270	$195	$95
July 6–July 29	$175	$295	$210	$105
August 3–August 15	$210	$310	$225	$120

All prices are per person. In addition to the rates there will be a total of $125 that covers all international and domestic taxes, fees, and surcharges.

Reservations and Payments

- Deposit: $200 per person, to be paid within 7 days of the reservation
- Final Payment: total balance due no less than 45 days before departure

Booking Changes

- A fee of $50 per transaction will be charged for any revision or alteration made after deposit has been paid provided that the revision or alteration is made at least 45 days before departure.

Cancellations

- 45 days or more before departure: nonrefundable deposit
- 45 to 22 days before departure: 25% of the total price in addition to the nonrefundable deposit
- 21–8 days before departure: 30% of the total price in addition to the nonrefundable deposit
- 7–1 days before departure: 50% of the total price in addition to the nonrefundable deposit
- Day of departure or no-show: 100% of the total price

Travel Protection

- $79.00 per person for trips (excluding taxes, fees, and surcharges) up to $1,000
- $99.00 per person for trips (excluding taxes, fees, and surcharges) over $1,000
- There is no charge for Travel Protection for children ages 8 through 16 traveling and sharing a room with two adults.
- Travel Protection must be paid with deposit

Single Supplement

- An additional charge of 25% of the Land or Land & Air price applies for single travelers

Triple Reduction

- A reduction from the Land or Land & Air price of $145 per person will apply for three adults sharing accommodations.
- A reduction from the Land or Land & Air price of $175 will apply for children ages 8 through 16 sharing accommodations with two adults.

2. One adult, August 3 departure, air from Pittsburgh, Travel Protection.
   - Total cost? _____
   - Total amount paid at deposit? _____
   - Total final payment amount? _____
   - Commission amount? _____

3. Two adults and one child, age 14, May 27 departure, land only, Travel Protection.
   - Total cost? _____
   - Total amount paid at deposit? _____
   - Total final payment amount? _____
   - Commission amount? _____

4. Three adults, July 6 departure, air from Tampa, no Travel Protection.
   - Total cost? _____
   - Total amount paid at deposit? _____
   - Total final payment amount? _____
   - Commission amount? _____

5. Your clients from question 4 cancel their trip on June 20. How much is the refund? _____

EXERCISE 14-5 Case Study Selling an Escorted Tour Package

Use the Web site http://www.caravantours.com to assist your client in planning an escorted tour to Mexico for his wife's sixtieth birthday. They have only two weeks for their trip and would like to spend around $1,500 per person, including transportation. They want a well-paced and unhurried itinerary and do not want to travel on any boats.

1. Of the Mexico tour offerings on the Web site, which tour meets your client's needs? Describe the itinerary features of this tour.

   _____
   _____
   _____
   _____

2. What is the total cost for a spring departure? _____

3. Is airfare included? _____

4. If your client books the tour today, when is the deposit due? What is the amount of the deposit? _____

5. What are the cancellation fees if the client cancels? _____

6. When is final payment due? _____

7. What is the amount of the final payment? _____

8. What is the cost to purchase the Travel Protection Plan for this tour? _____

9. List four benefits of the Travel Protection Plan:

   _____
   _____
   _____
   _____

10. What is included in the tour package? _____

11. List three reasons why you would consider this tour operator to be reputable:

   _____
   _____
   _____

12. How much luggage is allowed per person? _____

Review Questions

1. What do the letters ASTA stand for? _____

2. What do the letters USTOA stand for? _____

3. What do the letters NTA stand for? _____

4. What is a preferred vendor list? _____

5. In what way can you use the pictures in a tour brochure to learn about the vendor? _____
_____
_____

6. In what portion of a tour brochure do you usually find information about deposits and final payments? _____

7. In what ways do clients and travel counselors look at tour brochures differently? _____
_____

8. Why is understanding a tour's pace important? _____

9. What types of information should be learned during the qualification process? _____
_____
_____

10. Why should tours be booked in the GDS when possible? _____
_____

11. What items are usually kept in a tour client's file? _____
_____

12. What four areas should be covered in a confirmation letter? _____
_____

13. What two functions does a follow-up letter or phone call serve? _____
_____

14. Identify the appropriate term for each definition.

    a. The penalty amount for a cancelled tour. _____

    b. Transportation, transfers, accommodations, meals, and sightseeing. _____

    c. Down payment amount for a tour. _____

    d. Most structured type of tour; an escort is with the group throughout. _____

    e. The balance due after deposit. _____

    f. A tour that has been constructed by the travel counselor to fit the client's needs. _____

    g. The airport from which airfare is included. _____

    h. A company that arranges everything except air transportation. _____

    i. Moderately structured tour; a host is available at designated times. _____

    j. Least structured tour; participants are basically on their own. _____

k. The date by which the tour company must have the deposit. _____

l. A penalty amount for making changes to a booked tour. _____

m. A penalty amount for a single traveler on a tour. _____

n. A type of airfare that can only be used in conjunction with a tour. _____

o. A local tour employee who joins the group for short sightseeing excursions. _____

p. A company that creates and markets tours to travel counselors and the public. _____

q. An amount that is subtracted from the price when three people travel together. _____

SECTION V

Selling the Cruise Experience

CHAPTER 15
The Basics of Cruising

CHAPTER 16
Cruise Pricing and Selling

The Basics of Cruising

OBJECTIVES

At the conclusion of this chapter, you should be able to

- outline benefits and disadvantages of cruising.
- identify several sources for cruise information.
- list major cruise lines and types of cruise ships.
- identify popular world cruise areas, typical ports of call, points of embarkation, and cruise lines operating in each area.
- define terms associated with cruising.
- explain features and facilities onboard cruise ships.
- describe other types of sea travel.

KEY TERMS

aft	forward	roll
berths	galley	shore excursions
bow	inside cabins	special programs
bridge	keel	stabilizers
debarkation	midships	starboard
deck	outside cabins	staterooms
deck plan	port	stern
draft	ports of call	tender
embarkation	registry	theme cruises

In the early days of cruising, the thing to do was to sail from Southampton in England to New York in "the Colonies." Anyone who was anyone insisted on a port cabin (room on the ship's left side) on the westbound voyage. On the return trip, a starboard cabin (room on the ship's right side) was mandatory. In this way, these elite cruise passengers enjoyed a warm southern exposure in both directions. The importance of "port out, starboard home" added a new word to the English language—posh, and it meant luxurious.

These early cruisers were the beautiful people of their time. They would faint dead away were they to see how far cruising has come. Today, everyone cruises: young and old, famous and unknown, the idle rich and the blue-collar worker. The cruise industry is booming!

Nearly 70 new ships were introduced between 2000 and 2005, and an additional 20 will debut by 2008. By continuing to build new ships, the cruise industry is banking on its ability to attract new passengers for many years to come. If the past few years are any indication, that prediction is very likely to become reality. Statistics collected by the Cruise Lines International Association (CLIA) indicate that the cruise industry has been steadily increasing its number of passengers for several years. Although some experts think there may soon be too much capacity, most believe that steady growth will continue. Most cruises are sold by travel counselors (90 percent according to CLIA), and most travel professionals consider selling cruises a very important part of their overall business.

CRUISE BENEFITS AND DISADVANTAGES

There are many reasons why the cruise industry is growing. Cruise lines are continuing to enhance their product, appealing to a wider market. Besides building newer, bigger, and better ships, cruise lines are known for their ability to offer a variety of itineraries and activities to appeal to a wide range of interests. There are *niche* cruises that attract people interested in celebrities, music, sports, gourmet food, and much more. Cruise lines have also been extremely successful at offering a first-rate experience to customers. Customer satisfaction with cruises is exceptionally high.

Benefits to the Client

- high rate of satisfaction
- prepayment
- value
- service

One of the reasons travel counselors enjoy selling cruises is that this type of vacation has an exceptionally *high rate of satisfaction* (Figure 15–1). Cruise passengers

FIGURE 15–1 Customer satisfaction with cruises is exceptionally high.

who say that they would not cruise again are few and far between. In fact, many clients sail once or twice a year, year after year. Cruise lines have made a concerted effort to offer customers what they want in a vacation and to make certain that the vacation they promise is the vacation experienced by every ship's passenger.

As with purchasing packaged tours, *prepayment* is an advantage in purchasing a cruise. Although it may not be obvious to the client, prepayment allows her to see the overall vacation cost more clearly than if each feature is paid for individually throughout the trip. Determining whether a cruise fits within a client's budget is easy because so many of the features are included in a fixed price.

The fact that many of the cruise features are included means that this type of vacation has *value*. The typical cruise includes accommodations, meals, and a wide variety of entertainment and activities. Cruises around North America usually offer airfare add-ons from various U.S. and Canadian cities, whereas cruises to other areas may include airfare from major gateway cities. When airfare is included or added to the cruise cost, transfers from the airport to the pier may also be included. This can save the client $20 to $100 or more.

The *service* each passenger enjoys on a cruise is an unmistakable benefit. Many cruise ships have crew to passenger ratios of 1:1 or 1:2. Ratios like these usually result in exemplary service and a high degree of personal attention. Perhaps the best part of the service is that most crew members obviously enjoy what they do and are very eager to be of assistance.

Few vacations suit what is called the vertical traveler as well as the horizontal traveler—except, that is, for cruising. Vertical travelers enjoy a variety of activities and sightseeing, and cruising offers many opportunities for both pursuits. Horizontal travelers like nothing better than to relax by the pool with a good book and a cool beverage. On a cruise, the horizontal traveler can relax all day long if he wishes.

Benefits to the Travel Professional

Like selling tours, selling cruises affords the travel agency two very important benefits. Selling a cruise is *time efficient,* unlike selling trip components separately. Think about how much time it might take to sell five or six components individually compared to selling one product that includes everything. Obviously, spending less time on each sale means that more sales can be made each day.

Selling cruises can be very *profitable* for the travel agency, certainly more so than selling a trip consisting of air, car, and hotel. As we saw with tour packages, commission is paid on the entire cruise price, which includes meals and entertainment. Cruise lines pay a standard commission on the cruise, airfare, and trip protection insurance, and most pay additional percentage points to their high-volume producers.

Disadvantages of Cruising

Any type of travel product that has so many important benefits is likely to have some disadvantages, and cruising is no exception. Some disadvantages are:

- time at a destination
- storms
- size of accommodations
- seasickness

Most cruises include some days spent at sea and a different port of call on the alternate days. To some clients, these quick trips to a destination are a perfect way to experience several locations. Others want to spend a week on the beach or visit local museums and attractions, and a cruise provides too little time in port. Knowing the client is the best way to determine whether this is viewed as an advantage or a disadvantage.

The typical time for storms in the Caribbean is June through October. However, we all know that the weather does not always behave in a typical fashion. During bad weather, where can the passengers go while at sea? The answer is the ship's public rooms and their cabins. Cabins on many cruise ships are very small, much smaller than a typical hotel room. Being forced to remain inside during bad weather can make the cabins seem even smaller and some passengers may find that confinement a problem.

Seasickness can be a problem for some clients, and this condition can be exacerbated during stormy weather. Besides over-the-counter medication, such as Dramamine, some cruise passengers have obtained relief from the spice ginger taken in capsule form or mixed with tea. Another type of prevention is the acupressure bracelet. Of course, the travel counselor should suggest that the concerned client seek the advice of his personal physician before the trip.

If all of these precautions fail and the passenger becomes ill, he can call the ship's doctor. All major cruise ships have a physician onboard and a trip to the infirmary for an injection may turn a vacation disaster into a voyage to remember.

SOURCES FOR CRUISE INFORMATION

There are many excellent cruise references for travel agents. The Internet has made searching for and finding information much more efficient for busy professionals, and Web sites are, in general, able to provide more in-depth information. Cruise Lines International Association (CLIA) works to "ensure the highest caliber of cruise sales expertise" and therefore offers travel agents a wealth of information, both online and elsewhere.

CLIA

CLIA is an excellent resource for travel counselors. CLIA publishes the *CLIA Cruise Manual* annually, and they sponsor a Web site, http://www.cruising.org. The printed manual contains information on CLIA's 19 member cruise lines, including ships' profiles, sample menus, wine and beverage lists, sample daily activity sheets, deck plans, passenger services, and much more. CLIA's Web site provides the same information, but with the added conveniences of the Web. From CLIA's Web site you can use the "Cruise Finder" to search for a cruise by destination, cruise line, or length of the cruise, connect to any individual cruise line Web site, or locate a travel agency by zip code.

Although there is also a restricted section for member travel agents only, it is not necessary to be a member of CLIA to access much of the information on their Web site. A membership to CLIA does, however, have several advantages. CLIA boasts 17,000 member travel agencies that have access to many educational programs, promotional materials and direct marketing tools, market research, conferences, and other opportunities.

Other Information Sources

All cruise lines have printed brochures available for travel agents and customers highlighting their ships and sailings. In addition, most have extensive and informative Web sites. Some Web sites offer "virtual" tours of their ships, making it possible to get a 360-degree view of staterooms and other ship's features. Most Web sites offer booking capabilities as well.

You will remember Star Service Online (http://www.starserviceonline.com) as a hotel reference, but they also provide candid opinions of 250 cruise ships. It is necessary to be a member of Star Service to access their information.

The *Official Steamship Guide* is available to members either in print (published quarterly) or online at http://www.officialsteamshipguide.com. Members can locate information for over 70 ships, including schooner and river cruises, passenger freighters, barge and canal cruises, ferry links, and others.

The Web site http://www.smallshipcruises.com contains information about adventure and expedition cruises, wildlife and ecocruises, luxury ships, old and new sailing ships, barges, dive boats, as well as wheelchair-accessible vessels. There are more than 100 small ship companies and 400 vessels all over the world with 5 to 500 passengers. Their information is available to members only.

Several informative guidebooks and periodicals are available for cruisers, potential cruisers, and travel professionals. Most major bookstores carry guidebooks such as the Berlitz *Complete Guide to Cruising and Cruise Ships* and *Frommer's Cruises and Ports of Call*. These guidebooks contain information on specialty cruises, along with personal observations and recommendations of the authors. Periodicals are available by subscription. Two good choices are *Cruise Travel* (http://www.cruisetravelmag.com) and *Porthole* (http://www.porthole.com). Both feature articles on ships, ports of call, activities, and other topics of interest.

MAJOR CRUISE LINES AND CRUISE TYPES

Fortunately for travel counselors and cruise clients alike, there is a cruise line, ship, and itinerary to fit almost everyone's idea of a dream vacation. Perhaps the most important job a travel counselor has when working with a prospective cruise client is to match the client with the style of ship, type of cruise, and itinerary.

Each cruise line tends to focus on one style of ship: small yachtlike vessels, tall-masted sailing schooners, riverboats, or the mega ships that are like floating resorts. CLIA's Cruise Finder Web feature makes the following categorizations of its member cruise lines:

- Resort/Contemporary (examples are Carnival and Disney)
- Premium (examples are Holland America and Swan Hellenic)
- Luxury (examples are Radisson Seven Seas and Silversea Cruises)
- Niche/Specialty (examples are Norwegian Coastal Voyage and Windstar)
- Value/Traditional (examples are MSC Cruises and Norwegian Coastal Voyage)

The following is a list of cruise lines and their Web sites that a travel professional will most likely encounter. (Not all are CLIA members, nor is this list intended to be a comprehensive list of all cruise lines.)

American Cruise Lines	http://www.americancruiselines.com
American Hawaii Cruises	http://www.cruisehawaii.com
Carnival Cruise Line	http://www.carnival.com
Clipper Cruise Line	http://www.clippercruise.com
Costa Cruise Line	http://www.costacruises.com
Crystal Cruises	http://www.crystalcruises.com
Cunard Line, Ltd.	http://www.cunardline.com
Delta Queen Steamboat Company	http://www.deltaqueen.com
Disney Cruise Line	http://www.disneycruise.com
Holland America Line	http://www.hallandamerica.com
MSC Cruises	http://www.msccruises.com
Norwegian Coastal Voyage	http://www.coastalvoyage.com
Norwegian Cruise Line	http://www.ncl.com
Oceania Cruises	http://www.oceaniacruises.com
Princess Cruise Line	http://www.princesscruises.com
Radisson Seven Seas Cruises	http://www.rssc.com
Renaissance Cruise Line	http://www.renaissancecruises.com
Royal Caribbean International	http://www.rccl.com
Seabourn Cruise Line	http://www.seabourn.com
Silversea Cruise Line	http://www.silverseacruises.com
Swan Hellenic	http://www.swanhellenic.com
Windjammer Cruises	http://www.windjammer.com
Windstar Cruises	http://www.windstarcruises.com

CRUISE AREAS OF THE WORLD

The travel industry has divided the world into "cruise areas." If you were to mention any specific cruise area to an experienced travel counselor, certain cruise lines would come to mind. Although several cruise lines offer sailings throughout the world, many cruise lines concentrate on one or two specific areas. When a client says that he is interested in a cruise, the travel counselor should qualify the specific area in which he is interested.

Before looking at the areas of cruising, you should know some additional terms. Each cruise area contains certain port cities that are used as the point of embarkation. The point of embarkation is the port where the passengers get on or embark the ship to begin their cruise. Each cruise in a specific area offers ports of call; port cities where passengers may leave the ship for sightseeing, shopping, and so on. The port city where the cruise terminates is called the point of debarkation. The point of debarkation may or may not be the same port city as the point of embarkation. Passengers get off, or debark or disembark the ship at this port and begin the trip to their home city.

Let's examine the cruise areas, points of embarkation, ports of call, typical cruise lengths, and some of the cruise lines that offer cruises in each area.

1. Africa
   Point of embarkation: any major port.
   Cruise length: 3 to 24 days; 7- to 10-day cruises are the most common.
   Cruise lines: Costa, Crystal, Cunard, Princess, Seabourn, and Silversea.
   Ports of call: Tenerife, Canary Islands; Mombassa, Kenya; Casablanca, Tangier, Morocco; Cape Town, Durban, South Africa; and Dakar, Senegal.

2. Alaska
   Point of embarkation: Vancouver, British Columbia, Canada; San Francisco, California; Seward, Alaska.
   Cruise length: 3 to 14 days; 7-day cruises are the most popular.
   Cruise lines: Carnival, Crystal, Holland America, Norwegian, Princess, and Royal Caribbean.
   Ports of call: Juneau, Sitka, Ketchikan, Skagway, Alaska; cruising through College Fjord, Glacier Bay, Inside Passage, and Misty Fjords, Alaska.

3. Antarctica
   Point of embarkation: Ushuaia, Argentina.
   Cruise length: 8 to 18 days.
   Cruise lines: Clipper and Radisson Seven Seas.
   Ports of call: Deception Island, Drake Passage, and Paradise Bay.

4. Asia—North
   Point of embarkation: any major port.
   Cruise length: 3 to 14 days.
   Cruise lines: Crystal, Cunard, Holland America, Radisson Seven Seas, Seabourn, and Silversea.
   Ports of call: Chongqing, Hong Kong, People's Republic of China; Kagoshima, Osaka, Kobe, Tokyo, Japan; Taipei, Taiwan; and Seoul, Pusan, Inch' On, South Korea.

5. Asia—South
   Point of embarkation: any major port.
   Cruise length: 3 to 14 days; 7- to 10-day cruises are the most popular.

Cruise lines: Crystal, Cunard, Holland America, Renaissance, Royal Caribbean, Seabourn, and Silversea.
Ports of call: Bali, Komodo, Jakarta, Semarang, Indonesia; Bangkok, Phuket, Thailand; Da Nang, Haiphong, Ho Chi Minh City, Vietnam; Kuala Lumpur, Kuantan, Penang, Port Kelang, Malaysia; Manila, Philippines; and Singapore.

6. Australia and New Zealand
   Point of embarkation: Sydney, Australia and Auckland, New Zealand.
   Cruise length: 4 to 20 days; 10- to 14-day cruises are the most popular.
   Cruise lines: Crystal, Cunard, Holland America, Princess, Radisson Seven Seas, Royal Caribbean, and Silversea.
   Ports of call: Adelaide, Brisbane, Cairns, Darwin, Hobart, Melbourne, Sydney, Australia; and Auckland, Bay of Islands, Christchurch, Napier, Tauranga, Wellington, New Zealand.

7. Bahamas and Western Caribbean
   Point of embarkation: Miami, Tampa, Port Canaveral (Cocoa), Port Everglades (Ft. Lauderdale), Florida; and New Orleans, Louisiana.
   Cruise length: Bahamas only, 3 to 5 days; Western Caribbean, 7 to 14 days; 7-day cruises are the most popular.
   Cruise lines: Carnival, Celebrity, Costa, Cunard, Disney, Holland America, Norwegian, Princess, Radisson Seven Seas, Royal Caribbean, Seabourn, Silversea, and Windjammer.
   Ports of call: Castaway Cay, Cococay, Eleuthera, Freeport, Great Stirrup Cay, Half Moon Cay, Nassau, Bahamas; George Town, Cayman Islands; Labadee, Haiti; Montego Bay, Ocho Rios, Jamaica; and Santo Domingo, Dominican Republic.

8. Bermuda
   Point of embarkation: Boston, Massachusetts; New York City, New York; Philadelphia, Pennsylvania; and Baltimore, Maryland.
   Cruise length: 7 days
   Cruise lines: Celebrity, Cunard, Norwegian, Radisson Seven Seas, Royal Caribbean, Seabourn, and Silversea.
   Ports of call: King's Wharf, Hamilton, St. George's, Bermuda.

9. Canada and Eastern U.S. Seaboard
   Point of embarkation: any major port.
   Cruise length: 4 to 15 days; 7- to 10-day cruises are the most popular.
   Cruise lines: Celebrity, Clipper, Cunard, Holland America, Norwegian, Princess, Royal Caribbean, Seabourn, and Silversea.
   Ports of call: Campobello, St. Andrews, St. John, New Brunswick; Cape Harrison, Corner Brook,

St. Johns, Newfoundland; Charlottetown, Prince Edward Island; Gaspé, Province of Quebec; Halifax, Sydney, Nova Scotia, Canada; Alexandria, Norfolk, Virginia; Annapolis, Maryland; Bar Harbor, Maine; Boston, Massachusetts; Charleston, South Carolina; Ft. Lauderdale, Key West, Miami, Port Canaveral, Tampa, Florida; New York City, New York; Newport, Rhode Island; Philadelphia, Pennslvania; Savannah, Georgia.

10. Canada and U.S. West Coast

Point of embarkation: Seattle, Washington; Los Angeles, San Francisco, California; and Vancouver, British Columbia, Canada.

Cruise length: 3 to 8 days.

Cruise lines: Carnival, Celebrity, Clipper, Crystal, Cunard, Holland America, Norwegian, Princess, Royal Caribbean, Seabourn, and Silversea.

Ports of call: Prince Rupert, Princess Louisa, Vancouver, Victoria, British Columbia, Canada; Seattle, Washington; and Catalina Island, Los Angeles, San Diego, San Francisco, California.

11. Caribbean—Eastern

Point of embarkation: Miami, Tampa, Port Everglades (Ft. Lauderdale), Port Canaveral (Cocoa), FL.

Cruise length: 4 to 14 days; 7-day cruises are the most common.

Cruise lines: Carnival, Celebrity, Clipper, Costa, Crystal, Cunard, Holland America, Princess, Norwegian, Radisson Seven Seas, Royal Caribbean, Seabourn, Silversea, Windjammer, and Windstar.

Ports of call: Anguilla; Antigua; Guadeloupe; St. Kitts; Dominica; Puerto Rico; St. Croix, St. John, St. Thomas, U.S. Virgin Islands; St. Martin/St. Maarten; and Tortola, Virgin Gorda, British Virgin Islands.

12. Caribbean—Southern

Point of embarkation: Miami, Florida; San Juan, Puerto Rico; and Bridgetown, Barbados.

Cruise length: 7 to 14 days; 7-day cruises are the most common.

Cruise lines: same cruise lines as Caribbean—Eastern.

Ports of call: Aruba, Barbados, St. Vincent, Bonaire, Grenada, St. Lucia, Curacao, Martinique, and Trinidad.

13. Europe—Atlantic Coast

Point of embarkation: Lisbon, Portugal.

Cruise length: 7 to 15 days.

Cruise lines: Celebrity, Clipper, Costa, Crystal, Cunard, Holland America, Norwegian, Princess, Radisson Seven Seas, Royal Olympic, Seabourn, and Silversea.

Ports of call: Cádiz, La Coruña, Seville, Vigo, Spain; Cherbourg, Le Havre, St. Malo, France; Madeira Islands, Lisbon, Azore Islands, Portimao, Portugal; and Zeebrugge, Belgium.

14. Europe—Northern and Scandinavia

Point of embarkation: Amsterdam, Netherlands; Copenhagen, Denmark; and Stockholm, Sweden.

Cruise length: 5 to 15 days.

Cruise lines: Costa, Crystal, Cunard, Holland America, Norwegian, Princess, Radisson Seven Seas, Renaissance, Royal Caribbean, Seabourn, and Silversea.

Ports of call: Alesund, Bergen, Flam, Geiranger, Gudvangen, Hammerfest, Hellesylt, Honningsvag, Molde, Oslo, Stavanger, Trondheim, Norway; Amsterdam, Rotterdam, Netherlands; Copenhagen, Torshavn, Denmark; Gdańsk, Gdynia, Poland; Göteborg, Hälsingborg, Stockholm, Sweden; Hamburg, Keil, Rostock, Warnemünde, Germany; Helsinki, Finland; Reykjavík, Iceland; Riga, Latvia; St. Petersburg, Russia; and Tallinn, Estonia.

15. Great Britain and Ireland

Point of embarkation: Southampton, Dover, England and Edinburgh, Scotland.

Cruise length: 6 to 14 days; 6-day cruises are the most common.

Cruise lines: Clipper, Costa, Crystal, Cunard, Holland America, Norwegian, Princess, Radisson Seven Seas, Royal Caribbean, Seabourn, and Silversea.

Ports of call: Cobh, Cork, Dublin, Waterford, Ireland; Dover, Falmouth, Fowey, Harwich, Newcastle, Southampton, London, England, UK; Edinburgh, Greenock, Invergordon, Kirkwall, Lerwick, Rosyth, Scotland, United Kingdom; Fishguard, Holyhead, Wales, United Kingdom; and Londonderry, Northern Ireland, United Kingdom.

16. Hawaii

Point of embarkation: Honolulu, Hawaii and Los Angeles, California.

Cruise length: 4 to 16 days; 7-day cruises from Honolulu are the most popular.

Cruise lines: American Hawaii, Carnival, Crystal, Cunard, Holland America, Norwegian, Princess, Royal Caribbean, Silversea.

Ports of call: Hilo, Kailua-Kona, Hawaii; Honolulu, Oahu; Kauai; and Lahaina, Maui.

17. Mediterranean—Eastern

Point of embarkation: Piraeus (Athens), Greece and Istanbul, Turkey

Cruise length: 7 to 20 days; 7- to 10-day cruises are the most common.

Cruise lines: Clipper, Costa, Crystal, Cunard, First European, Holland America, Princess, Radisson Seven Seas, Royal Caribbean, Seabourn, and Silversea.

Ports of call: Alexandria, Egypt; Antalya, Bodrum, Canakkale, Dikili, Kusadasi, Istanbul, Turkey;

Corfu, Corinth Canal, Crete, Delos, Hydra, Mykonos, Patmos, Athens (Piraeus), Rhodes, Santorini (also known as Thira), Greece; Odessa, Yalta, Ukraine; and Cyprus.

18. Mediterranean—Western

Point of embarkation: Venice, Civitavecchia (Rome), Genoa, Italy; and Barcelona, Spain.

Cruise length: 7 to 20 days; 7- to 10-day cruises are the most common.

Cruise lines: same as Mediterranean—Eastern.

Ports of call: Barcelona, Ibiza, Málaga, Palma, Spain; Corsica Island, Cannes, Marseille, Nice, St. Tropez, Villefranche, France; Sardinia Island, Capri, Civitavecchia (Rome), Genoa, Livorno, Messina, Naples, Portofino, Sorrento, Venice, Italy; Dubrovnik, Croatia; Valletta, Malta; and Tunis, Tunisia.

19. Mexico

Point of embarkation: For Western Mexico: Los Angeles, San Diego, California; and Acapulco, Mexico. For Eastern Mexico: Miami, Tampa, Florida; and New Orleans, Louisiana.

Cruise length: 3 to 14 days; 7-day cruises are the most common.

Cruise lines: same as Caribbean—Eastern.

Ports of call: Acapulco, Cabo San Lucas, Ensenada, Huatulco, Ixtapa, Manzanillo, Mazatlán, Puerto Vallarta, Zihuatenjo, Cancun, Cozumel, Playa del Carmen, Mexico.

20. Nowhere

Point of embarkation: New York City, New York; Philadelphia, Pennsylvania; and New Orleans, Louisiana.

Cruise length: 2 or 3 days.

Cruise lines: varies.

Ports of call: none.

21. Panama Canal and Central America

Point of embarkation: Port Everglades (Ft. Lauderdale), Miami, Florida; Acapulco, Mexico; and San Juan, Puerto Rico.

Cruise length: 7 to 23 days; 10- to 12-day cruises are the most common.

Cruise lines: Carnival, Clipper, Crystal, Cunard, Holland America, Norwegian, Princess, Radisson Seven Seas, Royal Caribbean, Seabourn, Silversea, and Windstar.

Ports of call: Balboa, Colón, Isla de Coiba, Panama City, San Blas Island, Panama; Belize City, Belize; Caño Island, Golfo Dulce, Puerto Limón, Costa Rica; Puerto Cortés, Roatán, Honduras; and Puerto Quetzal, Santo Tomas, Guatemala.

22. River Cruising

North American rivers: Ohio, Mississippi, Cumberland, Tennessee—Delta Queen Steamboat Company; Columbia—Clipper; St. Lawrence—Clipper, Cunard, Norwegian, Princess, Royal Caribbean, Seabourn, and Silversea.

European rivers: Garonne, Loire, Seine, Saône, Rhône in France; Rhine, Main, Elbe in Germany; Volga in Russia; Danube in Switzerland, Germany, Austria, Hungary, Yugoslavia, and Romania.

South American rivers: Orinoco in Venezuela; Amazon in Brazil.

African rivers: Nile in Egypt.

Asian rivers: Yangtze and Pearl in the People's Republic of China.

23. South America

Point of embarkation: any major port.

Cruise length: 3 to 30 days; 7- to 14-day cruises are the most common.

Cruise lines: Carnival, Clipper, Crystal, Cunard, Holland America, Norwegian, Princess, Radisson Seven Seas, Royal Caribbean, Seabourn, Silversea, and Windstar.

Ports of call: Arica, Cape Horn, Coquimbo, Iquique, Puerto Montt, Punta Arenas, Santiago, Valparaiso, Chile; Belém, Boca do Valeria, Florianopolis, Recife, Rio de Janeiro, Salvador, Brazil; Galapagos Islands, Manta, Quito, Ecuador; Buenos Aires, Puerto Madryn, Ushuaia, Argentina; Callao, Peru; Caracas (La Guaira), Porlamar, Venezuela; Cartagena, Colombia; Devil's Island, French Guiana; and Montevideo, Uruguay.

24. South Pacific

Point of embarkation: Papeete, Tahiti.

Cruise length: 2 to 7 days.

Cruise lines: Crystal, Cunard, Holland America, Princess, Radisson Seven Seas, Renaissance, and Silversea.

Ports of call: Western Samoa; Pago Pago, American Samoa; Bora Bora, Moorea, French Polynesia; Papeete, Tahiti; Fiji; and Noumea, New Caledonia.

25. Transatlantic

Point of embarkation: New York City, New York; Port Everglades (Ft. Lauderdale), Miami, Florida; and Southampton, England, United Kingdom.

Cruise length: 6 to 25 days; 6-day sailings are the most common.

Cruise lines: several cruise lines offer occasional transatlantic crossings. Cunard Line's QM2 is the only ship that has routine crossings from spring through early fall.

Ports of call: none.

26. World Cruises

Cunard and Holland America offer world cruises annually. These cruises can be purchased in full or in segments. Embarkation can be any major port and ports of call are offered on all continents. World cruises are from 60 to 130 days long.

FIGURE 15–2 A ship's profile, like the one shown here for Carnival's GLORY, is an illustration of a ship's decks, it's configuration, and overall size.

THE LANGUAGE OF CRUISING

The Ship

Cruise ships come in all sizes, from vessels that carry 50 passengers to ones that carry 3,400 or more (Figure 15–2). Regardless of size, the terms used to identify areas of the ship, policies, and procedures are the same. The body or frame of the ship is called the hull and when looking at most ships head on, the hull is in the shape of the letter V. The bottom of the hull is the keel. Walls between primary sections of the ship are called *bulkheads,* just like on aircraft. On ships, especially older ones, bulkheads can create a short obstruction on the floor that must be stepped over. The portion of a ship that is below water is measured in feet and is call the ship's draft. Also below the water line on most ships are devices called stabilizers. These retractable devices are used to help reduce or eliminate the side-to-side motion of the ship, called roll.

Some ships, in fact many of today's larger vessels, have a draft that is too deep to allow mooring at the pier. In this situation, the ship drops anchor a short distance from the pier and uses a smaller vessel, called a tender, to transport passengers to shore. Tenders are usually fully enclosed and carry 60 to 100 passengers on each trip between the ship and shore. This process of reaching shore is called tendering, and travel counselors should explain this process, especially to first-time cruisers.

All ships are measured based on enclosed, revenue-producing space. This measurement is called gross registered tonnage (GRT). Today's cruise ships range from 1,000 to 150,000 GRT. By dividing a ship's GRT by the passenger capacity, space ratio is calculated. Theoretically, the higher the space ratio, the more spacious the ship, including the passenger cabins. Space ratios range from the low 20s to the high 60s. Many counselor reference sources list both the ship's GRT and space ratio.

Onboard

Unfortunately for new travel counselors, not much onboard a cruise ship is identified by a common name. Each floor or level on a ship is called a deck, and the diagram of each deck is the deck plan. The front of the ship is the bow and areas of the ship toward the bow are said to be forward. The back of a cruise ship is called the stern and areas near the stern are said to be aft. Even the left and right sides of the ship have special names; left is port, right is starboard. It is very common for a cruise line reservationist to ask the travel counselor if the client prefers a cabin fore (short for forward) or aft and to mention either the port or starboard side.

Experienced cruisers and travel counselors know that the answer to that question in most cases is neither. The reason is that the fore and aft sections of the ship experience more front-to-back motion, called pitch. Unfortunately, stabilizers do little to eliminate pitch and in rough seas, passengers accommodated in the fore and aft sections of the ship are aware of the weather conditions.

Most cruisers agree that the most stable accommodations are located midships; that is, toward the middle of the ship front-to-back. The laws of physics tell us that locations close to the center of gravity provide the most stability. On a ship, this means on a lower deck and midships. Travel counselors should be mindful of this when working with clients who express concern about the ship's motion.

Accommodations

Passenger accommodations on a cruise ship are called cabins or staterooms. Beds in passenger cabins are called berths and berths arranged in bunk-bed fashion are called upper/lower. Just to complicate things, the location at the pier where the ship is moored is also called a berth. Cabins that do not have a window, which is called a porthole if it is round, are said to be inside cabins, while those with windows are called outside cabins. As you might imagine, outside cabins are usually more expensive than inside cabins, and cabins with upper/lower berths are less expensive than those with a bed or beds on the floor.

Coming and Going

When passengers board a cruise ship, they use a walkway that links the ship to the pier and enter the ship through a doorway in the bulwark or side of the ship near the main deck. Both the walkway and the doorway are referred to as the gangway. Once onboard, passengers usually find themselves in the main lobby, known as the purser's lobby. The purser's lobby is where most business onboard is transacted, such as purchasing sightseeing trips ashore, called shore excursions, settling accounts at the end of the cruise, and so on.

Shore excursions are rarely included in the cost of the cruise. Cruises beyond North America may allow passengers to reserve and purchase shore excursions in advance, making them commissionable to the travel agency. Unfortunately, most cruises around North America do not offer this convenience and shore excursions are booked and paid for on a first-come, first-served basis onboard the ship.

Other Terms

The ship's navigational and command center is called the bridge. Some cruises offer tours of the bridge to passengers. A bridge tour is a real eye-opener of sophisticated technology. Another type of tour offered onboard some cruises is of the kitchen, known as the galley. When you think about the hundreds, perhaps thousands, of meals prepared every day on a cruise, it is easy to see why the galley must be the epitome of efficiency.

Every cruise ship is listed for legal and tax purposes in a specific country, known as the ship's registry. A ship's registry may not be in the same country as the home of the cruise line, and in fact, the countries are usually different. Ships that do not leave U.S. waters must be registered in the United States, and as such, are subject to U.S. laws, tax structures, and minimum wage considerations. Ships that leave or do not enter U.S. waters can be registered under any country, but the Bahamas, Panama, and Liberia are popular countries for ship registry.

Many cruise lines offer special programs for honeymooners, single travelers, children, and passengers with special dietary requirements. Some cruises offer a host program for unescorted women, while others provide fitness and spa programs. It is interesting to note that the more upscale the cruise line, the less likely it is to encourage travel with children.

Theme cruises have become very popular and are offered by a variety of cruise lines. Music lovers may favor a cruise that has a big band, music of the 1950s or 1960s, classical, or country theme. There are cruises focused around gourmet food and fine wine. Other types of theme cruises include sports, nature, history, art, and so on.

FACILITIES, FEATURES, AND FOOD

There are many aspects of the cruise experience that are quite different from every other mode of transportation and type of holiday. Without firsthand cruise experience or training in these differences, the travel counselor is hard pressed to accurately represent and sell cruises. Most potential cruise clients have many questions about what to expect from a cruise and the travel professional must be prepared to answer these questions.

Bars and Lounges

Are there bars onboard ship? When are they open? What is the minimum drinking age? Almost all cruise ships have more than one bar and lounge. In many cases, each one offers a different atmosphere; for example, a quiet piano bar, a dance club, a British pub, and so on. Most ships are not allowed by the country being visited to open the bars while the ship is in port.

The minimum drinking age is usually at the captain's discretion; however, 21 is typical. It is interesting to note that some countries do not have a minimum drinking age, and ships registered or traveling exclusively in those countries may not have a minimum drinking age either.

Alcoholic beverages on all cruises, except the most deluxe, are not included in the cost of the cruise. Most ships have extensive wine lists and offer all mixed drinks as well as domestic and imported beers and ales. Prices for alcoholic beverages onboard ship are similar to prices found in more upscale restaurants and bars. Tips for the bartender or waiter are appropriate on most cruises at the time of service or a standard tip may be automatically included in the bill.

Casino

Almost all cruise ships have a casino, although they can be very small, especially on older ships (Figure 15-3). Casinos onboard cruise ships usually offer slot machines and table games such as blackjack, roulette, and craps. Most cruise ships are not allowed by the country being visited to open the casino while the ship is in port. The minimum age for gambling onboard ship is at the captain's discretion; however, 21 is common.

Electricity

This is another subject rarely questioned by potential cruise clients but is very important to their enjoyment of

FIGURE 15–3 Almost all cruise ships have a casino.

Web Activity

1. Access Carnival Cruise Line's Web site and complete a comparison of the passenger capacity of each ship in the fleet.
2. Access Royal Caribbean International's Web site and complete a comparison of the casino size on each ship.
3. Access Cunard Line Ltd.'s Web site and list the health and sports facilities available.

the cruise. The United States is one of a handful of countries that use 110 volt; most of the world uses 220 volt. The difference in voltage is enough to rapidly burn up a hair dryer, razor, clothes steamer, curling iron, or other appliance. All of the cruise ships operating in and around North America are wired for 110 volt and possibly 220 volt as well. However, ships stationed in other areas of the world may be wired for 220 volt only and U.S. passengers must use a current converter.

To make matters worse, the plug configuration on many receptacles throughout the world is different from the standard two-prong style used in the United States. So, in addition to a current converter, passengers may also need plug adaptors. Current converters and plug adaptors can be purchased individually or in a set at any major retail outlet that handles luggage and other travel products. These items can also be obtained from Magellan's by mail order or through their Web site at http://www.magellans.com or from Orvis at http://www.orvis.com.

Entertainment

When it comes to activities and entertainment onboard a cruise ship, diversity is the word. During the daytime hours, a variety of activities is offered and passengers may participate in any or all of them. Skeet shooting, driving golf balls, gambling (while at sea), and bingo, for example, are available for an extra charge. Royal Caribbean International's ship, *Voyager of the Seas,* offers a rock-climbing wall, golf course, and inline skating track. Special activities such as these may be included in the price of a cruise. All of this is in addition to swimming pools, jogging tracks, and classes and discussions on various topics that are free.

Many cruise ships have a cinema that shows different films throughout the cruise. In the evening, stage performances are offered. These may be a full Broadway production, Las Vegas style revue, or comedy show. In one or more lounges, passengers enjoy a variety of music, from soft piano to country to rock. Most ships have a dance club that features all of the lights, bells, whistles, and hot music found at popular clubs ashore. All of these entertainment options are included in the cost of the cruise.

With all of this activity, how do passengers stay abreast of what is going on? Each morning, or during the previous night, a daily newsletter is slipped under each cabin door. This newsletter lists all activities of the day, as well as other types of information such as suggested dress for the evening meal, shore excursions, distance traveled, and the history of the next port of call.

More and more travelers see cruising as a perfect family vacation. But, what can the kids do for fun? Many cruise lines cater to families by providing child counselors and scheduled activities for children of different age groups at no extra charge. Special opportunities for children include escorted shore excursions, video games, a teen center or playroom, parties, movies, and menus. Cruise lines that cater to families may also offer reduced fares for children, babysitting service (for a fee), cribs, and quad or family cabins. It is important to note that some cruise lines offer these services and amenities only during the summer months, while other lines offer them year round.

The newer cruise ships are not to be left behind and are joining the technological revolution. It is common to find a computer center onboard where passengers can take a complimentary class or play the latest computer game. Some computer rooms have Internet access and passengers can check their e-mail while at sea. Depending on the ship, there may be an additional fee for Internet and e-mail use.

Finances

Have you ever considered that some cruises may not use U.S. dollars (USD) as the unit of currency onboard? Many potential cruise clients haven't either! Cruises that take place outside North America may use the currency of the country of registry, or the currency of the country of embarkation. For example, a cruise on the Rhine River in Germany may use the euro, shown with the symbol €. A cruise around the British Isles may use the pound sterling, symbol £, as the ship's unit of currency.

Some cruise ships are cashless; that is, everything purchased onboard is charged to the passenger's account. At the end of the cruise, the account is settled at the purser's desk, either in accepted currency or by credit card. Some cruise lines, especially the smaller ones, may not accept credit cards or perhaps they accept only a specific kind.

As with any other type of travel, it is advisable to leave valuables at home. If your client insists on taking the family jewels on his cruise, advise him to make use of a safe deposit box. On some ships, each cabin has a safe for the passengers' use at no extra cost. Other ships offer safe deposit boxes at the purser's desk, again at no extra charge. It is important to note that access to safe deposit boxes at the purser's desk is limited to the times the desk is open.

Understanding how and in what currency purchases are handled is very important so that the client can plan appropriately.

Food, Food, and More Food

For some cruise passengers, dining is one of the primary attractions of a cruise (Figure 15-4). You can look at any cruise brochure and see sumptuous delicacies pictured on almost every page. On many cruises there are six or more opportunities to eat during the day: breakfast, midmorning snack, luncheon, afternoon tea, dinner, and midnight buffet, all included in the cruise fare (sample dinner menu Figure 15-5).

Most of the larger cruise ships offer the main meals at two seatings, early and late, although some ships have instituted four times for each meal. Toward the back of each

FIGURE 15–4 For some cruise passengers dining is the primary attraction. Courtesy of Norwegian Cruise Line.

Dinner Menu

Starters

Vine Ripe Beefsteak Tomatoes and Fresh Buffalo Mozzarella
Marinated with Basil Leaves and Virgin Olive Oil

 Panko Crusted Crispy Shrimp Quenelles
Accompanied by Candied Carrots and Shiitake Mushroom

South Western Style Egg Roll
Marinated Baby Lettuce and Sweet & Sour Salsa

Cream of Garden Fresh Broccoli and Wisconsin Cheddar

Corn Chowder Maryland

Asparagus Vichyssoise
Chilled Potato Soup with Asparagus Tips

Salads

Mixed Garden and Field Greens
Tomatoes, Cucumbers and Carrots with Choice of Dressing

Curly Endive and Thinly Sliced Cucumbers
Marinated with a Low Calorie Lemon Dressing

These Items are Lower in Calories, Sodium, Cholesterol and Fat. Salads are prepared with Diet Dressing. Calorie Count and Fat Content can vary up to 10%.

Panko Crusted Crispy Shrimp Quenelles
Accompanied by Candied Carrots and Shiitake Mushroom
[194 Calories, 8 grams of Fat]

Asparagus Vichyssoise
Chilled Potato Soup with Asparagus Tips
[119 Calories, 3 grams of Fat]

Pan Fried Snapper
Crispy Fried Vegetables, Black Olives, Cauliflower Ragout, Grilled Tomato
Lemon and Caper Emulsion with Verbena Froth
[132 Calories, 5 grams of Fat]
 SAUVIGNON BLANC - NOBILO

FIGURE 15–5 Carnival's Total Choice Dining gives you more flexibility, more attentive service, and more choice. Sample menu courtesy of Carnival Cruise Lines' Web site, http://www.carnival.com.

cruise brochure, you may find a schedule of early and late dining times. For example,

Breakfast in port	6:45 A.M.	8:00 A.M.
Breakfast at sea	7:45 A.M.	9:00 A.M.
Luncheon	Noon	1:30 P.M.
Dinner	6:00 P.M.	8:00 P.M.

Both dining times have advantages and disadvantages. Early diners may not feel they can linger over coffee because passengers dining late are due to arrive. Passengers having breakfast late may feel rushed because of a scheduled shore excursion. Unfortunately, dining times cannot be combined; it's either an early or a late seating for the entire cruise.

Before making a cruise booking, travel counselors should discuss the pros and cons of the two meal seatings and learn which the client prefers. When making a cruise reservation by phone, the reservationist asks for a time preference. Clients may also specify their preference as to table size: a table for four, six, or eight. However, dining time and table size cannot be guaranteed and this should be made clear to the client. The cruise line assigns the dining time and table size, which may be indicated on the client's cruise documents, or be indicated at boarding.

Some cruise lines, particularly the more upscale ones, offer single, open seating. This dining program affords the passengers complete freedom to dine when they want (within specified hours) and to sit where and with whom they want. Single, open seating is by far the best type of meal program, but unfortunately, not many cruise lines can use this style because of passenger numbers.

Cunard Line's *Queen Elizabeth 2* (*QE2*) has a unique dining setup. There are four dining rooms onboard and each is linked to a particular cabin price range. In other words, the more expensive the cabin, the more upscale the dining room. Utilizing four dining rooms is a clever way to eliminate the need for two meal seatings; all dining rooms on *QE2* are single seating.

On most ships, passengers have other options for breakfast and lunch. Usually these meals are served buffet style near the pool or in a lounge. Room service is available on most ships and, generally, there is no extra charge. During meal times, soft drinks, coffee, and tea are included in the cruise fare. At other times of the day, there is a charge for soft drinks and tea on most ships. On more upscale cruise lines, certain wines may be complimentary with dinner, but on most ships, alcoholic beverages are at an additional cost.

The mention of the midnight buffet conjures up images of food too beautifully prepared to eat and those marvelous ice sculptures. Even if the passengers couldn't eat another bite, they should at least see the midnight buffet. Some passengers go to the midnight buffet just to take photographs of the incredible array of edibles, and then find that perhaps they are a bit hungry after all. As an added note, the average weight gain on a seven-day cruise is 10 pounds.

On a typical seven-day cruise, there are usually two formal dinners: the Captain's Gala, usually the second night, and the Farewell Dinner on the last night. For these evenings, men should wear dark suits, although some men will wear tuxedos. Ladies should wear cocktail dresses; however, some women prefer to wear floor-length gowns. The other nights are considered casual, but swimwear, shorts, jeans, and T-shirts are never appropriate for dinner.

Many ships today offer a variety of dining options in addition to the primary dining room. These include intimate dining areas, casual dining facilities, and ethnic food venues. A few cruise lines offer completely flexible dining in which the passenger may dine in any of the ship's facilities. A few ships now offer a pay-as-you-dine program, thereby giving cruise passengers greater choice.

Hair Salons

Most cruise ships have hair salons for both men and women. Cruise passengers can make an appointment by calling the salon from the phone in their cabin, or by contacting their cabin steward. The cost is very similar to the prices at salons in major cities. A tip of 15 to 20 percent is usually given to the hair stylist at the time of service.

Laundry

Laundry and dry cleaning services are available on almost all ships simply by contacting the cabin steward. The cabin steward picks up the laundry and returns it to the passengers' cabin. A tip to the cabin steward is not usually given at this time. Laundry and dry cleaning prices are comparable to those in any U.S. or Canadian city. Some ships have a launderette that passengers may use and depending on the ship, use of the launderette may be complimentary or coin operated.

Library

Many cruise ships, especially those sailing on longer voyages, offer a library. Books and videos are available to the passengers at no cost; however, a tip of a dollar or two to the attendant when returning the item is common.

Medical Services

Medical facilities onboard most cruise ships have advanced considerably over the past 10 years. Most major ships' infirmaries can handle routine illnesses and also perform many diagnostic tests as well. The cost of a visit to the ship's doctor ranges from $50 to $75. Medication or special treatments are usually in addition to the office call. An emergency air evacuation can cost as much as $15,000. Passengers can purchase insurance that covers must situations.

Phone, Fax, and Computer

Many passengers, especially those on extended cruises, may be concerned about communication with home or office while at sea. Each cruise line can provide passengers with an at-sea address, a phone number, the fax procedures, and an e-mail address. Telephones are standard in many cruise ship cabins; however, a ship-to-shore call can be expensive: $15.00 or more per minute. Sending a fax from the ship is more expensive than on land because all phone connections are via communication satellite links. Many ships have computer centers with Internet access for passenger use and e-mail may be complimentary.

Religious Services

Most cruises of a week in length or longer offer some type of worship service. Depending on the cruise area and country of registry, the service may be nondenominational Christian, Catholic, Jewish, or a service of any other major religion.

Ship's Shops

Duty-free (import tax-free) shopping can be enjoyed on many cruise ships. As a rule, these shops offer everything from aspirin to diamond jewelry. Everyday necessities are often higher priced than the same item is at the local store. Luxury items, especially imported items, tend to be lower priced than the same item is in the United States or Canada. Many cruise passengers shop for French perfumes, Austrian crystal, Swiss chocolate, Irish lace, and other international treasures without ever leaving the ship.

Many ships also offer a rental outlet, primarily for formalwear. Rental costs are similar to those found in any U.S. or Canadian city. Some passengers may want to wear tuxedos or long gowns but do not want the expense of buying these items. The rental outlet onboard ship is the perfect solution.

All of the larger ships have a photo shop and photographer. Passengers may find that their picture is taken as they board, as they shake hands with the captain before the Captain's Gala, and at varying times throughout the cruise. These photos are displayed in the photo shop and are available for purchase. The photo shop also sells a variety of film and other photographic supplies.

Spa, Sports, Health, and Fitness

Spas and fitness facilities have become an important part of most cruise ships. Visitors to these facilities will find a full range of health and beauty treatments, whirlpools, weight machines, cardio equipment, putting greens, water parks, jogging tracks, volleyball, shuffleboard, ping pong, and personal trainers. There are swimming pools, sports pools, and group fitness classes as well as fitness evaluations for those interested (Figure 15-6).

Tipping

Of all the questions asked by first-time cruise clients, inquiries about tipping procedures may be the most fre-

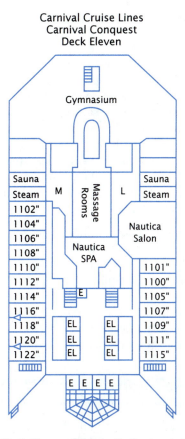

FIGURE 15–6 Deck Eleven of Carnival's Conquest shows spa facilities and gymnasium. Reprinted from http://www.carnival.com with permission from Carnival Cruise Lines.

quently asked. Generally, tipping falls into three categories, depending on the cruise ship.

Ultradeluxe cruise lines, such as Silversea and Seabourn, have a strict no-tipping policy. Passengers may be skeptical and feel that the cruise staff will accept tips anyway, but this is not the case. Any cruise line that has a no-tipping policy means just what it says; tips are not accepted.

Some upscale cruise lines, such as Cunard and Holland America, include tips in the cruise fare or have a "tipping not required" policy. Passengers on these lines may tip if they wish, but they should not feel obligated to do so. Fortunately, each cruise brochure and cruise line Web site usually discusses the topic of tipping.

All ships of Greek registry are required by law to pool all tips and divide them equally between the staff. On these ships, tips for the cabin steward, waiter, and assistant waiter are placed in an envelope (provided by the cruise ship) at the end of the cruise. The envelopes are either left behind in the cabin on debarkation or they are turned in at the purser's desk.

Most cruise lines accept, and in some cases blatantly encourage, tipping. Generally tips are handled in a three-step process:

1. Envelopes are provided, either at the purser's desk or they are slipped under each cabin door prior to the morning of the last day of the cruise.

2. The tip for the waiter and assistant waiter are combined, placed in an envelope, and given to the waiter after dinner on the last night of the cruise. Typical amounts suggested by many cruise lines are $3.50 per passenger per day for the waiter and $2.00 per passenger per day for the assistant waiter.

3. The tip for the cabin steward is placed in an envelope and left in the cabin at the end of the cruise. The typical amount suggested by many cruise lines is $3.50 per passenger per day.

Most seven-day cruises follow these three steps; however, tips may be prepaid on some cruise lines. Longer cruises may have more than one tipping occasion, usually after each week of the cruise.

As you have already learned, tips to other cruise staff takes place at the time of service. These cruise staff include hair stylist, library attendant, sommelier, masseuse, bartender, bar waiter, headwaiter, and maitre d'.

SELLING OTHER TYPES OF SEA TRAVEL

Sea travel is certainly not limited to luxury cruise ships, and many passengers are looking for a much different experience at sea. Throughout the world, there are cargo ships that carry passengers. Today's freighters are generally modern ships with stabilizers, air conditioning, modest but adequate quarters, plentiful (and sometimes quite excellent) cuisine, and interesting experiences. The extravagant entertainment found on a cruise ship is not a part of life on a freighter. Passengers must accept the fact that their presence on the vessel is second to that of the cargo. Therefore, ports of call are few and far between and are not scheduled for the passenger's benefit. Although freighters operate on a set schedule, certain conditions and situations may alter schedules drastically. Because freighters have so few passenger cabins, they are usually booked months in advance. Since most freighter companies do not pay commissions, it's necessary for the travel agent to add their profit on top of the cost of travel.

Around the world, ferries transport people, cargo, automobiles, and even livestock. Ferry crossings are not sold as a vacation, but rather as a form of transportation. However, they can be an interesting experience, and many can be reserved and prepaid for clients by a travel agent. Ferries come in all sizes and levels of luxury, from the size of a small cruise ship all the way down to a big rowboat. Although most ferry service is short distance, some have overnight accommodations. A common ferry crossing for U.S. travelers is from England to the Continent and from the United Kingdom to Ireland.

SUMMARY

Cruises come in all shapes, sizes, locations, and prices, so there is a cruise to fit everyone's idea of a dream vacation. It is the travel professional's responsibility to remember that a cruise is not a one-size-fits-all type of product, and a client's vacation can be ruined by selecting an inappropriate cruise line or ship. By understanding the various terms and programs associated with cruising, travel professionals are better able to explain the details to their clients, thus making the overall experience less stressful and more enjoyable.

 For additional Travel and Tourism resources, go to http://www.hospitality-tourism.delmar.com.

> ### Case Study
>
> Your clients, Clarence and Keesha Phillips, are interested in cruising the South Pacific. They want a smaller vessel (no mega-ships for them), but they are concerned that a smaller ship will be more subject to motion.
>
> 1. In what way might the size of the ship affect the amount of motion felt by the passengers?
> 2. What is the best recommendation you can make to clients who are concerned about motion sickness?
> 3. What cruise would you suggest for them and why?
> 4. What facilities onboard would you highlight for them?

PLEASE COMPLETE THE CHAPTER REVIEW QUESTIONS NOW.

EXERCISE 15-1 Lines, Ships, and Cruise Areas of the World

1. Identify the benefits clients enjoy by purchasing a cruise. _____
_____

2. Identify the benefits travel counselors enjoy by selling cruises. _____
_____

3. What possible disadvantages might there be to cruising? _____
_____

4. What would you say to a client who expresses concern about seasickness? _____
_____
_____

5. What are the typical points of embarkation for cruises to Bermuda? _____
_____

6. Identify the typical ports of call on Alaskan cruises. _____
_____

7. What are the special cruise areas on Alaskan cruises? _____
_____

8. How long are cruises in the Bahamas? _____

9. Identify the typical points of embarkation for cruises in the Southern Caribbean. ___
_____

10. What countries are often visited on Eastern Mediterranean cruises? _____
_____

11. How long are cruises in the Eastern Caribbean? _____

12. On what North American rivers are cruises offered? _____
_____

EXERCISE 15-2 The Language of Cruising

Define these cruise terms in your own words.

aft _____

berth _____

bow _____

bridge _____

bulkhead _____

deck plan _____

forward _____

galley _____

gangway _____

gross registered tonnage _____

hull _____

inside cabin _____

midships _____

outside cabin _____

pitch _____

port _____

registry _____

roll _____

shore excursions _____

stabilizers _____

starboard _____

stern _____

tender _____

upper/lower _____

Review Questions

1. Identify which are usually included (I) and are not included (N) in the cruise fare.

   _____ alcoholic beverages   _____ babysitting service   _____ bingo

   _____ breakfast, lunch, and dinner _____ children's activities   _____ cola by the pool

   _____ driving golf balls   _____ dry cleaning   _____ evening stage show

   _____ luncheon buffet by the pool   _____ massage   _____ movie in the cinema

   _____ phone call home   _____ room safe   _____ room service

   _____ roulette chips   _____ skeet shooting   _____ soft drink with lunch

   _____ tips to cruise staff   _____ use of computer center   _____ visit to ship's doctor

   _____ wash and style at the salon   _____ wine with dinner

2. Your clients are taking a cruise on the Seine River in France. Why would you ask the cruise line about electricity onboard?

   _____

   _____

3. How do passengers know what activities are being offered each day? _____

   _____

4. What type of cruise lines do not generally encourage travel with children? _____

5. How are onboard purchases handled on a "cashless" cruise? _____

   _____

6. What is a possible drawback to using safe deposit boxes that are located at the purser's desk? _____

   _____

7. Identify a pro and con to selecting the first or early meal seating. _____

   _____

8. Identify a pro and con of selecting the late meal seating. _____

   _____

9. Can a travel counselor guarantee the meal seating and table size for his clients? _____

10. Identify cruise staff members who are usually tipped at the time of service. _____

    _____

11. Why is buying luxury items onboard ship often less expensive than buying the same item at home? _____

    _____

12. Explain the three steps of tipping procedures that are applicable to most cruises. _____

    _____

    _____

13. Identify the typical points of embarkation on Alaskan cruises. _____

_____

14. What are the usual ports of call on Alaskan cruises? _____

_____

15. What is the typical length of Bahamian cruises? _____

16. Where do cruises to Bermuda usually begin? _____

_____

17. What is the most popular cruise length in the Eastern and Southern Caribbean? _____

18. Where do most cruises in the Eastern Mediterranean begin? _____

_____

19. What cruise lines offer Hawaiian cruises? _____

_____

20. Identify the North American rivers where cruises are offered. _____

_____

21. Identify the cruise term that fits each definition.

_____ toward the rear of the ship

_____ bed on a cruise ship

_____ ship's diagram showing all cabins, public rooms, and so on

_____ toward the front of the ship

_____ center part of a ship, front-to-back

_____ front-to-back motion of a ship

_____ left side of a ship when facing forward

_____ side-to-side motion of a ship

_____ optional sightseeing trips offered for purchase

_____ devices that help reduce or eliminate the ship's side-to-side motion

_____ right side of the ship when facing forward

_____ small vessel used to take passengers from the ship to the shore

_____ beds arranged in bunk-bed fashion on a cruise ship

22. What benefits do clients enjoy by purchasing a cruise? _____

_____

23. What benefits do travel counselors enjoy when selling cruises? _____

_____

24. What are the possible disadvantages to cruising? _____

_____

CHAPTER 16

Cruise Pricing and Selling

OBJECTIVES

At the conclusion of this chapter, you should be able to

- identify several ways to increase your knowledge of cruises.
- understand what influences the price of a cruise.
- accurately calculate the price of a cruise.
- identify elements necessary to make a cruise reservation.
- describe important after-sale functions for a travel agent.
- identify what is involved in embarking and debarking.
- explain cruise line security measures.
- understand other types of sea travel.

KEY TERMS

bon voyage gift	guaranteed share rate	reservation worksheet
cabin category	contraband	security
customs	passenger departure tax	travel season
discounts	port charges	

In Chapter 15, you learned that the cruise industry is booming. New ships with ever-increasing arrays of superior features mean growing numbers of cruisers every year. You now know the benefits and disadvantages of cruising, and that cruises have an exceptionally high percentage of satisfied customers. Yet, while more people are cruising, the percentage of vacationers who choose to cruise is relatively small. That means there is an enormous market of potential cruisers waiting to discover the romance, pampering, and value of a cruise.

Becoming as knowledgeable as possible about selling cruises is vital to tapping this vast resource and realizing an increase in profits. There are several things you can do to boost your cruise knowledge and become an effective cruise salesperson:

1. First-hand experience of every cruise ship would be the ideal way to develop your product knowledge. Unfortunately, though some try, it just isn't possible to achieve. Do take part in familiarization trips, ship inspections, and special events sponsored by cruise lines. These provide great hands-on experience.

2. Research individual cruise line Web sites and CLIA's Web site. Take a virtual ship's tour and investigate facilities available on each ship. Travel sites like Expedia.com or Travelocity.com allow you to compare and contrast cruises based on destination, cruise line, and length of cruise. The Internet has made information gathering much easier for travel planners. It's also easier for customers to do research. Travel counselors have to stay on their toes just to stay ahead of their customers.

3. Take advantage of training offered by CLIA, ASTA, and individual cruise lines. Whether it's a group training session or a video you can view at home, you will gain not only product knowledge, but also information on how to sell the cruise product.

4. Gather information from your clients. If they have cruised before, find out what they liked or didn't like about a particular ship. Most importantly, understand the importance of two-way communication. Is everyone a potential cruise client? Does everyone prefer a megaship? Does every client want the same cruise experience? Does every client want a "budget" cruise? The answer to all these questions is, obviously, "no." Because there are so many choices available, you can find a cruise product to fit almost any client. As with lodging and tour packages, a bad choice of product can lead to a ruined vacation for the client.

WHAT DOES A CRUISE COST?

Generally, the major determinants of the price of a cruise are cabin category and season. Other determinants include cruise length, the ship, and discounts.

All cruise pricing is based on a cabin category (see Figure 16–1). A cabin category is a group of cabins that have a common price. As with most other travel products, selecting the lowest priced product may not offer the value the client expects, so it is important to assist the client in selecting a cabin category that not only fits in his budget, but also his expectations.

At first glance, a lower cabin category may look good, but the least expensive cabin categories, while having the advantage of lower prices, have some disadvantages:

1. They usually have *upper and lower berths* instead of one or two beds on the floor. As you might imagine, cabins with upper/lower berths may not be practical for many clients, especially older clients, honeymoon couples, or travelers who are physically challenged.

2. They are *located in less favorable areas* of the ship. Unfortunately, lower priced cabins are often located in the forward and aft sections which experience more *pitch*. (Larger cabins and suites are usually located on the higher decks. These cabins provide wonderful views of the sea and the ports, but may experience more *roll* than cabins on lower decks.) Cabins that are located midship offer a smoother ride, plus they are closer to common areas. Lower priced cabins are also usually "inside," without a window or porthole. For a ship illustration see Figure 16–2.

3. They cannot *accommodate more than two* people. Anyone expecting to squeeze a third person, adult or child, into the least expensive cabin will find it's not possible. Three friends, or a family, simply can't qualify for the lowest priced cabins.

Cruise-only rates—rates include port charges		
Cabin Category	Value Season	Regular Season
Suites	$2,459	$2,679
Ocean View	$1,459	$1,659
Ocean View	$1,379	$1,589
Porthole	$1,289	$1,489
Interior	$1,269	$1,459
Interior	$1,239	$1,439
Interior	$1,189	$1,379
Upper/Lower	$1,129	$1,299
3rd & 4th guest	$879	$879
3rd & 4th guest	$989	$989
Vacation Protection	$59	$59
Vacation Protection	$99	$99

FIGURE 16–1 Two factors that affect cruise pricing are cabin category and seasons. This chart indicates the range of pricing.

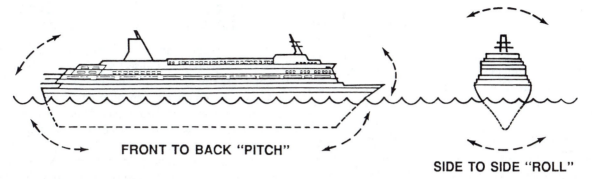

FRONT TO BACK "PITCH"

SIDE TO SIDE "ROLL"

FIGURE 16–2 Cabins on higher decks may experience more *roll* than those on lower decks, while lower priced cabins in the forward and aft sections experience more *pitch*.

Cruise prices are also based on travel season. Some cruises have two seasons, while others may have three. Generally, more popular travel seasons are higher in price and less favorable seasons are lower in cost.

Since *cruise length* is a variable in pricing, it's sometimes more meaningful to determine the cost per day by dividing the total cost by the number of days. By doing this, it's easier for a client to compare a four-day cruise price to a seven-day cruise price.

Another factor that affects cruise pricing is *the ship* itself. Newer ships often command higher prices, as do ships that offer more space or more crew members.

Yet another factor that affects the price of a cruise is discounting. Nearly all cruise lines offer discounts of varying amounts based on the cabin category. In fact, there are so many discounts that a cruise is seldom sold for the price printed on a Web site or in a brochure. *Early booking discounts* are available if a cruise is booked far in advance. How far in advance isn't always easy to tell from published information, so it often requires contacting the cruise line. *Special programs* are nearly always available for selected ships, sailing dates, and perhaps cabin categories. The reason for specials is to boost sales on ships and sailings that have low bookings. Specials can be a flat dollar discount or they can be something as impressive as a "two for one" offer. Some cruise lines have *loyalty programs* that offer discounts to past cruise customers. Others offer discounts to organizations such as the American Association of Retired Persons (AARP). Regardless of the nature of the discount, the fact is that the amount shown for a cabin category is the *maximum fare that could be applicable.*

BASICS OF CRUISE FARE CALCULATION

It would appear that establishing a client's cruise fare is a simple matter of selecting the ship, the season, the length of the cruise, and the cabin category, and then applying any applicable discounts. However, there is more to consider.

Prices quoted for a cabin category are *per person,* and usually assume that two people will occupy the cabin. A single person must pay a *single supplement,* or an additional charge to occupy the same room. If a single traveler wants to avoid paying this charge, some cruise lines offer a guaranteed share rate which pairs single travelers of the same sex in the same cabin. This often represents a big savings, but the idea of sharing a cabin with a total stranger usually outweighs the savings in the mind of most clients. When more than two passengers occupy a cabin, the third and fourth travelers pay a lower rate than the first two. Dividing the total cost by three or four will reduce the per person cost for all.

The current trend in cruise pricing is that the amount shown in the cabin category chart includes port charges but not airfare or other taxes. Port charges are taxes levied by the government of each port of call against the cruise line. These taxes are shown as a total per person, and are then included with the cruise price. Note that port charges are not commissionable and must be subtracted from the cruise sale before the agency commission can be calculated.

All cruises that depart from or return to a U.S. port are subject to other taxes as well and these taxes are not included in the cabin category price chart. As part of the travel counselor's fare calculation, a per-person passenger departure tax must be added. Passengers on cruises returning to the United States are subject to a customs fee per person. These taxes are established by the U.S. government and are, of course, subject to change. Like port charges, these items are not commissionable to the agency.

Cruises that begin and end outside the United States may be subject to a variety of other taxes and fees. These are not usually included in the cabin category price. Generally, the total of all other fees and taxes is shown somewhere on the same page as the cruise fares and must be added to the fare when calculating a client's total cost. Any tax or other government fee is not commissionable to the travel agency.

Most cruise passengers require air transportation from their hometown to the point of embarkation. This can be booked through the cruise lines, or it can be booked separately by the travel counselor. Most travel counselors find that the advantages of booking air transportation with the cruise line far outweigh the possibility of booking a somewhat lower fare obtained separately. Consider the following:

- Purchasing airfare from the cruise line usually includes transfers from the airport to the pier for cruises around North America and may include transfers for cruises in other parts of the world.

- Purchasing airfare from the cruise line safeguards the clients should there be flight delays. The cruise ship will delay departure as long as possible when flights are delayed. Should the ship sail, late arriving passengers will be transported to the ship's first port of call and the passengers may receive some form of compensation from the cruise line.

Making the Calculations

Because commission is not paid on the total amount, we have to divide the calculation into commissionable and noncommissionable totals. Use the following steps to calculate the total amount of the sale (the amount you will quote to your client):

1. Add all commissionable items together.
2. Subtract included port charges.
3. Multiply by two (assuming there are two passengers).
4. Add all noncommissionable items together and again multiply by two passengers.
5. Add the commissionable total and the noncommissionable totals together to obtain the total sale amount.

Your calculations will look like this:	
Per-person cruise fare	$1479
Per-person airfare	329
Per-person insurance	99
Per-person discount	−200
$1578 × 2 =	$3156.00
	(commissionable amount)
Per-person port charges	129.00
Per-person air charges	65.95
Per-person departure tax	3.00
Per-person customs fee	1.75
$199.70 × 2 =	$399.40
	(noncommissionable total)
$3156 + $199.70 =	$3555.40
	(total sale amount)

MAKING RESERVATIONS

A cruise reservation can be made by phone, in the agency GDS, or via individual cruise line Web sites. Most cruise bookings are still made with a phone call, but the GDS and Web sites are improving their offerings in order to attract more travel agents to make automated bookings. One example is Sabre Cruises, a browser-based cruise shopping and booking tool for travel agents that includes several cruise lines. In addition to being able to custom-fit a cruise to customer requirements, Sabre Cruises has more than 200,000 pages of graphical content, including descriptions of ports of call, ship views, deck plans, attraction information, maps, itineraries, and more. Several cruise line Web sites have agent-only sections that encourage agents to book online. The Web site http://www.vaxvacationaccess.com, which began as a tour booking tool, allows travel agents to make real-time bookings, access discounts, and search for cruises by customer interests for several major cruise lines.

Regardless of the method used to make a reservation, the travel agent must have all necessary information about the client and the selected cruise before beginning the booking process. Some agents prefer to use a reservation worksheet to make certain they collect everything that is necessary. Information needed includes the following:

- Names, exactly as shown on driver's license or passport.
- Age and citizenship.
- The ship, date of sailing, and departure city.
- Cabin preference.
- Special dietary requirements.
- Is air transportation required? If so, from where?
- Do they want trip insurance?
- Are they celebrating a special occasion, such as a birthday or anniversary? Many cruise lines provide special amenities, usually at no extra cost.
- What are their dining preferences?
- Shore excursions.

In general, cruises should be booked as far in advance as possible to ensure your client the best rates and first choice of cabin category. If a cabin category is sold out, the client may be offered a *guarantee* instead of an actual cabin. This means that the price is guaranteed, but a cabin will not be assigned until the day of sailing. If the client is willing to take this chance, they will receive a cabin that is at least equal to what they paid for but may be an upgraded (more expensive) cabin. Another booking option that leaves a great deal to chance is waiting until a few days or weeks prior to a sailing to book. If cabins are available, they may be offered at substantial discounts. On the other hand, if the departure is mostly filled, last-minute bookers won't receive any discount and will be assigned to whatever cabins are left.

After the reservation has been made, an *option date* is assigned. This is the date by which the cruise line must have the deposit. Option dates are usually seven days from the date of booking. Prior to the option date, the client can cancel without any penalty. A *confirmation number* is also assigned at the time of booking. This number makes it easier to access reservation information if changes need to be made.

Web Activity

Access the following cruise lines' Web sites to learn if they have an "agents-only" area: Carnival, Disney, Holland America, Norwegian, Premier, Princess, and Royal Caribbean.

KEEPING RECORDS

Most travel counselors create a file folder for each cruise sale. Within this folder should be the reservation worksheet, a hardcopy of an automated booking, and an action summary. The action summary is used to record all conversations, correspondence, payments, and transactions for the sale. In addition to being an ongoing record that covers all aspects of the sale, the action summary serves another important function. Should the booking counselor be out of the office, any other travel counselor can easily see what has been done, answer questions from the client, process payments, and so on.

As invoices are received from the cruise lines, these items should be kept in the folder as well. Keeping all paperwork about the sale together and in an orderly fashion substantially cuts down on the possibility of misplacing something, errors, and missing payment deadlines.

AFTER THE SALE

Once the cruise reservation is made, it's time to turn your attention to customer service. Cruisers have come to expect a superior level of service onboard and a total vacation that meets and exceeds expectations. Travel professionals know that offering this same value to their customers is key to retaining their business. Selling cruises offers many opportunities to enhance your value in the eyes of your client.

The first thing a travel agent should do after the reservation is send a follow-up letter to confirm to the client exactly what has been booked, what is included and not included in the price, cancellation policies, and trip insurance information. If a mistake has been made, it may very well be caught because of a confirmation letter. It's also important to thank the client for trusting you with his business. You might also include information on shore excursions, attire, weather forecasts, and the like.

Two to three weeks before the sailing date, the cruise line sends cruise documents to the travel agent. The documents include cruise tickets, air tickets, baggage tags, debarkation forms, general information about the cruise, and vouchers for transfers. E-documents are sometimes sent directly to the client, depending upon the cruise line. An e-document can be reproduced by the customer and contains all the components, including Web links to information about shore excursions and frequently asked questions.

Many travel agents like to send their cruise clients a **bon voyage gift**. These can be ordered through the cruise line. A bottle of wine makes a nice gift that can be delivered by the waiter at dinner. Snack trays, flowers, and fruit baskets can also be ordered and placed in the client's cabin.

A follow-up phone call or letter from you once your client has returned home is a great way to get feedback about the cruise experience, and it communicates to the client that you care. Most cruises are unqualified success stories, but if there were problems, this will give you an opportunity to deal with them. If the problem was a simple mishap that no one could control, sympathizing with the client may be all that's needed to soothe ruffled feathers. On the other hand, a problem of some severity that could have been avoided should be addressed. A letter to the cruise line, clearly identifying the problem and perhaps requesting compensation, may be in order.

Case Study

Your clients have decided to take a cruise and they have selected one of the least expensive cabin categories. They want to wait to make their reservation, thinking the rates may go down and they will be able to save a lot of money.

1. Is this reasoning justified?
2. Would you recommend that these clients wait to make their cruise reservation?
3. What risks do you see in waiting to make the booking and what advantages might there be in making the reservation now?

SETTING SAIL

Most cruise vacations begin with the passenger flying into the port city. What happens next? First, a passenger must claim their luggage. Near the baggage claim area of the airport, there is usually a cruise line representative holding a placard announcing the cruise line. The passenger should take their luggage to the representative. There may be several buses or vans outside the airport, and the representative advises the passenger which one to board. Baggage is usually taken to the pier in luggage trucks and is then delivered to the passenger's cabin. How does the cruise line know which baggage goes with which cabin? Remember the baggage tags that were part of the passenger's cruise packet? These tags identify the ship, sailing date, passenger's name, and cabin number.

Embarkation

Once at the pier, the passenger checks in. This procedure involves showing the cruise ticket to the cruise line agent on duty. Meal times and table assignments may also be made at this time. On some cruises, however, the meal time and table assignments are indicated on a card in the passenger's cabin.

The passenger is now ready to go onboard. In the movies, bon voyage parties are shown with friends and relatives celebrating the passenger's departure. In real life, most cruise lines do not allow nonpassengers onboard the ship. This policy is a security measure necessitated by the fact that we live in times of terrorism.

Debarkation

On completion of a cruise, most lines have a standard debarkation procedure. Each passenger is assigned a debarkation time, usually indicated by colored tags. This is to avoid having all passengers attempting to leave the ship at once.

When the ship arrives at her home port, the ship and crew members must clear customs (providing, of course, that the ship sailed into international waters). Customs officials board the ship for this procedure. Once the ship and crew have been cleared, it is the passengers' turn.

Some cities have customs offices at the port, others do not. In cities where there is a permanent customs office, passengers take their carry-on bags to the office for processing. In cities that do not have a port customs office, customs officials set up a temporary office, usually in the largest public room of the ship. Passengers and carry-on bags are processed in this temporary customs office.

Certain items are forbidden by the U.S. customs laws. Forbidden items are called contraband. Plant material is not allowed because insects and disease-causing bacteria and fungi may be present on organic products. For the same reason, fruits and vegetables are not allowed to be brought back into the United States.

On cruises throughout the Caribbean, passengers may purchase turtle shell products and Cuban cigars, both of which are contraband, but for different reasons. Turtle shell and all turtle products are forbidden because the turtle is on the endangered species list. Cuban cigars—and any other products of Cuba—cannot be brought into the United States because there are no diplomatic relations between Cuba and the United States.

Other examples of contraband include animals (without special licenses), certain ceramic tableware manufactured abroad with a high lead content, drugs and drug paraphernalia, medicines not approved by the Food and Drug Administration (FDA), firearms and ammunition, food products, and any animal or animal product on the endangered species list.

A very helpful booklet you can provide your client with is "Know Before You Go," published by the U.S. Customs Office. This free booklet contains information on duty-free allowances, restricted items, the percent of duty on excess purchases, and other helpful hints. Another method of accessing "Know Before You Go" is on the Internet. The Web site is http://www.cbp.gov, select "travel publications".

Cruise Line Security

As with other segments of the travel industry, the cruise lines have also responded to issues of safety and security. Many of their security procedures are confidential, but in general, passengers will be faced with additional luggage screenings and more visible security personnel, including canine inspections. According to CLIA's Web site, "cruise ships are inherently secure because they are a controlled environment with limited access."

At U.S. cruise terminals, procedures are similar to those found at airports, including requirements for photo identification and use of metal detectors for anyone who boards any ship. The following documents are required for all cruise passengers who are U.S. citizens: a passport or birth certificate (original or certified copy) plus a picture ID issued by a federal, state, or local government agency (except for children under age 16). Non-U.S. citizens are required to have a valid passport and visa (when needed) and an Alien Registration Card (ARC or "green" card) if the individual is a resident alien living in the United States.

In some parts of the world piracy has been an ongoing concern. Here again, the cruise lines have responded by placing additional people on watch and implementing strict policies to identify other vessels traveling close by.

SUMMARY

There is quite a large untapped market of potential cruisers offering travel professionals many possibilities for increased profitability. Selling cruises, however, requires a great deal of expertise. There are many ways that a travel professional can gain knowledge about cruising without

? What Would You Do?

Your clients are sailing in three weeks and the cruise documents have just arrived. Air transportation was booked through the cruise line and the tickets are in the document packet. The only problem is that the flights are departing from Kansas City instead of St. Louis (where your clients live).

1. Do you call your clients and explain that they must fly from Kansas City instead of St. Louis?
2. Do you book and sell separate air travel from St. Louis and try to get a refund on the other tickets?
3. Do you contact the cruise line and see if they can remedy the problem?

to his overall satisfaction. Calculating a cruise price involves understanding that prices are quoted per person and that many discounts are available.

A cruise reservation is most often made by phone; however, automated bookings are being encouraged by a number of innovations and improvements. Regardless of how the reservation is made, there are several things the travel agent must know about her client when making the reservation. Because cruises offer customers a superior level of service, clients expect no less from the travel agent who books their cruise. Adding value for your clients is the key to retaining their business.

 For additional Travel and Tourism resources, go to http://www.hospitality-tourism.delmar.com.

PLEASE COMPLETE THE CHAPTER REVIEW QUESTIONS NOW.

actually having to take every existing cruise. The price of a cruise is determined by several factors, primarily cabin category and the season. Matching the cruise, and especially the cabin category, with the customer is important

EXERCISE 16–1 Cruise Pricing and Selling

1. Define the following terms:

   Cabin category _____

   Confirmation number _____

   Customs fee _____

   Deposit _____

   Guarantee _____

   Guaranteed share rate _____

   Port charge _____

   Reservation worksheet _____

   Single supplement _____

2. Identify some possible disadvantages of selecting the lower priced cabin categories:

   _____
   _____
   _____

3. What cabin location would you suggest to a client who is concerned about seasickness? _____
   _____

4. Why is it often advantageous to purchase air transportation from the cruise line, even if it means paying a slightly higher fare?
   _____
   _____

5. List five things a travel agent needs from a client in order to make a reservation: _____
   _____
   _____
   _____

6. Use the information on the seven-day cruise from Miami in Figure 16–3 to answer the following questions. Your clients are two adults who are interested in the July 25 sailing in cabin category 4, including air from Erie, Pennsylvania.
   a. How much is the total cost? _____
   b. How much deposit is due? _____
   c. How much is the total final payment amount? _____
   d. How much commission will be earned? _____

7. Your clients are two adults who live in Miami and want to sail in cabin category 2 on the June 6 sailing.
   a. How much is the total cost? _____
   b. How much deposit is due? _____
   c. How much is the total final payment amount? _____
   d. How much commission will be earned? _____

7-day Cruises from Miami

Category & Deck	Value	Base	High
12 - Upper	2,039	2,139	2,239
11 - Verandah	1,839	1,939	2,039
9 - Empress	1,399	1,499	1,599
8 - Upper	1,379	1,479	1,579
7 - Verandah, Empress	1,359	1,459	1,559
6 - Upper, Riviera	1,339	1,439	1,539
5 - Main	1,239	1,339	1,439
4 - Riviera	1,219	1,319	1,419
3 - Empress	1,159	1,259	1,359
2 - Upper	1,139	1,239	1,339
1 - Riviera	1,119	1,219	1,319
3rd & 4th guest 12 & under*	599	599	599
3rd & 4th guest 13 & over*	649	649	649
Cruise Vacation Protection Plan	89	89	89

*Sharing stateroom with two full-fare guests.

All rates quoted in U.S. dollars, per guest, double occupancy (except as noted), and include Port Charges. For all guests, Passenger Departure Tax additional $3 per guest, Customs Fee additional $6.50 per guest.

Air transportation available from major cities throughout North America. See Air Program for details.

Holiday Sailings: December 19 and 27, add $500 per guest.

Special Single Guest Programs:

Categories 1–3: 150% of double occupancy rate
Categories 4–12: 200% of double occupancy rate
Guaranteed Share (4 guests per cabin) $770/guest

Cruise Vacation Protection Plan: children 16 years or less are covered at no extra charge providing the Plan is purchased by accompanying adults.

Value Sailings: May 2, 9; Sep. 5, 12, 26; Oct. 3, 10, 17, 24, 31; Nov 28

Base Sailings: Jan 4, 11; Apr. 25; May 16, 23, 30; Jun. 6; Aug. 29; Nov. 7, 14, 21

High Sailings: Jan. 18, 25; Feb. 1, 8, 15, 22, 29; Mar. 7, 14, 21, 28; Apr. 4, 11, 18; Jun. 13, 20, 27; Jul. 4, 11, 18, 25; Aug. 8, 15, 22; Dec. 19, 26

Deposit is $250 per guest.

Air Program

Departure City	Miami	Tampa/ Canaveral	Los Angeles	New Orleans	Alaska	San Juan	Hawaii	Panama Canal
Cincinnati, OH	309	319	459	279	699	479	659	479
Erie, PA	339	339	499	309	749	439	689	399
Fargo, ND	479	469	499	549	479	609	699	489
Indianapolis, IN	299	299	429	289	649	469	669	459

Note: The cruise rates shown in the chart include $119 port charges, which are not commissionable. Please subtract the port charges from the cruise rate, then add insurance (if applicable) before you calculate 10% commission. Air add-on is not commissionable.

FIGURE 16–3 Information contained in a typical cruise pricing section of a brochure or Web site that will be used to calculate cruise pricing.

8. Your client is a single adult who wants to travel in a cabin by herself on the September 12 sailing in cabin category 5, no air.

a. How much is the total cost? _____

b. How much deposit is due? _____

c. How much is the total final payment amount? _____

d. How much commission will be earned? _____

Review Questions

1. What methods can travel agents use to make cruise reservations?

_____

2. What should be included in a confirmation letter?

_____

_____

3. Why is agency follow-up important?

_____

_____

4. What type of person might be interested in traveling on a freighter?

_____

_____

5. List four things you can do to increase your knowledge of cruises:

_____

_____

_____

6. What five factors influence the price of a cruise?

_____

_____

7. Explain what a cabin category is and why it is important to match it to the client's budget and expectations.

_____

_____

_____

8. What are e-documents?

_____

_____

_____

9. Describe some cruise line security procedures that passengers will be faced with.

_____

_____

SECTION VI

International Air Travel

CHAPTER 17

Practical Advice for International Travelers

CHAPTER 18

International Air Travel Basics

CHAPTER 19

International Airfares, Taxes, Schedules, and Ticketing

Practical Advice for International Travelers

OBJECTIVES

At the conclusion of this chapter, you should be able to

- advise clients about proof of citizenship.
- advise clients how to obtain a passport.
- know where to obtain information about passports and visas.
- understand the importance of Consular Information Sheets.
- advise clients about security and terrorism issues.
- advise clients of health concerns for international travel.
- explain how monetary transactions might be handled.
- explain entry procedures into another country and the differences that might be encountered.
- advise clients about duty-free allowances and the procedures for returning to the United States.

KEY TERMS

altitude sickness	exchange rate	value added tax (VAT)
Consular Information Sheets	International Certificate of Vaccination	visa
consulate	jet lag	visa service or visa expediter
customs declaration form	passport	World Health Organization (WHO)
Department of Homeland Security	proof of citizenship	
embassy	tourist card	

Long before a client is ready to make international travel plans, he probably has many questions and concerns that must be addressed. He could request numerous publications from tourist bureaus and buy additional travel books at the local bookstore, search the Internet, or approach his travel counselor. The easiest of these methods, and the most beneficial for him and for the travel counselor, is making use of the counselor's expertise, experience, and vast reservoir of reference material.

International travelers often have many more questions and concerns than do domestic travelers. A good travel counselor can be of tremendous help to the international traveler—this is definitely added value for the client. Addressing the client's preliminary questions and concerns is actually the first step in the selling process. This is the time for the counselor to prove their worth as a travel counselor in anticipation of making the travel arrangements at the appropriate time. If the counselor successfully handles the client's questions and concerns, it is likely that this client will want the counselor to make the arrangements.

Suppose the client did all of this advance leg work himself at the bookstore, on his own initiative (or perhaps because the counselor offered no assistance with answering his questions). When he is ready to make his reservations, why should he return to this agency instead of the agency down the street, because all travel agencies sell basically the same products? In fact, he probably won't come back to this agency; he will use another travel counselor or deal directly with the suppliers for his travel arrangements.

If the counselor is armed with some specific knowledge and knows where to look for the answers and does not know (the counselor cannot know everything, but can try!), the above client scenario will be quite different.

A good travel professional is prepared for almost any question from the client—but what are the usual questions asked by international clients? Furthermore, what are the questions the international client *should* ask but may not think to ask? The unasked question should also be answered by the travel professional who is adept at understanding the travel situation and alleviating potential trouble spots and client anxiety.

On completion of this chapter, you should have a firm understanding of entry requirements for foreign countries, healthy international travel, money concerns with foreign currency, and immigration and customs procedures. These subjects are the topics that many clients ask about as they begin to consider traveling internationally. Sometimes, however, these important questions never cross the client's mind, and it is up to you to initiate the discussion of these matters.

ENTRY REQUIREMENTS FOR INTERNATIONAL TRAVEL

One of the first questions asked by many potential international travelers is about documentation needed to enter the foreign destination—as well it should be! As you will learn, obtaining the necessary types of documentation can be a time-consuming process and must be planned for well in advance of travel.

There are four basic types of documentation: *proof of citizenship, tourist card, passport,* and *visa.* Entry requirements vary by destination, but one or more of the four basic types of documentation is required by the government of the foreign destination. It is your responsibility as a travel counselor or airline reservationist to advise the client of the required entry documentation. So, how do you learn what documentation is needed for your client?

The most up-to-date reference source for entry requirements (aside from the State Department) is your airline computer system. Although the method of retrieving this information and the format in which it is displayed is slightly different in each system, the content of the data is basically the same. Your airline computer system is the most reliable source for this information because entry requirements can change daily, and computers have the flexibility to change quickly.

Two other excellent ways of learning about entry documentation are the U.S. State Department, Bureau of Consular Affairs and the consulate or embassy of the country being visited. Both of these sources can be contacted by phone. The U.S. State Department, Bureau of Consular Affairs maintains an excellent Web site and many foreign governments also have Web sites for their consulates or embassies. Because these sources are the "final word" with regard to entry documentation, they are extremely accurate and up-to-date.

Most countries have Web sites sponsored by the national tourist bureau, and although these sources are probably accurate with regard to entry documentation, the sources previously mentioned can always be relied on and are better choices. Printed reference sources should not be used for entry documentation. This type of information, like vaccination requirements, is time sensitive, something to which printed references cannot easily adapt.

Proof of Citizenship

Travelers to some Caribbean countries are required to carry proof of citizenship in addition to a photo ID, such as a driver's license. What is considered proof of citizenship?

1. original, state-issued birth certificate with raised seal
2. certified birth certificate copy with raised seal

Important Industry Web Sites

Centers for Disease Control: **http://www.cdc.gov**

Tourism Offices Worldwide: **http://www.towd.com**

U.S. State Department, Bureau of Consular Affairs:
http://travel.state.gov

U.S. State Department, Consular Information Sheets:
http://travel.state.gov/travel/warnings.html

U.S. Treasury, Customs Division, "Know Before You Go":
**http://www.customs.gov/xp/cgov/toolbox/
publications/travel/**

World Health Organization: **http://www.who.int**

3. naturalization certificate
4. valid passport or, in some cases, a passport expired less than eight years

It is important to note that if the traveler is using his birth certificate and his name has been changed, supporting documentation is required. If the name change is due to marriage, a marriage certificate must also be carried. Other types of name changes can be substantiated by a notarized affidavit.

A driver's license, marriage license, Social Security card, or baptismal record is *not* proof of citizenship. You do not have to be a U.S. citizen to drive, get married, get a Social Security card, or be baptized.

Tourist Card

In a handful of countries, Mexico being a prime example, a tourist card is required by all visitors in addition to a passport. Tourist cards may be obtained from the nearest consulate, but many travel agencies maintain a supply of Mexican tourist cards as a convenience to their clients. Travelers arriving by commercial means (e.g., airline, cruise ship) are given Mexican tourist cards en route.

Single or divorced parents traveling to Mexico with their children are required to carry an additional document. We have all read stories of children being kidnapped by one of their own parents, and Mexico has developed a policy in response to this unfortunate situation. A notarized letter (or death certificate) from the absent parent giving the child premission to travel must accompany the proof of citizenship and the tourist card. Other countries may also adopt this policy in the future, so it is always wise to check the agency's reference sources when children are to travel.

Passport

All countries except some Caribbean nations require U.S. travelers (including infants and children) to have valid passports. A passport is a multiple-page booklet, issued by the federal government, that states the traveler's citizenship. There are three types of U.S. passports:

1. regular (blue cover)
2. official (maroon cover)
3. diplomatic (black cover)

Who you are determines which type of passport you are issued; for most of us, it is a regular passport. For U.S. citizens 16 years of age and older, a passport is valid for 10 years; passports for citizens under the age of 16 are valid for five years.

To obtain any type of new passport, you need an application form. This tan-colored form may be obtained at designated post offices, any court clerk's offices, or the passport offices throughout the United States. Passport applications can also be printed from the Internet by accessing http://passport.unitedstates.org/. Many travel agencies maintain a supply of application forms as a convenience to their clients. Most applicants prefer to complete the application forms at home, and then proceed with the processing. Figure 17–1 reproduces an application form and gives you a good idea why many travelers would rather complete it at home. *Note:* Advise your client not to sign the application form at home! The traveler must sign the application form in front of a designated "passport agent." In addition to the application, the traveler is required to provide:

1. Proof of citizenship.
2. Proof of identity. This can be anything with both the applicant's name and photograph on it, such as a driver's license.
3. Two identical, full-face 2" × 2" photos, with white or off-white background, signed on the back. Photos taken at the local mall's automatic booth are not acceptable; only professional photographers and some travel agencies can provide passport photos.
4. New adult passport—$55 plus a $30 execution fee; new child (under 16 years old) passport—$40 plus a $30 execution fee. Additionally, there is a $12.00 security fee for an adult or a child's passport processing.

Special circumstances arise when one parent takes a child to obtain a passport. If the accompanying parent has sole custody of the child, the parent my bring evidence of this at the time application is made. If joint custody exists, the accompanying parent must bring a notarized written letter from the absent parent that gives consent for the passport issuance.

U.S. Department of State
APPLICATION FOR A US PASSPORT

OMB APPROVAL NO. 1405-0004
EXPIRATION DATE: 08/31/2008
ESTIMATED BURDEN: 85 Minutes
(See Instruction Page 3)

WARNING: False statements made knowingly and willfully in passport applications, including affidavits or other supporting documents submitted therewith, are punishable by fine and/or imprisonment under provisions of 18 U.S.C. 1001, 18 U.S.C. 1542 and/or 18 U.S.C. 1621. Alteration or mutilation of a passport issued pursuant to this application is punishable by fine and/or imprisonment under the provisions of 18 U.S.C 1543. The use of a passport in violation of the restrictions contained therein or of the passport regulations is punishable by fine and/or imprisonment under 18 U.S.C. 1544. All statements and documents are subject to verification.

When completing this form, PRINT IN BLUE OR BLACK INK ONLY

☐ 5 Yr. ☐ 10 Yr. Issue Date ___
☐ R ☐ D ☐ O ☐ DP
End. # ___ Exp. ___

1. Name of Applicant

Last

Suffix (Jr., Sr., III)

2. Date of Birth (mm-dd-yyyy)

First

Middle

3. Sex ☐ M ☐ F

4. Place of Birth (City & State OR City & Country)

5. Social Security Number (See Federal Tax Law Notice on Instruction Page 3)

6. Alien Registration No. (If applicable)

7. Height Feet Inches

8. Hair Color

9. Eye Color

10. Occupation

11. Employer

DS 11 06 2005

12. E-Mail Address (Optional)

13. Mailing Address

Street/RFD# OR Post Office Box

Apartment #

City

State

ZIP Code

Country (If outside the U.S.)

In Care of (If applicable)

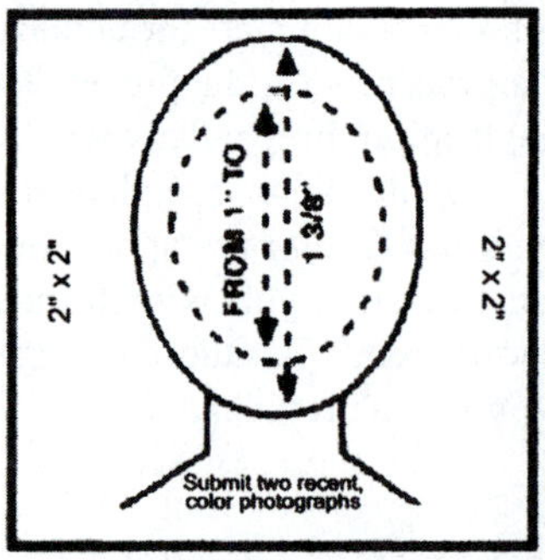

FROM 1" TO 1-3/8"
2" x 2"
2" x 2"
Submit two recent, color photographs

14. Permanent Address or Residence (If same as mailing address write "Same As Above")

Street / RFD # (DO NOT LIST P.O. BOX)

Apartment #

City

State

ZIP Code

15. Home Telephone (Include Area Code) (   )

16. Business Telephone (Include Area Code) (   )

17. Have you ever applied for or been issued a U.S. passport? ☐ YES ☒ NO If yes, complete the remaining items in block #17 and submit most recent passport.

Name in which your most recent passport was issued.

Status of recent passport ☐ Submitted ☐ Stolen ☐ Lost ☐ Other ___

Most recent passport number.

Approximate date your most recent U.S. passport was issued or date you applied. (mm-dd-yyyy)

18. Travel Plans

Date of Trip (mm-dd-yyyy)

Length of Trip

Countries to be Visited

19. Have you ever been married? ☐ YES ☐ NO If yes, complete the remaining items in block #19

Spouse's or Former Spouse's Full Name

Is your spouse (or former spouse) a U.S. citizen? ☐ YES ☐ NO

Date of Birth (mm-dd-yyyy)

Place of Birth

Date of Most Recent Marriage

Widowed? ☐   Divorced? ☐
Give Date:

20. What other names have you used? (Include name changes, maiden name, & former married names)

1)   2)   3)   4)

DS-11
09-2005

Page 1 of 2

FIGURE 17–1 Passport application (pages 1 and 2). Courtesy of U.S. Department of State, Bureau of Consular Affairs.

NAME OF APPLICANT (Last, First, Middle)				Date of Birth *(mm-dd-yyyy)*

21. Parental Information

Mother's Maiden Name			Date of Birth	Place of Birth
Last	First	Middle		

Father's Name			Date of Birth	Place of Birth
Last	First	Middle		

Is your mother a U.S. citizen? ☐ YES ☐ NO	Is your father a U.S. citizen? ☐ YES ☐ NO

22. Emergency Contact - Provide the information of a person not traveling with you to be contacted in the event of an emergency.

Name	Street / RFD #

Apartment #	City	State	ZIP Code

Telephone ( )	E-Mail Address *(Optional)*	Relationship

STOP   DO NOT SIGN APPLICATION UNTIL REQUESTED TO DO SO BY PERSON ADMINISTERING OATH.

23. Oath & Signature

I declare under penalty of perjury that I am a United States citizen (or non-citizen national) and have not, since acquiring United State citizenship (or U.S. nationality), performed any of the acts listed under "Acts or Conditions" on this application form (unless explanatory statement is attached). I declare under penalty that the statements made on this application are true and correct.

X _____
Applicant's Signature - age 14 and older

X _____
Mother's Legal Guardian's Signature *(If identifying minor)*

X _____
Father's Legal Guardian's Signature *(If identifying minor)*

Applicant's or Father's Identification Information

Type of Document	Issue Date _____
☐ Driver's License	Expiration Date _____
☐ Passport	Place of Issue _____
☐ Military Identification	
☐ Other (Specify) _____	

Name _____

ID Number _____

Mother's Identification Information

Type of Document	Issue Date _____
☐ Driver's License	Expiration Date _____
☐ Passport	Place of Issue _____
☐ Military Identification	
☐ Other (Specify) _____	

Name _____

ID Number _____

FOR ACCEPTANCE AGENT USE ONLY

Facility Identification Number _____

☐ Acceptance Agent; Facility Name & Location

_____

☐ (Vice) Consul USA; Location

_____

☐ Passport Services Staff Agent

Subscribed & sworn to (affirmed) before me

_____   Date *(mm-dd-yyyy)* _____
(Signature of person authorized to accept application)

(SEAL)

For Issuing Office Use Only

Name as it appears on citizenship evidence _____

☐ **Birth Certificate** ☐ SR ☐ CR ☐ City   File Date _____   Issue Date _____

☐ **Passport**   Issue Date: _____

☐ **Report of Birth** ☐ 240 ☐ 545 ☐ 1350   Issue Date _____

☐ **Naturalization Certificate**   Issue Date _____   Cert. # _____

☐ **Citizenship Certificate**   Issue Date _____   Cert. # _____

☐ **Other:** _____

☐ **Seen & Returned**

☐ **Attached** _____

APPLICATION APPROVAL

FEE _____ EXEC. _____ EF _____ OTHER _____

FIGURE 17–1 *Continued*

Once all the necessary forms have been obtained, the traveler is ready to begin the passport processing, achieved by one of two methods. Most travelers take all of the documents and the application to the nearest designated post office or court clerk's office. The passport officer verifies that all information is complete and then obtains the traveler's signature on the application form.

The traveler's application, proof of citizenship, and fee are sent to the nearest passport office. Currently, passport offices are located in Boston, Chicago, Honolulu, Houston, Los Angeles, Miami, New Orleans, Philadelphia, San Francisco, Seattle, Stamford, and Washington, D.C.

Depending on the time of the year and the passport office's workload, the proof of citizenship and passport are mailed to the traveler's home address in 1 to 12 weeks. The average return time is two to three weeks.

All U.S. passports issued after October 26, 2005 must be machine-readable and include a computer chip that contains biometric information about the passport holder. These new innovations greatly enhance and improve the gathering of information about the traveler and increase the effectiveness of security screening.

Countries who are part of the Visa Waiver Program (VWP) are also required to issue passports that are machine-readable with a computer chip. These countries allow for short-term travel between member countries without a visa and include Andorra, Australia, Austria, Belgium, Brunei, Denmark, Finland, France, Germany, Iceland, Ireland, Italy, Japan, Liechtenstein, Luxembourg, Monaco, the Netherlands, New Zealand, Norway, Portugal, San Marino, Singapore, Slovenia, Spain, Sweden, Switzerland, United Kingdom, and United States.

The passport office will handle application for a new passport in an expedited fashion for an additional fee of $60, plus overnight mailing costs. This special service results in a new passport being issued within three days of receipt of the application. If overnight mailing services are used, the total processing time is five business days; one day en route to the passport office, three days for processing, and one day en route to the traveler. It is important to note that a copy of the airline ticket should be sent with the passport application, substantiating the need for expedited handling.

The second method of processing is called "walking it through." In this procedure, *the traveler* takes the documents directly to a passport office. This method is used when a passport is needed immediately. The passport office advises travelers to arrive at the office early and be prepared to spend most of the day there. Sometimes the traveler carries the paperwork to each processing area of the office. Other times, the applicant begins the processing, leaves the passport office, and returns to the office at a specified time. In either case, the applicant returns home that same day with a passport in hand.

Advise your client to sign the passport as soon as it is received. The signature must be identical to the way the printed name appears on the passport.

A passport renewal is a much more convenient process, handled completely by mail. The traveler must obtain a pink renewal application from one of the same locations as for an original application. Once the renewal application form is completed and signed, it can be mailed, along with the old passport (issued within the last 15 years), two new photographs, and $67, to the nearest passport office. The addresses for the passport offices are listed on the back of the application form. When mailing a document as important as a passport, the passport office recommends using certified mail with return receipt requested. On receipt of the new passport, the traveler should immediately sign it exactly as the printed name appears.

As with new passport applications, the renewal process can take between 1 and 12 weeks, depending on the time of the year and the passport office's workload. The average return time is about two to three weeks on passport renewals.

PASSPORT TIPS Applicants for passports should begin the process as soon as possible. The processing time can be longer than average, especially if the passport office is overloaded by applications or its computers go down.

Advise your clients to make a copy of each printed page of the passport. Travelers should carry these copies and two extra passport photos separately when traveling. If the passport should be lost or stolen, these copies make replacement much easier.

Travelers should guard their passports when traveling just as though they were money. In several areas of the world, a U.S. passport is worth $1,000 or more on the local black market! When at home, keep the passport in a safety deposit box or safe.

Visa

Not all countries require U.S. travelers to obtain visas, but many countries in Central America, South America, Africa, Eastern Europe, the Middle East, and Asia do. A visa is a foreign government's written permission for a traveler to enter that country for a specific reason and length of time. Usually, a visa is a rubber stamp on one of the blank passport pages, rather than a separate document.

There are four basic types of visas: tourist, work, student, or business. A visa is issued by the foreign consulate of the country being visited. As mentioned earlier, foreign consulates are located in several U.S. cities. As a service to their clients, many travel agencies assist in obtaining visas.

To obtain a visa, the traveler must first be in possession of a valid passport. Other required paperwork, processing cost, and validity period for the visa depend on the country to be visited and the type of visa needed. A visa application is always needed, no matter what the reason for travel or the country being visited.

Unfortunately, no two visa application forms look the same. However, the information requested on one specific country's visa application is very similar to that of any other country's application form.

Other required items for obtaining a typical tourist visa, in addition to the visa application and valid passport, can include photos and a consular fee. Obtaining a business visa may also require a company letter stating the reason for travel and that sufficient funds have been provided by the company. In many cases, the traveler must also supply a copy of onward transportation.

Once all the required material has been gathered, the processing can be handled by one of three methods. The traveler or the travel counselor can send *all the material to the* consulate *of the country to be visited*. For safety, it is recommended that certified mail with return receipt requested be used. Overnight delivery, such as Federal Express, can be used when the visa is needed quickly. If the client is traveling to several countries that each require a visa, the procedure is repeated for each country's consulate.

The second method of processing is the use of a visa service or visa expediter. A visa service or expediter is very beneficial when the traveler needs several different visas. All paperwork is sent to the visa service or expediter instead of the consulate. A courier of the visa service or expediter hand-carries the paperwork to each consulate, obtains each visa, and returns the passport with all necessary visas intact. A fee per visa (usually $50 to $100) is charged, in addition to any applicable consular fees.

The third method is for the traveler who is part of an international group tour. Some *tour operators provide visa applications to tour members and handle processing*. The tour member or travel counselor sends the required documents and the traveler's passport to the tour operator. The tour operator then obtains all required visas on the traveler's behalf and returns the passport to the tour member. Some tour operators charge a small fee for this assistance, similar to that of a visa service or expediter.

Entry Documentation in the GDS

Most travel counselors rely on their GDS to obtain information about entry documentation, required vaccinations, and so on. Each GDS has a special format or command that is typed, resulting in a display of this information for the appropriate country. At the top of the next column is a sample display from Worldspan for Kenya.

As you can see in this example, basic information is given for both U.S. and Canadian citizens. Travelers from these countries entering Kenya as tourists and on business

```
> K E N Y A - ** TDS VISA GUIDE AND VISA SERVICE **

   *** USA ***              *** CANADA ***

   TOURIST—P V             TOURIST—P V

   BUSINESS—P V            BUSINESS—P V

   TWOV—CONNECT FLT        TWOV—CONNECT FLT

ENTRY AND VISA REQUIREMENTS . . . . . . . . .>GDOC KEVISA ( -

VISA INFO/FEES/SERVICE . . . . . . . . . . . . . .>GDOC KENOTE ( -

HEALTH REGULATIONS. . . . . . . . . . . . . . . .>GDOC KEHEALTH ( -

OTHER CITIZEN ENTRY REQUIREMENTS. . . . . .>GDOC KEOTHER ( -

CUSTOMS AND AIRPORT DEPT. TAX . . . . . . . .>GDOC KECUSTOMS ( -

U.S. STATE DEPARTMENT ADVISORY. . . . . . . .>GDOC KEADV ( -

CONSULATE ADDRESSES IN THE U.S. . . . . . . .>GDOC KEADDRESS ( -

FOR VISA APPLICATIONS SEE OUR WEBSITE—
HTTP://WWW.TRAVELDOCS.COM
```

need a passport (P) and a visa (V). Transit without a visa (TWOV) is allowed up to the time of the connecting flight. In other words, U.S. and Canadian citizens can change planes in Kenya without having a visa, but if they stay longer, a visa is needed.

Below the basic information, you can see menu options for several topics. Travel counselors can type the formats shown at the right of each topic, or they can use the "tab" key to select a specific topic. Notice that these topics include entry requirement specifics, information about health regulations, information for non-U.S. and non-Canadian citizens, U.S. State Department information, and the addresses of Kenyan consulates in the United States. An added feature is that visa applications can be obtained and printed from the TDS Web site.

STATE DEPARTMENT'S ROLE IN INTERNATIONAL TRAVEL

The State Department performs a very important function for international travelers by keeping abreast of changing political, business, and health situations around the world. The State Department publishes (on paper and in most airline computer systems) Consular Information Sheets for most countries of the world. These sheets contain a variety of useful information and, in some cases, much more.

Should a country or area within a country become dangerous for U.S. travelers, the State Department includes a statement of warning or caution within the Consular Information Sheet. The reason for the warning or caution could be anything from increased violence against tourists to a national strike to a shortage of medical supplies.

When diplomatic relations between the United States and a foreign country are severed, the State Department usually prohibits or restricts travel to that country.

If you pay attention to the news, you may know to which countries the State Department has advised against traveling. However, less severe incidents happen frequently and political situations may change without notice. It is your responsibility to check the State Department's Consular Information Sheet for every international trip you sell, and it is a good idea to provide your client with a copy of the information.

Everyone is aware that airport security has dramatically increased as a result of the September 11, 2001, terrorist attacks. The Department of Homeland Security is constantly reviewing and revising existing programs as well as implementing new policies and procedures. For example, items that were considered harmless a few years ago, such as manicure scissors and disposable lighters, may now be prohibited in carry-on baggage. A complete list of these items can be obtained on the Transportation Security Administration's Web site (http://www.tsa.gov).

TRAVELING IN GOOD HEALTH

When traveling abroad, many clients ask, "Do I need any shots?" The answer is, it depends on where the client is going. The World Health Organization (WHO), a division of the United Nations, monitors health standards throughout the world. In conjunction with foreign governments, the WHO determines if vaccinations are required and for which diseases.

Required and Recommended Vaccinations

Generally, travelers to Canada, the Caribbean, Europe, and Australia need not worry about vaccinations, as these areas are not considered "infected areas." When travel is to Central America, South America, Africa, or Asia, you should immediately determine if vaccinations are required or recommended. Travel to these areas may require or recommend vaccinations against yellow fever, cholera, or smallpox.

Yellow fever is usually found in African and South American countries, especially in rural areas. A yellow fever vaccination may be required for all visitors or just for those travelers coming from or traveling through an infected area.

Cholera vaccinations may be required, especially when travel is to some African and Asian countries. The disease is usually contracted from contaminated food and water. Depending on the destination, a cholera vaccination may

be required for all visitors, or a vaccination may be required for just those travelers who come from or travel through an infected area.

Worldwide eradication of smallpox has recently been achieved, but there is still a possibility that the disease could reappear. Therefore, you should verify the smallpox status occasionally.

How does a travel professional determine if vaccinations are required or recommended? Again, perhaps the most up-to-date reference source for world health standards is your airline computer system. Vaccination requirements can change quickly. Because a computer system has the capability of updating data whenever needed, the computer may provide more reliable data than does printed material. Travel publications issued by each foreign tourist office, as well as *Travel Planners,* also contain information about required vaccinations but, like all other printed material, can become outdated rather quickly.

Another avenue for information open to travelers and travel counselors is the Centers for Disease Control in Atlanta. The CDC can be reached at 404-329-3311, or by accessing their Web site.

Required vaccinations are administered by the client's physician and are logged on an International Certificate of Vaccination. A vaccination certificate is a multiple-page, yellow booklet that is supplied to physicians by the WHO. The booklet must be carried by the traveler along with her passport.

Many countries, especially those located in tropical, jungle areas, may recommend a vaccination against typhoid. In addition, these countries and local physicians strongly urge that travelers take malaria tablets before, during, and after the trip.

VACCINATION TIPS Not all doctors have vaccines on hand. The traveler may need to obtain the vaccination from a physician in a larger city or state capital.

Most vaccinations have an incubation period. This means that it takes some time before the vaccination is effective. The actual amount of time varies depending on the type of vaccination.

Some vaccinations are dangerous when given during pregnancy. Advise your client to ask a doctor before obtaining the vaccination.

Children less than six months old are usually exempt from cholera vaccinations. Yellow fever vaccinations are usually not given to children under one year of age. Certain existing medical conditions, such as heart disease and high blood pressure, may exempt a traveler from obtaining a particular vaccination.

If a traveler has been exempted from obtaining a specific vaccination, he should ask the doctor for a statement indicating the reason for exemption and the date. The doctor should use office letterhead and sign the statement.

U.S. travelers have usually been vaccinated against diphtheria, measles, mumps, polio, rubella, tetanus, and pertussis (whooping cough) as children. If they were not, or if they have not been given boosters, the counsel of their physicians should be sought before traveling to risky destinations.

With the ongoing AIDS epidemic, several countries are examining their policies for health requirements. These countries may require incoming visitors to provide a statement attesting that the traveler has tested negative for the HIV virus especially if the visitor is staying for an extended period of time.

Web Activity

1. Your client, Jackson Michaels, must travel to Singapore on business in August and it is his first trip to the Orient. He has to know about entry documentation and health regulations, but he also has asked about the local customs of the people, religion, and language. Using information obtained on the Internet, prepare a fact sheet for your client that includes this information as well as the practical data about travel to Singapore.

2. Ruben Rosenthal and Karen Weiss have come into your office to plan their honeymoon in May to Mexico. They are staying at an all-inclusive resort in Cancun and are renting a car to visit the Mayan archaeological sites on the Yucatan Peninsula. Using information obtained on the Internet, prepare a fact sheet for your clients, including all of the practical and cultural information you think they should know about their trip to Mexico.

Jet Lag (Desynchronosis)

During long flights that cross several time zones, some passengers may experience a condition known as jet lag. Symptoms of jet lag include extreme fatigue and alterations in waking and sleeping patterns. These symptoms may be worst on the second or third day of the trip. Passengers on westbound flights tend to feel the effects of jet lag more than do passengers on eastbound flights.

For example, a flight leaves JFK at 8:00 A.M. (Eastern Time) and arrives in LAX at 9:00 A.M. (Pacific Time). This flight appears to take only one hour because of the three-hour time difference between New York and California, but it actually takes four hours. Passengers have three additional hours before normal California bedtime. Imagine what the passenger on a 17-hour flight will experience!

There are, however, some things travelers can do to lessen the effects of jet lag.

1. If possible, schedule arrival time close to a normal bedtime (destination time). If the arrival time is in the middle of the day, don't retire for the night until your normal bedtime. A short nap upon arrival is fine, but it is wise to begin to function on the destination's time as soon as possible.
2. Experienced international travelers have learned not to plan strenuous activity on the first day in the destination; they use this day to relax and become acclimated to the environment.
3. Two to three days before departing on an international flight, begin to change your eating and sleeping times to those in the destination.
4. At the beginning of the flight, change your watch to the correct time in your destination. Your mind can sometimes trick your body into thinking that it is functioning on the destination's time.
5. During flight, drink plenty of nonalcoholic beverages. The air in an aircraft is very dry, which causes many passengers to retain water and feel excessively thirsty. Alcoholic beverages only compound the problem.
6. During the flight, exercise as frequently as possible. Stretch your arms and legs and walk around in the aircraft.

Intestinal Problems

Although it is known by many names (e.g., *turista* and Montezuma's Revenge), diarrhea is no laughing matter. Many doctors recommend that passengers carry anti-diarrhea medication, such as Lomotil or Imodium, when the destination has questionable health standards.

It is usually safe to drink the water in major world cities because the water is treated to kill harmful bacteria. However, disease-causing microorganisms thrive in the water supplies of many rural areas and less developed countries. In less than sanitary locations, bottled water or canned beverages should always be used for drinking.

Travelers may not think of it, but bottled water should also be used for something as simple as brushing teeth. Brewed tea and perked coffee are usually safe because they have been made with boiled water and the heat kills bacteria. The cup the tea or coffee is served in may not be safe because it was probably washed in tap water! Another problem area is ice made from regular tap water because bacteria can survive the cold.

In remote areas, travelers can purify local water by boiling it or treating it with tincture of iodine, chlorine, or Halazone tablets. Directions for these procedures are provided free of charge by the Centers for Disease Control in Atlanta, Georgia.

Fruits and vegetables also play host to disease-causing bacteria. It is recommended that travelers eat only cooked fruits and vegetables because the cooking heat kills the bacteria. If these foods must be eaten raw, they should at least be peeled.

Many bodies of water are terribly polluted. The Ganges River in India is a prime example. Advise your clients not to wade or swim in polluted rivers or lakes because these same disease-causing bacteria can enter the body through the skin.

Altitude Sickness

Many travelers and travel counselors are very aware of the problem of motion sickness, but what about altitude sickness? At destinations of 10,000 feet or more above sea level (e.g., Cuzco or La Paz), some travelers become quite ill. Symptoms of altitude sickness include shortness of breath, chest pain, nausea, dizziness, and extreme fatigue. In travelers with heart or lung problems, these symptoms are intensified. Advise your clients, especially older ones, to talk to their doctors before embarking on a journey to high altitudes.

Medical Assistance Abroad

Should all precautions for good health fail, there is help. Most hotel desk clerks and the U.S. Embassy can assist travelers in finding adequate medical treatment facilities. Many travel counselors provide the address of the destination's U.S. Embassy to their clients before the trip begins. This is especially important for those traveling on their own without a guide or escort.

Some travelers use the services offered by U.S. companies that were formed specifically to assist Americans traveling abroad. Once a traveler pays a membership fee to one of these companies, benefits can include medic alert identification, medical insurance, a directory of English-speaking health professionals abroad, and general health tips. Following are a few of these service companies:

- Assist-Card, 800-874-2223, http://www.assist-card.com
- International SOS Assistance, 800-523-8662, http://www.internationalsos.com

For more information about international insurance, the Health Insurance Association of America is an excellent source. The HIAA can be contacted by phone at 800-942-4242 or via their Web site at http://www.hiaa.org.

Another important organization is the International Association for Medical Assistance to Travelers. Travelers and counselors can contact IAMAT to obtain a list of English-speaking physicians and other health-related information for many countries worldwide. The phone number for IAMAT is 716-754-4883 and the Web site is http://www.iamat.org.

HEALTH TIPS Travelers with acute sinus conditions should consult their doctors before flying. The changing air pressure and dry air in an aircraft can cause extreme discomfort. Many physicians recommend taking a decongestant prior to and during the trip.

Infants and children with chronic ear trouble may suffer during air travel, especially at takeoff and landing. Air travel has a profound effect on the eustachian tubes in a child's ears. Swallowing helps equalize the pressure in the inner ear, reducing the pain. In adults, this condition can also occur, and sometimes chewing gum can help.

Advise your client to carry any medication in its original container. Immigration officials get nervous and are apt to ask questions when they see drugs (even prescription ones) in homemade packaging! All medication should be kept in the carry-on baggage; checked baggage can get lost, and replacing medication can be a problem in a foreign country.

International travelers should be advised to carry an extra pair of glasses or contact lenses. In fact, taking the prescription for eyewear is also a good idea. Should the glasses or lenses become lost or damaged, getting them replaced is much easier with the prescription.

Many enlightened travelers never go anywhere without a first aid kit that contains antiseptic, bandages, and baking soda. Baking soda? When mixed with water, baking soda makes an excellent paste remedy for insect bites and sunburns.

In several African countries, including Egypt, eye infections are prevalent. Never loan a camera or binoculars to local residents. Doing so can spread the infection.

MONEY MATTERS

Strange as it may seem, some travelers never question the type of currency used in a foreign country; they appear to think that the U.S. dollar is a global currency. The fact is that nearly every country has its own currency, which usually looks completely different from the currency of its neighbor countries. To compound the matter, each currency has a different buying power. For example, a hotel room that costs $100 per night in the United States might be expressed as 190 pounds sterling in the United Kingdom. In Japan, that same hotel room's rate might be expressed as 10,673 yen.

To compare U.S. dollars (USD) to any other world currency, you must first know the exchange rate. Most large newspapers and your airline computer system can provide the current exchange rate for most world currencies. But what do you do with the exchange rate? The answer to that question depends on whether you are converting *from* U.S. dollars or *to* U.S. dollars. For example,

To convert $100 USD to pounds sterling, exchange rate 1.5871:

100 USD ÷ 1.5871 = 63.01 pounds sterling

To convert 63.01 pounds sterling to USD, exchange rate 1.5871:

63.01 pounds sterling × 1.5871 = 100 USD

Some travel counselors provide clients with a list of exchange rates for the countries they will visit. The client can use a pocket calculator when shopping or doing business and figure the cost of an item in USD. The exchange rates can fluctuate daily, but the rates provided by the counselor help the client determine if he is getting a bargain, a fair price, or a raw deal.

Twenty-five European countries (Austria, Belgium, Cyprus, Czech Republic, Denmark, Estonia, Finland, France, Germany, Greece, Hungary, Ireland, Italy, Latvia, Lithuania, Luxembourg, Malta, The Netherlands, Poland, Portugal, Slovakia, Slovenia, Spain, Sweden, and United Kingdom) have formed a cooperative that affects a variety of business, governmental, and economic areas. One of the features that impacts European travelers the most is that these countries use a single currency, called the *euro,* divided into 100 euro cents. The symbol for the euro is €.

What this means to European travelers is that they will be dealing with only one currency, assuming of course, that the traveler confines his travels to countries within the cooperative union. Notable exceptions to the European cooperative include the United Kingdom (England, Scotland, Wales, and Northern Ireland), Switzerland, Norway, Sweden, and Denmark. These countries will continue to use their own national currencies.

Before beginning an international trip, the client should determine how to handle purchases in foreign countries. Here are five choices:

1. Buy foreign currency before leaving home.
2. Buy foreign-currency traveler's cheques before leaving home.
3. Buy USD traveler's cheques and exchange as needed.
4. Use a credit card or a debit card.
5. Use an ATM.

As with all choices, there is no one perfect answer. Each method of handling transactions abroad has advantages and disadvantages.

It is always helpful to have some small change on arrival for porters, taxis, and so forth. Large banks carry a small supply of only the major world currencies, such as British pounds sterling, the euro, and Japanese yen. If the client is traveling in other than major countries, they may not be able to purchase the correct currency. If the traveler is going to several countries, they should keep each currency separate, which is easier said than done.

Foreign-currency traveler's cheques are a good option, if the desired currency is offered in traveler's cheque form. Again, only major currencies, such as those listed previously, can be purchased in traveler's cheques. Imagine using a pound sterling traveler's cheque to purchase an item in euros, and then attempting to calculate the USD cost! There are three exchange rates at work in this situation. As in the United States, some smaller establishments may not be equipped to cash a traveler's cheque. Those that are may charge a small fee.

Another option is using an ATM (automated teller machine) to obtain local currency at the destination. ATMs can be found in major tourist destinations in the Caribbean and Europe and in some major cities worldwide. Most ATM transactions offer reasonable exchange rates and the typical fees for ATM use are charged. Because ATMs are not easily located in many countries, and don't exist at all in some areas, reliance on ATMs should not be recommended.

Money Tips

Many areas of the Caribbean, Canada, and Bermuda accept not only their own currencies but also U.S. dollars as payment on a one-to-one basis. If change is given, it's usually in local currency.

Advise your clients to keep receipts of all currency exchange transactions and purchases. Customs officials may ask to see them as the client departs the foreign country.

In some places, it is impossible to exchange leftover foreign currency back into dollars; travelers should attempt to spend all of that currency. Many countries will convert banknotes back into dollars, but not coins.

Many locations ask to see the traveler's passport before converting currency or cashing a traveler's cheque.

It is illegal in some countries to leave the country with local currency, even a few coins for souvenirs.

On entering some foreign countries, travelers are required to state how much cash and traveler's cheques they have. This declaration is compared to receipts when the traveler departs the country.

In some countries, independent travelers (not part of a tour group) are required by immigration officials immediately to convert a specific amount into local currency.

EMBASSIES AND CONSULATES

Many travelers are confused by embassies and consulates and believe them to be two completely different and separate agencies. An embassy is the office of the ambassador who is one country's representative stationed in another country. *Consulates* are regional offices of the embassy. The United States has embassies in more than 160 capital cities of the world as well as more than 80 consulates in other major world cities. Likewise, most countries have an embassy in Washington, D.C., and many countries have consulates in other major U.S. cities. The U.S. Embassy or its Consular Section's two primary functions are to:

1. Issue visas to foreign nationals visiting the United States.

2. Assist U.S. travelers in their international destinations, such as to:

- issue a replacement passport when it is lost or stolen
- assist with finding medical treatment
- help with an emergency situation at home
- help arrange for the transfer of funds from home
- assist with finding legal representation
- make arrangements when a traveler dies in a foreign country
- assist in a local disaster requiring evacuation

It is important to note that the U.S. Embassy or its Consular Section cannot get the traveler out of jail, settle disputes with local merchants or service providers, or act as a post office or message service.

Now, let's look at embassies and consulates in another way. For example, the Japanese Consulate located in the United States will issue visas to U.S. travelers to Japan. The Japanese Embassy or its Consular Section also provides similar services to citizens of Japan traveling in the United States.

Because of the assistance provided by the embassy, many travel counselors give their international clients the U.S. Embassy phone number and address for each country being visited. This information can be found in the GDS, on the Internet, and in many printed reference sources.

ENTRY INTO A FOREIGN COUNTRY

Many international travelers, especially novices, are unsure of what to do and where to go when they arrive at a foreign airport. This is understandable when you consider that everything is suddenly different. As a rule, though, most international airports are well marked, many times in English. Airport signs instruct incoming passengers how to get to an area called "Immigration," "Customs," or "Passport Control." Whatever this area is called, its purpose is the same.

One by one, each incoming passenger is asked to show their documentation. Depending on the country, this can be proof of citizenship or a passport. The immigration officer may ask the reason for the visit, how long the passenger will be in the country, and if the passenger has anything to declare. The immigration officer is referring to excess amounts of liquor, tobacco, and so forth. The *Travel Planner* has guidelines for each country's import allowances.

When the immigration officer decides that the traveler is harmless, he may place a stamp on the documentation, stating that the traveler has "cleared," or he may just verbally clear the passenger. Once cleared, the passenger is directed by signs to the baggage claim area.

AT THE DESTINATION

Travelers to another country may experience many differences: language, money, time, electricity, laws, social customs, history, art, and so on. In fact, some of these differences are what makes the destination interesting and probably helped the traveler choose the location. Unfortunately, some of these differences can cause the traveler a bit of anxiety. The travel counselor can easily eliminate this anxiety by doing some research and taking the time to explain to the client what they can expect.

In many countries, religion has a major impact on the lives of residents and the laws of the land. In countries where the majority of the citizens are Moslems (followers of Islam), shops may close during the times of prayer and certain foods and beverages may not be available, especially during Ramadan. Laws in Islamic countries can be very strict and punishment quite severe compared to U.S. norms.

Not knowing the social customs of a country can cause a traveler to put his foot in his mouth. For example, in some countries the left hand should never be used to hand something to another person, the U.S. hand sign for "okay" is considered an obscene gesture, and touching a person's head is the height of bad manners. And, there are dozens more mannerisms and gestures that are considered rude.

Many travel counselors rely on *Dos and Taboos Around the World* (ISBN 0-471-59528-4) written by Roger Axtell. This book is arranged alphabetically by country and gives a thorough account of the local customs as well as ways that travelers can cause offense. No one likes to "stick out" or appear rude while traveling abroad and this book is one of the best resources we have found.

Some countries, especially those in Europe, have a tax on products and services called a value added tax (VAT). This tax can be compared to a sales tax in the United States although the VAT can be as high as 30 percent. Because this tax is supposed to be for citizens of the country, it may be possible for travelers to get a tax rebate. Depending on the country, the rebate can be obtained at the airport before departure or it can be mailed to the traveler, less a processing fee. Some stores offer rebates for purchases over a certain value. Travel guides and national tourist bureaus are good sources for information about VAT rebates.

Using electrical appliances in an international destination is something that many travelers may not consider. The United States uses 110 volt whereas most of the rest of the world uses 220 volt. To compound the problem, the prong configuration in most countries is different than that in the United States. Travel counselors should always point out these differences to international travelers and explain that they will need plug adaptors and a current converter. Retail outlets that sell luggage often carry kits that include the adaptors and converter and they may also offer dual-voltage appliances. Travel supply vendors such as Magellan's and Orvis offer a full range of electrical products.

As you learned in the rental car section, many countries measure distance in kilometers (km) instead of miles (mi). This can cause problems when reading maps or looking at speed limit signs. Most countries use the metric system: liquids are measured in liters, solids are weighed in grams and kilos, centimeters are used instead of inches, meters are used instead of feet and yards, and so on. Many travel guides include conversion charts for these measurements as well as clothing and shoe size comparisons. Travel counselors should make sure their clients are aware of these facts and many counselors provide international travelers with conversion formulas.

At first glance, language may be the first difference noticed by international travelers. As a courtesy to the people of the country being visited, it is a good idea to learn a few simple phrases: please, thank you, yes, no, hello, excuse me, and so on. People who travel frequently to other countries have learned that knowing and attempting to use simple phrases in the local language is an important way to show respect for the country and her people.

Important Industry Web Sites

Convert It!: **http://www.onlineconversion.com**

Currency Conversion: **http://www.oanda.com**

Language Translator: **http://babel.altavista.com**

DUTY-FREE ALLOWANCE

Travelers who have been out of the United States for at least 48 hours can return with up to $400 in foreign purchases, free of duty (tax). If the traveler has been out of the United States less than 48 hours, the allowance is $200. When travel has been to the Caribbean, the *duty-free* allowance increases to $600. When travel has been to the U.S. Virgin Islands, American Samoa, or Guam, the allowance is $1,200. Travel to certain Third World and developing nations can also increase the allowance. The duty-free allowance is given once every 30 days.

The U.S. Customs Office allows international travelers to send gifts of less than $100 value ($200 from a U.S. Territory) to friends and relatives back home. A package can be sent once a day, to one address, duty free. The package must be marked "unsolicited gift" and the contents and value of the package must appear on the package.

In Chapter 16, on cruises, you learned about forbidden items called contraband. In many international airports, there are containers called *amnesty bins*. Customs officials hope that passengers with forbidden items in their possession will throw them away in the amnesty bins before they are found and confiscated. Custom officials have the right not only to confiscate the contraband but also to fine or arrest the offender.

RETURNING HOME

A client who is beginning a trip home may notice different security measures used in many international airports. In these airports, passengers do not walk through the familiar metal detector arch; instead, hand-held devices are used. Each passenger is asked to stand with legs and arms apart as the security officer moves the detector completely around the passenger's body. In many international airports, it is common to see security officers with rifles over their shoulders! At first glance, this may be unnerving, but to most travelers, these increased and visible security measures are a welcome sight.

At the first U.S. airport entered, each returning passenger must clear customs. This means that on a flight from Amsterdam via New York to Cedar Rapids, the passenger will clear customs in New York.

Incoming passengers are first directed to the baggage claim area. After claiming their luggage, signs direct them to the customs area. Most customs areas use the "red light–green light" system. If a passenger has exceeded his duty-free allowance, he must go to the red-light area. Passengers who have remained under the allowance go to the green-light area.

All passengers are asked to produce a customs declaration form. This document is provided to them en route by the airline.

Passengers exceeding the duty-free allowance have to pay duty, usually about 10 percent, on the excess amount. The exact percentages and other helpful information can be found in the U.S. Customs Office publication "Know Before You Go."

When the customs officer is convinced that the traveler is not a spy or a smuggler, he may or may not stamp the documentation. Passengers on connecting flights have to check their luggage for their trip home.

Advise your clients who are traveling with expensive jewelry or foreign-made electronic equipment to register these items with customs before leaving the United States. If these items are not registered, the customs officer on the return trip may think that they were purchased abroad on the current trip and charge duty on them.

? What Would You Do?

Hector Sanchez calls your office and says that his father has suffered a heart attack and is in the hospital. Mr. Sanchez wants to fly to Madrid as soon as possible to see his father but he doesn't have a passport (he is a U.S. citizen).

1. Would you tell Mr. Sanchez that travel to Madrid is not possible for at least two or three weeks?
2. Would you suggest that Mr. Sanchez mail his passport application in immediately?
3. Would you explain how a passport can be obtained in one day in an emergency situation?

SUMMARY

International travel by its very nature causes clients, especially first-time travelers, to have many questions. Some aspects of international travel are not questioned but should be. It is the travel counselor's responsibility to answer these questions and explain the less obvious concerns about international travel. By understanding and relating information about passports, visas, and health concerns, the travel professional is giving the client added service. Client anxiety is more common when considering international travel, and this can be greatly reduced by a few minutes of discussion between the travel professional and client.

For additional Travel and Tourism resources, go to http://www.hospitality-tourism.delmar.com.

PLEASE COMPLETE THE CHAPTER REVIEW QUESTIONS NOW.

Review Questions

1. What reference sources might you use to learn about entry documentation? _____

2. Identify the four basic types of entry documentation. _____

3. What constitutes "proof of citizenship"? _____

4. What is a passport? _____

5. What is a visa? _____

6. What items are needed for an adult to obtain a new U.S. passport? _____

7. Where can passport applications be obtained? _____

8. Identify the four types of visa. _____

9. What items are or might be needed in order to obtain a visa? _____

10. What is a Consular Information Sheet? _____

11. What three types of data are or can be included in a Consular Information Sheet? _____

12. Identify the organization that monitors health standards worldwide and determines which, if any, vaccinations are recommended or required. _____

13. What is jet lag? What causes it? _____

14. Your client is traveling to La Paz, Bolivia. Of what health situations will you caution them? What are the symptoms? _____

15. How can you obtain a list of English-speaking doctors for your client who is traveling to France? _____

16. Your client is traveling to Portugal and he takes medication for high blood pressure. Of what should you advise him? _____

17. Your client is traveling to England and Scotland. What suggestions could you make with regard to money? _____

_____

_____

18. What is the euro? _____

19. What is the value added tax? _____

20. In what ways might the U.S. Embassy assist your client while traveling in Brazil? _____

_____

_____

21. What agency would issue a visa for your client who will be traveling to Australia? _____

_____

22. Your client is traveling to Israel, Jordan, and Egypt. In addition to entry documentation and health standards, what other

topics should you discuss with your client? _____

_____

_____

23. How much is the duty-free allowance for a traveler returning from the U.S. Virgin Islands? _____

How much is the duty-free allowance for a traveler returning from Germany? _____

How much is the duty-free allowance for a traveler returning from Jamaica? _____

24. At what point in a client's trip is the customs declaration form completed and what information should be listed? _____

_____

International Air Travel Basics

OBJECTIVES

At the conclusion of this chapter, you should be able to

- explain the differences between domestic and international air travel.
- identify the IATA Traffic Conference Areas.
- convert 12-hour time to 24-hour time and vice versa.
- explain the effect the IDL has on travel.
- calculate time comparison.
- calculate elapsed flying time.
- identify many of the major international city, airport, and airline codes.

KEY TERMS

24-hour clock   Traffic Conference Areas

TRAVEL DIFFERENCES

There are many similarities between international air travel and what you have already learned about domestic air travel. Unfortunately, there are just as many differences. Perhaps the easiest way to learn about the differences is to compare each feature individually.

1. **Airports.** Although each domestic airport is different in design and layout, they seem somewhat familiar to most travelers. U.S. airports in international gateway and hub cities may be formidable, especially to inexperienced travelers.

Each international airport bears little resemblance to others, even in the same country. Within the airport, security may be more visible; it is not uncommon to see armed security guards patrolling the area. Customs, immigration, passport control, and duty-free shops are found only in international airports. The national airline in many foreign countries is given the preferred gates and check-in areas, unlike U.S. airports.

2. **Agency appointing body.** As you learned in Chapter 6, most U.S. travel agencies obtain ARC appointment, which is, in essence, approval to sell ARC-member airlines. ARC's appointment includes both domestic and international airlines. Many travel agencies also obtain International Airlines Travel Agency Network (IATAN) appointments as well. For travel agencies located outside of the United States, all appointments are handled by the International Air Transport Association (IATA).

3. **Baggage allowance.** Most domestic airlines allow two checked suitcases per passenger. The allowable weight of each suitcase varies among airlines, but generally each suitcase must weigh under 50 pounds. On domestic airlines, suitcases must also comply with a size limitation, usually 70 inches (length plus width plus height). Internationally, each suitcase is generally limited to less than 50 pounds (some carriers use kilos), but this can vary widely depending on airline. The length plus width plus height cannot usually exceed 107 inches.

4. **Check-in time.** Domestically, most airlines recommend that passengers check in no less than one hour prior to flight time. On international flights, checkin may be required at least two hours before the flight.

5. **Connection time.** On domestic connection service, a change of planes must be scheduled in under four hours. A domestic connection that exceeds four hours becomes a stopover, and the fare is usually higher. An international connection must take place in less than 24 hours; more than 24 hours is considered a stopover and the airfare may be increased.

6. **Equipment.** To remain cost effective, most domestic flights use narrow-body equipment and offer first-class and coach-class service. Wide-body aircraft are used on transcontinental flights and heavily traveled routes. Internationally, many narrow-body aircraft offer only one class of service. During high season, wide-body equipment is used more frequently for international travel, and coach class, business class, and first class are offered.

7. **Fares.** For domestic travel, fares are set by each airline, with little or no government interference. Travel counselors obtain most domestic fares from their airline computer systems, but sometimes they use the assistance of an airline rate desk. International fares must be negotiated between each foreign government and the IATA. International fares are also found in the airline computer systems; however, travel counselors may use an international airline rate desk more frequently.

8. **Infants.** Domestically, lap-held infants under two years of age travel free when accompanied by an adult. Internationally, the same infant under the same circumstances is charged 10 percent of the adult fare. Many domestic and international fares allow for an infant (under two years of age) to be in a carrier secured in the seat next to the adult for 50 percent of the adult fare.

9. **Pet acceptance.** Travel with pets is quite common on domestic flights, although the cost of pet travel varies among airlines. Because of many countries' laws against the importation of animals, travel with pets on international flights is seldom done. Consider the import law in the United Kingdom, which orders that the incoming pet must be held in quarantine at the owner's expense for six months!

10. **Reconfirmation.** Although reconfirming a domestic flight number and departure time (24 hours prior) is not required, reconfirming might prevent the client from missing his flight. Internationally, some airlines *require* reconfirmation 72 hours prior to flight time. These international airlines cancel any reservations that have not been reconfirmed by that time.

11. **Schedules.** Domestic flight schedules are available to travel counselors through their GDSs, in the *OAG Flight Guide–North American Edition,* and in the *OAG Flight Guide–Worldwide Edition.* Flight schedules involving city pairs outside of North America can be obtained in the GDS and the *OAG Flight Guide–Worldwide Edition* only.

12. **Ticketing.** Domestic airline tickets are almost always priced automatically and issued by computer; only about 1 percent of domestic airline tickets issued in the United States are handwritten. Internationally, a greater number of tickets are issued by hand. International tickets generally involve complicated fare ladders, may use the baggage allowance box, and may require pricing in foreign currency. Many times computer-generated international tickets must be priced manually by the travel counselor.

As you can see, some of the differences are subtle and others are major. One of the biggest differences between domestic and international air travel is the involvement of the IATA.

IATA AND TRAFFIC CONFERENCE AREAS

Founded in 1919, the *International Air Transport Association (IATA)* is jointly owned by approximately 77 international airlines. Prior to May 1985, IATA was responsible for, among other things, appointing U.S. travel agencies for the sale of international airline tickets. Now, IATA appoints travel agencies that are located outside of the United States.

IATA still plays a very important role in international air travel. One of IATA's responsibilities is the negotiation of airfares between its member airlines and the foreign governments for each route. Because many foreign airlines are owned in whole or in part by the country's government, IATA's role becomes one of foreign policy. To make the tasks of administration and setting airfares,

routes, airports used, and stopover points easier to manage, IATA has created three distinct Traffic Conference Areas (see Figure 18–1).

Each IATA Traffic Conference Area is identified as TC-1, TC-2, or TC-3. Traffic Conference Area 1 (TC-1) is the entire Western Hemisphere and includes the Bermuda Islands in the Atlantic Ocean, and the Hawaiian, Johnston, and Easter Islands in the Pacific Ocean.

Traffic Conference Area 2 (TC-2) includes the islands in the North Atlantic Ocean (except Bermuda), all of Europe (including the western part of Russia), Africa, and the Middle Eastern countries out to and inclusive of Iran.

Traffic Conference Area 3 (TC-3) includes the remaining countries in Asia, New Zealand, Australia, Fiji, Samoa, Tahiti, and all major islands of the Pacific Ocean except the Hawaiian, Johnston, and Easter Islands.

PLEASE TURN TO PAGE 287 AND COMPLETE EXERCISE 18–1 NOW.

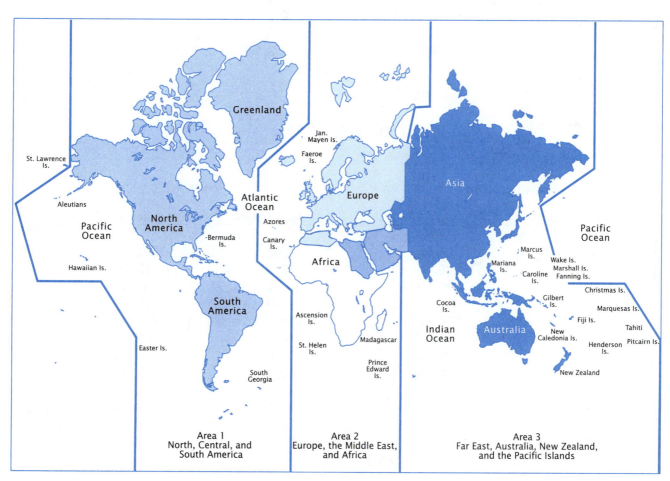

FIGURE 18–1 IATA Traffic Conference Areas.

Twenty-Four-Hour Clock

Before you can begin to plan international itineraries and obtain flight schedules from the *OAG Flight Guide–World-wide Edition*, you must first learn about the 24-hour clock. Flight schedules in the *OAG Flight Guide–Worldwide Edition* and almost all airline tickets written outside the United States indicate the flight departure time using the 24-hour clock. If you have lived abroad or been in the military, the 24-hour clock is not new to you. In Figure 18–2, you can easily see how time is expressed using this method.

Using the 24-hour clock avoids confusion and reduces errors in identifying A.M. and P.M. The 24-hour clock is always portrayed by four digits, to include both hours and minutes. The cycle begins at one minute past midnight (0001), progressing through the day and ending at midnight (2400). You never have a number higher than 2400.

Morning hours are fairly obvious. For P.M. times, the simplest thing to do is *add* 1200 to any of the morning hours, so they become the corresponding P.M. time.

$$\begin{array}{r} 0100 \\ +1200 \\ \hline 1300 \end{array} \quad \begin{array}{l} \text{(1:00 A.M.)} \\ \\ \text{(1:00 P.M.)} \end{array}$$

To convert the 24-hour clock back to the 12-hour clock, just subtract 1200 from the P.M. time.

$$\begin{array}{r} 2130 \\ -1200 \\ \hline 930 \end{array} \quad \begin{array}{l} \text{(19:30 P.M.)} \\ \\ \text{(becomes 9:30 A.M.)} \end{array}$$

PLEASE TURN TO PAGE 288 AND COMPLETE EXERCISE 18–2 NOW.

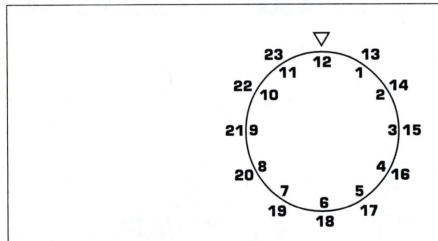

AM HOURS		PM HOURS	
24-hour clock	*12-hour clock*	*24-hour clock*	*12-hour clock*
0003	12:03 A.M.	1203	12:03 P.M.
0100	1:00 A.M.	1300	1:00 P.M.
0200	2:00 A.M.	1400	2:00 P.M.
0315	3:15 A.M.	1515	3:15 P.M.
0430	4:30 A.M.	1630	4:30 P.M.
0545	5:45 A.M.	1745	5:45 P.M.
0600	6:00 A.M.	1800	6:00 P.M.
0700	7:00 A.M.	1900	7:00 P.M.
0800	8:00 A.M.	2000	8:00 P.M.
0930	9:30 A.M.	2130	9:30 P.M.
1020	10:20 A.M.	2220	10:20 P.M.
1150	11:50 A.M.	2350	11:50 P.M.
1200	12:00 P.M. (noon)	2400	12:00 A.M. (midnight)

FIGURE 18–2 Time in 24-hour and 12-hour clocks.

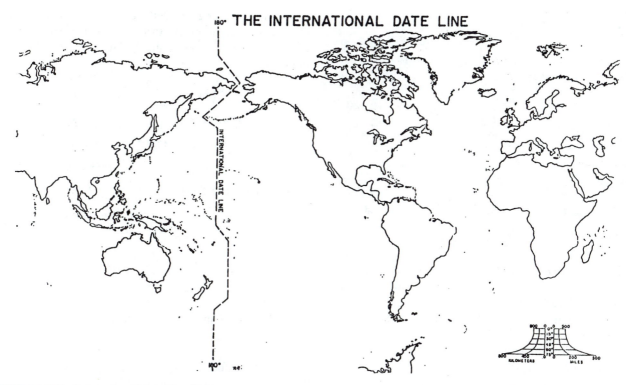

THE INTERNATIONAL DATE LINE

FIGURE 18–3 The International Date Line (IDL).

INTERNATIONAL DATE LINE (IDL)

You will remember that time around the world is figured in relation to Greenwich Mean Time (GMT). For international travel, the *International Date Line (IDL)* must also be considered. On the opposite side of the world from the GMT line is the imaginary vertical line known as the International Date Line (see Figure 18–3).

It is at the IDL that the calendar date changes from one day to the next. When a passenger is traveling from Los Angeles to Sydney, for example, the calendar changes from Sunday to Monday during the flight as the IDL is crossed. This means that a day is *lost*. The calendar has advanced one day, even though the passenger has not lived those 24 hours; therefore, the passenger has "lost" that day.

On the other hand, as the passenger crosses the IDL in an eastbound direction, a day is gained. The calendar regresses one day, but the passenger has already lived that day once; therefore, a day is "gained."

TIME COMPARISON

Time comparison for international cities is accomplished by following the same steps you learned for domestic time comparison. There are, however, two differences in the calculations that may arise when dealing with international cities.

1. Domestically, the IDL was not a factor; internationally, it may be.

2. Domestically, all cities were expressed as minus numbers in relationship to GMT. Internationally, both cities may be expressed as a negative number or a positive number, or one city might be a positive and the other city a negative number.

Steps to Calculate International Time Comparison

Step 1: Determine how each city is expressed in relationship to GMT.

Step 2: If both numbers are positive or both numbers are negative, subtract the smaller from the larger to obtain the number of hours difference between the two cities. If one city is a positive and the other a negative, add the two numbers together to obtain the number of hours difference in time.

Step 3: Put yourself in the city where you know the time. If you flew to the other city using the shortest route, do you cross the IDL? If yes, use "IDL Region"; if no, use "Basic Region" in Table 18–1. Which direction did you fly?

Step 4: Find the region and direction in Table 18–1. Go to the Time Comparison column to find the correct math step. Based on this math step, either add or subtract the number of hours difference between the two cities to the known time.

Basic:	Used when the shortest distance between the cities in question *does not cross the IDL*.
IDL:	Used when the shortest distance between the cities in question *does cross the IDL*.

Area and direction	Time comparison	Elapsed flying time
Basic east to west	Subtract	Add
Basic west to east	Add	Subtract
IDL east to west	Add	Subtract
IDL west to east	Subtract	Add

TABLE 18–1 Math steps for time calculation.

The *OAG Flight Guide–Worldwide Edition* contains a time chart that lists each country alphabetically. The chart on bottom of page 281 shows how each location is expressed in relationship to GMT, and if Daylight Savings Time is observed, the effective and discontinue dates are also shown. Please note that this text always indicates the expression for all cities.

PLEASE TURN TO PAGE 288 AND COMPLETE EXERCISE 18–3 NOW.

ELAPSED FLYING TIME

Calculating international elapsed flying time follows the same steps you learned for the domestic calculation. Because international flights often take much longer, some of the calculations may seem more difficult, especially when a flight arrives on a different day from when it departed.

Steps to Calculate Elapsed Flying Time

Step 1: Determine how each city is expressed in relation to GMT.

Step 2: If both numbers are positive or both numbers are negative, subtract the smaller from the larger to obtain the number of hours difference between the two cities. If one city is a positive and the other a negative, add the two numbers together to obtain the number of hours difference in time.

Step 3: Subtract the departure time from the arrival time to determine the apparent flying time.

Step 4: Using the shortest route, does the flight cross the IDL? Is the flight going east or west? Use your answers to these questions and the math chart in Table 18–1 to learn whether to add or subtract the number of hours difference between the two cities to the apparent flying time.

When subtracting the departure time from the arrival time, it may be necessary to borrow an hour, convert to a 24-hour clock, or even manipulate time. Consider the following:

Arrival Time	11:25 P.M.
− Departure Time	9:43 P.M.

You must borrow 1 hour:

Arrival Time	10:85 P.M.
− Departure Time	9:43 P.M.
=	1 hour 42 minutes

Arrival Time	2:15 P.M.
− Departure Time	10:15 A.M.

You must convert to 24-hour clock:

Arrival Time	14 15
− Departure Time	10 15
=	4 hours

Arrival Time	8:00 A.M. Wed.
− Departure Time	2:00 P.M. Tue.

You must convert to a 24-hour clock and manipulate time by adding 24 hours to the arrival time:

Arrival Time	32 00
− Departure time	14 00
=	18 hours

PLEASE TURN TO PAGE 289 AND COMPLETE EXERCISE 18–4 NOW.

INTERNATIONAL CITY, AIRPORT, AND AIRLINE CODES

Much as you might wish otherwise, there are still more codes that you have to become familiar with. Table 18–2 represents many of the major city, airport, and airline codes that you will come in contact with throughout your career. You can find a complete list of city/airport codes in the front of the *OAG Flight Guide–Worldwide Edition*. International airlines are a separate listing, also found in the front of the Worldwide edition.

Afghanistan
  Ariana Afghan—FG
    Kabul—KBL

Algeria
  Air Algérie—AH
    Algiers—ALG

Antigua
  Liat—LI
    Antigua (St. John's)—ANU

Argentina
  Aerolineas Argentinas—AR
    Buenos Aires—BUE
      Ministro Pistarini Airport—EZE
    San Carlos de Bariloche—BRC

Aruba
  Air Aruba—FQ
  ALM (Curacao)—LM
    Aruba (Oranjestad)—AUA

Australia
  Ansett Australia—AN
  Qantas—QF
    Adelaide—ADL
    Brisbane—BNE
    Darwin—DRW
    Hobart—HBA
    Melbourne—MEL
    Perth—PER
    Sydney—SYD

Austria
  Austrian Airlines—OS
  Lauda Air—NG
    Vienna—VIE

Bahamas
  Bahamasair—UP
    Freeport—FPO
    Nassau—NAS

Bahrain
  Gulf Air—GF
    Bahrain (Manama)—BAH

Bangladesh
  Biman Bangladesh—BG
  GMG Airlines—Z5
    Dhaka—DAC

Barbados
    Barbados (Bridgetown)—BGI

Belgium
  City Bird—H2
  Sabena—SN
    Brussels—BRU

Belize
  Maya Airways—MW
    Belize City—BZE

Bermuda
    Bermuda (Hamilton)—BDA

Bhutan
  Druk Airlines—KB
    Thimphu (Paro)—PBH

Bolivia
  Lloyd Aéreo Boliviano—LB
    La Paz—LPB

Bosnia Herzegovina
  Air Bosna—JA
    Sarajevo—SJJ

Brazil
  Varig—RG
  Vasp—VP
    Brasilia—BSB
    Rio de Janeiro—RIO
      Rio International—GIG
    São Paulo—SAO
      Congonhas Airport—CGH
      Guarulhos Airport—GRU
      Viracopos Airport—VCP

British Virgin Islands
    Tortola (Road Town)—TOV
    Virgin Gorda (Spanish Town)—VIJ

Brunei Darussalam
  Royal Brunei—BI
    Bandar Seri Begawan—BWN

Bulgaria
  Balkan-Bulgarian Airlines—LZ
    Sofia—SOF

Cambodia
  Kampuchea Airlines—KT
    Phnom Penh—PNH

Canada
  Air Canada—AC
  Canada 3000—2T
  Canadian Airlines—CP
  Pem-Air—PD
  Royal Aviation—QN
    Calgary—YYC
    Montreal—YMQ
      Dorval Airport—YUL
      Mirabel Airport—YMX
    Ottawa—YOW
    Quebec City—YQB

    Toronto—YTO
      Pearson International—YYZ
    Winnipeg—YWG
    Vancouver—YVR

Cayman Islands
  Cayman Airways—KX
    Grand Cayman (George Town)—GCM

Chile
  Ladeco Airlines—UC
  Lan Chile—LA
    Santiago—SCL

Colombia
  Aces—VX
  Avianca—AV
    Bogotá—BOG
    Cartagena—CTG

Côte d'Ivoire
  Air Afrique—RK
    Abidjan—ABJ

Congo, Democratic Republic of
  Congo Airlines—EO
    Kinshasa—FIH

Costa Rica
  Lacsa—LR
    San Jose—SJO

Croatia
  Croatia Airlines—OU
    Dubrovnik—DBV
    Zagreb—ZAG

Cuba
  Cubana—CU
    Havana—HAV

Cyprus
  Cyprus Airways—CY
    Larnaca—LCA

Czech Republic
  Czech Airlines CSA—OK
    Prague—PRG

Denmark
  Cimber Air—QI
  Maersk Air—DM
  Muk Air—ZR
    Copenhagen—CPH

Dominican Republic
  Queen Air—5G
    Santo Domingo—SDQ

(continued)

TABLE 18–2 International code list.

Ecuador
   Ecuatoriana—EU
      Guayaquil—GYE
      Quito—UIO

Egypt
   Egyptair—MS
      Cairo—CAI

El Salvador
   Taca International Airlines—TA
      San Salvador—SAL

Estonia
   Estonian Air—OV
      Tallinn—TLL

Fiji
   Air Fiji—PC
   Air Pacific—FJ
      Nadi—NAN
      Suva—SUV

Finland
   Finnair—AY
      Helsinki—HEL

France
   Air France—AF
   Air Liberte—IJ
   AOM French Airlines—IW
      Marseille—MRS
      Paris—PAR
         Charles de Gaulle Airport—CDG
         Orly Airport—ORY
      Nice—NCE

Ghana
   Ghana Airways—GH
      Accra—ACC

Georgia
   Air Georgia—DA
      Tbilisi—TBS

Germany
   Condor—DE
   Eurowings—EW
   Lufthansa—LH
      Berlin—BER
         Schoenfeld Airport—SXF
         Tegel Airport—TXL
      Dusseldorf—DUS
      Frankfurt—FRA
      Munich—MUC

Greece
   Olympic Airways—OA
      Athens—ATH

Guam
      Guam—GUM

Guatemala
   Aviateca—GU
      Guatemala City—GUA

Haiti
   Tropical Airways d'Haiti—M7
      Cap Haitien—CAP
      Port-au-Prince—PAP

Honduras
   Aero Lineas Sosa—P4
      La Ceiba—LCE
      Tegucigalpa—TGU

Hungary
   Malev Hungarian Airlines—MA
      Budapest—BUD

Iceland
   Icelandair—FI
      Reykjavik—REK
         Keflavik Airport—KEF

India
   Air India—AI
   Indian Airlines—IC
   Jet Airways India—9W
   Sahara Airlines—S2
      Calcutta—CCU
      Chennai (formerly Madras)—MAA
      Delhi/New Delhi—DEL
      Mumbai (formerly Bombay)—BOM

Indonesia
   Garuda Indonesia—GA
   Merpati Nusantara Airlines—MZ
      Denpasar—DPS
      Jakarta—JKT
         Soekarno-Hatta Airport—CGK

Ireland, Republic of
   Aer Lingus—EI
   Cityjet—WX
   Ryanair—FR
      Dublin—DUB
      Shannon—SNN

Israel
   El Al Israel—LY
      Jerusalem—JRS
      Tel Aviv—TLV

Italy
   Alitalia—AZ
      Florence—FLR
      Milan—MIL
         Linate Airport—LIN
         Malpensa Airport—MXP
      Rome—ROM
         Ciampino Airport—CIA
         Fiumincino (da Vinci) Airport—FCO
      Venice—VCE
         Marco Polo Airport—VCE
         Treviso Airport—TSF

Jamaica
   Air Jamaica—JM
      Kingston—KIN
      Montego Bay—MBJ
      Ocho Rios—OCJ

Japan
   All Nippon—NH
   Japan Air—JL
   Japan Asia—EG
      Nagoya—NGO
      Naha (Okinawa)—OKA
      Osaka—ITM
      Sapporo—OKD
      Tokyo—TYO
         Haneda Airport—HND
         Narita Airport—NRT

Jordan
   Royal Jordanian Airlines—RJ
      Amman—AMM

Kenya
   Kenya Airways—KQ
      Mombasa—MBA
      Nairobi—NBO

Korea, Democratic People's Republic of (North)
   Air Koryo—JS
      Pyongyang—FNJ

Korea, Republic of (South)
   Asiana Airlines—OZ
   Korean Air—KE
      Seoul—SEL

Kuwait
   Kuwait Airways—KU
      Kuwait—KWI

Laos
   Lao Aviation—QV
      Vientiane—VTE

TABLE 18–2 *Continued*

Lebanon
  MEA (Middle East Airlines)—ME
    Beirut—BEY

Libya
  Libyan Arab Airlines—LN
    Tripoli—TIP

Luxembourg
  Luxair—LG
    Luxembourg—LUX

Malaysia
  Malaysia Airlines—MH
    Kuala Lumpur—KUL
      Kuala Lumpur International—KUL
      Sultan Abdul Aziz Shah Airport—SZB
    Penang—PEN

Maldives
  Air Maldives—L6
    Male—MLE

Martinique
    Fort de France—FDF

Mexico
  Aeromexico—AM
  Mexicana—MX
  Taesa—GD
    Acapulco—ACA
    Cancun—CUN
    Cozumel—CZM
    Guadalajara—GDL
    Ixtapa/Zihuatenjo—ZIH
    Mazatlan—MZT
    Mexico City—MEX
    Puerto Vallarta—PVR

Morocco
  Royal Air Moroc—AT
    Casablanca—CAS
    Marrakech—RAK
    Rabat—RBA
    Tangier—TNG

Myanmar
  Air Mandalay—6T
  Myanmar Airways—UB
    Yangon—RGN

Nepal
  Royal Nepal Airlines—RA
    Kathmandu—KTM

Netherlands
  KLM Royal Dutch Airlines—KL
    Amsterdam—AMS

New Zealand
  Air New Zealand—NZ
  Ansett New Zealand—ZQ
    Auckland—AKL
    Christchurch—CHC
    Rotorua—ROT
    Wellington—WLG

Nicaragua
  Nica—6Y
    Managua—MGA

Nigeria
  Nigerian Airways—WT
    Lagos—LOS

Norway
    Bergen—BGO
    Oslo—OSL

Oman
  Oman Air—WY
    Muscat—MCT

Pakistan
  Pakistan International Airlines—PK
    Islamabad—ISB
    Karachi—KHI

Panama
  Copa—CM
    Panama City—PTY

Papua New Guinea
  Air Niugini—PX
    Port Moresby—POM

Paraguay
    Asuncion—ASU

People's Republic of China
  Air China—CA
  Air Macau—NX
  Cathay Pacific—CX
  Hong Kong Dragon Airlines—KA
    Beijing—PEK
    Guangzhou—CAN
    Hong Kong—HKG
    Shanghai—SHA

Peru
  Aero Continente—N6
  Aviandina—SJ
  Transportes Aereos Nacionales de Selva—TJ
    Cuzco—CUZ
    Lima—LIM

Philippines
  Philippine Air—PR
    Manila—MNL

Poland
  LOT Polish Airlines—LO
    Warsaw—WAW

Portugal
  TAP Air Portugal—TP
    Lisbon—LIS

Puerto Rico
  Dominair—YU
    San Juan—SJU

Qatar
  Qatar Airways—QR
    Doha—DOH

Romania
  Tarom—RO
    Bucharest—BUH
      Baneasa Airport—BBU
      Otopeni Airport—OTP

Russian Federation
  Aeroflot—SU
    Moscow—MOW
      Bykovo Airport—BKA
      Domodedovo Airport—DME
      Sheremetyevo Airport—SVO
      Vnukovo Airport—VKO
    St. Petersburg—LED

Saudi Arabia
  Saudi Arabian Airlines—SV
    Jeddah—JED
    Riyadh—RUH

Senegal
    Dakar—DKR

Seychelles
  Air Seychelles—HM
    Mahe Island—SEZ

Singapore
  Silk Air—MI
  Singapore Airlines—SQ
    Singapore—SIN

Slovakia
  Air Slovakia—GM
  Slovak Airlines—6Q
    Bratislava—BTS

South Africa
  South African Airways—SA
    Cape Town—CPT
    Johannesburg—JNB

(continued)

TABLE 18–2 *Continued*

Spain
    Iberia Airways—IB
    Spannair—JK
        Barcelona—BCN
        Madrid—MAD
        Seville—SVQ

Sri Lanka
    SriLankan Airlines—UL
        Colombo—CMB

St. Lucia
    Helenair—2Y
        St. Lucia (Castries)—SLU

St. Maarten / Sint Martin
    Windward Islands Airways—WM
        St. Maarten (Philipsburg)—SXM

Sweden
    SAS Scandinavian Airlines—SK
        Stockholm—STO
            Arlanda Airport—ARN
            Bromma Airport—BMA
            Skavsta Airport—NYO

Switzerland
    Swissair—SR
        Basel—BSL
        Geneva—GVA
        Zurich—ZRH

Syria
    Syrian Arab Airlines—RB
        Damascus—DAM

Tahiti and French Polynesia
    Air Tahiti—VT
    Air Tahiti Nui—TN
        Bora Bora—BOB
        Moorea—MOZ
        Papeete—PPT

Taiwan (Republic of China)
    China Airlines—CI
    Eva Airlines—BR
    Mandarin Airlines—AE
        Taipei—TPE

Tanzania
    Air Tanzania—TC
        Dar es Salaam—DAR

Trinidad and Tobago
    BWIA West Indies Airways—BW
        Port of Spain—POS

Thailand
    Thai Airways—TG
        Bangkok—BKK
        Phuket—HKT

Tunisia
    Tunis Air—TU
        Tunis—TUN

Turkey
    Turkish Airlines—TK
        Ankara—ANK
            Esenboga Airport—ESB
        Istanbul—IST

Ukraine
    Air Ukraine—6U
    Ukraine International Airlines—PS
        Kiev—IEV
        Odessa—ODS

United Arab Emirates
    Emirates—EK
        Abu Dhabi—AUH
        Dubai—DXB

United Kingdom
    British Airways—BA
    British Midland—BD
    Virgin Atlantic—VS
        Belfast, Northern Ireland—BFS
        Birmingham, England—BHX
        Cardiff, Wales—CWL
        Edinburgh, Scotland—EDI
        Glasgow, Scotland—GLA
            Glasgow International Airport—GLA
            Prestwick Airport—PIK
        Manchester, England—MAN
        London, England—LON
            Gatwick Airport—LGW
            Heathrow Airport—LHR
            London City Airport—LCY
            Luton Airport—LTN
            Stansted Airport—STN

Uruguay
    Pluna—PU
        Montevideo—MVD

U.S. Virgin Islands
        St. Croix (Christiansted)—STX
        St. Thomas (Charlotte Amalie)—STT

Venezuela
    Air Venezuela—7Q
    Avensa—VE
    Vensecar International—V4
        Caracas—CCS

Vietnam
    Vietnam Airlines—VN
        Hanoi—HAN
        Ho Chi Minh City—SGN

Yugoslavia
        Belgrade—BEG

TABLE 18–2 *Continued, end.*

As with U.S. cities, many international cities have a "generic" city code, as well as a specific code for each airport. In many cases, both types of codes are shown in Table 18–2. The table is shown alphabetically, first by country name, then by city name (a great way to practice your knowledge of world geography). You will also notice listings for airlines beside some countries. This is because many international airlines are associated with their respective governments. Many, in fact, are owned by the governments of their home countries. The airlines included here represent only the major carriers you will use on a routine basis.

PLEASE TURN TO PAGE 290 AND COMPLETE EXERCISE 18–5 NOW.

? **What Would You Do?**

Your client is flying to Sydney and you have told him that his flight arrives at 2:35 P.M., two days after he departs. He says that this simply cannot be correct.

1. Do you tell him that he is probably correct and that there is a mistake in the GDS flight schedule?
2. Do you explain that the flight simply takes more than 48 hours?
3. Do you show him how the International Date Line plus the actual flying time explains the arrival two days after departure?

SUMMARY

There are many differences between domestic and international air travel. Airport areas, agency appointing bodies, baggage allowance, check-in time, and pet acceptance are just a few. International airfares are established through collaboration between the airline, origin and destination countries, and the IATA. International air travelers appreciate a travel professional who is well versed in and willing to explain the various differences the client will encounter while traveling. It is also very important that travel professionals understand international fare construction and various pricing techniques. A client who feels that their travel counselor is using all of the applicable tools at his disposal to obtain the best airfare will return to this counselor again and again.

For additional Travel and Tourism resources, go to http://www.hospitality-tourism.delmar.com.

PLEASE COMPLETE THE CHAPTER REVIEW QUESTIONS NOW.

EXERCISE 18-1 IATA Traffic Conference Area

Directions: List the country, IATA Traffic Conference Area, and continent or geographical area for each city.

City	Country	TC Area	Continent/Geographical Area
Zurich			
Guatemala City			
Hong Kong			
Tel Aviv			
Copenhagen			
Toronto			
Nassau			
Kuala Lumpur			
Bombay			
Buenos Aires			
Quito			
Cancun			
Bangkok			
Paris			
Nairobi			
Cairo			
Bogotá			
Moscow			
Athens			
Tokyo			
Frankfurt			
Jakarta			
Glasgow			
Sydney			
Caracas			
St. Thomas			
Lagos			
Rome			
Nadi			
Basel			
Montreal			

EXERCISE 18-2 24-Hour Time

Directions: Convert either 12-hour or 24-hour time.

1230 _____	1750 _____	0035 _____
1420 _____	2300 _____	1010 _____
0005 _____	1330 _____	1645 _____
2020 _____	0955 _____	0345 _____
1906 _____	0222 _____	1530 _____
1150 _____	1212 _____	0007 _____
11:15 A.M. _____	2:23 P.M. _____	8:15 A.M. _____
11:29 P.M. _____	6:15 A.M. _____	1:01 A.M. _____
12:02 P.M. _____	3:15 P.M. _____	9:29 P.M. _____
12:15 A.M. _____	8:23 A.M. _____	10:05 A.M. _____
9:23 P.M. _____	3:58 A.M. _____	10:38 P.M. _____

EXERCISE 18-3 Time Comparison

1. It is 2:00 P.M. in New York (−5). What time is it in Honolulu (−10)? _____

2. It is 12:00 P.M. in Chicago (−6). What time is it in Paris (+1)? _____

3. It is 9:00 P.M. Tuesday in Los Angeles (−8). What time and day is it in Tokyo (+9)? _____

4. It is 10:00 A.M. in Denver (−7). What time is it in London (0)? _____

5. It is 3:00 A.M. in Honolulu (−10). What time is it in London (0)? _____

6. You have to call a tour operator in Paris (+1) at 4:00 P.M. Paris time. What time should you place the call, Des Moines (−6) time? _____

7. It is 3:00 A.M. Wednesday in Cairo (+2). What time and day is it in Chicago (−6)? _____

8. Your office is in New York City (−5) and your office hours are 8:00 A.M. to 5:00 P.M. You have to call a supplier in Athens (+2) at 3:30 P.M., Athens time. When should you place the call? _____

9. It is 9:03 P.M. in Zurich (+1). What time is it in Chicago (−6)? _____

10. It is 9:35 A.M. in Vancouver (−8). What time is it in Boston (−5)? _____

11. It is 9:25 P.M. in Santiago (−4). What time is it in Honolulu (−10)? _____

12. It is 8:30 P.M. in Paris (+1). What time is it in London (0)? _____

13. It is 2:15 P.M. in Miami (−5). What time is it in London (0)? _____

14. It is 10:45 P.M. in Madrid (+1). What time is it in Atlanta (−5)? _____

15. It is 12:33 P.M. in Manila (+8). What time is it in Houston (−6)? _____

16. It is 7:30 A.M. in Tokyo (+9). What time is it in London (0)? _____

17. It is 2:14 A.M. in Bogotá (−5). What time is it in Seattle (−8)? _____

18. It is 4:56 P.M. in Calcutta (+5½). What time is it in Lisbon (0)? _____

19. It is 12:15 A.M. in Singapore (+8). What time is it in Stockholm (+1)? _____

20. It is 11:07 A.M. in San Diego (−8). What time is it in Nassau (−5)? _____

EXERCISE 18-4 Elapsed Flying Time

1. A flight departs Chicago O'Hare (−6) at 6:00 P.M. Monday and arrives in Sydney (+10) at 6:20 A.M. Wednesday. What is the elapsed flying time? _____

2. A flight departs Istanbul (+2) at 11:20 A.M. and arrives in Berlin (+1) at 1:20 P.M. What is the elapsed flying time?

_____

3. A flight departs Hong Kong (+8) at 8:00 A.M. and arrives in Bangkok (+7) at 9:55 A.M. What is the elapsed flying time?

_____

4. A flight departs Boston (−5) at 7:10 P.M. Sunday and arrives in Athens (+2) at 2:25 P.M. Monday. What is the elapsed flying time? _____

5. A flight departs Rio de Janeiro (−3) at 2:30 P.M. and arrives at New York Kennedy (−5) at 8:30 P.M. What is the elapsed flying time? _____

6. A flight departs Los Angeles (−8) at 12:30 P.M. Tuesday and arrives in Seoul (+9) at 6:50 P.M. Wednesday. What is the elapsed flying time? _____

7. A flight departs Bogotá (−5) at 10:00 A.M. and arrives in Toronto (−5) at 4:50 P.M. What is the elapsed flying time?

_____

8. A flight departs Los Angeles (−8) at 10:00 P.M. on Monday and arrives in Sydney (+10) at 7:00 A.M. Wednesday. What is the elapsed flying time? _____

9. A flight departs London (0) at 10:45 A.M. and arrives in Nairobi (+3) at 9:15 P.M. What is the elapsed flying time?

_____

10. A flight departs Singapore (+8) at 9:45 P.M. on Friday and arrives in Rome (+1) at 5:55 A.M. on Saturday. What is the elapsed flying time? _____

11. A flight departs Los Angeles (−8) at 7:00 P.M. on Wednesday and arrives in London (0) at 1:00 P.M. Thursday. What is the elapsed flying time? _____

12. A flight departs Bogotá (−5) at 1:10 P.M. Sunday and arrives in Madrid (+1) at 7:35 A.M. on Monday. What is the elapsed flying time? _____

EXERCISE 18–5 International Codes

Directions: Indicate the city/airport code and the country name next to each city. Please print.

1. Bogotá _____

2. Belgrade _____

3. Dublin _____

4. Beijing _____

5. Santiago _____

6. Accra _____

7. Guam _____

8. Abidjan _____

9. Venice _____

10. Lima _____

11. Copenhagen _____

12. La Paz _____

13. Perth _____

14. Caracas _____

15. Cape Town _____

16. Calcutta _____

17. Budapest _____

18. Dakar _____

19. Edinburgh _____

20. Vienna _____

Directions: Indicate the city name, airport name where necessary, and country name. Please print.

21. CDG _____

22. FCO _____

23. NBO _____

24. BUE _____

25. LGW _____

26. SVO _____

27. NRT _____

28. LHR _____

29. ORY _____

30. YMX _____

Review Questions

1. Identify the IATA Traffic Conference Area for each country.

   _____ Peru   _____ Bahamas   _____ Indonesia   _____ Tanzania

   _____ New Zealand   _____ Spain   _____ Morocco   _____ Jamaica

   _____ Malaysia   _____ Norway   _____ Canada   _____ Finland

2. Convert these times into a 24-hour clock.

   _____ 10:15 A.M.   _____ 3:45 P.M.   _____ 2:05 A.M.

   _____ 11:37 P.M.   _____ 12:29 A.M.   _____ 9:35 A.M.

   _____ 2:19 A.M.   _____ 9:03 P.M.   _____ 12:04 P.M.

3. Convert these times into a 12-hour clock.

   _____ 0027   _____ 1455   _____ 0432

   _____ 1212   _____ 0221   _____ 2324

   _____ 1629   _____ 1812   _____ 0002

4. Identify the differences between domestic and international air travel.

Item	Domestic	International
Baggage		
Check-in		
Commission		
Connecting		
Time		
Infants		
Pets		
Reconfirmation		

5. It is 10:15 A.M. in Munich (+1). What time is it in Pittsburgh (−5)? _____

6. It is 9:45 P.M. Saturday in Auckland (+12). What time and day is it in Denver (−8)? _____

7. A flight departs Washington Dulles (−5) at 6:00 P.M. Monday and arrives at London Heathrow (0) at 6:25 A.M. Tuesday. What is the elapsed flying time? _____

8. A flight departs Los Angeles (−8) at 8:45 A.M. Friday and arrives in Tokyo (+9) at 4:25 P.M. on Saturday. What is the elapsed flying time? _____

9. Indicate the city name, airport name where necessary, and country name for these codes. Please print.

CAI _____

PRG _____

LGW _____

YUL _____

LED _____

BCN _____

HND _____

SNN _____

LHR _____

CUN _____

TPE _____

STT _____

IEV _____

CDG _____

ZRH _____

10. Indicate the city/airport code for these cities. Please print.

_____ Lima	_____ Montreal Mirabel	_____ Acapulco
_____ Johannesburg	_____ Tel Aviv	_____ St. Lucia
_____ Sydney	_____ Nassau	_____ Calgary
_____ Helsinki	_____ Hamilton, Bermuda	_____ Bogotá
_____ Oranjestad, Aruba	_____ Berlin, Tegel Airport	_____ Milan, Linate Airport
_____ Puerto Vallarta	_____ Amsterdam	_____ Toronto
_____ Barcelona	_____ San Juan, Puerto Rico	_____ Dar es Salaam

11. Indicate the airline name for each code. Please print.

BA _____   RG _____

QF _____   AF _____

SQ _____   JL _____

SR _____   VS _____

SK _____   AM _____

12. Indicate the code for these airlines. Please print.

_____ Iberia Airways   _____ Mexicana   _____ KLM Royal Dutch

_____ Lufthansa   _____ Air Canada   _____ Avianca

_____ Aer Lingus   _____ Cathay Pacific   _____ El Al Israel

_____ All Nippon   _____ Canadian Airlines   _____ Air New Zealand

International Airfares, Taxes, Schedules, and Ticketing

OBJECTIVES

At the conclusion of this chapter, you should be able to

- define and identify IATA trip classifications.
- explain the mechanics of and the reason for split ticketing.
- define the terms associated with international airfares.
- understand booking classes and fare basis codes.
- understand the taxes and other fees associated with international air travel.
- understand the differences between domestic and international ticketing.

KEY TERMS

airline rate desk
Advance Purchase Excursion (APEX)
  fares
Animal Plant and Health Inspection
  Service (APHIS) Fee
around-the-world fares
backhaul
bank buying rate (BBR)
budget fare
circle-trip minimum
combined tax item
double open-jaw

global indicator
higher intermediate point (HIP)
IATA trip classifications
logical geographical order
maximum permitted miles (MPM)
neutral unit of construction (NUC)
primary codes
security surcharge
Sold Inside, Ticketed/e-tkted Inside
  (SITI)
Sold Inside, Ticketed/e-tkted Outside
  (SITO)

Sold Outside, Ticketed/e-tkted Inside
  (SOTI)
Sold Outside, Ticketed/e-tkted Outside
  (SOTO)
stand-by fare
turnaround point
U.S. Arrival Tax
U.S. Customs Fee
U.S. Immigration Fee
youth fares
XT

Many travel counselors find that basic international fares are less complicated and are fewer in number than domestic airfares. This may be due to the fact that domestically, airlines can set fares at any amount and change them as often as they wish. Internationally, the airlines work together with governments and the International Air Transport Association (IATA) to establish fares. Therefore, international fares are more likely to remain the same, at least for a while.

IATA TRIP CLASSIFICATIONS

One of IATA's requirements for every international trip is that it must be classified, based on where travel is purchased and issued in relationship to where travel begins. Letters indicating this information identify each classification.

Sold Inside, Ticketed/e-tkted Inside (SITI) the country where travel originates is by far the most common type of trip. For example, your Boston agency collects money for and issues a ticket/e-tkt from Boston to Athens. As you can see, travel originates in the United States and the ticket/e-tkt is being sold and issued within the same country, hence the IATA classification of SITI.

Sold Outside, Ticketed/e-tkted Outside (SOTO) the country where travel originates is the second most common type of trip classification. For example, your Boston agency collects money for and issues a ticket/e-tkt from Athens to Boston. Now, the classification is based on the fact that travel originates in Greece. As you can see, travel is sold and the ticket/e-tkt is issued outside of Greece, hence the SOTO classification.

The other two IATA classifications, Sold Outside, Ticketed/e-tkted Inside (SOTI) the country where travel originates and Sold Inside, Ticketed/e-tkted Outside (SITO) the country where travel originates are quite rare.

An example of a SOTI might be the following: Your client's son is stationed at a military base near Frankfurt, Germany, and your client wants to bring his son home for the holidays. Your client purchases a Prepaid Ticket Advice (PTA) at your agency in Atlanta. Your client's son has Delta Airlines issue the ticket in Frankfurt.

An example of a SITO might be: Your Boston travel agency collects money for a trip from Boston to Dublin. The client picks up the ticket at a branch agency in London.

SITIs, SOTOs, and Split Ticketing

The ticketing technique known as split ticketing is used on some itineraries in an attempt to save the client money on airfare. This technique can only be done with normal fares, never when excursion fares are used. Split ticketing involves issuing two tickets as follows:

Ticket 1: Origin to destination, priced in U.S. dollars (USD)
Ticket 2: Destination to origin, priced in foreign currency, converted to USD

For example, your agency is located in New York City and your client is traveling from JFK to Cairo, round-trip, on business. She does not qualify for excursion fares and must use normal fares. How might split ticketing be used to this client's advantage (see Figure 19–1)?

Important Industry Web Sites

Airlines Around the World: **http://www.kls2.com/airlines/**

Currency Converter: **http://www.oanda.com**

International Airlines Travel Agents Network:
http://www.iatan.com

International Air Transport Association: **http://www.iata.org**

Mapblast: **http://www.mapblast.com**

Time Zone Converter: **http://www.worldtimeserver.com**

Weather Worldwide: **http://www.intellicast.com**

Worldclock: **http://www.timeanddate.com/worldclock**

World Tourism Offices: **http://www.towd.com**

New York to Cairo round-trip

Priced in U.S. dollars (USD)

$1,470 coach, each way

× 2

$2,940 coach, round-trip

Split Ticket Pricing

Ticket #1: NYC-CAI, $1,470
+
Ticket #2: CAI-NYC

3,656 Egyptian pounds (EGP)

× .290909 exchange rate (BBR)

$1,064 USD (rounded to nearest dollar)
=
$2,534 coach, round-trip

$406 savings by split ticketing

FIGURE 19–1 Sample split ticket calculations.

The exchange rate, officially called the bank buying rate (BBR), is found in the GDS as well as in many financial magazines and newspapers. For ticketing purposes, the BBR is set each Wednesday and is in effect until the following Wednesday. Each GDS has the capability of not only displaying the BBR but also converting any currency to any other currency within a fraction of a second.

You can see in Figure 19–1 that pricing the round-trip using normal fares in USD costs $2,940. However, by issuing two tickets, the client's total cost for the round trip is only $2,534: a savings of $406!

Now, consider the IATA trip classifications for each ticket. If one ticket is issued for the round-trip, the classification would be SITI. But, if split ticketing is used, there are two tickets and two classifications. Ticket 1 (JFK/CAI) is a SITI. Ticket 2 (CAI/JFK) is a SOTO.

As you might imagine, checking the viability of split ticketing takes a bit more time than simply looking at USD fares. In some cases, split ticketing may result in lower agency commission. However, never lose sight of the fact that doing the best possible job for the client should be the counselor's number one concern.

PLEASE TURN TO PAGE 305 AND COMPLETE
EXERCISE 19–1 NOW.

INTERNATIONAL FARE TERMS

At the beginning of their travel careers, most entry-level counselors do not handle complicated international fare calculations. Agency managers know that complex itineraries can be overwhelming to new counselors and, therefore, assign them to more experienced personnel. Even so, there are some new concepts you should become familiar with. Because a few of these terms are very complicated and difficult to understand, the explanations shown here are basic rather than comprehensive. With practice and a little patience, these terms will become clear to you.

A *gateway city* is the city or airport where an international flight begins or ends. As you might imagine, U.S. hub cities are also gateway cities in most cases. These include Boston, New York Kennedy, Washington Dulles, Miami, Dallas–Ft. Worth, Houston Bush Intercontinental, Los Angeles, San Francisco, and Chicago O'Hare. Keep in mind that just because an airport has the word "international" in its name does not mean it is a gateway city.

Most international airlines operate out of gateway cities only. As there are hundreds of nongateway cities, these airlines often work with local airlines with regard to fare. An airline that transports passengers from an interior city to the gateway city is called an *air add-on*. For example, Qantas may offer an add-on from Memphis to Los Angeles

on American, Delta, and United. Sometimes the air add-on is less expensive than the applicable excursion fare between these cities; other times the excursion fare is best. The travel counselor must know to consider both possibilities.

Many international fares indicate the routing as maximum permitted miles (MPM). This type of routing means that connections, and possibly stopovers, can be made anywhere, provided that the combined air mileage does not exceed the MPM for the fare. MPM fares are generally more expensive than fares with more limited routings. The fare rule display in all GDSs identifies the MPM for the fare.

All international airfare rules include a global indicator. The global indicator identifies the general route the flight must take in order to use the fare. Common sense tells us that a traveler going from Los Angeles to Sydney would fly transpacific, not transatlantic and, fortunately, global indicators follow the same logic. Standard global indicators include EH = Eastern Hemisphere, MA = Mid Atlantic, AT = North Atlantic, NP = North Pacific, PA = Pacific, and WH = Western Hemisphere.

It is not uncommon for a business client to present the travel counselor with a list of international cities and the length of time he requires in each city, and ask the counselor to arrange an itinerary. The travel counselor must be mindful of logical geographical order when arranging the cities. Itineraries that contain backtracking waste the client's time and usually increase the overall fare.

The farthest destination from the origin is usually called the turnaround point. It is at the turnaround point that the itinerary changes general direction and moves toward home. When establishing logical geographical order, some destinations are usually included on the way to the turnaround point; others may be included on the homeward bound direction. If your client was departing from Pittsburgh and needed to visit Cairo, London, Athens, Stockholm, and Madrid, how would you arrange the cities? Where would the turnaround point be?

Internationally, excursion fares are often referred to as Advance Purchase Excursion (APEX) fares. In today's airfare structure almost all excursion fares have an advance purchase requirement, but when APEX fares were first created, this was not true. Typically, APEX fares have the same restrictions and limitations of any excursion fare: advance purchase, minimum-stay requirement, maximum-stay limitation, same airline must be maintained, and there are penalties for change or cancellation.

Some airlines offer a budget fare from gateway cities. The budget fare is unique to international travel and is often less expensive than standard excursion fares because it requires some flexibility on the part of the passenger. When using a budget fare, the passenger selects the week of travel. Approximately one to two weeks before the selected week, the airline selects the actual flight and day of travel. The same procedure takes place for the return trip as well. As you might imagine, most travelers cannot use the budget fare because they cannot be as flexible as the fare requires.

Another type of fare that is unique to international travel is a stand-by fare. With this type of fare, the travel counselor does not make a reservation but does issue a ticket for a specific airline, flight, and date. The booking class for stand-by fares is usually U and the status box on the ticket shows "SA," meaning, space available. Stand-by fares may be the least expensive type of international fare because they require total flexibility from the passenger. The traveler goes to the airport, checks in with the airline, and hopes to be confirmed. Not many clients are willing or able to use stand-by fares.

Some airlines offer youth fares for travelers between the ages of 12 and 26. Generally, flight reservations for youth fares cannot be made any farther in advance than 24 hours. A travel agency specializing in college student travel may use youth fares, budget fares, and stand-by fares because these travelers may not be particular about which day they depart. However, for most clients, youth fares are not an option.

Around-the-world fares are just as the name implies: The traveler circumnavigates the globe. This fare can result in substantial savings when multiple destinations exist in both hemispheres. Typically, around-the-world fares are offered by several major airlines with specific prices for first-class, business-class, or coach-class travel. Rules for an around-the-world fare usually require that travel maintain a continuous east or west direction, all reservations must be made in advance, and there are penalties for change or cancellation.

As an example, an airline's around-the-world fare prices and rules might include

- $7,000 first class, $5,500 business class, $3,200 coach class
- 29,000 maximum miles for the entire trip
- 15 maximum stopovers
- only specified airlines can be used

Around-the-world fares are especially beneficial for first- and business-class travelers. Two or three destinations can easily add up to the around-the-world fare. For coach-class passengers usually five or more destinations are required before the around-the-world fare proves advantageous. Obviously, this type of fare is something all travel counselors should consider when the client has multiple international destinations.

Internationally, a *round-trip* is the same as domestic. If normal fares are used, different airlines and routings may be used on the outbound and inbound. When excursion fares are used, the typical restrictions and limitations must be met and followed. As with domestic airfares, international excursions can usually be split and combined or an excursion fare can be split and combined with a normal

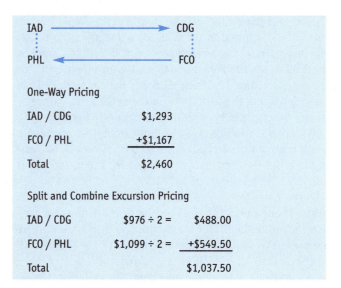

FIGURE 19–2 Sample double open-jaw trip price comparison.

fare. Excursion fares can never be sold on a one-way basis for half of the price.

Open-jaw and *circle trips* have the same definition internationally as they have domestically. As with round-trips, the airline(s) and routing used do not matter when normal fares are used on open-jaw and circle trips. As always, when excursion fares are to be split and combined, all of the rules must be followed. Internationally, these two types of trips have a new restriction when excursion fares are used: The cities on either end of the surface segment in an open-jaw trip and both destinations in a circle trip must be within Europe, or if outside Europe, be within the same country.

Internationally, there is a new type of trip called a double open-jaw. It is easy to mistake this type of trip as two one-way trips (see Figure 19–2). Doing so, however, results in using normal fares without considering the use of excursion fares.

The GDS fare rule display for each city pair indicates if excursions can be split and combined on a double open-jaw trip. Figure 19–2 shows that using excursion fares is substantially less expensive than pricing the trip with normal fares. As with a single open-jaw, both cities on either end of the surface segments must be within Europe or, if outside Europe, be within the same country.

Most international first- and business-class fares allow free, unlimited stopovers provided that the MPM is not exceeded. Theoretically, this means that a client could fly from Chicago O'Hare to London Heathrow, spend a few days, then fly to Amsterdam and pay the ORD/AMS fare. However, sometimes the stopover city has a higher fare than the destination. When this is true, the stopover city is called higher intermediate point (HIP) (see Figure 19–3) and the higher fare must be charged.

In Figure 19–3, you can see that the one-way business class British Airways fare from Chicago O'Hare to

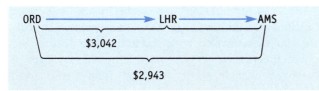

FIGURE 19–3 Illustration of a higher intermediate point (HIP).

Amsterdam is $2,943. Because the client is stopping over in London, that city pair's fare must be checked as well. The BA fare from ORD to LHR is $3,042. Therefore, LHR is a HIP and the higher fare must be charged for the ORD/LHR/AMS itinerary.

Logic might suggest that travel from ORD to LHR should be less expensive because, geographically, LHR is closer to ORD than AMS. Remember that the airline, each country's government, and IATA determine international fares jointly. Factors such as the cost of airport space, fuel, and flight catering are also considered. Just like fares between cities in the United States, the distance between international cities is not the sole determining factor for the fare.

When a HIP fare applies in one direction, the higher fare must be charged in both directions, regardless of the routing. This rule is called circle-trip minimum. In Figure 19–3, the client is charged $3,042 each way because of the LHR stopover on the outbound. Overall, she pays $198 more than the round-trip ORD/AMS fare. The $198 amount is called the backhaul.

When each international airfare is established, it is set in the currency of the country where the flight begins. It is also expressed in a generic amount, known as a neutral unit of construction (NUC). NUCs can be thought of as a world currency, not pertaining to any one country or currency. The purpose of NUCs is to simplify adding multiple currency fares together. All international airline tickets/e-tkts issued by computer show the NUC values in the fare ladder.

To obtain the NUC value, the airline multiplies the new fare by that country's rate of exchange (ROE), which is set by IATA. Each country's ROE is adjusted for inflation and other factors quarterly. The ROE for the United States is always 1.00; therefore, all fares expressed in USD have identical NUC values. For example, a fare rule from New York to Cairo might show

NYCCAI-MS

FBC	USD	NUC	PTC	FT	GI
Y	575.00	575.00	ADT	NL	AT

Because other countries' ROEs fluctuate, the fare and NUC amounts may not be equal. For example, a fare rule from Cairo to New York might show

CAINYC-ML

FBC	EGP	NUC	PTC	FT	GI
Y	4379.00	1273.09	ADT	NL	AT

Using NUCs instead of the actual fares may provide an advantage for travelers beginning their trip in the United States. For example, LAX to AKL, AKL to SYD, SYD to SIN, SIN to NRT, NRT to LAX. Because this itinerary begins in the United States, the travel counselor may use the NUC values for each city pair as the USD fare. This may prove to be less expensive than converting each foreign currency fare into USD and ticketing/e-tkting separately.

PLEASE TURN TO PAGE 305 AND COMPLETE EXERCISE 19–2 NOW.

BOOKING CLASSES AND FARE BASIS CODES

International booking classes and fare basis codes are much like those used for domestic travel. In fact, the *booking classes,* also called primary codes, are the same. Figure 19–4 illustrates most of the booking classes used today.

As with *domestic fare basis codes* (*FBCs*), the FBC may be just one letter (the booking class), or it may contain other letters and numbers. Either way, the booking class dictates the inventory that must be sold in order to obtain the desired fare.

International airfares are more apt to be designated by season than domestic fares. Typically, there are two or three seasons, each indicated by a letter within the fare basis code: H = *high season,* L = *low season,* and K or O = *shoulder (between high and low) season.*

Each fare rule explains when and how seasonal fares are to be used. Sometimes, the traveler's outbound date determines the applicable season for the entire trip. Other times, each travel date identifies each season, resulting in a splitting and combining of fares. Keep in mind that high season for one destination is not necessarily the same for a different destination.

P or F = first class

A = discounted first class

J or C = business class

D, I, or Z = discounted business class

Y, S, or W = coach class

B, H, K, L, M, N, Q, T, V, etc. = discounted coach class

U = air shuttle, reservation not required

E = air shuttle, reservation not allowed

FIGURE 19–4 International booking classes.

As with domestic airfares, the day of the week on which the client travels can have a bearing on the applicable fare. Typically, travel on Monday through Thursday is less expensive than flights on Friday, Saturday, and Sunday. Applicable days of travel may not be indicated in the fare basis code. Fare basis code indicators for applicable days of the week include *W = weekend* and *X = weekday.*

International fare basis codes may also include numbers, just like domestic FBCs. Numbers in international fare basis codes usually indicate maximum length of stay, although sometimes the numbers indicate advance purchase. *Maximum length of stay indicators include 30 = 30 days, 1M = 1 month, 45 = 45 days, 60 = 60 days.* Numbers indicating advance purchase include 1, 3, 7, 14, 21, and 30.

Many international fare basis codes include the letters *AP* or *AN,* both of which indicate APEX. The term APEX is used interchangeably with the term excursion. As discussed earlier, APEX fares have basically the same limitations and restrictions of any excursion fare: same airline, advance purchase, minimum-stay requirement, maximum-stay limitation, and penalties for change or cancellation.

PLEASE TURN TO PAGE 306 AND COMPLETE EXERCISE 19–3 NOW.

INTERNATIONAL TAXES AND FEES

When an airline quotes a fare or the travel counselor obtains a GDS fare display, all amounts are expressed as the base; taxes, PFCs, security fees, segment fees, fuel surcharges, and other international charges must be added.

For every flight that leaves or enters the United States, each passenger is charged a $5 security surcharge. So, for a round-trip, the security surcharge is $10 and appears in the fare ladder portion of a ticket/e-tkt with the code *Q.*

Every passenger departing the United States is charged a *U.S. Departure Tax* of $13.70 and all returning travelers are subject to a U.S. Arrival Tax of $13.70. These two taxes are shown in one of the tax boxes of a ticket/e-tkt with the code *US.*

Most passengers entering the United States from another country are subject to the U.S. Immigration Fee of $7, which appears in a ticket/e-tkt tax box with the code *XY.* Travelers returning to the United States from Guam, the U.S. Virgin Islands, and Puerto Rico are exempt from paying the U.S. Immigration fee.

The U.S. Customs Fee is $5 and is shown with the code *YC* in one of the tax boxes of a ticket/e-tkt for most travelers returning to the United States. Passengers arriving in the United States from a U.S. territory, Canada, Mexico, and the Caribbean are exempt from paying the U.S. Customs Fee.

The $3.10 Animal Plant and Health Inspection Service (APHIS) Fee, a division of the U.S. Department of Agriculture, applies to travelers returning to the United States and appears in a ticket/e-tkt tax box with the code *CA.* Exempt passengers include those returning from Canada and Puerto Rico.

You may remember that there are only three tax boxes on automated tickets/e-tkts and four boxes on the manual version. So, how can all of these taxes and fees appear on tickets/e-tkts? The answer is that they are combined. On automated tickets, the U.S. Immigration and U.S. Customs fees should be shown separately and all other items are combined in the third tax box. On manual tickets, the APHIS Fee should also be shown separately and all other items are combined in the fourth tax box. The code for combined taxes and fees is XT.

Depending on the client's destination, other taxes may also be collected as part of the ticket/e-tkt. Figure 19–5 lists some of these other taxes and fees for popular destinations.

Australia
  Australian Head Tax (domestic), varies by city
  Goods & Services Tax (GST) (domestic), code UO, 10 percent
  Noise Levy Tax (Sydney arrivals), code QK, AUD 3.40
  Passenger Movement Charge, code AAU, AUD 30

France
  Airport Tax, code FR, varies by city
  Aviation Civile Tax, code FR, to Europe FRF 23, beyond Europe FRF 39
  Domestic Tax, code FR, FRF 23
  Domestic Value Added Tax, code UI, 5.5 percent
  Passenger Service Charge, code QW or QX, varies by city

Germany
  Domestic Arrival Tax, code RD or RA, varies by city
  Security Charge, code DE, varies by city

Italy
  Embarkation Tax, code IT, varies by destination
  Security Charge, code VT, IRL 3,500

Japan
  Consumption Tax (domestic), code JP, 5 percent
  Passenger Facility Service Charge, code SW, varies by city

United Kingdom
  Air Passenger Duty, code GB, to Europe GBP 10, beyond Europe GBP 20
  Passenger Service Charge, code UB, varies by city

Please note these amounts are approximate and are subject to change.

FIGURE 19–5 Examples of taxes applicable for travel to countries outside America.

PFCs, segment fees, and domestic fuel surcharges are also part of the international air travel total costs. As always, clients departing a U.S. city that has a PFC or fuel surcharge are subject to the fee. Itineraries that include city pairs within the United States or buffer zone must include the applicable segment fees. The *ARC Industry Agents' Handbook* contains a thorough explanation of international taxes and fees. All GDSs include this information as well as complete lists of taxes and fees for each country.

AIRLINE RATE DESK

Many travel counselors calculate international fares on rare occasions. The GDSs have become so sophisticated that the computer automatically figures most rates. On complicated itineraries that the GDS cannot price, having an airline rate desk calculate the fare may be a practical alternative. Specialists who are trained in international fare calculation staff each international and major U.S. airline's rate desk.

When an airline rate desk calculates a rate, a rate desk number is given to the travel counselor. This number indicates the rate agent doing the calculation and the date the rate was figured. The rate desk number is the travel counselor's protection against errors. Should an airline dispute a ticket/e-tkt total from a rate desk price, providing the rate desk number puts the responsibility on the rate agent's shoulders.

Many travel agency managers suggest that the travel counselor calculate the rate before calling the airline rate desk. This step serves two purposes. First, it gives the travel counselor excellent practice at rate calculation. Second, the travel counselor may be able to catch an error made by the rate desk.

For example, the travel counselor calculates a rate of $2,500 and the rate desk arrives at a $2,875 figure. The travel counselor should ask the rate agent why the client would not qualify for the $2,500 fare. Perhaps the travel counselor miscalculated and the actual fare should be $2,875, or maybe the rate agent overlooked something that the travel counselor caught. Remember that human beings staff the airline rate desk, and all human beings are capable of errors.

PLEASE TURN TO PAGE 306 AND COMPLETE EXERCISE 19-4 NOW.

INTERNATIONAL FLIGHT SCHEDULES

Most U.S. travel counselors obtain international flight schedules in their GDSs, just as they do for domestic city pairs. All nonautomated U.S. travel agencies and some

What Would You Do?

A counselor in your office always calls the airline rate desk every time a client asks for an international airfare. The rate desk calculates the fare and the counselor then quotes the amount to the client.

1. Does calling the airline to obtain international airfares always result in the best price?
2. What are the disadvantages to this counselor who always uses the rate desk instead of calculating international airfares himself?
3. In what way(s) might the client's best interests not be served by relying exclusively on an airline rate desk?

agencies located outside of the United States rely on the *OAG Flight Guide* for obtaining schedules. Automated U.S. travel agencies may also subscribe to the *OAG Flight Guide* as a backup for the GDS. The *OAG* remains the foundation for the GDS flight availability displays.

OAG Flight Guide

The *OAG Flight Guide* is available in two versions: the North American edition, and the Worldwide edition. As you have already learned, the North American edition contains flight schedules between cities in North America. This includes the United States, Canada, Mexico, Central America, and the islands of the Caribbean. The Worldwide edition contains flight schedules between cities in all parts of the world, including those found in the North American edition. Each travel agency, depending on its type of business, may subscribe to one or both of the *OAG Flight Guides*.

Although the bulk of the *OAG Flight Guide–Worldwide Edition* contains flight schedules, there is a considerable amount of additional information as well. You have already learned about the Flight Routings section and how you can find a flight's origin, en route stops, and termination points. Other *OAG* information includes

- airline members of IATA
- airlines of the world, including two-character code, three-digit numeric code, headquarters address, phone, fax, and Web site URL
- airlines arranged numerically by their three-digit code
- code share airlines
- aircraft listed alphabetically by name and by code
- city and airport codes arranged alphabetically by code
- airport terminal information
- minimum connection time information by airport and airline combination

OAG also publishes a supplement to the Worldwide edition that includes bank and public holidays, airport diagrams, aircraft seating charts, airline club information, and baggage allowance information. Most of this information is available in the GDS and because it is, many U.S. travel agencies no longer subscribe to the *OAG*. The Worldwide edition, like the North American edition, is available online in addition to the printed versions.

GDS Flight Availability

To display flight availability in the GDS, the travel counselor enters the travel date, departure city/airport, arrival city/airport, and perhaps a desired departure time. GDS flight availability displays for international city pairs look just the same as for domestic travel (see Figure 19–6).

By looking at Figure 19–6 you can see that the overall layout of the GDS flight availability display appears the same as it does for a domestic city pair. However, notice the time zone indicators in the header line. The display shows Denver as MT (Mountain Time) but no time zone is shown for London. The double asterisks (**), called display symbols in the GDS, are used to indicate international time and appear for all cities outside North America.

Also notice how next-day arrivals are shown. The pound sign (#) is called an End Item in some GDSs, while other GDSs call it a Cross of Lorraine. It is used to mean "plus." Take a look at UA flight number 958. This is a change of gauge flight, indicated by "CHG" in the equipment column and by the comment immediately below the flight listing.

The meal indicators on international flights are a bit misleading in the GDS because of the limited space. UA flight number 906 indicates that lunch is served, but, in fact, dinner and breakfast are also served. There is no way to know this from the display; but because of the length of the flight, common sense tells you that more than just lunch will be served.

PLEASE TURN TO PAGE 307 AND COMPLETE EXERCISE 19–5 NOW.

REFERENCE SOURCES FOR ADDITIONAL INFORMATION

One of the most frequently used reference sources for general international information is the *OAG Business Travel Planner,* commonly called *Travel Planner.* This publication is available in three editions: the North America edition (includes the United States, Canada, Mexico, islands of the Caribbean, Central America, and South America); the Europe, Africa, and Middle East edition; and the Asia Pacific edition. You learned about the North America edition in the chapters on domestic air travel, so this section concentrates on the other two editions.

The Europe, Africa and Middle East edition is arranged in three sections based on the three geographical regions contained in the edition. Each section is then arranged alphabetically by country. The Asia Pacific edition is organized simply by country. Within each country's listing in both editions, you find

- a country map
- entry documentation requirements
- consulate offices in Canada and the United States
- U.S. Chamber of Commerce and Foreign Service Offices
- travel basics that include information on climate, communications, currency, electric current, import allowances, language, time, banking hours, business hours, shopping hours, and tipping policies
- public holidays
- where to write or call for more information

15JUN-SA-3P DENLHR (DENLON) MT** AC1

LHR ALTERNATE BQH LCY LGW LTN QQK QQP QQU SEN STN ZEP ZLX

1#UA	906	F5 C9 D1 Y0 B0 M0 H0 Q0	DENLHR-	1220P	730A#1	777	LL	1
2#AA	1376	F7 Y7 BR H4 K3 V1 M0 N0	DENORD-	222P	539P	7 M80	SS	0
3#AA	66	F7 J7 Y2 B0 H0 K0 V0 M0	LHR-	650P	825A#1	777	DD	0
4#UA	288	F9 C9 D9 Y0 B0 M0 H0 Q0	DENIAD-	320P	837P	7 747	DD	0
5#UA	924	F5 C9 D9 Y0 B0 M0 H0 Q0	LHR-	945P	950A#1	777	DD	0
6#UA	256	F9 Y9 B9 M9 H9 Q9 V9 W9	DENORD-	124P	444P	6 72S	LL	0
7#UA	928	F1 C9 D9 Y5 B5 M3 H0 Q0	LHR-	515P	655A#1	777	DD	0
8#UA	958	F5 C7 D7 Y0 B0 M0 H0 Q0	DENLHR-	225P	910A#1	CHG	DD	1

UA 958 PLANE CHANGE EN ROUTE

FIGURE 19–6 Sample GDS flight availability display.

Although some countries' listings contain only the most basic information, most major countries' listings continue with an alphabetical listing of cities. Each city's listing includes the nearest airport to the city and, possibly, alternate airports. Many cities also list the airlines that serve the city's airport, approximate transfer time and cost between the airport and city center, and basic hotel information. A city map, major attractions, convention and exhibition facilities, and airport car rental companies are included in listings for major cities.

The Internet has become an excellent source of information, and many travel counselors are using it to supplement printed reference sources. Most countries and major cities have Web sites, usually sponsored by the local visitor's bureau. Information from these sites is generally reliable and accurate. However, travel counselors should be cautious of information contained in "unofficial" Web sites. Remember, anyone can say anything on the Internet; there are no rules or regulations and there is no overseeing agency verifying truthfulness.

Travel counselors have found that using the visitor's bureau or tourist board's Web site has added value, both to the counselor and the client. Compiling a personalized fact sheet for the client from the Internet is much easier than retyping information from printed reference sources. Web site data that the travel counselor wants to include can simply be copied and pasted into any word processing program. Then, the travel counselor can easily add personal information, such as the client's name, travel date, agency and counselor's name, and so on. With some word processing skills, the travel counselor can format the document and add color text and graphics. The end result is a professional looking, personalized fact sheet.

Taking extra time with clients and providing them with added value, such as the fact sheet, may mean the difference between the client returning to the same counselor for future travel needs or finding another travel counselor. Remember, without excellent customer service, the agency loses clients, and without clients, the travel agency and its employees cannot survive.

Web Activity

Amanda and Kevin Layton have purchased airline tickets from you for their trip to Europe in July. They are traveling throughout France, Spain, and Portugal by train, and you have arranged for Eurail passes for Mr. and Mrs. Layton. Your clients are spending four nights in each of these cities: Paris, Lyon, Marseilles, Barcelona, Madrid, Seville, and Lisbon. You have explained the basics: money, language, electric current, and so on. Prepare a fact sheet for your clients focusing on what to see and do, city transportation, and popular hot spots.

In addition to the *Travel Planner* series and the Internet, there are many wonderful guidebooks available at most bookstores. These include *Michelin, Baedeker, Insight, Mobil,* and *Rough Guides*. Because of the limited geographical area covered by each book, most travel agencies may not have these guidebooks, or they may have only those for the destinations they sell the most. Like any other printed reference source, these guidebooks can become obsolete rather quickly. Fortunately, many of the guidebooks have a presence on the Internet.

BASIC INTERNATIONAL TICKETING

All rules for writing a ticket for travel within the United States apply to international tickets as well. There are, however, a few special requirements associated with international ticketing.

1. International tickets should be *validated* on the airline plate of the first major carrier providing international service. If the first flight on the itinerary is international, then that airline's plate is used for validation. If the first flight is from one U.S. city to another U.S. city and the second flight is international, the airline used on the second leg should be used for validation. The exception to this rule is KLM Royal Dutch Airlines. Because of KLM's agreement with Northwest Airlines, all tickets for KLM are validated on Northwest.

2. The letter X with a circle around it, ⊗, should be drawn in the airline validation box on a handwritten international ticket. The X is automatically printed on computer-generated tickets and it is not necessary to draw a circle around it. The X permits ARC to separate international sales from domestic for its monthly air sales statistical reports.

3. Fare ladders and validity dates for excursion fares must be used on all international tickets. If the passenger must make a change en route, this information assists the airline with the passenger's request.

4. The "allow" box on international tickets might have to be completed with the number of pieces or the weight of allowed baggage. Some small international airlines may limit free checked baggage to only one piece or to a very low weight. Baggage allowance information can be obtained in the CRS, by calling the airline, or by using the airline's Web site.

5. The IATA trip classifications of SITI, SITO, SOTI, or SOTO must appear on all international tickets next to the city codes in the "origin/destination" box.

6. Itineraries that begin outside of the United States may have to be priced in the currency of the country of origin. This amount appears in the "fare" box and includes the currency code. The "equiv. fare pd." box on the ticket

indicates the U.S. dollar equivalent to the fare. If the fare has been priced in NUCs, this amount appears in the "fare" box and the ROE must appear at the end of the fare ladder.

7. There are almost always more tax and other fee items than can be accommodated in the four tax boxes on a manual ticket (three on an automated ticket). Therefore, the use of a combined tax item, coded with XT, is common. When tax and fee items are combined, they must be listed separately in the fare ladder.

? What Would You Do?

Your clients are taking their first trip abroad and have come to you for advice. They are traveling to Damascus to visit relatives for three weeks in October.

1. Where do you obtain entry documentation requirements and where do you check for any State Department advisories?

2. What subjects do you research for your clients with regard to international travel differences?

3. Although your clients are staying with relatives while in Syria, they want to know about points of interest. Where do you look for this information?

SUMMARY

There are many terms associated with international airfares, some of which are very complex. The typical travel counselor usually handles fairly routine international intineraries and seldom comes in contact with the more difficult terms. Travel counselors who specialize in business travel or focus only on international air travel use these terms almost daily.

It is easy to see why a fare obtained from a GDS display should not be quoted to the client. There are several taxes and other fees that must be added on first. Depending on the client's origin and destination cities, taxes and fees for other countries may also apply, increasing the airfare even more.

Understanding the way in which international airfares can be used to the client's benefit is an important part of a travel professional's job. Becoming comfortable with fare techniques requires practice and the knowledge of how to find up-to-the-minute data on fares, taxes, and other fees that might apply.

Although most U.S. and Canadian travel agencies obtain flight schedules from the GDS, many other agencies rely on the *OAG Flight Guide* or individual airline Web sites. The *OAG Business Travel Planner* online can answer many of your questions. As with all other printed reference sources, they can become outdated rather quickly so most travel professionals of today prefer online reference sites.

For additional Travel and Tourism resources, go to http://www.hospitality-tourism.delmar.com.

PLEASE COMPLETE THE CHAPTER REVIEW QUESTIONS NOW.

EXERCISE 19-1 IATA Trip Classifications and Split Ticketing

Directions: Identify each trip as a SITI, SITO, SOTI, or SOTO.

1. Your client purchases a ticket from your Portland agency for a flight from Portland to Kuala Lumpur and back to Portland.

   _____

2. At your Boston agency, you have collected payment and issued a ticket for a flight from Zurich to Oslo. _____

3. Your client purchases a PTA at your Detroit agency for a flight from Luxembourg to Detroit. The passenger will pick up the ticket at the airport in Frankfurt. _____

4. Your Charleston agency collected payment and issued a ticket for flights from Atlanta to London Heathrow, London Heathrow to Paris Charles de Gaulle, and Paris Charles de Gaulle to Atlanta. _____

5. At your agency in San Antonio, you have issued a ticket and collected payment for a client who is traveling from San Antonio to Mexico City. _____

6. Your client has purchased a PTA at your Philadelphia office for a flight from Lima to Bogotá. However, the passenger is in Cuzco and wants to have the ticket issued there. _____

EXERCISE 19-2 International Fare Terms

Directions: In your own words, define each of these terms.

1. air add-on _____

   _____

2. APEX fare _____

   _____

3. around-the-world fare _____

   _____

4. backhaul _____

   _____

5. budget fare _____

   _____

6. circle-trip minimum _____

   _____

7. double open-jaw, when excursion fares are used _____

   _____

8. gateway city _____

_____

9. global indicator _____

_____

10. higher intermediate point _____

_____

11. logical geographical order _____

_____

12. maximum permitted miles _____

_____

13. neutral unit of construction _____

_____

14. open-jaw, when excursion fares are used _____

_____

15. turnaround point _____

_____

16. youth fare _____

_____

EXERCISE 19–3 Booking Classes and Fare Basis Codes

1. What booking classes are used to indicate coach class? _____

2. What letter in an FBC usually indicates weekend travel? _____

3. Give some examples of FBC maximum validity periods. _____

4. What booking classes are used to indicate business class? _____

5. What letters indicate an APEX fare in FBCs? _____

6. What letters are used to indicate season in FBCs? _____

7. What booking classes indicate first class? _____

8. What letter is used to indicate weekday travel in FBCs? _____

9. Give some examples of FBC advance purchase indicators. _____

10. Booking classes are also known as _____

EXERCISE 19–4 International Taxes and Fees

1. Identify by name and code these amounts that are added to most international round-trip airfares.

$13.70 _____

$13.70 _____

$10.00 _____

$7.00 _____

$5.00 _____

$3.10 _____

2. In addition to the items listed in question 1, identify by name and code three other U.S. fees or charges that might apply. What is the cost of each of these items?

   a. _____

   b. _____

   c. _____

3. What code is used on tickets/e-tkts to indicate a combined tax or fee item? _____

EXERCISE 19-5 CRS Flight Availability

Answer the following questions based on the GDS display below.

20NOV-TH-7P NYCBOM ET **

1#DL	106	J9 D9 I9 Y9 B9 M9 H9 Q9	JFKBOM-	745P	1155P#1	763	DD	1
2#NW	58	J9 C9 Y9 B9 M9 H9 Q9 V9	EWRBOM-	620P	1140P#1	D10	DD	1
3#AI	112	F2 J4 D4 W4 Y4 A4 Q4 K4	JFKBOM-	810P	135A#2	744	DD	2
4$AF	177	P4 F0 J4 C4 D4 N4 Y4 K4	JFKCDG-	750P	850A	744	MM	0
	AF 117 OPERATED BY CONTINENTAL							
5$AF	134	P4 F4 J4 C4 D4 N4 Y4 K0	BOM-	1015A	1125P#1	343	MM	0
6$SR	113	F0 J9 C9 D9 Y9 M9 L9 H9	EWRZRH-	845P	1015A	330		0
7$SR	192	F4 J9 C9 D9 Y9 M9 L9 H9	BOM-	1000A	1120A#2	M11	LL	0
8#BA	2172	F9 A9 J9 D9 Y9 B9 H9 K9	JFKLGW-	615P	605A	777	MM	0
9#BA	139	F9 A9 J9 D9 Y9 B9 H9 K9	LHRBOM-	945A	1159P#1	747	MM	0

1. How many nonstop flights from JFK to BOM are shown? _____

2. Which airline code and flight number represents the earliest direct departure from JFK to BOM? _____

3. Which airline codes and flight numbers represent the most convenient connection from JFK to BOM? _____

4. Which airline code and flight number represents the direct flight from EWR to BOM? _____

5. On which flights is first class not offered (identify by airline codes and flight numbers)? _____

   _____

6. If your client takes the Swissair connection and departs on Monday, on what day will she arrive in BOM? _____

7. Could your clients use K class on the Air France connection? _____

8. Which connection service is the least convenient and why do you think so (identify by airline codes and flight numbers)?

   _____

9. Which flight is a code share (identify by airline code and flight number)? _____

10. Which airline code and flight number represents the latest direct departure from JFK to BOM? _____

Review Questions

1. In detail, give a complete example of a transaction that is classified as a SITI. _____
   _____
   _____

2. In detail, give a complete example of a transaction that is classified as a SOTO. _____
   _____
   _____

3. In detail, explain the mechanics of split ticketing. _____
   _____
   _____

4. An international airline's supplemental fare on a different airline from an interior city to the gateway city is called _____
   _____

5. Another name for an international excursion fare is _____

6. The additional amount that applies when a HIP exists is called _____

7. The official name for the exchange rate that is used to convert one currency to another currency is called _____
   _____

8. A fare in which the client selects the week of travel and the airline selects the day and flight is called _____
   _____

9. Fly from SFO to NRT, fly from NRT to ITM, fly from ITM to SFO is an example of what type of trip? _____
   Could excursion fares be split and combined on this itinerary? _____

10. The rule that states that if a HIP fare applies in one direction, the HIP fare must be used in both directions is called _____
    _____

11. Fly from ATL to FRA, fly from LIS to MIA is an example of what type of trip? _____
    Could excursion fares be split and combined on this itinerary? _____

12. The city or airport from which an international flight begins or ends is called _____

13. The identifiers found in a fare rule display that indicate the general direction a flight schedule must take are called _____
    _____

14. A nearer stopover city that has a higher fare than the destination city is called _____
    _____

15. A generic currency that is used to add together fares of different currencies is called _____
    _____

16. Fly from IAH to BOG, fly from CCS to IAH is an example of what type of trip? _____
    Could excursion fares be split and combined on this itinerary? _____

17. The furthest destination from the origin and the city where the homeward-bound trip begins is called _____
_____

18. "R" represents what type of booking class? _____

19. "Y," "S," and "W" represent what type of booking class? _____

20. "A" represents what type of booking class? _____

21. "D," "I," and "Z" represent what type of booking class? _____

22. "B," "K," and "Q" represent what type of booking class? _____

23. What is indicated by the fare basis code HHWAP60? _____
_____

24. What is indicated by the fare basis code TKXAP1M? _____
_____

25. What is indicated by the fare basis code VLAN45? _____
_____

26. Your client is traveling to Kenya and Tanzania. Where would you learn about any taxes and fees that might apply to these
countries? _____
_____

27. Under what circumstances is the "equiv. fare pd." box used on an airline ticket? _____
_____

28. What symbol indicates that the ticket is for an international itinerary? _____

29. How might the amount of free checked baggage be indicated on an international ticket? _____
_____

30. In what ticket box is the IATA trip classification written? _____

31. How is the validating airline selected for international travel? _____
_____

SECTION VII

Selling and Servicing the Travel Client

CHAPTER 20

Sales Skills for the Travel Professional

CHAPTER 21

Customer Service for the Travel Professional

Sales Skills for the Travel Professional

OBJECTIVES

At the conclusion of this chapter, you will

- understand the importance of sales and communication.
- identify the steps in the sales process.
- describe appropriate ways to ask questions.
- make a sales-oriented proposal.
- handle customer objections.
- ask the customer for his business.
- understand and offer value-added products.
- understand the differences between in-person and telephone selling.
- understand specialty (niche) selling and its advantages.

KEY TERMS

buying signals	feeling-finding question	objections
closed-ended questions	niche market	open-ended questions
fact-finding question		

THE IMPORTANCE OF SALES

In most situations, travel is *discretionary*. In other words, people choose to spend their money on travel—or on something else. Customers have a further choice. They can choose to make their travel arrangements with a travel consultant—or not. If the choice is to work with a travel consultant, will it be you—or someone else? You are in a position to influence the prospective buyer's decision about not only *what* to buy, but also from *whom* to buy it (Figure 20–1).

Your *expertise* is what will make you a sought-after professional. It's a large part of the reason customers want to work with a travel agent instead of making an online booking. However, a travel consultant must rely on more than expertise. A travel consultant depends on income generated from the sale of travel products and services. If you don't make sales, you certainly won't be in business or employed for long, no matter how much product expertise you have.

Whether you are a travel counselor, airline reservation agent, or front desk clerk at a hotel, the sales process is the same, and the techniques you need can be learned. By understanding and using proven sales techniques, you will firmly increase the chances that choices are made in your favor.

BEING AN EFFECTIVE COMMUNICATOR

Selling is really about communication. The most effective salespeople are also effective communicators. The dictionary defines *communication* as "the exchange of thoughts,

FIGURE 20–1 You are in a position to influence a buyer's decisions about not only what to buy, but also from whom to buy it.

FIGURE 20–2 Effective communicators are able to put people immediately at ease by using techniques like a sincere greeting, a smile, a polished appearance, a friendly tone of voice, and a conversation opener.

messages, or information, as by speech, signals, writing, or behavior." A key part of this definition is *exchange*. Communication must go two ways. It is important to listen as well as talk. Listening involves not only hearing what is said, but also paying attention to nonverbal signals and behaviors.

Some successful salespeople will say they don't do anything special to make sales. They just carry on a conversation and the sales happen. To a certain extent this may be true for some people, but in reality, most successful salespeople have worked hard on their communication skills. Effective communicators are able to put people immediately at ease by using techniques like a sincere greeting, a smile, a polished appearance, a friendly tone of voice, and a conversation opener (Figure 20–2).

Effective communicators use skillful questioning to discover a great deal about their customers. People respond positively when you ask a question and give all of your attention to their response. When you really listen, it conveys to the customer that you are truly interested.

Our dictionary definition also mentions signals, writing, or behavior as ways to exchange information. It is also important to pay attention to nonverbal cues that provide clues to the customer's level of interest and receptiveness. We express many things with our bodies and facial expressions, and effective communicators are aware of what others are saying nonverbally.

THE SALES PROCESS

Throughout this text, you have picked up tips on selling a variety of travel products to potential travelers. In the cruise section, for example, you learned about the importance of matching customer wants and needs and likes and dislikes, with the features of a cruise. In the section on hotels, you learned it is necessary to ask the client questions regarding the type and location of the hotel she wants. In the rail section, you were introduced to features of rail travel that will assist you in helping a customer decide if a train trip meets his needs.

Each of these examples involves two important parts of the sales process:

1. The travel consultant *asks questions* of the potential customer to discover what her travel needs are.
2. The travel consultant uses his expertise to *match the product* to the customer's particular needs.

There are further steps in the sales process.

3. The travel consultant *makes her recommendations* to the customer.
4. The travel consultant *handles any questions or objections* the customer may have.
5. The travel consultant *asks the customer to buy*.
6. The travel consultant provides any other information or services that will serve to *support the customer*.

Each part of the sales process will be demonstrated in a short scene between a prospective customer and a travel counselor. Discussion of what took place in each scene will follow.

Initial Contact

Mrs. Traveler to her husband: We haven't had a vacation for two years. Couldn't we get away for a while?

Mr. Traveler: You know, that's a great idea. I can manage a week off in February or March. See what you can find for us to do. As long as it's someplace warm, I don't care where we go. Don't worry about the cost. Mom can watch the kids.

Mrs. Traveler thinks and thinks and finally decides she doesn't really care where they go either. Maybe a travel counselor will have a good package to suggest. So, she phones a travel counselor at random. Mrs. Traveler lays out her situation for the travel counselor.

Mrs. Traveler: We have seven days, just the two of us; we want to go to a warm climate, and we want a good price—maybe a package. Can you help us?

Travel Counselor to Mrs. Traveler: That's great! I'd love to help you, but I really need to know where you want to go.

Mrs. Traveler: We don't care. Can't you suggest something?

Travel Counselor: I'd really like to help, but there are so many places you could go that I really need to know where you want to go before I can suggest anything.

Mrs. Traveler: Oh. Well, I guess we'll have to decide and call again. Thanks anyway.

PLEASE TURN TO PAGE 323 AND COMPLETE EXERCISE 20–1 NOW.

Ask the Right Questions

If you said that the travel counselor in the preceding scene just blew a potential sale, you are absolutely correct! Mr. and Mrs. Traveler really didn't care about the destination as much as they did about getting away and having someone else attend to the details. The travel counselor's goal in this situation should have been to discover a little more about Mrs. and Mrs. Traveler and what they like to do, rather than focusing only on the destination. He could have asked questions like, "What do you like to do?" "How much do you want to spend?" "Have you considered taking a cruise?"

By asking a few questions about Mrs. Traveler's wants and needs, the travel counselor could have communicated a couple of things to Mrs. Traveler. First, he would have shown Mrs. Traveler that he was interested in Mrs. Traveler's needs. Second, he would have obtained information from Mrs. Traveler that could have resulted in a confirmed reservation. A confirmed reservation is the goal. Asking the right questions is the first step toward that goal.

Often a considerable amount of information is required from a prospective customer before a reservation can be made, but there are *always* four things the travel counselor needs:

1. name
2. date of travel
3. destination
4. number of travelers

The date is sometimes the most difficult piece of information to obtain, and a counselor cannot quote any price information until the date of travel is known. However, it is important to give the caller a reason to give you a date. Tell her truthfully that you are not able to give accurate information unless you have a specific date. If she still cannot or will not give you a date, suggest one to her and quote fares for that date.

Is asking, "When will you be traveling?" the same as asking, "What date will you be traveling?" No. The first question is too vague and may get a vague response, such as "next month." The way you ask a question can sometimes determine the answer. The travel counselor's goal is to get as much information as possible from the prospective customer. Asking questions that can be answered with a yes or no (closed-ended questions) usually elicits less information than questions that require the caller to phrase an answer (open-ended questions). "Do you like to play golf?" (closed-ended question). "What kind of activities do you and your husband like?" (open-ended question).

You may also ask questions requiring answers that deal with facts or with feelings. "What date do you want to return?" (fact-finding question). "What do you think about taking a cruise?" (feeling-finding question). With a customer like Mrs. Traveler, who gives you only minimal information, open-ended and feeling-finding questions can provide the travel counselor with a large amount of information that can then be used to turn the shopper into a buyer.

An additional purpose for asking appropriate questions is to determine the level of knowledge and experience of your potential customer. Many people are very knowledgeable about travel and travel products; many others are completely uninformed. Some are frequent travelers; others are not. Would you treat these different types of clients in the same way? Absolutely not! The first-time flyer may need considerable hand-holding and encouragement, as well as a large amount of information. The old pro won't need his hand held, and he may know exactly what he wants; you won't have to tell him. If you treat both of these customers in the same way, you will most likely lose them both.

PLEASE TURN TO PAGE 323 AND COMPLETE EXERCISE 20–2 NOW.

Can you see how the type of question you ask determines the type of information you receive in return? Develop good questioning skills early, and they will become a natural part of any conversation you have with a prospective customer.

Good questioning skills should be used to lead the conversation in a direction you want it to take. It is important that you have an agenda for every contact with a potential customer. Acquiring information you need is less difficult that way, and you can supply only the key information the customer actually wants and needs. The dialogue won't be the same with every customer, and some individuals require more time and skill than others, but keeping to an invisible agenda is a proven technique used by professional salespeople to keep conversations on track.

An effective way of maintaining your agenda is to answer the caller's question *briefly* and then follow with an information-building question. For example, if a prospective customer says, "Do you sell cruises?" your reply should be "Yes, we sell many different cruises. What part of the world are you interested in cruising?" You have answered the question briefly and asked a question intended to give a direction to the conversation. A poor response to this question is, "Yes, we do. We sell three-day, four-day, seven-day cruises to the Caribbean, Alaska, river cruises, . . ." This type of response gives neither you nor the customer any direction for the rest of the conversation.

You can also waste considerable time describing cruises in which the customer may not be interested.

Avoid answering a question with a question. This suggests to the customer that you did not hear his question, that you are not interested in his question, or that it was a dumb question. Always acknowledge a question by giving a brief answer but have your follow-up question ready to ask. If asked, "Do you sell cruises?" it is not appropriate to respond, "Where do you want to go?" Rather, acknowledge the inquiry by saying "You bet we do! Where are you interested in cruising?"

The best salespeople are great talkers, right? No way! The best salespeople are great *listeners*. How can you discover what you should know about your customer if you do all the talking? Especially in the initial stages of the contact with a customer, it is essential to say as little as possible and to really listen to what the customer has to say.

It isn't easy to be a good listener. Our thoughts move much faster than our speech, so we can lose concentration if we don't practice good listening habits. To be a good listener, you must first stop talking. Take notes if you have to so the caller is not forced to repeat. Be an *active* listener. Illustrate by your body posture (lean forward; don't turn your back even to use the computer), brief phrases of agreement ("Uh huh," "Yes, I see," "Really?"), and eye contact to show that you are involved in what the customer is saying.

Let's summarize what you have learned thus far. First, the customer has to feel that you are interested in her and that she can trust you to help her find what she wants. This trust may be affected by several factors: Your sincerity and enthusiasm, your friendliness, your greeting, and your level of interest all have an effect on the customer.

Second, ask questions to determine the customer's wants and needs. Sometimes a prospective customer is unable or unwilling to be specific about his needs. Don't do as the first travel counselor did and assume that being unspecific made Mrs. Traveler a less than serious caller. Rather, use your professional skills to help a potential customer articulate his needs. In the next scene, you will see how this is done.

Second Chance

Mrs. Traveler to her husband: I contacted a travel counselor today to get some suggestions for our trip.

Mr. Traveler: Did we get a good package vacation?

Mrs. Traveler: Well, the counselor must have been busy because she just gave me the brush-off. She said if I couldn't be more specific about where we want to go that she really couldn't suggest anything.

Mr. Traveler: Did you tell her what we wanted? Seven-day package? Warm weather? That should have given her enough to work with!

Mrs. Traveler: Yes, but she was no help at all. I don't think she really cared.

Mr. Traveler: Try another agency. Maybe you'll have better luck next time.

The next day, Mrs. Traveler phones another travel agency. After she identifies herself, she again lays out her situation for the counselor.

Mrs. Traveler: We have seven days, just the two of us; we want a warm climate and good price—maybe a package. Can you help us?

Travel Counselor to Mrs. Traveler: That's great! I have several ideas already, but first tell me what you like to do on vacation.

Mrs. Traveler: Let's see. We like to get away and really relax. You know, no deadlines, no hassles, time to get reacquainted with each other. We're fairly serious tennis players and like to be active, but there's never enough time for that, it seems. I love to shop!

Travel Counselor: That helps me a lot. How do you feel about the Caribbean?

Mrs. Traveler: We've never been there but have talked about going many times. Our friends have been to several islands. I guess my only concern would be where to go because I don't know anything about the islands. Do you have a suggestion?

Travel Counselor: Yes, I have a couple of things in mind that I think you will love, but tell me first, do you have a budget for this trip?

Mrs. Traveler: We didn't really talk about a specific amount. We were hoping that we could get a package or something with everything included that might be a little less expensive. When we went to Hawaii two years ago, we spent about $3,000 for a week. Can we do anything for around that amount?

Travel Counselor: We will certainly try! How would you feel about a cruise?

Mrs. Traveler: Hmmm! We've never thought about it. Sounds interesting if it's not too expensive.

Travel Counselor: We'll take a look and see. Cruising can be very economical. Are you flexible on your dates of travel?

Mrs. Traveler: Yes, my husband said he can get a week anytime in February or March.

Travel Counselor: Let's be sure I have all the information I need, Mrs. Traveler. You want to go someplace warm in February or March; you would be interested in the Caribbean, but destination isn't as important as a good package with a good price. You would consider a cruise if the price is comparable, and you like to play tennis and shop. Is there anything else you can tell me that might help?

Mrs. Traveler: No, I'll trust your judgment to find us something great.

Travel Counselor: It will take me a few minutes to collect this information for you. May I call you back?

We have come a long way in this scene! Notice how the travel counselor controlled the conversation by giving only brief answers to Mrs. Traveler's questions, and then was ready with her next question. She was enthusiastic and helpful without spending time discussing details. This travel counselor has discovered several things about the Travelers and has enough information to suggest some possibilities. She was able to find out

- when they can travel
- how many will travel
- how long they can travel
- what they like to do
- whether they might consider a destination in the Caribbean or a cruise

Progress! Because she was in control of the conversation and asked the right kind of questions, this travel counselor didn't take much time to get the information she needed.

Match the Product to the Need

Now that she has the information she needs, the counselor's next step is to use her product knowledge to find a product that matches Mr. and Mrs. Traveler's particular needs. This may require some research, and it will usually require putting your recommendations into some type of a proposal for your customer.

One caution should be made: Don't jump to conclusions and start telling the customer what she wants before you really know. It's sometimes tempting to assume that you know what's best for the customer. Let her finish telling you. If you offer something too early, it could be the wrong thing, and the customer will walk off thinking you don't have what she wants.

In response to Mrs. Traveler's opening statement, what if this travel counselor had said, "I'll send you some brochures on Mexico. Give me your address." How do you think Mrs. Traveler would have reacted? Did she say she wanted to go to Mexico? Maybe she doesn't like Mexico. If the counselor doesn't take the time to discover how Mrs. Traveler feels about Mexico, it's a waste of time to propose a trip to Mexico and to send a selection of brochures that probably won't be read. You can probably imagine Mrs. Traveler sighing and thinking to herself, "If Mexico is all this agency sells, I guess I'll have to call someone else."

PLEASE TURN TO PAGE 324 AND COMPLETE EXERCISE 20–3 NOW.

Recommend a Product

The travel counselor has so far discovered some very important information about Mr. and Mrs. Traveler. Without this information, it would not be possible to move one step further. Now, the travel counselor has a direction. She has done her research and used her expertise to come up with some suggestions for the Travelers, and she can now present them.

If this were a perfect world, Mrs. Traveler would think the travel counselor's recommendations were perfect. Her only concern would be which vacation to buy and whether to pay with cash or credit. Unfortunately, things don't always happen quite that smoothly. Let's see what happens next.

Answer Questions and Handle

The travel counselor phones Mrs. Traveler with her proposal the same afternoon. Mrs. Traveler loves both plans, but . . .

- I have to talk this over with my husband.
- That's too expensive for what we get.
- A cruise? I get motion sick and my husband's on a diet.
- We'll surely be bored on a cruise.
- Are you sure it's not hurricane season in the Caribbean?

What happened? Did the travel counselor do something wrong? Did Mrs. Traveler have a bad day? Is this sale doomed?

No, none of the above. What happened is a normal part of the sales process called objections. A customer's objections may be a legitimate request for more information, a lack of understanding of the product being offered, or a way of stalling the decision to buy. An objection does not mean that this customer is not going to buy. It simply means she needs a little more information and time. Objections can usually be anticipated, and you should be prepared to handle them.

The best way to handle any objection is to *listen* to it fully. Ask the customer for clarification if you do not completely understand the objection. Answer the objection by *giving additional information* or clearing up a misunderstanding, and *don't give up*. This sale is not lost. The customer has not said no.

Some techniques you can use to handle objections follow.

1. *Frankly admit* that the objection is a valid one. Then point out compensating features or ways to overcome it: "Motion sickness is a problem for some people, but there are excellent remedies now, and large ships are very stable."

2. *Agree with* the objection but offer facts to show that the objection is not true now. "Several years ago, this tour

company had some problems, but we sell many of their tours now and our clients tell us they are very satisfied."

3. *Restate the objection* as a question, then proceed to answer it. "Do you think this package is too expensive? It does look expensive, but let's look again at the features included in the price."

4. *Ask why* the customer feels the way he does. Sometimes it's difficult to tell what is behind a person's unexplained objection. "Why do you feel that you would not enjoy this tour?"

PLEASE TURN TO PAGE 324 AND COMPLETE EXERCISES 20–4 AND 20–5 NOW.

Ask for the Business

Up to this point, you have been developing a working relationship with the potential customer. You have asked questions and listened closely to the answers. You have let your expertise shine by finding just the right product to offer. You have handled all of the customer's objections, and the customer is agreeing with you about the benefits of the product you have offered. What's next?

Your next step is to *ask the customer to buy it*. This is the step that separates the sales professional from the mere order taker. Yet, many salespeople have difficulty asking for the business. It's difficult because every time you ask, you face potential rejection: The customer may say no. On the other hand, if you don't ask, you face the possibility that the customer may take the information you have given her and go elsewhere to buy the product.

It is important to recognize *when* the customer has made the decision to buy. It isn't necessary to wait until the end of the sales process to offer to make a reservation or ask the customer to buy. If he gives signs that he is ready early in the conversation, ask him then. Don't wait! How do you know when to ask? There are some buying signals you can look for to determine the client's readiness (Figure 20–3).

A buyer is ready if

- she is agreeing with what you say
- she is talking freely
- she is volunteering information
- she is asking pertinent questions
- she is smiling
- she is leaning forward and touching the brochure
- she is relaxed

A buyer is not ready if

- he is finding fault or criticizing
- he is making excuses
- he is bringing up objections
- he is sitting back in his chair with arms folded and eyes wandering

FIGURE 20–3 It is important to recognize when the customer has made the decision to buy. Look for buying signals to find out if she or he is ready to make a commitment to buy. If you're on the phone, is the customer agreeing with you or objecting?

If you are unsure about when to ask for the business, give it a *trial run*. For example, just assume the client is planning to buy. Ask, "In what name shall I hold the reservation?" "Because that date is right for you, shall I confirm it?" "There is space available on that date. May I make a tentative reservation for you?"

Another way you find out if the time is right is to offer the customer a *choice:* "Which flight do you prefer?" "Will this be cash or charge?"

The most common approach is the *direct approach.* Ask in a straightforward way if you can make the reservation. Most customers expect a good salesperson to ask for their business. It is not necessary to be annoying or high-pressure when asking for the business, and it will not be interpreted that way by the customer if she is ready to buy. The customer should be feeling comfortable with the counselor and asking for the business is the next logical step.

Mrs. Traveler to her husband (after describing the vacation plan she prefers): I found the most wonderful travel counselor. She really took her time and asked me a lot of questions about what we like to do, where we wanted to go, and how much we wanted to spend. She came up with a really great plan for us. It's a little more money than we spent last time, but I'm convinced it's what we should do. It's worth the extra money. I'll stop in the agency tomorrow and make the deposit if you agree.

Mr. Traveler: If you're that sold on it, let's go! Sounds like that travel counselor really knows her business.

Support the Customer

You did it! You made the sale. It's not time to rest yet, however. Customers have expectations of how they would like to be treated. If you are able to exceed those expectations in some way, you will have a happy customer. This is a principle of customer service, but it also applies to selling. Customers must feel they have gotten their money's worth. In addition to selling products and services, you are also selling your knowledge and expertise. Here are some ways to do it. Offer something extra—something you know about that may be something your customer hasn't even thought of! Develop a specialty in which you are *the* expert to keep customers coming back.

SELLING ADDITIONAL ITEMS A business makes more profit by convincing its existing customers to spend more money than by constantly trying to get new ones. The travel counselor who suggests to the customer that he purchase an option to make the trip better is not only performing a service for the customer but is also making additional commissions for the agency. Once the decision to purchase a tour package has been made, suggest an optional sightseeing trip. Once the decision to purchase a cruise has been made, suggest cruise insurance or an additional shore excursion. Customers don't always know about the little things that make their trip more memorable or more efficient.

SPECIALTY (NICHE) SELLING Some experts in travel believe that travel counselors may be redefined from *generalists* who sell every travel product and service to *specialists* selling only a particular travel specialty, often called a niche market. This is definitely a way to offer your customer something more. It is difficult to be all things to all people. By focusing on niche markets, travel agencies are identifying their unique interests, abilities, and attributes, and are offering these to clients with the same interests. For agencies that charge for their services, niche marketing provides a legitimate way for the customer to differentiate one agency from another based on an agency's specialization.

The Internet has been instrumental in supporting this move to niche marketing. Internet customers don't usually come into the office, so they don't know whether an agency with a great Web site is large or small. Your Web site serves to inform customers that you have the expertise they want. Likewise, doing business only in your "neighborhood" need not be a concern. An agency can develop a specialty that might not have much of a client base "at home" but can be supported by doing business globally on the Internet.

An area of specialization must be large enough to sustain a profitable level of business, but small enough to allow the counselor to become a true specialist. Specialties

FIGURE 20–4 A specialty or niche can be divided by activities such as skiing, golf, or tennis.

are sometimes divided by activity, customer type, destination, or product type.

- *Activities.* Choose an activity such as golf or tennis vacations, skiing, or scuba diving. Activities may also be subdivided by destination, so that you might choose to specialize in ski vacations in the Rocky Mountains or in Europe (Figure 20–4).

- *Customer type.* "Senior citizens" and "Baby Boomers" are both types of customers. Members of these groups are active, and travel is a product that surveys tell us is important to these groups. Some other customer types are families with children, people with disabilities, and honeymooners. Travel counselors have found good markets with all of these customer types.

- *Destinations.* Travel counselors have specialized in a country or region of the world for a long time. This particular specialty is one of the most successful. A destination specialty can be anything from Alaska to Zimbabwe.

- *Product type.* A counselor may choose to become an expert on cruising or train travel, adventure or spa vacations or luxury or economy tours. There are many types of travel products from which to choose.

If you are to be an expert in your chosen specialty, it is necessary to learn and understand everything about your product(s) and your market. Take advantage of any training that is offered in your specialty. Vendors, tourist boards, and travel associations are likely places to look for training. ASTA offers one-day and two-day niche marketing certification courses. Courses focus on adventure travel, the mature adult market, and family travel.

TELEPHONE SELLING

Sales by telephone, with no in-person contact, also follow the same process. Telephone sales do, however, have some special considerations that are addressed here. Many travel professionals spend considerable time doing business by phone; for many, it is a majority of their time (Figure 20–5). Just because we frequently do business by phone does not mean that we do it well. In fact, sales are lost because the travel professional did not present herself or the company effectively.

Approximately 55 percent of a communicated message is nonverbal or, in other words, visual. Thus, over half the message is lost when we do business over the telephone. This loss must be compensated for in other ways. The telephone salesperson has only his voice and the use of language at his disposal. He must, therefore, be adept at using words, word pictures, and vocal inflections to convey his message. Put a smile into your voice. Combined with the first opening words of a call, the smile you transmit to the customer sets the whole tone of the conversation. Your voice can convey more than you ever imagined. Your voice can reveal insecurity; it can display annoyance or impatience; it can irritate or discourage.

FIGURE 20–5 Many travel professionals spend considerable time doing business by phone.

On the other hand, it can express confidence and inspire and motivate.

1. Be enthusiastic. Reflect some of the excitement you feel about your job. (Sometimes you may not feel enthusiastic, but train your voice to convey it anyway.)

2. Concentrate on the conversation. If your thoughts are elsewhere, it isn't hard for the customer to detect the lack of interest.

3. Approach your job after proper rest. Fatigue and mental stress also show in your voice.

4. Make a real effort to vary the pitch of your voice. A communicated message is 38 percent tone of voice.

5. Speak at a comfortable rate and articulate your words.

6. Develop skill in using descriptive words so your customer can visualize the product or service you are offering.

7. Keep in mind that each caller is somebody special.

Each time the phone rings, you become an actor on stage appearing before a critical audience. You must play your role effectively. A large part of your effectiveness comes from the use of good telephone etiquette. Following are a few basics of telephone etiquette.

1. Be prepared before you answer a call. You cannot efficiently handle a caller if you are fumbling for a pencil and note paper or a clear spot on your desk.

2. Answer calls promptly. When the phone rings, it demands and should receive immediate attention. Answering by the second or third ring is preferred.

3. Use proper "on hold" techniques. If it is necessary to place a caller on hold, always ask, "Would you hold for a moment, please?" Explain why, and wait for the caller to respond; then thank her. When you resume the call, always begin with, "Thank you for waiting." Never answer a call and depress the hold button without acknowledging the caller.

4. Never pick up an incoming call and then finish a conversation with someone in the office before greeting the caller.

5. Be a good listener. It is an irritation to the caller to be asked to repeat information she has already given. Take notes.

6. Avoid interrupting the caller. Let him finish his own sentences. You may think you know what he is going to say, but don't anticipate. He may surprise you!

7. Enunciate clearly and speak slowly. Your caller may be hearing your information for the first time. Present it slowly and clearly.

8. Speak directly into the mouthpiece. If you cradle the receiver against your shoulder, your words may be muffled.

9. Never use slang or industry jargon. It doesn't make you look smart, it just confuses your caller.

10. Always thank the customer for calling.

Sales is a process that you can easily master. Develop good selling habits early in your career and you will be rewarded for a long time.

SUMMARY

You have seen the making of a sale. There are several things to remember about the situation involving the Travelers and most other situations you will encounter as a travel professional. Mrs. Traveler had every intention of buying a travel product from a travel counselor. The buying decision she had to make was which product and from which travel counselor. The first counselor she called did not understand the sales process well enough to know that by following a few simple rules, he might have gotten Mrs. Traveler's business. The second counselor understood this very well. The sales process can be summarized as follows.

1. Convey a sincere interest in the customer and her needs.

2. Qualify the customer by asking appropriate questions to help him articulate his needs.

3. Use your product knowledge and what you have learned about the customer to select some travel options that meet her needs.

4. Answer the customer's objections (if there are any).

5. Ask for a commitment: "May we make the reservation?"

6. Support the decision to buy. Reassure the customer, take care of details, offer additional value products, and follow up on the sale.

There are obviously many scenarios that a travel professional will encounter. A business traveler whose only need is an airline reservation and a hotel, a group leader who is responsible for taking 250 people to Las Vegas, and a family like the Travelers have individual needs that the travel professional must discover and fulfill. Selling is a process that nearly anyone can easily master. Developing good selling habits early in one's career will provide rewards for a long time.

A professional salesperson must strive to give his customers more than they expected to receive. Selling additional products and services that your customer may not have thought of purchasing is a way to create a satisfied customer *and* make more revenue for your agency at the same time. Specialty selling is becoming a much more important focus for agencies. Specializing gives a travel counselor the opportunity to identify unique attributes and interests and turn these into an asset for the customer. A counselor's specialty allows consumers to differentiate between the services offered by one travel agency over another. Follow-up after the sale is another way to give your customer more than she expected. It is also a way to gain some valuable information for you and for your agency.

Telephone selling has some special considerations because so much of what is communicated is lost when we do not have visual contact. Things like tone of voice and word selection become much more important.

For additional Travel and Tourism resources, go to http://www.hospitality-tourism.delmar.com.

PLEASE COMPLETE THE CHAPTER REVIEW QUESTIONS NOW.

EXERCISE 20-1 Initial Contact

1. Did this travel counselor just lose a possible sale? _____

2. You are the travel counselor. What do you say to Mrs. Traveler after she has given you the information about what she wants?

   _____

   _____

3. List all the information you can think of that a travel counselor needs from Mrs. Traveler to help her plan a vacation. _____

   _____

   _____

   _____

   _____

EXERCISE 20-2 Ask the Right Questions

Directions: Write an appropriate question that you would ask in response to the following statements. Your objective is to discover as much as possible about what the customer wants.

1. We had a bad experience on our last cruise.

   Closed-ended question: _____

   _____

   Open-ended question: _____

   _____

   Fact-finding question: _____

   _____

   Feeling-finding question: _____

   _____

2. I am interested in a tour of Hawaii.

   Closed-ended question: _____

   _____

   Open-ended question: _____

   _____

   Fact-finding question: _____

   _____

   Feeling-finding question: _____

   _____

EXERCISE 20-3 Match the Product to the Need and Make Your Recommendations

Directions: Using what you have learned about the Travelers, suggest two possible vacations for them to consider. They need dates of travel, mode of transportation, features included, and price.

1. _____
   _____
   _____

2. _____
   _____
   _____
   _____

EXERCISE 20-4 Handline Objections

Directions: Following are some common objections. Using the techniques for answering objections, write a response to each one.

1. "This resort is too expensive—much more than I want to spend." _____
   _____
   _____

2. "I have to check with my husband/wife." _____
   _____
   _____

3. "Group tours are only for senior citizens." _____
   _____
   _____

4. "A motorcoach? They're so uncomfortable and smelly." _____
   _____
   _____

5. "I've heard this airline is never on time." _____
   _____
   _____

6. "Our friends went there and it rained every day!" _____
   _____
   _____

7. "What if that airline goes out of business before I get home?" _____
   _____

8. "Trains are so slow." _____
   _____
   _____

EXERCISE 20-5 Objections

Directions: List three objections that Mrs. Traveler might have to the vacations you planned for her in your Proposal exercise, and explain how you answer her objections.

1. _____
   _____
   _____

2. _____
   _____
   _____

3. _____
   _____
   _____

EXERCISE 20-6 Role Play

Directions: The role play situation allows you to practice the selling techniques you have learned. You need at least three participants to complete this exercise. If you have more than three participants, divide your group into three smaller groups:

Group 1 will be the travel counselor.
Group 2 will be the customer.
Group 3 will be the observer.

If you have more than one person in each group, select a spokesperson in Groups 1 and 2. Group 3 will complete the checklist that follows. The spokesperson in Groups 1 and 2 may call a time-out to confer with the other members of the group at any time. The other group members should provide advice and assistance to the spokesperson.

GROUP 1—ASSIGNMENT:

Your goal as the travel counselor is to complete the six steps in the sales process. Review these steps. After determining what the customer wants, take several minutes to complete a proposal for the customer. Use any reference materials available. After presenting your information to the customer, your goal is to make a sale!

GROUP 2—ASSIGNMENT:

As the customer, you must have the following information:

1. Who will be traveling: name, address, phone; husband and wife? coworkers? friends?

2. Where you want to travel: area of the world.

3. For what purpose you are traveling: business, vacation, visit relatives, and so on.

4. How many are in your party?

5. When you will travel: a specific date or time of year.

6. How much do you want to spend?

7. What mode of travel you prefer: cruise, air, rail.

8. Other preferences: tour package? sightseeing options? shore excursions? rental car?

9. Objections you may have to the counselor's suggestions.

Decide on this information before beginning the role play. You should also decide how much of this information you wish to impart to the travel counselor. Hold back several key pieces of information so the travel counselor has to ask you about your needs.

GROUP 3–ASSIGNMENT:

You will observe this sales transaction between the travel counselor and the customer. Do not interfere but carefully watch for how well the travel counselor handles each step of the sales process. You will report at the end of the role play on what occurred and what might have been improved. Use the role play checklist for guidance in your evaluation.

Role Play Checklist

1. Did the travel counselor discover pertinent information about the customer's wants and needs? _____

2. What was discovered? _____

_____

_____

_____

_____

3. Did the travel counselor discover the customer's

   a. name, address, and phone number?   _____

   b. destination?   _____

   c. number traveling?   _____

   d. method of travel?   _____

   e. date of travel?   _____

   f. length of travel   _____

4. Did the counselor offer products that were in line with the customer's needs? _____

   a. What products were offered? _____

   _____

   _____

   _____

   b. What objections did the customer have? _____

   _____

   _____

   c. Was the counselor able to successfully answer the objections? _____

   d. Did the counselor ask the customer for his business? Offer to make a reservation? _____

   _____

   e. Did the counselor listen effectively? _____

   f. Suggestions or comments: _____

   _____

   _____

   _____

Review Questions

1. List the steps in the sales process:

   _____

   _____

   _____

   _____

   _____

   _____

2. How do you know if a prospective customer is ready to buy? _____

   _____

   _____

3. Why is a telephone sale different from an in-person sale? _____

   _____

   _____

4. If your prospective customer gives you very little information about what he wants, what is the best type of question to ask

   him? _____

   _____

5. What four pieces of information must you have from a customer before you can make a reservation? _____

   _____

   _____

6. When is it appropriate to suggest a product or service you think your customer might be interested in? _____

   _____

7. If a customer expresses an objection, does it mean she will not want to buy something? _____

   What three things can an objection mean?

   a. _____

   b. _____

   c. _____

8. One technique for handling an objection is to restate the objection as a question. List and explain three other objection-

   handling techniques. _____

   _____

   _____

   _____

9. If a customer is smiling and asking detailed questions about the tour you have proposed, is he probably ready to make a reservation? _____

What will you say to him? _____

_____

_____

_____

CHAPTER 21

Customer Service for the Travel Professional

OBJECTIVES

At the conclusion of this chapter, you will be able to

- define customer service.
- understand what customers want.
- recognize things you can do to improve customer service.
- utilize techniques to handle complaints and irate customers.
- utilize telephone etiquette.
- understand external things that affect how your customers see you.

KEY TERMS

customer expectations	follow-up	telephone etiquette
customer service	irate customers	

The Internet has assumed an increasing role in travel planning, to the point that some are asking if travel agents will survive. It is probably unlikely that we will ever see the demise of travel agents, because like everything, the Internet has its pros and cons. One of the biggest shortcomings reported by Internet users is the lack of customer service. There are times when a customer needs to have a question answered or a problem solved, things a travel agent does every day. A successful travel agent brings something special to every transaction—something only a travel agent can do. It might be expert *advice* on a destination, the *security* of knowing there's someone to help if something goes wrong, *saving time* for a business traveler because you did in 3 minutes what would have taken her 20, or a level of *customer service* that is difficult, if not impossible, to find online.

DEFINING CUSTOMER SERVICE

Customer service is a subject every one of us can discuss with authority because we are all customers. We know with certainty that being treated with respect and appreciation is preferable to being treated with indifference. We know exactly what should have been done better. Yet, can you define customer service?

Simply stated, customer service is whatever satisfies the customer. Satisfaction with a product or service is usually based on perceptions and expectations. A hotel guest who perceives that she should be treated royally because her hotel room costs $235 will depart unsatisfied if the service is anything less than superior. If, on the other hand, the hotel guest doesn't expect too much (perhaps because the hotel room cost $35), then she may be satisfied with much less service. The difference between how one expects to be treated and how one perceives the actual treatment determines one's satisfaction.

Product advertising is often intended to influence customer expectations. If an airline announces via advertising that its planes always depart on time, its customers are unhappy if a flight departs only 10 minutes late. The customer was expecting to depart on time, not 10 minutes late! A hotel that advertises its high level of personal service had better produce a high level of personal service. If not, it will produce many unsatisfied customers.

The difficulty with a definition of customer service is that each individual has his own personal definition. These are as diverse as levels of education, experience, personal preferences, and so on. Customer expectations also have a way of changing. As customers gain more experience with a particular product or service, the more exacting their expectations become.

What Do Customers Want?

The key to having satisfied customers is to ensure that service always exceeds expectations. When service falls short of expectations, the customer is invariably dissatisfied.

Although expectations are as individual as the customers, we can make a few generalizations about what customers expect. First, a customer wants to be treated courteously. Courtesy and etiquette are fundamental to any interpersonal relationship, whether business or personal. To overlook the basics such as "please" and "thank you" is inexcusable. We can list some other things customers want:

- to feel important
- to be kept informed, even if the news is bad
- to be treated fairly
- to know they are valued
- to feel that service is given willingly and they are not putting the server to too much trouble

The best way to discover what your customers want is to *ask them*. Previously, we discussed follow-up as an important way to get information and at the same time tell your customers that you care about them. The ability to provide for the needs and expectations of customers depends on our ability to develop an efficient system to feedback.

Many times travel counselors feel that providing good service to their customers is out of the individual counselor's control. The travel counselor cannot control canceled flights, lost deposits, overbooked hotels, storms at sea, and so on. What the counselor can offer is assurance that she will do everything possible to prevent problems, and that when things do go awry (and they will), the counselor will do everything possible to serve the best interests of the customer. Also, the counselor can (and should) prepare the customer to have realistic expectations about the products and services he is buying.

What the customer wants to know is what value she will receive for the money she is paying. What can her travel counselor do better than every other travel counselor? In our present market, differentiating between travel counselors is often difficult. Survival requires that your customers know what you will do for them.

Commitment to Excellence

Excellent customer service is not an accident. It doesn't just happen. Companies that have records of excellent customer service have worked hard to attain that reputation.

What have they done to get there? Why do the employees of one company seem to perform at a much higher level of customer service than the employees of another company? It takes leadership and support, beginning at the top of the organization. Everyone in the organization must be encouraged to practice truly excellent customer service. Many times the employees have the abilities and the proper attitudes toward customer service, but they lack the support from the management of their companies. An outstanding front desk clerk at a poorly managed motel won't single-handedly keep guests coming to the motel.

Companies that provide excellent customer service must also have a clear focus on their customers. As you have seen, customer expectations differ: A level of service that is superior for one group may fall short for another. Consider the example of automatic checkout from hotels. Business travelers generally appreciate the convenience of having in-room checkout procedures. An infrequent traveler on vacation may feel offended by this same service because he prefers the more personal attention he gets from the desk personnel when checking out. If the hotel doesn't provide for both of these groups of customers, one group is going to feel that the level of service at the hotel is inferior. Who your customers are and their level of experience and expectations define the service you should provide.

Customer service expectations usually parallel the price of a product or service. In other words, a first-class airline passenger expects to receive an enhanced level of service. If she receives the same level of service that a coach passenger does, she will be a dissatisfied customer. On the other hand, the coach passenger on the same aircraft may be extremely satisfied with his service because it was exactly what he expected to receive. The travel agency customer who buys a trip around the world has a much different expectation of his service than the customer who books a round-trip to Des Moines. When we spend more, we expect more service.

What Can Travel Professionals Do?

Some fascinating research suggests that even if effective customer service is impossible to render because of difficult circumstances, customers will be sympathetic and hold down their anger *if* they feel that the person who is providing the service is trying to do her best to make things right. The individual provider of customer service can make a difference! Ultimately, the customer service person is the entire organization in the customer's view.

There are several basics that each of us should follow:

- Acknowledge every customer as soon as possible, even if you are busy at the time.
- Get the customer's name and use it in your interaction.
- Make every customer feel special; even if he isn't buying much this time, there's always next time.

- Exhibit enthusiasm every time you serve a customer; it may be your hundredth customer, but you are that customer's first contact.
- Never, ever fight with a customer; remember, the customer is always right.
- Be conscious of how you say things; your tone of voice is sometimes more meaningful than the words you say.
- "I don't know" should always be followed by "but I'll be happy to find out."
- Provide more than the customer expects.
- Always thank the customer.

You can make a difference. Even if you don't receive the support you need, even if every other person the customer has contacted has been indifferent, you can provide a good experience for your customer and leave her feeling entirely differently about your company.

Follow-up

If your customer's trip was great, it's nice to hear the praise. If the trip was bad, you need to know that, too. The average dissatisfied customer tells 10 people about his trip. If the customer has an opportunity to tell his travel counselor, he will be less inclined to complain to friends, or the complaint may include a statement like "my travel counselor has really tried to help."

Follow-up requires considerable effort, and is often overlooked by busy travel professionals. Yet, the results are worth it. It can be done by phone, mail, or e-mail; it may be a formal questionnaire or an informal conversation, but it needs to be done. Following up conveys an important message to your customers: *I care!* Next time a customer is ready to make travel plans, she will remember you.

And by the way, if the reviews are good, don't forget to offer to book the next trip!

HANDLING COMPLAINTS

No matter what you do, there is always the possibility that circumstances will arise over which you have no control, and a customer will come to you with a complaint. It's important to look at a complaint for what it is—*feedback*. A complaint should provide the company with valuable information about the quality of the product or service it is providing. Keep in mind that people who complain represent less than 5 percent of all unsatisfied customers. Those who do complain should be listened to closely!

When you have a complaint, what do you want when you register that complaint? Usually, you want a little empathy, understanding, and an appreciation of the importance of your complaint and the inconvenience it has caused you. You probably want the service or product that was promised or a specific level of performance that was expected but has not yet been delivered. You may want compensation for damages, whether this is a refund or credit for errors or overcharges, or for the failure of the product or company to perform. Your customers are no different.

Sometimes, the customer wants *nothing!* A customer may simply wish to express dissatisfaction with a policy or procedure that has caused him inconvenience. Most people who take the time to frame a complaint of this nature are concerned and want to continue doing business with you. Just because they have not asked for a specific action does not mean you can ignore such a complaint. An incorrect response (such as no acknowledgement at all or a form letter that doesn't fit the situation) can result in serious alienation of a valued customer. The best response is a personal letter that restates the complaint and thanks the customer for bringing this information to your attention. If some action is planned, explain what that will be.

Handling complaints requires some special skills that can be easily learned. First, *listen* to everything the customer has to say, *without interrupting.* The customer has probably spent considerable time thinking about what she will say. Let her say it. Don't try to explain what happened or why it happened. Don't try to defend your position or that of your company. Remember, the customer is always right.

When she has finished, make a statement of *regret,* such as "I'm sorry you have had this problem." Then make a statement of *empathy,* such as "I can certainly understand your feelings."

Look for something you can *agree* with and say that you agree: "I certainly agree that four weeks is too long to wait for your confirmation."

The next step is to ask for additional information or clarification if you need it, then *offer a suggested solution.* Be sure to mention only what you can do or what you propose to do, *not* what you can't do. No one wants to be told about all the things you can't do. When an acceptable solution has been reached, thank the customer for calling (or coming in) and ask if there is anything else you can do to assist. If it is appropriate, follow up in a few days to be certain everything was settled to her satisfaction.

FIGURE 21-1 No matter how seasoned or how experienced you are, an irate person is hard to handle.

understanding of the situation. "How dare he? I'm trying to help! I didn't cause this situation!" We now have two angry people and a situation that's out of control. Somebody has to be in control, and that person is you. When you are in control, you benefit because it means you are not being controlled by this person's behavior toward you.

How do you gain control? First and foremost, do not take the attack as a personal assault. You personally were probably not responsible for the problem. Use the skills you learned for handling a complaint. Remain calm! Don't let yourself get angry or emotional.

In some companies, customer service representatives are asked to refer irate customers to a supervisor. This helps to give the customer a chance to cool down. Often, by the time a supervisor takes the call, the customer has calmed down considerably. The supervisor hasn't just been yelled at, so her thought processes may be clearer. The customer may be more inclined to listen to someone he perceives to be in authority.

Handle the situation in the best way you know how and forget about it. Move on to other things. You always think of the best things to say after the situation is over, but dwelling on it makes you less productive for the rest of the day and doesn't solve anything.

HANDLING IRATE CUSTOMERS

Sometimes a customer with a complaint is very angry. Although these irate customers are probably a minority of the complaints you will handle, they can seem like much more. No matter how seasoned or how experienced you are, an irate person is hard to handle (Figure 21-1).

Too often you, too, begin to react with your emotions. You may get angry at this person's total lack of

TELEPHONE ETIQUETTE

Because many travel professionals do a large portion of their customer contact by telephone, it is important to practice good telephone etiquette. Frequently the first impression a customer forms about a business is based on the person who answers the telephone. If that person exhibits an unfriendly attitude, an unwillingness to help, poor grammar, or just plain bad manners, the customer's first impression is likely to be justifiably unkind. That customer may never be back.

You will recall from the discussion of telephone sales in Chapter 20 that what you say is important, but how you say it is even more important. Put a smile into your voice. If you have any doubts about whether this is possible, just listen to any popular local radio personalities. Imagine how dull radio would be without projection of personality by the announcers. You can do the same thing over the phone. It may take some practice, but learning to project your personality through your voice can make a world of difference to your customers.

People become easily frustrated by numerous telephone transfers and interruptions. If you do not know who can assist the caller, take the information and a phone number and do the legwork yourself. This way the customer is not forced to make multiple explanations and endure being passed from person to person.

Answer the telephone by the second or third ring and answer in a way that can be understood by the caller. By the time you have answered the hundredth call, your greeting can become slurred. The customer is, however, hearing it for the first time.

If you initiate a call, don't make the other person wait to speak to you. Have your thoughts organized and your information at hand. If someone else places the call for you, be ready to speak to the person as soon as the call goes through.

Take notes so you don't have to make the caller repeat his needs, and so you don't have to trust your memory.

If you use an answering machine or voice mail when you are away from your phone, remember to check your outgoing message frequently. It should be clear and easily understood by the caller. Don't try to be cute. It usually does not come across well. Check for messages often and return your calls promptly.

Telephones are a major convenience, but they can also be a major source of frustration for a customer. Don't let your telephone procedures have a negative effect on the quality of customer service you provide.

CAN YOU JUDGE A BOOK BY ITS COVER?

Everything about you makes a statement to your customers. Advertisers have understood for many years that packaging is at least as important as the product inside the package. What kind of statement does your packaging make about you?

- *Your appearance.* "Dress for success" has become a common utterance among professionals. Whether you wear the traditional business suit, a uniform, or something more

individual, your attire makes a statement about you. Take your cue from the management of your company. Pay attention to who your customers are. If your offices are in a major metropolitan city, a conservative style may be most appropriate. If you work on or near a college campus, the style may be more casual. Your appearance must always be neat and clean. Never should your appearance detract from your customers' ability to relate to you.

- *Your desk.* Are you the neat and orderly type, or are you the disorganized type whose desk is piled 12 inches high at all times? Like your appearance, your desk makes a statement about you. A customer may not want to trust her travel plans to someone who appears to be disorganized. Personal items on your desk also make a statement. Think about what your personal items say about you to a customer.

- *Your office.* The arrangement of your office and the furnishings, style, and cleanliness all speak volumes to a customer (Figure 21–2). Is the coffeepot placed for customer access? Is it crusty with last year's coffee? Is the furniture tattered or elegant? Is the desk arrangement functional or cluttered? Look at these things through the eyes of your customers. Do they say what you would want them to say?

- *Your correspondence.* No letter or promotional material should leave your hands with misspelled words or grammatical errors. This conveys an attitude of not caring and of lack of attention to detail. The quality of business cards, stationery, and envelopes also has an impact upon your customers. These items are a reflection of you and how you do business. Do they speak well of you?

FIGURE 21–2 The arrangement of your office and the furnishings, style, and cleanliness all speak volumes to a customer.

SUMMARY

Customer service will be an integral part of careers in travel forever. How well you carry it through for your customers may well decide who survives and who does not. Because there is little differentiation in the products you provide, customer service is crucial to getting and retaining customers. Purchasing products over the Internet is often faulted for not providing the level of customer service that customers have come to expect. Only the travel professional that is able to provide a consistently high level of service can expect to continue to do business.

It is difficult to define customer service precisely because each individual customer has his own personal definition. Things like education, experience, and the amount of money spent for a product help to define customer expectations. Excellent customer service is based on your ability to exceed each customer's expectations.

Every person who is placed in a position to serve customers can make a difference. Research suggests that one customer service professional becomes the entire organization in the customer's view. That professional's attitude can make the difference between customer satisfaction or dissatisfaction.

Customers are the most important element of your career. Developing good customer service skills early in one's career is a good investment in the future.

For additional Travel and Tourism resources, go to http://www.hospitality-tourism.delmar.com.

PLEASE COMPLETE THE CHAPTER REVIEW QUESTIONS NOW.

Review Questions

1. List the steps you would take to handle a complaint. _____
   _____
   _____
   _____
   _____

2. Cite an example of excellent service that you have received and explain why you feel it was excellent. _____
   _____
   _____
   _____
   _____

3. Why do you feel it is important to maintain a reputation for excellent customer service? _____
   _____
   _____
   _____
   _____

4. List five basic things you can do to provide better customer service.
   a. _____
   b. _____
   c. _____
   d. _____
   e. _____

5. What effect can your appearance have on your customers? _____
   _____
   _____

6. Discuss three things you can do to make your telephone manner more pleasing to a customer. _____
   _____
   _____
   _____
   _____

7. Why should a business be concerned if its customers feel it is out of touch with the customer's needs? _____
   _____
   _____
   _____

8. Why is it important to know what your customers expect of your service? _____

_____

_____

_____

9. What percentage of customers complain? _____

10. Does the price of a product or service have an effect on the level of service the customer expects? If so, what?

_____

_____

_____

_____

Endnotes

CHAPTER 1

1. http://www.bls.gov
2. http://www.thetravelinstitute.com
3. http://www.ntaonline.com

CHAPTER 2

1. Jupiter Research Internet Travel Model, 2004

CHAPTER 3

1. http://www.tsa.gov/public
2. http://www.dhs.gov/dhspublic
3. http://www.tsa.gov/public
4. http://www.travelsense.org
5. http://www.ecotourism.org

References

Accommodations/Lodging

http://www.ahla.com
http://www.ichotelsgroup.com
http://www.hotelandtravelindex.com
http://www.travel-library.com

Air Travel

http://www.amadeus.com
http://www.galileo.com
http://www.genesistds.com
http://www.sabre.com
http://www.worldspan.com

Careers

http://www.bls.gov

Cruises

http://www.carnival.com
http://www.cruising.com
http://www.starserviceonline.com

Consolidators

http://www.usaca.com

Ecotourism

http://www.ecotourism.com
http://www.greenglobe21.com
http://www.audubon.org

Education

http://www.sustainabletravel.org
http://www.thetravelinstitute.com

Health

http://www.ccohs.com
http://www.cdc.gov
http://www.thesite.org.uk
http://www.tripprep.com

Independent and Home-Based Travel Professionals

http://www.hometravelagency.com/dictionary
http://www.ossn.com
http://www.sba.gov

Insurance

http://www.internationalbenefits.com
http://www.metlife.com
http://www.travelex-insurance.com
http://www.ustravelinsurance.com

Internet Travel Agencies

http://www.cendant.com
http://www.expedia.com
http://www.travelocity.com
http://www.travel2nytimes.com

Professional Organizations

http://www.arccorp.com
http://www.astanet.com
http://www.iata.org
http://www.iatan.com
http://www.m-travel.com
http://www.nacta.com
http://www.tia.org
http://www.travelsellers.com
http://www.wttc.org
http://www.idl-international.com

Publications

http://www.jaxfax.com

http://www.modernagent.com

http://www.nationalgeographic.com

http://www.thomascookpublishing.com

http://www.travelagentcentral.com

http://www.smartbrief.com

Rail Travel

http://www.americanorientexpress.com

http://www.amtrak.com

http://www.bluetrain.co.za

http://www.japanrail.com

http://www.orientexpress.com

http://www.railagent.com

http://www.raileurope.com

http://www.viarail.ca

Security/Safety

http://www.dhs.gov

http://www.english.safe-democracy.org

http://www.kevincoffey.com

http://www.state.gov

http://www.travelsense.org

http://www.travel.state.gov

http://www.tsa.gov

http://www.english.safe-democracy.org/keynotes/
terrorism-and-the-travel-industry.html

Technology

http://www.icann.org

http://www.precisecyberforensics.com/glossary.html

http://www.travelclick.net

http://www.wave.net

http://www.website101.com/define.html

Tours

http://www.ntaonline.com

http://www.ustoa.com

Travel News

http://www.northstartravelmedia.com

http://www.span.com

http://www.travelagewest.com

http://www.travelmole.net

Miscellaneous

http://www.ease.com

Glossary

24-hour clock: A method of keeping time that utilizes 24 numbers instead of using 12 hours in conjunction with a.m. and p.m.

A

AAD: See Agent Automated Deduction.

Acela: Amtrak's all-electric high-speed (up to 150 mph) trains that operate in the Northeast Corridor.

adjoining rooms: Accommodations that are side-by-side but do not have a communicating door between them.

Advance Purchase Excursion (APEX) fares: Another name for international excursion fares.

affiliated property: An independently owned accommodation property that uses the services of a representative, or rep., company.

aft: At or near the back of a ship.

agency identification plate: A metal plate that states the travel agency's name, location, and ARC number. It is provided by ARC at the time of appointment and is used in validation or imprinting devices.

air add-on: Special airfare between the traveler's home city and destination or gateway, offered by cruise lines, tour operators, and international airlines.

air traffic control: FAA employees who are responsible for a flight after it becomes airborne.

Air Transport Association (ATA): A trade association with members that include most of the airlines in the United States. ATA represents its members before Congress and promotes safety and efficiency in air travel.

airline clubs: Airport amenities sponsored by each airline. Benefits for club members include a private waiting area, business center, complimentary refreshments, and the service of an airline representative.

airline rate desk: A department of an airline that is staffed by employees who have been trained in the various details of fare construction.

Airlines Reporting Corporation (ARC): A conference consisting of member airlines, railroads, and other travel vendors. ARC is the appointing body for U.S. travel agencies selling air travel.

airport authority: The governing body of an airport, responsible for its operation and security.

airport hotel: A type of accommodation that is located on or near airport property.

Air–Rail: A combination of transportation that incorporates the advantages of train travel with the benefits of air travel. Usually offered as part of a unique vacation package, this feature provides the cost saving benefit of a round-trip fare.

Alaska/Hawaii International Travel Facilities Tax: a tax charged for air travel between the 48 contiguous states and Alaska or Hawaii.

Alaskan tax: A tax that applies to air travel from the 48 contiguous states to or from Alaska. The tax percentage is based on the traveler's origin and destination cities.

all-inclusive resort: A type of accommodation in which the room, meals, activities, and so on are included in the basic rate.

all-suite hotels: Accommodations that have separate rooms for sleeping, bathing, sitting, and dining/ cooking.

altitude sickness: A condition that affects many travelers at altitudes over 10,000 feet. Symptoms include extreme fatigue, shortness of breath, dizziness, and nausea.

amenities: Additional features, services, or extras offered by a travel supplier.

American Society of Travel Agents (ASTA): An organization with members that include travel agencies, tour operators, and others in the travel industry.

Animal Plant and Health Inspection Service (APHIS) Fee: A fee charged as part of the cost of air travel to passengers arriving in the United States from abroad. APHIS is a department of the U.S. Department of Agriculture.

APHIS: See Animal Plant and Health Inspection Service (APHIS) Fee

Apollo: The U.S. marketing division of the Galileo GDS.

ARC: See Airlines Reporting Corporation (ARC).

ARC appointment: The approval of a U.S. travel agency to sell air travel by the Airlines Reporting Corporation.

ARC number: The identifying number assigned by the Airlines Reporting Corporation to a U.S. travel agency upon appointment and used in validation of imprinting devices.

ARC report: A manual or electronic weekly report of a travel agency's sales.

Area Settlement Bank: ARC's processing center for a travel agency's weekly sales reports.

around-the-world fares: Fares designed for circumnavigation of the globe with multiple stopovers.

ARUNK or ARNK: A GDS term used to indicate a surface segment.

ASTA: See American Society of Travel Agents (ASTA).

ATA: See Air Transport Association (ATA).

attitude: The bearing assumed by a person indicative of feelings or opinions.

authorized amount: The maximum amount that the Area Settlement Bank may withdraw from a travel agency's bank account to cover its weekly sales report.

Auto Train: A special Amtrak train, operating between Lorton, Virginia, and Sanford, Florida, that transports automobiles and motorcycles in addition to passengers.

B

backhaul: The difference between a through fare and a HIP fare.

back-to-back excursion fares: A pricing technique for round-trip travel that has a connection in both directions. One excursion fare is calculated from origin to connection point, and back to the origin. The other excursion fare is calculated from the connection point to the destination, and back to the connection point. Then, the two excursion fares are added together.

back-to-back ticketing: An unethical practice in which two round-trips are scheduled, each with a fictitious return.

bank buying rate (BBR): The official exchange rate used to convert one currency to another currency when pricing air travel.

Base fare: An airfare that does not include tax.

BBR: See bank buying rate (BBR).

bed & breakfast: A type of accommodation, sometimes a private home, with a shared bathroom that includes a room and breakfast the following morning in the price.

berths: 1. The name for beds on a ship. 2. The location at the port where ships are moored.

bias: Preferential placement of airline information in a GDS.

biometrics: The digital analysis of biological characteristics such as facial structure, fingerprints, iris patterns, or voice recognition using cameras or scanners, then matching these characteristics to profiles contained in large databases.

boarding pass: A document, usually issued by an airline, that indicates a passenger's assigned seat for a flight.

bon voyage gift: A gift given by a travel counselor or other person to a cruise passenger.

booking classes: The first, or only, letters of the fare basis code that indicate first-class, business-class, or coach-class seating as well as the airfare being purchased. Also known as booking codes or primary codes.

booking code: The first, or only, letter of the fare basis code that indicates first-class, business-class, or coach-class seating as well as the airfare being purchased. Also known as booking class or primary code.

bow: The front of a ship.

breaking the fare: A pricing technique used for one-way travel with a connection. One fare is calculated from the origin to the connection point and is then added to the fare from the connection point to the destination.

bridge: The navigational and command center of a ship.

browser: A program such as Microsoft Internet Explorer or Netscape that provides easy access to the Internet.

budget fare: An international airfare in which the traveler selects the week of travel and the airline determines the actual day and flight.

bulk rates: Prices for a travel product that are applicable only when a minimum number is purchased.

bulkheads: Dividing walls or partitions between passenger cabins on an aircraft or ship.

Bullet Train: See Shinkansen

bumping: The airline practice of removing paid passengers from a flight when too many seats have been sold.

buying signals: The positive cues given by a customer who has made a decision to purchase a product or service.

C

cabin: 1. A room on a ship. 2. A section, such as first, business, and coach, on a flight.

cabin category: A group of cruise cabins that have a common price.

cancellation fee: The amount charged by a travel vendor when the traveler cancels his reservation.

cancellation policy: A travel vendor's schedule of fees for cancellation, based on how far in advance of travel the cancellation is made.

Canrailpass: A 30-day rail pass for unlimited train travel on Canada's Via Rail system.

carousels: Airport devices that transport baggage from the rear of the baggage handling area to the public area.

CDW: See collision damage waiver.

chain property: A type of accommodation, owned either privately or by the chain, that has the same name, general services, level of quality, and so on, as other properties in the chain.

change of gauge: A type of flight schedule in which a change of planes is required, but the flight number remains the same. Change of gauge flights are shown as direct service in the GDS and printed reference sources but include a symbol or notation that a change of aircraft is required.

child: 1. An air passenger who is over 2 and under 12. 2. A cruise or tour passenger, usually under the age of 16 or 18. 3. A hotel guest staying with a parent, usually under the age of 18.

churning: An unethical practice of repeatedly canceling and rebooking an airline reservation in the GDS.

circle trip: 1. When normal fares are used, a circle trip has more than one destination. 2. When excursion fares are used, a circle trip has two destinations—no more, no less. 3. Internationally, when excursion fares are used, both destinations must be (a) within Europe, or (b) within the same country.

circle-trip minimum: The airline fare rule that states that if a HIP fare applies in one direction, it must be charged in the other direction as well, regardless of the routing.

city-commercial hotel: A type of accommodation that is located in the city center or business district of a city.

city pair: The city where a passenger first boards and first deplanes a flight.

CLIA: See Cruise Lines International Association (CLIA).

closed-ended questions: Inquiries constructed to allow a response of only "yes" or "no."

code sharing: An airline practice of contracting with another airline to use the other airline's code designation.

collision damage waiver (CDW): A type of waiver offered by rental car companies, relieving the renter of responsibility if the vehicle is damaged.

combined tax item: The code used on ARC documents to indicate that various taxes and other fees have been combined into one figure, expressed as *XT*.

commission: Money paid by a travel vendor to a travel agency that sells its products.

commuter airlines: Small airlines, also known as regional airlines, that usually operate short-haul flights in one area of the country only.

compact: A rental car size group that is slightly larger than economy size, but slightly smaller than intermediate size.

components: Individual products and services that are included in a tour.

Computer Reservation Systems (CRS): Automation vendors such as Amadeus, Galileo, Sabre, and Worldspan. Now known as GDS.

concierge: 1. An accommodation property employee who is responsible for guest services. 2. A separate section of an accommodation property where only guests in that section have access to additional services.

concourse: The airport corridors where the gate areas are located.

conference: An organization such as the Airlines Reporting Corporation, International Airlines Travel Agent Network, and the International Air Transport Association.

confidentiality: The policy requiring that a travel professional never discuss a traveler's plans with anyone other than the traveler.

configuration: The interior design of an aircraft, or floor plan, that indicates seating areas, exit doors, wing area, lavatories, closets, galley, and flight deck.

confirmation number: The identifying number assigned by a travel vendor for a particular booking.

connecting rooms: Accommodations that are side-by-side and have a communicating door between them.

connection: 1. When travel is entirely within the United States, a connection is a change of planes that takes place in less than four hours. 2. When travel is international, a connection is a change of planes that takes place in less than 24 hours.

consolidator: A company that purchases air space at bulk rates and then resells the space to travel agencies and, sometimes, to the general public.

consortium: An organization with member travel agencies that combines sales volume for better negotiation with travel vendors.

Consular Information Sheets: U.S. State Department publications for each country that always include general information, possibly a statement of caution, or a restriction against travel.

consulate: A branch office of an embassy. Consulates issue travel visas to people visiting that country.

continents: Land masses that include Antarctica, Asia, Australia, Europe, North America, and South America.

contraband: Any item that cannot be legally imported into a country.

convention hotels: Accommodations that cater to convention attendees.

corridor trains: Amtrak trains that have a running time of less than six hours.

cover letter: A business letter written by a job applicant to a prospective employer that accompanies her resume.

Credit Memo: An airline issued document used to pay a travel agency's undercollected commission via the ARC report.

CRS: See Computer Reservation Systems (CRS).

cruise documents: A packet sent to the travel agency by the cruise line that contains the passenger's cruise ticket, baggage tags, itinerary, information on ports of call, cruise tips, and possibly airline tickets.

Cruise Lines International Association (CLIA): The official trade organization of the cruise industry, Cruise Lines International Association works in partnership with nearly 17,000 affiliated travel agencies throughout North America to ensure the highest caliber of cruise sales expertise and service for cruise vacationers. The function of CLIA is to promote the cruise product and raise awareness of cruising.

customer expectations: What the customer anticipates he will receive from the product or service purchased.

customer service: Whatever satisfies the customer based upon her perceptions and expectations.

customs: A department of the U.S. Treasury, or other country's government, that is responsible for monitoring incoming passengers, baggage, cargo, and freight.

customs declaration form: A U.S. Treasury document that must be completed by all U.S. citizens returning to the United States from abroad, indicating all items purchased during the trip. Other countries have similar requirements and forms for their citizens.

customs fee: A charge that is part of an airline ticket or e-tkt, made by the U.S. government for all passengers arriving in the United States from abroad.

D

daily rate: A rental car rate that is calculated per 24-hour period.

DBC: See denied boarding compensation (DBC).

debarkation: The process of leaving a ship.

Debit Memo: An airline issued document that is used to collect additional funds from a travel agency via the ARC report.

deck: A floor or level on a ship.

deck plan: The diagram or floor plan of a ship that indicates cabins, public rooms, elevators, and so on.

denied boarding compensation (DBC): A voucher given by the airline when a flight is overbooked to passengers who volunteer to take a later flight and bumped revenue passengers.

Department of Homeland Security (DHS): The Department of Homeland Security was created in 2002 as an executive department of the United States to safeguard the United States from terrorist attacks.

Department of Transportation (DOT): The U.S. government agency responsible for the regulation of air travel within the United States.

deposit: A down payment made on the purchase of a travel product.

direct flight: A flight that makes one or more en route stops but does not require a change of planes.

discounts: Price reductions commonly offered by cruise lines, based on variables such as early booking, special programs, loyalty, or membership in specified organizations.

document packet: A folder issued by a travel vendor that includes various materials for the traveler, such as cruise or tour tickets, airline tickets, general information, baggage tags, name tags, hotel lists, itinerary, and so on.

DOT: See Department of Transportation (DOT).

dot travel: A special domain for travel related Web sites for which domain owners must be prescreened to meet clear, standard, and objective criteria set by the travel industry.

double connections: Flight patterns that require two plane changes.

double open-jaw: An international trip that involves a surface segment at both the origin and destination ends.

draft: The depth of a ship's hull, measured in feet and inches, that is below the water line.

driving record check: The procedure of obtaining details about a traveler's driving record before the traveler's car rental transaction can be completed.

drop charge: A fee for renting a car in one city and returning it to a different location.

dry lease: The rental of a mode of transportation without the services of a crew.

dual-designated carrier: An airline that has contracted with and uses the two-character designator code of another airline.

duplicate bookings: An unethical practice of making more than one reservation for a traveler's trip.

duty-free: Import tax free.

dynamic packaging: The ability to quickly search a large group of suppliers, select tour components that meet customer needs and offer a customized travel package at the best price.

E

early booking discount: A price reduction offered by various cruise lines and tour operators when reservations are made a minimum number of days before travel.

e-commerce: The sale of products and services over a Web site.

economy: The smallest size group of rental cars; sometimes called subcompact.

ecotourism: The International Ecotourism Society (TIES) has defined ecotourism as *"responsible travel to natural areas that conserves the environment and improves the well-being of local people."* Also called sustainable tourism.

elapsed flying time: The actual number of minutes and hours a flight takes.

electronic ticket (e-tkt): A type of ticket transaction in which there are no flight coupons; accounting coupons are issued.

e-mail: Electronic mail that is sent and received via computer.

embarkation: The process of boarding a ship.

embassy: The office of one country's ambassador within a host country.

end transaction: The process of saving and filing a completed PNR.

en route stops: Stops between a flight's origin and destination for the purpose of boarding new passengers and taking on fuel, catering, baggage, and cargo.

entrepreneur: Business owner.

equator: The imaginary horizontal line that circles the globe at its center.

escort: An employee of a tour operator who travels with the group throughout the trip.

escorted tours: The most structured tours; all components are usually included and an escort is with the group throughout the trip.

e-tkt: See electronic ticket (e-tkt).

Eurailpass: A type of rail ticket that is valid in several European countries for a set number of days with unlimited stopover opportunities.

Europass: A type of rail ticket that provides unlimited rail travel in five of the most popular European countries within a two-month period.

exchange rate: See bank buying rate (BBR).

excursion fare: A round-trip airfare that can never be purchased on a one-way basis for half the amount.

Explore America: An Amtrak fare that is purchased for travel within one, two, three, or four zones. Other features include up to three stopovers, 30 or 45 days to complete travel, and no advance purchase is required.

F

FAA: See Federal Aviation Administration (FAA).

fact-finding question: An inquiry that requests specific information from the respondent.

familiarization (FAM) trip: A trip designed for the education of travel professionals that is sponsored by travel vendors or destinations.

fare based: A test used to determine if excursion fares can be split and combined on an open-jaw trip. For this test, the one-way coach fare between the surface segment cities must be equal to or less than one half of the excursion fare on each of the flown segments.

fare basis code (FBC): An airline's identification for a specific fare. An FBC can be a single letter (booking or primary code) or it can be a combination of letters and numbers.

fare ladder: The portion of an ARC document where base fares, PFCs, segment fees, and fuel surcharges are detailed.

FBC: See fare basis code (FBC).

FDA: See Food and Drug Administration (FDA).

Federal Aviation Administration (FAA): A department of the DOT that is responsible for air traffic control, aircraft certification, passenger safety, and pilot licensing.

feeling-finding question: An inquiry that requests the respondent to provide his perceptions about a product or service.

fictitious bookings: Unethical reservations made in case a passenger might travel.

fictitious return: The unethical practice of making up a return date so that a round-trip fare can be used instead of a more expensive one-way fare.

final payment: The balance due after a deposit has been made for the purchase of a travel product.

Flexipass: A rail pass offered by European Rail that permits rail travel for a specified number of days.

follow-up: Any contact with a customer after the initial contact.

Food and Drug Administration (FDA): A federal agency that regulates food and drugs entering or leaving the United States.

foreign independent tour (FIT): A customized tour where all components are arranged separately by the travel professional.

forward: At or near the front of a ship.

franchise properties: Accommodation properties that have purchased the right to belong to and use the name of a franchise group.

frequent flyer programs: Airline programs in which members accumulate miles from airlines and other travel vendors. The accumulated miles can be exchanged for airfare discounts, flight upgrades, free air travel, and other travel products.

frequent guest programs: Accommodation programs in which members accumulate points that can be used for discounts, upgrades, and other travel products.

fuel surcharge: An extra fee charged to boarding passengers by an airline at various airports because of fuel shortages or escalating fuel costs.

fuselage: The body of an aircraft.

G

Galileo: One of the four major GDSs; it is marketed in the United States as Apollo.

galley: The kitchen on an aircraft or ship.

gangway: The walkway leading up to a ship's entrance and the entrance itself.

gate: The waiting and boarding area located within a concourse of an airport.

gateway city: The city from which an international flight departs or arrives.

GDS: See Global Distribution System (GDS).

geotourism: Tourism that sustains or enhances the geographical character of a place—its environment, culture, aesthetics, heritage, and the well-being of its residents. Geotourism encompasses all tourism to the extent that residents of a location have a vested interest in protecting the resources that people are coming for, whether historic, cultural, gastronomic, environmental, or other.

Global Distribution System (GDS): A computer reservation system, typically owned jointly by airlines, that includes reservation databases of suppliers in many countries. The term *GDS* has largely replaced *CRS* as the term of choice within the industry.

global indicator: An international fare term that indicates the general route a trip must take in order to use a specific fare.

GMT: See Greenwich Mean Time (GMT).

Greenwich Mean Time (GMT): The time at the Greenwich Meridian (0 degrees, just outside of London). All locations around the word are expressed as being so many hours behind (-) or ahead (+) of GMT.

Greenwich Meridian: The imaginary vertical line that extends from the north to the south pole; identified as 0 degrees.

gross registered tonnage (GRT): A measurement of space on a ship equal to 100 cubic feet of enclosed, revenue-producing space.

ground control: Employees of the FAA who are responsible for flights before they become airborne.

ground operators: Vendors who arrange travel components such as hotels, sightseeing, transfers, and meals.

group: 1. Ten or more air passengers who are booked together for the same itinerary. 2. Ten or more rooms booked for the same dates at the same property. 3. Ten or more cabins booked for the same cruise and sailing date. 4. The size of a group varies with tour operators.

group presentation: A program to offer travel products to a group, club, or organization.

GRT: See gross registered tonnage (GRT).

guarantee: 1. With regard to accommodations, the process of giving the hotel the guest's credit card number, or mailing a deposit check or a check for full prepayment so that the room will be held all night. 2. A cruise policy in which the fare is guaranteed but the actual cabin assignment is made on the day of sailing. The cabin grade is of equal or greater value.

guaranteed share rate: A cruise price reduction for a single person based upon sharing a cruise cabin with another single person of the same sex.

guesthouses: Accommodations that are generally small, family-run properties offering a minimum of guest services. Also known as pensions.

Gulf Stream: An ocean current in the Northern Hemisphere that moves in a clockwise direction.

H

hardware: Physical computer equipment such as the monitor, CPU, keyboard, printer, and so on.

Hawaiian tax: A special tax that applies to air travel between the 48 contiguous states and Hawaii; the percentage is based on the traveler's origin city.

hemispheres: One half of the world; either north and south or east and west.

higher intermediate point (HIP): A nearer stopover city that has a higher fare than the destination city.

host: 1. The GDS developer or owner. 2. An employee of a tour operator who is available at the destination to the tour participants at specified times.

hosted tours: Moderately structured tours with a host who is available for assistance at specified times.

hostels: Accommodations that offer dormlike sleeping areas, shared bathroom facilities, and possibly shared kitchen facilities.

hotel: A type of accommodation in which room access is via a central corridor or hall. Hotels can be very basic with regard to facilities and amenities or they can offer a wide range of activities and dining options.

Hotel and Travel Index (HTI): a lodging reference, both printed and online, which lists basic information, such as location and rates, for thousands of hotels internationally; advertising space of varying sizes may be purchased by a hotel property; HTI online offers booking for 4,000 hotels.

housing bureau: An agency or division of a city's visitors' bureau that acts as a clearinghouse for accommodation space during a convention.

hubs: Unique collections of travel-related information and links to other useful and pertinent Web sites.

hub and spoke: An airline practice of using an airport as a home base (hub) and feeding flights from surrounding airports (spokes) into the hub.

hull: The outer shell of a cruise ship body.

I

IATA: See International Air Transportation Association (IATA).

IATA trip classifications: Identifiers used on airline tickets and e-tkts indicating where travel was purchased and issued in relation to where the itinerary begins. See SITI, SITO, SOTI, and SOTO.

IATAN: See International Airlines Travel Agent Network (IATAN).

IATAN ID card: An identification card offered by the International Airlines Travel Agent Network to qualifying travel professionals.

identity theft: A crime in which an imposter obtains key pieces of personal information, such as Social Security or driver's license numbers, in order to impersonate someone else. The information can be used to obtain credit, merchandise, or services in the name of the victim, or to provide the thief with false credentials.

IDL: See International Date Line (IDL).

inbound: The portion of an air trip that returns to the origin city. This term is usually used to indicate the return portion of a trip.

independent property: A type of accommodation that is privately owned and operated.

independent tours: The least structured tours; participants are basically on their own.

infants: Travelers who are under two years of age. Lap-held infants on flights within the United States travel free. Internationally, lap-held infants pay 10 percent of the adult fare. Most airlines will sell a seat to be used for an infant in a special carrier at 50 percent of the adult fare.

inside cabins: Passenger's rooms onboard ship that do not have a window or porthole.

insurance waiver: A legal release form used by some travel vendors and agencies, signed by the traveler, releasing the vendor or agency from liability.

Interactive Agent Reporting (IAR): ARC's automated travel agency reporting program.

interline agreements: Agreements between two airlines that cover ticketing, transference of passengers, baggage, and cargo.

intermediate: A rental car size category that is slightly larger than compact but slightly smaller than standard. Also known as midsize.

International Air Transport Association (IATA): A conference whose members include U.S. and international airlines. The appointing body for travel agencies outside the United States to sell air travel.

International Airlines Travel Agent Network (IATAN): A conference with members that include U.S. and international airlines. An appointing body for U.S. travel agencies selling air travel.

International Certificate of Vaccination: The official booklet that is completed by the physician who administers various vaccinations.

International Date Line (IDL): Imaginary line at 180° longitude, located on the opposite side of the earth from the Greenwich Meridian.

Internet: A global network of data, news, and opinions, connecting millions of computers and encompassing more than 100 countries.

Internet scam: Any type of fraud scheme that uses email, Web sites, chat rooms, or message boards to present fraudulent solicitations to prospective victims, to conduct fraudulent transactions, or to transmit the proceeds of fraud to financial institutions or to others connected with the scheme.

Internet Service Provider (ISP): A company that provides access to the Internet via phone lines.

inventory control: An airline policy that divides the total number of seats on a flight into price categories.

irate customers: Customers who are angry or enraged.

ISP: See Internet Service Provider (ISP).

itinerary field: The portion of a PNR that includes flights, surface segments, cars, hotels, cruises, tours, and other travel products.

J

Japanese National Railway: The railroad system that is operated by the government of Japan.

jet lag: A medical condition that may affect air travelers on some flights that cross several time zones. Symptoms include extreme fatigue and difficulty in adjusting waking and sleeping hours to the local time.

jet stream: An air current that moves in an eastwardly direction north of the Tropic of Cancer and south of the Tropic of Capricorn.

jetways: Devices that connect the airport gate door with the door of an aircraft and through which passengers board and deplane.

K

keel: The lowest portion of a ship's hull.

L

LDW: See loss damage waiver (LDW).

leg: The portion of a flight between stop points.

load factor: The percentage of filled seats on a flight to the total number of seats on the aircraft.

local guide: An employee of a tour operator who is a resident of the destination and joins the tour group for a short period of time.

logical geographical order: The process of arranging a traveler's destinations in such a way as to avoid backtracking and wide north–south deviations.

loss damage waiver (LDW): A waiver offered by rental car companies that releases the renter from liability when the vehicle is damaged.

M

major airline: A large airline that operates both short- and long-haul flights and has over $1 billion in annual sales.

markup: The process of adding profit to a price.

maximum permitted miles (MPM): An airfare term that limits the accumulated miles on a trip.

MCO: See Miscellaneous Charges Order (MCO).

meet and assist: An airline service in which an attendant meets a passenger and helps her to the next gate or other area of the airport.

Meridian of Longitude: Imaginary vertical lines that extend between the north and south poles.

Metroliner: Amtrak's high-speed electric train service that operates in the Northeast Corridor.

midships: The center portion of a ship, front to back.

mileage based: A test that determines whether or not excursion fares can be split and combined on an open-jaw trip. The air miles on the surface segment must be equal to or less than the miles on each of the flown segments.

minimum connecting time: The least amount of time that must be allowed for a change of planes.

Miscellaneous Charges Order (MCO): An accountable ARC document that can be used to pay for various travel services.

motel: A type of accommodation in which room access is via exterior doors. Motels usually have only one or two floors.

MPM: See maximum permitted miles (MPM).

N

name field: The portion of a PNR that includes the passenger's name and possibly titles and passenger type codes.

narrow-body aircraft: An aircraft that has a single aisle.

national airline: An airline that flies both long and short routes but within the borders of one country.

National Tour Association (NTA): An organization of tour suppliers and motorcoach operators who package trips and offer them to the public.

National Transportation Safety Board (NTSB): A government agency responsible for air accident investigations, safety recommendations, and statistical reports.

net amount: The portion of a traveler's final payment (less commission) that is sent to the vendor by agency check.

net rate: A rate that does not have travel agency commission built in.

neutral unit of construction (NUC): A generic currency used in calculating international airfares.

niche market: A particular travel specialty.

nonstop flight: A flight that does not stop in between the origin and the destination.

no-rec: A CRS term that means a PNR that was lost in transit to the airline being booked.

normal fare: A one-way airfare; if it is to be used on round-trip travel, the amount must be doubled.

North America Rail Pass: A type of rail ticket that allows for unlimited coach rail travel within the United States over a stated period of days. Stopovers are restricted and reservations are mandatory.

no-shows: Travelers who have reservations, but do not show up or cancel their booking.

NTA: See National Tour Association (NTA).

NTSB: See National Transportation Safety Board (NTSB).

NUC: See neutral unit of construction (NUC).

O

objections: Reasons expressed by a customer for not buying a product or service.

oceans: Major bodies of water that include Arctic, Atlantic, Indian, and Pacific.

offline connection: A type of flight pattern in which the traveler must change from one airline's flight to a different airline's flight.

one-way trip: A trip from origin to destination.

online: The act of being connected to the Internet via a phone line and Internet Service Provider (ISP).

online connection: A type of flight pattern in which the traveler must change planes but the airline remains the same.

open-ended questions: Inquiries constructed to encourage the respondent to provide as much information as possible.

open-jaw trip: A type of trip that involves the origin and two other cities, and travel between one city pair is by means other than commercial air.

open-jaw with side trip: A type of trip that involves the origin and three other cities, and travel between one city pair is by means other than commercial air.

option date: The date by which a vendor must receive a deposit.

optional PNR fields: Portions of a PNR that are not required to finalize and save the PNR. Optional fields include the traveler's address, seat assignments, remarks, and so on.

Orient Express: See Venice-Simplon Orient Express.

outbound: The portion of an air trip from the origin to a connection point or destination. This term is usually used to identify the first portion of an itinerary.

outside cabins: Passengers' rooms on a ship that have a window or porthole.

overbook: A policy in which more seats on a flight or rooms at an accommodation property are booked than are actually available.

override: Additional commission over and above the standard percentage.

P

PAI: See personal accident insurance (PAI).

parallels of latitude: Imaginary horizontal lines that circle the globe.

passenger contract: An agreement between the traveler and the vendor.

passenger departure tax: A tax imposed on cruise passengers departing a U.S. port.

Passenger Facility Charge (PFC): An airport fee of $1, $2, $3, or $4.50 that applies to all passengers boarding a flight at specified airports.

passenger name record (PNR): A reservation for air, rental car, hotel, cruise, tour, and other travel services.

passport: An official document issued by a national government that states the holder's citizenship.

PC: See personal computer (PC).

pensions: Accommodations in various countries that are similar to motels in the United States and Canada.

perks: Any additional service or feature that is given free.

personal accident insurance (PAI): A type of insurance offered by rental car companies that covers personal injury resulting from an accident.

personal computer (PC): Also called a desktop computer; a small computer that revolutionized the use of computers by individuals instead of only large corporations.

PFC: See Passenger Facility Charge (PFC).

phone field: The portion of a PNR that includes the travel agency's, passenger's home, passenger's business, and destination contact phone numbers.

pitch: 1. The distance between the rows of seats on an aircraft. 2. The side-to-side motion of a ship.

PNR: See passenger name record (PNR).

point-to-point fares: Airfares that are calculated from origin to the first stop point, from the first stop point to the second stop point, and so on.

port: 1. The left side of a ship or other vehicle when facing forward. 2. A harbor and docking area for ships.

port charges: Fees levied by each port of call applicable to all cruise passengers, paid as part of the cruise fare.

ports of call: Cities or islands where cruise ships stop and passengers may go ashore.

preexisting conditions: Medical conditions that existed prior to the purchase of insurance.

preferred vendor list: A list of travel vendors with which a travel agency prefers to do business.

Prepaid Ticket Advice (PTA): An accountable ARC document that is used to purchase air travel at a travel agency in one city and the airline issues the ticket for the passenger in a different city.

pressurize: The process of equalizing air pressure inside an aircraft while airborne to what it would be on the ground.

primary codes: The first, or only, letters of a fare basis code that indicate first-class, business-class, or coach-class seating as well as the airfare being purchased. Also known as a booking code or booking class.

private charter: The leasing of any mode of transportation by a group of individuals traveling together.

prohibited items: Certain items are prohibited from carry-on luggage for the overall security of air travelers. Prohibited items include weapons, explosives, and incendiaries, but also items that are seemingly harmless and may be used as weapons like hammers, bats, or mace. These items may not be carried to security checkpoints.

promotional fares: Special fares offered by airlines, Amtrak, and others that provide incentives to travel on specified days or to specified locations.

proposal: A suggestion or offer of a travel product to the client based on the information learned by the travel counselor during the qualification process.

proof of citizenship: Any document that proves the holder's citizenship: original birth certificate, certified copy of a birth certificate, passport, and naturalization certificate.

proof of financial responsibility: A requirement for renting a car, such as a major credit card or cash deposit.

pseudocity code: A travel agency's identification to a CRS.

PTA: See Prepaid Ticket Advice (PTA).

public charter: A packaged trip utilizing nonscheduled transportation that can be purchased by the public.

Q

qualify the traveler: The process of determining the traveler's wants, needs, level of travel experience, and knowledge.

R

rail fare: The basic fare paid on Amtrak for travel in coach or as an add-on for first-class travel.

received from field: A PNR field that contains the name of the person who made the reservation.

reconfirm: The process of contacting the airline to verify flight numbers, departure time, and arrival time of a reservation.

record locator: A unique identification for the particular PNR in a GDS.

refuel charge: An additional fee charged by some car rental companies for refueling.

Refund–Exchange Notice (REN): A nonaccountable ARC document used to process refunds and exchange transactions via the ARC report.

regional airlines: Small airlines, sometimes called commuter airlines, that operate short-haul routes.

registry: The listing of a ship with a specific country for tax purposes.

REN: See Refund–Exchange Notice (REN).

representative company: An organization that represents various independent accommodation properties with promotion and advertising, centralized booking capabilities, and commission processing.

reservation sales agents: Sales professionals for travel-related companies.

reservation worksheet: A form, usually designed by a travel agency, that is used to accumulate data about a client and the booking being made.

resorts: Accommodations that are designed to be destinations unto themselves.

restricted inventory: A limited number of seats on a flight that can be sold at a specified fare.

resume: A summary of a person's personal and professional qualifications, written in a specified format and used for the purpose of obtaining a job.

revision fee: A charge made by a travel vendor when a booking must be altered in some way.

rider: An addition to an existing insurance policy for a specific type of coverage.

roll: The side-to-side motion of a ship.

round-trip: A type of air trip from the origin to the destination and back to the origin.

S

Sabre: One of the major GDSs.

Sales Report Settlement Authorization: A nonaccountable ARC document that is used to report a travel agency's weekly sales.

search engine: An Internet function that allows a user to search Web sites by name or subject matter.

seat assignments: Automated identification of passengers' assigned row numbers and seats on a flight.

security: All measures taken by airlines, cruise lines, railroads, and others to protect travelers from danger or injury.

security fee: A special fee that is added to international base airfares for both outgoing and incoming passengers.

segment: The portion of an air itinerary between board and deplane points.

segment fee: A fee that applies to all passengers for each flight boarded and all en route stops.

self catering: a type of lodging that may be rented by the week and includes nearly everything that is necessary for daily living except food; the size may vary from one room to a suite of rooms

service fees: Fees charged by a travel agency to the client.

Shinkansen: The high speed train of Japan; also known as the bullet train.

shore excursions: Optional excursions and sightseeing trips at various ports of call offered for sale onboard cruises.

Sierra Madre Express: The Mexican train that passes through the Copper Canyon.

sine or sign: The user's identification to the GDS.

single connection: A type of flight pattern that involves a single change of planes.

single supplement: An additional charge for a travel product when one person is traveling alone.

single's policy: A vendor's policy for single travelers.

sister fares: Airfares with identical rules except for the day of the week, season, or time of day in which they are applicable.

skycaps: Airport employees who check baggage at the curbside.

socialized medicine: Government-funded (all or part) health care.

software: The program used by a computer to perform specific tasks.

Sold Inside, Ticketed/e-tkted Inside (SITI): An IATA trip classification that indicates a trip that is sold inside and ticketed inside the country where the itinerary begins.

Sold Inside, Ticketed/e-tkted Outside (SITO): An IATA trip classification that indicates a trip that is sold inside and ticketed outside the country where the itinerary begins.

Sold Outside, Ticketed/e-tkted Inside (SOTI): An IATA trip classification that indicates a trip that is sold outside and ticketed inside the country where the itinerary begins.

Sold Outside, Ticketed/e-tkted Outside (SOTO): An IATA trip classification that indicates a trip that is sold outside and ticketed outside the country where the itinerary begins.

special equipment: Additional features offered on rental cars such as ski racks, infant seats, hand controls, and so on.

special-interest tour: A type of tour designed to attract particular types of clients, or those interested in a specific subject or activity.

special programs: Discounts offered by cruise lines for a variety of reasons.

speculative bookings: Unethical bookings, sometimes called fictitious bookings, whereby a reservation is made in case the client might travel.

splitting and combining excursion fares: An airfare pricing technique in which one half of an excursion fare is used on the outbound, combined with one half of a different excursion fare on the inbound.

stabilizers: Devices on a ship that reduce or eliminate roll.

standard: The largest size category of rental cars.

stand-by fare: An international airfare in which the traveler purchases a ticket but does not have a reservation. The traveler waits at the airport in hopes of being confirmed.

starboard: The right side of a ship or vehicle when facing forward.

STAR Service (www.starserviceonline.com): an online reference covering 10,000 hotels in 100 countries; no advertising is accepted, and opinion and commentary on each property is done by its own correspondents

staterooms: Passengers' rooms on a cruise ship.

stern: The rear of a ship.

Superliner: Bi-level Amtrak equipment that operates on routes west of Chicago.

supply-and-demand: The relationship between the availability of a product to the desire for that product.

surface segment: A portion of a flight itinerary where no commercial flight exists.

sustainable tourism: See ecotourism.

T

TAP test: See Travel Agent Proficiency (TAP) test.

tarmac: The paved area around an airport.

TASF: See Travel Agency Service Fee (TASF) document.

taxiway: The connecting road between the tarmac and the runway.

TBA: See to be assigned (TBA).

telephone etiquette: The conventional rules of telephone usage.

tender: A small vessel, usually accommodating 100 people, that takes cruise passengers to shore while the ship is at anchor.

terminal: The central part of an airport.

TGV: See Train à Grande Vitesse (TGV).

theme cruises: Cruises that focus on a particular topic, activity, type of music, or other theme.

ticket date field: The portion of a PNR that includes the date tickets issued and paid for and possibly other ticketing-related information.

ticketless air travel: A type of air travel transaction in which the passenger has no flight coupons and the travel counselor does not issue any accounting documents.

time comparison: The process of determining the time in a different location, based on the local time.

timetable: A publication of departure and arrival times for various forms of transportation.

time zones: Divisions around the earth, all referenced to Greenwich Mean Time (GMT), that assist with calculating time comparison and elapsed flying time.

to be assigned (TBA): A cruise line policy in which the price is guaranteed but the cabin grade may be of equal or greater value. The actual cabin assignment is made on the day of sailing.

tour basing fare: A type of airfare that can only be purchased in conjunction with a tour.

tour escorts: Tour company employees who travel with tour groups throughout the trip.

tour guide: A tour company employee who joins the group for a short period of time.

tour operator: A company that packages and markets tour products.

tourist card: A type of documentation required of all incoming visitors by some countries.

trade publications: Magazines and Web sites designed for employees of the travel industry.

trade shows: Events for suppliers of travel products and services to promote their products to travel professionals.

trade winds: Air currents that flow in a westward direction.

Traffic Conference Areas: Divisions of the world that have been established by IATA.

Train à Grande Vitesse (TGV): High speed trains operated by the French National Railway.

transient: 1. A type of accommodation that caters to short stays and travelers "just passing through." 2. A traveler who stays only one or perhaps two nights in an accommodation.

Transportation Security Administration (TSA): The Transportation Security Administration is a government agency created in 2001 to "protect the nation's transportation systems by ensuring the freedom of movement for people and commerce."

Travel Agency Service Fee (TASF) document: A nonaccountable ARC document that is used to process travel agency service fees via a special ARC report.

Travel Agent Proficiency (TAP) test: A tool developed by several travel organizations to evaluate skills and knowledge required to be a travel counselor. The test is administered by ICTA.

travel counselor: Travel professional who sells travel products and services to the traveling public.

Travel Institute: A professional travel organization that provides continuing educational opportunities, testing, and identification for travel professionals.

travel insurance: An insurance policy designed to protect travelers against adverse events such as cancellation and interruption, and to reimburse medical expenses, the loss or damage of property, and transit delays. Travelers are compensated if they have to cancel or interrupt their travel, if they need emergency medical treatment or medical evacuation, and in other situations.

travel scams: Fraudulent travel schemes designed to convince potential travelers to pay for a product or service that is never rendered; an attempt to intentionally mislead travelers.

travel season: Various tour or cruise departure dates with a common price.

trip protection: An insurance package offered by a vendor or a major insurance company that usually covers trip cancellation or interruption, medical, flight, and baggage. Trip protection offered by major insurance companies may also include coverage against vendor bankruptcy.

triple reduction: A discount when more than two people are traveling together on a tour.

TSA: See Travel Security Administration (TSA).

turnaround point: The farthest destination from the origin on a flight itinerary.

U

U.S. Arrival Tax: A tax charged to all air passengers arriving in the United States from abroad.

U.S. Customs Fee: A charge levied to all air and cruise passengers arriving in the United States from abroad.

U.S. Departure Tax: A tax charged to all air passengers leaving the United States.

U.S. Immigration Fee: A fee levied against all air passengers arriving in the United States from abroad.

U.S. State Department: The United States Department of State, often referred to as the State Department, is the Cabinet-level foreign affairs agency of the United States government, equivalent to foreign ministries in other countries, administered by the United States Secretary of State.

U.S. Transportation Tax: A tax charged to all air passengers traveling within the 48 contiguous states, from the 48 contiguous states to cities in the Buffer Zone, entirely within Hawaii, and entirely within Alaska.

unaccompanied minors: Children over 5 and under 12 who are traveling alone.

Uniform Resource Locator (URL): The address of a Web site.

United States Air Consolidators Association (USACA): An organization of air consolidators and other affiliated companies.

United States Tour Operators Association (USTOA): An organization of travel vendors and sellers who promote reliability and security within the travel industry.

United States Travel Security Administration (TSA): See Travel Security Administration (TSA).

upper/lower: Bunk beds on a cruise ship.

URL: See Uniform Resource Locator (URL).

USACA: See United States Air Consolidators Association (USACA).

USTOA: See United States Tour Operators Association (USTOA).

V

vacation protection: See trip protection.

validation: The process of imprinting an ARC document with the date of issue, travel agency information, and vendor data.

value added tax (VAT): A type of tax that is charged on goods and services in some countries.

VAT: See value added tax (VAT).

vendors: Supplier of a travel products.

vendor bankruptcy: To operate under Chapter 11 or to cease operations under Chapter 7.

Venice-Simplon Orient Express: The refurbished Orient Express that travels between Venice and London.

VIA Rail Canada: The passenger rail system of Canada.

Viewliner: Amtrak equipment used on routes in the Eastern United States.

visa: Official written permission of a government for a traveler to enter that country for a specific reason and length of time.

visa service or visa expediter: A company that obtains a visa or visas for a traveler at a price.

W

wait-list: An airline list of passengers who hope to be confirmed on a specific flight as cancellations are received. Passengers using excursion fares cannot be placed on a wait-list.

waiver of responsibility: A legal document that relieves a travel agency or vendor of liability under certain circumstances.

walking the guest: An accommodation policy in which the guest is taken to another property of equal or greater value when the booked property is oversold.

Web banners: Unsolicited advertisements that appear on Web pages.

Web site: A location on the World Wide Web.

weekend rate: A rental car rate that is priced per 24-hour period and is applicable to rentals that begin after noon on Thursday and conclude before noon on Monday.

weekly rate: A rental car rate that is priced per five, six, or seven 24-hour periods.

wet lease: The leasing of transportation complete with a crew.

WHO: See World Health Organization (WHO).

wide-body aircraft: An aircraft that has two aisles.

World Health Organization (WHO): A department of the United Nations that is responsible for monitoring worldwide health standards and making recommendations accordingly.

Worldspan: One of the four major GDSs.

World Wide Web (www): The Internet function that manages the vast amount of information available to users.

www: See World Wide Web (www).

Y

youth fares: International airfares for travelers under 26 years old that cannot be booked more than 24 hours before departure.

Index

Note: Figures or tables are indicated by "f" or "t" following the page number.

A

AAA. *See* American Automobile Association
AAA Guidebooks, 150
Aberdare National Park, Kenya, 60
Abu Simbel, Egypt, 52
Accident insurance, 197
Accommodations
  charge codes, 151
  cruise ships, 234–235
  key concepts, 151–153
  lodging industry, 148
  property organization/ownership/
    management, 149–150
  rates, 151
  rating systems, 150–151
  reference tools, 153–154
  reservations, 155–156
  security in, 34, 156
  selection, 155
  tour, 207, 209
  types, 148–149
Accountable documents, 138
Acela, 175
Action summary, 249
Adjoining rooms, 152
Advance Purchase Excursion (APEX)
  fares, 297
Advertising
  careers in, 11
  of Web sites, 26
  on World Wide Web, 22–23
Affiliated property, 150
Africa, cruise area of, 231
Aft, 234
Agency identification plate, 138, 138f
AIDS, 267
Air add-on, 208, 297
Aircraft. *See* Commercial aircraft
Aircraft charters, 194–195
Airfares, 118–124
  basis codes, 119–120
  combinability rules, 123
  computer displays, 123, 124f
  construction of, 120–123
  inventory control, 118–119
  normal versus excursion, 118
  sister fares, 120
  See also International airfares
Airline clubs, 84
Airline Deregulation Act (1978), 77

Airline identification plate, 138
Airline rate desk, 301
Airlines
  agreements among, 77
  categories of, 77
  codes, 77–78, 280, 281–284t, 284
  operations of, 79–80
  policies of, 78–79
Airlines Reporting Corporation (ARC)
  Amtrak and, 175, 181
  appointment powers of, 7, 72–73
  area settlement bank, 140
  certification by, 16
  consolidators appointed by, 193
  credit memo, 140
  debit memo, 140
  functions of, 73
  Interactive Agent Reporting, 140
  organization of, 72–73
  reports of air sales, 140–141
  ticketless travel, 136
  ticket stock, 138, 138f
  VIA Rail Canada and, 181
  See also ARC Industry Agents' Handbook
Airline tickets
  information on, 139
  issuance of, 7
  See also Ticketing
Airport authority, 84
Airport codes, 84–85, 86f, 280, 281–284t, 284
Airport hotels, 149
Airports
  arrivals, 84
  cities served by multiple, 85
  codes for, 84–85, 86f, 280, 281–284t, 284
  departures, 83–84
  diagrams of, 83
  international versus domestic, 276
  ownership of, 84
  services offered by, 84
Air traffic control, 84
Air Transport Association (ATA), 77
Air travel
  for cruises, 248
  flight schedules, 99, 101, 104
  security for, 33–34, 34f, 76, 83–84, 266
  taxes, 125–127
Ajanta Caves, Mumbai, India, 63
À la carte, 153
Alamo, San Antonio, Texas, 59

Alaska
  cruise area of, 231
  Denali National Park, 61
  Inside Passage, 62
Alaska/Hawaii International Travel Facilities
  Tax, 125–126
Alaskan tax, 125–126
Alberta
  Banff National Park, 61
  Jasper National Park, 61
  Wood Buffalo National Park, 62
Alcazar, Segovia, Spain, 55
Alcohol, 235, 238
Alhambra Palace, Grenada, Spain, 55
Alien Registration Card, 250
All-inclusive resorts, 149
All-suite hotels, 149
Altitude sickness, 268
Altun Ha, Belize, 52
Amadeus, 20
Amazon River, Brazil, 62
Amboselli National Park, Kenya, 61
Amenities, 152, 155
American Association of Port Authorities
  (AAPA), 34
American Association of Retired Persons
  (AARP), 165, 247
American Automobile Association (AAA), 150,
  165, 166, 180
American Hotel and Lodging Association
  (AH&LA), 156
American Orient Express (train), 184
American Society of Travel Agents (ASTA), 15,
  22, 24, 36, 39, 193, 209, 246, 320
Amnesty bins, 271
Amtrak
  Auto Train, 179
  baggage, 180
  cell phones, 180
  corridor train service, 177–178
  discounted/promotional fares, 180–181
  fares, 179–180
  food, 178, 178f
  handicapped accommodations, 180
  history of, 174–175
  long-distance service, 178
  National Timetable, 175, 177, 177f
  pets, 180
  reservations, 181
  route system, 175, 176f, 177

Amtrak (*continued*)
  security on, 181
  sleeping accommodations, 179f
  smoking, 180
  stations, 180
  tipping, 180
Anasazi cliff dwellers, 52, 53
The Andalusian Express (train), 185
Angel Falls, Venezuela, 62
Animal Plant and Health Inspection Service
    (APHIS) Fee, 126, 300
Animals
  pets, 78–79, 155, 180, 276
  service, 79
Ankor Wat, Cambodia, 52
Ann Frank House, Amsterdam, Netherlands, 59
Antarctica, cruise area of, 231
Anuradhapura, Sri Lanka, 63
Anxiety, over international travel, 270, 272
Appearance, personal, 14, 333
ARC. *See* Airline Reporting Corporation
Arc de Triomphe, Paris, France, 59
Archeological sites, 52–54
Archipelago, 47
ARC Industry Agents' Handbook, 126, 141, 301
Area settlement bank, ARC, 140
Arizona, Grand Canyon National Park, 61
Arizona Memorial, Honolulu, Oahu, Hawaii, 59
Arlington, Virginia, 60
ARNK, 105, 139
Around-the-world fares, 298
Arrivals, 84
Art, 60
ARUNK. *See* ARNK
Asia, cruise areas of, 231
Athens, Greece, 53
ATMs (automated teller machines), 269
Atoll, 47
Atomium, Brussels, Belgium, 55
Attachments, e-mail, 22
Auschwitz, Poland, 59
Australia
  cruise area of, 231
  Kakadu National Park, 61
  outback, 63
  Uluru, 63
Aviation and Transportation Security Act
    (2001), 32, 76
Aztec civilization, 54

B
B&Bs, 148
Backhaul, 299
Back-to-back excursions, 106, 121, 121f
Back-to-back ticketing, 106
Baggage
  airline policies on, 79
  Amtrak policy on, 180
  cruises, 249–250
  insurance for, 197
  international versus domestic policies on,
    276, 303
Baha'i Temple, Haifi, Israel, 63
Bahamas, cruise area of, 231
Baltimore, Maryland, 60
Banff National Park, Alberta, Canada, 61

Bank buying rate (BBR), 297
Bankruptcies, insurance for, 197–198
Battle of the Bulge, Bastogne, Belgium, 59
Bay, 47
B.C.E., meaning of, 52
Beaches, 54–55
Bed & breakfasts (B&Bs), 148
Beijing, China, 53
Belize
  Altun Ha, 52
  Xunantunich, 54
*Berlitz Complete Guide to Cruising and Cruise
    Ships*, 230
Bermuda, cruise area of, 231
Berths, 234–235
Best Western, 150
Bias, 76
Big Ben, London, England, 55
Biltmore Mansion, Asheville, North
    Carolina, 55
Biometrics, 34
Black Forest, Germany, 62
Blarney Castle, Ireland, 55
Blenheim, England, 55
Blue Mosque, Istanbul, Turkey, 63
Blue Train (train), 185
Boarding pass, 79
Bognor Botanical Garden and Orchid House,
    Jakarta, Indonesia, 55
Bon voyage gift, 249
Booking. *See* Reservations
Booking class codes, 101, 119, 299
Border security, 35
Borobudur, Java, Indonesia, 63
Boston, Massachusetts
  Faneuil Hall Marketplace, 56
  historical sites, 59
Bow, 234
Brazil
  Amazon River, 62
  Christ the Redeemer, Rio de Janeiro, 63
  Iguazu Falls, 62
Breakers, Newport, Rhode Island, 55
Breaking the fare, 106, 121, 121f
Bridge, 235
British Columbia
  Butchart Gardens, Victoria, 55
  Capiland Suspension Bridge, Vancouver, 55
  Inside Passage, 62
Britrail pass, 184
Brochures
  cruise, 229
  tour, 206, 209–210
Brooklyn Bridge, New York City, New
    York, 55
Browsers, 21
Bryce Canyon National Park, Utah, 61
Buckingham Palace, London, England, 55
Buddha's Universal Church, San Francisco,
    California, 63
Budget fare, 297
Buffer zone, 126
Buildings and structures, 55–58
Bulkheads, 81, 83, 234
Bulk rates, 192
Bumping passengers, 80

Bush, George W., 32
Business-class cabin, 83
Business Enterprises for Sustainable Tourism
    (BEST), 38
Business Travel Planner, 106
Butchart Gardens, Victoria, British
    Columbia, 55
Buying signals, 318–319

C
Cabin category, 246
Cabins, 80
Calgary Airport Improvement Fee, 126
California
  Buddha's Universal Church, San Francisco,
    63
  Fisherman's Wharf, San Francisco, 56
  Golden Gate Bridge, San Francisco, 56
  Hearst Castle, California, 56
  Mann's Chinese Theatre, Hollywood, 56
  Yosemite National Park, 62
Cambodia, 52
Canada
  air travel taxes, 126
  Amtrak, 181
  cruise areas, 231–232
  rail travel, 181–182
Canadian (train), 182
Cancellation fee, 208
Cancellation policy, 153
Canrailpass, 181
Canyon, 47
Cape, 47
Capiland Suspension Bridge, Vancouver, British
    Columbia, 55
Cappadocia, Turkey, 62
Caraquet, New Brunswick, 59
Caravan Tours, 211f
Careers
  cruise industry, 10–11
  diversity of, 4, 5t
  event planners, 7–8
  flight attendants, 10
  job search, 11–15
  meeting facilitators, 7–8
  meeting planners, 7–8
  photographers, 11
  reservation sales agents, 8
  sales representatives, 8–9
  tour personnel, 9–10
  travel counselors, 6–7
  travel writers, 11
Cargo ships, 240
Caribbean, cruise areas of, 231–232
Carlsbad Caverns National Park, New
    Mexico, 61
Carousels, baggage, 84
Car rental. *See* Rental cars
Carthage, Tunisia, 52
Casinos, on cruises, 235
Cathedral of San Giovanni, Turin, Italy, 63
Cay (caye), 47
C.E., meaning of, 52
Cell phones, 36, 180
Celsius scale, 47
Cendant Corporation, 148

Centers for Disease Control, 266, 267
  International Travelers Hot Line, 36
Central America, cruise area of, 233
Certification, 15–16
Certified ARC specialist (CAS), 16
Certified Tour Professional (CTP) certificate, 9–10
Certified Travel Associate (CTA) program, 15
Certified Travel Counselor (CTC) program, 15
Certified Travel Specialist (CTS) program, 15
Chaco Ruins, New Mexico, 52
Chain property, 150
Chaleur (train), 182
Chambord, France, 55
Chan Chan, Peru, 52
Change, in travel industry, 4
Channel Tunnel train, 182f
Charters
  aircraft, 194–195
  association memberships of, 195
  booking private, 194
  drawbacks of, 194
  motorcoach/rail/cruise, 195
  private, 194–195
  public, 194–195
  travel agency, 195
Chartres Cathedral, Chartres, France, 63
Check-in time, international versus domestic, 276
Chenonceaux, France, 55
Chicago, Illinois, Sears Tower, 57
Chichén Itzá, Yucatán, Mexico, 52
Children
  accommodation rates for, 151
  airline policies on, 78
  Amtrak fares for, 180
  on cruises, 236
  ear pain during air travel, 268
  international airfares for, 298
  international versus domestic air policies on, 276
  Mexican travel with, 261
  passports for, 261
  rental car policies and, 166
  vaccinations for, 266
Chile
  Easter Island (Rapa Nui), 52
  Torres del Paine, 61
China
  Forbidden City, Beijing, 56
  Great Wall of China, 59
  Ming Tombs, Beijing, 53
  Tiananmen Square, Beijing, 60
  Wolong Natural Reserve, 62
  Xi'an Tomb, 54
  Yangtzee River Gorges, 63
Choice Hotels International, 150
Cholera, 266
Christ the Redeemer, Rio de Janeiro, Brazil, 63
Chrysler Building, New York City, New York, 56
Church of the Holy Sepulcher, Jerusalem, Israel, 63
Church of the Nativity, Bethlehem, Israel, 63
Churning, 105
Circle-trip minimum, 299

Circle trips, 100, 122, 122f, 298
City codes, 280, 281–284t, 284
City-commercial hotels, 149
City pair, 99
CLIA Cruise Manual, 229
Closed-ended questions, 315
Closing the sale, 318–319
Clothing, 14, 333
CN Tower, Toronto, Ontario, 56
Coach-class cabin, 83
Codes
  accommodations, 151
  airline, 77–78
  airport, 84–86
  booking class, 101, 119, 299
  city, 84–85
  fare basis, 119–120, 299–300
  international city/airport/airline, 280, 281–284t, 284
  primary, 299
Code sharing, 78, 78f
Cohosts, 74
College of Disney Knowledge, 16
Collision damage waiver (CDW), 166
Colorado
  Mesa Verde, 53
  Rocky Mountain National Park, 61
Colosseum, Rome, Italy, 52
Combinability rules, 123
Combined tax item, 300, 304
Commercial aircraft, 80–83
  international versus domestic, 276
  narrow-body, 80, 82, 82f, 276
  popular, 81f
  wide-body, 80, 82, 82f, 276
Commissions
  as agency revenue source, 75
  airlines not paying, 140, 141
  on charters, 194, 195
  compensation linked to, 6
  consolidators and, 193
  cruises, 229
  fees in relation to, 75
  freighter companies not paying, 240
  hotel sales, 148, 150, 151, 154, 155
  on insurance, 196
  for multiline sales reps, 9
  override, 75, 101
  rail travel, 181, 183, 184
  rates for, 6
  for rental counter agents, 166
  tours, 212
  vendor payments of, 75
Communication
  e-mail, 22
  telephone etiquette, 332–333
  telephone selling, 320–321
  travel counselors and, 314
  written, appearance of, 333
Commuter airlines, 77
Compact car, 164
Complaints, handling, 331–332
Computer reservations/ticketing, 20
Computer Reservation Systems (CRS), 20, 73
Computer skills, 5
Concierge, 152

Concourse, 83
Confidentiality, 5
Configuration, of aircraft, 80–82
Confirmation letter, for tour reservation, 214
Confirmation number, 152, 208, 249
Congo, Virunga National Park, 61
Connecting rooms, 152
Connection time
  international versus domestic, 276
  minimum, 99
Consolidators
  association memberships of, 193
  drawbacks of, 192
  evaluating, 192–193
  largest, 192
  operations of, 192
  policies of, 193
  profits for travel agencies from, 193
  reference source on, 192
Consortia, 75
Consular Information Sheets, 265–266
Consulates, 265, 269–270
Contact lenses, 268
Continents, 46
Continuing education, 15–16
Contraband, 250, 271
  See also Prohibited items
Convention hotels, 149
Convention rate, 151
Conventions, housing bureaus for, 153
Copan, Honduras, 52
Corporate rate, 151
Corporate travel counselors/managers, 7
Corridor trains, 175, 177–178
Couchette, 183
Cover letter, 14, 14f
Crater Lake, Oregon, 62
Credit cards
  insurance cover through, 198
  insurance provided by, 166, 198
  as proof of financial responsibility, 167
  security and, 21, 24–25, 36, 37
Crete (Kriti), Greece, 53
Crime, precautions against, 35–36
Cruise areas, 230–233
Cruise industry
  charters, 195
  employment advantages/disadvantages, 11
  growth of, 10, 228
  job descriptions, 10
  major lines, 230
  salary/benefits, 11
  training, 10–11, 16
  travel insurance sales by, 196
  See also Cruises
Cruise Lines International Association (CLIA), 193, 229, 246
  Cruise Counselor Certification Program, 16
Cruises
  accommodations, 234–235
  air travel for, 248
  bars/lounges, 235
  benefits of, 228–229
  casinos, 235
  cruise areas, 230–233
  departures, 249–250

Cruises (*continued*)
    disadvantages of, 229
    discounts, 247
    documents, 249
    electricity, 235–236
    entertainment, 236
    fare calculation, 247–249
    finances, 236–237
    follow-up, 249
    food, 237–238, 237f
    hair salons, 238
    information sources, 229–230
    key concepts, 234f
    laundry, 238
    library, 238
    loyalty programs, 247
    medical services, 238
    phone/fax/computer, 238–239
    pricing of, 246–247
    recordkeeping, 249
    religious services, 239
    reservations, 248–249
    security on, 34, 250
    selling, 246–249
    ships, 234, 234f
    shops, 239
    spas/fitness facilities, 239
    special programs, 235, 247
    theme, 235
    tipping, 239–240
    types, 230
    weight gain from, 238
    See also Cruise industry
Cruise Travel, 230
Cuba, 250
Currency
    on cruises, 236–237
    for international travel, 268–269
    neutral unit of construction, 299
    security involving, 36, 37
Customer expectations, 330–331
Customer service, 330–334
    business retention through, 76
    commitment to, 330–331
    communication skills, 314
    confirmation, 214
    on cruises, 228
    cruise sales, 249
    defining, 330
    expectations and, 330–331
    follow-up, 214, 331
    handling complaints, 331–332
    impression management, 333
    for irate customers, 332
    supporting the customer, 319–320
    telephone etiquette, 332–333
Customer service agents, 8
Customs, 250, 271
Customs, social, 270
Customs declaration form, 271

D
Dacau, Germany, 59
Daily rate, for rental cars, 165
Debarkation, 231, 250
Deck, 234

Deck plan, 234
Defaults, insurance for, 197–198
Delphi, Greece, 52
Delta, 47
Denali National Park, Alaska, 61
Denied boarding compensation (DBC), 80
Department of Homeland Security, 33, 33f, 34,
    76, 266
Department of Transportation (DOT), 76
Departures, 83–84
Deposit, for tours, 208
Destinations, 52–65
    archeological sites/mysterious places, 52–54
    beaches, 54–55
    buildings/structures/gardens, 55–58
    culture, 60
    gaming, 58
    golf, 58–59
    historical sites, 59–60
    national parks, 60–62
    natural treasures, 62–63
    religious sites, 63–64
    scuba and snorkeling, 64
    theme parks, 64–65
    winter sports, 65
Destination Specialist program, 15
Diamond Head, Honolulu, Oahu, Hawaii, 62
Diarrhea, 267
Direct access, 74
Direct flights, 99
Disney Specialist, 16
District sales managers (DSMs), 9
Documentation for international travel,
    260–264
    GDS information on, 265
    passport, 261, 262–263f, 264
    proof of citizenship, 260–261
    reference sources on, 260, 265
    tourist card, 261
    visa, 264–265
Document packet, 208
Doge's Palace, Venice, Italy, 56
Domains, Web, 25, 26
Dome of the Rock (Mosque of Omar),
    Jerusalem, Israel, 63
Dos and Taboos Around the World (Axtell), 270
Dot com, 26
Dot travel, 26
Double connections, 99
Double decker bus, 205f
Double open-jaw trips, 298
Draft, 234
Draft, of ship, 234
Dress, 14, 333
Driving regulations/customs, international, 166
Drop charge, 166
Dry lease, 195
Dual-designated carriers, 78
Duplicate bookings, 105
Duty-free allowance, 271
Dynamic packages, 204, 205–206

E
Easter Island (Rapa Nui), Chile, 52
E-commerce, 24–26
    advantages, 24

    travel agencies affected by, 24–25
    Web site development, 25–26
Economy car, 164
Ecotourism, 37–39
    certification of, 38–39
    defining, 38
    ecotourists, 39
    growth of, 32
    guidelines for, 39
    organizations concerned with, 38
Ecotourism Society, 39
Education, professional, 15–16
Egypt
    Abu Simbel, 52
    Great Pyramids, Giza, 53
    Khalili Bazaar, Cairo, 56
    Sphinx, Giza, 53
    St. Catherine's Monastery, Sinai, 64
    Temple of Karnak, Karnak, 54
    Temple of Luxor, Luxor, 54
    Valleys of the Kings, Queens, and
        Nobles, 54
Eiffel Tower, Paris, France, 56
Elapsed flying time, 104, 280, 280t
Electricity
    on cruises, 235
    on international travel, 270–271
Electronic ticket (e-tkt), 137
Ellis Island, New York City, New York, 56
E-mail, 22
E-marketing, 24–26
    advantages, 24
    travel agencies affected by, 24–25
    Web site development, 25–26
Embarkation, 250
Embarkation point, 231
Embassies, 269–270
Empire State Building, New York City, New
    York, 56
End transaction, 105
England
    Big Ben, London, 55
    Blenheim, 55
    Buckingham Palace, London, 55
    Hadrian's Wall, 59
    Oxford University, Oxford, 57
    Piccadilly Circus, London, 57
    Roman Baths, Bath, 60
    Stonehenge, 54
    Stratford-upon-Avon, 60
    Tower Bridge, London, 57
    Trafalgar Square, London, 58
    Warwick Castle, 58
    Westminster Abbey, London, 64
    Windsor Castle, 58
En route stops, 99
Entrepreneurs, 4
Ephesus, Turkey, 52
Equator, 46
Escort, 204
Escorted tours, 204–205
Ethics, and booking/ticketing practices,
    105–106
e-tkt, 137
Eurailpass, 183–184
Euro, 269

Europe
  cruise areas of, 232
  currency in, 269
  place names, 48
  rail travel, 182–184
Eurostar High Speed Train, 182f
Event planners, 7–8
Everglades National Park, Florida, 61
Exchange rate, 268–269, 297, 299
Exchanges, 140
Excursion fares, 99, 118, 122
Expertise, of travel counselors, 314
Eye infections, 268

F
Fact-finding questions, 316
Fahrenheit scale, 47
Familiarization (FAM) trips, 6, 15
Faneuil Hall Marketplace, Boston,
    Massachusetts, 56
Fare-based test, 121–122, 122f
Fare basis codes (FBCs), 119–120, 119f,
    299–300
Fare construction
  around-the-world travel, 298
  circle trip, 122, 298
  double open-jaw travel, 298
  international, 298–299
  one-way travel, 120
  open-jaw travel, 121–122, 298
  open-jaw with side trip, 122–123
  round-trip travel, 121, 298
  travel counselor knowledge of, 120
Fare ladder, 139
Farelogix, 20
Fares
  Amtrak, 179–180
  cruise, 247–249
  international versus domestic, 276
  See also Airfares
Federal Aviation Administration (FAA),
    34, 76
Federal Bureau of Investigation (FBI), 34
Federal Trade Commission (FTC), 35
Feeling-finding questions, 316
Fees
  air travel, 125–127, 127f (see Service fees)
  cruise, 247
  international, 300–301
  travel agency service, 140
Female-friendly hotels, 154
Fern Grotto, Kauai, Hawaii, 62
Ferries, 240
Fictitious bookings, 105
Fictitious return trips, 106
50/50 guideline, 105
First aid kit, 268
First-class cabin, 82
Fisherman's Wharf, San Francisco,
    California, 56
FIT (foreign independent tour), 205
Fjord, 47
Fjordland National Park, New Zealand, 61
Fjords, Norway, 62
Flam Line (train), 185
Flexipass, 183

Flight attendants
  advantages/disadvantages, 10
  career advancement, 10
  job description, 10
  qualifications, 10
  salary/benefits, 10
  training, 10
Flight availability displays, 101, 102f, 302, 302f
Flight insurance, 197
Flight itinerary planning
  elapsed flying time, 104
  flight patterns, 98–99
  flight schedule selection, 101
  information sources, 106
  priorities for, 98
  reservations, 105–106
  time comparison, 101–104
  trip types, 99–100
Flight patterns, 98–99
Flight schedules
  domestic, 99, 101, 104
  international, 276, 278, 301–302
Florence, Italy, Ponte Vecchio, 57
Florida
  Everglades National Park, 61
  Kennedy Space Center, Cape Canaveral, 59
Follow-up, 214, 249, 331
Fontainebleau Palace, Paris, France, 56
Food
  air travel, 79, 82–83
  Amtrak, 178, 178f
  cruises, 237–238
  European trains, 183
  safety of, 267
  tours, 207, 210
Food and Drug Administration, 250
Forbidden City, Beijing, China, 56
Fort Sumter, South Carolina, 59
Forward, 234
France
  Arc de Triomphe, Paris, 59
  Chambord, 55
  Chartres Cathedral, Chartres, 63
  Chenonceaux, 55
  Eiffel Tower, Paris, 56
  Fontainebleau Palace, Paris, 56
  Jardin du Luxembourg, Paris, 56
  Lourdes, 63
  Monet's House, Giverny, 57
  Normandy Beacues, 60
  Notre Dame Cathedral, Paris, 63
  Sacré-Coeur, Paris, 64
  Versailles Palace, Paris, 58
Franchise properties, 150
Freighters, 240
Frequent flyer programs, 79, 152
Frequent guest programs, 152
Frommer's Cruises and Ports of Call, 230
Front desk clerks, 8, 9f
Fuel surcharge, 125
Full-size car, 164
Fuselage, 81

G
Galapagos Islands, Ecuador, 62
Galileo, 20

Galley, 235
Gambia, West Africa, 59
Gaming, 58
Ganges River, India, 63
Gangway, 235
Gardens, 55–58
Gate, airport, 83–84
Gate agents, 8, 84
Gateway Arch, St. Louis, Missouri, 56
Gateway city, 208, 297
GDS. See Global Distribution System (GDS)
Genesis Travel Distribution, 20
Geography
  definition of, 46
  European place names, 48
  interest in, by travel professionals, 6
  logical flight order based on, 297
  maps, 46–47
Geotourism, 38
Germany
  Black Forest, 62
  Dacau, 59
  Linderhof Palace, 56
  Neuschwanstein, 57
  Nymphenburg Palace, Munich, 57
  Passion Play, Oberammergau, 64
  Tiergarten, Berlin, 57
  Würzburg Residence, 58
Gettysburg, Pennsylvania, 59
Giant's Causeway, Northern Ireland, 52
Glacier, 47
Glasses, 268
Global Distribution System (GDS)
  bank buying rate in, 297
  bias in, 76
  development of, 20
  entry documentation in, 265
  fare construction, 120
  fare displays, 123, 124f
  flight availability displays, 101, 102f,
    302, 302f
  flight schedules in, 99, 101, 104
  functions of, 73–74, 74f
  international flight schedules in, 276
  reports of air sales, 141
  reservations through, 105
  total fares, 125
  in U.S., 74f
Global indicator, 297
Global issues, 32
Golden Gate Bridge, San Francisco,
    California, 56
Golf, 58–59
Goods and Services Tax (GST), 126
Gorée Island, Senegal, 59
Gota Canal, Sweden, 56
Government, security role of, 32–33
Grand Canyon National Park, Arizona, 61
Grand Central Station, New York City, New
    York, 56
Graumann's Chinese Theatre. See Mann's
    Chinese Theatre, Hollywood
Great Britain. See United Kingdom
Great Pyramids, Giza, Egypt, 53
Great Smoky Mountains National Park,
    Tennessee/North Carolina, 61

Great South Pacific Express (train), 185
Great Wall of China, China, 59
Great Zimbabwe, Zimbabwe, 53
Greece
 Delphi, 52
 Mycenae, 53
 Parthenon, Athens, 53
Green Globe 21, 38
Greenwich, England, Old Royal Observatory, 60
Greenwich Mean Time (GMT), 101, 104f, 279
Greenwich Meridian, 46
Gross registered tonnage (GRT), 234
Ground control, 84
Ground operators, 207
Group rate, 151
Group sales, 195–196
Guarantee, for accommodations, 153
Guaranteed share rate, 247
Guesthouses, 149
Guidebooks, for international travel, 303
Gulf, 47
Gulf Stream, 47
Gunn, David L., 174

H
Hadrian's Wall, England, 59
Halifax Citadel, Halifax, Nova Scotia, 59
Handicapped travelers, Amtrak
 accommodations for, 180
Hannibal, 52
Harmonized Sales Tax (HST), 126
Hawaii
 Arizona Memorial, Honolulu, Oahu, 59
 cruise area of, 232
 Diamond Head, Honolulu, Oahu, 62
 Fern Grotto, Kauai, 62
 Mauna Kea, Hawaii Island, 62
 Mauna Loa, Hawaii Island, 62
Hawaiian tax, 125–126
Health
 international travel and, 266–268
 precautions concerning, 36
 tips for, 268
Health insurance, 36, 197, 268
Health Insurance Association of
 America, 268
Hearst Castle, California, 56
Hell's Canyon, Idaho, 62
Hemispheres, 46
Higher intermediate point (HIP), 298–299
High season, 151
High-speed trains, 175, 182, 184
Historical sites, 59–60
HIV, 267
Hofburg Palace, Vienna, Austria, 56
Hollywood, California, Mann's Chinese
 Theatre, 56
Home, working from, 7
Home-based travel counselors, 7
Hoover Dam, Nevada, 56
Horizontal travelers, 228–229
Hospitality Franchise Systems, 150
Host, 204
Hosted tours, 204
Hostels, 148
Hosts, 74

Hotel and Travel Index (HTI), 150,
 153–154, 154f
Hotels
 airport, 149
 all-suite, 149
 city-commercial, 149
 convention, 149
 definition of, 149
 female-friendly, 154
 resort, 149
 security in, 34, 156
Hotel safes, 37
Housing bureau, 153
Hub and spoke principle, 79, 80f, 175
Hubs, on World Wide Web, 22

I
IATA. *See* International Air Transport
 Association
IATAN. *See* International Airline Travel
 Agent Network
Identity theft, 35, 198
Iguazu Falls, Brazil/Argentina, 62
Image interpretation software, 34
Inbound portion of trip, 100
Incan civilization, 53
Independent property, 150
Independent tours, 204
Independent travel counselors, 7
India
 Ajanta Caves, Mumbai, 63
 Ganges River, 63
 Jantar Mantar, Jaipur, 56
 Taj Mahal, Agra, 57
 Vishvanatha Temple, Varanasi (Kasi, 64
Indonesia, 55
Infants, airline policies on, 78
Information sources, 106, 301–303
Inside cabins, 234–235
Inside Passage, British Columbia/Alaska, 62
Insurance
 accident, 197
 baggage, 197
 for bankruptcies and defaults, 197–198
 demand for, 196
 flight, 197
 health, 36, 197, 268
 identity theft, 198
 importance of, 196
 preexisting conditions for, 197
 rental car, 166
 terrorism, 198
 tours, 196, 208
 travel, 35, 196–198
 trip cancellation/interruption, 196–197
 waivers, 198
Intelliguide, 154, 154f
Interactive Agent Reporting (IAR), 140
Intercontinental Hotel Group, 148
Interline agreements, 77, 77f
Intermediate-size car, 164
International airfares, 296–300
 airline rate desk, 301
 booking classes, 299
 fare basis codes, 299–300
 IATA trip classifications, 296–297, 303

key concepts, 297–299
seasonal, 299
International Airlines Travel Agent Network
 (IATAN)
 appointment powers of, 73, 276
 consolidators appointed by, 193
 education program, 15–16
 identification cards, 73
International Air Transport Association
 (IATA)
 administrative duties of, 73, 277
 appointment powers of, 276
 consolidators appointed by, 193
 and security, 34
 trip classifications by, 296–297, 303
International air travel
 aircraft, 276
 airports, 276
 baggage, 276
 check-in time, 276
 city/airport/airline codes, 280, 281–284t, 284
 connection time, 276
 domestic versus, 276–277
 elapsed flying time, 280
 fares, 276
 flight schedules, 301–302
 IATA role in, 277
 infants, 276
 information sources, 301–303
 pets, 276
 reconfirmation, 276
 schedules, 276
 security for, 84, 271
 ticketing, 276, 303–304
 time and, 278–280
 See also International airfares
International Association for Medical
 Assistance to Travelers (IAMAT), 268
International Certificate of Vaccination, 266
International Date Line (IDL), 46, 102,
 279, 279f
International Driver's Permit (IDP), 166
The International Ecotourism Society
 (TIES), 38
International fees, 300–301
International Standards Organization (ISO), 84
International taxes, 300–301, 300f
International Tourism Partnership, 38
International travel
 anxiety over, 270, 272
 dangers of, 265–266
 at destination, 270–271
 duty-free allowance, 271
 embassies/consulates, 269–270
 entry into foreign country, 270
 entry requirements, 260–264
 health issues, 266–268
 money issues, 268–269
 return home, 271
 State Department role in, 265–266
 travel counselor as information source
  for, 260
 See also International air travel
International Travelers Hot Line, Centers for
 Disease Control, 36
International Year of Ecotourism (2002), 32, 37

Internet
   connection technology for, 21
   on cruises, 236, 238–239
   developments in, 20–21
   e-commerce/e-marketing, 24–26
   e-mail, 22
   lodging industry and, 148
   niche markets and, 319
   privacy and security on, 24–25
   as reference tool, 22
   scams on, 22, 24, 26, 36, 208
   security on, 21, 24–25
   significance of, 20
   travel professionals and, 21–22
   viruses, 22
   See also World Wide Web
Internet Corporation for Assigned Names and
   Numbers (ICANN), 26
Internet Service Providers (ISPs), 21
Interstitials, 22–23
Interviews, job, 14–15
Intestinal problems, 267
Inventory control, 118–119, 118f
Iran
   Persepolis, 53
   Ur, 54
Irate customers, 332
Ireland
   Blarney Castle, 55
   cruise area of, 232
   Ring of Kerry, 63
   See also Northern Ireland
Israel
   Baha'i Temple, Haifi, 63
   Church of the Holy Sepulcher,
      Jerusalem, 63
   Church of the Nativity, Bethlehem, 63
   Dome of the Rock (Mosque of Omar),
      Jerusalem, 63
   Masada, 63
   Western Wall (also Wailing Wall),
      Jerusalem, 64
Istanbul, Turkey
   Blue Mosque, 63
   Topkapi Palace, 57
Isthmus, 47
Itinerary field, 105
Itinerary planning. *See* Flight itinerary
   planning

J
Jantar Mantar, Jaipur, India, 56
Japan
   Meiji Shrine, 63
   Mt. Fuji, 62
   Nijo Castle, Kyoto, 57
   rail travel, 184
   Todai-ji Temple, Nara, 64
   Zen Garden of Emptiness, Kyoto, 58
Japanese National Railway, 184
Jardin Botanique, Montreal, Quebec, 56
Jardin du Luxembourg, Paris, France, 56
Jasper National Park, Alberta, 61
Jet lag, 267
Jet stream, 47
Jetways, 84

Job search, 11–15
   cover letter, 14
   interview skills, 14–15
   resume, 12, 13f
Jokhang, Lhasa, Tibet, 63
Journalists. *See* Travel writers
Juma Mosque, Durban, South Africa, 63

K
Kakadu National Park, Australia, 61
Kanchanaburi, Thailand, 59
Keel, 234
Kennedy Space Center, Cape Canaveral,
   Florida, 59
Kentucky, Mammoth Cave National Park, 61
Kenya
   Aberdare National Park, 60
   Amboselli National Park, 61
   Masai Mara Game Reserve, 61
Keukenhof (Kitchen) Garden, Netherlands, 56
Khalili Bazaar, Cairo, Egypt, 56
Kilometers, 46
Knossos, Crete (Kriti), Greece, 53
"Know Before You Go," 250, 271
Kruger National Park, South Africa, 61

L
Lake Titicaca, Peru/Bolivia, 62
Land-air price, 208
Land mass distortion, 46
Land-only price, 208
Language, 271
Lapse rate, 47
La Sagrada Familla, Barcelona, Spain, 63
Last seat availability, 74
Leading Hotels of the World, 150
Leaning Tower of Pisa, Pisa, Italy, 56
Leg, of flight, 99
Le Jet d'Eau, Geneva, Switzerland, 56
Leptis Magna, Libya, 53
Linderhof Palace, Germany, 56
Listening skills, 316
Little Big Horn National Monument,
   Montana, 60
Load factor, 79–80
Local guide, 204
Local transportation, scams involving, 37
Lodging. *See* Accommodations
Lodging industry, 148
Logical geographical order, 297
London, England
   Big Ben, 55
   Buckingham Palace, 55
   Piccadilly Circus, 57
   Tower Bridge, 57
   Trafalgar Square, 58
   Westminster Abbey, 64
London Plus Pass, 184
Loss damage waiver (LDW), 166
Lourdes, France, 63
Luggage. *See* Baggage
Luxury car, 165

M
Machu Picchu, Peru, 53
Major airlines, definition of, 77

Malaria, 266
Mammoth Cave National Park, Kentucky, 61
Manners, 270
Mann's Chinese Theatre, Hollywood,
   California, 56
Maps, 46–47
Marble House, Newport, Rhode Island, 56
Marketing
   e-mail for, 22
   e-marketing, 24–26
Marketing groups, 75f
Markup, 75
Masada, Israel, 63
Masai Mara Game Reserve, Kenya, 61
Matterhorn, Switzerland, 62
Mauna Kea, Hawaii Island, Hawaii, 62
Mauna Loa, Hawaii Island, Hawaii, 62
Maximum permitted miles (MPM), 297
Mayan civilization, 52, 53, 54
Meal plans, 153
Meal service
   decrease in, 83
   special requests, 79
Measurement systems, 271
Mecca, Saudi Arabia, 63
Medical assistance, during international travel,
   197, 268
Medications, 36, 268
Medina, Saudi Arabia, 63
Mediterranean, cruise areas of, 232–233
Meet and assist service, 79
Meeting facilitators, 7–8
Meeting planners, 7–8
Meiji Shrine, Tokyo, Japan, 63
Meridian of Longitude, 46
Mesa Verde, Colorado, 53
Metroliner, 175
Mexican airport departure tax, 126
Mexican Domestic Transportation Tax, 126
Mexican International Transportation Tax, 126
Mexican Tourist Tax, 126
Mexico
   air travel taxes, 126
   Chichén Itzá, Yucatán, 52
   cruise area of, 233
   Palenque, Chiapas, 53
   Teotihuacan, Mexico City, 54
   Tulum, Quintana Roo, 54
   Uxmal, Yucatán, 54
Midships, 234
Midsize car, 164
Mileage-based test, 121–122, 122f
Milford Sound, New Zealand, 62
Ming Tombs, Beijing, China, 53
Minimum connecting time, 99
Minivan, 165
Miscellaneous Charges Order (MCO), 76,
   136, 140
The Mobile Guide, 150
Modems, 21
Moenjodaro, Pakistan, 53
Monet's House, Giverny, France, 57
Money
   currency on cruises, 236–237
   foreign purchases, 269
   international currency, 268–269

Money (*continued*)
    scams and crime involving, 36, 37
    tips on, 269
Monteverde Cloud Forest Reserve, Costa
        Rica, 61
Montreal, Quebec, Jardin Botanique, 56
Monuments, security at, 35
Mormon Tabernacle, Salt Lake City, Utah, 63
Motels, 148–149
Motorcoach charters, 195
Mt. Cook National Park, New Zealand, 61
Mt. Everest, Nepal, 62
Mt. Fuji, Japan, 62
Mt. Kilimanjaro, Tanzania, 62
Mt. Rushmore, South Dakota, 60
Multiline sales representatives, 9
Museums, 60
Music, 60
Mycenae, Greece, 53
Mysterious places, 52–54

N

Name field, 105
Narrow-body aircraft, 80, 82, 82f, 276
National airlines, 77
National Association of Commissioned Agents
        (NACTA), 7
National Association of Retired Persons
        (NARP), 180
National Audubon Society, 39
National Geographic Society, 38
National parks, 60–62
National Railroad Passenger Corporation
        (Amtrak), 174
National Security Administration (NSA), 84
National Tour Association (NTA), 9, 193, 195,
        198, 208–209
National Transportation Safety Board (NTSB),
        76–77
Natural treasures, 62–63
Nazca Lines, Peru, 53
Negotiated hotel rates, 151
Nepal
    Mt. Everest, 62
    Royal Chitwan National Park, 61
Netherlands
    Ann Frank House, Amsterdam, 59
    Keukenhof (Kitchen) Garden, 56
    Space Tower, Rotterdam, 57
Net rate, 75
Neuschwanstein, Germany, 57
Neutral unit of construction (NUC), 299
New Mexico
    Carlsbad Caverns National Park, 61
    Chaco Ruins, 52
Newport, Rhode Island
    Breakers, 55
    Marble House, 56
New York City, New York
    Brooklyn Bridge, 55
    Chrysler Building, 56
    Ellis Island, 56
    Empire State Building, 56
    Grand Central Station, 56
    Statue of Liberty, 57
    St. Patrick's Cathedral, 64

New Zealand
    cruise area of, 231
    Fjordland National Park, 61
    Milford Sound, 62
    Mt. Cook National Park, 61
Ngorongoro Crater, Tanzania, 61
Niagara Falls, New York, 62
Niche markets, 319–320
Nigeria, Yankari National Park, 62
Nijo Castle, Kyoto, Japan, 57
Nonaccountable documents, 138
Nonstop flights, 98
No-rec, 74
Normal fares, 99, 118
Normandy Beacues, France, 60
North Carolina
    Biltmore Mansion, Asheville, 55
    Great Smoky Mountains National Park, 61
Northern Ireland, 52
Northstar Travel Media, 106, 153
No-shows, 80, 105–106
Notre Dame Cathedral, Paris, France, 63
Notre Dame de la Paix, Yamassoukro, Cote
        d'Ivoire, 64
Nymphenburg Palace, Munich, Germany, 57

O

OAG Business Travel Planner. See Travel
    Planner
OAG Flight Guide–Worldwide Edition, 276,
    280, 301
OAG (Official Airline Guide) Flight Guide
    airline codes, 77
    airport codes, 85
    airport diagrams, 83
    Alaska and Hawaii taxes, 126
    baggage information, 79
    commercial aircraft information, 80
    as information source, 106
    minimum connecting times, 99
    North American and worldwide editions, 101
    using, 101
Objections, handling, 318
Oceans, 46–47
Ocean (train), 182
Office skills, 5
Official Hotel Guide, 154
Official Steamship Guide, 230
Offline connections, 99
Old Royal Observatory, Greenwich,
        England, 60
One-way trips, 99–100, 120–121
Online Agency, 25
Online connections, 99
Open-ended questions, 315
Open-jaw trips, 100, 121–122, 121f,
        122f, 298
Open-jaw with side trip, 100, 122–123, 123f
Optional PNR fields, 105
Option date, 208, 249
Organizational skills, 5
Orient Express Hotels Group, 185
Orient Express (train), 184–185
Outback, Australia, 63
Outbound portion of trip, 100
Outside cabins, 234–235

Outside Sales and Support Network
        (OSSN), 7
Overbooking, 80
Override, 75, 101
Oxford University, Oxford, England, 57

P

Pacific Asia Travel Association (PATA), 193
Pagan, Myanmar, 64
Palenque, Chiapas, Mexico, 53
Pampas, Argentina, 63
Panama Canal, Panama, 57, 233
Paper ticket, 137
Parallels of latitude, 46
Paris, France
    Arc de Triomphe, 59
    Eiffel Tower, 56
    Fontainebleau Palace, 56
    Jardin du Luxembourg, 56
    Notre Dame Cathedral, 63
    Sacré-Coeur, 64
    Versailles Palace, 58
Parks, security at, 35
Parthenon, Athens, Greece, 53
Passenger agents, 8
Passenger contract, 195
Passenger departure tax, 247
Passenger Facility Charge (PFC), 125
Passenger names record (PNR), 73, 105,
        105f, 137
Passenger services agents, 8
Passion Play, Oberammergau, Germany, 64
Passports, 22, 34, 35, 181, 250
    applying for, 261, 262–263f, 264
    renewing, 264
    security for, 264
    tips on, 264
Payment arrangements
    agency fees and, 140
    charters, 194, 195
    cruises, 228
    lodging, 153
    Prepaid Ticket Advice, 139
    rental cars, 167, 168
    tours, 208, 212
Peninsula, 47
Pensions (accommodations), 149
People's Republic of China. *See* China
Perks, 196
Persepolis, Iran, 53
Personal accident insurance (PAI), 166
Personal computers (PCs), 21, 73
Peru
    Chan Chan, 52
    Lake Titicaca, 62
    Machu Picchu, 53
    Nazca Lines, 53
Petra, Jordan, 53
Pets
    accommodations for, 155
    airline policies on, 78–79
    Amtrak policy on, 180
    international versus domestic air policies
        on, 276
Philadelphia, Pennsylvania, 60
Phone field, 105

Photographers
  advantages/disadvantages, 11
  career advancement, 11
  job description, 11
  salary/benefits, 11
Piccadilly Circus, London, England, 57
Pickpockets, 36
Piracy, 250
Pitch
  of aircraft, 81
  of ship, 234, 246, 247f
Place names, European, 48
Plain, 47
Plateau, 47
Plaza Boliva, Caracas, Venezuela, 60
PNR. *See* Passenger names record
PNR fields, 105
Point-to-point fares, 121
Pompeii, Italy, 53
Ponte Vecchio, Florence, Italy, 57
Pop-up ads, 23
Port, 234
Port charges, 247
Porthole, 230
Ports of call, 231
Posh, origin of word, 228
Potala Palace, Lhasa, Tibet, 57
Praia do Carvoeira Beach, Portugal, 149f
Preexisting conditions, insurance and, 197
Preferred Hotels, 150
Preferred vendor list, 192, 208
Premium car, 165
Prepaid Ticket Advice (PTA), 139
Pressurization of cabins, 83
Priceline, 24
Primary codes, 299
Private charters, 194–195
Professional organizations, 15
Prohibited items, 35, 250, 266
Proof of citizenship, 260–261
Proof of financial responsibility, 166, 167
Pseudocity code, 74
Public charters, 194–195
Public relations, careers in, 11
Puffer machines, 34
Purser's lobby, 235

Q
Qualifying the traveler, 98, 207
Quebec Sales Tax, 126
Queen Elizabeth 2 (*QE2*) (ship), 238
Questions
  closed-ended, 315
  fact-finding, 316
  feeling-finding, 316
  open-ended, 315
  in sales process, 315–317

R
Railagent.com, 183
Rail fare, 179–180
Rail Passenger Service Act (1970), 174
Rail travel
  benefits of, 174
  in Canada, 181–182
  charters, 195

drawbacks of, 174
  in Europe, 182–184
  in Japan, 184
  luxury trains, 184–185
  private cars, 184–185
  in South Africa, 185
  See also Amtrak
Rail travel, security on, 34
Rating systems, for accommodations, 150–151
Received from field, 105
Reconfirmation of reservations, 79, 276
Recordkeeping, for cruise bookings, 249
Record locator, 105
Reef, 47
Refuel charge, 166
Refund-Exchange Notice (REN), 140
Refunds, 140
Regional airlines, 77
Registered Traveler program, 76
Registry, ship's, 235
Religion
  international travel and, 270
  services on cruises, 239
Religious sites, 63–64
Rental cars
  class and size groups, 164–165
  industry overview, 164
  insurance, 166
  international, 166
  locations for, 167
  pickup/dropoff, 167–168
  rate plans and extra charges, 165–166
  requirements, 167
  reservations, 167
Reporting air sales, 140–141
Representative company, 150
Reservation clerks, 8
Reservation form, 212, 213f
Reservations
  air travel, 105–106
  Amtrak, 181
  computerized, 20
  cruise, 248–249
  European trains, 183–184
  lodging, 155–156
  lost, 74
  passenger name records, 73
  rental car, 167
  timing of, 119
  tours, 212–214
  unethical practices, 105–106
  on World Wide Web, 23
Reservation sales agents
  advantages/disadvantages, 8
  career advancement, 8
  job description, 8
  related careers, 8
  salary/benefits, 8
  training, 8
Reservation worksheet, 248
Resorts, 149
Restricted inventory, 118
Restrictions, fare, 118–120, 122–123
Resume, 12, 13f
Revision fee, 208
Richmond, Virginia, 60

Rider, to insurance policy, 197
Ring of Kerry, Ireland, 63
River cruising, 233
Rocky Mountain National Park, Colorado, 61
Roll, of ship, 234, 246, 247f
Roman Baths, Bath, England, 60
Rome, Italy
  Colosseum, 52
  Roman Forum, 53
  Trevi Fountain, 58
Round-trips, 100, 121, 298
Royal Chitwan National Park, Nepal, 61
Royal Palace, Madrid, Spain, 57
Royal Palace, Stockholm, Sweden, 57
Runway, 84

S
Sabre, 20
Sacré-Coeur, Paris, France, 64
Safari, 207f
Sahara Desert, Northern Africa, 63
Sales, importance of, 314
Sales process, 314–320
  additional items, selling of, 319
  answering questions/handling
    objections, 318
  asking questions, 315–317
  closing the sale, 318–319
  customer support, 319–320
  initial contact, 315
  matching product to need, 317
  overview, 315
  product recommendation, 318
  specialty selling, 319–320
  telephone sales, 320–321
Sales Report Settlement Authorization, 140
Sales representatives, 8–9
  advantages/disadvantages, 9
  career advancement, 9
  job description, 9
  related careers, 9
  salary/benefits, 9
  training, 9
San Francisco, California
  Buddha's Universal Church, 63
  Fisherman's Wharf, 56
  Golden Gate Bridge, 56
Saudi Arabia
  Mecca, 63
  Medina, 63
Scams
  Internet, 22, 24, 26, 36, 208
  tour, 208
  travel, 35–37
Schönbrunn Palace, Vienna, Austria, 57
Screening Partnership Program (SPP), 76
Scuba and snorkeling, 64
Search engines
  advertising on, 23, 26
  overview of, 21
  Web site registration with, 26
Sears Tower, Chicago, Illinois, 57
Seasickness, 229, 234
Seat assignments
  airline policies on, 79
  passenger considerations for, 83

Sea travel, non-cruise, 240
Seattle, Washington, Space Needle, 57
Secretaries, travel arrangements handled by, 7
Security, 32–36
   air travel, 33–34, 34f, 76, 83–84, 266
   border, 35
   check points, 83
   cruise line, 34, 250
   government role in, 32–33
   hotels, 34, 156
   international air travel, 84, 271
   Internet, 21, 24–25
   parks/monuments, 35
   passports and, 264
   preparation by travelers, 35
   ships, 34, 250
   trains, 34, 181
   travel scams, 35–36
Security fees, 125
Security surcharge, 300
Seeing-eye dogs, 79
Segment, of flight, 99
Segment fees, 125
Self-catering accommodations, 149
Self-serve kiosks, 83
Serengeti National Park, Tanzania, 61
Servers, 25
Service animals, 79
Service fees, 75–76, 76f
Ships
   key concepts, 234–235
   profile, 234f
   security on, 34, 250
Shore excursions, 235
Sightseeing, 206
Sign, 74
Sine, 74
Single connections, 99
Single supplement, 208, 247
Sister fares, 120, 120f
Sistine Chapel, Vatican City, 64
SITI (Sold Inside, Ticketed/e-tkted Inside), 296
SITO (Sold Inside, Ticketed/e-tkted Outside), 296
Skycaps, 83
Smallpox, 266
Small ship companies, 230
Smoking
   Amtrak policy on, 180
   on international flights, 83
Social customs, 270
Socialized medicine, 197
Sold Inside, Ticketed/e-tkted Inside (SITI), 296
Sold Inside, Ticketed/e-tkted Outside (SITO), 296
Sold Outside, Ticketed/e-tkted Inside (SOTI), 296
Sold Outside, Ticketed/e-tkted Outside (SOTO), 296
SOTI (Sold Outside, Ticketed/e-tkted Inside), 296
SOTO (Sold Outside, Ticketed/e-tkted Outside), 296

South Africa
   Juma Mosque, Durban, 63
   Kruger National Park, 61
   rail travel, 185
South America, cruise area of, 233
Southern Mississippi River Valley, 60
South Pacific, cruise area of, 233
Space Needle, Seattle, Washington, 57
Space Tower, Rotterdam, Netherlands, 57
Spain
   Alcazar, Segovia, 55
   Alhambra Palace, Grenada, 55
   La Sagrada Familia, Barcelona, 63
   Royal Palace, Madrid, 57
Spanish Riding Academy, Vienna, Austria, 57
Special equipment, for rental cars, 165
Special-interest tours, 205
Specialization, by travel counselors, 319–320
Special meal requests, 79
Special rental vehicles, 165
Speculative bookings, 105
Sphinx, Giza, Egypt, 53
Split ticketing, 296–297
Splitting and combining excursions, 121–123, 122f
Sponsored links, 23f
Stabilizers, 234
Standard-size car, 164
Stand-by fare, 298
Starboard, 234
STAR Service, 153–154, 155f, 230
Staterooms, 234
Statue of Liberty, New York City, New York, 57
St. Basil's Cathedral, Moscow, Russia, 64
St. Catherine's Monastery, Sinai, Egypt, 64
Step-on guides, 9
Stern, 234
St. Louis, Missouri, Gateway Arch, 56
St. Mark's Square, Venice, Italy, 57
Stonehenge, England, 54
Stone Mountain, Atlanta, Georgia, 60
Stopover, 276
St. Patrick's Cathedral, New York City, New York, 64
St. Peter's Basilica, Vatican City, 64
St. Petersburg, Russia
   Summer Palace of Catherine the Great, 57
   Winter Palace, 58
Strait, 47
Stratford-upon-Avon, England, 60
Summer Palace of Catherine the Great, St. Petersburg, Russia, 57
Superliner train cars, 178, 179f
Supplemental liability insurance (SLI), 166
Supply-and-demand principle, 151
Surface segment, 100
Sustainable tourism, 38
Sweden
   Gota Canal, 56
   Royal Palace, Stockholm, 57
Switzerland
   Le Jet d'Eau, Geneva, 56
   Matterhorn, 62

T
Table d' hôte, 153
TA Edge, 25
Taj Mahal, Agra, India, 57
Tanzania
   Mt. Kilimanjaro, 62
   Ngorongoro Crater, 61
   Serengeti National Park, 61
Tarmac, 84
Taxes
   air travel, 125–127, 127f
   cruise, 247
   international travel, 270, 300–301, 300f
   rental car, 165
Taxiway, 84
Teams, working in, 4
Telemarketing, 36
Telephone etiquette, 332–333
Telephone selling, 320–321
Temperature, 47–48
Temple of Karnak, Karnak, Egypt, 54
Temple of Luxor, Luxor, Egypt, 54
Tender, 234
Tennessee, Great Smoky Mountains National Park, 61
Teotihuacan, Mexico City, Mexico, 54
Terminal building, 83
Terrorism, insurance against, 198
Texas, Alamo, San Antonio, 59
Theater, 60
Theme cruises, 235
Theme parks
   as destinations, 64–65
   security at, 35
Thomas Cook European Timetable, 182–183
Through flights, 99
Tiananmen Square, Beijing, China, 60
Tibet
   Jokhang, Lhasa, 63
   Potala Palace, Lhasa, 57
Ticket agents, 8
Ticket counters, 83
Ticket date field, 105
Ticketing
   basic ticket information, 139
   computerized, 20
   electronic, 137
   international, 303–304
   international versus domestic, 276
   paper, 137
   refunds/exchanges, 140
   ticketless, 136–137
   ticket stock, 138
   unethical practices, 105–106
   validation, 138–139
Ticketless travel, 136–137, 136f, 208
Tickets. See Airline tickets
Ticket sellers, 8
Ticket stock, 138, 138f
Ticket tax, 125
Tiergarten, Berlin, Germany, 57
Tikal, Guatemala, 54
Time comparison, 101–104, 104f, 279–280, 280t
Time management, 5
Time-shares, 36

Time zones, 101, 103f
Tipping
  on Amtrak, 180
  cruises, 235, 238, 239–240
  for meet-and-assist service, 79
  for wheelchair service, 79
Todai-ji Temple, Nara, Japan, 64
Toltec civilization, 52, 54
Topkapi Palace, Istanbul, Turkey, 57
Toronto, Ontario, CN Tower, 56
Torres del Paine, Chile, 61
Total fares, 125
Tour brochures, 206, 209–210
Tour conductors
  advantages/disadvantages, 10
  career advancement, 10
  job description, 9
  salary/benefits, 10
Tour coordinators, 10
Tour directors
  advantages/disadvantages, 10
  career advancement, 10
  job description, 9
  salary/benefits, 10
  training, 9–10
Tour escorts
  advantages/disadvantages, 10
  career advancement, 10
  job description, 9
  salary/benefits, 10
  training, 9–10
Tour guides
  advantages/disadvantages, 10
  career advancement, 10
  job description, 9
  salary/benefits, 10
Tourist card, 261
Tour operators
  association memberships of, 208–209
  policies of, 209, 210f, 211f
  responsibilities of, 204
  selection, 208–209
  travel insurance sales by, 196, 208
  visa service by, 265
Tours
  accommodation, 207
  accommodations, 209
  benefits of, 206–207
  confirmation/follow-up, 214
  dynamic packaging of, 204, 205–206
  escorted, 204–205
  food, 207, 210
  hosted, 204
  independent, 204
  industry changes, 205–206
  key concepts, 207–208
  operator selection, 208–209
  pace of, 210
  payment for, 208, 212
  pricing of, 207–210
  reservations, 212–214
  scams, 208
  selection, 207
  selling, 210–212
  special-interest, 205
  types, 204–206

Tower Bridge, London, England, 57
Trade publications, 15
Trade shows, 15
Trade winds, 47
Trafalgar Square, London, England, 58
Traffic Conference Areas, 277, 277f
Trains. See Amtrak; Rail travel
Transatlantic cruise area, 233
Transient guests, 149
Transportation Security Administration. See U.S.
  Transportation Security Administration
Travel agencies
  air travel, 72–73
  automation of, 73–74
  as consolidators, 192
  customer service, 76
  e-marketing impact on, 24–25
  GDS and, 74
  host agencies, 7
  lodging industry and, 148
  owners of, 7
  revenue of, 75–76
  sales authorization for, 72–73
  service fees, 140
  travel insurance sales by, 196
Travel agency owners, 7
Travel Agency Service Fee (TASF) document,
  76, 136, 140
Travel Agent Proficiency (TAP) test, 15
Travel agents. See Travel counselors
Travel Around the World, 46
Travel associations, 15
Travel clerks, 8
TravelCLICK, 26
Travel clubs, 36
Travel counselors
  advantages/disadvantages, 6
  appearance of, 333
  career advancement, 6–7
  communication skills for, 314
  cruise benefits for, 229
  customer service by, 330–333
  e-marketing impact on, 25
  expertise of, 314
  IATAN ID cards for, 73
  impression projected by, 333
  independent/home-based, 7
  "instant travel agent" scams, 37
  job description, 6
  related careers, 7
  salary/benefits, 6
  sales process for, 314–320
  specialization of, 319–320
  telephone etiquette for, 332–333
  telephone selling by, 320–321
  training, 6
Travel industry
  business segments of, 5t
  diversity within, 4
Travel Industry Association of America, 38
Travel Institute, 15
Travel insurance, 35
Travel Planner, 266, 270, 302–303
Travel professionals
  characteristics of, 4–5
  Internet and, 21–22

Travel Retailer Universal Enumeration
  (TRUE), 7
Travel scams, 35–36
Travel season, 247
Travel writers
  advantages/disadvantages, 11
  career advancement, 11
  job description, 11
  salary/benefits, 11
  training, 11
Trevi Fountain, Rome, Italy, 58
Trip cancellation/interruption insurance,
  196–197
Triple reduction, 208
Trip protection, 196, 208
Trunk airlines, 77
TSA. See U.S. Transportation Security
  Administration
Tulum, Quintana Roo, Mexico, 54
Turin, Italy, Cathedral of San Giovanni, 63
Turkey
  Blue Mosque, Istanbul, 63
  Cappadocia, 62
  Ephesus, Turkey, 52
  Topkapi Palace, Istanbul, 57
Turnaround point, 297
Tutankhamun, 54
24-hour clock, 278, 278f
Two-for-one scams, 36
Typhoid, 266

U
Uluru, Australia, 63
Unaccompanied minors, airline policies on, 78
Uniform Resource Locators (URLs), 21
United Kingdom
  cruise area of, 232
  rail travel in, 184
United Nations, 32, 37
United Nations Educational, Scientific, and
  Cultural Organization (UNESCO), 38, 52
United Nations Environmental Program
  (UNEP), 38
United States Air Consolidators Association
  (USACA), 193
United States Tour Operators Association
  (USTOA), 193, 198, 208–209
Unrestricted inventory, 118
Ur, Iran, 54
U.S. Arrival Tax, 300
U.S. Bureau of Consular Affairs, 35
U.S. Citizenship and Immigration
  Services, 34
U.S. Coast Guard, 34
U.S. Customs Fee, 300
U.S. Customs Service, 35, 250, 271
U.S. Embassy, 268, 269–270
U.S. Immigration Fee, 126, 300
U.S. State Department, 35, 36, 260, 265–266
U.S. Transportation Security Administration
  (TSA), 32–33, 35, 76, 181
U.S. Transportation Tax, 125
Utah
  Bryce Canyon National Park, 62
  Mormon Tabernacle, Salt Lake City, 63
  Zion National Park, 62

Utell, 150
Uxmal, Yucatán, Mexico, 54

V

Vacation protection, 196
Vaccinations, 266–267
Validating carrier, 138–139
Validation, 138–139, 303
Valleys of the Kings, Queens, and Nobles,
    Egypt, 54
Valuables
    air travel, 33
    cruises, 237
    hotels, 37, 156
    security of, 37
Value added tax (VAT), 270
Vanderbilt, Cornelius, 55
Vanderbilt, George W., 55
Vanderbilt, William K., 56
Vatican City
    Sistine Chapel, 64
    St. Peter's Basilica, 64
Vendors, 75
Venice, Italy
    Doge's Palace, 56
    St. Mark's Square, 57
Versailles Palace, Paris, France, 58
Vertical travelers, 228–229
VIA Rail Canada, 181–182
Victoria Falls, Zambia/Zimbabwe, 63
Vienna, Austria
    Hofburg Palace, 56
    Schönbrunn Palace, Vienna, 57
    Spanish Riding Academy, 57
Viewliner train cars, 178, 178f, 179f
Virunga National Park, Republic of Congo, 61
Viruses, Internet, 22
Visa expediters, 265
Visas, 264–265
Visa service, 265
Visa Waiver Program (VWP), 264
Vishvanatha Temple, Varanasi (Kasi), India, 64
Vouchers, air travel, 80

Wait-lists, 79
Waiver of responsibility, 194
Walking the guest, 153
Warwick Castle, England, 58
Washington, DC
    historical sites, 60
    White House, 58
Water
    oceans, 46
    weather and, 47
Water, safety of, 267–268
Waterloo, Belgium, 60
Wat Phra Keo (Temple of the Emerald Buddha),
    Bangkok, Thailand, 64
Weather, 47–48
Web banners, 22–23
Web sites
    design of, 25
    hosts for, 25
    naming and registering, 25
    promoting, 26
    types, 25
    See also World Wide Web
Weekend rate, for rental cars, 165
Weekly rate, for rental cars, 165
Weissmann Travel Reports, 46
Western Wall (also Wailing Wall), Jerusalem,
    Israel, 64
Westminster Abbey, London, England, 64
Wet lease, 195
Wheelchairs
    for air travel assistance, 79
    personal, not allowed on aircraft, 80
White House, Washington, DC, 58
Wide-body aircraft, 80, 82, 82f, 276
Winds, 47
Windsor Castle, England, 58
Winter Palace, St. Petersburg, Russia, 58
Winter sports destinations, 65
Wolong Natural Reserve, China, 62
Wood Buffalo National Park,
    Alberta, 62

World Conservation Union, 38
World cruises, 233
World Health Organization (WHO), 266
World Heritage Convention, 38
Worldspan, 20
World Tourism Organization (WTO), 38
World Travel and Tourism Council
    (WTTC), 38
World Wide Web
    advertising via, 22–23
    booking on, 23
    cruise information on, 229–230, 246
    developments in, 20–21
    domains on, 25, 26
    international travel information on, 303
    tour brochures on, 209–210
    See also Internet; Web sites
Würzburg Residence, Germany, 58

X

Xi'an Tomb, China, 54
XT (combined tax item), 300, 304
Xunantunich, Belize, 54

Y

Yangtzee River Gorges, China, 63
Yankari National Park, Nigeria, 62
Yellow fever, 266
Yellowstone National Park, Wyoming, 62
Yosemite National Park, California, 62
Youth fares, 298
Yucatán, Mexico
    Chichén Itzá, 52
    Uxmal, 54

Z

Zen Garden of Emptiness, Kyoto,
    Japan, 58
Zimbabwe
    Great Zimbabwe, 53
    Victoria Falls, 63
Zion National Park, Utah, 62